Criminal Justice and the American Constitution

H. Frank Way
University of California, Riverside

Duxbury Press
North Scituate, Massachusetts

Criminal Justice and the American Constitution
was produced by the following people:

Copy Editors: Barbara Bell Pitnof and Jacqueline M. Dormitzer
Interior Designer: K.B. Stevens
Cover Designer: Clifford Stoltze

Duxbury Press
A Division of Wadsworth, Inc.

Library of Congress Cataloging in Publication Data
Way, H. Frank.
    Criminal Justice and the American Constitution.

    Includes index.
    1. Criminal procedure—United States. 2. Due
    process of law—United States. I. Title.
KF9619.W32   345′.73′05   79-21395
ISBN 0-87872-238-6

Printed in the United States of America
1 2 3 4 5 6 7 8 9 — 84 83 82 81 80

For David, Madeline, and Deborah

Contents

Preface

Justice Frankfurter once observed that "the history of American freedom is, in no small measure, the history of procedure." This book is a study of one set of procedures, the constitutionally mandated rules of criminal procedure. The study proceeds on the assumption that these rules are important—that they address significant normative issues and have an operative reality beyond the pages of Supreme Court decisions. Undoubtedly, there is a gap in the legal-constitutional culture of the United States between the *is* of the daily operations of criminal justice and the *oughts* of constitutional rules. Yet it is equally certain that the oughts of due process coexist, albeit in tension, with the daily administration of criminal justice in the United States.

We prize due process rules or restraints for a number of reasons. First, they help to limit discretion and personal choice, thereby reducing the possibility of arbitrary rule and the abuse of power. But procedural rules in the area of criminal justice have other functions as well. Rules help to promote equal treatment, thereby increasing the likelihood of predictable and stable behavior. Finally, they protect individual freedoms. In short, the study of procedural rules is central to a complete understanding of how the system of criminal justice does work and should work in a constitutional society.

Still, procedural due process contains a gloomy paradox. Its commitment to criminal due process is one way society has of maintaining the ethic of restraint so essential to constitutionalism, to law, and to fundamental fairness. Yet the application of procedural due process may create the seeds of its own destruction, at least to the extent that rules—the procedural niceties—discredit the judiciary and thereby endanger the very Constitution that due process is attempting to preserve. Every time a criminal defendant who is factually guilty goes free in the name of due process, we create a little cynicism about our government. It may be expecting too much of the public to ask it to believe that the maintenance of the ethic of restraint occasionally requires that we grant freedom to those very individuals who are most heedless of ethical appeals.

Procedural due process often requires us to act in faithful commitment to our ideals and in the absence of scientifically tested propositions. Thus, as Justice Holmes observed, "Every year, if not every day, we have to wager our salvation upon some prophecy based upon imperfect knowledge." And so we proceed to model our system of criminal justice on a prophecy of imperfect knowledge, to wit, the Fourth, Fifth, Sixth, and Eighth Amendments to the Bill of Rights.

What follows, then, in the pages of this study is my attempt to present the normative model of criminal justice that we have come to call *due process of law*. The flaws of this volume are, of course, my own. However, I do express appreciation to Professors J. A. C. Grant and Don Brown, and equally to Marcus Leh, Ruth Langley, Tekla Morgan, Linda Jones, Chris Deviny, Sheryl Barton, and to my editor, Edward Francis. I also wish to acknowledge the reviews by Gregory Casey, University of Missouri; George F. Cole, University of Connecticut-Storrs; David Neubauer, American Judicature Society; Thomas Walker, Emory University; Marvin Zalman, Michigan State University; and Edwin C. Pearson.

The right of the people to be secure in their persons, houses, papers, and effects, against unreasonable searches and seizures, shall not be violated, and no Warrants shall issue, but upon probable cause, supported by Oath or affirmation, and particularly describing the place to be searched, and the persons or things to be seized.

—Fourth Amendment

No person shall be held to answer for a capital, or otherwise infamous crime, unless on a presentment or indictment of a Grand Jury, except in cases arising in the land or naval forces, or in the Militia, when in actual service in time of War or public danger; nor shall any person be subject for the same offence to be twice put in jeopardy of life or limb; nor shall be compelled in any criminal case to be a witness against himself, nor be deprived of life, liberty, or property, without due process of law; nor shall private property be taken for public use, without just compensation.

—Fifth Amendment

In all criminal prosecutions, the accused shall enjoy the right to a speedy and public trial, by an impartial jury of the State and district wherein the crime shall have been committed, which district shall have been previously ascertained by law, and to be informed of the nature and cause of the accusation; to be confronted with the witnesses against him; to have compulsory process for obtaining witnesses in his favor, and to have the Assistance of Counsel for his defence.

—Sixth Amendment

Excessive bail shall not be required, nor excessive fines imposed, nor cruel and unusual punishments inflicted.

—Eighth Amendment

. . . No State shall make or enforce any law which shall abridge the privileges or immunities of citizens of the United States; nor shall any State deprive any person of life, liberty, or property, without due process of law; nor deny to any person within its jurisdiction the equal protection of the laws.

—Section 1, Fourteenth Amendment

⊸§ 1 §⊷

Constitutional Politics and Criminal Justice

THE RULE OF LAW AND DISCRETIONARY POWER

There is a tension that necessarily exists in a free society between governmental power and personal liberty. Nowhere is that tension more evident than in the area of criminal justice. Controlling crime is an important responsibility of the state, and this means that the state must have sufficient powers to discharge this task—for its legislature, police, prosecutors, and trial courts to define, detect, prosecute, and punish criminal conduct. Yet free societies traditionally are chary of governmental power. James Madison, writing about the problems of framing a government, noted: "The great difficulty lies in this: you must first enable the government to control the governed; and in the next place oblige it to control itself."[1]

We oblige the government to control itself because of a deep conviction that power can and will be misused and abused, even in the discharge of compelling state responsibilities. The protection of life and property is certainly a compelling and often noble responsibility; still we have devised a host of constitu-

1

tional arrangements and devices that restrain the police, prosecutors, and judges. Common to all of these devices and arrangements is that the criminal power of the state must be exercised in a legal manner; that is, that the law is supreme, not the naked and unrestrained power of officers of the state.

The supremacy of the rule of law is an ancient heritage of free societies. From Aristotle's *Politics* (384–322 B.C.) to Cicero's *Laws* (106–43 B.C.) to John of Salisbury's *Policraticus* (1159), the rule of law had been a persistent ideal. But it was not until the late sixteenth century, in England, that the ideal began to gain a firm hold on the power of the state. By the seventeenth century, the rule of law and its offshoot, the common law, had both gained wide acceptance and proved to be sturdy weapons in the struggles against royal absolutism. Clearly, in the constitutional struggles of seventeenth-century England, the paramount issue was the division of power, the allocation of political responsibility. But it is equally clear that Englishmen and their American cousins were vitally concerned with preserving and improving the legal instruments for channeling the use of governmental power. In short, the rule of law had, by the seventeenth century, given rise to both substantive and procedural restraints on the state.

Of course, seventeenth-century procedural restraints in the area of criminal justice were relatively undeveloped, yet these restraints carried with them the same set of practical and ethical assumptions as does the rule of law. Procedural justice and the rule of law both assume that people have dignity that must be preserved as well as imperfections that must be recognized. These imperfections require that precautions be taken to control the use of power, so that individuals empowered to enforce the criminal law do not abuse that privilege. To this end, the rule of law attempts to limit the area of personal discretion in favor of fixed rules. Fixed rules constrain the choices of police officers, prosecutors, and judges—the presumption being that the potential for arbitrary rule is thereby reduced. The absence of fixed rules means that persons in the criminal justice network must exercise considerable personal judgment, or discretion. This judgment operates in an area of low visibility: The administration of criminal justice in a police station or in a prosecutor's office is neither public nor open to review by outside agencies. Discretion, then, in this context provides a natural environment for the arbitrary use and the misuse of the awesome power of criminal law.

Certainly we could argue that covering the landscape of the criminal process with fixed rules not only narrows the opportunity for the abuse of power, but lends predictability to the process and encourages fairness and equal treatment. This argument clearly has merit in a system committed to the rule of law. The difficulty with it is that it does not recognize the human condition: People are frequently unable not only to write rules of sufficient clarity to foreclose discretion, but to understand the wisdom of such foreclosure. For example, a rule of sufficient clarity in the area of arrest may lack the flexibility and adaptability that are necessary to meet the exigencies of human conduct. Human behavior is not always predictable, and one arrest situation may be totally unlike another. We must recognize then, as did Aristotle, that law as a system of rules is general or universal; it cannot "condescend upon particulars."[2]

The rule of law is, in a sense, extravagant. Even its strongest advocates recognize that it is impossible to squeeze all discretion out of the administration of justice. We cannot govern entirely by the rule of law; rather we must govern by a proper balance between a government of laws and a government of people—between rules and discretion. In fact, the choice is not between one or the other: In concrete areas, we must select the optimum point on the rules-to-discretion scale.[3] Discretion enables police officers, prosecutors, and judges to make justice individual, by taking into account those facts that cannot be anticipated. Finally, discretion in the criminal justice system, as in other areas, is often a product of the system's inability to formulate balanced rules. Although wisdom and knowledge can guide us in making difficult political choices, nonetheless the rational process assumes an information base that is often deficient or nonexistent in crucial procedural areas. For example, the data base necessary to select the optimum point on the rules-to-discretion scale in many questions of search and arrest procedures is quite small.[4]

This does not mean that we accept without question all discretionary powers that exist in the criminal justice system. Where discretion is unnecessary because it serves neither the goals of law enforcement nor individual freedom, it should be eliminated; where discretion is too broad, it should be narrowed. Discretion may well be crucial in an overloaded system of criminal justice, but it is equally true that discretion is the handmaiden of injustice.[5] We must structure judicial and executive discretion in problem areas (search and seizure, interrogation of suspects, arrest, bail, sentencing) where a reasonable case can be made that the existing discretion is dangerous and harmful to a free and safe society.

Models of Criminal Justice

Implicit in the discussion above is the assumption that formal procedural rules do make a difference: The behavior of police officers, prosecutors, and judges can be and is confined by rules. Of course, formal restraints on the actors in the criminal justice system do not give the entire scenario. Still, formal procedural requirements, especially those that have come to be accepted as requirements of due process of law, offer insight into our system of justice.

Due process of law suggests an adversary model of justice, in which the assumption of legal innocence dictates that the powers of the state be balanced by the procedural rights of the defendant. It is a cautious model, skeptical of power and especially skeptical of the reliability of administrative fact-finding.[6] It is a model that allows for few shortcuts and one that has little tolerance for factual error. The typical case under the due process model ends in the adversary trial, with the full panoply of defendants' rights.

That the criminal justice system does not always, or even generally, operate in the manner of the due process model is widely recognized.[7] For a number of reasons, the operative model of criminal justice in America closely resembles what has been called the *bureaucratic,* or *crime control, model.* This model emphasizes speed and efficiency in the processing of a large workload. It is generally skeptical of formal procedural rules, seeing them as obstacles to the rapid processing of those suspects who have been screened and thought to be guilty in fact. The reliance on and faith in the quality of administrative fact-finding enables the bureaucratic model to process large numbers of cases by summary methods. The typical case here ends not in a trial of disputed facts, but in a plea of guilty, often in conjunction with bargaining over the number and level of charges, and about a sentencing recommendation.

Although it may be true that the bureaucratic model most accurately conforms to the realities of criminal justice in America, still the model is influenced in some degree by the restraints of procedural due process. Even the plea-bargained case must at several junctures answer to the formal requirements of due process. Furthermore, it is entirely plausible that the due process model has subtle effects on the daily administration of criminal justice. Perhaps the conduct of the actors in the system is circumscribed in subtle degree by a legal culture that has traditionally given some recognition to the formal rights of defendants.

The Separation of Powers

If formal procedural requirements do have impact on the system, who should make the rules? The separation of powers, to the extent that it is based on the allocation of competences and the differentiation of functions, seems to suggest that the executive and legislative branches of government should assume the major responsibility for developing formal rules of criminal procedure. Many rules of procedure do in fact originate in the executive branch and are enacted by the legislature. The bulk of these formal rules, however, are technical and generally are not constitutional requirements. They express a policy choice by the legislative branch and, of course, are subject to amendment and repeal at the will of the legislature.

We do not intend to suggest that the legislature is not empowered to enact formal rules of procedure that are based on constitutional requirements. However, the line separating rules that are constitutionally mandated and those that are simply matters of legislative preference is not always easy to draw. Indeed, certain statutory rules of procedure that once were considered to be constitutionally mandated have subsequently, through judicial interpretation, lost their constitutional status. For example, consider the twelve-juror requirement of the Judiciary Act of 1789.[8] Finally, certain statutory rules of procedure, such as those governing federal jury selection and the right of speedy trial in federal criminal cases, blend legislative preferences with constitutional requirements.

Although the legislative branch does periodically address itself to problems of criminal procedure, the courts have long played the major role in this area. The reason lies partly with legislative default and partly with judicial competence gained through experience in the system. Judicial rule making may be based on constitutional requirements or it may simply be a reflection of the supervisory powers exercised by appellate courts over trial courts in a given jurisdiction. We are, of course, not immediately concerned here with procedural rules, of whatever origin, that are not considered a part of the broad fabric of constitutional due process. It is in the area of due process requirements that the judiciary, in particular the Supreme Court of the United States, has played its most creative and controversial role.

The Role of the Supreme Court

Charles Evan Hughes's aphorism, "The Constitution is what the Supreme Court says it is,"[9] surely says too much. The Constitution is more than judicial fiat. Yet Hughes was correct if he meant that the Supreme Court has a central and even decisive role in giving meaning to the Constitution. Through the remarkable institution of judicial review, the Court is often the constitutional authority of last resort. By virtue of the doctrine propounded in *Marbury v. Madison*,[10] it may hear appeals in both state and federal cases that raise federal questions. Criminal cases often give rise to claims of violations of rights that are arguably protected under the Constitution. These cases, if accepted for review by the Supreme Court,[11] become the convenient vehicles for constitutional pronouncements in the area of criminal procedure. In a sense, the Clarence Gideons and the Ernesto Mirandas are historical accidents, individuals whose ordinary lawsuits became the means for extraordinary judicial pronouncements.

The accidental quality of constitutional developments in criminal procedure is powerful testimony to those features of the Supreme Court that delineate and distinguish it from other political agencies in American government. Although the Supreme Court has carved out a broad charter for itself in constitutional law, it often has the appearance of being a remarkably fragile institution, quite incapable of discharging its broad charter. For example, the judicial power of the United States extends only to litigated cases,[12] which locks the Court into the adversary system of law. The Court must wait for the adversaries to come to it, and to do so the adversaries must pass through a series of restraints designed to keep them away. Once the adversaries are admitted to the Court—that is, once the Court agrees to hear a case—the adversary process continues to restrain the Court's orbit. The information available to the Court is generally limited to what is contained in the briefs submitted by the adversaries (supplemented occasionally by an amicus brief).[13] Furthermore, the adversary process limits the Court's technical power of enforcement only to those who are parties to the suit. Thus, in a case that becomes the occasion for announcing a new rule of criminal procedure, the Court has neither the technical power nor the physical resources to immediately impose that rule on others. The Court lacks the power of the sword and the power of the purse; it has neither a bureaucracy to monitor its rules nor traditional sanctions to enforce them. Then, can this institution, called by the late Alexander Bickel "the least dangerous branch" of government,[14] hope to reach into the precinct stations, prosecutors' offices, and trial courts of a far-flung federal system? The honest answer is no: Constitutional rules of criminal procedure are not self-executing; they often do not have the impact that authoritative pronouncements of the Court are presumed to have.[15]

To the extent that criminal rules of procedure attempt to restrain populations over which the judiciary has no direct contact, the restraints may not be effective. The Supreme Court has only limited power to respond to violations, particularly violations of rules by the police. For example, the Supreme Court may require trial courts not to admit evidence obtained in violation of a rule, or it may require appellate courts to reverse convictions obtained in violation of a rule. But exclusionary rules and reversals are indirect sanctions; generally they do not impose a penalty on those immediately responsible for the violations. Even in lower courts—where the Supreme Court might be expected to exercise tremendous authority—its power is far from self-evident.[16]

The absence of direct sanctions alone, however, does not explain sufficiently the often perplexing nature of the power of the judiciary in general and the Supreme Court in particular. Even when the Supreme Court has direct supervisory authority, as it does in the case of lower federal courts, the relationship is far from hierarchical. Although supervisory authority may add measurably to the Court's power over the federal judiciary, nonetheless the lower courts have often demonstrated a remarkable ability to evade Supreme Court policy.

The Court's power is reduced even more when we introduce the element of federalism. There is no criminal justice system in the United States; rather, there is a network of agencies concerned with criminal justice, agencies that are only partially linked, if at all, by jurisdictional ties. Each of the fifty states, as well as the national government, has its own criminal law, separate law enforcement agencies, and separate judicial systems. Furthermore, the states have the major responsibility in the area of criminal law, and therefore they carry the major burden of criminal cases. Under a system of reserved powers, each state historically has been free to develop not only its own substantive criminal law, but also its own criminal procedure. As Justice Harlan reminded his colleagues, "The specifics of trial procedure, which in every mature legal system will vary greatly in detail, are within the sole competence of the States."[17]

THE SUPREME COURT, FEDERALISM,
AND THE INCORPORATION DOCTRINE

For many years, the Supreme Court by policy did not hear appeals in state criminal cases. In general, this policy stemmed from the Court's reluctance to impose on the states the same procedural requirements that are constitutionally mandated in federal criminal cases. To some commentators, the Court's reluctance was merely another manifestation of an excessively narrow view of the constitutional theory of federalism. Considerations of federalism are not entirely inappropriate; in point of fact, the Bill of Rights does not apply to the states.[18]

There is little question that at the time the Fourth, Fifth, Sixth and Eighth Amendments were adopted they were intended to be imposed only on the national government. Yet it is equally certain that in some measure the Fourteenth Amendment, adopted in 1868, altered the original theory of federalism. The proscriptions of the Fourteenth Amendment are directed at the states, denying to them, among other things, the power to deprive any person of life, liberty, or property without due process of law. On numerous occasions after 1868, the Court was pressed to declare that the Fourteenth Amendment's due process clause[19] incorporated the procedural constraints of the Fourth, Fifth, Sixth, and Eighth Amendments. These requests were repeatedly turned back.[20] Indeed, in *Palko v. Connecticut* (1937),[21] the Court flatly rejected the contention that the Fourteenth Amendment incorporates or absorbs the prohibition of the First through the Eighth Amendments. Instead, the Court declared that the defendant was entitled only to a "fair trial" and that appellate court review of state criminal procedures should simply assess whether a claimed denial of a procedural right violated those "fundamental principles of liberty and justice which lie at the base of all civil and political institutions."[22] The fair-trial standard provided little specific guidance to trial or appellate courts, and in consequence the battle over incorporation continued. Although the *Palko* rationale was reaffirmed in 1947,[23] there were an increasing number of judicial chinks in the fair-trial doctrine.[24] Finally, in the early 1960s, the Warren Court, sometimes by narrow majorities, began the process of incorporating the major procedural protections of the Bill of Rights into the Fourteenth Amendment's due process clause. By 1971 the following specific procedural guarantees had been incorporated:

1. The right under the Fourth Amendment to exclude evidence illegally obtained[25]
2. The protection against cruel and unusual punishment[26]
3. The right to counsel[27]
4. The right against compulsory self-examination and a complementary exclusionary rule[28]
5. The right to confrontation of witnesses[29]
6. The right to compulsory process[30]
7. The right to speedy trial[31]

8. The right to trial by jury[32]
9. The protection against double jeopardy[33]
10. The protection against excessive bail[34]
11. The notice and certainty of charge[35]

In short, the Court has incorporated into the due process clause all of those specific protections and guarantees in criminal procedure that are constitutionally mandated in various parts of the Bill of Rights except the right to indictment by grand jury. This is not to suggest that the federal rules of criminal procedure now apply to the states. When the Court "nationalizes," or incorporates a broad constitutional guarantee, it does not necessarily mandate that the states must implement that guarantee through federal criminal procedure.[36]

However wise the process of incorporation has been, the Court must still face the reality that the decentralization of the operations of criminal justice is a corollary of the constitutional arrangements agreed to in 1787. The process of incorporation cannot mask the fact that the daily administration of criminal justice is still largely a state and local responsibility. Attempts by the Court to modify this condition often are met not only with vocal opposition, but more significantly with the natural lethargy and apathy of the federal system. The Court does not have the power to enforce or to reward, so local actors in the criminal justice network, who are not even in formal communication with the Court, can hardly be expected to march in step with its decisions.

The role of the Supreme Court in criminal justice is shaped by the realities of judicial power. Without the power or resources to rule, the judiciary is more dependent on the power of the word than are the other branches of government. The search for the right words—words that convey legitimacy and command respect—is central to the judicial task. No other branch of government is under as great an obligation to publicly explain and justify its decisions. The judicial role, then, is intertwined with legitimacy, and judicial legitimacy rests almost exclusively on the rationale of judicial decisions.

Although legal realists recognize that mechanical jurisprudence is a myth, we continue to cling to the view that courts are disinterested and that justices deserve their titles. As Justice Frankfurter once noted, the judicial task must not rest on whim or will; rather, "it must be an overriding judgment founded on something much deeper and more justifiable than personal preference. As far as it lies within human limitations, it must be an impersonal judgment. It must rest on fundamental presuppositions rooted in history to which widespread acceptance may be attributed."[37]

Constitutional adjudication, whether in criminal justice or any other area, must rest on the conventional sources of the law. The rationale of the Supreme Court's decisions must be explicable in terms of the conventional legal criteria of history, precedent, and constitutional exegesis and principles. Only when the Supreme Court is able to anchor its rulings in this way will they convey the legitimacy implicit in Aristotle's definition of law (reason free of all passion). Behaviorists and legal realists may counter that what we expect of the justices is an ideal—that service on the bench does not transform people into Olympian gods. Of course, the Supreme Court is not a mystical fountain of justice, nor are the justices neutral instruments for the discovery of preexisting law. The Supreme Court makes law for the simple reason that there are few constitutional absolutes; that, as Justice Holmes noted, the provisions of the Constitution "are not mathematical formulas having their essence in their form; . . . their significance is vital, not formal."[38]

Yet to recognize that the Court is a political instrument, that it mixes will and judgment, is not to say that judicial decisions should be devoid of principles or unmindful of the historical and legal context of constitutional adjudication. However elusive constitutional principles may be and however uncertain precedent and history are, they form the path to judicial legitimacy. Former Solicitor General Archibald Cox noted:

> The Court's power to give its decisions the force of legitimacy ultimately depends in large measure on its professional artistry in weaving wise statecraft into the fabric of law . . . if the capacity of judge-made law to command free assent depends upon the proposition that the decisions of the judges rest upon principles more enduring and more general than the wills of individual judges— then the effectiveness of the Court . . . is eroded by any failure to show how novel decisions required by changes in human condition and the realization of bolder aspirations nonetheless draw their sanction from a continuing community of principle.[39]

The Continuing Community of Principle: The Bill of Rights

The process of resolving constitutional issues on the basis of principled adjudication is not easy. There is no clear set of constitutional principles that enable a justice to match a factual problem with a principle and in some mechanical manner arrive at a decision.[40]

Justice Holmes was correct when he observed that general propositions do not decide concrete cases. Still, there are some general propositions that, although they are not predictive of results in specific cases, do provide a philosophical and intellectual framework for procedural questions in criminal justice. No Supreme Court justice can ignore the Bill of Rights, particularly the Fourth, Fifth, Sixth, and Eighth Amendments. By adopting these instruments as part of the basic instrument of government, the founders foreclosed the possibility that questions about criminal procedure would be open-ended. The language of the amendments leaves considerable room for interpretation or, as Justice Brandeis said, the Constitution possesses the capacity for adaptation by an ever-developing people.[41] But the capacity for adaptation through judicial interpretation does not mean that the amendments are without contemporary relevance. To some persons the Bill of Rights may be nothing more than a series of pious platitudes, quaint and antique language to which only passing and occasional reference need be made. This position makes a mockery of constitutional law. The constitutional provisions on the rights of criminal defendants are as much a part of the constitutional fabric as is any other provision of the Constitution. The meaning of these provisions and their implications for criminal law enforcement cannot be dismissed, even though one implication is that ease and efficiency must at times be sacrificed to the higher priority the Constitution accords to the rights of criminal suspects and defendants. This priority stems from a set of assumptions and beliefs, however untested they may be, that are fundamental principles of a free society—principles so central that they are necessarily standards of constitutional adjudication.

The libertarian principles that flow from the Fourth, Fifth, Sixth, and Eighth Amendments stem from a basic commitment to the preservation and enforcement of individual liberty. This libertarian perspective recognizes that all people share a common core of humanity and dignity that must not be violated by the state. Finally, it views the state and its power with a large measure of skepticism because that power is subject to abuse, both subtle and obvious. Therefore, power must be checked by placing restraints, like those in the Constitution, on its use. Because it stresses the primacy of the individual, the libertarian philosophy also holds that the function of the law is to promote human liberty; the function of the criminal law is to provide a measure of protection against behavior that threatens human liberty and to forestall resorting to violence to satisfy wrongs. But the libertarian view accords the criminal law only guarded acceptance, fearing that the single-minded pursuit of safety and order would create a condition in which all are safe and none are free.

The libertarian perspective does not lead automatically to a simple prodefendant conclusion in concrete cases. All it suggests is that the Bill of Rights mandates that judicial inquiry in matters of criminal procedure begin with the same assumptions about people and the same measured skepticism about governments that are implicit in the Fourth, Fifth, Sixth, and Eighth Amendments. This means when the Supreme Court is requested by the state to place its imprimatur on a particular criminal procedure or to legitimate discretionary conduct by criminal justice agencies that the Court must respond with the same measured skepticism about the criminal sanction that is implicit in the Bill of Rights. At a minimum, this requires that the Court's opinions take public account of the broad mandates that stem from the Fourth, Fifth, Sixth, and Eighth Amendments, and the Court's adjustment to them; anything less falls short of the craftsmanship we expect of the judiciary.

CONCLUSION

Although the Supreme Court is not the only agency capable of shaping procedural justice, it has come to be the chief constitutional agency for checking and examining existing practices and procedures against the durable principles of the Bill of Rights. The Court's task is obviously a difficult one, not only because the principles are not easy to apply, but because the Court is constitutionally a weak branch of government. Madison may have recognized the need to set ambition against ambition, but he did not anticipate how the Supreme Court could act as an effective check on the power of the government in the area of criminal justice. Without effective power to establish rules, especially for the pretrial stage of state and federal criminal cases, and with only limited controls over state proceedings generally, the Court is often forced to adopt methods that create doubt about the legitimacy of its role. When the Court disallows probative evidence because the methods used to obtain that evidence offend a constitutional guarantee, it risks being criticized for being "soft" on criminals. Similarly, when convictions are reversed because of a violation of a procedural right, for example, the right to confrontation or cross-examination, it risks being accused of being "overly technical," especially if the procedural flaw occurred in what appears to have been an otherwise orderly and fair trial. Letting probable felons go free because of police or prosecutor blunders, or judicial errors, can discredit the Court. Yet if the Court is to play more than a trivial role in giving shape and substance to constitutional protections, then it must assume these risks. The Court does not have an array of options: It cannot persuade or cajole with methods more appropriate to the executive and legislative bodies. With rare exceptions, the judicial message must be the by-product of an appeal in an ordinary lawsuit. Within the limited confines of the judicial arena, often the only way the Court has to vindicate constitutional guarantees is to reverse the conviction of a defendant who is probably guilty. The Court does not, thereby, endorse criminal behavior. Only if it fails to present a valid rationale rooted in a constitutional provision is there a risk that the Court's action will be misunderstood—appearing to endorse a criminal action rather than to protect a constitutional value. In a similar vein, when the Court sustains a conviction and confers legitimacy on a particular practice or procedure, it is equally obligated to demonstrate that its position is consonant with the Constitution. In either context, then, the function of the Court, in the words of Judge Charles Wyzanski, is to "mold the people's view of durable principles of government."[42]

NOTES

1. *Federalist Papers* No. 51.
2. *Ethics*, bk. 5, chap. 105 quoted in George Sabine, *A History of Political Theory*, 3d ed. New York: Holt, Rinehart & Winston, 1961), p. 367.
3. See Kenneth Culp Davis, *Discretionary Justice* (Baton Rouge: Louisiana State University Press, 1969), chap. 2.
4. Furthermore, in selecting the optimum point, we would be trying to predict the consequences of such a choice on the values implicit and explicit in law enforcement and

privacy. This raises not only difficult data problems, but extremely difficult measurement problems.

5. Davis, *Discretionary Justice,* p. 25.

6. For a discussion of the due process model, see Herbert Packer, *The Limits of the Criminal Sanction* (Stanford, Calif.: Stanford University Press, 1968), chap. 8.

7. E.g., ibid.; and Abraham Blumberg, *Criminal Justice* (Chicago: Quadrangle, 1967).

8. See below, pp. 346–347.

9. Quoted in Alfred H. Kelley and Winfred A. Harbison, *The American Constitution,* 3d ed. (New York: Norton, 1963), p. 142.

10. 1 Cranch 137 (1803); and by the power of § 25 of the Judiciary Act of 1789, 1 Stat. 81. See also *Martin v. Hunter's Lessee,* 7 Wheat. 304 (1816).

11. The Court has discretionary power to accept or reject a petition in a criminal case from a state or federal appellate court.

12. The precise language of Article III, section 2, is "The judicial power shall extend to all cases, in law and equity, arising under this Constitution, the laws of the United States, and treaties made, or which shall be made, under their authority."

13. The Court, at its discretion, may allow a friend of the court, *amicus curiae,* who is not a party to the suit but who may have special competence, to submit a brief. In criminal procedures cases, amicus briefs are sometimes offered by the American Civil Liberties Union, the International Association of Chiefs of Police, the National Defender League, or by an interested state attorney general.

14. Alexander Bickel, *The Least Dangerous Branch* (New York: Bobbs-Merrill, 1962).

15. See generally Stephen L. Wasby, *The Impact of the United States Supreme Court* (Homewood, Ill.: Dorsey Press, 1970).

16. Walter Murphy, "Lower Court Checks on Supreme Court Power," 53 *Am. Pol. Sci. Rev.* 1017 (1959).

17. Dissenting in *Mapp v. Ohio,* 367 U.S. 643, 682 (1961).

18. *Brown v. Baltimore,* 7 Pet. 243 (1833).

19. The privileges and immunities clause of the same amendment was an alternative.

20. E.g., *Hurtado v. California,* 110 U.S. 516 (1884); *Maxwell v. Dow,* 176 U.S. 581 (1900); and cases listed in *Twining v. New York,* 211 U.S. 78 (1908).

21. *Palko v. Connecticut,* 302 U.S. 319 (1937).

22. Quoting from *Herbert v. Louisiana,* 272 U.S. 319 (1926).

23. *Adamson v. California,* 332 U.S. 46 (1947); see the dissenting opinion of Justice Black at 68.

24. E.g., *Wolf v. Colorado,* 338 U.S. 25 (1949); and *Moore v. Michigan,* 355 U.S. 155 (1957).

25. *Mapp v. Ohio.*

26. *Robinson v. California,* 370 U.S. 660 (1962).

27. *Gideon v. Wainwright,* 372 U.S. 335 (1963).

28. *Malloy v. Hogan,* 378 U.S. 1 (1964); and *Miranda v. Arizona,* 384 U.S. 436 (1966).

29. *Pointer v. Texas,* 380 U.S. 400 (1964).

30. *Washington v. Texas,* 388 U.S. 14 (1967).

31. *Klopfer v. North Carolina,* 386 U.S. 21 (1967).

32. *Duncan v. Louisiana,* 391 U.S. 145 (1968).

33. *Benton v. Maryland,* 395 U.S. 784 (1969).

34. Dicta in *Schilb v. Kuebel,* 404 U.S. 357, 365 (1971).

35. Dicta in *Twining v. New Jersey,* 211 U.S. 78, 112 (1908); and *Cole v. Arkansas,* 333 U.S. 196, 201 (1948).

36. See Henry J. Friendly, "The Bill of Rights as a Code of Criminal Procedure," 53 *Calif. L. Rev.* 929 (1965).

37. Concurring in *Sweezy v. New Hampshire,* 354 U.S. 234, 266–267 (1957).

38. *Gompers v. United States,* 233 U.S. 604, 610 (1914).

39. Archibald Cox, *The Warren Court* (Cambridge, Mass.: Harvard University Press, 1968), pp. 48–49.

40. For a summary of the principled-adjudication controversy of the 1950s and 1960s, see Martin Shapiro, *Law and Politics in the Supreme Court* (New York: Free Press, 1964), chap. 1.

41. See Bickel, *Least Dangerous Branch*, p. 107.

42. Quoted in Arthur E. Sutherland, *Government Under Law* (Cambridge, Mass.: Harvard University Press, 1956), p. 486.

2

The
Principle
of
Legality

Fundamental to our understanding of the constitutional rights of criminal defendants is the threshold principle of legality. The heart of the principle is the initial restraint placed on the state whenever it attempts to bring a criminal action against an individual. The principle is embodied in a cluster of constitutional provisions, doctrines, and canons. Collectively these restraints require that the state conform to the requirements of the maxim, *nulla poena sine lege—* no punishment without law.[1] This means that from the outset of a criminal case the state must proceed only according to a previously authorized and precisely defined penal law. The threshold limitations placed on the state are based on the constitutional prohibition against ex post facto laws, the vagueness doctrine, and its corollary canon, the canon of strict construction.

Broadly speaking, the purpose of the principle of legality is to reduce the possibility of arbitrary and oppressive action by the government in the enforcement of criminal laws. It does this by requiring that individuals be given advance and fair notice of the kinds of conduct subject to criminal sanctions. These constraints do more than reduce the element of surprise in the criminal law; they also ensure a proper allocation or division of competences among the legislative, executive, and judicial branches.[2] Because many criminal laws are written in general terms, the principle of legality attempts to keep the discretion of judges and executive officers within tolerable limits, and keeps the legislature on constant notice that the lawmaking function is distinct from enforcement, interpretation, and judgment. The principle goes to the very heart of constitutionalism—namely, a division of political power that prevents undue concentration in the hands of one set of authorities.[3]

EX POST FACTO LAWS

In a sense, the constitutional prohibition against ex post facto laws seems archaic. Today there is little concern that legislatures would try to punish conduct that was perfectly legal at the time it was committed. The principle of legality is so widely accepted, and the constitutional proscriptions so much a part of our governmental order, that the willful disregard by legislatures of the prohibition against ex post facto laws is remote. Yet the framers of the Constitution were sufficiently concerned about the problem of retroactive legislation that the prohibitions against ex post facto laws and bills of attainder were among the few procedural limitations that were placed in the Constitution, as drafted and ratified, and that applied to both state legislatures and to the Congress.[4]

The constitutional proscription against ex post facto laws is stated in simple language: Neither Congress nor any state shall pass retroactive legislation. Like all constitutional provisions, the proscription offers no definition of an ex post facto law. Within a short time, however, a judicial definition was made: Whatever the original intention of the framers may have been, since Justice Chase's opinion in *Calder v. Bull* (1798) the prohibition has applied only to criminal laws.[5] Indeed, Justice Chase's opinion remains the cornerstone for all subsequent judicial interpretation:

> 1st.   Every law that makes an action done before the passing of the law; and which was innocent when done, criminal; and punishes such action. 2d. Every law that changes the punishment, and inflicts a greater punishment, than the law annexed to the crime when committed. . . . 4th. Every law that alters the legal rules of evidence, and receives less, or different, testimony, than the law required at the time of the commission of the offense, in order to convict the offender.[6]

Justice Chase's first ruling restricts the protection to criminal laws, rather than to both criminal and civil laws. Although his interpretation has been disputed,[7] it continues to be accepted by subsequent Courts.[8] Only rarely has controversy arisen, generally over whether a retroactive law that is civil on its face operates in fact as a criminal law. In 1878, in a case involving an excise tax on tobacco, the Supreme Court did rule that the ex post facto effect of a law cannot be evaded by giving a civil form to that which is essentially criminal.[9] However, some years later, in a case involving forfeiture of land for nonpayment of taxes, the Court ignored the 1878 ruling and upheld a retroactive tax law.[10]

The sense of public legitimacy that must support the criminal law would be severely eroded if legislatures set about retroactively punishing otherwise innocent acts or retroactively increasing the punishment for conduct proscribed by the criminal law. In fact, this has never been a problem in the United States. What does occasionally happen is that legislatures change punishments associated with previously defined criminal conduct, which can raise the ex post facto issue, but only if the punishment is increased and applied to acts already committed. For example, the Court has held that retroactively adding a period of solitary confinement prior to the execution of a death sentence is ex post facto,[11] since the changed punishment was of an infamous and painful character. However, when South Carolina changed its punishment for murder from hanging to electrocution and applied it to those awaiting execution, the Court concluded that, because electrocution was less painful and more humane than hanging, the change did not make the punishment harsher and thus did not violate the ex post facto provision.[12] Similarly, in *Rooney v. North Dakota*, the retroactive addition of several months' imprisonment prior to the execution of a death sentence was not ex post facto. The Court contended that rational people want to live as long as they can, and consequently the change did not work to the disadvantage of the defendant.[13] If, however, a law alters the indeterminate-sentence statute and requires a maximum sentence where previously the law allowed a range from minimum to maximum, then it may not be applied retroactively to prior conduct.[14] In so ruling, Justice Stone noted that "the Constitution forbids the application of any new punitive measure to a crime already consummated, to the detriment or material disadvantage of the wrongdoer."[15]

The major problem with ex post facto laws involves retroactive changes in trial procedures, including changes in the rules of evidence. Unfortunately the Supreme Court's cases do not provide a clear answer to problems in this area. Revision of the criminal law is an ongoing process: Legislative changes in trial procedures, practices, and rules of evidence are common and not infrequently raise substantial questions under the prohibitions against ex post facto legislation. Although *Calder v. Bull* indicated that laws altering the rules of evidence by requiring less or different testimony than required at the time of the commission of the offense were ex post facto, subsequent decisions have tended to cast doubt on this ruling. In *Hopt v. Utah,* the prosecution was allowed to take advantage of a change in the law enlarging the class of witnesses competent to testify, although the change occurred after the commission of the offense and although the particular testimony worked to Hopt's disadvantage. Justice Harlan, speaking for a unanimous Court, noted:

> Any statutory alteration of the legal rules of evidence which would authorize conviction upon less proof, in amount or degree, than was required when the offense was committed, might, in respect of that offense, be obnoxious to the constitutional inhibition upon *ex post facto laws.* But alterations which do not increase the punishment nor change the ingredients of the offense or the ultimate facts necessary to establish guilt, but, leaving untouched the nature of the crime and the amount or degree of proof essential to conviction, only removes existing restrictions upon the competency of certain classes of persons as witnesses, relate to modes of procedure only, in which no one can be said to have a vested right, and which the State, upon grounds of public policy, may regulate at pleasure. Such regulations of the mode in which the facts constituting guilt may be placed before the jury, can be made applicable to prosecutions or trials thereafter had, without reference to the date of the commission of the offense charged.[16]

Yet one year before *Hopt,* the Court had unanimously reversed a conviction against a claim that the contested law was merely a procedural change.[17] In that same case, favorable reference was made to an earlier conclusion by Justice Washington that an ex post facto law is one that alters the situation to an individual's disadvantage.[18]

Of course, we could argue that enlarging the scope of admissible evidence increases the likelihood that a jury will discover the truth and that the defendant (in the abstract) is not disadvantaged by the truth. This was apparently the basis not only for the *Hopt* decision, but also for the decision in *Thompson v. Missouri.* There, the rules of evidence were altered and retroactively applied so as to admit a comparison of disputed handwriting, allowing the prosecution to tie the defendant to a prescription for strychnine and a threatening letter.[19] Justice Harlan, author of the *Hopt* opinion, concluded in *Thompson* that "the statute did nothing more than remove an obstacle arising out of a rule of evidence that withdrew from the consideration of the jury testimony which, in the opinion of the legislature, tended to elucidate the ultimate, essential fact to be established, namely, the guilt of the accused."[20] It is difficult to square Justice Harlan's reasoning with earlier decisions. Enlarging the area of admissible testimony and evidence undoubtedly worked to the disadvantage of the accused in both *Hopt* and *Thompson.*

True, no one should have a vested right in procedure: The state should be free to alter criminal procedure and apply the changes to pending trials. As Justice Harlan wrote in *Gibson v. Mississippi,* "The inhibition upon the passage of ex post facto laws does not give a criminal a right to be tried, in all respects, by the law in force when the crime charged was committed."[21] But it is one thing to change the qualifications for a member of the grand jury (as was accepted in *Gibson*) or to alter the membership of an appellate tribunal;[22] it is quite another to alter procedure in such a way as to deprive and disadvantage the defense in a substantial manner. For example, there may be no constitutionally mandated size to a trial jury,[23] but to reduce the size of the jury, and to apply that reduction retroactively, would be a procedural change that would deny the accused a substantial and previously existing right.[24]

To suggest that no one has a vested right in any particular procedure does little to clarify the issue. Rather, we should begin with the proposition that retroactive changes in the criminal law are suspect and proceed, on a case-by-case basis, to determine whether their application works a serious prejudice on the accused. If the changes ameliorate existing law or if the changes are neutral or insignificant, then the constitutional issue can be dismissed. Although the weight of the Supreme Court's record in this area is in the direction of allowing almost any change that does not retroactively increase punishment or retroactively apply a new criminal offense, still the principle of legality is not well served by retroactive procedural changes that disadvantage the accused. For example, in *Dobbert v. Florida* (1977), the defendant was tried and convicted of murder.[25] At the time the offense was committed, Florida law provided that a person convicted of a capital felony was to be punished by death unless the jury, by majority vote, recommended mercy, in which case the defendant would receive a life sentence. However, Dobbert was not sentenced according to this 1971 provision, but according to an amended law, enacted in 1972, that allowed the trial judge to override the jury's recommendation. The *Dobbert* jury, by a vote of 10 to 2, recommended a life sentence; the trial judge overruled and sentenced Dobbert to death.[26] Dobbert contended that, because the law in effect at the time of the offense did not allow the judge to override a recommendation of mercy, the new sentencing law harmed him. Justice Rehnquist, writing for the majority, concluded "that the changes in the law are procedural, and on the whole ameliorative"[27]—not in violation of the ex post facto provision.

Unquestionably, the Florida legislation was "on the whole ameliorative." It was passed in response to the decision in *Furman v. Georgia*,[28] and its improved procedures for the imposition of the death penalty were subsequently upheld by the Supreme Court.[29] But a question remains: Clearly the 1972 provision worked to Dobbert's grave disadvantage. Finally, to imply that procedural changes do not come within the orbit of the prohibition against ex post facto legislation is to engage in semantics. As Justice Miller stated for the Court in an 1882 case: "Can any substantial right which the law gave the defendant at the time to which his guilt relates, be taken away from him by ex post facto legislation, because, in the use of a modern phrase, it is called a law of procedure? We think it cannot."[30]

The retroactive application of the Florida statute gave rise to problems; the prospective application of procedural change is quite appropriate. For example, when Congress changed the defense of insanity in the District of Columbia, shifting the burden from the prosecution to the defense, the Court of Appeals for the District of Columbia appropriately ruled that the new law could not be retroactively applied.[31] Its prospective application would be both wise and just, but to apply the change retroactively would undermine public confidence in the legitimacy and fairness of the criminal law. Similarly, when the state of Florida attempted retroactively to apply stricter standards for obtaining severance, it was ruled ex post facto.[32]

When we consider the oppression that could result from the retroactive application of changes in criminal procedure, the small number of felons that go free as a result of prospective application is not a high price to pay. Legislatures must be able to make necessary changes in procedure, even those that repeal an unfair advantage given to the defense, but only consistent with constitutional protections. By making the changes prospectively, they eliminate the possibility of charges that the government has taken unfair advantage of its power to alter the rules of the system.

THE VAGUENESS DOCTRINE

The prohibition against ex post facto laws alone would not ensure that the principle of legality obtains throughout the system of criminal justice. Of equal importance is the constitutional doctrine of *void for vagueness*.[33] The doctrine attempts to resolve the problems of linguistic uncertainty so common to criminal statutes. Vagueness may be the result of sloppy drafting or it may be the result of the general imprecision of the language. Whatever the cause, the rule is reasonably clear: The criminal law, the set of guidelines proscribing and prescribing certain conduct, must, insofar as the language permits, enable people of ordinary intelligence to know whether their conduct comes within its limits.

> No one may be required at peril of life, liberty or property to speculate as to the meaning of penal statutes. All are entitled to be informed as to what the State commands or forbids.[34]

Perhaps the best general statement of the doctrine appears in *Connally v. General Construction Co.* (1926). There the Court said:

> The dividing line between what is lawful and unlawful cannot be left to conjecture. The citizen cannot be held to answer charges based upon penal statutes whose mandates are so uncertain that they will reasonably admit of different constructions. A criminal statute cannot rest upon an uncertain foundation. The crime, and the elements constituting it, must be so clearly expressed that the ordinary person can intelligently choose, in advance, what course it is lawful for him to pursue. Penal statutes prohibiting the doing of certain things, and providing a punishment for their violation, should not admit of such a double meaning that the citizen may act upon the one conception of its requirements and the courts upon another.[35]

The vagueness doctrine does more than provide individuals with a reasonable standard against which to measure their conduct; it also provides courts and juries with an ascertainable standard of guilt. In the absence of standards, the triers of facts effectively become legislative bodies. As the Court noted many years ago,

> it would certainly be dangerous if the Legislature could set a net large enough to catch all possible offenders and leave it to the courts to step inside and say who could be rightfully detained and who could be set at large. This would, to some extent, substitute the Judicial for the Legislative Department of the Government.[36]

The doctrine also precludes judicial enlargement of an otherwise narrowly drafted criminal law. Here the problem is not an ambiguous law that raises speculation as to its meaning nor a vague law that has been given a narrow judicial gloss, but a narrow law that is enlarged retroactively by judicial decision. As the Court noted in *Pierce v. United States*: "Judicial enlargement of a criminal act is at war with a fundamental concept of the common law that crimes must be defined with appropriate definiteness."[37] To unexpectedly broaden the scope of a criminal act and apply it retroactively is to provide a judicial parallel to ex post facto laws.[38]

Of course criminal statutes must be drafted with a degree of generality; to do otherwise would limit their utility. Due process does not require excessively narrow criminal laws, and the Court has stated that the Constitution does not present an obstacle to defining criminal conduct.[39]

Some criminal laws are vague not because generality is a property of the criminal law, but rather by legislative intent. This is particularly true of vagrancy- and loitering-type laws, which are aimed at suspected rather than observed criminal conduct and are used by the police as a means of preventing crime by removing "undesirables" from public places.[40] These laws, with their dragnet approach to public order, provide no clear guidelines to citizens, police, or courts. The conduct prohibited by vagrancy-loitering laws is so vague that pretextual arrests become their common vice.[41] As Judge Robinson noted in a District of Columbia vagrancy case, "We have before us a blunderbuss statute without a bead-sight enforcement policy."[42]

Aside from the problem of vagueness, there is a certain charm about vagrancy laws. The Florida statute, along with similar laws in other states, evokes nostalgia:

> (1) Rogues and vagabonds, (2) idle or dissolute persons who go about begging, (3) common gamblers, (4) persons who use juggling, or unlawful games or plays, (5) common pipers and fiddlers, (6) common drunkards, (7) common night walkers, (8) thieves, (9) pilferers, (10) traders in stolen property, 11) lewd, wanton and lascivious persons, (12) keepers of gambling places, (13) common railers and brawlers, (14) persons who neglect their calling or employment, or (15) are without reasonably continuous employment

or regular income and who have not sufficient property to sustain them, and misspend what they earn without providing for themselves or the support of their families, (16) persons wandering or strolling around from place to place without any lawful purpose or object, (17) habitual loafers, (18) idle and disorderly persons, (19) persons neglecting all lawful business and habitually spending their time by frequenting houses of ill fame, gaming houses or tippling shops, (20) persons able to work but habitually living upon the earnings of their wives or minor children, and (21) all able bodied male persons over the age of eighteen years who are without means of support and remain in idleness, shall be deemed vagrants.[43]

Fortunately, vagrancy-loitering laws appear to be falling rapidly under the vagueness doctrine.[44] In 1971 in *Palmer v. Euclid,* the Supreme Court refused to uphold the enforcement of the town's suspicious-person ordinance. The ordinance defined a "suspicious person" as "any person who wanders about the streets or other public ways or who is found abroad at late or unusual hours in the night without any visible or lawful business and who does not give satisfactory account of himself."[45] In the following year, the Court unanimously declared a Jacksonville, Florida, vagrancy law void. Justice Douglas, speaking for the Court, observed that the Jacksonville ordinance was void not only because it failed to give persons of ordinary intelligence fair notice that their contemplated conduct is illegal, but because the statute encouraged arbitrary and erratic arrests and convictions. Investigatory, or preventive, arrests run afoul not only of the vagueness doctrine, but of the Fourth Amendment as well.[46]

THE CANON OF STRICT CONSTRUCTION

The third facet in the principle of legality is the canon of strict construction of the sanctions of penal statutes. The canon is an extension of the requirement of fair notice and regard for the proper allocation of competences in the branches of government. Briefly stated, strict construction demands that before a penal law may be applied to the conduct of the accused, it must be clear that the law covers the specific conduct of the accused; ambiguity must be decided in favor of the accused.[47] Thus the term *motor vehicle* as used in the National Motor Vehicle Theft Act could not be construed to apply to the theft of an airplane.[48] In other words, in the judicial construction of penal laws, the canon of strict construction would appear to preclude reasoning by recourse to analogies. Although legislative intent is not to be ignored, statutory interpretation must be by reference to the clear and ordinary meaning of the words and not by analogy to acts similar in kind to the evil proscribed by the letter of the law. This point was ably stated by Chief Justice Marshall:

The rule that penal laws are to be construed strictly, is perhaps not much less old than construction itself. It is founded on the tenderness of the law for the rights of individuals; and on the plain principle that the power of punishment is vested in the legislative, not in the judicial department. It is the legislature, not the court, which is to define a crime, and ordain its punishment.[49]

Chief Justice Marshall's acceptance of the policy of strict construction has been reiterated on numerous occasions since 1820. For example, when the Court was confronted with a provision of the 1968 Omnibus Crime Control and Safe Streets Act regarding possession of firearms by convicted felons, it adopted a narrow interpretation of the provision. Justice Marshall, speaking for the majority, reasoned that a narrow construction was appropriate because

first, "a fair warning should be given to the world in language that the common world will understand, of what the law intends to do if a certain line is passed. To make the warning fair, so fair as possible the line should be clear." . . . Second, because of the seriousness of criminal penalties, and because criminal punishment usually represents the moral condemnation of the community, legislatures and not courts should define criminal activity. This policy embodies "the instinctive distastes against men languishing in prison unless the lawmaker has clearly said they should." . . . Thus, where there is ambiguity in a criminal statute, doubts are resolved in favor of the defendant.[50]

Not only does the policy of strict construction apply to the elements of the crime, it also applies to any ambiguities regarding the prescribed punishment. For example, the Court held in *Bell v. United States* that the Mann Act did not expressly make the simultaneous interstate transportation of more than one woman for the purpose of prostitution liable to cumulative punishment for each woman transported, thus deciding against turning a single transaction into multiple offenses with cumulative punishment. There, Justice Frankfurter observed, "When Congress leaves to the Judiciary the task of imputing to Congress an undeclared will, the ambiguity should be resolved in favor of lenity."[51]

We should not conclude from Justice Frankfurter's comment that legislative determination to refrain from ambiguity will necessarily result in clear and precise penal laws. There are areas of the penal law that are plagued with problems of ambiguity, among them inchoate crimes (conspiracy), the law of attempts, and obscenity laws. But the problems of strict construction are by no means limited to these areas. Problems of ambiguity in penal law run the course of the traditional substantive criminal law (murder, armed robbery, auto theft, burglary). Ambiguity does become a more pressing issue when state legislatures and the Congress attempt to control socially and technologically complex problems by use of the criminal sanction, for example, in the new areas of consumer fraud, environmental pollution, and racketeering in interstate commerce.[52]

CONCLUSION

As the late Herbert Packer pointed out, the difficulty with the entire doctrinal web of legality is that the doctrines and canons come at the wrong point in the process.[53] The principle of legality is aimed primarily at legislatures and to some extent at police and prosecutors. Unless these agencies take the principle seriously, its impact will be slight. Careful, precise craftsmanship in legal drafting is the essential first step. The prospective application of new and revised criminal laws, particularly when they disadvantage the defense, is another. Finally, the principle of legality suggests that legislatures should approach with caution the expansion of the criminal law, especially expansion into areas where the mischief to be controlled has no set meaning or where the technological problems involved necessarily compound the issue of clarity.

NOTES

1. See Jerome Hall, *General Principles of Criminal Law*, 2d ed. (Indianapolis: Bobbs-Merrill, 1960), pp. 27–69.

2. See Herbert Packer, *The Limits of the Criminal Sanction* (Stanford, Calif.: Stanford University Press, 1968), pp. 87–97.

3. See Carl J. Friedrich, *Constitutional Government and Democracy* (Boston: Ginn, 1946), pp. 3–34.

4. Art. I, § 9, cl. 3; and art. I, § 10, cl. 1. The limitation on the suspension of the writ of habeas corpus and the provision for trial by jury in criminal cases were also part of the original Constitution, but the language applies only to the national government.

5. *Calder v. Bull*, 3 Dall. 386 (1798). Also see William W. Crossky, "The True Meaning of the Constitutional Prohibition of *Ex post Facto Laws*," 14 *U. Chi. L. Rev.* 539 (1947).

6. *Calder v. Bull*, 3 Dall. at 390.

7. See Crossky, "True Meaning."

8. Cf. Chief Justice Marshall's opinion in *Fletcher v. Peck*, 6 Cranch 87, 137–139 (1812); and the test oath cases, *Ex parte Garland*, 4 Wall. 333 (1867), and *Cummings v. Missouri*, 4 Wall. 277 (1867).

9. *Burgess v. Salmon*, 97 U.S. 381 (1878).

10. *Kentucky Union Co. v. Kentucky*, 219 U.S. 140 (1911).

11. *In re Medley*, 134 U.S. 160 (1890).

12. *Malloy v. South Carolina*, 237 U.S. 180 (1915).

13. *Rooney v. North Dakota*, 196 U.S. 319 (1905).

14. *Lindsey v. Washington*, 301 U.S. 397 (1937).

15. Ibid. at 401. Cf. *Eason v. Dunbar*, 367 F.2d 381 (1966); and *James v. Twomey*, 466 F.2d 718 (1972).

16. *Hopt v. Utah*, 110 U.S. 574, 590 (1884).

17. *Kring v. Missouri*, 107 U.S. 221, 232 (1883).

18. See *United States v. Hall*, 26 F. Cas No. 15, 285 C.C.D. Pa. (1809).

19. *Thompson v. Missouri*, 171 U.S. 380 (1898).

20. Ibid. at 387–388.

21. *Gibson v. Mississippi*, 162 U.S. 565, 590 (1896).

22. *Duncan v. Missouri*, 152 U.S. 377 (1894).

23. See *Williams v. Florida*, 399 U.S. 78 (1970).

24. *Thompson v. Utah*, 170 U.S. 343 (1897).

25. *Dobbert v. Florida*, 432 U.S. 282 (1977).

26. The change in the Florida law was made necessary by U.S. Supreme Court decisions that cast constitutional doubt on the state's existing death penalty law. See *Donaldson v. Sack*, 265 So.2d 499 (1972).

27. *Dobbert v. Florida*, 432 U.S. at 292.

28. *Furman v. Georgia*, 408 U.S. 238 (1972).

29. *Proffitt v. Florida*, 428 U.S. 242 (1976).

30. *Kring v. Missouri*, 107 U.S. 221, 232 (1882).

31. *United States v. Williams*, 475 F.2d 355 (1973).

32. *Talavera v. Wainwright*, 468 F.2d 1013 (1972); cf. *Beazell v. Ohio*, 269 U.S. 167 (1925).

33. The vagueness doctrine is a due process doctrine that applies to both state and federal criminal cases.

34. *Lanzetta v. New Jersey*, 306 U.S. 451, 453 (1939).

35. *Connally v. General Construction Co.*, 269 U.S. 385, 393 (1926).

36. *United States v. Reese*, 92 U.S. 214, 221 (1876).

37. *Pierce v. United States*, 314 U.S. 306, 311 (1941).

38. *Bouie v. City of Columbia*, 378 U.S. 347, 353 (1964).

39. *United States v. Petrillo*, 332 U.S. 1, 7 (1947).

40. See generally Forrest Lacey, "Vagrancy and Other Crimes of Personal Condition," 66 *Harv. L. Rev.* 1203 (1953).

41. See *United States ex rel. Newsome v. Malcolm*, 492 F.2d 1166 (1974).

42. *Recks v. United States*, 414 F.2d 1111 (1968).

43. Quoted in *Lazarus v. Faircloth*, 301 F. Supp. 266 (1969), vacated sub nom. *Shevin v. Lazarus*, 401 U.S. 987 (1971).

44. E.g., *New York v. Berck*, 300 N.E.2d 411 (1973), cert. denied, 94 S.Ct. 724 (1973); cf. *Pennsylvania v. Duncan*, 321 A.2d 917 (1974), upholding a state loitering law.

45. *Palmer v. Euclid*, 402 U.S. 544 (1971).

46. *Papachristou v. City of Jacksonville*, 405 U.S. 156 (1972). Vagrancy and breach of the peace laws may also raise First Amendment issues; see *Gooding v. Wilson*, 405 U.S. 518 (1972); *Coates v. City of Cincinnati*, 402 U.S. 611 (1971); and *Cox v. Louisiana*, 379 U.S. 536 (1965). Cf. *Colten v. Kentucky*, 407 U.S. 104 (1972), where the Supreme Court upheld a conviction under a disorderly conduct statute against a challenge of vagueness. The majority opinion noted that "the root of the vagueness doctrine is a rough idea of fairness. It is not a principle designed to convert into a constitutional dilemma the practical difficulties in drawing criminal states both general enough to take into account the variety of human conduct and sufficiently specific to provide fair warning that certain kinds of conduct are prohibited" (p. 111). But see *Ellis v. Dyson*, 421 U.S. 426 (1975), where the Court upheld the standing of petitioners to seek declaratory relief against an allegedly unconstitutional city loitering ordinance.

47. *Strict construction* relates to ambiguous penal laws and not to vague penal laws. *Vague penal laws* do not have ascertainable standards and are thus constitutionally unenforceable. *Ambiguous penal laws* are constitutionally enforceable once the judiciary has resolved the ambiguity by placing a narrow construction on the law. Furthermore, strict construction is not a due process doctrine, and, although it is generally followed in all criminal jurisdictions, it is not directly applied by the Supreme Court to state cases, presumably because as a general rule federal courts do not interpret state laws, but rather accept the construction of the highest state court. See Hall, *General Principles*, pp. 41–42.

48. *McBoyle v. United States*, 283 U.S. 25 (1931); cf. *McReynolds v. City of Ottumwa*, 207 N.W.2d 792 (1973).

49. *United States v. Wiltberger,* 5 Wheat. 73, 95 (1820).

50. *United States v. Bass,* 404 U.S. 336, 347–348 (1971).

51. *Bell v. United States,* 349 U.S. 81, 83 (1955).

52. E.g., *New Jersey v. Angelo's Motor Sales, Inc.,* 310 A.2d 97 (1973); *Mourning v. Family Publications,* 411 U.S. 356 (1973); and *United States v. Emmons,* 410 U.S. 396 (1973).

53. Packer, *Limits of the Criminal Sanction,* pp. 95–96.

JUDICIAL DECISIONS

Procedural Changes and Ex post Facto Laws:
Dobbert v. Florida, 432 U.S. 282 (1977)

Mr. Justice REHNQUIST delivered the opinion of the Court.

Petitioner was convicted of murder in the first degree, murder in the second degree, child abuse, and child torture. The victims were his children. Under the Florida death penalty statute then in effect he was sentenced by the trial judge to death. The Florida Supreme Court affirmed and we granted certiorari to consider whether changes in the Florida death penalty statutes subjected him to trial under an ex post facto law. . . . We conclude that petitioner has not shown the deprivation of any federal constitutional right, and affirm the judgment of the Florida Supreme Court.

I

Petitioner was convicted of murdering his daughter Kelly Ann, age 9, and his son Ryder Scott, age 7. He was also found guilty of torturing his son Ernest John, age 11, and of abusing his daughter Honore Elizabeth, age 5. The brutality and heinousness of these crimes are relevant both to petitioner's motion for a change of venue due to pretrial publicity and to the trial judge's imposition of the sentence of death. The trial judge, in his factual findings at the sentencing phase of the trial, summarized petitioner's treatment of his own offspring as follows:

> "The evidence and testimony showed premeditated and continuous torture, brutality, sadism and unspeakable horrors committed against all of the children over a period of time."

. . .

This sordid tale began to unravel in early 1972 when Ernest John III was found battered and wandering in Jacksonville, Fla. An arrest warrant was issued for petitioner, who evidently fled the area. About a year later, Honore Elizabeth was found in a Ft. Lauderdale hospital with a note pinned to her clothing asking that she be sent to her mother in Wisconsin. Shortly thereafter petitioner's abandoned automobile was found near a bridge with a suicide note on the front seat. Petitioner, however, had fled to Texas, where he was eventually arrested and extradited to Florida.

. . .

Trial was had and the jury found petitioner guilty of inter alia, murder in the first degree. Pursuant to the Florida death penalty statute then in effect, a sentencing hearing was held before the judge and jury. The jury by a 10-to-2 majority found sufficient mitigating circumstances to outweigh any aggravating circumstances and recommended a sentence of life imprisonment. The trial judge, pursuant to his authority under the amended Florida statute, overruled the jury's recommendation and sentenced petitioner to death. The Florida Supreme Court affirmed over two dissents.

II

Petitioner makes three separate claims based on the prohibition against ex post facto laws. . . . His first ex post facto claim is addressed to the change in the function of judge and jury in the imposition of death sentences in Florida between the time he committed the acts charged and the time he was tried for them. The second ex post facto claim is grounded on his contention that at the time he acted there was no valid death penalty statute in effect in Florida. The third claim relates to the more stringent parole requirements attached to a life sentence under the new law. A discussion of the relevant changes in Florida death sentencing procedures brings these claims into focus.

The murders for which petitioner was convicted were alleged to have occurred on December 31, 1971 (Kelly Ann) and between January 1 and April 8, 1972 (Ryder Scott). During that period of time, F.S.A. §§ 775.082 (1971) and 921.141 (1971), as then written, provided that a person convicted of a capital felony was to be punished by death unless the verdict included a recommendation of mercy by a majority of the jury.*

On June 22, 1972, this Court struck down a Georgia death penalty statute as violative of the Eighth and Fourteenth Amendments. *Furman v. Georgia,* 408 U.S. 238 (1972). Shortly thereafter, on July 17, 1972, in *Donaldson v. Sack,* 265 So.2d 499 (Fla. 1972), the Florida Supreme Court found the 1971 Florida death penalty statutes inconsistent with *Furman.* Late in 1972 Florida enacted a new death penalty procedure, Chapter 72–724, Laws of Florida (1972), amending, inter alia, §§ 775.082 and 921.141.

The opinion . . . in *Proffitt v. Florida,* 428 U.S. 242 (1976), in which the constitutionality of this statute was upheld, details at length the operation of the revised § 921.141. After a defendant is found guilty of a capital felony, a separate sentencing hearing is held before the trial judge and the trial jury. Any evidence that the judge deems relevant to sentencing may be admitted, and certain evidence relating to aggravating or mitigating circumstances must be admitted. The jury, by a majority vote, then renders an advisory decision, not binding on the court, based upon these aggravating and mitigating circumstances. The court must then also weigh the aggravating and mitigating circumstances. If the court imposes a sentence of death, it must set forth written findings of fact regarding the aggravating and mitigating circumstances. A judgment of conviction and sentence of death is then subject to an automatic, priority review by the Florida Supreme Court. It is in the light of these changes that we must adjudge petitioner's ex post facto claims.

A

Petitioner argues that the change in the role of the judge and jury in the imposition of the death sentence in Florida between the time of the murders and the time of the trial constitutes an ex post facto violation. Petitioner views the change in the Florida death sentencing procedure as depriving him of a substantial right to have

* The text of those statutes is as follows: "Recommendation to mercy.—A defendant found guilty by a jury of an offense punishable by death shall be sentenced to death unless the verdict includes a recommendation to mercy by a majority of the jury. When the verdict includes a recommendation to mercy by a majority of the jury, the court shall sentence the defendant to life imprisonment. A defendant found guilty by the court of an offense punishable by death on a plea of guilty or when a jury is waived shall be sentenced by the court to death or life imprisonment." Fla. Stat., § 921.141 (1971).

the jury determine, without review by the trial judge, whether that penalty should be imposed. We conclude that the changes in the law are procedural, and on the whole ameliorative, and that there is no ex post facto violation.

Article I, § 10, of the United States Constitution prohibits a State from passing any "ex post facto Law." Our cases have not attempted to precisely delimit the scope of this Latin phrase, but have instead given it substance by an accretion of case law. In *Beazell v. Ohio*, 269 U.S. 167, 169 (1925), Mr. Justice Stone summarized for the Court the characteristics of an ex post facto law:

> "It is settled, by decisions of this Court so well known that their citation may be dispensed with, that any statute which punishes as a crime an act previously committed, which was innocent when done; which makes more burdensome the punishment for a crime, after its commission, or which deprives one charged with crime of any defense available according to law at the time when the act was committed, is prohibited as ex post facto."

It is equally well settled, however, that "the inhibition upon the passage of ex post facto laws does not give a criminal a right to be tried, in all respects, by the law in force when the crime charged was committed." *Gibson v. Mississippi*, 162 U.S. 565, 590 (1896). . . .

Even though it may work to the disadvantage of a defendant, a procedural change is not ex post facto. For example, in *Hopt v. Utah*, 110 U.S. 574 (1884), as of the date of the alleged homicide a convicted felon could not have been called as a witness. Subsequent to that date, but prior to the trial of the case, this law was changed; a convicted felon was called to the stand and testified, implicating Hopt in the crime charged against him. Even though this change in the law obviously had a detrimental impact upon the defendant, the Court found that the law was not ex post facto because it neither made criminal a theretofor innocent act, nor aggravated a crime previously committed, nor provided greater punishment, nor changed the proof necessary to convict.

. . .

In the case at hand, the change in the statute was clearly procedural. The new statute simply altered the methods employed in determining whether the death penalty was to be imposed; there was no change in the quantum of punishment attached to the crime. . . .

In this case, not only was the change in the law procedural, it was ameliorative. It is axiomatic that for a law to be ex post facto it must be more onerous than the prior law. Petitioner argues that the change in the law harmed him because the jury's recommendation of life imprisonment would not have been subject to review by the trial judge under the prior law. But it certainly cannot be said with assurance that, had his trial been conducted under the old statute, the jury would have returned a verdict of life.

Hence, petitioner's speculation that the jury would have recommended life were the prior procedure in effect is not compelling. We must compare the two statutory procedures in toto to determine if the new may be fairly characterized as more onerous. Under the old procedure, the death penalty was "presumed" unless the jury, in its unbridled discretion, made a recommendation for mercy. The Florida Legislature enacted the new procedure specifically to provide the constitutional procedural protections required by *Furman*, thus providing capital defendants with more, rather than less, judicial protection. These protections, upheld by this Court in *Proffitt,* provided are substantial. A separate hearing is held; the defendant is allowed to present any relevant mitigating evidence. The jury renders an advisory verdict based upon its perception of aggravating and mitigating factors in the case. The court makes the final determination, but may impose death only after making a written finding that there are insufficient mitigating circumstances to outweigh the aggravating circumstances.

Finally, in what may be termed a tripartite review, the Florida Supreme Court is required to review each sentence of death. This required review, not present under the old procedure, is by no means perfunctory; . . . This crucial protection demonstrates that the new statute affords significantly more safeguards to the defendant than did the old. Death is not automatic, absent a jury recommendation of mercy, as it was under the old procedure. . . .

B

Petitioner's second ex post facto claim is based on the contention that at the time he murdered his children there was no death penalty "in effect" in Florida. This is so, he contends, because the earlier statute enacted by the legislature was, after the time he acted, found by the Supreme Court of Florida to be invalid under our decision in *Furman v. Georgia,* supra. Therefore, argues petitioner, there was no "valid" death penalty in effect in Florida as of the date of his actions. But this sophistic argument mocks the substance of the ex post facto clause. Whether or not the old statute would in the future, withstand constitutional attack, it clearly indicated Florida's view of the severity of murder and of the degree of punishment which the legislature wished to impose upon murderers. The statute was intended to provide maximum deterrence, and its existence on the statute books provided fair warning as to the degree of culpability which the State ascribed to the act of murder.

. . .

C

Petitioner's third ex post facto contention is based on the fact that the new Florida statute provides that anyone sentenced to life imprisonment under that section must serve at least 25 years before becoming eligible for parole. The prior section contained no such limitation. The Florida Supreme Court in *Lee v. State,* 294 So.2d 305 (1974), found that this provision restricting parole could not constitutionally be applied to crimes committed prior to its effective date. Petitioner contends that nonetheless its enactment by the Florida Legislature amounts to an ex post facto law, and that because of this he may successfully challenge the death sentence imposed upon him.

Petitioner, of course, did not receive a life sentence, and so any added onus attaching to it as a result of the change in Florida law had no effect on him. In *Lindsey v. Washington,* 301 U.S. 397, 400–401, the Court stated:

> ". . . The Constitution forbids the application of any new punitive measure to a crime already consummated, to the detriment or material disadvantage of the wrongdoer. *It is for this reason that an increase in the possible penalty is ex post facto,*

regardless of the length of the sentence actually imposed, since the measure of punishment prescribed by the later statute is more severe than that of the earlier." (Emphasis added.)

Lifted from their context and read expansively, the italicized portions of the quoted language would lend some support to petitioner's claim. But we think that consideration of the *Lindsey* language in the factual context in which that case was decided does not lead to the result sought by petitioner.

. . .

Petitioner here can make no claim comparable to Lindsey's. Under the new law, both life imprisonment and death remain as possible alternative sentences. Only if we were to read the excerpted portion of the quoted language from *Lindsey* to confer standing on the defendant to complain of an added burden newly attached to a sentence which was never imposed on him would that language assist him. But we hold that petitioner, having been sentenced to death, may not complain of burdens attached to the life sentence under the new law which may not have attached to it under the old.

. . . The judgment of the Supreme Court of Florida is therefore

Affirmed.

Mr. Justice STEVENS, with whom Mr. Justice BRENNAN and Mr. Justice MARSHALL join, dissenting.

Only a few simple facts are relevant to the question of law presented by this case. At the time of petitioner's offense, there was no constitutional procedure for imposing the death penalty in Florida. Several months after his offense, Florida enacted the death penalty statute that was upheld in *Proffitt v. Florida,* 428 U.S. 242. Before this statute was passed, as a matter of Florida law, the crime committed by petitioner was not a capital offense. It is undisputed, therefore, that a law passed after the offense is the source of Florida's power to put petitioner to death.

The Court holds that Florida may apply this law to petitioner without violating the ex post facto clause. In its view, the unconstitutional law which was on the Florida statute books at the time of the offense "clearly indicated Florida's view of the severity of murder and of the degree of punishment which the legislature wished to impose upon murderers." The Court concludes that the "fair warning" provided by the invalid statute "was sufficient compliance with the ex post facto provision of the United States Constitution."

This conclusion represents a clear departure from the test the Court has applied in past cases construing the ex post facto clause. That test was stated in *Lindsey v. Washington,* 301 U.S. 397, 401, in language that might have been written with the present case in mind:

"The Constitution forbids the application of any new punitive measure to a crime already consummated, to the detriment or material disadvantage of the wrongdoer."

. . . In the case before us the new standard created the possibility of a death sentence that could not have been lawfully imposed when the offense was committed. A more dramatically different standard of punishment is difficult to envision.

. . .

The Vagueness Doctrine:
Papachristou v. Jacksonville, 405 U.S. 156 (1972)

Mr. Justice DOUGLAS delivered the opinion of the Court.

This case involves eight defendants who were convicted in a Florida municipal court of violating a Jacksonville, Florida, vagrancy ordinance. Their convictions, entailing fines and jail sentences (some of which were suspended), were affirmed by the Florida Circuit Court in a consolidated appeal, and their petition for certiorari was denied by the District Court of Appeal, 236 So.2d 141, on the authority of *Johnson v. State*, Fla., 202 So.2d 852. The case is here on a petition for certiorari, which we granted. For reasons which will appear, we reverse.

At issue are five consolidated cases. Margaret Papachristou, Betty Calloway, Eugene Eddie Melton, and Leonard Johnson were all arrested early on a Sunday morning, and charged with vagrancy—"prowling by auto."

Jimmy Lee Smith and Milton Henry were charged with vagrancy—"vagabonds."

Henry Edward Heath and a codefendant were arrested for vagrancy—"loitering" and "common thief."

Thomas Owen Campbell was charged with vagrancy—"common thief."

Hugh Brown was charged with vagrancy—"disorderly loitering on street" and "disorderly conduct—resisting arrest with violence."

The facts are stipulated. Papachristou and Calloway are white females. Melton and Johnson are black males. Papachristou was enrolled in a job-training program sponsored by the State Employment Service at Florida Junior College in Jacksonville. Calloway was a typing and shorthand teacher at a state mental institution located near Jacksonville. She was the owner of the automobile in which the four defendants were arrested. Melton was a Vietnam war veteran who had been released from the Navy after nine months in a veterans' hospital. On the date of his arrest he was a part-time computer helper while attending college as a full-time student in Jacksonville. Johnson was a tow-motor operator in a grocery chain warehouse and was a lifelong resident of Jacksonville.

At the time of their arrest the four of them were riding in Calloway's car on the main thoroughfare in Jacksonville. They had left a restaurant owned by Johnson's uncle where they had eaten and were on their way to a nightclub. The arresting officers denied that the racial mixture in the car played any part in the decision to make the arrest. The arrest, they said, was made because the defendants had stopped near a used-car lot which had been broken into several times. There was, however, no evidence of any breaking and entering on the night in question.

Of these four charged with "prowling by auto" none had been previously arrested except Papachristou who had once been convicted of a municipal offense.

Jimmy Lee Smith and Milton Henry (who is not a petitioner) were arrested between 9 and 10 a.m. on a weekday in downtown Jacksonville, while waiting for a friend who was to lend them a car so they could apply for a job at a produce company. Smith was a part-time produce worker and part-time organizer for a Negro political group. He had a common-law wife and three children supported by him and his wife. He had been arrested several times but convicted only once. Smith's companion, Henry, was an 18-year-old high school student with no previous record of arrest.

This morning it was cold, and Smith had no jacket, so they went briefly into a dry cleaning shop to wait, but left when requested to do so. They thereafter walked back and forth two or three times over a two-block stretch looking for their friend. The store owners, who apparently were wary of Smith and his companion, summoned two police officers who searched the men and found neither had a weapon. But they were arrested because the officers said they had no identification and because the officers did not believe their story.

Heath and a codefendant were arrested for "loitering" and for "common thief." Both were residents of Jacksonville, Heath having lived there all his life and being employed at an automobile body shop. Heath had previously been arrested but his codefendant had no arrest record. Heath and his companion were arrested when they drove up to a residence shared by Heath's girlfriend and some other girls. Some police officers were already there in the process of arresting another man. When Heath and his companion started backing out of the driveway, the officers signaled to them to stop and asked them to get out of the car, which they did. Thereupon they and the automobile were searched. Although no contraband or incriminating evidence was found, they were both arrested, Heath being charged with being a "common thief" because he was reputed to be a thief. The codefendant was charged with "loitering" because he was standing in the driveway, an act which the officers admitted was done only at their command.

Campbell was arrested as he reached his home very early one morning and was charged with "common thief." He was stopped by officers because he was traveling at a high rate of speed, yet no speeding charge was placed against him.

Brown was arrested when he was observed leaving a downtown Jacksonville hotel by a police officer seated in a cruiser. The police testified he was reputed to be a thief, narcotics pusher, and generally opprobrious character. The officer called Brown over to the car, intending at that time to arrest him unless he had a good explanation for being on the street. Brown walked over to the police cruiser, as commanded, and the officer began to search him, apparently preparatory to placing him in the car. In the process of the search he came on two small packets which were later found to contain heroin. When the officer touched the pocket where the packets were, Brown began to resist. He was charged with "disorderly loitering on street" and "disorderly conduct—resisting arrest with violence." While he was also charged with a narcotics violation, that charge was nolled.

Jacksonville's ordinance and Florida's statute were "derived from early English law," *Johnson v. State,* 202 So.2d, at 854, and employ "archaic language" in their definitions of vagrants. Id., at 855. The history is an often-told tale. The breakup of feudal estates in England led to labor shortages which in turn resulted in the Statutes of Laborers, designed to stabilize the labor force by prohibiting increases in wages and prohibiting the movement of workers from their home areas in search of improved conditions. Later vagrancy laws became criminal aspects of the poor laws. The series of laws passed in England on the subject became increasingly severe. But "the theory of the Elizabethan poor laws no longer fits the facts." *Edwards v. California,* 314 U.S. 160, 174. The conditions which spawned these laws may be gone, but the archaic classifications remain.

This ordinance is void for vagueness, both in the sense that it "fails to give a person of ordinary intelligence fair notice that his contemplated conduct is forbidden by the statute," *United States v. Harriss,* 347 U.S. 612, 617, and because it encourages arbitrary and erratic arrests and convictions.

Living under a rule of law entails various suppositions, one of which is that "[all persons] are entitled to be informed as to what the State commands or forbids." *Lanzetta v. New Jersey,* 306 U.S. 451, 453.

Lanzetta is one of a well-recognized group of cases insisting that the law give fair notice of the offending conduct. In the field of regulatory statutes governing business activities, where the acts limited are in a narrow category, greater leeway is allowed.

The poor among us, the minorities, the average householder are not in business and not alerted to the regulatory schemes of vagrancy laws; and we assume they would have no understanding of their meaning and impact if they read them. Nor are they protected from being caught in the vagrancy net by the necessity of having a specific intent to commit an unlawful act.

The Jacksonville ordinance makes criminal activities which by modern standards are normally innocent. "Nightwalking" is one. Florida construes the ordinance not to make criminal one night's wandering, *Johnson v. State,* 202 So.2d, at 855, only the "habitual" wanderer or, as the ordinance describes it, "common night walkers." We know, however, from experience that sleepless people often walk at night, perhaps hopeful that sleep-inducing relaxation will result.

. . .

"Persons able to work but habitually living upon the earnings of their wives or minor children"—like habitually living "without visible means of support"—might implicate unemployed pillars of the community who have married rich wives.

"Persons able to work but habitually living upon the earnings of their wives or minor children" may also embrace unemployed people out of the labor market, by reason of a recession or disemployed by reason of technological or so-called structural displacements.

Persons "wandering or strolling" from place to place have been extolled by Walt Whitman and Vachel Lindsay. The qualification "without any lawful purpose or object" may be a trap for innocent acts. Persons "neglecting all lawful business and habitually spending their time by frequenting . . . places where alcoholic beverages are sold or served" would literally embrace many members of golf clubs and city clubs.

Walkers and strollers and wanderers may be going to or coming from a burglary. Loafers or loiterers may be "casing" a place for a holdup. Letting one's wife support him is an intra-family matter, and normally of no concern to the police. Yet it may, of course, be the setting for numerous crimes.

The difficulty is that these activities are historically part of the amenities of life as we have known them. They are not mentioned in the Constitution or in the Bill of Rights. These unwritten amenities have been in part responsible for giving our people the feeling of independence and self-confidence, the feeling of creativity. These amenities have dignified the right of dissent and have honored the right to be nonconformists and the right to defy submissiveness. They have encouraged lives of high spirits rather than hushed, suffocating silence.

They are embedded in Walt Whitman's writings, especially in his "Song of the Open Road." They are reflected too, in the spirit of Vachel Lindsay's "I Want to Go Wandering," and by Henry D. Thoreau.

This aspect of the vagrancy ordinance before us is suggested by what this Court said in 1876 about a broad criminal statute enacted by Congress: "It would certainly be dangerous if the legislature could set a net large enough to catch all possible offenders, and leave it to the courts to step inside and say who could be rightfully detained, and who should be set at large." *United States v. Reese*, 92 U.S. 214, 221.

While that was a federal case, the due process implications are equally applicable to the States and to this vagrancy ordinance. Here the net cast is large, not to give the courts the power to pick and choose but to increase the arsenal of the police. In *Winters v. New York*, 333 U.S. 507, the Court struck down a New York statute that made criminal the distribution of a magazine made up principally of items of criminal deeds of bloodshed or lust so massed as to become vehicles for inciting violent and depraved crimes against the person. The infirmity the Court found was vagueness —the absence of "ascertainable standards of guilt" in the sensitive First Amendment area. . . .

Where the list of crimes is so all-inclusive and generalized as the one in this ordinance, those convicted may be punished for no more than vindicating affronts to police authority:

> "The common ground which brings such a motley assortment of human troubles before the magistrates in vagrancy-type proceedings is the procedural laxity which permits 'conviction' for almost any kind of conduct and the existence of the House of Correction as an easy and convenient dumping-ground for problems that appear to have no other immediate solution." Foote, "Vagrancy-Type Law and Its Administration," 104 U. Pa. L. Rev. 603, 631.

Another aspect of the ordinance's vagueness appears when we focus, not on the lack of notice given a potential offender, but on the effect of the unfettered discretion it places in the hands of the Jacksonville police. Caleb Foote, an early student of this subject, has called the vagrancy-type law as offering "punishment by analogy." Id., at 609. Such crimes, though long common in Russia, are not compatible with our constitutional system. We allow our police to make arrests only on "probable cause," a Fourth and Fourteenth Amendment standard applicable to the States as well as to the Federal Government. Arresting a person on suspicion, like arresting a person for investigation, is foreign to our system, even when the arrest is for past criminality. Future criminality, however, is the common justification for the presence of vagrancy statutes. . . .

A direction by a legislature to the police to arrest all "suspicious" persons would not pass constitutional muster. A vagrancy prosecution may be merely the cloak for a conviction which could not be obtained on the real but undisclosed grounds for the arrest. *People v. Moss*, 309 N.Y. 429. But as Chief Justice Hewart said in *Frederick Dean*, 18 Crim. App. 133, 134 (1924):

> "It would be in the highest degree unfortunate if in any part of the country those who are responsible for setting in motion the criminal law should entertain, connive at or coquette with the idea that in a case where there is not enough evidence to charge the prisoner with an attempt to commit a crime, the prosecution may, nevertheless, on such insufficient evidence, succeed in obtaining and upholding a conviction under the Vagrancy Act, 1824."

Those generally implicated by the imprecise terms of the ordinance—poor people, nonconformists, dissenters, idlers—may be required to comport themselves according to the life style deemed appropriate by the Jacksonville police and the courts. Where, as here, there are no standards governing the exercise of the discretion granted by the ordinance, the scheme permits and encourages an arbitrary and discriminatory enforcement of the law. It furnishes a convenient tool for "harsh and discriminatory enforcement by local prosecuting officials, against particular groups deemed to merit their displeasure." *Thornhill v. Alabama,* 310 U.S. 88, 97–98. It results in a regime in which the poor and the unpopular are permitted to "stand on a public sidewalk . . . only at the whim of any police officer." *Shuttleworth v. Birmingham,* 382 U.S. 87, 90. . . .

A presumption that people who might walk or loaf or loiter or stroll or frequent houses where liquor is sold, or who are supported by their wives or who look suspicious to the police are to become future criminals is too precarious for a rule of law. The implicit presumption in these generalized vagrancy standards—that crime is being nipped in the bud—is too extravagant to deserve extended treatment. Of course, vagrancy statutes are useful to the police. Of course, they are nets making easy the roundup of so-called undesirables. But the rule of law implies equality and justice in its application. Vagrancy laws of the Jacksonville type teach that the scales of justice are so tipped that even-handed administration of the law is not possible. The rule of law, evenly applied to minorities as well as majorities, to the poor as well as the rich, is the great mucilage that holds society together.

The Jacksonville ordinance cannot be squared with our constitutional standards and is plainly unconstitutional.

Reversed.

3

Arrest,
Search,
and
Seizure

The right of the people to be
secure in their persons, houses, papers, and effects, against
unreasonable searches and seizures, shall not be violated, and
no Warrants shall issue, but upon probable cause, supported
by Oath or affirmation, and particularly describing the place
to be searched, and the persons or things to be seized.

—Fourth Amendment

THE FOUNDATIONS OF THE FOURTH AMENDMENT

The security we enjoy against unreasonable searches and seizures and the
procedures that effectuate reasonable process did not come to us suddenly and
in perfect form. Like many of the provisions that reduce arbitrary actions of
the government and protect liberty, the rights of privacy protected under the
Fourth Amendment have evolved slowly and somewhat unevenly. Even today,
controversy surrounds the Fourth Amendment. Its critics see it as a shield for
criminals, as indeed at times it is. Yet the liberty embodied in this amendment
is essential to a constitutional government. The privacy we have come to expect
in our homes and offices against unreasonable invasion by the government and
the freedom from arbitary arrest are central to our liberty. However cumbersome and complex the laws of arrest, search, and seizure may have become, its
historical foundations suggest that a measure of privacy has long been a goal
of Western societies.

Long before the modern state assumed major responsibilities for social control, Biblical writers recorded a strong respect for the privacy of the dwelling.[1] Roman law also protected the privacy of the dwelling and developed rather elaborate procedures for the recovery of stolen goods alleged to be hidden in private homes.[2] And even the somewhat undeveloped legal system of Anglo-Saxon England recognized the crime of *hamsocn,* the forcible invasion of a home. In Norman England, as the King assumed increasing responsibilities for maintaining the peace, procedures evolved for both empowering an army to put down violence (the *posse comitatus* of the sheriff) and a more formal system of warrants for searches, seizures, and arrests.[3] Although the modern concept of unreasonable searches and seizures clearly has some historical foundation in these earlier procedures, it was not formalized until after the Glorious Revolution of 1689—that is, until after the broad outlines of the modern state were firmly established and the Whigish notion of limited government had become accepted political theory. In short, it is in eighteenth century England and America that we find the rapid development of the doctrines associated with unreasonable searches and seizures.

Although the law associated with the writ of habeas corpus was well established by the end of the seventeenth century, the great writ provided only the machinery to obtain release or bail after the fact of arrest. The protection against illegal arrest had to await the abuses of executive power during the reign of George III, both in England and America. In England, in the early 1760s, the catalyst was a series of searches and arrests under general, rather than specific, warrants, which had been issued by an officer of the crown rather than by a magistrate. These executive warrants were aimed at what the crown felt were seditious libels that had been printed in several journals, among them John Wilkes's *North Briton.* The arrest of Wilkes, a member of the House of Commons, and the seizure of various articles and pamphlets gave rise to a number of civil suits for damages, which Wilkes and several printers were awarded.[4] Perhaps the most famous opinion delivered in all of these eighteenth-century cases was that of Lord Camden in *Entick v. Carrington* (1765). Entick's home was broken into by messengers of the King on the authority of a general warrant issued by Lord Halifax. The messengers seized a quantity of private papers and pamphlets. Camden's judgment against Carrington has given shape to the law of search and seizure for over two hundred years. He wrote:

> To search, seize, and carry away all the papers of the subject upon the first warrant: that such a right should have existed from the time whereof the memory of man runneth not to the contrary, and never yet have found a place in any book of law; is incredible. But if so strange a thing could be supposed, I do not see how we could declare the law upon such evidence.
>
> But still it is insisted, that there has been a general submission, and no action brought to try the right.
>
> I answer, there has been a submission of guilt and poverty to power and the terror of punishment. But it would be strange doctrine to assert that all the

people of this land are bound to acknowledge that to be universal law, which a few criminal booksellers have been afraid to dispute.[5]

Lord Camden's opinion won him popular acclaim, and he was shortly made lord chancellor. But his support of Wilkes and especially his liberal views on the American colonies finally cost him the post. Indeed, there is some irony in the fact that Camden's career had been promoted by his good friend William Pitt. It was Pitt who followed up Camden's condemnation of general warrants by successfully leading the House of Commons in 1766 to declare that general warrants were universally invalid. It was Pitt, who, in the course of debate, declared: "The poorest man may, in his cottage, bid defiance to all the forces of the Crown. It may be frail; its roof may shake; the wind may blow through it; the storm may enter; the rain may enter; but the King of England may not enter; all his force dares not cross the threshold of the ruined tenement."[6]

Yet it was this same Pitt who, as Secretary of State in 1760, had instructed the Colonial governors to enforce the Acts of Trade, thus precipitating the writs of assistance case in Boston in 1761. The writs were general warrants for the seizure of smuggled goods and were the American analogue to the general warrants involved in Wilkes's case. The colonists deeply resented these writs, not only because they were neither specific nor backed by probable cause, or oath, but more importantly because they were an attempt by London to end the lucrative trade in uncustomed goods with the West Indies. Although James Otis lost in his defense of the Boston merchants, John Adams, a young courtroom spectator, was later to say: "Then and there was the first scene of the first act of opposition. . . . Then and there the child Independence was born."[7] Perhaps. But more likely, the writs were to contribute directly to several of the newly independent states' adopting provisions against general warrants and, ultimately, to the proposal by James Madison in 1789 to include a similar provision in the Bill of Rights. Madison's proposal was broadened to include not only a proscription against general warrants, but a proscription against all unreasonable searches and seizures. It was adopted as the Fourth Amendment.[8]

THE SCOPE OF PROTECTED PRIVACY

It was not until 1886, in *Boyd v. United States*, that the Supreme Court handed down an opinion interpreting the Fourth Amendment. In that year, the Court struck down a portion of an act of Congress that required a defendant to produce in court private books, papers, and invoices—the functional equivalent of a *subpoena duces tecum*. The case involved forfeiture proceedings under a revenue act that provided that a refusal to produce the requested documents would be considered a confession to the government's allegations. In effect, there was no actual search and seizure, but rather what the Court called a constructive search and seizure. This did not deter Justice Bradley, who proceeded to tie together the Fourth Amendment and the self-incrimination clause of the Fifth Amendment. Relying on *Entick v. Carrington,* he wrote:

> The principles laid down in this opinion affect the very essence of constitutional liberty and security. They reach farther than the concrete form of the case then before the court, with its adventitious circumstances; they apply to all invasions, on the part of the Government and its employees, of the sanctity of a man's home and the privacies of life. It is not the breaking of his doors and the rummaging of his drawers that constitutes the essence of the offense; but it is the invasion of his indefensible right of personal security, personal liberty and private property, where that right has never been forfeited by his conviction of some public offense; it is the invasion of this sacred right which underlies and constitutes the essence of Lord Camden's judgment. Breaking into a house and opening boxes and drawers are circumstances of aggravation; but any forcible and compulsory extortion of a man's own testimony or of his private papers to be used as evidence to convict him of crime or to forfeit his goods is within the condemnation of that judgment. In this regard the Fourth and Fifth Amendments run almost into each other.[9]

The importance of *Boyd* lies not so much in the narrow ruling on documents and invoices, [10] but in the sweeping view of the protection against unreasonable intrusions adopted by the Court. At least until the advent of the Burger Court, this liberal interpretation influenced later doctrinal developments in all areas with the exception of those associated with automobiles.

After *Boyd,* the Court frequently turned its attention to delineating the specific areas or places protected by the amendment. The protection has extended beyond the home to hotel rooms,[11] to garages adjacent to homes,[12] to offices,[13] to automobiles,[14] and to sealed letters.[15] Yet the scope of protection of the Fourth Amendment cannot be determined by mere reference to constitutionally protected areas. Whether a given place, even a home,[16] is protected depends on whether a person has demonstrated an expectation of privacy in the place and whether society is prepared to recognize the expectation as reasonable.[17] To expect constitutional privacy in an open field, for example, is unreasonable.[18] In 1967, the Court held that under certain conditions one has a right to expect privacy in a public phone booth. Justice Stewart, writing for the majority in this case, approached the issue of scope in the following manner:

> . . . The correct solution of Fourth Amendment problems is not necessarily promoted by incantation of the phrase "constitutionally protected area." . . . The Fourth Amendment cannot be translated into a general constitutional "right to privacy." That Amendment protects individual privacy against certain kinds of governmental intrusion, but its protections go further, and often have nothing to do with privacy at all. Other provisions of the Constitution protect

personal privacy from other forms of governmental invasion. But the protection of a person's right to privacy—his right to be left alone by other people—is, like the protection of his property and of his very life, left largely to the law of the individual States.

. . . This effort to decide whether or not a given "area," viewed in the abstract, is "constitutionally protected" deflects attention from the problem presented by this case. For the Fourth Amendment protects people, not places. What a person knowingly exposes to the public, even in his own home or office, is not a subject of Fourth Amendment protection.

. . . But what he seeks to preserve as private, even in an area accessible to the public, may be constitutionally protected.[19]

Although one's expectation of privacy is undoubtedly crucial to the application of the Fourth Amendment, as a standard for police conduct it is too abstract, based as it is, to a great extent, on a person's state of mind. A standard for law enforcement behavior must rest on the more generalized and widely accepted expectation of privacy that people have in certain places and things, in particular, in the privacy of the home.

Dwellings and Other Private Areas

One of the hallmarks of a free society is the expectation that the government will respect the privacy of the home. Indeed, long before there was a fully developed law of search and seizure, English law recognized that the home was normally to be protected against governmental invasion.[20] Contemporary law has incorporated this expectation by generally requiring that the reasonable search of a home must be by either warrant or consent. The Fourth Amendment, of course, does not preclude the government from making a reasonable search of a home, but the beginning point in determining whether a search is reasonable is the presence of a valid search warrant. Indeed, in a 1925 case, the Supreme Court noted: "The search of a private dwelling without a warrant is, in itself, unreasonable and abhorrent to our laws."[21] This does not deny police officers the right to enter and search: "The point of the Fourth Amendment, which often is not grasped by zealous officers, is not that it denies law enforcement the support of the usual inferences which reasonable men draw from evidence. Its protection consists in requiring that those inferences be drawn by a neutral and detached magistrate instead of being judged by the officer engaged in the often competitive enterprise of ferreting out crime."[22]

In short, the home is a constitutionally protected area—an area that has such a widely held expectation of privacy that reasonable governmental intrusion must normally be accomplished only by means of a search warrant. The major exceptions to this warrant requirement are the incidental search and the search in hot pursuit.

The Incidental Search

Although delay and inconvenience are not accepted as justification for dispensing with a warrant, the Court has recognized a limited number of exceptional circumstances that do justify dispensing with a search warrant. The most widely reported exception is the limited search incidental to an otherwise valid arrest. In *Agnello v. United States,* the Court rejected the warrantless search of Agnello's home as incidental to an earlier arrest that occurred several blocks away. However, the Court did note that "the right without a search warrant contemporaneously to search persons lawfully arrested while committing crime, and to search the place where the arrest is made in order to find and seize things connected with the crime as its fruits, or as the means by which it was committed, as well as weapons and other things to effect an escape from custody, is not to be doubted."[23]

Incidental search of a protected area raises two issues. The first concerns the validity of the initial entry into a protected area. By common-law doctrine, codified in a majority of the states, a police officer may enter a protected area without a search warrant in order to make an arrest. The validity of the so-called arrest entries has never been directly ruled on by the Supreme Court. Rather, both federal and state courts have subsumed the issue of entry under the incidental-search doctrine.[24] On the other hand, the mere execution of a valid arrest does not immediately appear to fall within the exceptional circumstances that would justify dispensing with a search warrant to enter a home.

Clearly, if an arrest entry is used as a pretext for gaining entry in order to search, then the Fourth Amendment's protection of privacy would appear to be defeated. For example, if there is a deliberate delay in an arrest so as to enable officers to gain entry into a protected area, then a resulting search is clearly not incidental to the arrest.[25] But beyond this issue is the whole question of whether arrest entry can be justified. In the 1960s, in one instance, a valid arrest warrant on a murder charge was used as justification for the warrantless search of more than three hundred private homes.[26] Certainly, the immediate historical background of the adoption of the Fourth Amendment makes it clear that general warrants were proscribed. Calling a warrant a specific arrest warrant does not alter this constitutional proscription.

Of course, there can be a practical problem: In many situations, the police do not know the exact location of an individual to be arrested and cannot stipulate an address in the warrant. Yet short of voluntary consent, the Constitution appears to preclude a general search of homes in order to make an arrest. Where an address is known, the limited arrest entry at one location still seems to require that the officers submit their probable cause to a magistrate and allow him or her to determine whether entry is necessary in order to effectuate an arrest or to protect the lives of those in proximity to the arrest.[27]

The second problem arising under the doctrine of incidental search concerns the physical scope of the search. There is little controversy when the incidental search is limited to the body of the person arrested; controversy begins when the incidental search moves beyond. As noted above, *Agnello* rejected the contention that incidental search could move beyond the body to the arrestee's home, located several blocks away. But when an arrest has been made in a protected area (a home, an office), the physical scope of the incidental search has been a hotly contested issue, producing a variety of responses from the Supreme Court. At times the Court has sanctioned only a limited incidental search; at other times it has permitted what amounts to general fishing expeditions.[28] In 1969, however, the Court held that a warrantless search of an entire house as incidental to a valid arrest was unreasonable. This decision in *Chimel v. California,* which repudiates earlier cases, sharply reduces the allowable area of incidental search and presumably minimizes the possibilities of general exploratory searches. Justice Stewart, speaking for the majority, gave the following guidelines:

> When an arrest is made, it is reasonable for the arresting officer to search the person arrested in order to remove any weapons that the latter might seek to use in order to resist arrest or effect his escape. Otherwise, the officer's safety might well be endangered, and the arrest itself frustrated. In addition, it is entirely reasonable for the arresting officer to search for and seize any evidence on the arrestee's person in order to prevent its concealment or destruction. And the area into which an arrestee might reach in order to grab a weapon or evidentiary items must, of course, be governed by like rule. A gun on a table or in a drawer in front of one who is arrested can be as dangerous to the arresting officer as one concealed in the clothing of the person arrested. There is ample justification, therefore, for a search of the arrestee's person and the area "within his immediate control"—construing that phrase to mean the area from within which he might gain possession of a weapon or destructible evidence.
>
> There is no comparable justification, however, for routinely searching any room other than that in which an arrest occurs—or, for that matter, for searching through all the desk drawers or other closed or concealed areas in that room itself. Such searches, in the absence of well-recognized exceptions, may be made only under the authority of a search warrant. The "adherence to judicial processes" mandated by the Fourth Amendment requires no less.[29]

Undoubtedly, *Chimel* imposes a more stringent standard by which to judge the scope of incidental search than had prevailed throughout most of the post–World War II era. *Chimel* and its companion cases make it clear that incidental search cannot be the basis for either a general exploratory search or a search beyond the immediate area of arrest.[30] The Court reiterated this position a year after *Chimel* in a Louisiana case, and more recently in *Mincey v. Arizona*.[31] (In the latter case, the Tucson police conducted a warrantless four-day search of an apartment, the scene of an apparent murder. The Court agreed that the exigent circumstances of danger to life or the possible destruction of evidence can justify a warrantless search. However, the Court rejected

the theory of a murder scene exception to the Fourth Amendment and noted
that the four-day search, which included opening dresser drawers and ripping
up carpet, could not be rationalized in terms of an emergency search.) The
decision in *Chimel* means that the circumstances of each case must determine
the reasonableness of an incidental search. Furthermore, it does not limit the
existing doctrine that an officer may seize illegal or contraband items in plain
view, assuming always the officer's view is based on a valid intrusion. As the
Court noted in *Coolidge v. New Hampshire*, "Where . . . the arresting officer
inadvertently comes within plain view of a piece of evidence, not concealed,
although outside the area under the immediate control of the arrestee, the
officer may seize it, so long as the plain view was obtained in the course of an
appropriately limited search of the arrestee."[32]

Exceptional Circumstances and Hot Pursuit

The doctrine of incidental search is widely acknowledged, but other exceptions
to the general requirement of a warrant to search a dwelling are less clearly
articulated. In a 1948 opinion, Justice Jackson noted that "there are exceptional
circumstances in which, on balancing the need for effective law enforcement
against the right of privacy, it may be contended that a magistrate's warrant
for search may be dispensed with."[33] In the same year, Justice Douglas offered
an example of an exceptional circumstance: An officer, passing by on the
street and hearing a shot and a cry for help, demands entrance into a dwelling.[34] However, even though the Court has noted the abstract *possibility* of
exceptional circumstances, it has never delineated any such circumstances other
than incidental search and the so-called doctrine of hot pursuit. Indeed, it is
dubious constitutional theory to suggest that emergencies or the exigencies of
a situation could carve out additional exceptions.[35]

The final exception, then, is the doctrine of hot pursuit. This elusive doctrine
appears to be of early English origin[36] and is related broadly to what might be
called the doctrine of necessity. The parameters of hot pursuit are far from
clear. At least on two occasions, the Supreme Court has implicitly endorsed
the doctrine,[37] but, other than to suggest that necessity or emergency justifies
dispensing with a search warrant, the Court has failed to address itself to a
firm definition. Presumably, the pursuit must be fresh (or "hot") and the officers must know that an escaped prisoner or a person eluding arrest has taken
refuge in a specific house or other protected area. For example, in *United
States v. Santana*, the police approached Santana's home and, finding her
standing in the doorway, shouted, "Police," and displayed their badges. Santana
retreated into the vestibule of the house, and the police followed her inside.
The Supreme Court ruled that the open doorway was a public place, an area
where Santana had no expectation of privacy, and that the pursuit into the
vestibule was a "hot pursuit." The Court's opinion noted that "the fact that

the pursuit here ended almost as soon as it began did not render it any less a 'hot pursuit' sufficient to justify the warrantless entry."[38]

Santana did not resolve all the questions that continue to surround this area. Does the doctrine apply to all arrestable offenses? What firsthand knowledge, if any, is required of pursuing officers? How specific must the knowledge of the precise location of the escaped prisoner or fleeing felon be? (For example, does hot pursuit allow a general search of all units of an apartment building, or must the officers have prior knowledge of a precise unit?)

Announcement and Entry

Charles Dickens once observed that "no room is private to his Majesty when the street door's once passed. That's law. Some people maintain that an Englishman's house is his castle. That's gammon."[39] Dickens was a better novelist than a lawyer, but his point is well taken. The Fourth Amendment assumes there is a reasonable procedure for invading the privacy of a protected area. Whether the intrusion is by arrest entry or by a search warrant, the law has long required that officers pause before entry in order to announce their identity and lawful purpose. The precise development of the announcement requirement is somewhat clouded, but Sir Edward Coke took notice of it in the widely cited *Semayne's Case* in 1603. The case involved a civil process, but Coke's dictum is worth noting:

> In all cases when the King is party, the sheriff (if the doors be not open) may break the party's house to arrest him, or to do other execution of the K.'s process, if otherwise he cannot enter. But before he breaks it, he ought to signify the cause of his coming, and to make request to open doors.[40]

The announcement rule continues to serve the same basic purposes that it did in the early seventeenth century: the protection of privacy, the reduction of possible violence, and the protection of property from unnecessary destruction. However, the exact constitutional contours of the rule are far from clear. In part, this is a result of the exceptions to the rule; in part, it is a result of the general failure to distinguish between statutory and common-law requirements of the rule and those aspects of the rule that have constitutional dimensions.

With some exceptions, announcement by federal officers is governed by the following provision in the federal code: "The officer may break open any outer or inner door or window of a house, or any part of a house, or anything therein, to execute a search warrant, if, after notice of his authority and purpose, he is refused admittance or when necessary to liberate himself or a person aiding him in the execution of the warrant."[41] To what extent the federal requirement is based on the Fourth Amendment, and thus applies to all state and federal police officers, is uncertain. In *Ker v. California,* it was assumed by both the majority and the dissenters that notice of authority and purpose had constitutional status.[42] In any event, many states have a rule similar to the federal code provision.[43]

The controversy over the announcement rule centers not around its constitutional status, but rather on the circumstances that can justify entry without announcement and the quantity of evidence that is necessary to trigger the exceptions. Justice Brennan's opinion in *Ker* lists three circumstances that would justify a no-knock entry: "(1) where the persons within already know of the officers' authority and purpose, or (2) where the officers are justified in the belief that persons within are in imminent peril of bodily harm, or (3) where those within, made aware of the presence of someone outside (because, for example, there has been a knock at the door), are then engaged in activity which justifies the officers in the belief that an escape or the destruction of evidence is being attempted."[44] To these, we add the obvious exception that the requirement does not apply to unoccupied premises.[45] There is also authority for including peril of bodily harm to the officers, a corollary to Justice Brennan's second exception.[46] Finally, the exception pertaining to the destruction of evidence is generally limited to those situations in which the officers have probable cause to believe that the destruction is in progress;[47] it does not cover situations in which evidence is only likely to be destroyed or is easily destructible.

Justice Brennan's position in *Ker* stressed that the occupants must be aware of the officers' presence. He based this on the constitutional grounds that an exception runs counter to the presumption of innocence and that the

> practical hazards of law enforcement militate strongly against any relaxation of the requirement of awareness. First, cases of mistaken identity are surely not novel in the investigation of crime. The possibility is very real that the police may be misinformed as to the name or address of a suspect, or as to other material information. That possibility is itself a good reason for holding a tight rein against judicial approval of unannounced police entries into private homes. Innocent citizens should not suffer the shock, fright or embarrassment attendant upon an unannounced police intrusion. Second the requirement of awareness also serves to minimize the hazards of the officers' dangerous calling. We expressly recognized . . . that compliance with the federal notice statute "is also a safeguard for the police themselves who might be mistaken for prowlers and be shot down by a fearful householder." Indeed, one of the principal objectives of the English requirement of announcement of authority and purpose was to protect the arresting officers from being shot as trespassers.[48]

Experience under the no-knock provisions of the 1970 Drug Abuse and Control Act[49] and the District of Columbia Court Reform and Criminal Procedure Act of 1970[50] appears to underscore Justice Brennan's practical concerns. Carelessness and overzealousness led to a growing number of cases of mistaken addresses, often with cruel results for the innocent victims. Narcotic officers invaded the wrong homes so many times that in 1974 Congress repealed the no-knock provision of the drug abuse law.[51] However, no-knock entries by state officers continue to be governed by *Ker,* which is to say that there are few explicit constitutional standards that govern a police officer's dispensing with the announcement rule. The Court has not made clear either the quantity of probable cause necessary to dispense with announcement or the degree, if any, of prior judicial involvement.[52] The situation in regard to federal standards is equally uncertain:[53] There is little agreement among federal courts of appeal as to whether both identity and purpose must be announced and as to how much delay is reasonable prior to entry.[54]

THE GENERAL REQUIREMENTS OF PROCESS

Since Lord Camden's decision in *Entick v. Carrington,* there has been common agreement that warrants, either for search and seizure or for arrest, must be judicially issued and specific.[55] The need for judicial oversight of arrest, search, and seizure has been stressed in numerous decisions of the Supreme Court.[56] However, it was not until the early 1970s that the Court had occasion to rule directly on what constitutes a judicial officer for purposes of issuing warrants.

Judicial Warrants

In *Coolidge v. New Hampshire* (1971), the Court struck down a warrant that had been issued by a state attorney general because the attorney general, who was also a law enforcement officer, lacked the neutrality and detachment envisioned in the requirement.[57] In the following year, the Court confronted an arrest warrant issued by a clerk of a municipal court. Noting that United States commissioners (people who are not judges) had long issued warrants, the Court unanimously upheld the warrant.

> The substance of the Constitution's warrant requirements does not turn on the labeling of the issuing party. The warrant traditionally has represented an independent assurance that a search and arrest will not proceed without probable cause to believe that a crime has been committed and that the person or place named in the warrant is involved in the crime. Thus, an issuing magistrate must meet two tests. He must be neutral and detached, and he must be capable of determining whether probable cause be drawn by "a neutral and detached magistrate instead of being judged by the officer engaged in the often competitive enterprise of ferreting out crime." . . .
>
> The requisite detachment is present in the case at hand. Whatever else neutrality and detachment might entail, it is clear that they require severance and disengagement from activities of law enforcement. There has been no showing whatever here of partiality, or affiliation of these clerks with prosecutors or police. The record shows no connection with any law enforcement

activity or authority which would distort the independent judgment the Fourth Amendment requires.[58]

Although in theory clerks of courts are not directly responsible to law enforcement officers, in practice the system may not be quite so compartmentalized as the opinion suggests.[59] Presumably, the opinion leaves open the question of whether a given clerk or office has functioned in a detached and neutral manner. However, the Court has made it clear that neutrality is not maintained if the issuing officer receives a personal fee for issuing warrants but no fee when a warrant application is turned down.[60]

Behind the warrant requirement is the expectation that the judiciary will balance the needs of law enforcement against the rights protected under the Fourth Amendment. Typical of the defense of the requirement is Justice Douglas's statement in *McDonald v. United States*:

> We are not dealing with formalities. The presence of a search warrant serves a high function. Absent some grave emergency, the Fourth Amendment has interposed a magistrate between the citizen and the police. This was done not to shield criminals nor to make the home a safe haven for illegal activities. It was done so that an objective mind might weigh the need to invade that privacy in order to enforce the law. The right of privacy was deemed too precious to entrust to the discretion of those whose job is the detection of crime and the arrest of criminals. Power is a heady thing; and history shows that the police acting on their own cannot be trusted. And so the Constitution requires a magistrate to pass on the desires of the police before they violate the privacy of the home.[61]

The expectation, however, is based on a model of criminal justice that may contradict reality. It assumes that magistrates play an active, rather than reactive, role in controlling the police: it assumes that a neutral and detached judiciary can temper police zeal. In short, it places judicial control at the center of guarding against unreasonable searches and seizures. But the reality of the warrant process does not support the judiciary as a control agency. Warrants are issued ex parte (without benefit of adversary proceedings) by magistrates who frequently play a passive, reactive role and are seldom inclined or able to supervise police officers or prosecutors. In such situations, the judicial examination of requests is pro forma; the judge is a rubber stamp.[62]

We might conclude, then, that the warrant has been accorded an unduly central role in protecting privacy under the Fourth Amendment. In fact, we could argue that the language of the Fourth Amendment accords no such central role to the warrant, because the warrant clause is substantively independent of the clause prohibiting unreasonable searches and seizures.[63] Clearly the text of the amendment does not say that a reasonable search or seizure may be made only by process of a warrant; the warrant clause was probably a reflection of the general condemnation of the writs of assistance rather than a clearly stated broad policy. Textual analysis and history aside, however, we still confront the major substantive policy of the amendment—a clear prohibition against arbitrary governmental searches and seizures. The fact is that the amendment only suggests how that policy can be attained, and judicially issued warrants based on probable cause seem to be consistent with this broad goal. If there is an inconsistency between the theory and the practice of judicial warrants, scrapping the warrant requirement is not the best method for securing the objectives of the amendment. Without the ancillary requirement of warrants, probable cause, and particularity, there would be little flesh left to the bare and elusive phrase "unreasonable searches and seizures." Indeed, the Supreme Court has recently reaffirmed the warrant requirement. In *Arkansas v. Sanders* (1979), the Court ruled that a warrantless seizure of luggage from an automobile, even in the presence of probable cause, could not be conducted in the absence of a warrant or of exigent circumstances.[64]

The Proscription Against General Warrants

The language of the Fourth Amendment, if not its historical background, makes it abundantly clear that general warrants are proscribed. Persons, places, and things to be searched or seized must be particularly described in a warrant. The reason for this is to prevent police officers from conducting general searches or dragnet arrests in the *hope* of finding something illegal. Keeping police discretion within reasonable limits does not mean, however, that an impossible degree of particularity is required.

> The "particularity" demanded by the Fourth Amendment has never been thought by this Court to be reducible "to formula"; . . . it has instead been made plain that its measurement must take fully into account the character both of the materials to be seized and of the purposes of the seizures.
> . . . The degree of particularity necessary is best measured by that requirement's purpose. The central purpose of the particularity requirement is to leave "nothing . . . to the discretion of the officer executing the warrant" . . . by describing the materials to be seized with precision sufficient to prevent "the seizure of one thing under a warrant describing another."[65]

Although there is no formula for particularity, the Supreme Court has made it clear that when there is an overlap with the First Amendment the required degree of specificity increases. In *Stanford v. Texas* (1965), the Court held invalid a Texas search warrant that authorized the seizure in a designated house of books, pamphlets, records, cards, pictures, recordings, and other written instruments of the Communist party of Texas held in violation of the state's Suppression Act of 1955. After a five-hour search, the police left with some two thousand items. Speaking for a unanimous Court, Justice Stewart reviewed the historical background of the Fourth Amendment and concluded:

"Two centuries have passed since the historic decision in *Entick v. Carrington,* almost to the very day. The world has greatly changed, and the voice of non-conformity now sometimes speaks a tongue which Lord Camden might find hard to understand. But the Fourth Amendment guarantees to John Stanford that no official of the State shall ransack his home and seize his books and papers under the unbridled authority of a general warrant—no less than the law 200 years ago shielded John Entick from the messengers of the King."[66]

In situations where there is no overlap with freedom of expression, the requirement is less exacting. Thus, while a single search warrant would not normally suffice to authorize the search of a multiple-unit dwelling or apartment house, a single search warrant to search an entire five-story commercial garage, operated as a single business enterprise, was held valid when Chief Justice Taft observed that "it is enough if the description is such that the officer with a search warrant can, with reasonable effort, ascertain and identify the place intended."[67] A specific street address normally will satisfy the requirement for a single-unit dwelling; in cases where a street address is not available, a warrant should give other particulars that indicate a reasonably precise location. Similarly, in an arrest warrant, a name, alias, or nickname is sufficient;[68] in the absence of a name, a John or Jane Doe warrant may issue, which should describe the individual with a reasonable degree of particularity.[69]

Probable Cause

Of central importance to the Fourth Amendment is the requirement that a reasonable search or seizure, including arrest, be based on prior probable cause. The general purpose of the requirement is to reduce the possibility of arbitrary searches and arrests. The first point of the requirement is that the probable cause be established *prior* to the search or seizure: A search or seizure that is unreasonable at the outset is not made reasonable by what it turns up.[70] For a precise definition of *probable cause,* the Court has generally followed the pattern established in *Stacey v. Emery*: Probable cause exists when "the facts and circumstances before the officer are such as to warrant a man of prudence and caution in believing that the offense has been committed."[71] The quantity and quality of information necessary to establish probable cause are not the same as are required to establish guilt. For example, in *Brinegar v. United States* (1949), Brinegar, a resident of the "dry" state of Oklahoma, was arrested on an open highway for illegal transportation of liquor. The arresting officer had four bases for probable cause: He had previously arrested Brinegar on the same charge, he had recently seen Brinegar loading liquor into a car in the nearby "wet" state of Missouri, Brinegar was driving away from Missouri into Oklahoma, and the rear end of the car appeared to be heavily loaded. In concluding that these were sufficient grounds to believe that Brinegar was illegally transporting liquor, the Court observed:

In dealing with probable cause . . . as the very name implies, we deal with probabilities. These are not technical; they are the factual and practical considerations of everyday life on which reasonable and prudent men, not legal technicians, act. The standard of proof is accordingly correlative to what must be proved.

. . . Since Marshall's time, at any rate, it has come to mean more than bare suspicion: Probable cause exists where "the facts and circumstances within their [the officers'] knowledge, and of which they had reasonably trustworthy information, [are] sufficient in themselves to warrant a man of reasonable caution in the belief that "an offense has been or is being committed."[72]

Can mere suspicion establish probable cause? The answer is a qualified no. Mere suspicion, or a so-called information and belief warrant, has never been accepted by the Supreme Court as the basis for either an arrest or a search.[73] Somewhat typical of a suspicion arrest was the case of *Beck v. Ohio*. There the arresting officer testified that he knew what Beck looked like and knew that he had a prior record for gambling charges. Beyond this, the officer had no information other than a generalized statement that someone had told him something about Beck. The Court held this insufficient to establish probable cause.[74] Similarly, the Court held that officers could not justify a gambling search where they acted merely on the presence of a large number of automobiles and the unidentified tips of street informants.[75]

Probable cause may well begin with suspicion, but suspicion must be transformed into probable cause by underlying circumstances or by credible information.[76] This information may be partly the hearsay of a reliable informer,[77] but it must describe the suspected criminal activity in sufficient detail so that a magistrate knows that he or she is relying on something more than casual rumor.[78]

Obviously, the Court's position on probable cause is still ambiguous. This ambiguity stems largely from disagreements about the use of informers' tips, an issue that has divided the Court since at least *Draper v. United States* (1959).[79] The problem is not whether informers' tips may be used to establish probable cause, but rather the degree of independent corroboration that should be required to support hearsay information. Justice Douglas, the strongest critic of the informer system, has rejected as probable cause hearsay built on hearsay.[80] His position was supported in *Aguilar v. Texas* (1964), where a majority held:

Although an affidavit may be based on hearsay information and need not reflect the direct personal observations of the affiant . . . the magistrate must be informed of some of the underlying circumstances from which the informant concluded that the narcotics were where he claimed they were, and some of the underlying circumstances from which the officer concluded that the informant, whose identity need not be disclosed . . . was "credible" or his information "reliable."[81]

The *Aguilar* test has had some difficulty in surviving changes in Court personnel and opinion.[82] Indeed, by the early 1970s, the Court was hopelessly divided on the informant issue.[83] Until the Court can agree on a standard, lower courts are effectively free to select from the *Draper-Jones-McCray* line of cases or from the *Nathanson-Aguilar-Spinelli* group.[84] Like so many divisions in the area of criminal justice, these cases reflect the reasonable disagreement of justices who do not always share the same values. Justice Douglas's position, clearly reflected in his dissent in *Draper*, stresses the need to limit police discretion in order to reduce the likelihood of unreasonable invasions of individual liberty. This position is contrary to the one adopted by many justices, including Chief Justice Burger, which stresses the practical needs of law enforcement and eschews "hypertechnicality" and "elaborate specificity."[85]

Arrest

The constitutional law governing arrests is perhaps the most widely neglected area of the Fourth Amendment. One reason for this is that, except insofar as an arrest results in an incidental seizure, it has not been the subject of extensive judicial review, either in suits for false arrest or under exclusionary rules.[86] For whatever reason, there remains confusion as to the restraints placed on arrest by the Fourth Amendment. Generally, the Supreme Court has limited discussion of the issue to prior probable cause without considering whether there are other constitutional-level restraints on arrest.

COMMON-LAW ARREST.   At common law, officers have the right to arrest without a warrant for (1) a felony committed in their presence or (2) if they have reasonable grounds to believe that the person has committed or is committing a felony. For misdemeanors, the common law provides that officers cannot arrest without a warrant unless the misdemeanor is committed in their presence. At least on three occasions, the Supreme Court has applied the common law of arrest to warrantless arrests.[87] However, whether the Court intended to establish a constitutional doctrine in these areas is not clear.[88] The question is important: In the absence of exigent circumstances, must an arrest warrant be obtained? Certainly, the clear weight of authority and practice is that no warrant is constitutionally required when the felony arrest is based on probable cause and occurs in a public place. Thus, in *United States v. Watson* (1976), the Court upheld Watson's warrantless arrest in a public restaurant on the grounds of probable cause, noting that "the cases construing the Fourth Amendment thus reflect the ancient common-law rule that a peace officer was permitted to arrest without a warrant for a misdemeanor or felony committed in his presence as well as for a felony not committed in his presence if there was reasonable grounds for making the arrest."[89] The *Watson* opinion leaves open the question of warrantless arrests in private areas; furthermore, it casts doubt on the current practice of warrantless arrests for misdemeanors that are not committed in the presence of the arresting officers. This doubt must be resolved because it is in conflict with current practice under several federal and state statutes.[90] There are, of course, both federal and state statutes governing arrest,[91] and the Court has indicated on several occasions that arrest without warrant is governed by the law of the state in which the arrest takes place.[92] This apparently applies to both state and federal arrests and to either state or federal offenses.[93]

CUSTODIAL ARREST AND INCIDENTAL SEARCH.   Anglo-American law has long recognized the right of officers, when executing a valid arrest, to undertake a self-protective "pat-down" for weapons, to seize items that might be used to effectuate an escape, and to prevent the destruction of evidence of the crime.[94] But, traditionally, these incidental searches limited the unrestrained discretion of the arresting officers: Without further probable cause (produced by the pat-down), they could search only a suspect's outer clothing.[95] However, in two cases in 1973, the Supreme Court greatly widened the discretion of arresting officers to conduct a full search. Both cases involved relatively minor vehicle code offenses. (In fact, in one of the cases, state law allowed the offense to be handled by citation rather than arrest.)[96] In rejecting the idea that an incidental search is limited by its self-protective justification, the majority held that

> the authority to search the person incident to a lawful custodial arrest, while based upon the need to disarm and to discover evidence, does not depend on what a court may later decide was the probability in a particular arrest situation that weapons or evidence would in fact be found upon the person of the suspect. A custodial arrest of a suspect based on probable cause is a reasonable intrusion under the Fourth Amendment; that intrusion being lawful, a search incident to the arrest requires no additional justification. It is the fact of the lawful arrest which establishes the authority to search, and we hold that in the case of a lawful custodial arrest a full search of the person is not only an exception to the warrant requirement of the Fourth Amendment, but it is also a "reasonable" search under that Amendment.[97]

Thus a full search, following a valid arrest, and taking the prisoner into custody, is per se reasonable and does not subject the particulars of the search to a post hoc judicial examination.[98] Of course any contraband discovered in the course of such a search is subject to seizure.

Some months after these decisions, the Court upheld, in a 5 to 4 decision, the right of the police to defer incidental search after a valid custodial arrest. In *United States v. Edwards*, the Court held that, once an arrestee is in lawful custody, the personal effects subject to incidental search at the time of arrest may be searched and with a warrant seized, even after a lapse of time for administrative processing of the arrestee.[99]

These cases may well give an added measure of protection to arresting officers, but they also give rise to serious questions about the unrestrained use of discretionary powers on the part of the police. Not only do these cases open the door to searches of such personal effects as wallets and purses,[100] but they also open the door to possible abuses of the power of arrest in minor traffic offenses. Given the vast number of daily traffic violations, certainly there is a risk that custodial arrest (for a minor offense) could be misused as a pretext for a full body search. A general and nonjudicially supervised arrest may well aid the police in discovering evidence of crimes, particularly of narcotic offenses, but the price to be paid in certain areas may be higher than is reasonably necessary.

Stop and Frisk and Investigatory Stops

From the perspective of police officers, much of the case law under the Fourth Amendment probably seems unrelated to reality. In the area of arrest, this unreality stems from conflicting assumptions. Until the late 1960s, constitutional interpretation had limited police officers' power to arrest without warrant to those situations in which they had prior probable cause to believe that a crime had been committed or that the arrestee was in the process of committing a crime. The case law of the Supreme Court did not address itself to preventive law enforcement, and, by stressing prior probable cause, there was a strong constitutional inference that preventive arrest was unconstitutional. To the police, preventing a criminal act is as important as investigating completed criminal activity. One of the most common techniques in preventive law enforcement is the *investigatory stop*—the stopping of individuals engaged in suspicious behavior or who are found in suspicious circumstances. The purpose of an investigatory stop is to prevent a crime, not to make a traditional arrest on probable cause, but the method raises serious constitutional issues.

The Court first addressed these issues in 1968, in *Terry v. Ohio* and two companion cases.[101] In *Terry*, a plainclothes officer, patrolling a downtown area of Cleveland, observed three individuals acting in a suspicious manner and concluded that they were contemplating a daytime robbery of a store. After watching them, the officer approached the individuals, identified himself, and asked for their names. Receiving a mumbled response, he seized one of the men and conducted a pat-down of the man's outer clothing. When he felt what seemed to be a pistol, he reached inside the suspect's coat and seized a revolver. The Court, in upholding Terry's conviction for carrying a concealed weapon, held that the so-called stop and frisk was within the scope of the Fourth Amendment, though not covered by the requirement of probable cause but, instead, by the standard of reasonableness. Still, the majority opinion never directly addressed itself to the issue of the stop, only to the issue of the frisk.[102]

To balance between the government's interest in search and seizure and the constitutionally protected interest of the individual, the majority focused on the limited nature of the intrusion of a pat-down: Officers must "be able to point to specific and articulable facts, which, taken together with other reasonable inferences from those facts, reasonably warrant that intrusion."[103] The opinion made clear that the element of a dangerous crime alone justified the officer in conducting a *limited pat-down of the outer clothing,* in order to protect himself and those in the immediate vicinity from violence.[104] Furthermore, the majority opinion stressed that the justification for the search inside Terry's clothing was predicated on the reasonable inference that the officer felt a gun during the pat-down, noting that the officer's search,

> unlike a search without a warrant incident to a lawful arrest, is not justified by any need to prevent the disappearance or destruction of evidence of crime. . . . The sole justification of the search in the present situation is the protection of the police officer and others nearby, and it must therefore be confined in scope to an intrusion reasonably designed to discover guns, knives, clubs, or other hidden instruments for the assault of the police officer.[105]

The refusal of the Court in *Terry* to rule on the issue of forcible stop, or "investigatory seizure," left undefined the constitutional restraints that are imposed on the police in forestalling an incipient criminal act by recourse to a forcible field stop; the Court only hinted at what might be involved.[106] However, four years after *Terry,* a new majority treated the unanswered issue as if it had been decided. In *Adams v. Williams,* Justice Rehnquist, writing for a six-person majority, upheld the right of a Connecticut police officer, acting on a tip supplied moments before, to investigate the informant's statement that a certain individual seated in a nearby parked car had narcotics on him and that he had a gun in his possession. The officer approached the car and asked the individual to get out. When, instead, the individual rolled down the window, the officer reached inside and seized a gun, arrested the individual for unlawful possession, and made an incidental search that revealed a quantity of narcotics. The majority opinion upheld the officers' initial response by the following rationale:

> The Fourth Amendment does not requires a policeman who lacks the precise level of information necessary for probable cause to arrest to simply shrug his shoulders and allow a crime to occur or a criminal to escape. On the contrary, *Terry* recognizes that it may be the essence of good police work to adopt an intermediate response.
> . . . A brief stop of a suspicious individual, in order to determine his identity or to maintain the status quo momentarily while obtaining more information, may be most reasonable in light of the facts known to the officer at the time.[107]

Rejecting an earlier test of probable cause in situations where an informant's tip is involved, the majority simply concluded that there must be some indication that the tip is reliable. They discovered that indication in a Connecticut law that makes it a misdemeanor to knowingly give a false report to a police officer, implying that statements against penal interest have greater credibility than might otherwise be assumed.[108]

Adams still left undefined the standard of forcible stop. There is, of course, no question about the right, indeed the responsibility, of police officers to ask questions. Yet presumably *Terry* and *Adams* have not foreclosed the right of an individual to ignore a question and to walk away. The issue is not one of cooperation between police and citizens, but rather the constitutional standard against which we must judge those situations in which citizens are obliged to answer and the reasonable consequences of their failure to respond. *Terry* and *Adams* appeared to sanction boundless police discretion. If the contours of probable cause for arrest were unclear, then those of reasonable suspicion were even less well defined. It was to this problem that the Court turned its attention in 1979.

The facts in *Brown v. Texas* seem typical of citizen-police encounters in urban areas. Brown was noticed by patrol officers at mid-day in an alley; he was walking away from another man. The area was known for its serious drug problem, and the officers had never before seen Brown. Because the situation looked suspicious, they stopped Brown and asked him to identify himself. When he refused, he was arrested and subsequently convicted for violating a Texas law that makes it an offense to refuse to give an officer one's name and address. In unanimously reversing the conviction, the Court pointed out that the patrol officers had no reason to suspect Brown was involved in criminal activity. The Court noted that the standard of reasonable suspicion in an investigatory stop requires that officers base their seizure on specific, objective facts "indicating that society's legitimate interests require the seizure of the particular individual. . . ."[109]

Brown does not suggest that the police have no authority to ask questions; but it does indicate that when a seizure has occurred, the Fourth Amendment comes into play. Given the desire of many police departments to assert a police presence in high-crime areas, *Brown* will probably not reduce the incidence of police stops. Finally, Brown did not answer the question of whether the state may punish individuals who are *lawfully* stopped and who refuse to give their names and addresses.

Consent Searches

NONCUSTODIAL.   It is axiomatic that a right guaranteed under the Constitution may, in most circumstances, be waived by voluntary consent. The right to privacy under the Fourth Amendment is no exception. Voluntary citizen-police cooperation is essential to law enforcement, and such cooperation frequently includes consent to searches and seizures. Voluntary consent may be motivated by self-interest, particularly in those situations where the citizen initiates the police activity, or by some commitment to the welfare of the community. But regardless of the motivation, the consent must be voluntary—that is, it must be the product of a free and unconstrained choice and not the product of implicit or explicit coercion nor of direct, implied, or covert threat.

How can the state demonstrate that a search was in fact voluntary? The most direct way is by reference to the circumstances immediately surrounding the search. The Supreme Court, in *Schneckloth v. Bustamonte*, rejected the argument that the beginning point in such an inquiry is a demonstration that consent is based on knowledge of the right to refuse a request to search or seize.[110] Rejecting the requirement of a *Miranda*-type warning, [111] the Court chose to use the broader "totality-of-circumstances" test that had characterized the determination of voluntariness in pre-*Miranda* confession cases.[112] The Court reasoned that requiring proof of knowledge would be impractical because

> consent searches are part of the standard investigatory techniques of law enforcement agencies. They normally occur on the highway, or in a person's home or office, and under informal and unstructured conditions. The circumstances that prompt the initial request to search may develop quickly or be a logical extension of investigative police questioning.[113]

The totality-of-circumstances approach stresses the inferences that can be drawn from such factors as time, place, age, education, emotional maturity, and race. In *Schneckloth*, the majority recited the minimal facts of the case: In the early morning, an automobile was stopped for a routine, minor vehicle code violation, which revealed that the driver did not have a license. At that point, the officer requested to search the car. The owner of the car was not present, but his brother was a passenger and gave his consent; it was said both freely and casually. The majority opinion never returned to the facts, nor did it suggest how voluntary consent had been established.

Of course, lack of knowledge of the constitutional right to refuse does not ipso facto preclude a voluntary choice. It is conceivable that in the absence of knowledge one could make a free choice: For example, a person could conclude that, because the police asked for it, failing to receive consent they would defer to the refusal.[114] On the other hand, we might argue that this reasoning ignores the social reality of requests for consent. More often than not, requests are made of those individuals in society—the poor, the ignorant, the ethnic minorities—who are most susceptible to intimidation by the mere presence of police authority. They may infer, rightly or wrongly, that they will in some sense suffer the consequences of any refusal to cooperate with the police. Or we might argue that, regardless of the social setting of the search, mere acquiescence to police authority is not a voluntary consent, as indeed the Court had argued at an earlier date.[115] This last may approximate the reality of the typical situation, but it raises a question: How can a rule be shaped in such a way that it relieves individuals of the fears that may stem from a variety of causes, including social and economic deprivation?

THIRD-PARTY.   The decision in *Schneckloth* was limited to the issue of the voluntary consent of one who is the subject of the search and not to consent to searches by third parties. A subject of a search, in making a choice whether or not to consent, is more likely to be aware of the consequences of the choice than might be the case in a third-party consent. On several occasions, the Court has been confronted with third-party consent searches. In two of these cases, the Court simply ruled that the consent had not been voluntary, without formulating any rule to govern the process.[116] In two other cases, the Court ruled that a night clerk in a hotel could not waive a guest's protection against an unreasonable search of his room[117] and that a tenant does not surrender his rights under the Fourth Amendment to the landlord.[118] But again, the Court did not establish any well-defined guidelines governing third-party consent.

Presumably there are situations in which a third party could reasonably grant consent, and still other situations in which a waiver would be unreasonable. The first indication of how the Court might approach the issue came in 1969. Clothing, left in a third party's home in a jointly used duffel bag, was seized with the third party's consent. The elements of joint use and possession were deemed sufficient to grant consent.[119] Some years later, the Court elaborated on these points: It held that if a woman jointly occupied a bedroom with a man, her common authority over the premises or effects would be sufficient to make a binding consent to search as against an absent nonconsenting party.[120] Justice White, in a footnote to his majority opinion, cautioned, however, that common authority was not to be implied from the mere property interest a third party has in the property. Rather the authority of the third party must rest on "mutual use of the property by persons generally having joint access or control for most purposes, so that it is reasonable to recognize that any of the co-inhabitants has the right to permit the inspection in his own right and that the others have assumed the risk that one of their number might permit the common area to be searched."[121]

The common-authority test appears to be an appropriate beginning in third-party consent. It may be necessary, however, to further refine the test in order to clarify the position of those who frequently exercise a form of temporary common authority over a dwelling (visiting relatives, employees). Temporary and subordinate access or control of a dwelling should not constitute sufficient authority to counter the expectation of privacy that normally accompanies permanent control.[122]

Seizable Items

For a number of years, there was more than a little confusion as to the kinds of things that could validly be seized without running afoul of the Fourth and

Fifth Amendments. The confusion stemmed from passages in *Entick* and *Boyd* that tied the protection against unreasonable seizure to the privilege against self-incrimination. Justice Bradley's dictum, "the 'unreasonable searches and seizures' condemned in the Fourth Amendment are almost always made for the purpose of compelling a man to give evidence against himself, which in criminal cases is condemned in the Fifth Amendment,"[123] led the Court in *Gouled v. United States* (1921) to unanimously adopt the so-called mere-evidence rule, which prohibited the seizure of items of evidential value only. Building on *Boyd, Gouled* held that warrants

> may not be used as a means of gaining access to a man's house or office and papers solely for the purpose of making search to secure evidence to be used against him in a criminal or penal proceeding, but that they may be resorted to only when a primary right to such search and seizure may be found in the interest in which the public or the complainant may have in the property to be seized, or in the right to the possession of it, or when a valid exercise of the police power renders possession of the property by the accused unlawful, and provides that it may be taken.[124]

Later cases expanded the mere-evidence rule and formalized it, allowing the government to seize under warrants only stolen goods, fruits of a crime (including contraband), and instrumentalities of a crime. The rule assumed that before the government could seize an item, it had to have a possessory right or superior interest in the item. The rule failed to accord the government any interest in evidence that would help identify and punish criminal violators. As one commentator suggested, the rule was both historically and analytically unsound.[125]

In *Warden v. Hayden* (1967), the Court overturned the mere-evidence rule. In sustaining the seizure of clothing alleged to have been worn by an armed robber, Justice Brennan noted:

> The premise in Gouled that government may not seize evidence simply for the purpose of proving crime has likewise . . . been discredited. The requirement that the Government assert in addition some property interest in material it seizes has long been a fiction, obscuring the reality that government has an interest in solving crime. There must, of course, be a nexus—automatically provided in the case of fruits, instrumentalities or contraband—between the item to be seized and criminal behavior. Thus in the case of "mere evidence," probable cause must be examined in terms of cause to believe that the evidence sought will aid in a particular apprehension or conviction. In so doing, consideration of police purposes will be required.[126]

Justice Brennan's opinion was in line with the distinction then emerging between testimonial, or communicative, evidence, protected under the Fifth Amendment, and real, or physical, evidence.[127] Subsequent lower-court decisions have tended to focus on the issue of compulsory self-incrimination,[128] personal letters,[129] and gambling records,[130] and have not returned to his statement that there must be a nexus between the items seized and the criminal. Nor have subsequent cases returned to the issue specifically not decided in *Hayden*—that is, "whether there are items of evidential value whose very nature precludes them from being the object of a reasonable search and seizure."[131]

Because *Hayden* leaves uncertain what restraints remain on the scope of seizable items, it may be necessary in the future to provide more sharply defined boundaries. The end of the mere-evidence rule should not grant the police a blank check to seize any item during the course of a valid search. *Hayden* suggests that the beginning point in setting the boundary is a requirement that there must be probable cause to believe that the evidence sought will aid in apprehension or conviction. Implicit in that requirement is a proscription against general seizures in the mere hope that at some future point the items may aid the prosecution. Finally, any boundary rule under *Hayden* must be compatible with the proscription against general searches. As Judge Learned Hand suggested, the real evil is the "rummaging about" among an individual's personal effects.[132] If privacy rather than property is the central value of the Fourth Amendment, then the death of *Gouled* should require close attention to the constraints placed on the police under *Chimel*.

AUTOMOBILES

One of the unfortunate consequences of the common-law approach is a tendency to ignore rules and doctrine and instead to allow some unique fact of each case to govern. This so-called white horse approach is not a stranger to arrest, search, and seizure and positively abounds in the law of automobile searches. As Justice Rehnquist has observed, the law of automobile searches "is something less than a seamless web."[133] Almost from the outset, the automobile, because of its ambulatory character, has been accorded some exception to the warrant requirement. In *Carroll v. United States* (1925), one of the many Prohibition cases, the Supreme Court declared:

> Having thus established that contraband goods concealed and illegally transported in an automobile or other vehicle may be searched for without a warrant, we come now to consider under what circumstances such search may be made. It would be intolerable and unreasonable if a prohibition agent were authorized to stop every automobile on the chance of finding liquor, and thus subject all persons lawfully using the highways to the inconvenience and indignity of such a search. Travelers may be so stopped in crossing an international boundary, because of national self-protection reasonably requiring one entering the country to identify himself as entitled to come in, and his belongings as effects which may be lawfully brought in. But those lawfully within the country, en-

titled to use the public highways, have a right to free passage without inter-
ruption or search unless there is known to a competent official authorized to
search, probable cause for believing that their vehicles are carrying contraband
or illegal merchandise.[134]

From 1925 until the 1960s, the Court only occasionally considered the issue
of automobile searches, and when it did the issue related to probable cause[135]
rather than to exigent circumstances justifying a warrantless search. The
Carroll doctrine (the ambulatory character of the automobile can create a
practical necessity for dispensing with a warrant) was widely accepted
throughout the 1940s and 1950s. But the doctrine had extended well beyond
the common-sense approach to a point of almost no protection against police
searches. As Justice Jackson had forecast in his dissent in *Brinegar* in 1949,
exemptions to the warrant requirement are interpreted and applied by the
police and will be pushed to the limit.[136] So long as there was probable cause,
the mere potential for mobility created an almost blanket exemption from the
warrant requirement.

Until 1979, automobile cases generally centered on the absence of warrants
and the scope of searches. The issue of automobile stops had been addressed
only in conjunction with border patrol stop-and-search cases. However, in
Delaware v. Prouse (1979), the Court addressed the issue of the degree of police
authority to randomly stop automobiles to check a driver's license and/or a
car's registration.[137] The *Prouse* majority concluded that the police do not have
discretionary power to make random and unconstrained spot checks. To stop
an automobile, the police officer must have either probable cause to believe
that the vehicle or an occupant is subject to seizure for a violation of the law
or reasonable suspicion that the driver is unlicensed or the automobile is unregistered. The majority suggested, however, that the state may subject motorists to routine roadblock stops or checks if they are conducted in accordance
with plans embodying explicit neutral limitations on an officer's discretion. In
short, if the state wishes to check motorists at roadblocks, it may do so by a
plan that constrains the discretion of officers (for example, stopping all oncoming traffic at a designated spot).

Impoundment and Custody

Although undoubtedly automobiles have a potential for flight, still they are
part of one's personal effects within the meaning of the Fourth Amendment.
In 1964 in *Preston v. United States*, a unanimous Court held that once the
police had towed a car to a police garage, after arresting its occupants at a
different location, they could not conduct an incidental search of the car,
noting that "even in the case of motorcars, the test still is, was the search

unreasonable."[138] Because the search was remote in time and place from the arrest, it was held not to be an incidental search.

Three years after *Preston,* the Court began a pattern of checkered decisions in automobile searches. In *Cooper v. California,* a case almost on all fours with *Preston,* a five-justice majority allowed the warrantless search of a towed car, remote in time and place from the arrest, distinguishing its decision from *Preston* on the basis that, because the *Cooper* car was possibly used in a narcotic offense, it was subject to a forfeiture proceeding under California law.[139] Justice Black's opinion, however, failed to explain how a state could gain such dominion over a personal effect merely because the personal effect was the future subject of a judicial determination of forfeiture. Presumably a limited interest in privacy survives an involuntary transfer of property. This *sub silentio* overruling of *Preston* was given further confirmation in *Harris v. United States* (1968), where the Court upheld the right of the police, subsequent to arrest, to enter an impounded automobile in order to inventory the contents and secure any valuables therein.[140] The mere lawful custody of an automobile was becoming the basis for justifying a warrantless search, even though the Court had expressly rejected that argument in *Preston.* In *Chambers v. Marony* (1970), with only Justice Harlan dissenting, the Court upheld another warrantless search of an in-custody automobile, remote in time and place from the arrest.[141] The Court held that, because the police had probable cause to search the car and because a car is readily movable, it was of little practical difference whether the police temporarily seized the car and sought a judicial search warrant, or merely conducted an immediate search. What the majority ignored was that the *Carroll* rationale carried with it the element of open highways. If *Chambers* is limited to open-highway situations, then it becomes *Carroll* after arrest, at the station house.[142] Thus, *Chambers* held that, whenever the police make a legal search of an automobile under the *Carroll* doctrine, they may also seize it and take it elsewhere for purposes of the search.

Shortly after *Chambers,* the Court was again confronted with a situation in which the police towed away a car after an arrest and made several subsequent searches of the contents of the car. This time, the car was parked on a private driveway. The Court was so divided in *Coolidge v. New Hampshire* (1971) that it was unable to agree on the validity of the warrantless seizure. Two years after *Coolidge,* following changes in Court personnel, a new five-justice majority emerged. In *Cady v. Dombrowski* (1973), recently appointed Justice Rehnquist led the majority to adopt a new strategy in automobile cases. A car, disabled in what initially appeared to be a drunk-driving case, was towed away and subsequently searched. In upholding what was called a "caretaking search," the majority opinion eschewed formulas for refining the determination of reasonableness and instead focused on the reasonableness of automobile searches within the practical confines of the extensive, and often noncriminal, contact that state and local police have with automobiles.[143] The practicality of obtaining a warrant in a circumstance where it was apparent that neither the automobile nor its contents were likely to take flight or disappear was ignored, and the issue of privacy was cast in the doubtful context of noncriminal, or caretaking, contact. Such benign inventories may well protect personal property, but if the purpose is benign, it would seem more appropriate to ask the vehicle's owner whether he or she wishes to forego privacy in order to protect the contents of the vehicle. Otherwise, why not allow the owner to assume what is likely to be an insurable risk?

By 1974, the fact-specific approach was in full swing. The *Harris* search was justified in order to protect valuables; the *Cooper* search was justified to protect the safety of the officers; the *Cady* search was justified by the need to protect the general public. In *Cardwell v. Lewis* (1974), the new majority held a warrantless search reasonable because it occurred in a public parking lot and the search was limited to the exterior of the car.[144] *Cardwell* also introduced another distinguishing factor—the lesser expectation of privacy in an automobile. Attempting to build on *Katz v. United States* (whatever a person knowingly exposes to the public is not a subject of constitutional protection),[145] Justice Blackmun concluded:

> One has a lesser expectation of privacy in a motor vehicle because its function is transportation and it seldom serves as one's residence or as the repository of personal effects. A car has little capacity for escaping public scrutiny. It travels public thoroughfares where both its occupants and its contents are in plain view.
>   . . . This is not to say that no part of the interior of an automobile has Fourth Amendment protection; the exercise of a desire to be mobile does not, of course, waive one's right to be free of unreasonable government intrusion. But insofar as Fourth Amendment protection extends to a motor vehicle, it is the right to privacy that is the touchstone of our inquiry.[146]

But Justice Blackmun's final caveat about the expectation of privacy in the interior of an automobile has apparently been abandoned. In *South Dakota v. Opperman* (1976), an illegally parked automobile was impounded and an inventory was made of the contents, including the contents of the closed but unlocked glove compartment. The glove compartment contained a quantity of marihuana. The Court ruled that, where an automobile has been lawfully impounded and the police have conducted a standard inventory, such caretaking procedures are reasonable under the Fourth Amendment.[147]

Border Searches

As early as *Carroll*, the Supreme Court had observed that border searches were exceptional, implying that they did not come within the zone of the Fourth Amendment. But the *Carroll* dicta spoke only of searches at the point of crossing an international boundary. In addition to permanent inspection stations at points of entry, either at the border or at airport terminals, the border patrol has had roving as well as permanent checkpoints located at some distance from the border. In *Almeida-Sanchez v. United States,* a five-justice majority ruled that, in the absence of warrants or probable cause, it was invalid for a roving patrol unit to search an automobile at a distance of some twenty miles from the border. Justice Stewart, writing for the majority, pointed out that "the *Carroll* doctrine does not declare a field day for the police in searching automobiles. Automobile or no automobile, there must be probable cause for the search."[148]

Although the *Almeida-Sanchez* rule requiring probable cause was subsequently extended to permanent border checkpoints, the Court has now substantially retreated from its inflexible position. Roving border patrols may briefly stop an automobile and question the occupants about their citizenship and immigration status based on a standard of reasonable suspicion that the car contains aliens, but further detention or search must be based on probable cause.[149] Routine stops and questioning about citizenship at inland permanent checkpoints do not even require individualized reasonable suspicion, but searches of automobiles continue to require consent or probable cause.[150]

WIRETAPPING AND EAVESDROPPING

In 1890, Louis Brandeis, then a Boston attorney, wrote that "numerous mechanical devices threaten to make good the prediction that 'what is whispered in the closet shall be proclaimed from the house-tops.' "[151] In our age of parabolic microphones, sonic-wave listening devices, and Watergate, there is a kind of Orwellian ring to Brandeis's comment. Brandeis sensed then that technology could outstrip the legal protection of privacy, and his prediction did not fall far short.

The advent of the telephone and its widespread use, coupled with later technological advances, made a constitutional battle over privacy in this area inevitable. The constitutional law of search and seizure was property oriented, unprepared to cope with such challenges to privacy as the telephone and its adaptation to criminal investigations through wiretapping. A wiretap did not necessarily involve a physical intrusion into a protected area, and this lack of property trespass prompted the Supreme Court in 1928 to rule that such wiretaps were not covered by the Fourth Amendment.[152] The majority opinion in *Olmstead v. United States* provoked strong dissents, particularly from Justices Holmes and Brandeis. Holmes called wiretapping by the government "dirty business" and concluded that "for my part I think it a lesser evil that some criminals should escape than that the government should play an ignoble part."[153] Brandeis in his dissent, anticipating the search for a broader definition of the Fourth Amendment by a quarter of a century, stated:

The makers of our Constitution undertook to secure conditions favorable to the pursuit of happiness. They recognized the significance of man's spiritual nature, of his feelings and of his intellect. They knew that only a part of the pain, pleasure and satisfactions of life are to be found in material things. They sought to protect Americans in their beliefs, their thoughts, their emotions and their sensations. They conferred, as against the government, the right to be let alone— the most comprehensive of rights and the right most valued by civilized men. To protect that right, every unjustifiable intrusion by the government upon the privacy of the individual, whatever the means employed, must be deemed a violation of the 4th Amendment.[154]

In less than ten years, the Court returned to the wiretapping issue. In *Nardone v. United States* (1937), the Court seized on section 605 of the Federal Communications Act of 1934 and interpreted the statute to ban federal officers from intercepting and divulging telephone messages.[155] Whatever the merits of the case against wiretapping, the fact was that many law enforcement agencies, including the FBI, favored its use, and these agencies continued to wiretap after the ruling.[156] In fact, the case for wiretapping as an essential tool of law enforcement gained numerous supporters, particularly in Congress, and pressure mounted to legalize controlled wiretapping and electronic eavesdropping. Within a few years, the Court retreated from its implications in the *Nardone* cases, returning to a more traditional analysis in government wiretapping and eavesdropping cases.[157]

In *Goldman v. United States* (1942), its first eavesdropping case, the Court upheld the use of evidence obtained by placing a detectaphone against a wall and listening to a telephone conversation in an adjoining room.[158] This was followed some years later by *On Lee v. United States* (1952), a decision upholding the use of evidence obtained by a radio transmitter concealed on the body of an undercover agent.[159] In both of these cases the majority ruled that there had been no illegal physical invasion of a protected area. Moreover, Justice Jackson, writing for the majority in *Lee*, took up the challenge of "dirty business" and argued:

> The use of informers, accessories, accomplices, false friends, or any of the other betrayals which are "dirty business" may raise serious questions of credibility. To the extent that they do, a defendant is entitled to broad latitude to probe credibility by cross-examination. . . . But to the extent that the argument for exclusion departs from such orthodox evidentiary canons as relevancy and credibility, it rests solely on the proposition that the Government shall be arbitrarily penalized for the low morals of its informers. However unwilling we as individuals may be to approve conduct such as that of Chin Poy, such disapproval must not be thought to justify a social policy of the magnitude necessary to arbitrarily exclude otherwise relevant evidence.[160]

The underlying values that separate Justice Jackson's position from Justice Frankfurter's dissent are reasonably typical of the broad and often conflicting policy differences that have separated the Court in this area and other areas of criminal justice. The gulf is most apparent in the following passage from the dissent:

> Suppose it be true that through "dirty business" it is easier for prosecutors and police to bring an occasional criminal to heel. It is most uncritical to assume that unless the Government is allowed to practice "dirty business" crime would become rampant or would go unpunished.
>
> In the first place, the social phenomena of crime are imbedded in the texture of our society. Equally deep-seated are the causes of all that is sordid and ineffective in the administration of our criminal law. These are outcroppings, certainly in considerable part, of modern industrialism and of the prevalent standards of the community, related to the inadequacy in our day of early American methods and machinery for law enforcement and to the small pursuit of scientific inquiry into the causes and treatment of crime. My deepest feeling against giving legal sanction to such "dirty business" as the record in this case discloses is that it makes for lazy ·and not alert law enforcement. It puts a premium on force and fraud, not on imagination and enterprise and professional training.[161]

The dirty business of wiretapping and eavesdropping raises serious questions, and the Court has struggled with these manifold problems unsuccessfully for over a quarter of a century. Justice Frankfurter's dissent appears to suggest that electronic surveillance is constitutionally and morally wrong. But what was the basis of the wrong? Had the informer in *Lee* obtained his information without a radio transmitter, he would have been allowed to testify, subject to cross-examination regarding his credibility. The electronic recording of the conversation would seem to increase its reliability. Police frequently use informers as well as undercover agents to obtain information. They may gain information by misrepresentation, by deception, and by consent. They may use electronic devices or they may rely on their memory. Yet merely because the police are searching for evidence would seem to be an insufficient basis for coverage under the Fourth Amendment, unless the amendment is broadened to cover not only unreasonable searches and seizures, but also unreasonable investigations.[162] For example, is it unreasonable for an officer to gain entrance by consent—a consent given as an attempted bribe—and then surreptitiously to record the attempted bribe? The Supreme Court has answered no.[163] And the Court has also said that even when a defendant was unaware that the incriminating conversation was being made to an informer the use of a recording device was not unconstitutional.[164] If, however, governmental access to a conversation was gained by intrusion into a protected area, then the Court held that the recorded conversation was not admissible as evidence.[165]

As we can see, there was some confusion in the Supreme Court's decisions in the wiretapping–electronic eavesdropping area during the 1950s and early 1960s. Beginning in 1957[166] there was some movement in the direction of bringing wiretapping and electronic eavesdropping within the scope of the Fourth Amendment. This was finally accomplished in 1967, first in *Berger v. New York*[167] and then in *Katz v. United States*. In *Berger*, the Court struck down New York's eavesdropping statute, but explicitly held that electronic eavesdropping was subject to Fourth Amendment protection and consequently a statute meeting the requirements of the amendment would be valid. Some months later, in *Katz*, the Court held that the decisions in *Olmstead* and *Goldman* were no longer controlling. *Katz* involved an electronic recording of a conversation in a public phone booth. The Court held that when one enters a phone booth and shuts the door, one is "entitled to assume that the words he utters into the mouthpiece will not be broadcast to the world."[168] Having brought electronic recording within the limitations of the Fourth Amendment, the Court then proceeded to implicitly invite legislative authorization of judicial warrants in wiretapping and electronic eavesdropping by noting that "it is clear that this surveillance was so narrowly circumscribed that a duly authorized magistrate, properly notified of the need for such investigation, specifically informed of the basis on which it was to proceed, and clearly apprised of the precise intrusion it would entail, could constitutionally have authorized, with appropriate safeguards, the very limited search and seizure that the Government asserts in fact took place."[169]

One year after *Katz*, Congress passed the Omnibus Crime Control and Safe Streets Act of 1968.[170] Title III of this act bans the unauthorized interception of wire and oral communications and prohibits the use as evidence of such in any legislative, executive, or judicial proceedings. Certain exceptions are made to exempt presidential foreign-intelligence operations and presidential efforts to protect against the unlawful overthrow of the government or against any clear and present danger to the structure and existence of the government. However, in *United States v. United States District Court*,[171] the Supreme Court held that this exemption was not a grant of authority to conduct warrantless taps in cases of domestic-security surveillance. Noting that there is some convergence of the First and Fourth Amendments in national-security cases, the Court cautioned:

> History abundantly documents the tendency of Government—however benevolent and benign its motives—to view with suspicion those who most fervently dispute its policies. Fourth Amendment protections become the more necessary when the targets of official surveillance may be those suspected of unorthodoxy in their political beliefs. The danger to political dissent is acute where the Government attempts to act under so vague a concept as the power to protect "domestic security." Given the difficulty of defining the domestic security interest, the danger of abuse in acting to protect that interest becomes apparent.[172]

The majority did suggest, however, that Congress could provide for different standards and procedures for judicial taps in domestic-security cases as distinct from "ordinary crime."[173] After placing certain limitations on the manufacture and sale of listening devices, the 1968 act authorizes federal judicial warrants for taps for selected criminal offenses and similarly allows states to pass legislation authorizing taps.[174] The procedures for application and issuance of wiretap-eavesdrop warrants are similar to those that apply to regular warrants, with two exceptions: Wiretap-eavesdrop warrants do not specify a specific conversation to be intercepted, nor do they require that a warrant be served. A judge, on proper application, is authorized to issue the warrant if:

3.   (a) there is probable cause for belief that an individual is committing, has committed, or is about to commit a particular offense enumerated in section 2516 of this chapter;

(b) there is probable cause for belief that particular communications concerning that offense will be obtained through such interception;

(c) normal investigative procedures have been tried and have failed or reasonably appear to be unlikely to succeed if tried or to be too dangerous;

(d) there is probable cause for belief that facilities from which, or the place where, the wire or oral communications are to be intercepted are being used, or are about to be used, in connection with the commission of such offense, or are leased to, listed in the name of, or commonly used by such person.

4.   Each order authorizing or approving the interception of any wire or oral communication shall specify—

(a) the identity of the person, if known, whose communications are to be intercepted;

(b) the nature and location of the communications facilities as to which, or the place where, authority to intercept is granted;

(c) a particular description of the type of communication sought to be intercepted, and a statement of the particular offense to which it relates;

(d) the identity of the agency authorized to intercept the communications, and of the person authorizing the application; and

(e) the period of time during which such interception is authorized, including a statement as to whether or not the interception shall automatically terminate when the described communication has been first obtained.[175]

Although judicial controls in the area of wiretapping and eavesdropping may well be preferred to the chaos that obtained in this area before 1968, wiretapping legislation in general and the 1968 act in particular present several problems. The legislation is difficult to square with the Fourth Amendment because warrants here lack the degree of particularity thought to be essential in normal warrants. As Justice Douglas remarked:

If a statute were to authorize placing a policeman in every home or office where it was shown that there was probable cause to believe that evidence of crime would be obtained, there is little doubt that it would be struck down as a bald invasion of privacy, far worse than the general warrants prohibited by the Fourth Amendment. I can see no difference between such a statute and one

authorizing electronic surveillance, which, in effect, places an invisible policeman in the home. If anything, the latter is more offensive because the home-
owner is completely unaware of the invasion of privacy.[176]

The act requires that an application must contain a particular description and
location of a proposed tap and a particular description of the type of communications sought to be intercepted as well as the identity (if known), of the
person whose communications are to be intercepted. However, the Court has
upheld a warrant that specified conversations between a named individual and
"persons as yet unknown."[177] When the "person as yet unknown" turned out
to be the wife of the individual named in the warrant, Justice Douglas, dissenting, observed, "Under today's decision a wiretap warrant apparently need
specify but one name and a national dragnet becomes operative. Members of
the family of the suspect, visitors in his home, doctors, ministers, merchants,
teachers, attorneys, and everyone having any possible connection . . . are
caught up in this web."[178]

Beyond the broad constitutional question of generality, certain provisions
in the 1968 act are of dubious constitutionality. For example, under Title III
police may undertake an emergency forty-eight-hour tap without judicial authorization. The act fails to define *emergency* or to provide any protection against
using an emergency tap as a fishing expedition in order to obtain probable
cause for the issuance of a judicial warrant.

Of course it can be argued that tapping is a useful if not indispensable tool
of law enforcement—an argument that has been made many times.[179] Still,
however strong the argument for electronic eavesdropping, its efficacy has yet
to be demonstrated. At least on the basis of annual reports, wiretapping could
not be endorsed as an efficient tool in law enforcement. For example, in 1972
there were 841 installed state and federal taps,[180] leading to 2,861 arrests.[181]
However, the average cost of a tap was $5,435, and only 402 convictions were
reported, a hardly impressive conviction rate of 14 percent.[182]

The question of efficacy aside, it does not seem likely that a ban on the use
of wiretapping will be passed at the national level. On the other hand, efforts
to introduce additional controls over "judge shopping" and "emergency taps"
may be in order.

MINOR INTRUSIONS

Over a quarter of a century ago, Justice Frankfurter wrote one of the most
cherished passages in constitutional rhetoric. *Rochin v. California* (1952) involved a defendant who had swallowed capsules thought by police to contain
illegal drugs. When their own physical force was unsuccessful in obtaining the
capsules, the officers took the defendant to a hospital and ordered his stomach
pumped. In reversing the conviction, Justice Frankfurter wrote:

We are compelled to conclude that the proceedings by which this conviction was obtained do more than offend some fastidious squeamishness or private sentimentalism about combatting crime too energetically. This is conduct that shocks the conscience. Illegally breaking into the privacy of the petitioner, the struggle to open his mouth and remove what was there, the forcible extraction of his stomach's contents—this course of proceeding by agents of government to obtain evidence is bound to offend even hardened sensibilities. They are methods too close to the rack and the screw to permit of constitutional differentiation.[183]

In the absence of the element of force that was present in the conduct of the officers in *Rochin*, it is by no means certain that the Court today would hold stomach pumping without consent to be unconstitutional.[184] Indeed, just five years after *Rochin*, a majority of the Court at least indirectly sanctioned the involuntary taking of a sample of blood in a drunk-driving case against a claim that the procedure violated, among other things, the Fourth Amendment.[185] Some years later, after the application of the exclusionary rule to the states, the Court again confronted the issue of the involuntary blood sample and the Fourth Amendment.

In *Schmerber v. California* (1966), a five-justice majority held that although compulsory blood tests are governed by the Fourth Amendment, they are "minor intrusions."[186] The Court stressed that a test must be justified by the circumstances, here the apparent intoxication of the defendant, and that no warrant was required because delay would have destroyed the evidence (the alcohol content of the blood would diminish with the passage of time necessary to secure a warrant). The majority qualified its holding by noting that the test had been conducted by qualified medical personnel in a medical environment.[187]

Following *Schmerber*, the Court has also upheld investigative seizures of evidence without a warrant for fingernail scrapings,[188] handwriting examples,[189] and voice exemplars.[190] Unfortunately, the rationale of the Court in these cases is far from clear. In the fingernail-scraping case, the majority relied on *Chimel*, that a limited search incidental to arrest for evidence was reasonable even though the scrapings were taken at a time when the defendant was not under arrest. In one of the voice exemplar cases, the majority held that requiring a witness before a grand jury to produce a voice exemplar did not come within the protection of the Fourth Amendment because

the Fourth Amendment provides no protection for what "a person knowingly exposes to the public, even in his own home or office."
. . . The physical characteristics of a person's voice, its tone and manner, as opposed to the content of a specific conversation, are constantly exposed to the public. Like a man's facial characteristics, or handwriting, his voice is repeatedly produced for others to hear. No person can have a reasonable expec-

tation that others will not know the sound of his voice, any more than he can reasonably expect that his face will be a mystery to the world.[191]

Thus in the absence of an expectation of privacy, there was no requirement that the grand jury request satisfy a test of reasonableness.[192]

Although one case involved the seizure of fingernail scrapings and the other case the seizure of a voice sample, making the former subject to the Fourth Amendment and the latter not would appear to rest on a trivial distinction. Why are fingernails less public than a voice? The fact is that the Court has been unable to agree on a standard to control police identification procedures. The voice exemplar case comes closest to providing a satisfactory justification: The Fourth Amendment has its limits and ought not to be expected to provide protections that stretch language beyond those limits.[193]

THE EXCLUSIONARY RULE

Considering the extraordinary extent of the law of arrest, search, and seizure, only briefly detailed above, it is sometimes startling to realize that little of this law would exist but for the exclusionary rule. It is largely through the exclusionary rule that the law of search and seizure has been developed. The rule, first announced at the federal level in *Weeks v. United States* in 1914[194] and applied to the states in *Mapp v. Ohio* in 1961, allows a defendant in a criminal trial, who satisfies the standing requirement, to make a timely (generally pretrial) motion for the return and/or trial suppression of illegally seized evidence.[195]

Almost from the outset, the rule has been the subject of great controversy. Its critics have noted that it violates the common-law practice of not stopping in a criminal case to determine a collateral issue, here, the legality of the evidence.[196] However, the more convincing argument is twofold: first, that the costs of the rule are too high, and second, that the rule does not accomplish its goal.

The cost argument is really two separate arguments. The original argument was simply that by allowing felons to go free, the rule undermines the deterrent purpose of the criminal law: "By every unnecessary limitation the judges place on police efficiency, and by every discovered criminal they protect from deserved punishment, those judges are derogating from the force of deterrence and contributing to the country's already too heavy and increasing burden of crime."[197] Or, as Justice Cardozo succinctly put it, by excluding illegally seized evidence "the criminal is to go free because the Constable has blundered."[198] Undoubtedly the rule *does* allow felons to go free; generally, it is asserted by those defendants who, in the absence of the rule, would likely be convicted. This, in turn, gives rise to the second part of the cost argument, that the political costs to the judiciary are too high. The rule is unpopular not only with the police and many lower-court judges, but additionally it is a rule that the public finds difficult to accept. In practical terms it makes the vindication of the rights of innocent people dependent on their assertion by a felon, a condition not likely to generate much public confidence. Any judicial rule that has the appearance of coddling criminals is likely to be suspect to the public,[199] and in turn, through the loss of confidence, may weaken the judiciary.[200]

The second argument against the exclusionary rule, and the one most debated today, is that the rule has failed to achieve its goal of deterring illegal conduct by the police. Perhaps the foremost judicial exponent of this argument is Chief Justice Burger, who wrote:

> Some clear demonstration of the benefits and effectiveness of the exclusionary rule is required to justify it in view of the high price it extracts from society—the release of countless guilty criminals. . . . But there is no empirical evidence to support the claim that the rule actually deters illegal conduct of law enforcement officials. . . .
>
> There are several reasons for this failure. The rule does not apply any direct sanction to the individual official whose illegal conduct results in the exclusion of evidence in a criminal trial. With rare exceptions law enforcement agencies do not impose direct sanctions on the individual officer responsible for a particular judicial application of the suppression doctrine. . . . Thus there is virtually nothing done to bring about a change in his practices. The immediate sanction triggered by the application of the rule is visited upon the prosecutor whose case against a criminal is either weakened or destroyed. The doctrine deprives the police in no real sense; except that apprehending wrongdoers is their business, police have no more stake in successful prosecutions than prosecutors or the public.
>
> . . . But the prosecutor who loses his case because of police misconduct is not an official in the police department; he can rarely set in motion any corrective action or administrative penalties. Moreover, he does not have control or direction over police procedures or police actions that lead to the exclusion of evidence.
>
> . . . Suppressing unchallenged truth has set guilty criminals free but demonstrably has neither deterred deliberate violations of the Fourth Amendment nor decreased those errors in judgment that will inevitably occur given the pressures inherent in police work having to do with serious crimes.[201]

Although empirical data on the impact of the exclusionary rule are inconclusive,[202] the case against the deterrent goal of the rule is perhaps even stronger than suggested by the chief justice. For example, it has been suggested that deterrence does not work unless two factors are present: first, a desire to prosecute and, second, a need to introduce some item that has been seized illegally. Thus thousands of illegal arrests are beyond the deterrence of the rule, either because they were intended as harassment with no intent to prosecute or because they did not involve a seizure of evidence needed for prosecution.[203] In short, the efficacy of the rule may depend on the police-prosecutor disposition of a case. In cases where no prosecution takes place, or where illegally seized evidence is not used in a prosecution, or where pleas of guilty are entered, the rule simply does not come into operation.

Furthermore, the rule may have undesirable side effects, among them a tendency to induce the police to commit perjury,[204] particularly in regard to whether the items seized were in plain view. A reliance on the rule may also forestall the development of other mechanisms for the control of illegal searches and seizures, such as practical tort remedies.

It is evident that the arguments against the *Mapp* exclusionary rule have received an increasingly sympathetic response from the Supreme Court. The Court's generally hostile and critical position is evident in its increasingly permissive response to police latitude in street and automobile searches. Such a critical position almost of necessity precludes any expansion of the scope of the exclusionary rule, and this was made clear in a 1974 decision that refused to extend the *Mapp* rule to the proceedings of a grand jury. A witness who had been the probable victim of an illegal search challenged the grand jury's questions on the grounds that they violated the Fourth Amendment because they were predicated on an illegal seizure. The Court concluded that applying the rule would have little deterrent effect.[205]

Finally, in *Stone v. Powell,* the Court reversed a policy dating back to the early 1960s, which allowed state prisoners to obtain a federal writ of habeas corpus if illegally seized evidence was admitted in their trials. In this 1976 decision, the Court ruled that where a state has provided a defendant with an opportunity for full and fair litigation of a Fourth Amendment claim, the defendant may not, on conviction, collaterally attack the conviction in a federal habeas proceeding solely on the basis that illegally seized evidence was admitted at defendant's trial. Of course, a few state prisoners are still able to seek review of a Fourth Amendment claim by appeal from the state's highest appellate court directly to the Supreme Court. The decision, however, now forecloses federal district courts from backstopping the Supreme Court in the area of the Fourth Amendment. The Court's opinion again indicated its disenchantment with *Mapp's* exclusionary rule:

> Application of the rule . . . deflects the truthfinding process and often frees the guilty. The disparity in particular cases between the error committed by the police officer and the windfall afforded a guilty defendant by application of the rule is contrary to the idea of proportionality that is essential to the concept of justice. Thus, although the rule is thought to deter unlawful police activity in part through the nurturing of respect for Fourth Amendment values, if applied indiscriminately it may well have the opposite effect of generating disrespect for the law and administration of justice. These long-recognized costs of the rule persist when a criminal conviction is sought to be overturned on collateral review on the ground that a search-and-seizure claim was erroneously rejected by two or more tiers of state courts.[206]

Further evidence of the current Court's disapproval of the exclusionary rule came in *Rakas v. Illinois* (1978).[207] Rakas had been a passenger in a suspected armed-robbery getaway car. The car was stopped and searched, and rifle shells from the glove compartment and a sawed-off shotgun were seized. At Rakas's trial, the judge denied his motion to exclude the seized evidence, maintaining that as a mere passenger Rakas did not have standing to move exclusion. A narrow majority of five justices, led by Justice Rehnquist, upheld the trial court's position. Had the majority limited its opinion to the issue of standing, it would have been noteworthy only for its almost total disregard of the body of case law in the area of standing.[208] Instead, Justice Rehnquist's opinion became the occasion for yet another retreat in Fourth Amendment jurisprudence. Claiming adherence to the *Katz* formula of expectation of privacy and eschewing a narrow property basis for its conclusion, the opinion nonetheless tied the Fourth Amendment to property interests. Justice Rehnquist argued that, because Rakas had neither a property nor a possessory interest in the car or the items seized, he had no legitimate expectation of privacy. The opinion did indicate that legitimate expectations of privacy are tied to both real and personal property as well as to understandings that are recognized and permitted by society;[209] still the opinion did not address the question of whether society has recognized as legitimate a passenger's expectation of privacy in a private automobile. The implications in *Rakas* for automobile passengers, however, appear to go well beyond the facts of the case, seeming to undermine the generally accepted formulations of defense standing to exclude illegally seized evidence. As such, the decision constitutes yet another erosion of the exclusionary rule.

Although a majority of the Burger Court has indicated a strong distaste for the decision in *Mapp*, still a case can be made for the exclusionary rule. The argument generally begins with a negative; that is, no practical alternative to the rule exists, either in the form of tort liability against the police or in the form of internal procedures to discipline illegal law enforcement.[210] Although civil remedies are not necessarily precluded,[211] the immediate prospects are far from promising. Assuming that violations of the Fourth Amendment by the police should have some measurable consequence, then, in the absence of effective alternatives, exclusion is a needed if regrettable rule.

However, casting the argument about the exclusionary rule solely in terms of deterrence ignores the moral raitonale that has also been used in its justification.[212] At least since the time of *Weeks*, when the rule was first applied to the federal courts, a sense of judicial integrity has been associated with the rule.[213] The "clean-hands" argument asserts that "nothing can destroy a government more quickly than its failure to observe its own laws, or worse, to disregard the character of its own existence."[214] Justice Brandeis stated it in this manner: "Our government is the potent, the omnipresent teacher. For good or for ill, it teaches the whole people by its example. . . . If the government becomes a lawbreaker, it breeds contempt for law; it invites every man to become a law unto himself; it invites anarchy."[215]

Breeding contempt for law generally, and in particular for those restraints on government that have been placed in the Constitution, is not an argument that can be dismissed lightly. Although there is little empirical evidence regarding socialization and the law, it is reasonable to assume that illegal searches and seizures increase cynicism and contempt, for both the criminal law and the police, among the groups most likely to come into contact with the criminal justice system.[216]

Of course, if a viable alternative to the exclusionary rule existed—that is, an alternative that demonstrably reduced illegal searches and seizures—then the contempt-of-law argument would be greatly weakened. Still, even a viable alternative would leave unsolved the problem of whether it is proper for a judicial body under any circumstance to sanction police violation of a constitutionally protected right. As Professor Dallin Oaks noted, "It would be intolerable if the guarantees against unreasonable search and seizure could be violated without practical consequence. . . . By demonstrating that society will attach serious consequences to the violation of constitutional rights, the exclusionary rule invokes and magnifies the moral and educational force of the law."[217]

CONCLUSION

Short of a total retreat from the exclusionary rule or the unlikely possibility of new legislative interest in protecting the rights guaranteed by the Fourth Amendment, we shall continue to face a series of unfortunate but largely unavoidable problems. The reasonableness standard of the Fourth Amendment creates a continuing problem in judicial interpretation. Given the reasonableness standard and the fact that arrest, search, and seizure are at once widely invoked and invoked under myriad conditions, it is not particularly surprising that these areas of the law are plagued by uncertainty. A degree of ambiguity is a necessary consequence not only of conceptual and environmental constraints, but additionally of the judiciary's unwillingness to adopt extreme measures.

Uncertainty would quickly be diminished if the judiciary were to adopt excessively narrow rules aimed at virtually eliminating the need for police discretion in effectuating an arrest, search, or seizure. This could be done, for example, by adopting demanding and exacting warrant requirements or by increasing the quantity and quality of information needed to support probable cause. At the other extreme, the judiciary could increase police discretion to a point where uncertainty would also disappear simply because discretion would justify virtually any conduct. Surely the language of the Fourth Amendment demands that the judiciary define a reasonable pattern for arrest, search, and seizure, a pattern that protects individual privacy and freedom of movement and still enables the police to be reasonably effective in enforcing the criminal laws.

Even though a measure of uncertainty is a necessary by-product of the reasonableness standard, the standard alone does not account for the meandering path of the Supreme Court's decisions in this area. As is true in other areas of constitutional disputes, the Court has avoided comprehensive doctrinal development by the simple expedient of narrowly addressing particular categories of fact (the automobile, the home). By focusing on the ever-shifting facts of arrest, search, and seizure, the Court has failed to provide a minimum conceptual framework that could act as an intellectual bridge from one problem to another. A compromise is necessary: Certainly the law should not be locked into the concrete of excessively narrow principles, but the need for a convincing conceptual framework that would keep uncertainty within tolerable limits must be recognized.

NOTES

1. Gen. 19:4–11; Deut. 24:10; and Josh. 7:10–26.
2. See generally Nelson B. Lasson, *The History and Development of the Fourth Amendment* (Baltimore: Johns Hopkins Press, 1937), chap. 1.
3. See generally James Fitzjames Stephen, *A History of the Criminal Law in England* (London: Macmillan, 1883), vol. 1.
4. See generally William Holdsworth, *A History of English Law* (London: Methuen, 1938), vol. 10, pp. 658–672.
5. *Entick v. Carrington,* 19 How. St. Tr. 1030, 1066–1074 (1765).
6. Quoted in Lasson, *History and Development,* pp. 49–50.
7. Quoted in William Tudor, *Life of James Otis* (Boston: Wells and Lilly, 1823), pp. 56–57.
8. Lasson, *History and Development,* pp. 79–105.
9. *Boyd v. United States,* 116 U.S. 616, 630 (1886).
10. Indeed, although a *subpoena duces tecum* is broadly covered by the Fourth Amendment, see *FTC v. American Tobacco Co.,* 264 U.S. 298 (1924), the required production of private documents having a public aspect to them or public documents in private custody raises substantially different issues than those decided in *Boyd.* See *Wilson v. United States,* 221 U.S. 361 (1911), corporate records; *Doris v. United States,* 328 U.S. 582 (1946), ration coupons; and *Shapiro v. United States,* 335 U.S. 1 (1947), records under Emergency Price Control Act. More recent opinions have diverged even further from *Boyd.* See *Anderson v. Maryland,* 425 U.S. 435 (1976), upholding a subpoena of bank records.
11. *United States v. Jeffers,* 342 U.S. 48 (1951).
12. *Taylor v. United States,* 286 U.S. 1 (1932).
13. *Gouled v. United States,* 255 U.S. 298 (1921).
14. *Carroll v. United States,* 267 U.S. 132 (1925).
15. *Ex parte Jackson,* 96 U.S. 727 (1878).
16. See *Lewis v. United States,* 385 U.S. 206, 211 (1966).
17. Justice Harlan concurring in *Katz v. United States,* 389 U.S. 347, 361 (1967).
18. *Hester v. United States,* 265 U.S. 57 (1924).
19. *Katz v. United States,* 389 U.S. at 350–351.

20. See *Accarino v. United States,* 179 F.2d 456 (1949).

21. *Agnello v. United States,* 269 U.S. 20, 32 (1925).

22. *Johnson v. United States,* 333 U.S. 10, 13–14 (1948); see also *McDonald v. United States,* 335 U.S. 451 (1948), and *United States v. Jeffers,* 342 U.S. 48 (1951).

23. *Agnello v. United States,* 269 U.S. at 30.

24. See note, "The Neglected Fourth Amendment Problem in Arrest Entries," 23 *Stan. L. Rev.* 995 (1971).

25. See *McKnight v. United States,* 183 F.2d 977 (1950).

26. See *Lankford v. Schmidt,* 240 F. Supp. 550 (1965), rev. on other grounds, 364 F.2d 197 (1966).

27. For a lengthy discussion of the issue of warrantless arrest entry into a dwelling, see Justice Stewart's opinion in *Coolidge v. New Hampshire,* 403 U.S. 443, 476–481, joined only by Justices Douglas, Brennan, and Marshall; and rebuttal by Justice White, at 510–515 (see especially n. 1 at 510).

28. See *Marron v. United States,* 275 U.S. 192 (1927); *Go-Bart v. United States,* 282 U.S. 134 (1931); *United States v. Lefkowitz,* 285 U.S. 452 (1932); *United States v. Harris,* 331 U.S. 145 (1947); and *United States v. Rabinowitz,* 339 U.S. 56 (1950).

29. *Chimel v. California,* 395 U.S. 752, 762–763 (1969).

30. *Shipley v. California,* 395 U.S. 818 (1969); and *Von Cleef v. New Jersey,* 395 U.S. 814 (1969).

31. *Mincey v. Arizona,* 434 U.S. 1343 (1978); see also *Vale v. Louisiana,* 399 U.S. 30, 34 (1970).

32. *Coolidge v. New Hampshire,* 403 U.S. at 466, n. 24; see also *Harris v. United States,* 390 U.S. 234 (1968).

33. *Johnson v. United States,* 333 U.S. at 14.

34. *McDonald v. United States,* 335 U.S. at 454.

35. A dwelling that is a moving vehicle, such as a motor home in mobile condition, might be so considered; see *Johnson v. United States,* 333 U.S. at 15.

36. See Horace Wilgus, "Arrest Without a Warrant," 22 *Mich. L. Rev.* 798, 804 (1924).

37. *Ker v. California,* 374 U.S. 23 (1963); and *Warden v. Hayden,* 387 U.S. 294 (1967).

38. *United States v. Santana,* 427 U.S. 38, 43 (1976).

39. Charles Dickens, *Pickwick Papers,* chap. 24.

40. *Semayne's Case,* 77 Eng. Rep. 194, 195 (1603). See also *Case of Richard Curtis,* 168 Eng. Rep. 67 (1756).

41. 18 U.S.C. 3109 (1964).

42. *Ker v. California,* 374 U.S. at 38, 53.

43. See *Miller v. United States,* 357 U.S. 301, 308 at n. 8 (1958).

44. Concurring and dissenting in *Ker v. California,* 374 U.S. at 47.

45. See note, "No-Knock and the Constitution," 25 *Minn. L. Rev.* 871 (1971).

46. Ibid. at 878–879.

47. E.g., *California v. Costello,* 432 P.2d 706 (1967).

48. *Ker v. California,* 374 U.S. at 55–58.

49. 21 U.S.C. 879(b).

50. Pub. L. 91-358, § 23-522(c)–(2).

51. For an interesting account of events in 1973, see Andrew Malcolm, "Violent Drug Raids," *New York Times,* June 25, 1973, p. 1.

52. See note, "Announcement in Police Entries," 80 *Yale L.J.* 139, 155–174 (1970).

53. See *Sabbath v. United States,* 391 U.S. 585 (1968).

54. See *United States v. Pratter,* 465 F.2d 227 (7th Cir. 1972); *United States v. Artieri,* 491 F.2d 440 (2d Cir. 1974); and *United States v. Wylie,* 462 F.2d 1178 (D.C. Cir. 1972).

55. The warrant requirement both in law and in practice is largely confined to searches and seizures, rather than arrests, that can be made with or without a warrant.

56. E.g., *McDonald v. United States* and *United States v. Jeffers.*

57. *Coolidge v. New Hampshire*, 403 U.S. at 449–450.

58. *Shadwick v. City of Tampa*, 407 U.S. 345, 350-351 (1972).

59. See Abraham S. Blumberg, *Criminal Justice* (Chicago: Quadrangle, 1967), chap. 3.

60. *Connally v. Georgia*, 429 U.S. 245 (1977).

61. *McDonald v. United States*, 335 U.S. at 455.

62. See Warren LaFave, *Arrest: The Decision to Take a Suspect into Custody* (Boston: Little, Brown, 1965), pp. 502–503; and Abraham Goldstein, "Reflections on Two Models," 26 *Stan. L. Rev.* 1009, 1024 (1974).

63. Lasson, *History and Development*, pp. 100–101; and Telford Taylor, *Two Studies in Constitutional Interpretation* (Columbus: Ohio State University Press, 1969), pp. 42–43.

64. *Arkansas v. Sanders*, _____ U.S. _____ (1979).

65. Dissenting in *Berger v. New York*, 388 U.S. 41, 98–99 (1967).

66. *Stanford v. Texas*, 379 U.S. 476, 485–486 (1965). See also *Lo-Ji Sales, Inc. v. New York*, _____ U.S. _____ (1979), where the Court held that the Fourth Amendment does not countenance open-ended warrants (completed during the search or after the seizure).

67. *Steele v. United States*, 267 U.S. 498, 503 (1925).

68. *United States v. Curtis*, 427 F.2d 630, 632 (1970).

69. Cf. *West v. Cabell*, 153 U.S. 78 (1894), where the court indicated that the arrest of one Vandy West on a warrant specifying James West would make the officers liable on the official bond.

70. E.g., *Johnson v. United States* and *Henry v. United States*, 361 U.S. 98 (1959).

71. *Stacey v. Emery*, 97 U.S. 642, 645 (1878).

72. *Brinegar v. United States*, 338 U.S. 160, 175–176 (1949). Although not directly relevant to the area of criminal justice, note should be made of the flexibility of probable cause in the area of administrative searches and regulatory inspections. In two cases in 1967, the Supreme Court extended the scope of the Fourth Amendment to routine area inspections in the enforcement of municipal codes, such as health and safety codes, *Camara v. Municipal Court*, 387 U.S. 523, and *See v. City of Seattle*, 387 U.S. 541. However, the Court balanced the public interest in such routine inspections against the level of intrusion and concluded that, although warrants would be required, probable cause for area warrants could be less than would be considered sufficient in criminal cases. In effect, *Camara* introduced a sliding scale of probability, depending on the level of intrusion. See Peter S. Greenberg, "The Balance of Interests Theory and the Fourth Amendment," 61 *Calif. L. Rev.* 1011 (1973). For subsequent case developments, see *Colonnade Catering v. United States*, 397 U.S. 72 (1970); and *United States v. Biswell*, 406 U.S. 311 (1972).

73. See *Nathanson v. United States*, 290 U.S. 41, 47 (1933); and *Go-Bart v. United States*, 282 U.S. at 355.

74. *Beck v. Ohio*, 379 U.S. 89 (1964).

75. *Recznik v. City of Lorain*, 393 U.S. 166 (1968).

76. *Aguilar v. Texas*, 378 U.S. 188 (1964).

77. *Draper v. United States*, 358 U.S. 307 (1959).

78. *Spinelli v. United States*, 393 U.S. 410 (1969). Cf. *McCray v. United States*, 386 U.S. 300 (1967).

79. *Draper v. United States*. The dispute has its origins in the different approaches to probable cause taken in *Husty v. United States*, 282 U.S. 694 (1931), and *Nathanson v. United States*.

80. Dissenting in *United States v. Ventresca*, 380 U.S. 102, 121 (1965).

81. *Aguilar v. Texas*, 378 U.S. at 114–115.

82. See such reversals in the positions of Justices Harlan, White, and Fortas in *McCray, Aguilar,* and *Spinelli.*

83. See *United States v. Harris,* 403 U.S. 573 (1971), in which a majority could not agree on an opinion.

84. At least insofar as arrest is concerned, a consensus may be emerging based on *Terry v. Ohio,* 392 U.S. 1 (1968), and *Adams v. Williams,* 407 U.S. 143 (1972). Both cases are treated here on pp. 53–55.

85. See Chief Justice Burger's opinion in *United States v. Harris,* 403 U.S. at 479–580.

86. Of course, absent a seizure, the exclusionary rule would not come into play in an arrest because there is nothing to be excluded at trial. Nor may a defendant claim that a court lacks jurisdiction to try him or her because the arrest was illegal, *Ker v. Illinois* and *Frisbe v. Collins,* 342 U.S. 519 (1952). However, if during the period of illegal detention an otherwise valid confession is obtained, the confession must be excluded as tainted, *Brown v. Illinois,* 422 U.S. 590 (1975).

87. *Kurz v. Moffitt,* 115 U.S. 487 (1885); *Bad Elk v. United States,* 177 U.S. 529 (1900); and *Carroll v. United States,* 267 U.S. 132 (1925).

88. See *Street v. Surdyka,* 492 F.2d 368, 371 (1974).

89. *United States v. Watson,* 423 U.S. 411, 418 (1976). Although the quoted portion of the *Watson* opinion does not limit warrantless arrests to public places, the concurring opinions specifically noted such a limited ruling; see also concurring opinions in *Coolidge v. New Hampshire,* 403 U.S. at 477–478. The *Watson* opinion leaves open the question of warrantless arrests in private areas. It also casts doubt on the current practice of warrantless arrests for misdemeanors not committed in the presence of the arresting officer. This doubt will have to be resolved because it is in conflict with state and local practice.

90. See Drug Abuse Prevention and Control Act 1970, 21 U.S.C. 872 and 26 U.S.C. 7607; *United States v. Grosso,* 225 F. Supp. 161 (1964). In addition to these questions, whether the common law of arrest has constitutional status raises questions about the right to resist unlawful arrest; see *United States v. Moore,* 4837 F.2d 1361 (1973), and cases cited at 1364, n. 1.

91. E.g., 18 U.S.C. 3052, authorizing FBI arrests.

92. *Miller v. United States,* 357 U.S. 301, 305 (1958); and *United States v. Di Re,* 332 U.S. 581, 589 (1948).

93. Unless, in the case of federal officers, there is an applicable federal statute that supersedes state process; see 18 U.S.C. 3041.

94. E.g., *Preston v. United States,* 376 U.S. 364 (1964).

95. See *Peters v. New York,* 392 U.S. 40, 67 (1968); *Minnesota v. Curtis,* 190 N.W.2d 631 (1971); on *Oregon v. O'Neal,* 444 P.2d 951 (1968).

96. Indeed, in most jurisdictions the majority of traffic offenses may be handled by arrest or citation, at the discretion of the officer.

97. *United States v. Robinson,* 414 U.S. 218, 235 (1973).

98. *Gustafson v. Florida,* 414 U.S. 260 (1973).

99. *United States v. Edwards,* 415 U.S. 800 (1974).

100. E.g., *United States v. Basurto,* 497 F.2d 781 (1974).

101. *Sibron v. New York* and *Peters v. New York,* 392 U.S. 40 (1968).

102. Justice Harlan's concurring opinion in *Terry* did touch on the stop issue, 392 U.S. at 32–33.

103. Ibid. at 21.

104. The reversal of the conviction in *Sibron* underscored the majority's understanding that the initial intrusion must be limited to a pat-down.

105. *Terry v. Ohio,* 392 U.S. at 29.

106. Ibid. at 20, n. 16. It is interesting, however, that *Terry* was decided just in time to provide a constitutional rationale for certain airport antiskyjacking procedures that

were adopted in the early 1970s. E.g., see *United States v. Cyzewski,* 484 F.2d 509 (1973), for a review of the cases.

107. *Adams v. Williams,* 407 U.S. at 145–146.

108. See *United States v. Harris.*

109. *Brown v. Texas,* _____ U.S. _____ (1979). See also *Dunaway v. New York,* _____ U.S. _____ (1979), where the Court attempted to forestall expanding the definition of *investigatory stop* from a momentary intrusion to a seizure that is an arrest in everything but name. Dunaway was stopped, seized, and taken to a police station for questioning. Since the Dunaway intrusion was equivalent to an arrest, not an investigatory stop, the Court ruled that the standard of probable cause applied.

110. *Schneckloth v. Bustamonte,* 412 U.S. 218 (1973).

111. *Miranda* warnings are required only in custodial situations; *Schneckloth* was limited to noncustodial searches.

112. *Schneckloth v. Bustamonte,* 412 U.S. 218, 232.

113. Ibid. at 231–232.

114. See note, "The Supreme Court, 1972 Term," 87 *Harv. L. Rev.* 213–221 (1973).

115. See, *Johnson v. United States,* 333 U.S. at 13.

116. *Amos v. United States,* 255 U.S. 314 (1921); and *Bumper v. North Carolina,* 391 U.S. 543 (1968).

117. *Stoner v. California,* 376 U.S. 483 (1964).

118. *Chapman v. United States,* 365 U.S. 610 (1961).

119. *Frazier v. Cupp,* 294 U.S. 731 (1969).

120. *United States v. Matlock,* 415 U.S. 164 (1974).

121. Ibid. at 171, n. 7.

122. For a proposed propertied privacy list, see Virginia Cook, "Third-Party Consent Searches," 41 *U. Chi. L. Rev.* 121 (1973).

123. *Boyd v. United States,* 116 U.S. at 633.

124. *Gouled v. United States,* 255 U.S. at 309.

125. Taylor, *Two Studies,* pp. 59–70.

126. *Warden v. Hayden,* 387 U.S. 294, 306–307 (1967).

127. Ibid. at 302–303. See note, "Supreme Court 1966 Term," 81 *Harv. L. Rev.* 112–114 (1967).

128. E.g., *United States v. De Marsh,* 360 F. Supp. 132 (1973).

129. *United States v. Blank,* 459 F.2d 383 (1972).

130. *United States v. Murray,* 492 F.2d 172 (1973).

131. *Warden v. Hayden,* 387 U.S. at 303.

132. *United States v. Poller,* 43 F.2d 911, 914 (1930).

133. *Cady v. Dombrowski,* 413 U.S. 433, 440 (1973).

134. *Carroll v. United States,* 267 U.S. at 153–154.

135. *Brinegar v. United States; Husty v. United States,* 282 U.S. 699 (1931); and *Henry v. United States,* 361 U.S. 98 (1959).

136. *Brinegar v. United States,* 338 U.S. at 182.

137. *Delaware v. Prowe,* _____ U.S. _____ (1979).

138. *Preston v. United States,* 376 U.S. 364, 367 (1964).

139. *Cooper v. California,* 386 U.S. 58 (1967).

140. *Harris v. United States,* 390 U.S. 234 (1968).

141. *Chambers v. Marony,* 399 U.S. 42 (1970).

142. See note, "Warrantless Searches and Seizures of Automobiles," 87 *Harv. L. Rev.* 835, 845 (1974).

143. *Cady v. Dombrowski,* 413 U.S. at 436.

144. *Cardwell v. Lewis,* 417 U.S. 583.

145. *Katz v. United States,* 389 U.S. at 351.

146. *Cardwell v. Lewis,* 94 S. Ct. at 2469–2470.

147. *South Dakota v. Opperman,* 428 U.S. 364 (1976). See also *Texas v. White,* 423 U.S. 67 (1975).

148. *Almeida-Sanchez v. United States,* 413 U.S. 266 (1975).

149. *United States v. Brignoni-Ponce,* 422 U.S. 873 (1975).

150. *United States v. Martinez-Fuerte,* 428 U.S. 543 (1976).

151. Louis Brandeis and Samuel Warren, "The Right to Privacy," 4 *Harv. L. Rev.* 190, 193 (1890).

152. *Olmstead v. United States,* 277 U.S. 438, 465 (1928).

153. Ibid. at 470.

154. Id.

155. *Nardone v. United States,* 302 U.S. 379 (1937); and 308 U.S. 338 (1939). See Alan F. Westin, "The Wire-Tapping Problem," 52 *Colum. L. Rev.* 165 (1952).

156. The FBI reasoned that § 605 banned only the interception and divulgence of telephone messages; hence, interception alone was thought to be valid.

157. E.g., *Goldstein v. United States,* 316 U.S. 114 (1942).

158. *Goldman v. United States,* 316 U.S. 129 (1942).

159. *On Lee v. United States,* 343 U.S. 747 (1952).

160. Ibid. at 757.

161. Ibid. at 760–761.

162. E.g., *Massiah v. United States,* 377 U.S. 201 (1964).

163. *Lopez v. United States,* 373 U.S. 427 (1963).

164. *Osborn v. United States,* 385 U.S. 323 (1966). See also *Hoffa v. United States,* 385 U.S. 293 (1966); and *United States v. White,* 401 U.S. 745 (1971).

165. *Silverman v. United States,* 365 U.S. 505 (1961), the so-called spike-mike case. Cf. *Irvine v. California,* 347 U.S. 128 (1954).

166. See *Benanti v. United States,* 355 U.S. 96 (1957); *Silverman v. United States;* and *Hoffa v. United States.*

167. *Berger v. New York,* 388 U.S. 41 (1967).

168. *Katz v. United States,* 389 U.S. 352.

169. Ibid. at 356–357.

170. 18 U.S.C. 2510.

171. *United States v. United States District Court,* 407 U.S. 297 (1972).

172. Ibid. at 314.

173. On the issue of the convergence of the First and Fourth Amendments, see Alan Westin, *Privacy and Freedom* (New York: Atheneum, 1967), p. 398.

174. The limits of specific federal crimes are broad. In regard to state offenses, the act permits states to include all offenses dangerous to life, limb, or property, and punishable by imprisonment of more than one year.

175. 18 U.S.C. 2520. Warrants can be issued for a maximum of thirty days and are renewable, on reapplication, for an additional thirty days.

176. Concurring in *Berger v. New York,* 388 U.S. at 64–65.

177. *United States v. Kahn,* 415 U.S. 143 (1974).

178. Ibid. at 163. See *United States v. Donovan,* 429 U.S. 413 (1977), where the Court ruled that a warrant application must identify all potential targets for which the government has probable cause but held that failure to totally comply with this requirement does not require the suppression of evidence.

179. See, e.g., Robert Blakey, "Aspects of the Evidence Gathering Process," in *Task Force Report: Organized Crime,* President's Commission on Law Enforcement and Administration of Justice (Washington, D.C.: GPO, 1967), pp. 91–97; cf. Herman Schwartz, "The Legitimation of Electronic Eavesdropping," 67 *Mich. L. Rev.* 455 (1969).

180. This included 779 phone taps, 29 microphone taps, and 33 combination taps.

181. Director of the Administrative Office of the U.S. Courts, *Annual Report, 1973* (Washington, D.C.: GPO, 1974), pp. 590–595.

182. The greatest use was in the areas of gambling and narcotic offenses, and the federal government and the states of New York and New Jersey accounted for 86 percent of the taps installed in 1972. Fifteen other states had statutes authorizing taps.

183. *Rochin v. California,* 342 U.S. 165, 172 (1952).

184. E.g., *United States v. Owens,* 475 F.2d 759 (1973), upholding a nonconsent stomach pumping for a narcotic drug.

185. *Breithaupt v. Abram,* 352 U.S. 432 (1957), decided before *Mapp v. Ohio.*

186. *Schmerber v. California,* 384 U.S. 757, 772 (1966).

187. *Schmerber* also raised the question of noncompulsory self-discrimination, with the majority ruling that the privilege does not apply to physical evidence, such as a blood sample; see the dissent of Justice Black, 384 U.S. at 773.

188. *Cupp v. Murphy,* 412 U.S. 291 (1973).

189. *Gilbert v. California,* 388 U.S. 263 (1967).

190. *United States v. Dionisio,* 410 U.S. 1 (1973); and *United States v. Mara,* 410 U.S. 19 (1973).

191. *United States v. Dionisio,* 410 U.S. at 14.

192. Cf. *Davis v. Mississippi,* 394 U.S. 721 (1969), disallowing fingerprinting in the context of an illegal detention. But see *United States v. Bridges,* 499 F.2d 179 (1974), upholding chemical analysis of hands; and *United States v. D'Amico,* 400 F.2d 331 (1969), upholding the seizure of a hair sample.

193. This is not to suggest, however, that the majority has given a satisfactory answer to the more weighty issues of self-incrimination involved in all of these so-called minor intrusion cases.

194. *Weeks v. United States,* 232 U.S. 383 (1914).

195. For the requirement of standing to assert the rule, see *Jones v. United States,* 362 U.S. 257 (1960), and *Mancusi v. DeForte,* 392 U.S. 364 (1968); for a general discussion of the background of the rule, see H. Frank Way, "Exclusion of Evidence Illegally Obtained," 26 *Tenn. L. Rev.* 332 (1959).

196. The rule, as it relates to illegal evidence, was first announced in the United States in 1841 in *Commonwealth v. Dana,* 2 Met. 329 (Mass).

197. John B. Waite, "Judges and the Crime Burden," 54 *Mich. L. Rev.* 169, 186 (1955).

198. *People v. Defore,* 150 N.E. 585, 587 (1926).

199. E.g., *Gallup Opinion Index,* no. 98 (August 1973): 8–13; and *Gallup Opinion Index,* no. 45 (March 1969): 12.

200. On the political costs of the rule, see John Kaplan, "The Limits of the Exclusionary Rule," 26 *Stan. L. Rev.* 1027, 1035 (1974).

201. Dissenting in *Bivens v. Six Unknown Named Agents,* 403 U.S. 388, 415–418 (1971). Chief Justice Burger wrote this in 1971, and at that time he indicated that he would oppose abandoning the *Mapp* rule until a meaningful substitute was developed. By 1976, concurring in *Stone v. Powell,* 428 U.S. at 500–501, he concluded that the existence of the exclusionary rule inhibits a legislative search for rational alternatives:

> It can no longer be assumed that other branches of government will act while judges cling to this Draconian, discredited device in its present absolutist form. Legislatures are unlikely to create statutory alternatives, or impose direct sanctions on errant police officers or on the public treasury by way of tort actions so long as persons who commit serious crimes continue to reap the enormous and undeserved benefits of the exclusionary rule. And of course, by definition the direct beneficiaries of this rule can be none but persons guilty of crimes.

202. See Dallin Oaks, "Studying the Exclusionary Rule in Search and Seizure," 37 *U. Chi. L. Rev.* 665 (1970); James Spiotto, "Search and Seizure: An Empirical Study," 2 *J. Leg. Stud.* 243 (1973); Michael Ban, "The Impact of *Mapp v. Ohio* on Police Behavior" (Paper delivered at the 1973 meeting of the Midwest Political Science Asso-

ciation meeting); and Bradley Canon, "Taking Advantage of a Quasi-Experiment: The Impact of *Mapp v. Ohio*" (Paper delivered at the 1974 meeting of the American Political Science Association). However, studies by the Government Accounting Office released in 1979 indicated that less than 1 percent of potential federal felony cases were administratively screened out because of the exclusionary rule, and in only 1.3 percent of the cases filed was evidence excluded. A similar study of thirteen state and local jurisdictions concluded that only a small portion of prosecutions were rejected at the screening stage for reasons of due process. See *Los Angeles Times,* July 1, 1979, part I, p. 3.

203. See note, "Search and Seizure in Illinois," 47 *Nw. U. L. Rev.* 493 (1952); and LaFave, *Arrest,* p. 5.

204. Oaks, "Studying the Exclusionary Rule," pp. 739–742.

205. *United States v. Calandra,* 414 U.S. 338, 351 (1974).

206. *Stone v. Powell,* 428 U.S. at 489.

207. *Rakas v. Illinois,* 435 U.S. 922 (1978).

208. As a general rule, a defendant has legal standing to request the exclusion of illegally seized evidence only if the seizure violated the defendant's rights under the Fourth Amendment. But the Court has long held that whether a personal right has been violated does not necessarily depend on a property or possessory interest in the place searched or the items seized; see *Jones v. United States* and *Mancusi v. DeForte,* 392 U.S. 364.

209. *Rakas v. Illinois,* _____ U.S. at n. 12.

210. See Way, "Exclusion of Evidence," pp. 346–349.

211. See *Monroe v. Pape,* 365 U.S. 167 (1961), action under Civil Rights Act, 42 U.S.C. 1983; and *Bevins v. Six Unknown Named Agents.*

212. See Fred G. Bennett, "Judicial Integrity and Judicial Review: An Argument for Expanding the Scope of the Exclusionary Rule," 20 *U.C.L.A. L. Rev.* 1129 (1973).

213. *Weeks v. United States* 232 U.S. at 392.

214. *Mapp v. Ohio,* 367 U.S. at 659.

215. Dissenting in *Olmstead v. United States,* 277 U.S. at 485.

216. See Herbert Jacob, "Black and White Perceptions of Justice in the City" (Paper delivered at the 1970 meeting of the American Political Science Association), pp. 4–6; and Albert Beisel, *Control over Illegal Enforcement of the Criminal Law* (Boston: Boston University Press, 1955), p. 8.

217. Oaks, "Studying the Exclusionary Rule," p. 756.

JUDICIAL DECISIONS

The Scope of the Search:
Chimel v. California, *395 U.S. 752 (1969)*

Mr. Justice STEWART delivered the opinion of the Court.

This case raises basic questions concerning the permissible scope under the Fourth Amendment of a search incident to a lawful arrest.

The relevant facts are essentially undisputed. Late in the afternoon of September 13, 1965, three police officers arrived at the Santa Ana, California, home of the petitioner with a warrant authorizing his arrest for the burglary of a coin shop. The officers knocked on the door, identified themselves to the petitioner's wife, and asked if they might come inside. She ushered them into the house, where they waited 10 or 15 minutes until the petitioner returned home from work. When the petitioner entered the house, one of the officers handed him the arrest warrant and asked for permission to "look around." The petitioner objected, but was advised that "on the basis of the lawful arrest," the officers would nonetheless conduct a search. No search warrant had been issued.

Accompanied by the petitioner's wife, the officers then looked through the entire three-bedroom house, including the attic, the garage, and a small workshop. In some rooms the search was relatively cursory. In the master bedroom and sewing room, however, the officers directed the petitioner's wife to open drawers and "to physically move contents of the drawers from side to side so that [they] might view any items that would have come from [the] burglary." After completing the search, they seized numerous items—primarily coins, but also several medals, tokens, and a few other objects. The entire search took between 45 minutes and an hour.

At the petitioner's subsequent state trial on two charges of burglary, the items taken from his house were admitted into evidence against him, over his objection that they had been unconstitutionally seized. He was convicted, and the judgments of conviction were affirmed by both the California Court of Appeal and the California Supreme Court. Both courts accepted the petitioner's contention that the arrest warrant was invalid because the supporting affidavit was set out in conclusory terms, but held that since the arresting officers had procured the warrant "in good faith," and since in any event they had had sufficient information to constitute probable cause for the petitioner's arrest, that arrest had been lawful. From this conclusion the appellate courts went on to hold that the search of the petitioner's home had been justified, despite the absence of a search warrant, on the ground that it had been incident to a valid arrest. We granted certiorari in order to consider the petitioner's substantial constitutional claims.

Without deciding the question, we proceed on the hypothesis that the California courts were correct in holding that the arrest of the petitioner was valid under the Constitution. This brings us directly to the question whether the warrantless search of the petitioner's entire house can be constitutionally justified as incident to that arrest. The decisions of this Court bearing upon that question have been far from consistent, as even the most cursory review makes evident.

Approval of a warrantless search incident to a lawful arrest seems first to have been articulated by the Court in 1914 as dictum in *Weeks v. United States,* 232 U.S. 383, in which the Court stated:

> "What then is the present case? Before answering that inquiry specifically, it may be well by a process of exclusion to state what it is not. It is not an assertion of the right on the part of the Government, always recognized under English and American law, to search the person of the accused when legally arrested to discover and seize the fruits or evidences of crime." Id., at 392.

That statement made no reference to any right to search the *place* where an arrest occurs, but was limited to a right to search the "person." Eleven years later the case of *Carroll v. United States,* 267 U.S. 132, brought the following embellishment of the *Weeks* statement:

> "When a man is legally arrested for an offense, whatever is found upon his person *or in his control* which it is unlawful for him to have and which may be used to prove the offense may be seized and held as evidence in the prosecution." Id., at 158.

Still, that assertion too was far from a claim that the "place" where one is arrested may be searched so long as the arrest is valid. Without explanation, however, the principle emerged in expanded form a few months later in *Agnello v. United States,* 269 U.S. 20—although still by way of dictum:

> "The right without a search warrant contemporaneously to search persons lawfully arrested while committing crime and to search the place where the arrest is made in order to find and seize things connected with the crime as its fruits or as the means by which it was committed, as well as weapons and other things to effect an escape from custody, is not to be doubted." Id., at 30.

And in *Marron v. United States,* 275 U.S. 192, two years later, the dictum of *Agnello* appeared to be the foundation of the Court's decision. In that case federal agents had secured a search warrant authorizing the seizure of liquor and certain articles used in its manufacture. When they arrived at the premises to be searched, they saw "that the place was used for retailing and drinking intoxicating liquors." Id., at 194. They proceeded to arrest the person in charge and to execute the warrant. In searching a closet for the items listed in the warrant they came across an incriminating ledger, concededly not covered by the warrant, which they also seized. The Court upheld the seizure of the ledger by holding that since the agents had made a lawful arrest, "they had a right without a warrant contemporaneously to search the place in order to find and seize the things used to carry on the criminal enterprise." Id., at 199.

That the *Marron* opinion did not mean all that it seemed to say became evident, however, a few years later in *Go-Bart Importing Co. v. United States,* 282 U.S. 344, and *United States v. Lefkowitz,* 285 U.S. 452. In each of those cases the opinion of the Court was written by Mr. Justice Butler, the author of the opinion in *Marron.* In *Go-Bart,* agents had searched the office of persons whom they had lawfully arrested, and had taken several papers from a desk, a safe, and other parts of the office. The Court noted that no crime had been committed in the agents' presence, and that although the agent in charge "had an abundance of information and time to swear out a valid [search] warrant, he failed to do so." 282 U.S., at 358. In holding the search and seizure unlawful, the Court stated:

"Plainly the case before us is essentially different from *Marron v. United States,* 275 U.S. 192. There, officers executing a valid search warrant for intoxicating liquors found and arrested one Birdsall who in pursuance of a conspiracy was actually engaged in running a saloon. As an incident to the arrest they seized a ledger in a closet where the liquor or some of it was kept and some bills beside the cash register. These things were visible and accessible in the offender's immediate custody. There was no threat of force or general search or rummaging of the place." 282 U.S., at 358.

This limited characterization of *Marron* was reiterated in *Lefkowitz,* a case in which the Court held unlawful a search of desk drawers and a cabinet despite the fact that the search had accompanied a lawful arrest.

The limiting views expressed in *Go-Bart* and *Lefkowitz* were thrown to the winds, however, in *Harris v. United States,* 331 U.S. 145, decided in 1947. In that case, officers had obtained a warrant for Harris' arrest on the basis of his alleged involvement with the cashing and interstate transportation of a forged check. He was arrested in the living room of his four-room apartment, and in an attempt to recover two canceled checks thought to have been used in effecting the forgery, the officers undertook a thorough search of the entire apartment. Inside a desk drawer they found a sealed envelope marked "George Harris, personal papers." The envelope, which was then torn open, was found to contain altered Selective Service documents, and those documents were used to secure Harris' conviction for violating the Selective Training and Service Act of 1940. The Court rejected Harris' Fourth Amendment claim, sustaining the search as "incident to arrest."

Only a year after *Harris,* however, the pendulum swung again. In *Trupiano v. United States,* 334 U.S. 699, agents raided the site of an illicit distillery, saw one of several conspirators operating the still, and arrested him, contemporaneously "seiz-[ing] the illicit distillery." The Court held that the arrest and others made subsequently had been valid, but that the unexplained failure of the agents to procure a search warrant—in spite of the fact that they had had more than enough time before the raid to do so—rendered the search unlawful. The opinion stated:

"It is a cardinal rule that, in seizing goods and articles, law enforcement agents must secure and use search warrants wherever reasonably practicable. . . ." Id., at 705, 708.

In 1950, two years after *Trupiano,* came *United States v. Rabinowitz,* 339 U.S. 56, the decision upon which California primarily relies in the case now before us. In *Rabinowitz,* federal authorities had been informed that the defendant was dealing in stamps bearing forged overprints. On the basis of that information they secured a warrant for his arrest, which they executed at his one-room business office. At the time of the arrest, the officers "searched the desk, safe, and file cabinets in the office for about an hour and a half," and seized 573 stamps with forged overprints. The stamps were admitted into evidence at the defendant's trial, and this Court affirmed his conviction, rejecting the contention that the warrantless search had been unlawful. The Court held that the search in its entirety fell within the principle giving law enforcement authorities "the right 'to search the place where the arrest is made in order to find and seize things connected with the crime. . . .'" *Harris* was regarded as "ample authority" for that conclusion. The opinion rejected the rule of *Trupiano* that "in seizing goods and articles, law enforcement agents must secure and use search warrants wherever reasonably practicable." The test, said the Court, "is not whether it is reasonable to procure a search warrant, but whether the search was reasonable."

Rabinowitz has come to stand for the proposition, inter alia, that a warrantless search "incident to a lawful arrest" may generally extend to the area that is considered to be in the "possession" or under the "control" of the person arrested. And it was on the basis of that proposition that the California courts upheld the search of the petitioner's entire house in this case. That doctrine, however, at least in the broad sense in which it was applied by the California courts in this case, can withstand neither historical nor rational analysis.

Even limited to its own facts, the *Rabinowitz* decision was, as we have seen, hardly founded on an unimpeachable line of authority. As Mr. Justice Frankfurter commented in dissent in that case, the "hint" contained in *Weeks* was, without persuasive justification, "loosely turned into dictum and finally elevated to a decision." And the approach taken in cases such as *Go-Bart, Lefkowitz,* and *Trupiano* was essentially disregarded by the *Rabinowitz* Court.

Nor is the rationale by which the State seeks here to sustain the search of the petitioner's house supported by a reasoned view of the background and purpose of the Fourth Amendment. . . . The Amendment was in large part a reaction to the general warrants and warrantless searches that had so alienated the colonists and had helped speed the movement for independence. In the scheme of the Amendment, therefore, the requirement that "no Warrants shall issue, but upon probable cause," plays a crucial part. As the Court put it in *McDonald v. United States,* 335 U.S. 451:

> "We are not dealing with formalities. The presence of a search warrant serves a high function. Absent some grave emergency, the Fourth Amendment has interposed a magistrate between the citizen and the police. This was done not to shield criminals nor to make the home a safe haven for illegal activities. It was done so that an objective mind might weigh the need to invade that privacy in order to enforce the law. The right of privacy was deemed too precious to entrust to the discretion of those whose job is the detection of crime and the arrest of criminals. . . ." Id., at 455–456.

Even in the *Agnello* case the Court relied upon the rule that "belief, however well founded, that an article sought is concealed in a dwelling house, furnishes no justification for a search of that place without a warrant. And such searches are held unlawful notwithstanding facts unquestionably showing probable cause." 269 U.S., at 33. Clearly, the general requirement that a search warrant be obtained is not lightly to be dispensed with, and "the burden is on those seeking [an] exemption [from the requirement] to show the need for it. . . ." *United States v. Jeffers,* 342 U.S. 48, 51.

. . . When an arrest is made, it is reasonable for the arresting officer to search the person arrested in order to remove any weapons that the latter might seek to use in order to resist arrest or effect his escape. Otherwise, the officer's safety might well be endangered, and the arrest itself frustrated. In addition, it is entirely reasonable for the arresting officer to search for and seize any evidence on the arrestee's person in order to prevent its concealment or destruction. And the area into which an arrestee might reach in order to grab a weapon or evidentiary items must, of course, be governed by a like rule. A gun on a table or in a drawer in front of one who is arrested can be as dangerous to the arresting officer as one concealed in the clothing of the person arrested. There is ample justification, therefore, for a search of the arrestee's person and the area "within his immediate control"—construing that phrase to mean the area from within which he might gain possession of a weapon or destructible evidence.

There is no comparable justification, however, for routinely searching any room other than that in which an arrest occurs—or, for that matter, for searching through all the desk drawers or other closed or concealed areas in that room itself. Such searches, in the absence of well-recognized exceptions, may be made only under the authority of a search warrant. The "adherence to judicial processes" mandated by the Fourth Amendment requires no less.

. . .

It is argued in the present case that it is "reasonable" to search a man's house when he is arrested in it. But that argument is founded on little more than a subjective view regarding the acceptability of certain sorts of police conduct, and not on considerations relevant to Fourth Amendment interests. Under such an unconfined analysis, Fourth Amendment protection in this area would approach the evaporation point. It is not easy to explain why, for instance, it is less subjectively "reasonable" to search a man's house when he is arrested on his front lawn—or just down the street—than it is when he happens to be in the house at the time of arrest. As Mr. Justice Frankfurter put it:

> "To say that the search must be reasonable is to require some criterion of reason. It is no guide at all either for a jury or for district judges or the police to say that an 'unreasonable search' is forbidden—that the search must be reasonable. What is the test of reason which makes a search reasonable? The test is the reason underlying and expressed by the Fourth Amendment: the history and experience which it embodies and the safeguards afforded by it against the evils to which it was a response." *United States v. Rabinowitz,* 339 U.S., at 83 (dissenting opinion).

Thus, although "the recurring questions of the reasonableness of searches" depend upon "the facts and circumstances—the total atmosphere of the case," id., at 63, 66 (opinion of the Court), those facts and circumstances must be viewed in the light of established Fourth Amendment principles.

It would be possible, of course, to draw a line between *Rabinowitz* and *Harris* on the one hand, and this case on the other. For *Rabinowitz* involved a single room, and *Harris* a four-room apartment, while in the case before us an entire house was searched. But such a distinction would be highly artificial. The rationale that allowed the searches and seizures in *Rabinowitz* and *Harris* would allow the searches and seizures in this case. No consideration relevant to the Fourth Amendment suggests any point of rational limitation, once the search is allowed to go beyond the area from which the person arrested might obtain weapons or evidentiary items. The only reasoned distinction is one between a search of the person arrested and the area within his reach on the one hand, and more extensive searches on the other.

The petitioner correctly points out that one result of decisions such as *Rabinowitz* and *Harris* is to give law enforcement officials the opportunity to engage in searches not justified by probable cause, by the simple expedient of arranging to arrest suspects at home rather than elsewhere. We do not suggest that the petitioner is necessarily correct in his assertion that such a strategy was utilized here, but the fact remains that had he been arrested earlier in the day, at his place of employment rather than at home, no search of his house could have been made without a search warrant. In any event, even apart from the possibility of such police tactics, the general point so forcefully made by Judge Learned Hand in *United States v. Kirschenblatt*, 2 Cir., 16 F.2d 202, remains:

> "After arresting a man in his house, to rummage at will among his papers in search of whatever will convict him, appears to us to be indistinguishable from what might be done under a general warrant; indeed, the warrant would give more protection, for presumably it must be issued by a magistrate. True, by hypothesis the power would not exist, if the supposed offender were not found on the premises; but it is small consolation to know that one's papers are safe only so long as one is not at home."

Rabinowitz and *Harris* have been the subject of critical commentary for many years, and have been relied upon less and less in our own decisions. It is time, for the reasons we have stated, to hold that on their own facts, and insofar as the principles they stand for are inconsistent with those that we have endorsed today, they are no longer to be followed.

Application of sound Fourth Amendment principles to the facts of this case produces a clear result. The search here went far beyond the petitioner's person and the area from within which he might have obtained either a weapon or something that could have been used as evidence against him. There was no constitutional justification, in the absence of a search warrant, for extending the search beyond that area. The scope of the search was, therefore, "unreasonable" under the Fourth and Fourteenth Amendments and the petitioner's conviction cannot stand.

Reversed.

Hot Pursuit:
United States v. Santana, 427 U.S. (1976)

Mr. Justice REHNQUIST delivered the opinion of the Court.

I

On August 16, 1974, Michael Gilletti, an undercover officer with the Philadelphia Narcotics Squad arranged a heroin "buy" with one Patricia McCafferty (from whom he had purchased narcotics before). McCafferty told him it would cost $115 "and we will go down to Mom Santana's for the dope."

Gilletti notified his superiors of the impending transaction, recorded the serial numbers of $110 [*sic*] in marked bills, and went to meet McCafferty at a prearranged location. She got in his car and directed him to drive to 2311 North Fifth Street, which, as she had previously informed him, was respondent Santana's residence.

McCafferty took the money and went inside the house, stopping briefly to speak to respondent Alejandro who was sitting on the front steps. She came out shortly afterwards and got into the car. Gilletti asked for the heroin; she thereupon extracted from her bra several glassine envelopes containing a brownish-white powder and gave them to him.

Gilletti then stopped the car, displayed his badge and placed McCafferty under arrest. He told her that the police were going back to 2311 North Fifth Street and wanted to know where the money was. She said, "Mom has the money." At this point Sergeant Pruitt and other officers came up to the car. Gilletti showed them the envelope and said "Mom Santana has the money." Gilletti then took McCafferty to the police station.

Pruitt and the others then drove approximately two blocks back to 2311 North Fifth Street. They saw Santana standing in the doorway of the house with a brown paper bag in her hand. They pulled up to within 15 feet of Santana and got out of their van, shouting "police," and displaying their identification. As the officers approached, Santana retreated into the vestibule of her house.

The officers followed through the open door, catching her in the vestibule. As she tried to pull away, the bag tilted and "two bundles of glazed paper packets with a white powder" fell to the floor. Respondent Alejandro tried to make off with the dropped envelopes but was forcibly restrained. When Santana was told to empty her pockets she produced $135, $70 of which could be identified as Gilletti's marked money. The white powder in the bag was later determined to be heroin.

An indictment was filed in the United States District Court for the Eastern District of Pennsylvania charging McCafferty with distribution of heroin, in violation of 21 U.S.C. § 841, and respondents with possession of heroin with intent to distribute in violation of the same section. McCafferty pleaded guilty. Santana and Alejandro moved to suppress the heroin and money found during and after their arrests.

The District Court granted respondents' motion. In an oral opinion the court found that "there was strong probable cause that Defendant Santana had participated in the transaction with Defendant McCafferty." However the court continued:

"One of the police officers . . . testified that the mission was to arrest Defendant Santana. Another police officer testified that the mission was to recover the bait money. Either one would require a warrant, one a warrant of arrest under ordinary circumstances and one a search warrant."

The court further held that Santana's "reentry from the doorway into the house" was not grounds for allowing the police to make a warrantless entry into the house on the grounds of "hot pursuit," because it took "hot pursuit" to mean "a chase on and about public streets." The court did find, however, that the police acted under "extreme emergency" conditions. The Court of Appeals affirmed this decision without opinion.

II

In *United States v. Watson,* 423 U.S. 411 (1976), we held that the warrantless arrest of an individual in a public place upon probable cause did not violate the Fourth Amendment. Thus the first question we must decide is whether, when the police first sought to arrest Santana, she was in a public place.

While it may be true that under the common law of property the threshold of one's dwelling is "private," as is the yard surrounding the house, it is nonetheless clear that under the cases interpreting the Fourth Amendment Santana was in a "public" place. She was not in an area where she had any expectation of privacy. "What a person knowingly exposes to the public, even in his own house or office, is not a subject of Fourth Amendment protection." *Katz v. United States,* 389 U.S. 347, 351 (1967). She was not merely visible to the public but as exposed to public view, speech, hearing and touch as if she had been standing completely outside her house.

Hester v. United States, 265 U.S. 57, 59 (1924). Thus, when the police, who concededly had probable cause to do so, sought to arrest her, they merely intended to perform a function which we have approved in *Watson.*

The only remaining question is whether her act of retreating into her house could thwart an otherwise proper arrest. We hold that it could not. In *Warden v. Hayden,* 387 U.S. 294 (1967), we recognized the right of police, who had probable cause to believe that an armed robber had entered a house a few minutes before, to make a warrantless entry to arrest the robber and to search for weapons. This case, involving a true "hot pursuit," is clearly governed by *Warden;* the need to act quickly here is even greater than in that case while the intrusion is much less. The District Court was correct in concluding that "hot pursuit" means some sort of a chase, but it need not be an extended hue and cry "in and about [the] public streets." The fact that the pursuit here ended almost as soon as it began did not render it any the less a "hot pursuit" sufficient to justify the warrantless entry into Santana's house. Once Santana saw the police, there was likewise a realistic expectation that any delay would result in destruction of evidence. Once she had been arrested the search, incident to that arrest, which produced the drugs and money was clearly justified.

We thus conclude that a suspect may not defeat an arrest which has been set in motion in a public place, and is therefore proper under *Watson,* by the expedient of escaping to a private place. The opinion of the Court of Appeals is

Reversed.

The Warrant Requirement:
Arkansas v. Sanders, ——— U.S. ——— (1979)

Mr. Justice POWELL delivered the opinion of the Court.

This case presents the question whether, in the absence of exigent circumstances, police are required to obtain a warrant before searching luggage taken from an automobile properly stopped and searched for contraband. We took this case by writ of certiorari to the Supreme Court of Arkansas to resolve some apparent misunderstanding as to the application of our decision in *United States v. Chadwick,* 433 U.S. 1 (1977), to warrantless searches of luggage seized from automobiles.

I

On April 23, 1976, Officer David Isom of the Little Rock, Ark., Police Department received word from an informant that at 4:35 that afternoon respondent would arrive aboard an American Airlines flight at gate number one of the Municipal Airport of Little Rock, Ark. According to the informant, respondent would be carrying a green suitcase containing marihuana. Both Isom and the informant knew respondent well, as in January of 1976 the informant had given the Little Rock Police Department information that had led to respondent's arrest and conviction for possession of marihuana. Acting on the tip, Officer Isom and two other police officers placed the airport under surveillance. As the informant had predicted, respondent duly arrived at gate one. The police watched as respondent deposited some hand luggage in a waiting taxicab, returned to the baggage claim area, and met a man whom police subsequently identified as David Rambo. While Rambo waited, respondent retrieved from the airline baggage service a green suitcase matching that described by the informant. Respondent gave this suitcase to his companion and went outside, where he entered the taxi into which he had put his luggage. Rambo waited a short while in the airport and then joined respondent in the taxi, after placing the green suitcase in the trunk of the vehicle.

When respondent's taxi drove away carrying respondent, Rambo, and the suitcase, Officer Isom and one of his fellow officers gave pursuit and, with the help of a patrol car, stopped the vehicle several blocks from the airport. At the request of the police, the taxi driver opened the trunk of his vehicle, where the officers found the green suitcase. Without asking the permission of either respondent or Rambo, the police opened the unlocked suitcase and discovered what proved to be 9.3 pounds of marihuana packaged in 10 plastic bags.

On October 14, 1976, respondent and Rambo were charged with possession of marihuana with intent to deliver in violation of Ark. Stat. Ann. § 82–2617 (1976). Before trial, respondent moved to suppress the evidence obtained from the suitcase, contending that the search violated his rights under the Fourth and Fourteenth Amendments. The trial court held a hearing on January 31, 1977, and denied the suppression motion without explanation. After respondent's conviction by a jury on February 3, 1977, he was sentenced to 10 years in prison and was fined $15,000.

On appeal the Supreme Court of Arkansas reversed respondent's conviction, ruling that the trial court should have suppressed the marihuana because it was obtained through an unlawful search of the suitcase. 262 Ark. 595 (1977). Relying upon *United States v. Chadwick,* supra, and *Coolidge v. New Hampshire,* 403 U.S. 443 (1971), the court concluded that a warrantless search generally must be supported by "probable cause coupled with exigent circumstances." In the present case, the court found there was ample probable cause for the police officers' belief that contraband was contained in the suitcase they searched. The court found to be wholly lacking, however, any exigent circumstance justifying the officers' failure to secure a warrant for the search of the luggage. With the police in control of the automobile and its occupants, there was no danger that the suitcase and its contents would be rendered unavailable to due legal process. The court concluded, therefore, that there was "nothing in this set of circumstances that would lend credence to an assertion of impracticality in obtaining a search warrant."

II

Although the general principles applicable to claims of Fourth Amendment violations are well settled, litigation over requests for suppression of highly relevant evidence continues to occupy much of the attention of courts at all levels of the state and federal judiciary. Courts and law enforcement officials often find it difficult to discern the proper application of these principles to individual cases, because the circumstances giving rise to suppression requests can vary almost infinitely. Moreover, an apparently small difference in the factual situation frequently is viewed as a controlling difference in determining Fourth Amendment rights. The present case presents an example. Only two Terms ago, we held that a locked footlocker could not lawfully be searched without a warrant, even though it had been loaded into the trunk of an automobile parked at a curb. *United States v. Chadwick,* supra. In earlier cases, on the other hand, the Court sustained the constitutionality of warrantless searches of automobiles and their contents under what has become known as the "automobile exception" to the warrant requirement. See, e.g., *Chambers v. Maroney,* 399 U.S. 42 (1970); *Carroll v. United States,* 267 U.S. 132 (1925). We thus are presented with the task of determining whether the warrantless search of respondent's suitcase falls on the *Chadwick* or the *Chambers/Carroll* side of the Fourth Amendment line. Although in a sense this is a line-drawing process, it must be guided by established principles.

We commence with a summary of these principles. The Fourth Amendment protects the privacy and security of persons in two important ways. First, it guarantees "the right of the people to be secure in their persons, houses, papers, and effects, against unreasonable searches and seizures." In addition, this Court has interpreted the amendment to include the requirement that normally searches of private property be performed pursuant to a search warrant issued in compliance with the warrant clause. In the ordinary case, therefore, a search of private property must be both reasonable and performed pursuant to a properly issued search warrant. The mere reasonableness of a search, assessed in the light of the surrounding circumstances, is not a substitute for the judicial warrant required under the Fourth Amendment. . . . The prominent place the warrant requirement is given in our decisions reflects the "basic constitutional doctrine that individual freedoms will best be preserved through a separation of powers and division of functions among the different branches and levels of Government." *United States v. United States District Court,* supra, 407 U.S., at 317.

Nonetheless, there are some exceptions to the warrant requirement. These have been established where it was concluded that the public interest required some flexibility in the application of the general rule that a valid warrant is a prerequisite for a search. Thus, a few "jealously and carefully drawn" exceptions provide for those cases where the societal costs of obtaining a warrant, such as danger to law officers or the risk of loss or destruction of evidence, outweigh the reasons for prior recourse to a neutral magistrate. But because such exception to the warrant requirement invariably impinges to some extent on the protective purpose of the Fourth Amendment, the few situations in which a search may be conducted in the absence of a warrant have been carefully delineated and "the burden is on those seeking the exemption to show the need for it." *United States v. Jeffers,* 342 U.S. 48, 51 (1951). Moreover, we have limited the reach of each exception to that which is necessary to accommodate the identified needs of society.

One of the circumstances in which the Constitution does not require a search warrant is when the police stop an automobile on the street or highway because they have probable cause to believe it contains contraband or evidence of a crime. . . . There are essentially two reasons for the distinction between automobiles and other private property. First, as the Court repeatedly has recognized, the inherent mobility of automobiles often makes it impracticable to obtain a warrant. In addition, the configuration, use, and regulation of automobiles often may dilute the reasonable expectation of privacy that exists with respect to differently situated property.

III

In the present case, the State argues that the warrantless search of respondent's suitcase was proper under *Carroll* and its progeny. The police acted properly—indeed commendably—in apprehending respondent and his luggage. They had ample probable cause to believe that respondent's green suitcase contained marihuana. A previously reliable informant had provided a detailed account of respondent's expected arrival at the Little Rock Airport, which account proved to be accurate in every detail, including the color of the suitcase in which respondent would be carrying the marihuana. Having probable cause to believe that contraband was being driven away in the taxi, the police were justified in stopping the vehicle, searching it on the spot, and seizing the suitcase they suspected contained contraband. . . .

The only question, therefore, is whether the police, rather than immediately searching the suitcase without a warrant, should have taken it, along with respondent, to the police station and there obtained a warrant for the search. A lawful search of luggage generally may be performed only pursuant to a warrant. In *Chadwick* we declined an invitation to extend the *Carroll* exception to all searches of luggage, noting that neither of the two policies supporting warrantless searches of automobiles applies to luggage. Here, as in *Chadwick*, the officers had seized the luggage and had it exclusively within their control at the time of the search. Consequently, "there was not the slightest danger that [the luggage] or its contents could have been removed before a valid search warrant could be obtained." 433 U.S., at 13. And, as we observed in that case, luggage is a common repository for one's personal effects, and therefore is inevitably associated with the expectation of privacy.

The State argues, nevertheless, that the warrantless search of respondent's suitcase was proper, not because the property searched was luggage, but rather because it was taken from an automobile lawfully stopped and searched on the street. In effect, the State would have us extend *Carroll* to allow warrantless searches of everything found within an automobile, as well as of the vehicle itself. . . .

We conclude that the State has failed to carry its burden of demonstrating the need for warrantless searches of luggage properly taken from automobiles. A closed suitcase in the trunk of an automobile may be as mobile as the vehicle in which it rides. But as we noted in *Chadwick*, the exigency of mobility must be assessed at the point immediately before the search—after the police have seized the object to be searched and have it securely within their control. Once police have seized a suitcase, as they did here, the extent of its mobility is in no way affected by the place from which it was taken. Accordingly, as a general rule there is no greater need for warrantless searches of luggage taken from automobiles than of luggage taken from other places.

Similarly, a suitcase taken from an automobile stopped on the highway is not necessarily attended by any lesser expectation of privacy than is associated with luggage taken from other locations. One is not less inclined to place private, personal possessions in a suitcase merely because the suitcase is to be carried in an automobile rather than transported by other means or temporarily checked or stored. Indeed, the very purpose of a suitcase is to serve as a repository for personal items when one wishes to transport them. Accordingly, the reasons for not requiring a warrant for the search of an automobile do not apply to searches of personal luggage taken by police from automobiles. We therefore find no justification for the extension of *Carroll* and its progeny to the warrantless search of one's personal luggage merely because it was located in an automobile lawfully stopped by the police.

In sum, we hold that the warrant requirement of the Fourth Amendment applies to personal luggage taken from an automobile to the same degree it applies to such luggage in other locations. Thus, insofar as the police are entitled to search such luggage without a warrant, their actions must be justified under some exception to the warrant requirement other than that applicable to automobiles stopped on the highway. Where—as in the present case—the police, without endangering themselves or risking loss of the evidence, lawfully have detained one suspected of criminal activity and secured his suitcase, they should delay the search thereof until after judicial approval has been obtained. In this way, constitutional rights of suspects to prior judicial review of searches will be fully protected.

The judgment of the Arkansas Supreme Court is

Affirmed.

Arrest:
United States v. Watson, *423 U.S. 411 (1976)*

Mr. Justice WHITE delivered the opinion of the Court.

This case presents questions under the Fourth Amendment as to the legality of a warrantless arrest and of an ensuing search of the arrestee's automobile carried out with his purported consent.

I

The relevant events began on August 17, 1972, when an informant, one Khoury, telephoned a postal inspector informing him that respondent Watson was in possession of a stolen credit card and had asked Khoury to cooperate in using the card to their mutual advantage. On five to 10 previous occasions Khoury had provided the inspector with reliable information on postal inspection matters, some involving Watson. Later that day Khoury delivered the card to the inspector. On learning that Watson had agreed to furnish additional cards, the inspector asked Khoury to arrange to meet with Watson. Khoury did so, a meeting being scheduled for August 22. Watson cancelled that engagement, but at noon on August 23, Khoury met with Watson at a restaurant designated by the latter. Khoury had been instructed that if Watson had additional stolen credit cards, Khoury was to give a designated signal. The signal was given, the officers closed in and Watson was forthwith arrested. He was removed from the restaurant to the street where he was given the warnings required by *Miranda v. Arizona,* 384 U.S. 436 (1966). A search having revealed that Watson had no credit cards on his person, the inspector asked if he could look inside Watson's car, which was standing within view. Watson said, "Go ahead," and repeated these words when the inspector cautioned that "if I find anything, it is going to go against you." Using keys furnished by Watson, the inspector entered the car and found under the floor mat an envelope containing two credit cards in the names of other persons. These cards were the basis for two counts of a four-count indictment charging Watson with possessing stolen mail in violation of 18 U.S.C. § 1708.

Prior to trial, Watson moved to suppress the cards, claiming that his arrest was illegal for want of probable cause and an arrest warrant and that his consent to search the car was involuntary and ineffective because he had not been told that he could withhold consent. The motion was denied, and Watson was convicted of illegally possessing the two cards seized from his car.

A divided panel of the Court of Appeals for the Ninth Circuit reversed, 504 F.2d 849 (1974), ruling that the admission in evidence of the two credit cards found in the car was prohibited by the Fourth Amendment. . . . We granted certiorari. 420 U.S. 924 (1975).

II

A major part of the Court of Appeals' opinion was its holding that Watson's warrantless arrest violated the Fourth Amendment. Although it did not expressly do so, it may have intended to overturn the conviction on the independent ground that the two credit cards were the inadmissible fruits of an unconstitutional arrest. However that may be, the Court of Appeals treated the illegality of Watson's arrest as an important factor in determining the voluntariness of his consent to search his car. We therefore deal first with the arrest issue.

Contrary to the Court of Appeals' view, Watson's arrest was not invalid because executed without a warrant. Section 3061(a) of Title 18 U.S.C. expressly empowers the Board of Governors of the Postal Service to authorize Postal Service officers and employees "performing duties related to the inspection of postal matters" to

"(3) make arrests without warrant for felonies cognizable under the laws of the United States if they have reasonable grounds to believe that the person to be arrested has committed or is committing such a felony."

By regulation, 39 CFR § 232.5(a) (1975), and in identical language the Board of Governors has exercised that power and authorized warrantless arrests. There being probable cause in this case to believe that Watson had violated § 1708, the inspector and his subordinates, in arresting Watson, were acting strictly in accordance with the governing statute and regulations. The effect of the judgment of the Court of Appeals was to invalidate the statute as applied in this case and as applied to all the situations where a court fails to find exigent circumstances justifying a warrantless arrest. We reverse that judgment.

Under the Fourth Amendment, the people are to be "secure in their persons, houses, papers, and effects, against unreasonable searches and seizures . . . and no Warrants shall issue, but upon probable cause. . . ." Section 3061 represents a judgment by Congress that it is not unreasonable under the Fourth Amendment for postal inspectors to arrest without a warrant provided they have probable cause to do so. This was not an isolated or quixotic judgment of the legislative branch. Other federal law enforcement officers have been expressly authorized by statute for many years to make felony arrests on probable cause but without a warrant. . . .

Because there is a "strong presumption of constitutionality due to an Act of Congress, especially when it turns on what is 'reasonable' . . . obviously the Court should be reluctant to decide that a search thus authorized by Congress was unreasonable and that the Act was therefore unconstitutional." *United States v. Di Re,* 332 U.S. 581, 585 (1948). Moreover, there is nothing in the Court's prior cases indicating that under the Fourth Amendment a warrant is required to make a valid arrest for a felony. Indeed, the relevant prior decisions are uniformly to the contrary.

"The usual rule is that a police officer may arrest without warrant one believed by the officer upon reasonable cause to have been guilty of a felony. . . ." *Carroll v. United States,* 267 U.S. 132, 156 (1925). In *Henry v. United States,* 361 U.S. 98 (1959), the Court dealt with an FBI agent's warrantless arrest under 18 U.S.C. § 3052 which authorizes a warrantless arrest where there are reasonable grounds to believe that the person to be arrested has committed a felony. The Court declared that "the statute states the constitutional standard. . . ." Id., at 100. The necessary inquiry, therefore, was not whether there was a warrant or whether there was time to get one but whether there was probable cause for the arrest. In *Abel v. United States,* 362 U.S. 217, 232 (1960), the Court sustained an administrative arrest made without "a judicial warrant within the scope of the Fourth Amendment." The crucial question in *Draper v. United States,* 358 U.S. 307 (1959), was whether there was probable cause for the warrantless arrest. If there was, the Court said, "the arrest, though without a warrant, was lawful. . . ." Id., at 310. . . . Just last Term, while recognizing that maximum protection of individual rights could be assured by requiring a magistrate's review of the factual justification prior to any arrest, we stated that "such a requirement would constitute an intolerable handicap for legitimate law enforcement" and noted that the Court "has never invalidated an arrest supported by probable cause solely because the officers failed to secure a warrant." *Gerstein v. Pugh,* 420 U.S. 103, 113 (1975).

The cases construing the Fourth Amendment thus reflect the ancient common-law rule that a peace officer was permitted to arrest without a warrant for a misdemeanor or felony committed in his presence as well as for a felony not committed in his presence if there was reasonable grounds for making the arrest. This has also been the prevailing rule under state constitutions and statutes. "The rule of the common law, that a peace officer or a private citizen may arrest a felon without a warrant, has been generally held by the courts of the several States to be in force in cases of felony punishable by the civil tribunals." *Kurtz v. Moffitt,* 115 U.S. 487, 504 (1885). . . .

Because the common-law rule authorizing arrests without warrant generally prevailed in the States, it is important for present purposes to note that in 1792 Congress invested United States Marshals and their deputies with "the same powers in executing the laws of the United States, as sheriffs and their deputies in their several states have by law, in executing the laws of their respective states." Act of May 2, 1792, c. 28, § 9, 1 Stat. 265. The Second Congress thus saw no inconsistency between the Fourth Amendment and giving United States Marshals the same power as local peace officers to arrest for a felony without a warrant. This provision equating the power of federal marshals to those of local sheriffs was several times re-enacted and is today § 570 of Title 28. That provision, however, was supplemented in 1935 by § 504a of the Judicial Code, which in its essential elements is now 18 U.S.C. § 3053 and which expressly empowered marshals to make felony arrests without warrant and on probable cause. . . .

The balance struck by the common law in generally authorizing felony arrests on probable cause, but without warrant, has survived substantially intact. It appears in almost all of the States in the form of express statutory authorization. . . .

This is the rule Congress has long directed its principal law enforcement officers to follow. Congress has plainly decided against conditioning warrantless arrest power on proof of exigent circumstances. Law enforcement officers may find it wise to seek arrest warrants where practicable to do so, and their judgments about probable cause may be more readily accepted where backed by a warrant issued by a magistrate. But we decline to transform this judicial preference into a constitutional rule when the judgment of the Nation and Congress has for so long been to authorize warrantless public arrests on probable cause rather than to encumber criminal prosecutions with endless litigation with respect to the existence of exigent circumstances, whether it was practicable to get a warrant, whether the suspect was about to flee, and the like.

Watson's arrest did not violate the Fourth Amendment, and the Court of Appeals erred in holding to the contrary.

III

Because our judgment is that Watson's arrest comported with the Fourth Amendment, Watson's consent to the search of his car was not the product of an illegal arrest. To the extent that the issue of the voluntariness of Watson's consent was resolved on the premise that his arrest was illegal, the Court of Appeals was also in error.

We are satisfied in addition that the remaining factors relied upon by the Court of Appeals to invalidate Watson's consent are inadequate to demonstrate that, in the totality of the circumstances, Watson's consent was not his own "essentially free and unconstrained choice" because his "will had been overborne and his capacity for self-determination critically impaired." *Schneckloth v. Bustamonte*, 412 U.S. 218, 225 (1973). There was no overt act or threat of force against Watson proved or claimed. There were no promises made to him and no indication of more subtle forms of coercion that might flaw his judgment. He had been arrested and was in custody, but his consent was given while on a public street, not in the confines of the police station. Moreover, the fact of custody alone has never been enough in itself to demonstrate a coerced confession or consent to search. Similarly, under Schneckloth, the absence of proof that Watson knew he could withhold his consent, though it may be a factor in the overall judgment, is not to be given controlling significance. There is no indication in this record that Watson was a newcomer to the law, mentally deficient or unable in the face of a custodial arrest to exercise a free choice. He was given *Miranda* warnings and was further cautioned that the results of the search of his car could be used against him. He persisted in his consent.

In these circumstances, to hold that illegal coercion is made out from the fact of arrest and the failure to inform the arrestee that he could withhold consent would not be consistent with *Schneckloth* and would distort the voluntariness standard that we reaffirmed in that case.

In consequence, we reverse the judgment of the Court of Appeals.

So ordered.

Reversed.

Incidental Search:
United States v. Robinson, *414 U.S. 218 (1973)*

Mr. Justice REHNQUIST delivered the opinion of the Court.

Respondent Robinson was convicted in United States District Court for the District of Columbia of the possession and facilitation of concealment of heroin. . . . He was sentenced to concurrent terms of imprisonment for these offenses. . . . The Court of Appeals en banc reversed the judgment of conviction, holding that the heroin introduced in evidence against respondent had been obtained as a result of a search which violated the Fourth Amendment to the United States Constitution. . . .

On April 23, 1968, at approximately 11 p.m., Officer Richard Jenks, a 15-year veteran of the District of Columbia Metropolitan Police Department, observed the respondent driving a 1965 Cadillac near the intersection of 8th and C Streets, N.E., in the District of Columbia. Jenks, as a result of previous investigation following a check of respondent's operator's permit four days earlier, determined there was reason to believe that respondent was operating a motor vehicle after the revocation of his operator's permit. This is an offense defined by statute in the District of Columbia which carries a mandatory minimum jail term, a mandatory minimum fine, or both.

Jenks signaled respondent to stop the automobile, which respondent did, and all three of the occupants emerged from the car. At that point Jenks informed respondent that he was under arrest for "operating after revocation and obtaining a permit by misrepresentation." It was assumed by the Court of Appeals, and is conceded by the respondent here, that Jenks had probable cause to arrest respondent, and that he effected a full-custody arrest.

In accordance with procedures prescribed in police department instructions, Jenks then began to search respondent. He explained at a subsequent hearing that he was "face-to-face" with the respondent, and "placed [his] hands on [the respondent], my right hand to his left breast like this (demonstrating) and proceeded to pat him down thus [with the right hand]." During this patdown, Jenks felt an object in the left breast pocket of the heavy coat respondent was wearing, but testified that he "couldn't actually tell the size of it." Jenks then reached into the pocket and pulled out the object, which turned out to be a "crumpled up cigarette package." Jenks testified that at this point he still did not know what was in the package:

> "As I felt the package I could feel objects in the package but I couldn't tell what they were. . . . I knew they weren't cigarettes."

The officer then opened the cigarette pack and found 14 gelatin capsules of white powder which he thought to be, and which later analysis proved to be, heroin. Jenks then continued his search of respondent to completion, feeling around his waist and trouser legs, and examining the remaining pockets. The heroin seized from the respondent was admitted into evidence at the trial which resulted in his conviction in the District Court.

. . . We conclude that the search conducted by Jenks in this case did not offend the limits imposed by the Fourth Amendment, and we therefore reverse the judgment of the Court of Appeals.

I

It is well settled that a search incident to a lawful arrest is a traditional exception to the warrant requirement of the Fourth Amendment. This general exception has historically been formulated into two distinct propositions. The first is that a search may be made of the *person* of the arrestee by virtue of the lawful arrest. The second is that a search may be made of the area within the control of the arrestee.

Examination of this Court's decisions shows that these two propositions have been treated quite differently. The validity of the search of a person incident to a lawful arrest has been regarded as settled from its first enunciation, and has remained virtually unchallenged until the present case. The validity of the second proposition, while likewise conceded in principle, has been subject to differing interpretations as to the extent of the area which may be searched.

. . .

Throughout the series of cases in which the Court has addressed the second proposition relating to a search incident to a lawful arrest—the permissible area beyond the person of the arrestee which such a search may cover—no doubt has been expressed as to the unqualified authority of the arresting authority to search the person of the arrestee. In *Chimel*, where the Court overruled *Rabinowitz* and *Harris* as to the area of permissible search incident to a lawful arrest, full recognition was again given to the authority to search the person of the arrestee. . . .

Three years after the decision in *Chimel*, supra, we upheld the validity of a search in which heroin had been taken from the person of the defendant after his arrest on a weapons charge, in *Adams v. Williams*, 407 U.S. 143 (1972), saying:

> "Under the circumstances surrounding Williams' possession of the gun seized by Sgt. Connolly, the arrest on the weapons charge was supported by probable cause, and the search of his person and of the car incident to that arrest was lawful." Id., at 149.

Thus the broadly stated rule, and the reasons for it, have been repeatedly affirmed in the decisions of this Court. . . . Since the statements in the cases speak not simply in terms of an exception to the warrant requirement, but in terms of an affirmative authority to search, they clearly imply that such searches also meet the Fourth Amendment's requirement of reasonableness. . . .

III

Virtually all of the statements of this Court affirming the existence of an unqualified authority to search incident to a lawful arrest are dicta. We would not, therefore, be foreclosed by principles of stare decisis from further examination into history and practice in order to see whether the sort of qualifications imposed by the Court of Appeals in this case were in fact intended by the Framers of the Fourth Amendment or recognized in cases decided prior to *Weeks*. Unfortunately such authorities as exist are sparse. Such common-law treatises as Blackstone's Commentaries and Holmes' Common Law are simply silent on the subject. . . .

While these earlier authorities are sketchy, they tend to support the broad statement of the authority to search incident to arrest found in the successive decisions of this Court, rather than the restrictive one which was applied by the Court of Appeals in this case. The scarcity of case law before *Weeks* is doubtless due in part to the fact that the exclusionary rule there enunciated had been first adopted only 11 years earlier in Iowa; but it would seem to be also due in part to the fact that the issue was regarded as well settled.

The Court of Appeals in effect determined that the *only* reason supporting the authority for a *full* search incident to lawful arrest was the possibility of discovery of evidence or fruits. Concluding that there could be no evidence or fruits in the case of an offense such as that with which respondent was charged, it held that any protective search would have to be limited by the conditions laid down in *Terry* for a search upon less than probable cause to arrest. Quite apart from the fact that *Terry* clearly recognized the distinction between the two types of searches, and that a different rule governed one than governed the other, we find additional reason to disagree with the Court of Appeals.

The justification or reason for the authority to search incident to a lawful arrest rests quite as much on the need to disarm the suspect in order to take him into custody as it does on the need to preserve evidence on his person for later use at trial. *Agnello v. United States,* 269 U.S. 20 (1925). The standards traditionally governing a search incident to lawful arrest are not, therefore, commuted to the stricter *Terry* standards by the absence of probable fruits or further evidence of the particular crime for which the arrest is made.

Nor are we inclined, on the basis of what seems to us to be a rather speculative judgment, to qualify the breadth of the general authority to search incident to a lawful custodial arrest on an assumption that persons arrested for the offense of driving while their licenses have been revoked are less likely to possess dangerous weapons than are those arrested for other crimes. It is scarcely open to doubt that the danger to an officer is far greater in the case of the extended exposure which follows the taking of a suspect into custody and transporting him to the police station than in the case of the relatively fleeting contact resulting from the typical *Terry*-type stop. This is an adequate basis for treating all custodial arrests alike for purposes of search justification.

But quite apart from these distinctions, our more fundamental disagreement with the Court of Appeals arises from its suggestion that there must be litigated in each case the issue of whether or not there was present one of the reasons supporting the authority for a search of the person incident to a lawful arrest. We do not think the long line of authorities of this Court dating back to *Weeks,* or what we can glean from the history of practice in this country and in England, requires such a case-by-case adjudication. A police officer's determination as to how and where to search the person of a suspect whom he has arrested is necessarily a quick ad hoc judgment which the Fourth Amendment does not require to be broken down in each instance into an analysis of each step in the search. The authority to search the person incident to a lawful custodial arrest, while based upon the need to disarm and to discover evidence, does not depend on what a court may later decide was the probability in a particular arrest situation that weapons or evidence would in fact be found upon the person of the suspect. A custodial arrest of a suspect based on probable cause is a reasonable intrusion under the Fourth Amendment; that intrusion being lawful, a search incident to the arrest requires no additional justification. It is the fact of the lawful arrest which establishes the authority to search, and we hold that in the case of a lawful custodial arrest a full search of the person is not only an exception to the warrant requirement of the Fourth Amendment, but is also a "reasonable" search under that Amendment.

IV

The search of respondent's person conducted by Officer Jenks in this case and the seizure from him of the heroin, were permissible under established Fourth Amendment law. While thorough, the search partook of none of the extreme or patently abusive characteristics which were held to violate the Due Process Clause of the Fourteenth Amendment in *Rochin v. California*, 342 U.S. 165 (1952). Since it is the fact of custodial arrest which gives rise to the authority to search, it is of no moment that Jenks did not indicate any subjective fear of the respondent or that he did not himself suspect that respondent was armed. Having in the course of a lawful search come upon the crumpled package of cigarettes, he was entitled to inspect it; and when his inspection revealed the heroin capsules, he was entitled to seize them as "fruits, instrumentalities, or contraband" probative of criminal conduct. The judgment of the Court of Appeals holding otherwise is reversed.

Reversed.

Stop and Frisk:
Terry v. Ohio, 392 U.S. 1 (1968)

Mr. Chief Justice WARREN delivered the opinion of the Court.

This case presents serious questions concerning the role of the Fourth Amendment in the confrontation on the street between the citizen and the policeman investigating suspicious circumstances.

Petitioner Terry was convicted of carrying a concealed weapon and sentenced to the statutorily prescribed term of one to three years in the penitentiary. Following the denial of a pretrial motion to suppress, the prosecution introduced in evidence two revolvers and a number of bullets seized from Terry and a codefendant, Richard Chilton, by Cleveland Police Detective Martin McFadden. At the hearing on the motion to suppress this evidence, Officer McFadden testified that while he was patrolling in plain clothes in downtown Cleveland at approximately 2:30 in the afternoon of October 31, 1963, his attention was attracted by two men, Chilton and Terry, standing on the corner of Huron Road and Euclid Avenue. He had never seen the two men before, and he was unable to say precisely what first drew his eye to them. However, he testified that he had been a policeman for 39 years and a detective for 35 and that he had been assigned to patrol this vicinity of downtown Cleveland for shoplifters and pickpockets for 30 years. He explained that he had developed routine habits of observation over the years and that he would "stand and watch people or walk and watch people at many intervals of the day." He added: "Now, in this case when I looked over they didn't look right to me at the time."

His interest aroused, Officer McFadden took up a post of observation in the entrance to a store 300 to 400 feet away from the two men. "I get more purpose to watch them when I seen their movements," he testified. He saw one of the men leave the other one and walk southwest on Huron Road, past some stores. The man paused for a moment and looked in a store window, then walked on a short distance, turned around and walked back toward the corner, pausing once again to look in the same store window. He rejoined his companion at the corner, and the two conferred briefly. Then the second man went through the same series of motions, strolling down Huron Road, looking in the same window, walking on a short distance, turning back, peering in the store window again, and returning to confer with the first man at the corner. The two men repeated this ritual alternately between five and six times apiece—in all, roughly a dozen trips. At one point, while the two were standing together on the corner, a third man approached them and engaged them briefly in conversation. This man then left the two others and walked west on Euclid Avenue. Chilton and Terry resumed their measured pacing, peering and conferring. After this had gone on for 10 to 12 minutes, the two men walked off together, heading west on Euclid Avenue, following the path taken earlier by the third man.

By this time Officer McFadden had become thoroughly suspicious. He testified that after observing their elaborately casual and oft-repeated reconnaissance of the store window on Huron Road, he suspected the two men of "casing a job, a stick-up," and that he considered it his duty as a police officer to investigate further. He added that he feared "they may have a gun." Thus, Officer McFadden followed Chilton and Terry and saw them stop in front of Zuckers' store to talk to the same man who had conferred with them earlier on the street corner. Deciding that the situation was ripe for direct action, Officer McFadden approached the three men, identified himself as a police officer and asked for their names. At this point his knowledge was confined to what he had observed. He was not acquainted with any of the three men by name or by sight, and he had received no information concerning them from any other source. When the men "mumbled something" in response to his inquiries, Officer McFadden grabbed petitioner Terry, spun him around so that they were facing the other two, with Terry between McFadden and the others, and patted down the outside of his clothing. In the left breast pocket of Terry's overcoat Officer McFadden felt a pistol. He reached inside the overcoat pocket, but was unable to remove the gun. At this point, keeping Terry between himself and the others, the officer ordered all three men to enter Zucker's store. As they went in, he removed Terry's overcoat completely, removed a .38-caliber revolver from the pocket and ordered all three men to face the wall with their hands raised. Officer McFadden proceeded to pat down the outer clothing of Chilton and the third man, Katz. He discovered another revolver in the outer pocket of Chilton's overcoat, but no weapons were found on Katz. The officer testified that he only patted the men down to see whether they had weapons, and that he did not put his hands beneath the outer garments of either Terry or Chilton until he felt their guns. So far as appears from the record, he never placed his hands beneath Katz' outer garments. Officer McFadden seized Chilton's gun, asked the proprietor of the store to call a police wagon, and took all three men to the station, where Chilton and Terry were formally charged with carrying concealed weapons.

. . .

After the court denied their motion to suppress, Chilton and Terry waived jury trial and pleaded not guilty. The court adjudged them guilty, and the Court of Appeals for the Eighth Judicial District, Cuyahoga County, affirmed. The Supreme Court of Ohio dismissed their appeal. . . . We granted certiorari, 387 U.S. 929 (1967), to determine whether the admission of the revolvers in evidence violated petitioner's rights under the Fourth Amendment. . . . We affirm the conviction.

. . .

II.

Our first task is to establish at what point in this encounter the Fourth Amendment becomes relevant. That is, we must decide whether and when Officer Mc-Fadden "seized" Terry and whether and when he conducted a "search." There is some suggestion in the use of such terms as "stop" and "frisk" that such police conduct is outside the purview of the Fourth Amendment because neither action rises to the level of a "search" or "seizure" within the meaning of the Constitution. We emphatically reject this notion. It is quite plain that the Fourth Amendment governs "seizures" of the person which do not eventuate in a trip to the station house and prosecution for crime—"arrests" in traditional terminology. It must be recognized that whenever a police officer accosts an individual and restrains his freedom to walk away, he has "seized" that person. And it is nothing less than sheer torture of the English language to suggest that a careful exploration of the outer surfaces of a person's clothing all over his or her body in an attempt to find weapons is not a "search." Moreover, it is simply fantastic to urge that such a procedure performed in public by a policeman while the citizen stands helpless, perhaps facing a wall with his hands raised, is a "petty indignity." It is a serious intrusion upon the sanctity of the person, which may inflict great indignity and arouse strong resentment, and it is not to be undertaken lightly.

The danger in the logic which proceeds upon distinctions between a "stop" and an "arrest," or "seizure" of the person, and between a "frisk" and a "search" is two-fold. It seeks to isolate from constitutional scrutiny the initial stages of the contact between the policeman and the citizen. And by suggesting a rigid all-or-nothing model of justification and regulation under the Amendment, it obscures the utility of limitations upon the scope, as well as the initiation, of police action as a means of constitutional regulation. This Court has held in the past that a search which is reasonable at its inception may violate the Fourth Amendment by virtue of its intolerable intensity and scope. *Kremen v. United States*, 353 U.S. 346 (1957). The scope of the search must be "strictly tied to and justified by" the circumstances which rendered its initiation permissible. *Warden v. Hayden*, 387 U.S. 294, 310 (1967) (Mr. Justice Fortas, concurring).

The distinctions of classical "stop-and-frisk'" theory thus serve to divert attention from the central inquiry under the Fourth Amendment—the reasonableness in all the circumstances of the particular governmental invasion of a citizen's personal security. "Search" and "seizure" are not talismans. We therefore reject the notions that the Fourth Amendment does not come into play at all as a limitation upon police conduct if the officers stop short of something called a "technical arrest" or a "full-blown search."

In this case there can be no question, then, that Officer McFadden "seized" petitioner and subjected him to a "search" when he took hold of him and patted down the outer surfaces of his clothing. We must decide whether at that point it was reasonable for Officer McFadden to have interfered with petitioner's personal security as he did. And in determining whether the seizure and search were "unreasonable" our inquiry is a dual one—whether the officer's action was justified at its inception, and whether it was reasonably related in scope to the circumstances which justified the interference in the first place.

III.

If this case involved police conduct subject to the Warrant Clause of the Fourth

Amendment, we would have to ascertain whether "probable cause" existed to justify the search and seizure which took place. However, that is not the case. We do not retreat from our holdings that the police must, whenever practicable, obtain advance judicial approval of searches and seizures through the warrant procedure, see e.g., *Katz v. United States*, 389 U.S. 347 (1967). . . . But we deal here with an entire rubric of police conduct—necessarily swift action predicated upon the on-the-spot observations of the officer on the beat—which historically has not been, and as a practical matter could not be, subjected to the warrant procedure. Instead, the conduct involved in this case must be tested by the Fourth Amendment's general proscription against unreasonable searches and seizures.

Nonetheless, the notions which underlie both the warrant procedure and the requirement of probable cause remain fully relevant in this context. In order to assess the reasonableness of Officer McFadden's conduct as a general proposition, it is necessary "first to focus upon the governmental interest which allegedly justifies official intrusion upon the constitutionally protected interests of the private citizen," for there is "no ready test for determining reasonableness other than by balancing the need to search [or seize] against the invasion which the search [or seizure] entails." *Camara v. Municipal Court*, 387 U.S. 523, 534–535, 536–537 (1967). And in justifying the particular intrusion the police officer must be able to point to specific and articulable facts which, taken together with rational inferences from those facts, reasonably warrant that intrusion. The scheme of the Fourth Amendment becomes meaningful only when it is assured that at some point the conduct of those charged with enforcing the laws can be subjected to the more detached, neutral scrutiny of a judge who must evaluate the reasonableness of a particular search or seizure in light of the particular circumstances. And in making that assessment it is imperative that the facts be judged against an objective standard: would the facts available to the officer at the moment of the seizure or the search "warrant a man of reasonable caution in the belief" that the action taken was appropriate? Anything less would invite intrusions upon constitutionally guaranteed rights based on nothing more substantial than inarticulate hunches, a result this Court has consistently refused to sanction. . . .

Applying these principles to this case, we consider first the nature and extent of the governmental interests involved. One general interest is of course that of effective crime prevention and detection; it is this interest which underlies the recognition that a police officer may in appropriate circumstances and in an appropriate manner approach a person for purposes of investigating possible criminal behavior even though there is no probable cause to make an arrest. It was this legitimate investigative function Officer McFadden was discharging when he decided to approach petitioner and his companions. He had observed Terry, Chilton, and Katz go through a series of acts, each of them perhaps innocent in itself, but which taken together warranted further investigation. There is nothing unusual in two men standing together on a street corner, perhaps waiting for someone. Nor is there anything suspicious about people in such circumstances strolling up and down the street, singly or in pairs. Store windows, moreover, are made to be looked in. But the story is quite different where, as here, two men hover about a street corner for an extended period of time, at the end of which it becomes apparent that they are not waiting for anyone or anything; where these men pace alternately along an identical route, pausing to stare in the same store window roughly 24 times; where each completion of this route is followed immediately by a conference between the two men on the corner; where they are joined in one of these conferences by a third man who leaves swiftly; and where the two men finally follow the third and rejoin him a couple of blocks away. It would have been poor police work indeed for an officer of 30 years' experience in the detection of thievery from stores in this same neighborhood to have failed to investigate this behavior further.

The crux of this case, however, is not the propriety of Officer McFadden's taking steps to investigate petitioner's suspicious behavior, but rather, whether there was justification for McFadden's invasion of Terry's personal security by searching him for weapons in the course of that investigation. We are now concerned with more than the governmental interest in investigating crime; in addition, there is the more immediate interest of the police officer in taking steps to assure himself that the person with whom he is dealing is not armed with a weapon that could unexpectedly and fatally be used against him. Certainly it would be unreasonable to require that police officers take unnecessary risks in the performance of their duties. American criminals have a long tradition of armed violence, and every year in this country many law enforcement officers are killed in the line of duty, and thousands more are wounded. Virtually all of these deaths and a substantial portion of the injuries are inflicted with guns and knives.

In view of these facts, we cannot blind ourselves to the need for law enforcement officers to protect themselves and other prospective victims of violence in situations where they may lack probable cause for an arrest. When an officer is justified in believing that the individual whose suspicious behavior he is investigating at close range is armed and presently dangerous to the officer or to others, it would appear to be clearly unreasonable to deny the officer the power to take necessary measures to determine whether the person is in fact carrying a weapon and to neutralize the threat of physical harm.

We must still consider, however, the nature and quality of the intrusion on individual rights which must be accepted if police officers are to be conceded the right to search for weapons in situations where probable cause to arrest for crime is lacking. Even a limited search of the outer clothing for weapons constitutes a severe, though brief, intrusion upon cherished personal security, and it must surely be an annoying, frightening, and perhaps humiliating experience. . . .

Our evaluation of the proper balance that has to be struck in this type of case leads us to conclude that there must be a narrowly drawn authority to permit a reasonable search for weapons for the protection of the police officer, where he has reason to believe that he is dealing with an armed and dangerous individual, regardless of whether he has probable cause to arrest the individual for a crime. The officer need not be absolutely certain that the individual is armed; the issue is whether a reasonably prudent man in the circumstances would be warranted in the belief that his safety or that of others was in danger. And in determining whether the officer acted reasonably in such circumstances, due weight must be given, not to his inchoate and unparticularized suspicion or "hunch," but to the specific reasonable inferences which he is entitled to draw from the facts in light of his experience.

IV.

We must now examine the conduct of Officer McFadden in this case to determine whether his search and seizure of petitioner were reasonable, both at their inception and as conducted. He had observed Terry, together with Chilton and another man, acting in a manner he took to be preface to a "stick-up." We think on the facts and circumstances Officer McFadden detailed before the trial judge a reasonably prudent man would have been warranted in believing petitioner was armed and thus presented a threat to the officer's safety while he was investigating his suspicious behavior. The actions of Terry and Chilton were consistent with McFadden's hypothesis that these men were contemplating a daylight robbery—which, it is reasonable to assume, would be likely to involve the use of weapons—and nothing in their conduct from the time he first noticed them until the time he confronted them and identified himself as a police officer gave him sufficient reason to negate that hypothesis. Although the trio had departed the original scene, there was nothing to indicate abandonment of an intent to commit a robbery at some point. Thus when Officer McFadden approached the three men gathered before the display window at Zucker's store he had observed enough to make it quite reasonable to fear that they were armed; and nothing in their response to his hailing them, identifying himself as a police officer, and asking their names served to dispel that reasonable belief. We cannot say his decision at that point to seize Terry and pat his clothing for weapons was the product of a volatile or inventive imagination, or was undertaken simply as an act of harassment; the record evidences the tempered act of a policeman who in the course of an investigation had to make a quick decision as to how to protect himself and others from possible danger, and took limited steps to do so.

The manner in which the seizure and search were conducted is, of course, as vital a part of the inquiry as whether they were warranted at all. The Fourth Amendment proceeds as much by limitations upon the scope of governmental action as by imposing preconditions upon its initiation. The entire deterrent purpose of the rule excluding evidence seized in violation of the Fourth Amendment rests on the assumption that "limitations upon the fruit to be gathered tend to limit the quest itself." Thus, evidence may not be introduced if it was discovered by means of a seizure and search which were not reasonably related in scope to the justification for their initiation.

We need not develop at length in this case, however, the limitations which the Fourth Amendment places upon a protective seizure and search for weapons. These limitations will have to be developed in the concrete factual circumstances of individual cases. Suffice it to note that such a search, unlike a search without a warrant incident to a lawful arrest, is not justified by any need to prevent the disappearance or destruction of evidence of crime. The sole justification of the search in the present situation is the protection of the police officer and others nearby, and it must therefore be confined in scope to an intrusion reasonably designed to discover guns, knives, clubs, or other hidden instruments for the assault of the police officer.

The scope of the search in this case presents no serious problems in light of these standards. Officer McFadden patted down the outer clothing of petitioner and his two companions. He did not place his hands in their pockets or under the outer surface of their garments until he had felt weapons, and then he merely reached for and removed the guns. He never did invade Katz' person beyond the outer surfaces of his clothes, since he discovered nothing in his pat-down which might have been a weapon. Officer McFadden confined his search strictly to what was minimally necessary to learn whether the men were armed and to disarm them once he discovered the weapons. He did not conduct a general exploratory search for whatever evidence of criminal activity he might find.

V.

We conclude that the revolver seized from Terry was properly admitted in evidence against him. At the time he seized petitioner and searched him for weapons, Officer McFadden had reasonable grounds to believe that petitioner was armed and dangerous, and it was necessary for the protection of himself and others to take swift measures to discover the true facts and neutralize the threat of harm if it materialized. The policeman carefully restricted his search to what was appropriate to the discovery of the particular items which he sought. Each case of this sort will, of course, have to be decided on its own facts. We merely hold today that where a police officer observes unusual conduct which leads him reasonably to conclude in light of his experience that criminal activity may be afoot and that the persons with whom he is dealing may be armed and presently dangerous, where in the course of investigating this behavior he identifies himself as a policeman and makes reasonable inquiries, and where nothing in the initial stages of the encounter serves to dispel his reasonable fear for his own or others' safety, he is entitled for the protection of himself and others in the area to conduct a carefully limited search of the outer clothing of such persons in an attempt to discover weapons which might be used to assault him. Such a search is a reasonable search under the Fourth Amendment, and any weapons seized may properly be introduced in evidence against the person from whom they were taken.

Affirmed.

Investigatory Stops:
Adams v. Williams, 407 U.S. 143 (1972)

Mr. Justice REHNQUIST delivered the opinion of the Court.

Respondent Robert Williams was convicted in a Connecticut state court of illegal possession of a handgun found during a "stop and frisk," as well as of possession of heroin that was found during a full search incident to his weapons arrest. After respondent's conviction was affirmed by the Supreme Court of Connecticut, seems Williams' petition for federal habeas corpus relief was denied by the District Court and by a divided panel of the Second Circuit, but on rehearing en banc the Court of Appeals granted relief. That court held that evidence introduced at Williams' trial had been obtained by an unlawful search of his person and car, and thus the state court judgments of conviction should be set aside. Since we conclude that the policeman's actions here conformed to the standards this Court laid down in *Terry v. Ohio*, 392 U.S. 1 (1968), we reverse.

Police Sgt. John Connolly was alone early in the morning on car patrol duty in a high-crime area of Bridgeport, Connecticut. At approximately 2:15 a.m. a person known to Sgt. Connolly approached his cruiser and informed him that an individual seated in a nearby vehicle was carrying narcotics and had a gun at his waist.

After calling for assistance on his car radio, Sgt. Connolly approached the vehicle to investigate the informant's report. Connolly tapped on the car window and asked the occupant, Robert Williams to open the door. When Williams rolled down the window instead, the sergeant reached into the car and removed a fully loaded revolver from Williams' waistband. The gun had not been visible to Connolly from outside the car, but it was in precisely the place indicated by the informant. Williams was then arrested by Connolly for unlawful possession of the pistol. A search incident to that arrest was conducted after other officers arrived. They found substantial quantities of heroin on Williams' person and in the car, and they found a machete and a second revolver hidden in the automobile.

Respondent contends that the initial seizure of his pistol, upon which rested the later search and seizure of other weapons and narcotics, was not justified by the informant's tip to Sgt. Connolly. He claims that absent a more reliable informant, or some corroboration of the tip, the policeman's actions were unreasonable under the standards set forth in *Terry v. Ohio*, supra.

In *Terry* this Court recognized that "a police officer may in appropriate circumstances and in an appropriate manner approach a person for purposes of investigating possibly criminal behavior even though there is no probable cause to make an arrest." Id., at 22. The Fourth Amendment does not require a policeman who lacks the precise level of information necessary for probable cause to arrest to simply shrug his shoulders and allow a crime to occur or a criminal to escape. On the contrary, *Terry* recognizes that it may be the essence of good police work to adopt an intermediate response. See id., at 23. A brief stop of a suspicious individual, in order to determine his identity or to maintain the status quo momentarily while obtaining more information, may be most reasonable in light of the facts known to the officer at the time. Id., at 21–22.

The Court recognized in *Terry* that the policeman making a reasonable investigatory stop should not be denied the opportunity to protect himself from attack by a hostile suspect. "When an officer is justified in believing that the individual whose suspicious behavior he is investigating at close range is armed and presently dangerous to the officer or to others," he may conduct a limited protective search for concealed weapons. 392 U.S., at 24. The purpose of this limited search is not to discover evidence of crime, but to allow the officer to pursue his investigation without fear of violence, and thus the frisk for weapons might be equally necessary and reasonable, whether or not carrying a concealed weapon violated any applicable state law. So long as the officer is entitled to make a forcible stop, and has reason to believe that the suspect is armed and dangerous, he may conduct a weapons search limited in scope to this protective purpose. Id., at 30.

Applying these principles to the present case, we believe that Sgt. Connolly acted justifiably in responding to his informant's tip. The informant was known to him personally and had provided him with information in the past. This is a stronger case than obtains in the case of an anonymous telephone tip. The informant here came forward personally to give information that was immediately verifiable at the scene. Indeed, under Connecticut law, the informant might have been subject to immediate arrest for making a false complaint had Sgt. Connolly's investigation proved the tip incorrect. Thus, while the Court's decisions indicate that this informant's unverifiable tip may have been insufficient for a narcotics arrest or search warrant, see *e.g.,* *Spinelli v. United States*, 393 U.S. 410 (1969); *Aguilar v. Texas*, 378 U.S. 108 (1964), the information carried enough indicia of reliability to justify the officer's forcible stop of Williams.

In reaching this conclusion, we reject respondent's argument that reasonable cause for a stop and frisk can only be based on the officer's personal observation, rather than on information supplied by another person. Informants' tips, like all other clues and evidence coming to a policeman on the scene, may vary greatly in their value and reliability. One simple rule will not cover every situation. Some tips, completely lacking in indicia of reliability, would either warrant no police response or require further investigation before a forcible stop of a suspect would be authorized. But in some situations—for example, when the victim of a street crime seeks immediate police aid and gives a description of his assailant, or when a credible informant warns of a specific impending crime—the subtleties of the hearsay rule should not thwart an appropriate police response.

While properly investigating the activity of a person who was reported to be carrying narcotics and a concealed weapon and who was sitting alone in a car in a high-crime area at 2:15 in the morning, Sgt. Connolly had ample reason to fear for his safety. When Williams rolled down his window, rather than complying with the policeman's request to step out of the car so that his movements could more easily be seen, the revolver allegedly at Williams' waist became an even greater threat. Under these circumstances the policeman's action in reaching to the spot where the gun was thought to be hidden constituted a limited intrusion designed to insure his safety, and we conclude that it was reasonable. The loaded gun seized as a result of this intrusion was therefore admissible at Williams' trial. *Terry v. Ohio*, 392 U.S., at 30.

Once Sgt. Connolly had found the gun precisely where the informant had predicted, probable cause existed to arrest Williams for unlawful possession of the weapon. Probable cause to arrest depends "upon whether, at the moment the arrest was made . . . the facts and circumstances within [the arresting officers'] knowledge and of which they had reasonably trustworthy information were sufficient to warrant a prudent man in believing that the [suspect] had committed or was committing an offense." *Beck v. Ohio*, 379 U.S. 89, 91 (1964). In the present case the policeman found Williams in possession of a gun in precisely the place predicted by the informant. This tended to corroborate the reliability of the informant's further report of narcotics and, together with the surrounding circumstances, certainly suggested no lawful explanation for possession of the gun. Probable cause does not require the same type of specific evidence of each element of the offense as would be needed to support a conviction. Rather, the Court will evaluate generally the circumstances at the time of the arrest to decide if the officer had probable cause for his action:

> "In dealing with probable cause, however, as the very name implies, we deal with probabilities. These are not technical; they are the factual and practical considerations of everyday life on which reasonable and prudent men, not legal technicians, act." *Brinegar v. United States*, 338 U.S. 160, 175 (1949).

Under the circumstances surrounding Williams' possession of the gun seized by Sgt. Connolly, the arrest on the weapons charge was supported by probable cause, and the search of his person and of the car incident to that arrest was lawful. See *Brinegar v. United States*, supra; *Carroll v. United States*, 267 U.S. 132 (1925). The fruits of the search were therefore properly admitted at Williams' trial, and the Court of Appeals erred in reaching a contrary conclusion.

Reversed.

Pedestrian Investigatory Stops:
Brown v. Texas, —— *U.S.* —— *(1979)*

Mr. Chief Justice BURGER delivered the opinion of the Court.

This appeal presents the question whether appellant was validly convicted for refusing to comply with a policeman's demand that he identify himself pursuant to a provision of the Texas Penal Code which makes it a crime to refuse such identification on request.

I

At 12:45 on the afternoon of December 9, 1977, officers Venegas and Sotelo of the El Paso Police Department were cruising in a patrol car. They observed appellant and another man walking in opposite directions away from one another in an alley. Although the two men were a few feet apart when they first were seen, officer Venegas later testified that both officers believed the two had been together or were about to meet until the patrol car appeared.

The car entered the alley, and officer Venegas got out and asked the appellant to identify himself and explain what he was doing there. The other man was not questioned or detained. The officer testified that he stopped appellant because the situation "looked suspicious and we had never seen that subject in that area before." The area of El Paso where appellant was stopped has a high incidence of drug traffic. However, the officers did not claim to suspect appellant of any specific misconduct, nor did they have any reason to believe that he was armed.

Appellant refused to identify himself and angrily asserted that the officers had no right to stop him. Officer Venegas replied that he was in a "high drug problem area"; officer Sotelo then "frisked" appellant, but found nothing.

When appellant continued to refuse to identify himself, he was arrested for violation of Texas Penal Code Ann. § 38.02(a), which makes it a criminal act for a person to refuse to give his name and address to an officer "who has lawfully stopped him and requested the information." Following the arrest the officers searched appellant; nothing untoward was found.

While being taken to the El Paso County Jail appellant identified himself. Nonetheless, he was held in custody and charged with violating § 38.02(a). When he was booked he was routinely searched a third time. Appellant was convicted in the El Paso Municipal Court and fined $20 plus court costs for violation of § 38.02. He then exercised his right under Texas law to a trial de novo in the El Paso County Court. There, he moved to set aside the information on the ground that § 38.02(a) of the Texas Penal Code violated the First, Fourth, and Fifth Amendments and was unconstitutionally vague in violation of the Fourteenth Amendment. The motion was denied. Appellant waived jury, and the court convicted him and imposed a fine of $45 plus court costs.

. . . We reverse.

II

When the officers detained appellant for the purpose of requiring him to identify himself, they performed a seizure of his person subject to the requirements of the Fourth Amendment. In convicting appellant, the County Court necessarily found as a matter of fact that the officers "lawfully stopped" appellant. See Texas Penal Code Ann. § 38.02. The Fourth Amendment, of course, "applies to all seizures of the person, including seizures that involve only a brief detention short of traditional arrest. *Davis v. Mississippi*, 394 U.S. 721 (1969). . . .

The reasonableness of seizures that are less intrusive than a traditional arrest, depends " 'on a balance between the public interest and the individual's right to personal security free from arbitrary interference by law officers.' " *Pennsylvania v. Mimms*, 434 U.S. 106, 109 (1977). Consideration of the constitutionality of such seizures involves a weighing of the gravity of the public concerns served by the seizure, the degree to which the seizure advances the public interest, and the severity of the interference with individual liberty.

A central concern in balancing these competing considerations in a variety of settings has been to assure that an individual's reasonable expectation of privacy is not subject to arbitrary invasions solely at the unfettered discretion of officers in the field. See *Delaware v. Prouse*, 440 U.S. _____, _____ (1979). To this end, the Fourth Amendment requires that a seizure must be based on specific, objective facts indicating that society's legitimate interests require the seizure of the particular individual, or that the seizure must be carried out pursuant to a plan embodying explicit, neutral limitations on the conduct of individual officers. *Delaware v. Prouse*, supra, at _____.

The State does not contend that appellant was stopped pursuant to a practice embodying neutral criteria, but rather maintains that the officers were justified in stopping appellant because they had a "reasonable, articulable suspicion that a crime had just been, was being, or was about to be committed." We have recognized that in some circumstances an officer may detain a suspect briefly for questioning although he does not have "probable cause" to believe that the suspect is involved in criminal activity, as is required for a traditional arrest. *United States v. Brignoni-Ponce*, supra, 422 U.S., at 880–881. However, we have required the officers to have a reasonable suspicion, based on objective facts, that the individual is involved in criminal activity. *Delaware v. Prouse*, supra, at _____.

The flaw in the State's case is that none of the circumstances preceding the officers' detention of appellant justified a reasonable suspicion that he was involved in criminal conduct. Officer Venegas testified at appellant's trial that the situation in the alley "looked suspicious," but he was unable to point to any facts supporting that conclusion. There is no indication in the record that it was unusual for people to be in the alley. The fact that appellant was in a neighborhood frequented by drug users, standing alone, is not a basis for concluding that appellant himself was engaged in criminal conduct. In short, the appellant's activity was no different from the activity of other pedestrians in that neighborhood. When pressed, officer Venegas acknowledged that the only reason he stopped appellant was to ascertain his identity. The record suggests an understandable desire to assert a police presence; however that purpose does not negate Fourth Amendment guarantees.

In the absence of any basis for suspecting appellant of misconduct, the balance between the public interest and appellant's right to personal security and privacy tilts in favor of freedom from police interference. The Texas statute under which appellant was stopped and required to identify himself is designed to advance a weighty social objective in large metropolitan centers: prevention of crime. But even assuming that purpose is served to some degree by stopping and demanding identification from an individual without any specific basis for believing he is involved in criminal activity, the guarantees of the Fourth Amendment do not allow it. When such a stop is not based on objective criteria, the risk of arbitrary and abusive police practices exceeds tolerable limits.

The application of Texas Penal Code Ann. § 38.02 to detain appellant and require him to identify himself violated the Fourth Amendment because the officers lacked any reasonable suspicion to believe appellant was engaged or had engaged in criminal conduct. Accordingly, appellant may not be punished for refusing to identify himself, and the conviction is reversed.

Reversed.

Automobile Investigatory Stops:
Delaware v. Prouse, —— U.S. —— (1979)

Mr. Justice WHITE delivered the opinion of the Court.

The question is whether it is an unreasonable seizure under the Fourth and Fourteenth Amendments to stop an automobile, being driven on a public highway, for the purpose of checking the driving license of the operator and the registration of the car, where there is neither probable cause to believe nor reasonable suspicion that the car is being driven contrary to the laws governing the operation of motor vehicles or that either the car or any of its occupants is subject to seizure or detention in connection with the violation of any other applicable law.

I

At 7:20 p.m. on November 30, 1976, a New Castle County, Del., patrolman in a police cruiser stopped the automobile occupied by respondent. The patrolman smelled marihuana smoke as he was walking toward the stopped vehicle, and he seized marihuana in plain view on the car floor. Respondent was subsequently indicted for illegal possession of a controlled substance. At a hearing on respondent's motion to suppress the marihuana seized as a result of the stop, the patrolman testified that prior to stopping the vehicle he had observed neither traffic or equipment violations nor any suspicious activity, and that he made the stop only in order to check the driver's license and registration. The patrolman was not acting pursuant to any standards, guidelines, or procedures pertaining to document spot checks, promulgated by either his department or the State Attorney General. Characterizing the stop as "routine," the patrolman explained, "I saw the car in the area and was not answering any complaints so I decided to pull them off." The trial court granted the motion to suppress, finding the stop and detention to have been wholly capricious and therefore violative of the Fourth Amendment.

The Delaware Supreme Court affirmed. . . .

III

The Fourth and Fourteenth Amendments are implicated in this case because stopping an automobile and detaining its occupants constitute a "seizure" within the meaning of those Amendments, even though the purpose of the stop is limited and the resulting detention quite brief. . . . Thus, the permissibility of a particular law-enforcement practice is judged by balancing its intrusion on the individual's Fourth Amendment interests against its promotion of legitimate governmental interests. Implemented in this manner, the reasonableness standard usually requires, at a minimum, that the facts upon which an intrusion is based be capable of measurement against "an objective standard," whether this be probable cause or a less stringent test. In those situations in which the balance of interests precludes insistence upon "some quantum of individualized suspicion," other safeguards are generally relied upon to assure that the individual's reasonable expectation of privacy is not "subject to the discretion of the official in the field."

In this case, however, the State of Delaware urges that patrol officers be subject to no constraints in deciding which automobiles shall be stopped for a license and registration check because the State's interest in discretionary spot checks as a means of ensuring the safety of its roadways outweighs the resulting intrusion on the privacy and security of the persons detained.

IV

We have only recently considered the legality of investigative stops of automobiles where the officers making the stop have neither probable cause to believe nor reasonable suspicion that either the automobile or its occupants are subject to seizure under the applicable criminal laws. . . .

Although not dispositive, these decisions undoubtedly provide guidance in balancing the public interest against the individual's Fourth Amendment interests implicated by the practice of spot checks such as occurred in this case. We cannot agree that stopping or detaining a vehicle on an ordinary city street is less intrusive than a roving patrol stop on a major highway and that it bears greater resemblance to a permissible stop and secondary detention at a checkpoint near the border. In this regard, we note that *Brignoni-Ponce* was not limited to roving patrol stops on limited access roads, but applied to any roving patrol stop by border patrol agents on any type of roadway on less than reasonable suspicion. See 422 U.S. at 882–883 (1975). We cannot assume that the physical and psychological intrusion visited upon the occupants of a vehicle by a random stop to check documents is of any less moment than that occasioned by a stop by border agents on roving patrol. Both of these stops generally entail law-enforcement officers signaling a moving automobile to pull over to the side of the roadway, by means of a possibly unsettling show of authority. Both interfere with freedom of movement, are inconvenient, and consume time. Both may create substantial anxiety. For Fourth Amendment purposes, we also see insufficient resemblance between sporadic and random stops of individual vehicles making their way through city traffic and those stops occasioned by roadblocks where all vehicles are brought to a halt or to a near halt, and all are subjected to a show of the police power of the community. "At traffic checkpoints, the motorist can see that other vehicles are being stopped, he can see visible signs of the officer's authority, and he is much less likely to be frightened or annoyed by the intrusion." Id., 422 U.S. at 894–895.

V

But the State of Delaware urges that even if discretionary spot checks such as occurred in this case intrude upon motorists as much as or more than do the roving patrols held impermissible in *Brignoni-Ponce,* these stops are reasonable under the Fourth Amendment because the State's interest in the practice as a means of promoting public safety upon its roads more than outweighs the intrusion entailed. Although the record discloses no statistics concerning the extent of the problem of lack of highway safety, in Delaware or in the Nation as a whole, we are aware of the danger to life and property posed by vehicular traffic and of the difficulties that even a cautious and an experienced driver may encounter. We agree that the States have a vital interest in ensuring that only those qualified to do so are permitted to operate motor vehicles, that these vehicles are fit for safe operation, and hence that licensing, registration, and vehicle inspection requirements are being observed. Automobile licenses are issued periodically to evidence that the drivers holding them are sufficiently familiar with the rules of the road and are physically qualified to operate a motor vehicle. The registration requirement and, more pointedly, the related annual inspection requirement in Delaware are designed to keep dangerous automobiles off the road. Unquestionably, these provisions, properly administered, are essential elements in a highway safety program. . . .

The question remains, however, whether in the service of these important ends the discretionary spot check is a sufficiently productive mechanism to justify the intrusion upon Fourth Amendment interests which such stops entail. On the record before us, that question must be answered in the negative. Given the alternative mechanisms available, both those in use and those that might be adopted, we are unconvinced that the incremental contribution to highway safety of the random spot check justifies the practice under the Fourth Amendment.

The foremost method of enforcing traffic and vehicle safety regulations, it must be recalled, is acting upon observed violations. Vehicle stops for traffic violations occur countless times each day; and on these occasions, licenses and registration papers are subject to inspection and drivers without them will be ascertained. Furthermore, drivers without licenses are presumably the less safe drivers whose propensities may well exhibit themselves. Absent some empirical data to the contrary, it must be assumed that finding an unlicensed driver among those who commit traffic violations is a much more likely event than finding an unlicensed driver by choosing randomly from the entire universe of drivers. If this were not so, licensing of drivers would hardly be an effective means of promoting roadway safety. It seems common sense that the percentage of all drivers on the road who are driving without a license is very small and that the number of licensed drivers who will be stopped in order to find one unlicensed operator will be large indeed. The contribution to highway safety made by discretionary stops selected from among drivers generally will therefore be marginal at best. Furthermore, and again absent something more than mere assertion to the contrary, we find it difficult to believe that the unlicensed driver would not be deterred by the possibility of being involved in a traffic violation or having some other experience calling for proof of his entitlement to drive but that he would be deterred by the possibility that he would be one of those chosen for a spot check. In terms of actually discovering unlicensed drivers or deterring them from driving, the spot check does not appear sufficiently productive to qualify as a reasonable law-enforcement practice under the Fourth Amendment.

Much the same can be said about the safety aspects of automobiles as distinguished from drivers. Many violations of minimum vehicle safety requirements are observable, and something can be done about them by the observing officer, directly and immediately. . . .

The marginal contribution to roadway safety possibly resulting from a system of spot checks cannot justify subjecting every occupant of every vehicle on the roads to a seizure—limited in magnitude compared to other intrusions but nonetheless constitutionally cognizable—at the unbridled discretion of law-enforcement officials. To insist upon neither an appropriate factual basis for suspicion directed at a particular automobile nor upon some other substantial and objective standard or rule to govern the exercise of discretion "would invite intrusions upon constitutionally guaranteed rights based on nothing more substantial than inarticulate hunches. . . ." *Terry v. Ohio,* supra, 392 U.S. at 22. By hypothesis, stopping apparently safe drivers is necessary only because the danger presented by some drivers is not observable at the time of the stop. When there is not probable cause to believe that a driver is violating any one of the multitude of applicable traffic and equipment regulations—nor other articulable basis amounting to reasonable suspicion that the driver is unlicensed or his vehicle unregistered—we cannot conceive of any legitimate basis upon which a patrolman could decide that stopping a particular driver for a spot check would be more productive than stopping any other driver. This kind of standardless and unconstrained discretion is the evil the Court has discerned when in previous cases it has insisted that the discretion of the official in the field be circumscribed, at least to some extent.

VI

The "grave danger" of abuse of discretion, *United States v. Martinez-Fuerte,* supra, 428 U.S. at 559, does not disappear simply because the automobile is subject to state regulation resulting in numerous instances of police-citizen contact, *Cady v. Dombrowski,* 413 U.S. 433, 441 (1973). . . .

An individual operating or travelling in an automobile does not lose all reasonable expectation of privacy simply because the automobile and its use are subject to government regulation. Automobile travel is a basic, pervasive, and often necessary mode of transportation to and from one's home, workplace, and leisure activities. Many people spend more hours each day travelling in cars than walking on the streets. Undoubtedly, many find a greater sense of security and privacy in travelling in an automobile than they do in exposing themselves by pedestrian or other modes of travel. Were the individual subject to unfettered governmental intrusion every time he entered an automobile, the security guaranteed by the Fourth Amendment would be seriously circumscribed. . . .

VII

Accordingly, we hold that except in those situations in which there is at least articulable and reasonable suspicion that a motorist is unlicensed or that an automobile is not registered, or that either the vehicle or an occupant is otherwise subject to seizure for violation of law, stopping an automobile and detaining the driver in order to check his driver's license and the registration of the automobile are unreasonable under the Fourth Amendment. This holding does not preclude the State of Delaware or other States from developing methods for spot checks that involve less intrusion or that do not involve the unconstrained exercise of discretion. Questioning of all oncoming traffic at roadblock-type stops is one possible alternative. We hold only that persons in automobiles on public roadways may not for that reason alone have their travel and privacy interfered with at the unbridled discretion of police officers. The judgment below is affirmed.

So ordered.

Mr. Justice REHNQUIST, dissenting.

The Court holds, in successive sentences, that absent an articulable, reasonable suspicion of unlawful conduct, a motorist may not be subjected to a random license check, but that the States are free to develop "methods for spot checks that . . . do not involve the unconstrained exercise of discretion," such as "questioning . . . all oncoming traffic at roadblock-type stops. . . ." Because motorists, apparently like sheep, are much less likely to be "frightened" or "annoyed" when stopped en masse, a highway patrolman needs neither probable cause nor articulable suspicion to stop *all* motorists on a particular throughfare, but he cannot without articulable suspicion stop *less* than all motorists. The Court thus elevates the adage "misery loves company" to a novel role in Fourth Amendment jurisprudence. The rule becomes "curiouser and curiouser" as one attempts to follow the Court's explanation for it.

The Plain-view Doctrine:
Harris v. United States, *390 U.S. 234 (1968)*

PER CURIAM.

Petitioner was charged with robbery under the District of Columbia Code. At his trial in the United States District Court for the District of Columbia, petitioner moved to suppress an automobile registration card belonging to the robbery victim, which the Government sought to introduce in evidence. The trial court, after a hearing, ruled that the card was admissible. Petitioner was convicted of the crime charged and sentenced to imprisonment for a period of two to seven years. On appeal . . . the full Court of Appeals affirmed petitioner's conviction, with two judges dissenting. We granted certiorari to consider the problem presented under the Fourth Amendment. We affirm.

Petitioner's automobile had been seen leaving the site of the robbery. The car was traced and petitioner was arrested as he was entering it near his home. After a cursory search of the car, the arresting officer took petitioner to a police station. The police decided to impound the car as evidence, and a crane was called to tow it to the precinct. It reached the precinct about an hour and a quarter after petitioner. At this moment, the windows of the car were open and the door unlocked. It had begun to rain.

A regulation of the Metropolitan Police Department requires the officer who takes an impounded vehicle in charge to search the vehicle thoroughly, to remove all valuables from it, and to attach to the vehicle a property tag listing certain information about the circumstances of the impounding. Pursuant to this regulation, and without a warrant, the arresting officer proceeded to the lot to which petitioner's car had been towed, in order to search the vehicle, to place a property tag on it, to roll up the windows, and to lock the doors. The officer entered on the driver's side, searched the car, and tied a property tag on the steering wheel. Stepping out of the car, he rolled up an open window on one of the back doors. Proceeding to the front door on the passenger side, the officer opened the door in order to secure the window and door. He then saw the registration card, which lay face up on the metal stripping over which the door closes. The officer returned to the precinct, brought petitioner to the car, and confronted petitioner with the registration card. Petitioner disclaimed all knowledge of the card. The officer then seized the card and brought it into the precinct. Returning to the car, he searched the trunk, rolled up the windows, and locked the doors.

The sole question for our consideration is whether the officer discovered the registration card by means of an illegal search. We hold that he did not. The admissibility of evidence found as a result of a search under the police regulation is not presented by this case. The precise and detailed findings of the District Court, accepted by the Court of Appeals, were to the effect that the discovery of the card was not the result of a search of the car, but of a measure taken to protect the car while it was in police custody. Nothing in the Fourth Amendment requires the police to obtain a warrant in these narrow circumstances.

Once the door had lawfully been opened, the registration card, with the name of the robbery victim on it, was plainly visible. It has long been settled that objects falling in the plain view of an officer who has a right to be in the position to have that view are subject to seizure and may be introduced in evidence. *Ker v. State of California*, 374 U.S. 23, 42–43 (1963).

Affirmed.

Automobile Inventories:
South Dakota v. Opperman, *428 U.S. 364 (1976)*

Mr. Chief Justice BURGER delivered the opinion of the Court.

We review the judgment of the Supreme Court of South Dakota, holding that local police violated the Fourth Amendment to the Federal Constitution, as applicable to the States under the Fourteenth Amendment, when they conducted a routine inventory search of an automobile lawfully impounded by police for violations of municipal parking ordinances.

(1)

Local ordinances prohibit parking in certain areas of downtown Vermillion, S.D., between the hours of 2 a.m. and 6 a.m. During the early morning hours of December 10, 1973, a Vermillion police officer observed respondent's unoccupied vehicle illegally parked in the restricted zone. At approximately 3 a.m., the officer issued an overtime parking ticket and placed it on the car's windshield. The citation warned:

"Vehicles in violation of any parking ordinance may be towed from the area."

At approximately 10 a.m. on the same morning, another officer issued a second ticket for an overtime parking violation. These circumstances were routinely reported to police headquarters, and after the vehicle was inspected, the car was towed to the city impound lot.

From outside the car at the impound lot, a police officer observed a watch on the dashboard and other items of personal property located on the back seat and back floorboard. At the officer's direction, the car door was then unlocked and, using a standard inventory form pursuant to standard police procedures, the officer inventoried the contents of the car, including the contents of the glove compartment which was unlocked. There he found marihuana contained in a plastic bag. All items, including the contraband, were removed to the police department for safekeeping. During the late afternoon of December 10, respondent appeared at the police department to claim his property. The marihuana was retained by police.

Respondent was subsequently arrested on charges of possession of marihuana. His motion to suppress the evidence yielded by the inventory search was denied; he was convicted after a jury trial and sentenced to a fine of $100 and 14 days' incarceration in the county jail. On appeal, the Supreme Court of South Dakota reversed the conviction. The court concluded that the evidence had been obtained in violation of the Fourth Amendment prohibition against unreasonable searches and seizures. We granted certiorari, and we reverse.

(2)

This Court has traditionally drawn a distinction between automobiles and homes or offices in relation to the Fourth Amendment. Although automobiles are "effects" and thus within the reach of the Fourth Amendment, warrantless examinations of automobiles have been upheld in circumstances in which a search of a home or office would not.

The reason for this well-settled distinction is twofold. First, the inherent mobility of automobiles creates circumstances of such exigency that, as a practical necessity, rigorous enforcement of the warrant requirement is impossible. *Carroll v. United States*, 267 U.S. 132, 153–154(1925). But the Court has also upheld warrantless searches where no immediate danger was presented that the car would be removed from the jurisdiction. *Chambers v. Maroney*, 399 U.S., at 51–52 (1967). Besides the element of mobility, less rigorous warrant requirements govern because the expectation of privacy with respect to one's automobile is significantly less than that relating to one's home or office. In discharging their varied responsibilities for ensuring the public safety, law enforcement officials are necessarily brought into frequent contact with automobiles. Most of this contact is distinctly noncriminal in nature. Automobiles, unlike homes, are subjected to pervasive and continuing governmental regulation and controls, including periodic inspection and licensing requirements. As an everyday occurrence, police stop and examine vehicles when license plates or inspection stickers have expired, or if other violations, such as exhaust fumes or excessive noise, are noted, or if headlights or other safety equipment are not in proper working order.

The expectation of privacy as to autos is further diminished by the obviously public nature of automobile travel. Only two Terms ago, the Court noted:

> "One has a lesser expectation of privacy in a motor vehicle because its function is transportation and it seldom serves as one's residence or as the repository of personal effects. A car has little capacity for escaping public scrutiny. It travels public thoroughfares where both its occupants and its contents are in plain view." *Cardwell v. Lewis*, 417 U.S., at 590.

In the interests of public safety and as part of what the Court has called "community caretaking functions," *Cady v. Dombrowski*, supra, 413 U.S. at 441, automobiles are frequently taken into police custody. Vehicle accidents present one such occasion. To permit the uninterrupted flow of traffic and in some circumstances to preserve evidence, disabled or damaged vehicles will often be removed from the highways or streets at the behest of police engaged solely in caretaking and traffic-control activities. Police will also frequently remove and impound automobiles which violate parking ordinances and which thereby jeopardize both the public safety and the efficient movement of vehicular traffic. The authority of police to seize and remove from the streets vehicles impeding traffic or threatening public safety and convenience is beyond challenge.

When vehicles are impounded, local police departments generally follow a routine practice of securing and inventorying the automobiles' contents. These procedures developed in response to three distinct needs: the protection of the owner's property while it remains in police custody; the protection of the police against claims or disputes over lost or stolen property; and the protection of the police from potential danger. The practice has been viewed as essential to respond to incidents of theft or vandalism. In addition, police frequently attempt to determine whether a vehicle has been stolen and thereafter abandoned.

These caretaking procedures have almost uniformly been upheld by the state courts, which by virtue of the localized nature of traffic regulation have had considerable occasion to deal with the issue. Applying the Fourth Amendment standard of "reasonableness," the state courts have overwhelmingly concluded that, even if an inventory is characterized as a "search," the intrusion is constitutionally permissible. . . .

The majority of the federal Courts of Appeals have likewise sustained inventory procedures as reasonable police intrusions. . . .

(3)

The decisions of this Court point unmistakably to the conclusion reached by both federal and state courts that inventories pursuant to standard police procedures are reasonable. In the first such case, Justice Black made plain the nature of the inquiry before us:

> "But the question here is not whether the search was *authorized* by state law. The question is rather whether the search was *reasonable* under the Fourth Amendment." *Cooper v. California*, 386 U.S. 58, 61 (1967) (emphasis added).

. . .

In applying the reasonableness standard adopted by the Framers, this Court has consistently sustained police intrusions into automobiles impounded or otherwise in lawful police custody where the process is aimed at securing or protecting the car and its contents. In *Cooper v. California*, supra, the Court upheld the inventory of a car impounded under the authority of a state forfeiture statute. Even though the inventory was conducted in a distinctly criminal setting and carried out a week after the car had been impounded, the Court nonetheless found that the car search, including examination of the glove compartment where contraband was found, was reasonable under the circumstances. This conclusion was reached despite the fact that no warrant had issued and probable cause to search for the contraband in the vehicle had not been established. The Court said in language explicitly applicable here:

> "It would be unreasonable to hold that the police, having to retain the car in their custody for such a length of time, had no right, even for their own protection, to search it." 386 U.S., at 61–62.

. . .

Finally, in *Cady v. Dombrowski*, supra, the Court upheld a warrantless search of an auto towed to a private garage even though no probable cause existed to believe that the vehicle contained fruits of a crime. The sole justification for the warrantless incursion was that it was incident to the caretaking function of the local police to protect the community's safety. Indeed, the protective search was instituted solely because the local police "were under the impression" that the incapacitated driver, a Chicago police officer, was required to carry his service revolver at all times; the police had reasonable grounds to believe a weapon might be in the car, and thus available to vandals. 413 U.S., at 436. The Court carefully noted that the protective search was carried out in accordance with *standard procedures* in the local police department, ibid., a factor tending to ensure that the intrusion would be limited in scope to the extent necessary to carry out the caretaking function. In reaching this result, the Court in *Cady* distinguished *Preston v. United States*, 376 U.S. 364 (1964), on the grounds that the holding, invalidating a car search conducted after a vagrancy arrest, "stands only for the proposition that the search challenged there could not be justified as one incident to an arrest." 413 U.S., at 444. *Preston* therefore did not raise the issue of the constitutionality of a protective inventory of a car lawfully within police custody.

The holdings in *Cooper* . . . and *Cady* point the way to the correct resolution of this case. None of the . . . cases, of course, involves the precise situation presented here; but, as in all Fourth Amendment cases, we are obliged to look to all the facts and circumstances of this case in light of the principles set forth in these prior decisions. . . .

The Vermillion police were indisputably engaged in a caretaking search of a lawfully impounded automobile. The inventory was conducted only after the car had been impounded for multiple parking violations. The owner, having left his car illegally parked for an extended period, and thus subject to impoundment, was not present to make other arrangements for the safekeeping of his belongings. The inventory itself was prompted by the presence in plain view of a number of valuables inside the car. As in *Cady*, there is no suggestion whatever that this standard procedure, essentially like that followed throughout the country, was a pretext concealing an investigatory police motive.

On this record we conclude that in following standard police procedures, prevailing throughout the country and approved by the overwhelming majority of courts, the conduct of the police was not "unreasonable" under the Fourth Amendment.

The judgment of the South Dakota Supreme Court is therefore reversed and the case is remanded for further proceedings not inconsistent with this opinion.

Reversed and remanded.

The Exclusionary Rule:
Mapp v. Ohio, 367 U.S. 643 (1961)

Mr. Justice CLARK delivered the opinion of the Court.

Appellant stands convicted of knowingly having had in her possession and under her control certain lewd and lascivious books, pictures, and photographs in violation of § 2905.34 of Ohio's Revised Code. As officially stated in the syllabus to its opinion, the Supreme Court of Ohio found that her conviction was valid though "based primarily upon the introduction in evidence of lewd and lascivious books and pictures unlawfully seized during an unlawful search of defendant's home. . . ." 170 Ohio St. 427–428.

On May 23, 1957, three Cleveland police officers arrived at appellant's residence in that city pursuant to information that "a person [was] hiding out in the home, who was wanted for questioning in connection with a recent bombing, and that there was a large amount of policy paraphernalia being hidden in the home." Miss Mapp and her daughter by a former marriage lived on the top floor of the two-family dwelling. Upon their arrival at that house, the officers knocked on the door and demanded entrance but appellant, after telephoning her attorney, refused to admit them without a search warrant. They advised their headquarters of the situation and undertook a surveillance of the house.

The officers again sought entrance some three hours later when four or more additional officers arrived on the scene. When Miss Mapp did not come to the door immediately, at least one of the several doors to the house was forcibly opened and the policemen gained admittance. Meanwhile Miss Mapp's attorney arrived, but the officers, having secured their own entry, and continuing in their defiance of the law, would permit him neither to see Miss Mapp nor to enter the house. It appears that Miss Mapp was halfway down the stairs from the upper floor to the front door when the officers, in this highhanded manner, broke into the hall. She demanded to see the search warrant. A paper, claimed to be a warrant, was held up by one of the officers. She grabbed the "warrant" and placed it in her bosom. A struggle ensued in which the officers recovered the piece of paper and as a result of which they handcuffed appellant because she had been "belligerent" in resisting their official rescue of the "warrant" from her person. Running roughshod over appellant, a policeman "grabbed" her, "twisted [her] hand," and she "yelled [and] pleaded with him" because "it was hurting." Appellant, in handcuffs, was then forcibly taken upstairs to her bedroom where the officers searched a dresser, a chest of drawers, a closet and some suitcases. They also looked into a photo album and through personal papers belonging to the appellant. The search spread to the rest of the second floor including the child's bedroom, the living room, the kitchen and a dinette. The basement of the building and a trunk found therein were also searched. The obscene materials for possession of which she was ultimately convicted were discovered in the course of that widespread search.

At the trial no search warrant was produced by the prosecution, nor was the failure to produce one explained or accounted for. At best, "There is, in the record, considerable doubt as to whether there ever was any warrant for the search of defendant's home." 170 Ohio St. at page 430, 166 N.E.2d at page 389. The Ohio Supreme Court believed a "reasonable argument" could be made that the conviction should be reversed "because the 'methods' employed to obtain the [evidence] were such as to 'offend "a sense of justice,"'" but the court found determinative the fact that the evidence had not been taken "from defendant's person by the use of brutal or offensive physical force against defendant." 170 Ohio St. at page 431, 166 N.E.2d at pages 389–390.

The State says that even if the search were made without authority, or otherwise unreasonably, it is not prevented from using the unconstitutionally seized evidence at trial, citing *Wolf v. People of State of Colorado*, 338 U.S. 25, at page 33 (1949), in which this Court did indeed hold "that in a prosecution in a State court for a State crime the Fourteenth Amendment does not forbid the admission of evidence obtained by an unreasonable search and seizure." On this appeal . . . it is urged once again that we review that holding.

. . .

IV.

Since the Fourth Amendment's right of privacy has been declared enforceable against the States through the Due Process Clause of the Fourteenth, it is enforceable against them by the same sanction of exclusion as is used against the Federal Government. Were it otherwise, then just as without the *Weeks* rule the assurance against unreasonable federal searches and seizures would be "a form of words," valueless and undeserving of mention in a perpetual charter of inestimable human liberties, so too, without that rule the freedom from state invasions of privacy would be so ephemeral and so neatly severed from its conceptual nexus with the freedom from all brutish means of coercing evidence as not to merit this Court's high regard as a freedom "implicit in 'the concept of ordered liberty.'" At the time that the Court held in *Wolf* that the Amendment was applicable to the States through the Due Process Clause, the cases of this Court, as we have seen, had steadfastly held that as to federal officers the Fourth Amendment included the exclusion of the evidence seized in violation of its provisions. Even *Wolf* "stoutly adhered" to that proposition. The right to privacy, when conceded operatively enforceable against the States, was not susceptible of destruction by avulsion of the sanction upon which its protection and enjoyment had always been deemed dependent under the *Boyd, Weeks* and *Silverthorne* cases. Therefore, in extending the substantive protections of due process to all constitutionally unreasonable searches—state or federal—it was logically and constitutionally necessary that the exclusion doctrine—an essential part of the right to privacy—be also insisted upon as an essential ingredient of the right newly recognized by the *Wolf* case. In short, the admission of the new constitutional right by *Wolf* could not consistently tolerate denial of its most important constitutional privilege, namely, the exclusion of the evidence which an accused had been forced to give by reason of the unlawful seizure. To hold otherwise is to grant the right but in reality to withhold its privilege and enjoyment. Only last year the Court itself recognized that the purpose of the exclusionary rule "is to deter—to compel respect for the constitutional guaranty in the only effectively available way—by removing the incentive to disregard it." *Elkins v. United States,* supra, 364 U.S. at page 217.

Indeed, we are aware of no restraint, similar to that rejected today, conditioning the enforcement of any other basic constitutional right. The right to privacy, no less important than any other right carefully and particularly reserved to the people, would stand in marked contrast to all other rights declared as "basic to a free society." *Wolf v. People of State of Colorado,* supra, 338 U.S. at page 27. This Court has not hesitated to enforce as strictly against the States as it does against the Federal Government the rights of free speech and of a free press, the rights to notice and to a fair, public trial, including, as it does, the right not to be convicted by use of a coerced confession, however logically relevant it be, and without regard to its reliability. *Rogers v. Richmond,* 365 U.S. 534 (1961). And nothing could be more certain than that when a coerced confession is involved, "the relevant rules of evidence" are overridden without regard to "the incidence of such conduct by the police," slight or frequent. Why should not the same rule apply to what is tantamount to coerced testimony by way of unconstitutional seizure of goods, papers, effects, documents, etc.? We find that, as to the Federal Government, the Fourth and Fifth Amendments and, as to the States, the freedom from unconscionable invasions of privacy and the freedom from convictions based upon coerced confessions do enjoy an "intimate relation" in their perpetuation of "principles of humanity and civil liberty [secured] . . . only after years of struggle." *Bram v. United States,* 168 U.S. 532, 543–544 (1897). They express "supplementing phases of the same constitutional purpose—to maintain inviolate large areas of personal privacy." *Feldman v. United States,* 322 U.S. 487, 489–490 (1944). The philosophy of each Amendment and of each freedom is complementary to, although not dependent upon, that of the other in its sphere of influence—the very least that together they assure in either sphere is that no man is to be convicted on unconstitutional evidence.

V.

Moreover, our holding that the exclusionary rule is an essential part of both the Fourth and Fourteenth Amendments is not only the logical dictate of prior cases, but it also makes very good sense. There is no war between the Constitution and common sense. Presently, a federal prosecutor may make no use of evidence illegally seized, but a State's attorney across the street may, although he supposedly is operating under the enforceable prohibitions of the same Amendment. Thus the State, by admitting evidence unlawfully seized, serves to encourage disobedience to the Federal Constitution which it is bound to uphold. Moreover, as was said in Elkins, "the very essence of a healthy federalism depends upon the avoidance of needless conflict between state and federal courts." 364 U.S. at page 221. Such a conflict, hereafter needless, arose this very Term, in *Wilson v. Schnettler*, 365 U.S. 381 (1961), in which, and in spite of the promise made by *Rea,* we gave full recognition to our practice in this regard by refusing to restrain a federal officer from testifying in a state court as to evidence unconstitutionally seized by him in the performance of his duties. Yet the double standard recognized until today hardly put such a thesis into practice. In non-exclusionary States, federal officers, being human, were by it invited to and did, as our cases indicate, step across the street to the State's attorney with their unconstitutionally seized evidence. Prosecution on the basis of that evidence was then had in a state court in utter disregard of the enforceable Fourth Amendment. If the fruits of an unconstitutional search had been inadmissible in both state and federal courts, this inducement to evasion would have been sooner eliminated. There would be no need to reconcile such cases as *Rea* and *Schnettler,* each pointing up the hazardous uncertainties of our heretofore ambivalent approach.

Federal-state cooperation in the solution of crime under constitutional standards will be promoted, if only by recognition of their now mutual obligation to respect the same fundamental criteria in their approaches. "However much in a particular case insistence upon such rules may appear as a technicality that inures to the benefit of a guilty person, the history of the criminal law proves that tolerance of shortcut methods in law enforcement impairs its enduring effectiveness." *Miller v. United States,* 357 U.S. 301, 313 (1958). Denying shortcuts to only one of two cooperating law enforcement agencies tends naturally to breed legitimate suspicion of "working arrangements" whose results are equally tainted. *Byars v. United States,* 273 U.S. 28 (1927).

There are those who say, as did Justice (then Judge) Cardozo, that under our constitutional exclusionary doctrine "the criminal is to go free because the constable has blundered." *People v. Defore,* 242 N.Y. at page 21. In some cases this will undoubtedly be the result. But, as was said in *Elkins,* "there is another consideration—the imperative of judicial integrity." 364 U.S. at page 222. The criminal goes free, if he must, but it is the law that sets him free. Nothing can destroy a government more quickly than its failure to observe its own laws, or worse, its disregard of the charter of its own existence. As Mr. Justice Brandeis, dissenting, said in *Olmstead v. United States,* 277 U.S. 438, 485 (1928): "Our government is the potent, the omnipresent teacher. For good or for ill, it teaches the whole people by its example. . . . If the government becomes a lawbreaker, it breeds contempt for law; it invites every man to become a law unto himself; it invites anarchy." Nor can it lightly be assumed that, as a practical matter, adoption of the exclusionary rule fetters law enforcement. Only last year this Court expressly considered that contention and found that "pragmatic evidence of a sort" to the contrary was not wanting. *Elkins v. United States,* supra, 364 U.S. at page 218. The Court noted that

> "The federal courts themselves have operated under the exclusionary rule of *Weeks* for almost half a century; yet it has not been suggested either that the Federal Bureau of Investigation has thereby been rendered ineffective, or that the administration of criminal justice in the federal courts has thereby been disrupted. Moreover, the experi-

ence of the states is impressive. . . . The movement towards the rule of exclusion has been halting but seemingly inexorable." Id., 364 U.S. at pages 218–219.

The ignoble shortcut to conviction left open to the State tends to destroy the entire system of constitutional restraints on which the liberties of the people rest. Having once recognized that the right to privacy embodied in the Fourth Amendment is enforceable against the States, and that the right to be secure against rude invasions of privacy by state officers is, therefore, constitutional in origin, we can no longer permit that right to remain an empty promise. Because it is enforceable in the same manner and to like effect as other basic rights secured by the Due Process Clause, we can no longer permit it to be revocable at the whim of any police officer who, in the name of law enforcement itself, chooses to suspend its enjoyment. Our decision, founded on reason and truth, gives to the individual no more than that which the Constitution guarantees him, to the police officer no less than that to which honest law enforcement is entitled, and, to the courts, that judicial integrity so necessary in the true administration of justice.

The judgment of the Supreme Court of Ohio is reversed and the cause remanded for further proceedings not inconsistent with this opinion.

Reversed and remanded.

Standing:
Rakas v. Illinois, —— U.S. —— (1978)

Mr. Justice REHNQUIST delivered the opinion of the Court.

Petitioners were convicted of armed robbery in the Circuit Court of Kankakee County, Ill., and their convictions were affirmed on appeal. At their trial, the prosecution offered into evidence a sawed-off rifle and rifle shells that had been seized by police during a search of an automobile in which petitioners had been passengers. Neither petitioner is the owner of the automobile and neither has ever asserted that he owned the rifle or shells seized. The Illinois Appellate Court held that petitioners lacked standing to object to the allegedly unlawful search and seizure and denied their motion to suppress the evidence. We granted certiorari in light of the obvious importance of the issues raised to the administration of criminal justice and now affirm.

I

Because we are not here concerned with the issue of probable cause, a brief description of the events leading to the search of the automobile will suffice. A police officer on a routine patrol received a radio call notifying him of a robbery of a clothing store in Bourbonnais, Ill., and describing the getaway car. Shortly thereafter, the officer spotted an automobile which he thought might be the getaway car. After following the car for some time and after the arrival of assistance, he and several other officers stopped the vehicle. The occupants of the automobile, petitioners and two female companions, were ordered out of the car and after the occupants had left the car, two officers searched the interior of the vehicle. They discovered a box of rifle shells in the glove compartment, which had been locked, and a sawed-off rifle under the front passenger seat. App. 10–11. After discovering the rifle and the shells, the officers took petitioners to the station and placed them under arrest.

Before trial petitioners moved to suppress the rifle and shells seized from the car on the ground that the search violated the Fourth and Fourteenth Amendments. They conceded that they did not own the automobile and were simply passengers; the owner of the car had been the driver of the vehicle at the time of the search. Nor did they assert that they owned the rifle or the shells seized. The prosecutor challenged petitioners' standing to object to the lawfulness of the search of the car because neither the car, the shells nor the rifle belonged to them. The trial court agreed that petitioners lacked standing and denied the motion to suppress the evidence. . . .

II

Petitioners first urge us to relax or broaden the rule of standing enunciated in *Jones v. United States,* 362 U.S. 257 (1960), so that any criminal defendant at whom a search was "directed" would have standing to contest the legality of that search and object to the admission at trial of evidence obtained as a result of the search. Alternatively, petitioners argue that they have standing to object to the search under *Jones* because they were "legitimately on [the] premises" at the time of the search.

The concept of standing discussed in *Jones* focuses on whether the person seeking to challenge the legality of a search as a basis for suppressing evidence was himself the "victim" of the search or seizure. Id., at 261. Adoption of the so-called "target" theory advanced by petitioners would in effect permit a defendant to assert that a violation of the Fourth Amendment rights of a third party entitled him to have evidence suppressed at his trial. If we reject petitioners' request for a broadened rule of standing such as this, and reaffirm the holding of *Jones* and other cases that Fourth Amendment rights are personal rights that may not be asserted vicariously, we will have occasion to re-examine the "standing" terminology emphasized in *Jones.* . . .

A

We decline to extend the rule of standing in Fourth Amendment cases in the manner suggested by petitioners. As we stated in *Alderman v. United States,* 394 U.S. 165 (1969), "Fourth Amendment rights are personal rights which, like some other constitutional rights, may not be asserted vicariously." Id., at 174. A person who is aggrieved by an illegal search and seizure only through the introduction of damaging evidence secured by a search of a third person's premises or property has not had any of his Fourth Amendment rights infringed. *Alderman,* supra, at 174. And since the exclusionary rule is an attempt to effectuate the guaranties of the Fourth Amendment, *United States v. Calandra,* 414 U.S. 338, 347 (1974), it is proper to permit only defendants whose Fourth Amendment rights have been violated to benefit from the rule's protections. . . .

B

Had we accepted petitioners' request to allow persons other than those whose own Fourth Amendment rights were violated by a challenged search and seizure to suppress evidence obtained in the course of such police activity, it would be appropriate to retain *Jones'* use of standing in Fourth Amendment analysis. Under petitioners' target theory, a court could determine that a defendant had standing to invoke the exclusionary rule without having to inquire into the substantive question of whether the challenged search or seizure violated the Fourth Amendment rights of that particular defendant. However, having rejected petitioners' target theory and reaffirmed the principle that the "rights assured by the Fourth Amendment are personal rights, [which] . . . may be enforced by exclusion of evidence only at the instance of one whose own protection was infringed by the search and seizure," *Simmons v. United States*, 390 U.S., at 389, the question necessarily arises whether it serves any useful analytical purpose to consider this principle a matter of standing, distinct from the merits of a defendant's Fourth Amendment claim. We can think of no decided cases from this Court that would have come out differently had we concluded, as we do now, that the type of standing requirement discussed in *Jones* and reaffirmed today is more properly subsumed under substantive Fourth Amendment doctrine. Rigorous application of the principle that the rights secured by this Amendment are personal, in place of a notion of "standing," will produce no additional situations in which evidence must be excluded. The inquiry under either approach is the same. But we think the better analysis forthrightly focuses on the extent of a particular defendant's rights under the Fourth Amendment, rather than on any theoretically separate, but invariably intertwined concept of standing. . . .

C

Here petitioners, who were passengers occupying a car which they neither owned nor leased, seek to analogize their position to that of the defendant in *Jones v. United States*, 362 U.S. 257 (1960). In *Jones*, petitioner was present at the time of the search of an apartment which was owned by a friend. The friend had given Jones permission to use the apartment and a key to it, with which Jones had admitted himself on the day of the search. He had a suit and shirt at the apartment and had slept there "maybe a night," but his home was elsewhere. At the time of the search, Jones was the only occupant of the apartment because the lessee was away for a period of several days. Id., at 259. Under these circumstances, this Court stated that while one wrongfully on the premises could not move to suppress evidence obtained as a result of searching them, "anyone legitimately on premises where a search occurs may challenge its legality." 362 U.S., at 267. Petitioners argue that their occupancy of the automobile in question was comparable to that of Jones in the apartment and that they therefore have standing to contest the legality of the search—or as we have rephrased the inquiry, that they, like Jones, had their Fourth Amendment rights violated by the search.

We do not question the conclusion in *Jones* that the defendant in that case suffered a violation of his personal Fourth Amendment rights if the search in question were unlawful. Nonetheless, we believe that the phrase "legitimately on premises" coined in *Jones* creates too broad a gauge for measurement of Fourth Amendment rights. For example, applied literally, this statement would permit a casual visitor who has never seen, or been permitted to visit the basement of another's house to object to a search of the basement if the visitor happened to be in the kitchen of the house at the time of the search. Likewise, a casual visitor who walks into a house one minute before a search of the house commences and leaves one minute after the search ends would be able to contest the legality of the search. The first visitor would have absolutely no interest or legitimate expectation of privacy in the basement, the second would have none in the house, and it advances no purpose served by the Fourth Amendment to permit either of them to object to the lawfulness of the search.

We think that *Jones* on its facts merely stands for the unremarkable proposition that a person can have a legally sufficient interest in a place other than his own home so that the Fourth Amendment protects him from unreasonable governmental intrusion into that place. See 362 U.S., at 263, 265. In defining the scope of that interest, we adhere to the view expressed in *Jones* and echoed in later cases that arcane distinctions developed in property and tort law between guests, licensees, invitees, and the like, ought not to control. Id., at 266. But the *Jones* statement that a person need only be "legitimately on premises" in order to challenge the validity of the search of a dwelling place cannot be taken in its full sweep beyond the facts of that case.

Katz v. United States, 389 U.S. 347 (1967), provides guidance in defining the scope of the interest protected by the Fourth Amendment. In the course of repudiating the doctrine derived from *Olmstead v. United States*, 277 U.S. 438 (1928), and *Goldman v. United States*, 316 U.S. 129 (1942), that if police officers had not been guilty of a common-law trespass they were not prohibited by the Fourth Amendment from eavesdropping, the Court in *Katz* held that capacity to claim the protection of the Fourth Amendment depends not upon a property right in the invaded place but upon whether the person who claims the protection of the Amendment has a legitimate expectation of privacy in the invaded place. 389 U.S., at 353. Viewed in this manner, the holding in *Jones* can best be explained by the fact that Jones had a legitimate expectation of privacy in the premises he was using and therefore could claim the protection of the Fourth Amendment with respect to a governmental invasion of those premises, even though his "interest" in those premises might not have been a recognized property interest at common law.*

Our Brother White in dissent expresses the view that by rejecting the phrase

---

*Obviously, however, a "legitimate" expectation of privacy by definition means more than a subjective expectation of not being discovered. A burglar plying his trade in a summer cabin during the off season may have a thoroughly justified subjective expectation of privacy, but it is not one which the law recognizes as "legitimate." His presence, in the words of *Jones*, 362 U.S., at 267, is "wrongful"; his expectation is not "one that society is prepared to recognize as 'reasonable.'" *Katz v. United States*, 389 U.S. 347, 361 (1967) (Harlan, J., concurring). And it would, of course, be merely tautological to fall back on the notion that those expectations of privacy which are legitimate depend primarily on cases deciding exclusionary rule issues in criminal cases. Legitimation of expectations of privacy by law must have a source outside of the Fourth Amendment, either by reference to concepts of real or personal property law or to understandings that are recognized and permitted by society. One of the main rights attaching to property is the right to exclude others, see W. Blackstone, Commentaries, Book II, Ch. I, and one who owns or lawfully possesses or controls property will in all likelihood have a legitimate expectation of privacy by virtue of this right to exclude. Expectations of privacy protected by the Fourth Amendment, of course, need not be based on a common-law interest in real or personal property, or on the invasion of such an interest. These ideas were rejected both in *Jones*, supra, and *Katz*, supra. But by focusing on legitimate expectations of privacy in Fourth Amendment jurisprudence, the Court has not altogether abandoned use of property concepts in determining the presence or absence of the privacy interests protected by that Amendment. . . .

"legitimately on [the] premises" as the appropriate measure of Fourth Amendment rights, we are abandoning a thoroughly workable, "bright line" test in favor of a less certain analysis of whether the facts of a particular case give rise to a legitimate expectation of privacy. *Post*, at 12. If "legitimately on premises" were the successful litmus test of Fourth Amendment rights that he assumes it is, his approach would have at least the merit of easy application, whatever it lacked in fidelity to the history and purposes of the Fourth Amendment. But a reading of lower court cases that have applied the phrase "legitimately on premises," and of the dissent itself, reveals that this expression is not a shorthand summary for a bright line rule which somehow encapsulates the "core" of the Fourth Amendment's protections.

. . . In abandoning "legitimately on premises" for the doctrine that we announce today, we are not foresaking a time-tested and workable rule, which has produced consistent results when applied, solely for the sake of fidelity to the values underlying the Fourth Amendment. We also are rejecting blind adherence to a phrase which at most has superficial clarity and which conceals underneath that thin veneer all of the problems of line drawing which must be faced in any conscientious effort to apply the Fourth Amendment. Where the factual premises for a rule are so generally prevalent that little would be lost and much would be gained by abandoning case-by-case analysis, we have not hesitated to do so. But the phrase "legitimately on premises" has not shown to be an easily applicable measure of Fourth Amendment rights so much as it has proved to be simply a label placed by the courts on results which have not been subjected to careful analysis. We would not wish to be understood as saying that legitimate presence on the premises is irrelevant to one's expectation of privacy, but it cannot be deemed controlling.

D

Judged by the foregoing analysis, petitioners' claims must fail. They asserted neither a property nor a possessory interest in the automobile, nor an interest in the property seized. And as we have previously indicated, the fact that they were "legitimately on [the] premises" in the sense that they were in the car with the permission of its owner is not determinative of whether they had a legitimate expectation of privacy in the particular areas of the automobile searched. It is unnecessary for us to decide here whether the same expectations of privacy are warranted in a car as would be justified in a dwelling place in analogous circumstances. We have on numerous occasions pointed out that cars are not to be treated identically with houses or apartments for Fourth Amendment purposes. But here petitioners' claim is one which would fail even in an analogous situation in a dwelling place since they made no showing that they had any legitimate expectation of privacy in the glove compartment or area under the seat of the car in which they were merely passengers. Like the trunk of an automobile, these are areas in which a passenger qua passenger simply would not normally have a legitimate expectation of privacy. Ante, at 14.

Jones v. United States, 362 U.S. 257 (1960) and *Katz v. United States*, 389 U.S. 347 (1967), involved significantly different factual circumstances. Jones not only had permission to use the apartment of his friend, but had a key to the apartment with which he admitted himself on the day of the search and kept possessions in the apartment. Except with respect to his friend, Jones had complete dominion and control over the apartment and could exclude others from it. Likewise in *Katz,* the defendant occupied the telephone booth, shut the door behind him to exclude all others and paid the toll, which "entitled him to assume that the word he utter[ed] into the mouthpiece would not be broadcast to the world." 389 U.S., at 352. Katz and Jones could legitimately expect privacy in the areas which were the subject of the search and seizure they sought to contest. No such showing was made by these petitioners with respect to those portions of the automobile which were searched and from which incriminating evidence was seized.

IV

The Illinois courts were therefore correct in concluding that it was unnecessary to decide whether the search of the car might have violated the rights secured to someone else by the Fourth and Fourteenth Amendments to the United States Constitution. Since it did not violate any rights of these petitioners, their judgment of conviction is

Affirmed.

Mr. Justice WHITE, with whom Mr. Justice BRENNAN, Mr. Justice MARSHALL, and Mr. Justice STEVENS join, dissenting.

The Court today holds that the Fourth Amendment protects property, not people, and specifically that a legitimate occupant of an automobile may not invoke the exclusionary rule and challenge a search of that vehicle unless he happens to own or have a possessory interest in it. Though professing to acknowledge that the primary purpose of the Fourth Amendment's prohibition of unreasonable searches is the protection of privacy—not property—the Court nonetheless effectively ties the application of the Fourth Amendment and the exclusionary rule in this situation to property law concepts. Insofar as passengers are concerned, the Court's opinion today declares an "open season" on automobiles. However unlawful stopping and searching a car may be, absent a possessory or ownership interest, no "mere" passenger may object, regardless of his relationship to the owner. Because the majority's conclusion has no support in the Court's controlling decisions, in the logic of the Fourth Amendment, or in common sense, I must respectfully dissent. If the Court is troubled by the practical impact of the exclusionary rule, it should face the issue of that rule's continued validity squarely instead of distorting other doctrines in an attempt to reach what are perceived as the correct results in specific cases. Cf. *Stone v. Powell,* 428 U.S. 465, 536 (White, J., dissenting).

. . .

In sum, one consistent theme in our decisions under the Fourth Amendment has been, until now, that "the Amendment does not shield only those who have title to the searched premises." *Mancusi v. DeForte,* 392 U.S. 364, 367 (1968). Though there comes a point when use of an area is shared with so many that one simply cannot reasonably expect seclusion, see id., at 377 (White, J., dissenting), short of that limit a person legitimately on private premises knows the others allowed there and, though his privacy is not absolute, is entitled to expect that he is sharing it only with those persons and that governmental officials will intrude only with consent or by complying with the Fourth Amendment.

It is true that the Court asserts that it is not limiting the Fourth Amendment bar against unreasonable searches to the protection of property rights, but in reality it is doing exactly that. Petitioners were in a private place with the permission of the owner, but the Court states that that is not sufficient to establish entitlement to a legitimate expectation of privacy. Ante, at 17. But if that is not sufficient, what would be? We are not told, and it is hard to imagine anything short of a property interest that would satisfy the majority. Insofar as the Court's rationale is concerned, no passenger in an automobile, without an ownership or possessory interest and regardless of his relationship to the owner, may claim Fourth Amendment protection against illegal stops and searches of the automobile in which he is rightfully present. The Court approves the result in *Jones*, but it fails to give any explanation why the facts in *Jones* differ, in a fashion material to the Fourth Amendment, from the facts here. More importantly, how is the Court able to avoid answering the question why presence in a private place with the owner's permission is insufficient? If it is "tautological to fall back on the notion that those expectations of privacy which are legitimate depend primarily on cases deciding exclusionary rule issues in criminal cases," ante, at 15 n. 12, then it surely must be tautological to decide that issue simply by unadorned fiat.

As a control on governmental power, the Fourth Amendment assures that some expectations of privacy are justified and will be protected from official intrusion. That should be true in this instance, for if protected zones of privacy can only be purchased or obtained by possession of property, then much of our daily lives will be unshielded from unreasonable governmental prying, and the reach of the Fourth Amendment will have been narrowed to protect chiefly those with possessory interests in real or personal property. I had thought that *Katz* firmly established that the Fourth Amendment was intended as more than simply a trespass law applicable to the government. Katz had no possessory interest in the public telephone booth, at least no more than petitioners had in their friend's car; Katz was simply legitimately present. And the decision in *Katz* was based not on property rights but on the theory that it was essential to securing "conditions favorable to the pursuit of happiness" that the expectation of privacy in question be recognized.

At most, one could say that perhaps the Constitution provides some degree less protection for the personal freedom from unreasonable governmental intrusion when one does not have a possessory interest in the invaded private place. But that would only change the extent of the protection; it would not free police to do the unreasonable, as does the decision today. And since the accused should be entitled to litigate the application of the Fourth Amendment where his privacy interest is merely arguable, the failure to allow such litigation here is the more incomprehensible.

IV

The Court's holding is contrary not only to our past decisions and the logic of the Fourth Amendment, but also to the everyday expectations of privacy that we all share. Because of that, it is unworkable in all the various situations that arise in real life. If the owner of the car had not only invited petitioners to join her but had said to them, "I give you a temporary possessory interest in my vehicle so that you will share the right to privacy that the Supreme Court says that I own," then apparently the majority would reverse. But people seldom say such things, though they may mean their invitation to encompass them if only they had thought of the problem.

If the nonowner were the spouse or child of the owner, would the Court recognize a sufficient interest? If so, would distant relatives somehow have more of an expectation of privacy than close friends? What if the nonowner were driving with the owner's permission? Would nonowning drivers have more of an expectation of privacy than mere passengers? What about a passenger in a taxicab? *Katz* expressly recognized protection for such passengers. Why should Fourth Amendment rights be present when one pays a cabdriver for a ride but be absent when one is given a ride by a friend?

The distinctions the Court would draw are based on relationships between private parties, but the Fourth Amendment is concerned with the relationship of one of those parties to the government. Divorced as it is from the purpose of the Fourth Amendment, the Court's essentially property-based rationale can satisfactorily answer none of the questions posed above. That is reason enough to reject it. The *Jones* rule is relatively easily applied by police and courts; the rule announced today will not provide law enforcement officials with a bright line between the protected and the unprotected. Only rarely will police know whether one private party has or has not been granted a sufficient possessory or other interest by another private party. Surely in this case the officers had no such knowledge. The Court's rule will ensnare defendants and police in needless litigation over factors that should not be determinative of Fourth Amendment rights.

More importantly, the ruling today undercuts the force of the exclusionary rule in the one area in which its use is most certainly justified—the deterrence of bad-faith violations of the Fourth Amendment. See *Stone v. Powell*, 428 U.S. 465, 537–542 (1976) (White, J., dissenting). This decision invites police to engage in patently unreasonable searches every time an automobile contains more than one occupant. Should something be found, only the owner of the vehicle, or of the item, will have standing to seek suppression, and the evidence will presumably be usable against the other occupants. The danger of such bad faith is especially high in cases such as this one where the officers are only after the passengers and can usually infer accurately that the driver is the owner. The suppression remedy for those owners in whose vehicles something is found and who are charged with crime is small consolation for all those owners *and* occupants whose privacy will be needlessly invaded by officers following mistaken hunches not rising to the level of probable cause but operated on in the knowledge that someone in a crowded car will probably be unprotected if contraband or incriminating evidence happens to be found. After this decision, police will have little to lose by unreasonably searching vehicles occupied by more than one person.

Of course, most police officers will decline the Court's invitation and will continue to do their jobs as best they can in accord with the Fourth Amendment. But the very purpose of the Bill of Rights was to answer the justified fear that governmental agents cannot be left totally to their own devices, and the Bill of Rights is enforceable in the courts because human experience teaches that not all such officials will otherwise adhere to the stated precepts. Some policemen simply do act in bad faith, even if for understandable ends, and some deterrent is needed. In the rush to limit the applicability of the exclusionary rule somewhere, anywhere, the Court ignores precedent, logic, and common sense to exclude the rule's operation from situations in which, paradoxically, it is justified and needed.

4

No
Compulsory
Self-Incrimination

FREEBORN JOHN LILBURNE AND NEMO TENETUR

Of all the characters that have helped to shape Anglo-American liberties, perhaps none was as colorful as Freeborn John Lilburne, a flinty and contentious Englishman who did so much to secure the right against compulsory self-incrimination. A man of modest origins, Lilburne was forever suspicious of authority. He was one of those insufferable, quarrelsome, fractious, God-fearing people who appear at the right time and place to make an important contribution to liberty. A Puritan independent and leader of the democratic Levellers, he first came up against the government of Charles I and then against the protectorate of Oliver Cromwell. His cause was the defense of freedom and justice, and his outrage was directed particularly against the infamous oath ex officio.

The oath ex officio was a remnant of the inquisitional system of criminal justice. It was first introduced from the Continent to England in 1236 and met with immediate opposition.[1] But the judicial arm of the king's council, the Court of Star Chamber, adopted the inquisitional oath, and it was widely used in ecclesiastical courts and by the courts of Star Chamber and High Commission as a device for the discovery of heresy. The oath required a defendant to answer all questions truly on pain of perjury, without knowing either the accusers or the charges. A failure to take the oath resulted in a judgment of guilty. In short, the defendant was between a rock and a hard place!

By Lilburne's time, the oath had fallen into disuse. Sir Edward Coke had discoursed against it, and at least as early as 1589 he had propounded the maxim *"nemo tenetur prodere seipsum"*—no one is bound to accuse himself.[2] Archbishop Loud reactivated the Court of High Commission and along with it the oath ex officio, with new patents from Charles I. In 1637, the commission arrested Lilburne, thereby setting on stage, at just the right historical moment, someone prepared to take advantage of the odium of Star Chamber and a growing body of legal opinion in support of *nemo tenetur*. He was examined by the attorney general, Sir John Banks, and ordered to appear before the Star Chamber. At age twenty-seven, Lilburne was already as cantankerous as many eighty-year-olds.[3] With the underground press and his own keen sense of propaganda, he became a hero for his defiance of the oath and Star Chamber. Lilburne's own account of his first trial reads in part:

Upon Friday, the 9th of February, in the morning, one of the officers of the Fleet came to my chamber, and bid me get up and make me ready to go to the Star-Chamber-Bar. . . . And being at the bar, sir John Banks laid a verbal accusation against me; which was, that I refused to answer, and also to enter my appearance, and that I refused to take the Star-Chamber oath: and then was read the affidavit of one Edmond Chillington, button-seller, made against Mr. John Wharton and myself: the sum of which was, that he and I had printed at Rotterdam, in Holland, Dr. Bastwick's Answer, and his Litany, and divers other scandalous Books. And then after I obtained leave to speak, I said, My noble lords, as for that affidavit, it is a most false lye and untrue.

LORD-KEEPER.   Why will you not answer?

LILBURNE.   My honourable lord, I have answered fully before sir John Banks to all things that belong to me to answer unto: and for other things, which concern other men, I have nothing to do with them.—But why do you refuse to take the Star-Chamber oath? Most noble lord, I refused upon this ground, because that when I was examined, though I had fully answered all things that belonged to me to answer unto, and had cleared myself of the thing for which I am imprisoned, which was for sending Books out of Holland, yet that would not satisfy and give content, but other things were put unto me, concerning other men, to insnare me, and get further matter against me; which I perceiving refused, being not bound as to answer to such things as do not belong unto me. And withal I perceived the oath to be an oath of inquiry; and for the lawfulness of which oath I have no warrant; and upon these grounds I did and do still refuse the oath. . . .

LORD-KEEPER.   Well; tender him the book.

. . . Unto whom I replied, Sir, I will not swear. . . .

Then said the Lord-Keeper, Thou art a mad fellow, seeing things are thus, that thou wilt not take thine Oath, and answer truly.

My honourable lord, I have declared unto you the real truth; but for the oath, it is an oath of inquiry, and of the same nature as the High-Commission Oath; which oath I know to be unlawful; and withal I find no warrant in the Word of God for an oath of inquiry, and it ought to be the director of me in all things that I do: and therefore, my lords, at no hand, I dare not take the oath.[4]

Lilburne pressed on after 1637, and, although he was acquitted in two subsequent trials, he met his match in the Cromwell protectorate. Cromwell refused to release him from prison, even though he had been acquitted by a jury, and Lilburne spent his remaining years in jail. The glorious thing, however, about this fractious man was that his life had made a difference. He had asked the important question: Was the state supreme, or was it "Governed, Bounded, and Limitted by Laws and Liberties"?[5] There was never a moment when anyone doubted his answer; there was never a moment when he would not have volunteered it.

Within three years after Lilburne's first trial, the prerogative courts of Star Chamber and High Commission were abolished and the oath ex officio met a similar fate.[6] *Nemo tenetur* was recognized in the ecclesiastical courts, and throughout the remaining years of the seventeenth century the common-law courts began to accept it fully. By the early eighteenth century, *nemo tenetur* was an acknowledged trial right in England.[7] Curiously enough, in an extension of the right, in the early eighteenth century the courts adopted in criminal cases the civil rule of disqualification for interest: For the next hundred years, an accused was prohibited in England and America from becoming a sworn witness![8]

The seventeenth-century acceptance of *nemo tenetur*, and its expansion to include witnesses as well as the accused[9] and the right against self-infamy,[10] was no accidental development. *Nemo tenetur* was part of a gradual humanizing of English criminal justice, particularly after the Restoration. The unfair advantages enjoyed by the Crown in criminal cases were giving way to an accusatory system that afforded the defense more precise rules of evidence,[11] the right to present witnesses (at first unsworn), and even in some situations to have the assistance of counsel.[12]

In the American colonies, *nemo tenetur* was settled common law by 1776;[13] and the Revolution raised it to constitutional status in eight states. In June 1789, James Madison included the right in his package of proposals for a federal Bill of Rights. As finally adopted, *nemo tenetur* became part of the Fifth Amendment. The language—"No person . . . shall be compelled in any criminal case to be a witness against himself"—was not a restatement of the existing common law but rather a reaffirmation of a principle.[14] Like other provisions of the Bill of Rights, it was not intended to be a precise code. It was a reflection of the political morality that gradually developed in England and America—a morality that held that, regardless of the importance of enforcing the criminal laws, the government must abide by procedures consonant with the goals of administrative and judicial integrity and a proper regard for the privacy of the guilty as well as of the innocent.

THE PURPOSES OF THE RIGHT

Concern about rising crime rates and the possible negative impact of the Warren Court's decisions on the resolution of the crime problem has led some critics to suggest that *nemo tenetur* ought to be curtailed.[15] The debate over the Fifth Amendment reveals a lack of consensus both in the Supreme Court and in the legal community about the basic purposes of the right. The policies thought to be served by *nemo tenetur* are almost as numerous as there are commentators. For example, the Lilburne trial offers an insight into the policies that stand behind the protection. Yet when we recall this trial or the earlier trial of dissident minister John Udall,[16] it is apparent that other political values were at least as prominent as fairness in criminal procedure. Clearly Udall and Lilburne were fighting for freedom of expression and a degree of religious liberty at least as much as for the right to refuse to incriminate themselves. To wrench the Lilburne and Udall trials out of context and to postulate a general right against self-incrimination is both historically inaccurate and illogical.[17] Today, the First Amendment is available to protect freedom of expression and religion, or at least it is a more suitable principle for the protection of dissent than is the Fifth Amendment.[18]

It has also been suggested that *nemo tenetur* is justified as a protection for the innocent. Justice Field once wrote that timidity and nervousness could easily work against an innocent defendant forced to take the witness stand.[19] We can agree with Justice Field that there are possible instances where the innocent might appropriately need the protection of *nemo tenetur*[20] and still conclude that it is largely the guilty, not the innocent, who seek the protection of the clause.[21]

If there were substantial evidence that the innocent needed the protection of the clause, that would, in itself, be sufficient foundation for the continued acceptance of *nemo tenetur*. If, however, the clause largely protects the guilty, then we can reasonably ask if the clause does not serve other and better purposes than that of providing a shield for the guilty. Justice Goldberg has supplied a catalog of policies served by no compulsory self-incrimination. Speaking for the majority in a 1964 opinion, he wrote that the clause

> reflects many of our fundamental values and most noble aspirations: our unwillingness to subject those suspected of crime to the cruel trilemma of self-accusation, perjury or contempt; our preference for an accusatorial rather than

an inquisitional system of criminal justice; our fear that self-incriminating state-ments will be elicited by inhumane treatment and abuses; our sense of fair play which dictates "a fair state-individual balance by requiring the government to leave the individual alone until good cause is shown for disturbing him and by requiring the government in its contest with the individual to shoulder the entire load" . . . our respect for the inviolability of the human personality and of the right of each individual "to a private enclave where he may lead a private life" . . . our distrust of self-deprecatory statements; and our realization that the privilege, while sometimes "a shelter to the guilty," is often "a pro-tection to the innocent."[22]

Within two years, however, Justice Stewart, writing for the majority, re-jected protection of the innocent as a basic purpose of the clause: "The basic purposes that lie behind the privilege against self-incrimination do not relate to protecting the innocent from conviction, but rather to preserving the in-tegrity of a judicial system in which even the guilty are not to be convicted unless the prosecution 'shoulder the entire load.' "[23]

Although we may concede that the protection of the innocent is not greatly served by the protection against self-incrimination, to cast the policy debate in terms of guilty and innocent probably does not shed much light on the topic. Of course, the protection at times acts as a roadblock to the ascertain-ment of truth. Yet to acknowledge this is not to say that the protection does not serve other socially useful purposes.[24] The protection of privacy, the preservation of the integrity of the judicial system, and the discouragement of inhumane treatment of suspects may all, on occasion, be served by *nemo tene-tur*. It does not follow, however, that any particular policy goal is served automatically by every application of the protection, any more than that truth is served by its absence. The social values of the protection are not self-evident: We must examine the applications of the rule to ascertain whether *nemo tenetur* has constitutional value in our society.

APPLICATIONS OF THE RIGHT

Trial

Perhaps the least debatable application of the right against self-incrimination is the absolute and unqualified right of criminal defendants not to testify at trial (including arraignment and preliminary hearing). Having said that, we must immediately note that most defendants do testify at their trials, not out of legal compulsion, but because their failure to directly answer charges, pre-sumably in most situations, would have a negative impact on the judge and jury. (The untutored instinct of a jury often is to draw an inference of guilt from a defendant's failure to come forward and explain the charges.)[25] Gen-erally, prosecutors do not go to trial with weak cases; in consequence, most criminal defendants, should they elect to go to trial, must present a convincing argument to counter the state's case.[26] In short, although defendants are under no legal compulsion to testify, they will often face the practical necessity of testifying.

Defendants who choose to testify in their own behalf become subject to cross-examination and impeachment. As Justice Brown wrote in *Fitzpatrick v. United States* (1900):

> Where an accused party waives his constitutional privilege of silence, takes the stand in his own behalf and makes his own statement, it is clear that the prosecution has a right to cross-examine upon such statement with the same latitude as would be exercised in the case of an ordinary witness, as to the circumstances connecting him with the alleged crime. While no inference of guilt can be drawn from his refusal to avail himself of the privilege of testifying, he has no right to set forth to the jury all the facts which tend in his favor without laying himself open to cross-examination upon those facts.[27]

If a defendant's testimony were not subject to cross-examination, there would be the risk that perjurious testimony by the defendant would not be subject to challenge. At some point, a balance must be struck between a defendant's right against compulsory self-incrimination and the criminal trial as a forum for the determination of truth. Cross-examining a defendant who voluntarily testifies and restricting that cross-examination *to matters raised on direct examination* do not appear to be inconsistent with the goals of privacy, judicial integrity, or humane treatment of the accused.[28]

The No-comment Rule

In order to further underscore the trial right to silence, prosecutors and judges are precluded under the no-comment rule from remarking on a defendant's silence.[29] When the rule was first applied to state criminal trials in *Griffin v. California* (1965), Justice Douglas justified the rule by reasoning that

> comment on the refusal to testify is a remnant of the "inquisitorial system of criminal justice." . . . It is a penalty imposed by courts for exercising a constitutional privilege. It cuts down on the privilege by making its assertion costly. It is said, however, that the inference of guilt for failure to testify as to facts peculiarly within the accused's knowledge is in any event natural and irresistible, and that comment on the failure does not magnify that inference into a penalty for asserting a constitutional privilege.
>   . . . What the jury may infer, given no help from the court, is one thing. What it may infer when the court solemnizes the silence of the accused into evidence against him is quite another.[30]

Justice Stewart did not agree. In his dissent in *Griffin,* he wrote that a carefully phrased comment rule, to include judicial cautions to the jury about burden of proof, reasonable doubt, and no interference of guilt per se from silence, would, as a practical matter, provide a better protective shield for defendants than a situation in which the jury is left to "roam at large with only its un-tutored instincts to guide it."[31]

Because the *Griffin* decision did not rule on the issue of whether a state trial court is under a positive obligation to instruct the jury that the defendant's silence creates no presumption of guilt, Justice Stewart's point is well taken.[32] A carefully limited comment rule that protects the presumption of innocence might be an adequate compromise with the no-comment rule.

INCONSISTENT STATEMENTS AND THE NO-COMMENT RULE.   If a defendant waives the right to silence and testifies, the waiver is complete and the defendant may "not resume it at will, whenever cross-examination may be inconvenient or embarrassing."[33] Thus, if the defendant has made a prior statement incon-sistent with current testimony, his or her credibility may be impeached by introducing the inconsistent statement, even if that statement was obtained in violation of the *Miranda* rules.[34] However logical and reasonable the incon-sistent-statement rule may be, it has been applied occasionally in a manner that undermines the right to silence. In *Raffel v. United States* (1926), the Supreme Court allowed the silence of the defendant in his first trial to be used against him when he elected to testify in a second trial.[35] Some years after *Raffel,* the Court ruled that a defendant who elects to testify and who during the course of cross-examination momentarily claims the right against self-incrimination (which claim is upheld by the trial judge) is not later subject to adverse com-ment by the prosecutor for asserting the right. The majority reasoned as follows:

> If advised by the court that his claim of privilege though granted would be employed against him, he well might never claim it. If he receives assurance that it will be granted if claimed, or if it is claimed and granted outright, he has every right to expect that the ruling is made in good faith and that the rule against comment will be observed.[36]

However, this decision stopped short of holding that any prior assertion of the right is consistent with innocence. Thus in 1957, the Court, although it ruled that it was prejudicial error to allow a prosecutor to comment on a defendant's assertion of the right before the grand jury, left open the possibility that a prior assertion of the right could be inconsistent with the defendant's trial testimony and thus properly placed before the jury.[37]

We may not quarrel with the rule allowing prior inconsistent statements to be used to attack a defendant's credibility, but we can question whether constitutionally protected silence is ever an untruth. For example, for a number of years the federal courts of appeals were in conflict as to whether the prosecution could comment during cross-examination on a defendant's silence at the time of arrest.[38] Finally, in 1975, the Supreme Court attempted to resolve the conflict. In *United States v. Hale,* defendant had received a *Miranda* warning at the time of arrest and did not respond to police questioning. When the defendant testified at trial, the government, relying on *Raffel,* sought on cross-examination to reveal the defendant's earlier silence. Although the Supreme Court held that the prosecutor's question carried with it an intolerable prejudicial impact, the majority rested its decision on nonconstitutional grounds.[39] It held that, where the prosecution fails to establish a threshold of inconsistency between silence at the police station and later exculpatory testimony at trial, proof of silence lacks any significant probative value and must therefore be excluded.[40] The opinion noted that "not only is evidence of silence at the time of arrest generally not very probative of a defendant's credibility, but it also has a significant potential for prejudice. The danger is that the jury is likely to assign much more weight to the defendant's previous silence than is warranted."[41]

Finally, in *Doyle v. Ohio* (1976), the Court closed the door on the prosecution's use of silence for impeachment of a defendant's testimony. In *Doyle,* the defendant was arrested shortly after he had allegedly sold a quantity of marihuana to an undercover agent. Immediately after Doyle's arrest, he was read his *Miranda* rights. A search of his car revealed a large quantity of money, the exact amount the undercover agent claimed to have paid Doyle for the marihuana. Doyle made no effort at this time, however, to explain where he had obtained the money. At his trial, Doyle testified that the money was intended to be used to purchase marihuana from the agent, but that the agent refused to sell Doyle the marihuana because Doyle indicated that he wanted a smaller quantity than they had previously agreed to. If Doyle's testimony were believed, then he could not be convicted of selling the illegal substance. Because the arresting officers had not actually seen the transaction and thus could not testify about the actual exchange, Doyle's testimony was not entirely implausible. The state's case would, in such a situation, be greatly strengthened if it could undermine the credibility of a defendant's version by inferring that the failure to give such an explanation to arresting officers suggests that the trial testimony was fabricated to meet the contours of the state's case. In short, the state claimed that Doyle's trial testimony was inconsistent with his silence at the time of his arrest. In reversing the conviction, the Supreme Court argued that, given the warning requirements of *Miranda,*

silence in the wake of these warnings may be nothing more than the arrestee's exercise of these *Miranda* rights. Thus, every post-arrest silence is insolubly ambiguous because of what the State is required to advise the person arrested.

Moreover, while it is true that the *Miranda* warnings contain no express assurance that silence will carry no penalty, such assurance is implicit to any person who receives the warnings. In such circumstances, it would be fundamentally unfair and a deprivation of due process to allow the arrested person's silence to be used to impeach an explanation subsequently offered at trial.[42]

THE SCOPE OF THE RIGHT

Persons

Historically, the scope of the right applied only to defendants; witnesses have had no such immunity from testifying, assuming a valid request. The right is available to witnesses only at a point in the testimony where a witness is requested to respond to a question that could be self-incriminating. However, the right cannot be invoked as a shield to protect a witness from personal shame or disgrace.[43] Nor may a witness invoke the right on behalf of others. The right is personal, applying only to people, not corporations,[44] and cannot be used on behalf of third parties.[45] Furthermore, if a witness fails to invoke the right and answers freely to incriminating questions, the witness may not at some later point invoke the right, at least not in regard to factual issues about which the witness has already offered an incriminating response.[46] Nor may a witness be the sole judge as to whether a truthful response would be self-incriminating, nor may the witness invoke the right on the remote possibility that the response would incriminate. Ultimately, a judge must determine whether the right is properly invoked.[47] The Supreme Court has quoted with approval the rule laid down in the nineteenth century by Lord Chief Justice Cockburn:

> To entitle a party called as a witness to the privilege of silence, the court must see, from the circumstances of the case and the nature of the evidence which the witness is called to give, that there is reasonable ground to apprehend danger to the witness from his being compelled to answer. Further than this, we are of opinion that the danger to be apprehended must be real and appreciable, with reference to the ordinary operation of law in the ordinary course of things,—not a danger of an imaginary and unsubstantial character, having reference to some extra-ordinary and barely possible contingency, so improbable that no reasonable man would suffer it to influence his conduct. We think that a merely remote and naked possibility, out of the ordinary course of law and such as no reasonable man would be affected by, should not be suffered to obstruct the administration of justice.[48]

If the trial judge determines whether the right is being properly invoked, how much must a witness reveal in order for the court to make a decision?

If a witness must hazard incrimination simply in order to establish the right, then "he would be compelled to surrender the very protection which the privilege is designed to guarantee. To sustain the privilege, it need only be evident from the implications of the question, in the setting in which it is asked, that a responsive answer to the question or an explanation of why it cannot be answered might be dangerous because injurious disclosure could result."[49] In short, if a response would provide a "link in the chain of evidence" necessary to prosecute, then the witness need not respond.[50]

The Forum

The obvious setting for invoking the right is the criminal trial, and some would restrict the right to the trial setting.[51] However, there is common agreement that the right may be invoked in any setting where testimony is compelled and where a response would be incriminating, including, then, civil proceedings.[52]

IMMUNITY STATUTES

At times, the government's need for information is so urgent or essential to the prosecution of certain types of crimes that some accommodation with the right to silence is reached through immunity statutes. These statutes, in various forms, date back to the middle of the nineteenth century,[53] and were first tested in the Supreme Court in *Counselman v. Hitchcock* (1892). Immunity statutes confer, generally on an unwilling witness, varying degrees of immunity in regard to compelled testimony, either before grand juries, courts, or legislative committees, or at administrative hearings. Usually on pain of contempt, the unwilling witness is forced to testify about matters relevant to the inquiry even though the response would, in the absence of the immunity, tend to incriminate the witness. The Court in *Counselman* unanimously held that the immunity statute was invalid because it did not forbid the indirect use of compelled testimony in any future prosecution against the witness: "A statutory enactment, to be valid, must afford absolute immunity against future prosecution for the offense to which the question relates."[54] By forbidding only the direct use of compelled testimony, the statute left the witness exposed to a prosecution based on leads obtained from the compelled testimony.

Counselman opened the door to a properly drafted immunity statute, and in the following year Congress passed a new statute conferring immunity from prosecution on account of any transaction to which a witness testifies.[55] Transactional immunity appeared to have met the objections raised in *Counselman*, but in 1896 the issue was once again before the Court in *Brown v. Walker*. This time the decision was split with only a bare majority voting to uphold transactional immunity. Justice Brown, speaking for the majority, reasoned:

> The clause of the Constitution in question is obviously susceptible of two interpretations. If it be construed literally, as authorizing the witness to refuse to disclose any fact which might tend to incriminate, disgrace, or expose him to unfavorable comments, then, as he must necessarily to a large extent determine upon his own conscience and responsibility whether his answer to the proposed question will have that tendency . . . the practical result would be that no one could be compelled to testify to a material fact in a criminal case, unless he chose to do so, or unless it was entirely clear that the privilege was not set up in good faith. If, upon the other hand, the object of the provision be to secure the witness against a criminal prosecution, which might be aided directly or indirectly by his disclosure, then, if no such prosecution became possible,—in other words, if his testimony operate as a complete pardon for the offense to which it relates,—a statute absolutely securing to him such immunity from prosecution would satisfy the demands of the clause in question.[56]

The dissenters replied that it would be virtually impossible to provide an adequate statutory substitute for the right because of the evidentiary uncertainty in any subsequent prosecution related to a witness's testimony and because a witness is forced to expose himself or herself to the hazards of perjury.[57] Justice Field, in dissent, challenged the majority's contention that exposure to injury is not a fatal element in an immunity statute. To those who contended that the sole purpose of the amendment was to protect against self-incrimination, Justice Field replied:

> It is true, as counsel observes, that both the safeguard of the Constitution and the common-law rule spring alike from that sentiment of personal self-respect, liberty, independence, and dignity which has inhabited the breasts of English-speaking peoples for centuries, and to save which they have always been ready to sacrifice many governmental facilities and conveniences. In scarcely anything has that sentiment been more manifest than in the abhorrence felt at the legal compulsion upon witnesses to make concessions which must cover the witness with lasting shame and leave him degraded both in his own eyes and those of others. What can be more abhorrent . . . than to compel a man who has fought his way from obscurity to dignity and honor to reveal crimes of which he had repented and of which the world was ignorant?[58]

Although Field's argument was long on emotional appeal and short on analysis, the fact remains that the protection against self-incrimination has, in the absence of a grant of immunity, effects other than that of protecting a witness against self-incrimination. By protecting a person against self-infamy, a measure of protection against such consequences as the loss of professional reputation and the loss of employment is added to *nemo tenetur*. Many years after *Brown*, Justice Douglas dissented from a decision upholding the 1954 Immunity Act,[59] echoing Field's broad view of the right. The dissent, written in *Ullmann v. United States* (1956), at the end of the McCarthy era, noted:

> The Fifth Amendment stands between the citizen and his government. When public opinion casts a person into the outer darkness, as happens today when a person is exposed as a Communist, the government brings infamy on the head of the witness when it compels disclosure. That is precisely what the Fifth Amendment prohibits.[60]

Non-immunized Losses

When Justice Douglas wrote his dissent in *Ullman*, he may have been prompted to stretch the right of silence under the Fifth Amendment because of the failure of the Supreme Court to give adequate First Amendment protection to political dissenters,[61] particularly when the dissenters chose to avail themselves of the right of silence. Yet the attempt to protect political dissent by an excessively broad interpretation of *nemo tenetur* could lead to consequences of doubtful propriety. It is one thing to assert that a public schoolteacher ought not to be summarily dismissed for refusing on grounds of self-incrimination to answer questions about political associations;[62] it is quite another thing to say that there can be no negative consequences to a witness who asserts the right of self-incrimination. Official investigations into the conduct of public employees or administrative proceedings in professional licensing frequently encounter refusals to cooperate. In *Garrity v. New Jersey* (1967), the Court overturned the conviction of a police officer, who at an earlier stage had been confronted with the choice of testifying about possible criminal conduct or the loss of his position. When he chose to testify, the Court concluded that his testimony was coerced by the threatened loss of position and that therefore the confession could not be used against him in a subsequent prosecution.[63] One year later, the Court made it clear that a city could not discharge a police officer who had been confronted with a choice of either waiving the right against self-incrimination or facing discharge for refusing to do so; yet the Court made it equally clear that, if public employees choose to assert the right in response to questions relating to the performance of their official duties, then they could validly be dismissed.[64] So long as an employee does not face coercion to relinquish the constitutional right, any refusal to account for the performance of official duties could be a basis for discharge.[65]

In these cases, none of the employees had been offered statutory immunity from criminal prosecution. The issue yet to be resolved is whether a public employee who has been granted immunity and reveals misconduct in the performance of official duties may be discharged on the basis of the immunized testimony. Unless we accept the Field-Douglas view of *nemo tenetur,* there appears to be little doubt about the right to discharge such an employee.

Use and Derivative-use Immunity

Since the *Counselman* decision in 1892, it was assumed that a federal statutory grant of immunity had to be as broad in scope and effect as the constitutional right and that the statute must provide "absolute immunity against future prosecution for the offense to which the question relates."[66] In effect, this amounted to transactional immunity; that is, immunity from any prosecution, penalty, or forfeiture "on account of any transaction, matter or thing concerning which . . . the witness may testify or produce evidence."[67] Transactional immunity—the absolute immunity from prosecution relating in any substantial manner to the immunized testimony—remained the basic form of federal immunity statutes for almost eighty years. In 1970, after a recommendation of the National Commission on Reform of Federal Criminal Laws, Congress enacted the so-called use and derivative-use immunity statute.[68] Use and derivative-use statutes prohibit the direct or indirect use of compelled testimony, including investigatory leads, but they do not preclude prosecution for the offense or a related offense if the prosecution is based on evidence obtained wholly independently of the compelled testimony. In 1972, in a 5 to 2 decision, the Supreme Court upheld the statute:

> The privilege has never been construed to mean that one who invokes it cannot subsequently be prosecuted. Its sole concern is to afford protection against being "forced to give testimony leading to the infliction of penalties affixed to . . . criminal acts." Immunity from the use of compelled testimony, as well as evidence derived directly and indirectly therefrom, affords this protection. It prohibits the prosecutorial authorities from using the compelled testimony in any respect, and it therefore insures that the testimony cannot lead to the infliction of criminal penalties on the witness.[69]

In order to ensure no use of compelled testimony, the majority also ruled that the prosecution would have the responsibility to establish, in any subsequent prosecution of the witness, that there was no taint in the evidence, and an affirmative duty to "prove that the evidence it proposes to use is derived from a legitimate source wholly independent of the compelled testimony."[70]

This prosecutorial responsibility did not satisfy Justice Brennan, who in an earlier case noted:

> In dealing with a single jurisdiction, we ought to recognize the enormous difficulty in attempting to ascertain whether a subsequent prosecution of an individual, who has previously been compelled to incriminate himself in regard to the offense in question, derives from the compelled testimony or from an

"independent source." For one thing, all the relevant evidence will obviously be in the hands of the government—the government whose investigation included compelling the individual involved to incriminate himself. Moreover, this argument does not depend upon assumptions of misconduct or collusion among government officers. It assumes only the normal margin of human fallibility. Men working in the same office or department exchange information without recording carefully how they obtained certain information; it is often impossible to remember in retrospect how or when or from whom information was obtained.[71]

Justice Brennan's point is clearly valid in those situations where it is impossible for the prosecution to discharge its affirmative responsibility of demonstrating wholly independent evidence. On the other hand, there are situations where the responsibility is relatively easy to discharge, particularly where the evidence was obtained prior to the compelled testimony.[72] Rather than adopting a rule that suggests that uncertainty would necessarily prevail in all cases, perhaps the better rule would be to require that all subsequent prosecutions be based on previously discovered evidence, thus precluding any prosecution based on evidence obtained subsequent to compelled testimony.[73]

Federalism and Immunity Statutes

Once the Supreme Court decided that the protection against self-incrimination applied to the states,[74] it was necessary to resolve the question of federal-state immunity. Can a witness be prosecuted on the basis of immunized testimony in another jurisdiction? Although the Court had held in *Brown* that Congress had authority under the supremacy clause to prohibit a state from using federally immunized testimony in a state prosecution, the opposite was not possible so long as the constitutional protection was not incorporated into the Fourteenth Amendment. This issue was finally addressed in *Murphy v. Waterfront Commission* (1964), where the Court ruled that witnesses who had been granted statutory immunity by a state could not be prosecuted under federal law on the basis of their incriminating testimony, nor could federally immunized witnesses be prosecuted by a state on the basis of their compelled federal testimony.[75]

CONFESSIONS

Obtaining needed information by granting statutory immunity is not a routine practice. On the other hand, interrogating suspects is common grist in the daily administration of justice. Asking questions about unsolved crimes is absolutely essential to the discharge of justice, but the legal right, indeed the *responsibility,* to ask questions can give birth to the idea that the interrogator is entitled to a response. As the late Dean Wigmore wrote:

> The exercise of the power to extract answers begets a forgetfulness of the just limitations of that power. The simple and peaceful process of questioning breeds a readiness to resort to bullying and to physical force and torture. If there is a right to an answer, there soon seems to be a right to the expected answer,—that is, to a confession of guilt. Thus the legitimate use grows into the unjust abuse.[76]

The product of "the unjust abuse," of course, is a coerced confession.

Originally, the constraint against coerced confessions and the right of no compulsory self-incrimination were quite separate, both in origin and in practice. Historically, the rule against coerced confessions was based on the invalidity of a confession that was not voluntarily given; it had no immediate relationship to *nemo tenetur.*[77] But testimonial compulsion and confessions have become intertwined. Indeed, the process began in the late nineteenth century, when the Supreme Court handed down its decision in *Bram v. United States* (1897).[78]

The facts of *Bram* are straightforward: On the night of July 14, 1896, on an American vessel bound from Boston to South America, the captain of the vessel, his wife, and the ship's second mate were murdered in their beds. Bram, the ship's first officer, was accused by a co-suspect, one Brown, of committing the murders. The vessel finally landed at Halifax, Nova Scotia, where Bram was taken into custody and interrogated by a member of the Halifax police department. During the otherwise normal interrogation, the detective ordered Bram to remove all of his clothing. In the course of the brief interrogation and the physical examination of Bram's clothing, the officer testified that the following exchange took place:

> When Mr. Bram came into my office, I said to him: "Bram, we are trying to unravel this horrible mystery." I said: "Your position is rather an awkward one. I have had Brown in this office and he made a statement that he saw you do the murder." He said: "He could not have seen me; where was he?" I said: "He states he was at the wheel." "Well," he said, "he could not have seen me from there." I said: "Now look here, Bram. I am satisfied that you killed the captain from all I have heard from Mr. Brown. But," I said, "some of us here think you could not have done all that crime alone. If you had an accomplice, you should say so, and not have the blame of this horrible crime on your own shoulders." He said, "Well, I think and many others on board the ship think, that Brown is the murderer; but I don't know anything about it." He was rather short in his replies.[79]

The Court reversed Bram's conviction, saying in an extraordinary but almost casual statement:

In criminal trials, in the Courts of the United States wherever a question arises whether a confession is incompetent because not voluntary, the issue is controlled by that portion of the 5th Amendment to the Constitution of the United States, commanding that no person "shall be compelled in any criminal case to be a witness against himself."[80]

It is by no means apparent from the opinion that the Court recognized that it was joining *nemo tenetur* and the heretofore separate rule against the admission of untrustworthy statements. Some years later, Dean Wigmore called the Court's position in *Bram* "radically erroneous."[81]

A close reading of the opinion is instructive, not because it introduced a new certainty into the judicial determination of a voluntary confession, but rather because of the uncertainty of the rule. The *Bram* rule was so subtle that it proved to be of little use in controlling the problem of coerced confessions. In the determination of voluntariness, the Court said:

> The rule is not that in order to render a statement admissible the proof must be adequate to establish that the particular communications contained in a statement were voluntarily made, but it must be sufficient to establish that the making of the statement was voluntary: that is to say, that from causes, which the law treats as legally sufficient to engender in the mind of the accused hope or fear in respect to the crime charged, the accused was not involuntarily impelled to make a statement, when but for the improper influences he would have remained silent.[82]

Applied to a case of physical coercion (torture, brutality), the rule is of some utility. But the more typical case involves psychological coercion, and such coercion is based on the fine distinctions drawn, as in *Bram*, from the totality of the circumstances surrounding it.

Bram was to remain an obscure decision until the 1940s. When the Supreme Court first served notice on the states that the use of involuntary confessions violated due process, *Bram* was not even noted.[83] However, in the 1940s and 1950s, when the Court confronted an increasing number of state confession cases, it attempted, rather unsuccessfully, to apply a *Bram*-type rule to the setting of psychological coercion.[84]

The weakness in *Bram* is that it offers little in the way of prospective guidance to the police. It was entirely dependent on a postmortem examination of the total circumstances of each case and inevitably led to a series of conflicting decisions. The decisions were notable for their long recitation of the facts and the judicial conclusions, with little attention to any relationship between the facts and the conclusions.[85]

The heart of the problem in psychological-coercion cases was that the Court kept asking the wrong question; that is, the Court continued to try to discover factual answers to the question of voluntariness. Presumably, the determination of voluntariness must be clear, but retrospective determinations rarely lead to straightforward answers. Certainly, physical circumstances can be shown absolutely, but states of mind, of necessity, are equivocal, and equivocal situations are an open invitation to the misuse, and even abuse, of power. Thus, in one case, the Court upheld a confession obtained after the accused had been forced to hold a pan containing the bones of the deceased; yet two years later, the Court threw out the confession of a defendant who had been stripped naked during several hours of interrogation.[86]

By the 1960s, it was apparent that decisions in this area were clouded. In 1964, the Supreme Court made a sharp break in the area of confessions. In *Escobedo v. Illinois,* a five-justice majority ruled that

> where, as here, the investigation is no longer a general inquiry into an unsolved crime but has begun to focus on a particular suspect, the suspect has been taken into police custody, the police carry out a process of interrogations that lends itself to eliciting incriminating statements, the suspect has requested and been denied an opportunity to consult with his lawyer, and the police have not effectively warned him of his absolute constitutional right to remain silent . . . that no statement elicited by the police during the interrogation may be used against him at a criminal trial.[87]

In short, *Escobedo* addressed itself to the central problems in the confession issue: the incommunicado setting of police interrogation, the absence of counsel, and the inadequate warnings of the right to silence. Although *Escobedo* provided a foundation for settling the endless disputes over voluntariness, it did not offer a final solution. It left unanswered numerous questions concerning the timing of warnings and the relationship of legal counsel to confession.

Two years later, the Court elaborated on the issue of interrogation and confessions. In *Miranda v. Arizona* (1966), the five-justice majority began with a conclusion about police interrogation:

> An interrogation environment is created for no purpose other than to subjugate the individual to the will of his examiner. . . . Unless adequate protective devices are employed to dispel the compulsion inherent in custodial surroundings, no statement obtained from the defendant can truly be the product of his free choice.[88]

Based on this conclusion, the majority then spelled out in detail the protective devices necessary to ensure that a confession does not violate a defendant's Fifth Amendment right against self-incrimination. The opinion began by limiting the protective devices to custodial interrogation; that is, to "questioning initiated by law enforcement officers after a person has been taken into custody or otherwise deprived of his freedom of action in any significant way."[89] Assuming, then, the context of a custodial interrogation, the majority summarized the required procedures as follows:

As for the procedural safeguards to be employed, unless other fully effective means are devised to inform accused persons of their right of silence and to assure a continuous opportunity to exercise it, the following measures are required. Prior to any questioning, the person must be warned that he has a right to remain silent, that any statement he does make may be used as evidence against him, and that he has a right to the presence of an attorney, either retained or appointed. The defendant may waive effectuation of these rights, provided the waiver is made voluntarily, knowingly and intelligently. If, however, he indicates in any manner and at any stage of the process that he wishes to consult with an attorney before speaking there can be no questioning. Likewise, if the individual is alone and indicates in any manner that he does not wish to be interrogated, the police may not question him. The mere fact that he may have answered some questions on his own does not deprive him of the right to refrain from answering any further inquiries until he has consulted with an attorney and thereafter consents to be questioned.[90]

Whatever the merits of Chief Justice Warren's opinion in *Miranda,* and the craftsmanship was not always equal to the task, the policy objectives of the opinion are clear. By detailing these procedural requirements, the majority hoped to eliminate some if not all of the imponderables associated with the determination of voluntariness. To accomplish this, the majority developed one of the most detailed sets of procedures ever contained in an opinion of the Supreme Court. By tying the admission of confessions to specific procedural requirements, the majority presumably anticipated that the requirements would be less subject to factual disputes than had heretofore been true in confession cases. Additionally, the majority wished to ensure that the right against self-incrimination would be available not just in formal proceedings, but also in contacts with the police. Here the majority seemed to be motivated not only by considerations of no compulsory self-incrimination, but also by a desire to cut down the abuse of police power.[91]

The opinion in *Miranda* also makes clear those things that the majority did not want to accomplish. It did not question the use of confessions,[92] the interrogation of suspects, nor the general questioning of nonsuspects.[93] Finally, it acknowledged that the procedures adopted by the Court were not the only solutions to the problem and that, therefore, Congress and the states were free to develop other measures, subject to judicial review, so long as those measures were as effective as those adopted by the Court.[94]

The reaction to *Escobedo* and *Miranda* was far from uniform, but law enforcement agencies and legislative bodies were generally unhappy with the decisions.[95]

Whether any of the goals of *Miranda* have been reached is an open question. Initial research appears to challenge not only police fears of being shackled by the decision, but also any expectation that there would be a dramatic decrease in the number of confessions obtained.[96] Nor has the decision appeared to reduce the number of disputes over the admissibility of confessions; on the contrary, the number has probably increased. However, by focusing attention on specific requirements, *Miranda* may have reduced the problem to one of more manageable proportions. Still, the procedures are by no means free of the same imponderable questions that characterized pre-*Miranda* disputes. Probably the most difficult is what constitutes "in custody" or "significantly deprived of freedom of action" for purposes of triggering *Miranda* warnings. The decision correctly assumes that not all police questioning should trigger a warning, and, given the variety of situations in which questioning can occur, disputes are inevitable.[97]

The Court has held that noncustodial interrogation by Internal Revenue agents does not require a *Miranda* warning because the setting is not coercive.[98] Similarly, a person who voluntarily appears at a police station and submits to questioning, even though the appearance is in response to a police call, is not entitled to a *Miranda* warning. If a defendant appears voluntarily and is free to leave, the interrogation is not custodial. [99] On the other hand, the police may not make arrests without probable cause—the so-called investigatory arrests—and then by the mere expedient of giving a *Miranda* warning, use confessions that are a by-product of the tainted arrests. Fourth Amendment considerations require that confessions that are the by-product of illegal arrests be admitted only after a trial court determines both that the confessions were voluntary and that no causal connection exists between the illegal arrests and the confessions. In short, where both the Fourth and Fifth Amendments come into play, trial courts must go beyond the question of voluntariness and examine such things as the temporal proximity of the arrest and confession and the purpose and flagrancy of the official misconduct.[100]

The lower courts have developed at least two tests to determine whether, short of formal arrest, the circumstances of a given case require a *Miranda* warning:

1. The "objective reasonable man test" which holds that custody exists if the action of the interrogating officers and the surrounding circumstances, fairly construed, would reasonably have led him to believe he could not leave freely. . . . In some jurisdictions the intent of the officer and the belief of the person interrogated are both rejected in favor of an objective standard which considers the officer's statements and acts and the surrounding circumstances gauged by a reasonable man test.
2. A subjective test in which custody occurs if a suspect is led to believe as a reasonable person that he is being deprived or restricted of his freedom of action or movement under pressure of official authority.[101]

Another area left undecided by *Miranda* is the protective devices in regard to the right to counsel.[102] Similarly, questions have been raised as to whether all elements of the *Miranda* warnings are essential: For example, may the warning leave out notice of the right to the presence of an attorney during the interrogation?[103]

Given the detailed nature of the *Miranda* guidelines, it is not surprising that some of the language used in the opinion has been challenged. For example, the *Miranda* opinion indicated that "once warnings have been given the subsequent procedure is clear. If the individual indicates in any manner, at any time prior to or during questioning, that he wishes to remain silent, the interrogation must cease."[104] Does this mean that one who has invoked the right to silence is thereby given a blanket immunity of indefinite duration from further interrogation? This issue was frequently raised in the lower federal courts, and in 1975, in *Michigan v. Mosley,* the Court attempted to resolve the problem.[105] Mosley had been arrested in the early afternoon on a robbery charge and, after receiving the *Miranda* warning, indicated that he did not want to be interrogated. The officer then placed Mosley in a cell. Some hours later, another officer, investigating an unrelated offense, gave Mosley another *Miranda* warning and interrogated him. The interrogation led to an incriminating statement. The Court, in upholding the admission of the statement, reasoned that *Miranda* does not create a per se proscription of indefinite duration against further questioning on any subject once the person in custody indicates a desire to remain silent. Instead, the Court ruled that the issue of admissibility after a person in custody has indicated a desire to remain silent depends "on whether his right to cut off questioning was 'scrupulously honored.' "[106]

Surely the Court was correct in indicating that the right to silence does not create a blanket immunity of indefinite duration. But to rule that the issue of admissibility is to be determined by, in effect, the voluntariness of the defendant's submitting to subsequent interrogation is a step backwards to the vague contours of pre-*Miranda* confession cases. *Miranda* represented an attempt to avoid post hoc inquiries into the voluntariness of statements, electing instead to establish concrete steps to dispel the vagaries necessarily inherent in a judicial inquiry into voluntariness. Furthermore, the *Mosley* opinion fails to consider the centrality of custody to the rationale of *Miranda*. Custody is the triggering device that brings into operation the *Miranda* warnings. Thus, there would be some logic in ruling that only the termination of custody or a defense initiative would allow interrogation to resume or a new interrogation to begin. So long as custody continues, or so long as a defendant remains uncounseled, the coercive atmosphere is not dispelled. The *Mosley* opinion ignores the coercive atmosphere of the isolated interrogation, and thereby ignores the foundation of *Miranda*.

Given the adverse reaction to *Miranda,* it was not surprising that the Burger Court was less than enthusiastic in its support. In *Harris v. New York* (1971), a five-justice majority ruled that when a defendant elects to testify at trial, the prosecution may introduce a prior confession in order to impeach the credibility of the defendant's conflicting testimony, even though that testimony was obtained in violation of the *Miranda* requirements. Chief Justice Burger, speaking for the majority, ruled:

Having voluntarily taken the stand, petitioner was under an obligation to speak truthfully and accurately, and the prosecution here did no more than utilize the traditional truth-testing devices of the adversary process. Had inconsistent statements been made by the accused to some third person, it could hardly be contended that the conflict could not be laid before the jury by way of cross-examination and impeachment.

The shield provided by *Miranda* cannot be perverted into a license to use perjury by way of a defense, free from the risk of confrontation with prior inconsistent utterances. We hold, therefore, that petitioner's credibility was appropriately impeached by use of his earlier conflicting statements.[107]

Justice Brennan, in dissent, observed:

The Court today tells the police that they may freely interrogate an accused incommunicado and without counsel and know that although any statement they obtain in violation of *Miranda* cannot be used on the State's direct case, it may be introduced if the defendant has the temerity to testify in his own defense. This goes far toward undoing much of the progess made in conforming police methods to the Constitution. I dissent.[108]

In 1975, the Burger Court underscored its ruling in *Harris*. In *Oregon v. Hass*, the majority again ruled that although incriminating statements obtained in violation of *Miranda* requirements are not admissible in the prosecution's case-in-chief, they can be used to impeach the credibility of a defendant who elects to testify. Again the majority reasoned that the *Miranda* rules were not to be perverted into a "license to testify inconsistently or even perjuriously, free from the risk of confrontation with prior inconsistent utterances."[109]

Hass, after being arrested and after receiving proper *Miranda* warnings, had requested a lawyer. The arresting officer said that Hass could phone an attorney once they reached the police station. In the meantime, Hass made an incriminating admission, presumably in response to the officer's further questioning.[110] Justice Brennan, again writing in dissent, argued that the majority had gone beyond *Harris* in allowing such an admission to be used on cross-examination:

Even after *Harris*, police had some incentive for following *Miranda* by warning an accused of his right to remain silent and his right to counsel. If the warnings were given, the accused might still make a statement which could be used in the prosecution's case-in-chief. Under today's holding, however, once the warnings are given, police have almost no incentive for following *Miranda*'s requirement that "if the individual states that he wants an attorney, the interrogation must cease until an attorney is present." If the requirement is followed there will almost surely be no statement since the attorney will advise the accused to remain silent. If, however, the requirement is disobeyed, the police may obtain a statement which can be used for impeachment if the accused has the temerity to testify in his own defense. Thus, after today's decision, if an individual states that he wants an attorney, police interrogation will doubtless now be vigorously pressed to obtain statements before the attorney arrives.[111]

Although *Harris* and *Hass* were probably intended to take some of the sting out of *Miranda,* they do not constitute a silent overturning of *Miranda.* Although most defendants do testify at their trials, few would do so if the case against them rested solely on an improperly obtained confession. The state is obliged to make a case against a defendant independently of an improperly obtained confession. If a prosecutor failed to make such an independent case and relied, instead, on impeaching a defendant's testimony, the state's case against the defendant would probably not survive a defense motion for directed acquittal.

A principal difficulty in achieving the goals of *Miranda* lies in the fact that *Miranda* places the initial defense of a suspect's rights on the shoulders of the police. Given the adversary-accusatory nature of criminal law, it is unlikely that this responsibility can be effectively discharged by the police. Without casting doubt on the honesty of the police, the procedures appear to be calculated to give rise to disputes over what occurred. By the time police officers are required to give a *Miranda* warning, they are likely to be confronted with a suspect whom they have concluded is factually guilty. Most of the forces that influence their behavior, both in the police department and externally, encourage officers to conclude that their responsibility is to bring a suspect to the bar of justice and not to protect the suspect's right to silence. Thus, warnings can become perfunctory, casual, and even cryptic.

We will continue to experience retreats and advances in the *Miranda* procedure with changes in judicial personnel, but *Miranda* will never produce a satisfactory solution to the problem of protecting a constitutional right so long as the environment of isolation continues to surround the interrogation of suspects. Some accommodation must be made between the real needs of the police to interrogate suspects and the suspects' right to silence. This accommodation will never be reached so long as interrogations are conducted in isolation, which, despite its advantages, breeds factual doubt and suspicion. This doubt and suspicion must infect subsequent judicial determinations and often leads to judicial conclusions that are at best equivocal.

IDENTIFICATION PROCEDURES

Both state and federal courts have long held that defendants may be compelled to give nontestimonial assistance to the prosecution. The rationale in supoprt of this began with the long-accepted practice of in-court identification (by witnesses) of the accused. In England, at least since the seventeenth century, the courts have accepted this type of physical identification.[112] And in 1910, the Supreme Court ruled that the protection against compulsory self-incrimination does not extend to the compelled exhibition of the person of the defendant: "The prohibition of compelling a man in a criminal court to be a witness against himself is a prohibition of the use of physical or moral compulsion to extort communications from him, not an exclusion of his body as evidence when it may be material. The objection in principle would forbid a jury to look at a prisoner and compare his features with a photograph in proof."[113]

The rule that bodily exhibition (which includes clothes, physical characteristics, and fingerprints) is not protected by the Fifth Amendment does not rest on any assumption that such exhibition may not be the result of compulsion or that it does not force defendants to aid in their own prosecution. Rather, it rests on the premise that the right against compulsory self-incrimination is limited to testimonial compulsion.

In *Schmerber v. California* (1966), the Supreme Court attempted to distinguish between testimonial compulsion on the one hand and real, or physical, evidence (in this case, a compulsory blood test) on the other. Writing for the majority Justice Brennan argued that the privilege

> offers no protection against compulsion to submit to fingerprinting, photographing, or measurements, to write or speak for identification, to appear in court, to stand, to assume a stance, to walk, or to make a particular gesture. The distinction which has emerged, often expressed in different ways, is that the privilege is a bar against compelling "communications" or "testimony," but that compulsion which makes a suspect or accused the source of "real or physical evidence" does not violate it.[114]

Justice Black, writing in dissent, objected to what he considered to be the majority's labored distinction:

> [It is a] strange hierarchy of values that allows the State to extract a human being's blood to convict him of a crime because of the blood's content but proscribes compelled production of his lifeless papers. Certainly there could be few papers that would have any more "testimonial" value to convict a man of drunken driving than would an analysis of the alcoholic content of a human being's blood introduced in evidence at a trial for driving while under the influence of alcohol. In such a situation blood, of course, is not oral testimony given by an accused but it can certainly "communicate" to a court and jury the fact of guilt.[115]

In the years following *Schmerber,* the Court has applied its ruling to police lineups,[116] situations requiring the accused to speak,[117] and the taking of handwriting samples[118] and voice exemplars.[119]

Although compulsory self-incrimination has not been applied to various techniques for the identification of an accused, the Warren Court did rule that, at certain stages, counsel is required in identification lineups, and that in-court identifications based on suggestive pretrial lineups violate the right to cross-examination[120] and may also violate due process.[121] Because of the grave risk of mistaken identification, the trial court must determine on the basis of all the circumstances whether a given lineup or other identification procedure was unnecessarily suggestive and conducive to irreparable mistaken identification.[122] The Burger Court has indicated less concern over suggestive identification procedures. In 1972 Justice Powell, speaking for the majority, upheld a suggestive show-up, in which there was both visual and voice identification by the victim. In that show-up, the defendant was walked past the victim by two detectives. In sustaining the show-up, Justice Powell observed:

> Some general guidelines emerge . . . as to the relationship between suggestiveness and misidentification. It is, first of all, apparent that the primary evil to be avoided is "a very substantial likelihood of irreparable misidentification."
> . . . While the phrase was coined as a standard for determining whether an in-court identification would be admissible in the wake of a suggestive out-of-court identification, with the deletion of "irreparable" it serves equally well as a standard for the admissibility of testimony concerning the out-of-court identification itself. It is the likelihood of misidentification which violates a defendant's right to due-process, and it is this which was the basis of the exclusion of evidence in *Foster*. Suggestive confrontations are disapproved because they increase the likelihood of misidentification, and unnecessarily suggestive ones are condemned for the further reason that the increased chance of misidentification is gratuitous. But as *Stovall* makes clear, the admission of evidence of a showup without more does not violate due process.[123]

SELF-REPORTING AND DISCLOSURES

The conceptual strain on the right against self-incrimination is nowhere more evident than in the area of self-reporting and compulsory disclosures. Twentieth-century American government has attempted to regulate an enormous number of activities. Many of the regulatory devices in economic and consumer-oriented areas are not directly aimed at controlling antisocial behavior, but rather at gathering information, regulating the economy, and protecting citizens. It is not unusual for a regulatory device to mandate a certain measure of self-reporting or compulsory disclosure by those engaged in regulated activities. Not infrequently, legislatures have attached both civil and criminal penalties for substantive violations. The Fifth Amendment becomes involved when self-reporting or compulsory disclosure exposes an individual to the risk of self-incrimination.

On the other hand, legislatures have tried to use compulsory disclosure and registration devices as a means of directly controlling antisocial behavior. Dangerous drugs, certain weapons, certain organizations, and gambling have all been subjected to such control. In these areas, the regulation is primarily through the use of the criminal sanction, although the legislation, at least at the federal level, may be offered under the rubric of tax legislation.

The Supreme Court first addressed the issue of compulsory disclosure in 1886. In *Boyd v. United States,* the Court held that a *subpoena duces tecum* that required an individual to produce private papers in a forfeiture proceeding was subject to the constraints of both the Fourth and Fifth Amendments.[124] However, it was not until 1927 that the Court had occasion to rule on a self-reporting device. In *United States v. Sullivan,* the defendant refused to divulge his net income as requested by federal income tax law. Sullivan, who said that a large part of his income had been obtained in violation of the National Prohibition Act, claimed he was exonerated from reporting this income because to do so would violate his right against compulsory self-incrimination. Justice Holmes, speaking for a unanimous Court, quickly dismissed Sullivan's contention:

> It would be an extreme if not an extravagant application of the 5th Amendment to say that it authorized a man to refuse to state the amount of his income because it had been made in crime. But if the defendant desired to test that or any other point he should have tested it in return so that it could be passed upon. He could not draw a conjurer's circle around the whole matter by his own declaration that to write any word upon the government blank would bring him into danger of the law.[125]

Although the *Sullivan* opinion indicated that a taxpayer might refuse on grounds of self-incrimination to answer a specific question, the opinion did not address the question of whether the mere act of filing a tax return could be a link in the chain of evidence leading to a criminal prosecution. The government clearly is entitled to collect those taxes that are due under valid tax laws. However, does the interest in collecting taxes outweigh other constitutional considerations? Income tax evasion is a criminal offense, and a summons to appear before an IRS agent and to respond to inquiries can, for some taxpayers, pose a serious threat of criminal prosecution. If one underlying principle of the Fifth Amendment is the preservation of an accusatory, rather than inquisitional, system of criminal law, then we must guard against tax proceedings that are inquisitions.[126]

After *Sullivan,* the Court did not return to the issue of compulsory disclosure until its decision in *Albertson v. Subversive Activities Control Board* (1965).[127] Acting under the authority of the Subversive Activities Control Act of 1950, the federal government ordered members of the Communist party to register. Members of the organization countered that to do so would violate their right against compulsory self-incrimination. In upholding their refusal to register, the Supreme Court unanimously ruled that, unlike the case in *Sullivan,* the claim here was substantial and far from frivolous:

> In *Sullivan* the questions in the income tax return were neutral on their face and directed at the public at large, but here they are directed at a highly selective group inherently suspect of criminal activities. Petitioners' claims are

not asserted in an essentially noncriminal and regulatory area of inquiry, but against an inquiry in an area permeated with criminal statutes, where response to any of the form's questions in context might involve the petitioners in the admission of a crucial element of a crime.[128]

The rationale of placing a regulatory measure in an essentially noncriminal area, with minimal risk of criminal prosecution, was to be adopted in later decisions as one means of determining the validity of a claim under the Fifth Amendment. Where the risk is substantial, the Court has upheld a defense of self-incrimination. For example, in 1968 the Court held that a claim of self-incrimination was a complete defense to a federal prosecution for failure to pay an occupational tax on wagering and failure to register before engaging in the business of accepting wagers as required by federal law.[129] The majority opinion noted:

> Petitioner was confronted by a comprehensive system of federal and state prohibitions against wagering activities; he was required, on pain of criminal prosecution, to provide information which he might reasonably suppose would be available to prosecuting authorities, and which would surely prove a significant "link in a chain" of evidence tending to establish his guilt. Unlike the income tax return in question in *United States v. Sullivan* . . . every portion of these requirements had the direct and unmistakable consequence of incriminating petitioner; the application of the constitutional privilege to the entire registration procedure was in this instance neither "extreme" nor "extravagant."[130]

On the same day, the Court also ruled on the registration requirement for certain weapons under the National Firearms Act.[131] In *Haynes v. United States*, the Court again used the rationale of suspect activity and substantial risk in order to sustain a claim of self-incrimination. The Court reasoned that the firearms registration requirement was "directed principally at those persons who have obtained possession of a firearm without complying with the Act's other requirements, and who therefore are immediately threatened by criminal prosecution. . . . They are unmistakably persons 'inherently suspect of criminal activities.' "[132]

One year later, the same rationale was applied to a provision of the Marihuana Tax Act that required a purchaser of marihuana to obtain an order and to pay a transfer tax.[133] Because compliance with the statutory scheme would require one to identify oneself with a selective and suspect group, the Court found the claim of self-incrimination was real and appreciable.[134]

The conceptual problems in the compulsory-registration cases were relatively minor and, indeed, prompted only Chief Justice Warren to dissent in three of the cases. Compulsory disclosure by a highly suspect class provided a convenient, if not convincing, rationale for triggering the right against self-incrimination. Also, there was no shortage of decided cases that had ruled in a similar vein, so a simple process of inductive reasoning allowed the Court to dispose of the cases without recourse to the more hazardous and onerous task of deducing a decision on the basis of principles.

But the problems of self-reporting and disclosure are not always so conveniently resolved. The weakness of the craftsmanship in the registration cases was fully exposed when the Court undertook to examine California's hit-and-run law. Hit-and-run statutes have been around almost as long as the automobile.[135] Such statutes customarily require the operator of an automobile involved in an accident that causes injury to persons or property to stop and give his or her name and address. Failure to do so normally constitutes a criminal offense. In *California v. Byers* (1971), the Court was confronted with the following provision of the California Vehicle Code:

> The driver of any vehicle involved in an accident resulting in damage to any property including vehicles shall immediately stop the vehicle at the scene of the accident and shall then and there . . . locate and notify the owner or person in charge of such property of the name and address of the driver and owner of the vehicle involved.[136]

Byers demurred to the charge and pleaded the protection against self-incrimination. The California Supreme Court upheld the statute but imposed a use restriction that banned the state from using the disclosed information in a criminal prosecution against the discloser.[137] The U.S. Supreme Court also upheld the statute, but without the use restriction. In a plurality opinion, Chief Justice Burger reasoned that Byers was not confronted with a substantial hazard of self-incrimination, and furthermore that what the statute required of Byers was not testimonial and thus not properly subject to the limitations of the Fifth Amendment. He reasoned:

> It is difficult to consider this group as either "highly selective" or "inherently suspect of criminal activities." Driving an automobile, unlike gambling, is a lawful activity. Moreover, it is not a criminal offense under California law to be a driver "involved in an accident." An accident may be the fault of others; it may occur without any driver having been at fault. No empirical data are suggested in support of the conclusion that there is a relevant correlation between being a driver and criminal prosecution of drivers. So far as any available information instructs us, most accidents occur without creating criminal liability even if one or both of the drivers are guilty of negligence as a matter of tort law.[138]

Separate dissents by Justices Black and Brennan, joined by Justices Douglas and Marshall, rejected the plurality's conclusion and argued that Byers was confronted with a substantial risk and that the disclosure was of a testimonial nature. Only the concurring opinion of Justice Harlan attempted to come to grips with the conceptual problems. Although his opinion briefly explored the relevance of the underlying principles of privacy and the preservation of the accusatory system, he rejected this approach in favor of a balancing test. In weighing the character and urgency of the public interest, his opinion appeared to rest on a fear that, given society's needs in other socio-economic areas for self-reporting, to strike down the statute would "embark us on uncharted and treacherous seas."[139]

CONCLUSION

It is pointless to search in contemporary Fifth Amendment cases for constitutional principles that support the decisions. Privacy, humane treatment, and the maintenance of the accusatory system are at best relegated to an occasional note in a concurring or dissenting opinion. The Court has avoided principles, relying instead on narrow tests ("an inherently suspect class") or broad concepts (testimonial evidence versus real evidence).[140] Of course, the task of decision making is easier when the majority is not compelled to confine a decision by extant constitutional principles. In the absence of confining constitutional principles, the Court has been free to make such accommodations to social interests as can command the support of at least five justices. The freewheeling hypotheses of legal realism are at home in such an atmosphere. The *Harris* and *Hass* rulings simply become the current majority's analog to *Schmerber*.

Result-oriented decisions with their reasonably narrow rationales have, of course, the great advantage that they are directed to discrete issues and do not tend to bind the future options of the judiciary. As social and economic conditions change, the judiciary, unconstrained by carefully constructed and developed principles, is free to chart a new course in response to the exigencies of practicality. And, in fairness to the judiciary, constitutional principles of sufficient clarity to be useful in decision making are at once notably few and often in conflict with other principles. At least in their present state, privacy, humane treatment, and the preservation of the accusatory system are principles of such breadth that they are understandably useless in providing a working framework for adjudication.

Finally, principles can get the Court into trouble. As Martin Shapiro remarked, "Standing on principle, in international, barroom, or legislative-judicial relations, is likely to lead to a fight."[141] A strict application of the principles of privacy and maintenance of the accusatory system might well have precluded judicial acceptance of immunity statutes and certain forms of compulsory disclosures, which almost certainly would have embroiled the Supreme Court in fights with Congress and the states. Yet even accepting the political realities of the Court's institutional setting, we cannot excuse its failure to develop convincing arguments or reasoned elaboration in justification for such decisions as *Schmerber, Byers,* and *Harris.*

The *Schmerber* opinion fails not only because it rests on a highly dubious test of "real evidence," but because it suggests that the intrusion was small, which is a conclusion, not an argument. Similarly, the *Byers* opinion never explains why, in an accusatory system, a defendant should be required to help the prosecution meet the burden of proof. Nor did the Court suggest there why the adjustment made by the California Supreme Court (adding a use limitation to the statute) was not a better accommodation to the Fifth Amendment right than the Court's own unsupported conclusion.

Given the uncertain mandate of the self-incrimination clause, a degree of adjustment and balance between individual and societal interests is to be expected. In balancing, however, the Court is under a heavy obligation to explain why the individual interests protected by the Fifth Amendment must give way to the larger interests of society.

NOTES

1. See Leonard Levy, *Origins of the Fifth Amendment: The Right Against Self-Incrimination* (New York: Oxford University Press, 1968), pp. 43–82.

2. Ibid. at 229. In 1607, as chief justice of common pleas, Coke spoke out against the oath; see Edward S. Corwin, "The Supreme Court's Construction of the Self-Incrimination Clause," 29 *Mich. L. Rev.* 7 (1930).

3. For an excellent account of his life, see Pauline Gregg, *Free-Born John: A Biography of John Lilburne* (London: George Harrap, 1961).

4. *The Trial of John Lilburne and John Wharton for Printing and Publishing Seditious Books*, 13 Car. I 1637, 3 How. St. Tr. 1315–1343 (1637).

5. Quoted in Levy, *Origins*, p. 331.

6. In 1662, Parliament specifically prohibited the oath ex officio; Corwin, "Supreme Court's Construction," p. 9, n. 16.

7. Although it was not yet recognized in the pretrial preliminary examination. In 1848, by an act Parliament required the examining magistrate to inform a suspect of the right to silence; Levy, *Origins*, p. 329.

8. This rule prevailed in England until 1898; in the United States it prevailed at the state level until the 1880s and at the federal level until 1870. One state, Georgia, continued the practice at least until 1961; see *Ferguson v. Georgia*, 365 U.S. 570 (1961).

9. See *Rex v. Reading*, 7 How. St. Tr. 296 (1679); and William Holdsworth, *A History of English Law* (London: Methuen, 1938), vol. 9, pp. 198–201.

10. Levy, *Origins*, pp. 317–318. The self-infamy rule fell into disuse in the nineteenth century.

11. Holdsworth, *History of English Law*, vol. 9, pp. 217–219.

12. James Fitzjames Stephen, *A History of the Criminal Law in England* (London: Macmillan, 1883), vol. 1, pp. 424, 453–454.

13. For a somewhat contrary view, see Julius Goebel, Jr., and T. Raymond Naughton, *Law Enforcement in Colonial New York* (New York: Commonwealth Fund, 1944), p. 656. Cf. Levy, *Origins*, pp. 333–404.

14. Ibid. at 430. On the Bill of Rights generally, see Robert A. Rutland, *The Birth of the Bill of Rights, 1776–1791* (New York: Collier, 1962); and Irving Brant, *The Bill of Rights: Its Origins and Meaning* (New York: New American Library, 1965).

15. See Lewis Mayers, *Shall We Amend the Fifth Amendment?* (New York: Harper,

1959); and Henry J. Friendly, "The Fifth Amendment Tomorrow: The Case for Constitutional Change," 37 *U. Cin. L. Rev.* 671 (1968).

16. *The Trial of John Udall,* How. St. Tr. 1271 (1590). Udall refused the oath ex officio, was found guilty of seditious libel, and died in prison.

17. See Walter Schaefer, *The Suspect and Society: Criminal Procedure and Converging Constitutional Doctrines* (Evanston, Ill.: Northwestern University Press, 1967), p. 72.

18. However, one could argue that the First Amendment was of little use in protecting left-wing political dissent before legislative committees in the McCarthy era; see *Wilkerson v. United States,* 365 U.S. 399 (1961). Cf. *Gibson v. Florida Legislative Investigating Comm.,* 372 U.S. 539 (1963).

19. *Wilson v. United States,* 149 U.S. 60, 66 (1893).

20. See examples proposed in Erwin N. Griswold, *The Fifth Amendment Today* (Cambridge, Mass.: Harvard University Press, 1955), pp. 14–20. Cf. Erwin Griswold, "The Right to Be Let Alone," 55 *Nw. U. L. Rev.* 216, 223 (1960).

21. See Schaefer, *Suspect and Society,* p. 66; and Robert McKay, "Self-Incrimination and the New Privacy," in *The Supreme Court Review, 1967* (Chicago: University of Chicago Press, 1967), pp. 206–209.

22. *Murphy v. Waterfront Comm'n.,* 378 U.S. 52, 55 (1964).

23. *Tehan v. United States,* 382 U.S. 406, 415–416 (1966).

24. See Douglas Thompson, "Judge Friendly's Amendments to the Fifth Amendment," 38 *U. Cin. L. Rev.,* 488, 499 (1969).

25. Dissenting in *Griffin v. California,* 380 U.S. 609, 621 (1965).

26. See Frank W. Miller, *Prosecution: The Decision to Charge a Suspect with a Crime* (Boston: Little, Brown, 1969), pp. 21–43.

27. *Fitzpatrick v. United States,* 178 U.S. 304, 315 (1900). And see *McGautha v. California,* 402 U.S. 183, 215 (1971); impeachment of a defendant poses perhaps a greater threat to conviction because it opens the door to proof of bad character, including prior convictions. For a recommendation of a change in impeachment of defendant's character, see Schaefer, *Suspect and Society,* pp. 67–68.

28. The permissible scope of impeachment raises a more serious issue; see above, note 27.

29. *Wilson v. United States,* 149 U.S. 60 (1893); and *Griffin v. California,* 380 U.S. 609 (1965).

30. Ibid. at 614; in *Lockett v. Ohio,* 434 U.S. 889 (1978), the Court upheld a prosecutor's closing comment in which the prosecutor made references to the "unrefuted" and "uncontradicted" evidence presented by the state.

31. *Griffin v. California,* 380 U.S. at 621.

32. However, federal courts are obligated to give such an instruction; *Brund v. United States,* 308 U.S. 287 (1939).

33. *Raffel v. United States,* 271 U.S. 494, 497 (1926). Cross-examination, of course, is limited to the charges at issue and to matters raised on direct examination.

34. *Harris v. New York,* 401 U.S. 222 (1971). Cf. *Simmons v. United States,* 390 U.S. 377 (1968), where the Supreme Court refused to allow a pretrial admission of ownership in a motion for exclusion of illegally obtained evidence to be admitted at trial on the issue of guilt.

35. *Raffel v. United States,* 271 U.S. 494 (1926).

36. *Johnson v. United States,* 318 U.S. 189, 197–199 (1943). The right was asserted in response to a prosecutor's question about an event not related to the indictment and one that might have been subject of a future prosecution.

37. *Halperin v. United States,* 353 U.S. 391, 415 (1957); and see *Stewart v. United States,* 366 U.S. 1 (1961), reversing a conviction where prosecution commented during cross examination about the defendant's failure to testify in previous trials for the same offense.

38. E.g., *United States v. Ramirez*, 441 F.2d 950 (5th Cir. 1971). Cf. *Johnson v. Patterson*, 475 F.2d 1066 (10th Cir. 1973).

39. *United States v. Hale*, 422 U.S. 171 (1975).

40. Ibid., at 175.

41. Ibid. at 179.

42. *Doyle v. Ohio*, 426 U.S. 610, 617–618 (1976).

43. *Brown v. Walker*, 161 U.S. 591, 605 (1896).

44. *Hale v. Henkel*, 201 U.S. 43 (1906).

45. *Rogers v. United States*, 340 U.S. 367, 371 (1951). Nor may it be invoked on behalf of corporations or other collective entities; *Bellis v. United States*, 417 U.S. 85 (1974).

46. *Rogers v. United States.*

47. *Mason v. United States*, 244 U.S. 362, 365 (1917).

48. *Regina v. Boyes*, 121 Eng. Rep. 730 (1861); and see *Mason v. United States*, 244 U.S. at 365.

49. *Hoffman v. United States*, 341 U.S. 479, 486–487 (1951).

50. *Blau v. United States*, 340 U.S. 159, 161 (1950).

51. Mayers, *Shall We Amend?*

52. *Arndstein v. McCarthy*, 254 U.S. 71 (1920); before a grand jury, *Counselman v. Hitchcock*, 142 U.S. 547 (1892); before a legislative committee, *Slochower v. Board of Education*, 350 U.S. 551 (1956); or in administrative proceedings, *Murphy v. Waterfront Comm.*

53. See note, "Immunity Statutes and the Constitution," 68 *Colum. L. Rev.* 959, 960–961 (1968).

54. *Counselman v. Hitchcock*, 142 U.S. at 585–586 .

55. Act of February 11, 1893, 27 Stat. 443.

56. *Brown v. Walker*, 161 U.S. 591, 595–606 (1896).

57. Justice Shiras, with Justices Gray and White concurring, dissenting; ibid. at 622–623.

58. Ibid. at 631–632.

59. 68 Stat. 745, 18 U.S.C. 3486.

60. *Ullmann v. United States*, 350 U.S. 422, 453–454 (1956).

61. See, e.g., *Adler v. Board of Education*, 342 U.S. 485 (1952); *Lerner v. Casey*, 357 U.S. (1958); and *Nelson v. Los Angeles*, 326 U.S. 1 (1960). Cf. *Slochower v. Board of Education.*

62. *Slochower v. Board of Education.*

63. *Garrity v. New Jersey*, 385 U.S. 493 (1967); see also *Spevack v. Klein*, 385 U.S. 511 (1967).

64. *Gardner v. Broderick*, 392 U.S. 273 (1968).

65. *Uniformed Sanitation Men v. Commissioner of Sanitation*, 392 U.S. 280, 284–285 (1968). See also *Confederation of Police v. Conlisk*, 489 F.2d 891 (7th Cir. 1973); and *Wormer v. Hampton*, 496 F.2d 99 (5th Cir. 1974). The principle of *Garrity* and *Gardner* was later applied to private, nonimmunized contractors in *Lefkowitz v. Turley*, 414 U.S. 79 (1973), and to state political party officers in *Lefkowitz v. Cunningham*, 431 U.S. 801 (1977).

66. *Counselman v. Hitchcock*, 142 U.S. at 586.

67. Act of February 11, 1893.

68. 18 U.S.C. 6002.

69. *Kastigar v. United States*, 406 U.S. 441, 453 (1972).

70. Ibid. at 460.

71. Dissenting in *Piccarello v. New York*, 400 U.S. 548, 567–569 (1971). See also *Zicarelli v. New Jersey State Comm.*, 406 U.S. 472 (1972), upholding the "responsive" limitation in a use and derivative use immunity statute.

72. E.g., *United States v. First Western State Bank,* 491 F.2d 780 (8th Cir. 1974).

73. E.g., *United States v. McDaniel,* 482 F.2d 305 (8th Cir. 1973).

74. *Malloy v. Hogan,* 378 U.S. 1 (1964).

75. *Murphy v. Waterfront Comm'n,* 378 U.S. at 77–78.

76. John Henry Wigmore, *A Treatise on Evidence,* 2d ed., vol. 4, § 2251 (Boston: Little, Brown, 1923), p. 824.

77. Ibid., § 2266, pp. 879–880.

78. *Bram v. United States,* 168 U.S. 532 (1897).

79. Ibid. at 539.

80. Ibid. at 542.

81. Wigmore, *On Evidence,* vol. 4, § 2266, p. 879.

82. *Bram v. United States,* 168 U.S. at 549.

83. *Brown v. Mississippi,* 279 U.S. 278 (1936).

84. E.g., *Ward v. Texas,* 316 U.S. 547 (1942); and *Thomas v. Arizona,* 356 U.S. 390 (1958). See generally H. Frank Way, "The Supreme Court and State Coerced Confessions," 12 *J. Pub. L.* 53 (1963).

85. At the same time, the Supreme Court was attempting, in federal cases, to impose more specific guidelines for federal officers; *McNabb v. United States,* 318 U.S. 332 (1943); *Mallory v. United States,* 354 U.S. 449 (1957). Under the *McNabb-Mallory* rule, confessions obtained during a period of illegal detention were inadmissible in federal courts.

86. *Lyons v. Oklahoma,* 320 U.S. 732 (1943); and *Malinski v. New York,* 324 U.S. 401 (1945).

87. *Escobedo v. Illinois,* 378 U.S. 478, 490–491 (1964).

88. *Miranda v. Arizona,* 384 U.S. 436, 457–458 (1966).

89. Ibid. at 444. The immediate setting of *Miranda* was a station house interrogation. In *Orozco v. Texas,* 394 U.S. 324 (1969), the Court extended the parameter of custodial interrogation to field interrogation if the suspect is under arrest or otherwise significantly deprived of freedom of action.

90. *Miranda v. Arizona,* 384 U.S. at 444–445.

91. Ibid. at 482.

92. Ibid. at 478.

93. Ibid at 477.

94. Ibid. at 490.

95. E.g., see title II, Omnibus Crime Control and Safe Streets Act of 1968, Pub. L. 90–351 (June 19, 1968). Section 3501-b of this act was an attempt by Congress to undermine the thrust of *Miranda* in federal prosecutions. Subsection (b) reads as follows:

> (b)   The trial judge in determining the issue of voluntariness shall take into consideration all the circumstances surrounding the giving of the confession, including (1) the time elapsing between arrest and arraignment of the defendant making the confession, if it was made after the arrest and before the arraignment, (2) whether such defendant knew the nature of the offense with which he was charged or of which he was suspected at the time of making the confession, (3) whether or not such defendant was advised or knew that he was not required to make any statement and that any such statement could be used against him, (4) whether or not such defendant had been advised prior to questioning of his right to the assistance of counsel, and (5) whether or not such defendant was without the assistance of counsel when questioned and when giving such confession.
>
> The presence or absence of any of the above-mentioned factors to be taken into consideration by the judge need not be conclusive on the issue of voluntariness of the confession.

96. See Michael Wald et al., "Interrogations in New Haven: The Impact of *Miranda*," 76 *Yale L.J.* 1534 (1967); Richard Medalie et al., "Custodial Interrogation in Our Nation's

Capital," 66 *Mich. L. Rev.* 1363 (1968); and Richard H. Seeburger and R. Stanton Wettick, Jr., "*Miranda* in Pittsburgh," 29 *U. Pitt. L. Rev.* 1 (1967).

97. E.g., *Government of Virgin Islands v. Kirnan,* 377 F. Supp. 601 (1974); and *United States v. Bettenhausen,* 499 F.2d 1223 (10th Cir. 1974). Cf. *Williams v. Brewer,* 375 F. Supp. 170 (1974).

98. *Beckwith v. United States,* 425 U.S. 341 (1976).

99. *Oregon v. Mathiason,* 429 U.S. 492 (1977).

100. *Brown v. Illinois,* 422 U.S. 590 (1975); accord, *Dunaway v. New York,* _____ U.S. _____ (1979).

101. Noted in *New Jersey v. Godfrey,* 329 A.2d 75, 79 at n. 1 (1974).

102. E.g., *United States v. Clark,* 499 F.2d 802 (4th Cir. 1974). See also *Brewer v. Williams,* 430 U.S. 387 (1977), where the Court ruled that once adversary proceedings have commenced a defendant has a right to legal representation when the government interrogates him or her.

103. E.g., *United States v. Floyd,* 496 F.2d 982 (2d Cir. 1974). It should be noted that hearings on the voluntariness of confessions are not limited to the threshold questions raised by the *Miranda* requirements because it may also be necessary to determine whether a given confession was voluntary even though the *Miranda* requirements were satisfied. In short, a *Miranda* warning does not per se create an irrebuttable presumption that a confession is voluntary or free of taint; see *Brown v. Illinois,* 422 U.S. 590 (1975).

104. *Miranda v. Arizona,* 384 U.S. at 473.

105. *Michigan v. Mosley,* 423 U.S. 96 (1975).

106. Ibid. at 104.

107. *Harris v. New York,* 401 U.S. 222, 225–226 (1971).

108. Ibid. at 232.

109. *Oregon v. Hass,* 420 U.S. 714 (1975). See also *Mincey v. Arizona,* 437 U.S. 385 (1978), where the Court ruled that an interrogation was involuntary, despite *Miranda* warnings, and could not be used to impeach Mincey's testimony at trial.

110. The opinion does not make it clear whether the admission was in direct response to a question.

111. *Oregon v. Hass,* 420 U.S. at 725.

112. E.g., *Trial of Captain Thomas Vaughan,* 13 How. St. Tr. 486, 517 (1696).

113. *Holt v. United States,* 218 U.S. 245, 252–253 (1910). See also *Wigmore on Evidence,* vol. 4, § 2265.

114. *Schmerber v. California,* 384 U.S. 757, 761–765 (1966). Cf. *Rochin v. California,* 342 U.S. 165 (1952).

115. *Schmerber v. California,* 384 U.S. at 774–775.

116. *United States v. Wade,* 388 U.S. 218 (1967). The Court in *Wade* did rule that a post-indictment lineup required the aid of counsel; see below, pp. 299–301.

117. *Stovall v. Denno,* 388 U.S. 293 (1967).

118. *Gilbert v. California,* 388 U.S. 263 (1967).

119. *United States v. Dionisio,* 410 U.S. 1 (1973). Cf. *Davis v. Mississippi,* 394 U.S. 721 (1969), where fingerprint evidence, taken in a lawless wholesale arrest, was held inadmissible under the Fourth Amendment.

120. *United States v. Wade.*

121. *Stovall v. Denno.*

122. *Foster v. California,* 394 U.S. 440 (1969).

123. *Neil v. Biggers,* 409 U.S. 188, 198–199 (1972). The Burger Court has also limited *Wade* to postindictment lineups, *Kirby v. Illinois,* 406 U.S. 682 (1972), and has refused to extend the right to counsel to photographic displays, *United States v. Ash,* 413 U.S. 300 (1973).

124. *Boyd v. United States,* 116 U.S. 616 (1886).

125. *United States v. Sullivan,* 274 U.S. 259, 263–264 (1927).

126. For additional problems, see *Reisman v. Caplan,* 375 U.S. 440 (1964); *Donaldson v. United States,* 400 U.S. 517 (1971); and *Couch v. United States,* 409 U.S. 322 (1973). See also Paul Lipton, "Constitutional Rights in Criminal Tax Investigations," 45 *F.R.D.* 323 (1968); and note, "Constitutionally Privileged False Statements," 22 *Stan. L. Rev.* 783 (1970).

127. *Albertson v. Subversive Activities Control Board,* 382 U.S. 70 (1965). In *Shapiro v. United States,* 335 U.S. 1 (1948), the Supreme Court upheld a section of the Emergency Price Control Act requiring persons to keep records and make them available to the price administrator. In *Shapiro,* a bare majority further held that there could be no valid claim of statutory or constitutional immunity from self-incrimination if the records and documents were required to be kept by law. Justice Frankfurter, in dissent, wrote:

> The underlying assumption of the Court's opinion is that all records which Congress in the exercise of its constitutional powers may require individuals to keep in the conduct of their affairs, because those affairs also have aspects of public interest, become "public" records in the sense that they fall outside the constitutional protection of the Fifth Amendment. The validity of such a doctrine lies in the scope of its implications. The claim touches records that may be required to be kept by federal regulatory laws, revenue measures, labor and census legislation in the conduct of business which the understanding and feeling of our people still treat as private enterprise, even though its relations to the public may call for governmental regulation, including the duty to keep designated records.
>
> . . . But the notion that whenever Congress requires an individual to keep in a particular form his own books dealing with his own affairs his records cease to be his when he is accused of crime, is indeed startling. . . .
>
> The fact of the matter, then is that records required to be kept by law are not necessarily public in any except a word-playing sense. . . .
>
> . . . If Congress by the easy device of requiring a man to keep the private papers that he has customarily kept can render such papers "public" and non-privileged, there is little left to either the right of privacy or the constitutional privilege (335 U.S. 1, 53–70).

128. *Albertson v. Subversive Activities Control Board,* 382 U.S. at 77–79.

129. 26 U.S.C. 4411 & 4412.

130. *Marchetti v. United States,* 390 U.S. 39, 48–49 (1968), overruling *United States v. Kahriger,* 345 U.S. 22 (1953), and *Lewis v. United States,* 348 U.S. 419 (1955). See also *Grosso v. United States,* 390 U.S. 62 (1968), decided with *Marchetti,* upholding, under a claim of self-incrimination, the failure of a defendant to pay excise tax on wagering.

131. 26 U.S.C. 5841.

132. *Haynes v. United States,* 390 U.S. 85, 96–97 (1968).

133. 26 U.S.C. 4741.

134. *Leary v. United States,* 395 U.S. 6, 18 (1969). Cf. *Minor v. United States,* 396 U.S. 77 (1969), where the Court held that, in contrast to a buyer, the seller of narcotics did not expose himself to the risk of self-incrimination because he had the option not to sell to any buyer who did not have a proper order form. See also *United States v. Knox,* 396 U.S. 77 (1969), disallowing a claim of self-incrimination in a prosecution for making a false statement in a wagering registration form.

135. See *Ex parte Kneedler,* 147 S.W. 983 (1912).

136. *California v. Byers,* 402 U.S. 424, 426 (1971).

137. *People v. Byers,* 458 F.2d 465 (1969).

138. *California v. Byers,* 402 U.S. at 429–433.

139. Ibid. at 458. See also *California Bankers Association v. Schultz,* 416 U.S. 21 (1974), where the Supreme Court upheld a provision of the Bank Secrecy Act of 1970 requiring a bank to report to the federal government certain private-depositor currency transactions that would be useful in criminal, tax, or regulatory investigations against a claim by a bankers'

association that the law violated both the First, Fourth and Fifth Amendments. In part, the Court relied on the required-records doctrine of *Shapiro v. United States.*

140. One is reminded by the broadness of the testimonial-evidence test of Justice Holmes's warning that "too broadly generalized conceptions are a constant source of fallacy," *Lorenzo v. Wirth,* 170 Mass. 596 (1898).

141. Martin Shapiro, *Law and Politics in the Supreme Court* (New York: Free Press, 1964), p. 28.

JUDICIAL DECISIONS

Application to the States:
Malloy v. Hogan, 378 U.S. 1 (1964)

Mr. Justice BRENNAN delivered the opinion of the Court.

In this case we are asked to reconsider prior decisions holding that the privilege against self-incrimination is not safeguarded against state action by the Fourteenth Amendment. *Twining v. New Jersey,* 211 U.S. 78.

The petitioner was arrested during a gambling raid in 1959 by Hartford, Connecticut, police. He pleaded guilty to the crime of pool selling, a misdemeanor, and was sentenced to one year in jail and fined $500. The sentence was ordered to be suspended after 90 days, at which time he was to be placed on probation for two years. About 16 months after his guilty plea, petitioner was ordered to testify before a referee appointed by the Superior Court of Hartford County to conduct an inquiry into alleged gambling and other criminal activities in the county. The petitioner was asked a number of questions related to events surrounding his arrest and conviction. He refused to answer any question "on the grounds it may tend to incriminate me." The Superior Court adjudged him in contempt, and committed him to prison until he was willing to answer the questions. Petitioner's application for a writ of habeas corpus was denied by the Superior Court, and the Connecticut Supreme Court of Errors affirmed. The latter court held that the Fifth Amendment's privilege against self-incrimination was not available to a witness in a state proceeding, that the Fourteenth Amendment extended no privilege to him, and that the petitioner had not properly invoked the privilege available under the Connecticut Constitution. We granted certiorari. We reverse. We hold that the Fourteenth Amendment guaranteed the petitioner the protection of the Fifth Amendment's privilege against self-incrimination, and that under the applicable federal standard, the Connecticut Supreme Court of Errors erred in holding that the privilege was not properly invoked.

The extent to which the Fourteenth Amendment prevents state invasion of rights enumerated in the first eight Amendments has been considered in numerous cases in this Court since the Amendment's adoption in 1868. Although many Justices have deemed the Amendment to incorporate all eight of the Amendments, the view which has thus far prevailed dates from the decision in 1897 in *Chicago, B & Q. R. Co. v. Chicago,* 166 U.S. 226, which held that the Due Process Clause requires the States to pay just compensation for private property taken for public use. It was on the authority of that decision that the Court said in 1908 in *Twining v. New Jersey,* supra, that "it is possible that some of the personal rights safeguarded by the first eight Amendments against national action may also be safeguarded against state action, because a denial of them would be a denial of due process of law." 211 U.S., at 99.
. . .

We hold today that the Fifth Amendment's exception from compulsory self-incrimination is also protected by the Fourteenth Amendment against abridgement by the States. Decisions of the Court since *Twining* and *Adamson* have departed from the contrary view expressed in those cases. . . .

The respondent Sheriff concedes in its brief that under our decisions, particularly those involving coerced confessions, "the accusatorial system has become a fundamental part of the fabric of our society and, hence, is enforceable against the States." The State urges, however, that the availability of the federal privilege to a witness in a state inquiry is to be determined according to a less stringent standard than is applicable in a federal proceeding. We disagree. We have held that the guarantees of the First Amendment, the prohibition of unreasonable searches and seizures of the Fourth Amendment, and the right to counsel guaranteed by the Sixth Amendment are all to be enforced against the States under the Fourteenth Amendment according to the same standards that protect those personal rights against federal encroachment. In the coerced confession cases, involving the policies of the privilege itself, there has been no suggestion that a confession might be considered coerced if used in a federal but not a state tribunal. The Court thus has rejected the notion that the Fourteenth Amendment applies to the States only a "watered-down, subjective version of the individual guarantees of the Bill of Rights," *Ohio ex rel. Eaton v. Price,* 364 U.S. 263, 275. If *Cohen v. Hurley,* 366 U.S. 117, and *Adamson v. California,* supra, suggest such an application of the privilege against self-incrimination, that suggestion cannot survive recognition of the degree to which the *Twining* view of the privilege has been eroded. What is accorded is a privilege of refusing to incriminate one's self, and the feared prosecution may be by either federal or state authorities. It would be incongruous to have different standards determine the validity of a claim of privilege based on the same feared prosecution, depending on whether the claim was asserted in a state or federal court. Therefore, the same standards must determine whether an accused's silence in either a federal or state proceeding is justified.

We turn to the petitioner's claim that the State of Connecticut denied him the protection of his federal privilege. It must be considered irrelevant that the petitioner was a witness in a statutory inquiry and not a defendant in a criminal prosecution, for it has long been settled that the privilege protects witnesses in similar federal inquiries. *Counselman v. Hitchcock,* 142 U.S. 547. We recently elaborated the content of the federal standard in *Hoffman:*

> "The privilege afforded not only extends to answers that would in themselves support a conviction . . . but likewise embraces those which would furnish a link in the chain of evidence needed to prosecute. . . . If the witness, upon interposing his claim, were required to prove the hazard . . . he would be compelled to surrender the very protection which the privilege is designed to guarantee. To sustain the privilege, it need only be evident from the implications of the question, in the setting in which it is asked, that a responsive answer to the question or an explanation of why it cannot be answered might be dangerous because injurious disclosure could result." 341 U.S., at 486–487.

We also said that, in applying that test, the judge must be

> " '*perfectly clear,* from a careful consideration of all the circumstances in the case, that the witness is mistaken, and that the answer[s] *cannot possibly* have such tendency' to incriminate." 341 U.S., at 488.

The State of Connecticut argues that the Connecticut courts properly applied the federal standards to the facts of this case. We disagree.

The investigation in the course of which petitioner was questioned began when the Superior Court in Hartford County appointed the Honorable Ernest A. Inglis, formerly Chief Justice of Connecticut, to conduct an inquiry into whether there was reasonable cause to believe that crimes, including gambling, were being committed in Hartford County. Petitioner appeared on January 16 and 25, 1961, and in both instances he was asked substantially the same questions about the circumstances surrounding his arrest and conviction for pool selling in late 1959. The questions which petitioner refused to answer may be summarized as follows: (1) for whom did he work on September 11, 1959; (2) who selected and paid his counsel in connection with his arrest on that date and subsequent conviction; (3) who selected and paid his bondsman; (4) who paid his fine; (5) what was the name of the tenant of the apartment in which he was arrested; and (6) did he know John Bergoti. The Connecticut Supreme Court of Errors ruled that the answers to these questions could not tend to incriminate him because the defenses of double jeopardy and the running of the one-year statute of limitations on misdemeanors would defeat any prosecution growing out of his answers to the first five questions. As for the sixth question, the court held that petitioner's failure to explain how a revelation of his relationship with Bergoti would incriminate him vitiated his claim to the protection of the privilege afforded by state law.

The conclusions of the Court of Errors, tested by the federal standard, fail to take sufficient account of the setting in which the questions were asked. The interrogation was part of a wide-ranging inquiry into crime, including gambling, in Hartford. It was admitted on behalf of the State at oral argument—and indeed it is obvious from the questions themselves—that the State desired to elicit from the petitioner the identity of the person who ran the pool-selling operation in connection with which he had been arrested in 1959. It was apparent that petitioner might apprehend that if this person were still engaged in unlawful activity, disclosure of his name might furnish a link in a chain of evidence sufficient to connect the petitioner with a more recent crime for which he might still be prosecuted.

Analysis of the sixth question, concerning whether petitioner knew John Bergoti, yields a similar conclusion. In the context of the inquiry, it should have been apparent to the referee that Bergoti was suspected by the State to be involved in some way in the subject matter of the investigation. An affirmative answer to the question might well have either connected petitioner with a more recent crime, or at least have operated as a waiver of his privilege with reference to his relationship with a possible criminal. We conclude, therefore, that as to each of the questions, it was "evident from the implications of the question, in the setting in which it [was] asked, that a responsive answer to the question or an explanation of why it [could not] be answered might be dangerous because injurious disclosure could result," *Hoffman v. United States*, 341 U.S., at 486–487.

Reversed.

Use and Derivative-use Immunity:
Kastigar v. United States, *406 U.S. 441 (1972)*

Mr. Justice POWELL delivered the opinion of the Court.

This case presents the question whether the United States Government may compel testimony from an unwilling witness, who invokes the Fifth Amendment privilege against compulsory self-incrimination, by conferring on the witness immunity from use of the compelled testimony in subsequent criminal proceedings, as well as immunity from use of evidence derived from the testimony.

Petitioners were subpoenaed to appear before a United States grand jury in the Central District of California on February 4, 1971. The Government believed that petitioners were likely to assert their Fifth Amendment privilege. Prior to the scheduled appearances, the Government applied to the District Court for an order directing petitioners to answer questions and produce evidence before the grand jury under a grant of immunity conferred pursuant to 18 U.S.C. §§ 6002, 6003. Petitioners opposed issuance of the order, contending primarily that the scope of the immunity provided by the statute was not coextensive with the scope of the privilege against self-incrimination, and therefore was not sufficient to supplant the privilege and compel their testimony. The District Court rejected this contention, and ordered petitioners to appear before the grand jury and answer its questions under the grant of immunity.

Petitioners appeared but refused to answer questions, asserting their privilege against compulsory self-incrimination. They were brought before the District Court, and each persisted in his refusal to answer the grand jury's questions, notwithstanding the grant of immunity. The court found both in contempt, and committed them to the custody of the Attorney General until either they answered the grand jury's questions or the term of the grand jury expired. The Court of Appeals for the Ninth Circuit affirmed. This Court granted certiorari to resolve the important question whether testimony may be compelled by granting immunity from the use of compelled testimony and evidence derived therefrom ("use and derivative use" immunity), or whether it is necessary to grant immunity from prosecution for offenses to which compelled testimony relates ("transactional" immunity).

I

The power of government to compel persons to testify in court or before grand juries and other governmental agencies is firmly established in Anglo-American jurisprudence. The power with respect to courts was established by statute in England as early as 1562, and Lord Bacon observed in 1612 that all subjects owed the King their "knowledge and discovery." While it is not clear when grand juries first resorted to compulsory process to secure the attendance and testimony of witnesses, the general common-law principle that "the public has a right to every man's evidence" was considered an "indubitable certainty" that "cannot be denied" by 1742. The power to compel testimony, and the corresponding duty to testify, are recognized in the Sixth Amendment requirements that an accused be confronted with the witnesses against him, and have compulsory process for obtaining witnesses in his favor. The first Congress recognized the testimonial duty in the Judiciary Act of 1789, which provided for compulsory attendance of witnesses in the federal courts. . . .

But the power to compel testimony is not absolute. There are a number of exemptions from the testimonial duty, the most important of which is the Fifth Amendment privilege against compulsory self-incrimination. The privilege reflects a complex of our fundamental values and aspirations, and marks an important advance in the development of our liberty. It can be asserted in any proceeding, civil or criminal, administrative or judicial, investigatory or adjudicatory; and it protects against any disclosures which the witness reasonably believes could be used in a criminal prosecution or could lead to other evidence that might be so used. This Court has been zealous to safeguard the values which underlie the privilege.

Immunity statutes, which have historical roots deep in Anglo-American jurisprudence, are not incompatible with these values. Rather, they seek a rational accommodation between the imperatives of the privilege and the legitimate demands of government to compel citizens to testify. The existence of these statutes reflects the importance of testimony, and the fact that many offenses are of such a character that the only persons capable of giving useful testimony are those implicated in the crime. Indeed, their origins were in the context of such offenses, and their primary use has been to investigate such offenses. Congress included immunity statutes in many of the regulatory measures adopted in the first half of this century. Indeed, prior to the enactment of the statute under consideration in this case, there were in force over 50 federal immunity statutes. In addition, every State in the Union, as well as the District of Columbia and Puerto Rico, has one or more such statutes. The commentators, and this Court on several occasions, have characterized immunity statutes as essential to the effective enforcement of various criminal statutes. . . .

II

Petitioners' contend, first, that the Fifth Amendment's privilege against compulsory self-incrimination, which is that "no person . . . shall be compelled in any criminal case to be a witness against himself," deprives Congress of power to enact laws that compel self-incrimination, even if complete immunity from prosecution is granted prior to the compulsion of the incriminatory testimony. In other words, petitioners assert that no immunity statute, however drawn, can afford a lawful basis for compelling incriminatory testimony. They ask us to reconsider and overrule *Brown v. Walker*, 161 U.S. 591 (1896). . . .

We find no merit to this contention and reaffirm the decisions in *Brown* and *Ullmann*.

III

Petitioners' second contention is that the scope of immunity provided by the federal witness immunity statute, 18 U.S.C. § 6002, is not coextensive with the scope of the Fifth Amendment privilege against compulsory self-incrimination, and therefore is not sufficient to supplant the privilege and compel testimony over a claim of the privilege. The statute provides that when a witness is compelled by district court order to testify over a claim of the privilege:

"the witness may not refuse to comply with the order on the basis of his privilege against self-incrimination; but no testimony or other information compelled under the order (or any information directly or indirectly derived from such testimony or other information) may be used against the witness in any criminal case, except a prosecution for perjury, giving a false statement, or otherwise failing to comply with the order." 18 U.S.C. § 6002.

. . .

The statute's explicit proscription of the use in any criminal case of "testimony or other information compelled under the order (or any information directly or indirectly derived from such testimony or other information)" is consonant with Fifth Amendment standards. We hold that such immunity from use and derivative use is coextensive with the scope of the privilege against self-incrimination, and therefore is sufficient to compel testimony over a claim of the privilege. While a grant of immunity must afford protection commensurate with that afforded by the privilege, it need not be broader. Transactional immunity, which accords full immunity from prosecution for the offense to which the compelled testimony relates, affords the witness considerably broader protection than does the Fifth Amendment privilege. The privilege has never been construed to mean that one who invokes it cannot subsequently be prosecuted. Its sole concern is to afford protection against being "forced to give testimony leading to the infliction of 'penalties affixed to . . . criminal acts.' " Immunity from the use of compelled testimony, as well as evidence derived directly and indirectly therefrom, affords this protection. It prohibits the prosecutorial authorities from using the compelled testimony in *any* respect, and it therefore insures that the testimony cannot lead to the infliction of criminal penalties on the witness.

. . .

IV

Although an analysis of prior decisions and the purpose of the Fifth Amendment privilege indicates that use and derivative-use immunity is coextensive with the privilege, we must consider additional arguments advanced by petitioners against the sufficiency of such immunity. We start from the premise, repeatedly affirmed by this Court, that an appropriately broad immunity grant is compatible with the Constitution.

Petitioners argue that use and derivative-use immunity will not adequately protect a witness from various possible incriminating uses of the compelled testimony: for example, the prosecutor or other law enforcement officials may obtain leads, names of witnesses, or other information not otherwise available that might result in a prosecution. It will be difficult and perhaps impossible, the argument goes, to identify, by testimony or cross-examination, the subtle ways in which the compelled testimony may disadvantage a witness, especially in the jurisdiction granting the immunity.

This argument presupposes that the statute's prohibition will prove impossible to enforce. The statute provides a sweeping proscription of any use, direct or indirect, of the compelled testimony and any information derived therefrom:

> "No testimony or other information compelled under the order (or any information directly or indirectly derived from such testimony or other information) may be used against the witness in any criminal case . . ." 18 U.S.C. § 6002.

This total prohibition on use provides a comprehensive safeguard, barring the use of compelled testimony as an "investigatory lead," and also barring the use of any evidence obtained by focusing investigation on a witness as a result of his compelled disclosures.

A person accorded this immunity under 18 U.S.C. § 6002, and subsequently prosecuted, is not dependent for the preservation of his rights upon the integrity and good faith of the prosecuting authorities. . . . This burden of proof, which we reaffirm as appropriate, is not limited to a negation of taint; rather, it imposes on the prosecution the affirmative duty to prove that the evidence it proposes to use is derived from a legitimate source wholly independent of the compelled testimony.

This is very substantial protection, commensurate with that resulting from invoking the privilege itself. The privilege assures that a citizen is not compelled to incriminate himself by his own testimony. It usually operates to allow a citizen to remain silent when asked a question requiring an incriminatory answer. This statute, which operates after a witness has given incriminatory testimony, affords the same protection by assuring that the compelled testimony can in no way lead to the infliction of criminal penalties. The statute, like the Fifth Amendment, grants neither pardon nor amnesty. Both the statute and the Fifth Amendment allow the government to prosecute using evidence from legitimate independent sources.

The statutory proscription is analogous to the Fifth Amendment requirement in cases of coerced confessions. A coerced confession, as revealing of leads as testimony given in exchange for immunity, is inadmissible in a criminal trial, but it does not bar prosecution. Moreover, a defendant against whom incriminating evdence has been obtained through a grant of immunity may be in a stronger position at trial than a defendant who asserts a Fifth Amendment coerced-confession claim. One raising a claim under this statute need only show that he testified under a grant of immunity in order to shift to the government the heavy burden of proving that all of the evidence it proposes to use was derived from legitimate independent sources. On the other hand, a defendant raising a coerced-confession claim under the Fifth Amendment must first prevail in a voluntariness hearing before his confession and evidence derived from it become inadmissible.

There can be no justification in reason or policy for holding that the Constitution requires an amnesty grant where, acting pursuant to statute and accompanying safeguards, testimony is compelled in exchange for immunity from use and derivative use when no such amnesty is required where the government, acting without colorable right, coerces a defendant into incriminating himself.

We conclude that the immunity provided by 18 U.S.C. § 6002 leaves the witness and the prosecutorial authorities in substantially the same position as if the witness had claimed the Fifth Amendment privilege. The immunity therefore is coextensive with the privilege and suffices to supplant it. The judgment of the Court of Appeals for the Ninth Circuit accordingly is

Affirmed.

The Exclusionary Rule:
Miranda v. Arizona, 384 U.S. 436 (1966)

Mr. Chief Justice WARREN delivered the opinion of the Court.

The cases before us raise questions which go to the roots of our concepts of American criminal jurisprudence: the restraints society must observe consistent with the Federal Constitution in prosecuting individuals for crime. More specifically, we

deal with the admissibility of statements obtained from an individual who is subjected to custodial police interrogation and the necessity for procedures which assure
that the individual is accorded his privilege under the Fifth Amendment to the Constitution not to be compelled to incriminate himself.

We dealt with certain phases of this problem recently in *Escobedo v. State of
Illinois,* 378 U.S. 478 (1964). There, as in the four cases before us, law enforcement
officials took the defendant into custody and interrogated him in a police station for
the purpose of obtaining a confession. The police did not effectively advise him of
his right to remain silent or of his right to consult with his attorney. Rather, they
confronted him with an alleged accomplice who accused him of having perpetrated
a murder. When the defendant denied the accusation and said "I didn't shoot
Manuel, you did it," they handcuffed him and took him to an interrogation room.
There, while handcuffed and standing, he was questioned for four hours until he
confessed. During this interrogation, the police denied his request to speak to his
attorney, and they prevented his retained attorney, who had come to the police
station, from consulting with him. At his trial, the State, over his objection, introduced
the confession against him. We held that the statements thus made were constitutionally inadmissible.

This case has been the subject of judicial interpretation and spirited legal debate
since it was decided two years ago. Both state and federal courts, in assessing its
implications, have arrived at varying conclusions. A wealth of scholarly material has
been written tracing its ramifications and underpinnings. Police and prosecutor have
speculated on its range and desirability. We granted certiorari in these cases in order
further to explore some facets of the problems, thus exposed, of applying the privilege against self-incrimination to in-custody interrogation, and to give concrete constitutional guidelines for law enforcement agencies and courts to follow.

We start here, as we did in *Escobedo,* with the premise that our holding is not
an innovation in our jurisprudence, but is an application of principles long recognized and applied in other settings. We have undertaken a thorough re-examination
of the *Escobedo* decision and the principles it announced, and we reaffirm it. That
case was but an explication of basic rights that are enshrined in our Constitution—that
"No person . . . shall be compelled in any criminal case to be a witness against
himself," and that "the accused shall . . . have the Assistance of Counsel"—rights
which were put in jeopardy in that case through official overbearing. These precious
rights were fixed in our Constitution only after centuries of persecution and struggle.
And in the words of Chief Justice Marshall, they were secured "for ages to come,
and . . . designed to approach immortality as nearly as human institutions can
approach it."

. . .

I.

The constitutional issue we decide in each of these cases is the admissibility of
statements obtained from a defendant questioned while in custody or otherwise
deprived of his freedom of action in any significant way. In each, the defendant was
questioned by police officers, detectives, or a prosecuting attorney in a room in which
he was cut off from the outside world. In none of these cases was the defendant

given a full and effective warning of his rights at the outset of the interrogation process. In all the cases, the questioning elicited oral admissions, and in three of them, signed statements as well which were admitted at their trials. They all thus share salient features—incommunicado interrogation of individuals in a police-dominated atmosphere, resulting in self-incriminating statements without full warnings of constitutional rights.

An understanding of the nature and setting of this in-custody interrogation is essential to our decisions today. The difficulty in depicting what transpires at such interrogations stems from the fact that in this country they have largely taken place incommunicado. From extensive factual studies undertaken in the early 1930's, including the famous Wickersham Report to Congress by a Presidential Commission, it is clear that police violence and the "third degree" flourished at that time. In a series of cases decided by this Court long after these studies, the police resorted to physical brutality—beatings, hanging, whipping—and to sustained and protracted questioning incommunicado in order to extort confessions. The Commission on Civil Rights in 1961 found much evidence to indicate that "some policemen still resort to physical force to obtain confessions." The use of physical brutality and violence is not, unfortunately, relegated to the past or to any part of the country. Only recently in Kings County, New York, the police brutally beat, kicked and placed lighted cigarette butts on the back of a potential witness under interrogation for the purpose of securing a statement incriminating a third party.

The examples given above are undoubtedly the exception now, but they are sufficiently widespread to be the object of concern. Unless a proper limitation upon custodial interrogation is achieved—such as these decisions will advance—there can be no assurance that practices of this nature will be eradicated in the foreseeable future. . . . We stress that the modern practice of in-custody interrogation is psychologically rather than physically oriented. As we have stated before, "Since *Chambers v. State of Florida,* 309 U.S. 227, this Court has recognized that coercion can be mental as well as physical, and that the blood of the accused is not the only hallmark of an unconstitutional inquisition." *Blackburn v. State of Alabama,* 361 U.S. 199, 206 (1960). Interrogation still takes place in privacy. Privacy results in secrecy and this in turn results in a gap in our knowledge as to what in fact goes on in the interrogation rooms. A valuable source of information about present police practices, however, may be found in various police manuals and texts which document procedures employed with success in the past, and which recommend various other effective tactics. These texts are used by law enforcement agencies themselves as guides. It should be noted that these texts professedly present the most enlightened and effective means presently used to obtain statements through custodial interrogation. . . .

From these representative samples of interrogation techniques, the setting prescribed by the manuals and observed in practice becomes clear. In essence, it is this: To be alone with the subject is essential to prevent distraction and to deprive him of any outside support. The aura of confidence in his guilt undermines his will to resist. He merely confirms the preconceived story the police seek to have him describe. Patience and persistence, at times relentless questioning, are employed. To obtain a confession, the interrogator must "patiently maneuver himself or his quarry into a position from which the desired objective may be attained." When normal procedures fail to produce the needed result, the police may resort to deceptive stratagems such as giving false legal advice. It is important to keep the subject off balance, for example, by trading on his insecurity about himself or his surroundings. The police then persuade, trick, or cajole him out of exercising his constitutional rights.

Even without employing brutality, the "third degree" or the specific stratagems described above, the very fact of custodial interrogation exacts a heavy toll on individual liberty and trades on the weakness of individuals. . . .

It is obvious that such an interrogation environment is created for no purpose other than to subjugate the individual to the will of his examiner. This atmosphere carries its own badge of intimidation. To be sure, this is not physical intimidation, but it is equally destructive of human dignity. The current practice of incommunicado interrogation is at odds with one of our Nation's most cherished principles—that the individual may not be compelled to incriminate himself. Unless adequate protective devices are employed to dispel the compulsion inherent in custodial surroundings, no statement obtained from the defendant can truly be the product of his free choice.
. . .

The question in these cases is whether the privilege is fully applicable during a period of custodial interrogation. In this Court, the privilege has consistently been accorded a liberal construction. We are satisfied that all the principles embodied in the privilege apply to informal compulsion exerted by law-enforcement officers during in-custody questioning. An individual swept from familiar surroundings into police custody, surrounded by antagonistic forces, and subjected to the techniques of persuasion described above cannot be otherwise than under compulsion to speak. As a practical matter, the compulsion to speak in the isolated setting of the police station may well be greater than in courts or other official investigations, where there are often impartial observers to guard against intimidation or trickery.
. . .

III.

Today, then, there can be no doubt that the Fifth Amendment privilege is available outside of criminal court proceedings and serves to protect persons in all settings in which their freedom of action is curtailed in any significant way from being compelled to incriminate themselves. We have concluded that without proper safeguards the process of in-custody interrogation of persons suspected or accused of crime contains inherently compelling pressures which work to undermine the individual's will to resist and to compel him to speak where he would not otherwise do so freely. In order to combat these pressures and to permit a full opportunity to exercise the privilege against self-incrimination, the accused must be adequately and effectively apprised of his rights and the exercise of those rights must be fully honored.

It is impossible for us to foresee the potential alternatives for protecting the privilege which might be devised by Congress or the States in the exercise of their creative rule-making capacities. Therefore we cannot say that the Constitution necessarily requires adherence to any particular solution for the inherent compulsions of the interrogation process as it is presently conducted. Our decision in no way creates a constitutional straitjacket which will handicap sound efforts at reform, nor is it intended to have this effect. We encourage Congress and the States to continue their laudable search for increasingly effective ways of protecting the rights of the individual while promoting efficient enforcement of our criminal laws. However, unless we are shown other procedures which are at least as effective in apprising accused persons of their right of silence and in assuring a continuous opportunity to exercise it, the following safeguards must be observed.

At the outset, if a person in custody is to be subjected to interrogation, he must first be informed in clear and unequivocal terms that he has the right to remain silent. For those unaware of the privilege, the warning is needed simply to make them aware of it—the threshold requirement for an intelligent decision as to its exercise. More important, such a warning is an absolute prerequisite in overcoming the inherent pressures of the interrogation atmosphere. It is not just the subnormal or woefully ignorant who succumb to an interrogator's imprecations, whether implied or expressly stated, that the interrogation will continue until a confession is obtained or that silence in the face of accusation is itself damning and will bode ill when presented to a jury. Further, the warning will show the individual that his interrogators are prepared to recognize his privilege should he choose to exercise it.

. . .

The warning of the right to remain silent must be accompanied by the explanation that anything said can and will be used against the individual in court. This warning is needed in order to make him aware not only of the privilege, but also of the consequences of forgoing it. It is only through an awareness of these consequences that there can be any assurance of real understanding and intelligent exercise of the privilege. Moreover, this warning may serve to make the individual more acutely aware that he is faced with a phase of the adversary system—that he is not in the presence of persons acting solely in his interest.

The circumstances surrounding in-custody interrogation can operate very quickly to overbear the will of one merely made aware of his privilege by his interrogators. Therefore, the right to have counsel present at the interrogation is indispensable to the protection of the Fifth Amendment privilege under the system we delineate today. Our aim is to assure that the individual's right to choose between silence and speech remains unfettered throughout the interrogation process. A once-stated warning, delivered by those who will conduct the interrogation, cannot itself suffice to that end among those who most require knowledge of their rights. A mere warning given by the interrogators is not alone sufficient to accomplish that end. . . .

An individual need not make a pre-interrogation request for a lawyer. While such request affirmatively secures his right to have one, his failure to ask for a lawyer does not constitute a waiver. No effective waiver of the right to counsel during interrogation can be recognized unless specifically made after the warnings we here delineate have been given. The accused who does not know his rights and therefore does not make a request may be the person who most needs counsel. . . .

Accordingly we hold that an individual held for interrogation must be clearly informed that he has the right to consult with a lawyer and to have the lawyer with him during interrogation under the system for protecting the privilege we delineate today. As with the warnings of the right to remain silent and that anything stated can be used in evidence against him, this warning is an absolute prerequisite to interrogation. No amount of circumstantial evidence that the person may have been aware of this right will suffice to stand in its stead. Only through such a warning is there ascertainable assurance that the accused was aware of this right.

If an individual indicates that he wishes the assistance of counsel before any interrogation occurs, the authorities cannot rationally ignore or deny his request on the basis that the individual does not have or cannot afford a retained attorney. The financial ability of the individual has no relationship to the scope of the rights involved here. . . .

In order fully to apprise a person interrogated of the extent of his rights under this system then, it is necessary to warn him not only that he has the right to consult with an attorney, but also that if he is indigent a lawyer will be appointed to represent him. Without this additional warning, the admonition of the right to consult with counsel would often be understood as meaning only that he can consult with a lawyer if he has one or has the funds to obtain one. The warning of a right to counsel would be hollow if not couched in terms that would convey to the indigent—the person most often subjected to interrogation—the knowledge that he too has a right to have counsel present. As with the warnings of the right to remain silent and of the general right to counsel, only by effective and express explanation to the indigent of this right can there be assurance that he was truly in a position to exercise it.

Once warnings have been given, the subsequent procedure is clear. If the individual indicates in any manner, at any time prior to or during questioning, that he wishes to remain silent, the interrogation must cease. At this point he has shown that he intends to exercise his Fifth Amendment privilege; any statement taken after the person invokes his privilege cannot be other than the product of compulsion, subtle or otherwise. Without the right to cut off questioning, the setting of in-custody interrogation operates on the individual to overcome free choice in producing a statement after the privilege has been once invoked. If the individual states that he wants an attorney, the interrogation must cease until an attorney is present. At that time, the individual must have an opportunity to confer with the attorney and to have him present during any subsequent questioning. If the individual cannot obtain an attorney and he indicates that he wants one before speaking to police, they must respect his decision to remain silent.

. . .

If the interrogation continues without the presence of an attorney and a statement is taken, a heavy burden rests on the government to demonstrate that the defendant knowingly and intelligently waived his privilege against self-incrimination and his right to retained or appointed counsel. . . . Since the State is responsible for establishing the isolated circumstances under which the interrogation takes place and has the only means of making available corroborated evidence of warnings given during incommunicado interrogation, the burden is rightly on its shoulders.

An express statement that the individual is willing to make a statement and does not want an attorney followed closely by a statement could constitute a waiver. But a valid waiver will not be presumed simply from the silence of the accused after warnings are given or simply from the fact that a confession was in fact eventually obtained. . . . Moreover, where in-custody interrogation is involved, there is no room for the contention that the privilege is waived if the individual answers some questions or gives some information on his own prior to invoking his right to remain silent when interrogated.

. . .

The warnings required and the waiver necessary in accordance with our opinion today are, in the absence of a fully effective equivalent, prerequisites to the admissibility of any statment made by a defendant. No distinction can be drawn between statements which are direct confessions and statements which amount to "admissions" of part or all of an offense. The privilege against self-incrimination protects the individual from being compelled to incriminate himself in any manner; it does not distinguish degrees of incrimination. . . .

The principles announced today deal with the protection which must be given to the privilege against self-incrimination when the individual is first subjected to police interrogation while in custody at the station or otherwise deprived of his freedom of action in any significant way. It is at this point that our adversary system of criminal proceedings commences, distinguishing itself at the outset from the inquisitorial system recognized in some countries. Under the system of warnings we delineate today or under any other system which may be devised and found effective, the safeguards to be erected about the privilege must come into play at this point.

Our decision is not intended to hamper the traditional function of police officers in investigating crime. When an individual is in custody on probable cause, the police may, of course, seek out evidence in the field to be used at trial against him. Such investigation may include inquiry of persons not under restraint. General on-the-scene questioning as to facts surrounding a crime or other general questioning of citizens in the fact-finding process is not affected by our holding. It is an act of responsible citizenship for individuals to give whatever information they may have to aid in law enforcement. In such situations the compelling atmosphere inherent in the process of in-custody interrogation is not necessarily present.

In dealing with statements obtained through interrogation, we do not purport to find all confessions inadmissible. Confessions remain a proper element in law enforcement. Any statement given freely and voluntarily without any compelling influences is, of course, admissible in evidence. . . . There is no requirement that police stop a person who enters a police station and states that he wishes to confess to a crime, or a person who calls the police to offer a confession or any other statement he desires to make. Volunteered statements of any kind are not barred by the Fifth Amendment and their admissibility is not affected by our holding today.

To summarize, we hold that when an individual is taken into custody or otherwise deprived of his freedom by the authorities in any significant way and is subjected to questioning, the privilege against self-incrimination is jeopardized. Procedural safeguards must be employed to protect the privilege and unless other fully effective means are adopted to notify the person of his right of silence and to assure that the exercise of the right will be scrupulously honored, the following measures are required. He must be warned prior to any questioning that he has the right to remain silent, that anything he says can be used against him in a court of law, that he has the right to the presence of an attorney, and that if he cannot afford an attorney one will be appointed for him prior to any questioning if he so desires. Opportunity to exercise these rights must be afforded to him throughout the interrogation. After such warnings have been given, and such opportunity afforded him, the individual may knowingly and intelligently waive these rights and agree to answer questions or make a statement. But unless and until such warnings and waiver are demonstrated by the prosecution at trial, no evidence obtained as a result of interrogation can be used against him.

IV.

. . .

In announcing these principles, we are not unmindful of the burdens which law enforcement officials must bear, often under trying circumstances. We also fully recognize the obligation of all citizens to aid in enforcing the criminal laws. This Court, while prosecuting individual rights, has always given ample latitude to law enforcement agencies in the legitimate exercise of their duties. The limits we have placed on the interrogation process should not constitute an undue interference with a proper system of law enforcement. As we have noted, our decision does not in any way preclude police from carrying out their traditional investigatory functions. Although confessions may play an important role in some convictions, the cases before us present graphic examples of the overstatement of the "need" for confessions. . . .

Therefore, in accordance with the foregoing, the judgments of the Supreme Court of Arizona in No. 759, of the New York Court of Appeals in No. 760, and of the Court of Appeals for the Ninth Circuit in No. 761 are reversed. The judgment of the Supreme Court of California in No. 584 is affirmed.

It is so ordered.

Custodial Interrogation:
Michigan v. Mosley, 423 U.S. 96 (1975)

Mr. Justice STEWART delivered the opinion of the Court.

The respondent, Richard Bert Mosley, was arrested in Detroit, Mich., in the early afternoon of April 8, 1971, in connection with robberies that had recently occurred at the Blue Goose Bar and the White Tower Restaurant on that city's lower east side. The arresting officer, Detective James Cowie of the Armed Robbery Section of the Detroit Police Department, was acting on a tip implicating Mosley and three other men in the robberies. After effecting the arrest, Detective Cowie brought Mosley to the Robbery, Breaking and Entering Bureau of the Police Department, located on the fourth floor of the departmental headquarters building. The officer advised Mosley of his rights under this Court's decision in *Miranda v. Arizona*, 384 U.S. 436, and had him read and sign the department's constitutional rights notification certificate. After filling out the necessary arrest papers, Cowie began questioning Mosley about the robbery of the White Tower Restaurant. When Mosley said he did not want to answer any questions about the robberies, Cowie promptly ceased the interrogation. The completion of the arrest papers and the questioning of Mosley together took approximately 20 minutes. At no time during the questioning did Mosley indicate a desire to consult with a lawyer, and there is no claim that the procedures followed to this point did not fully comply with the strictures of the *Miranda* opinion. Mosley was then taken to a ninth-floor cell block.

Shorty after 6 p.m., Detective Hill of the Detroit Police Department Homicide Bureau brought Mosley from the cell block to the fifth-floor office of the Homicide Bureau for questioning about the fatal shooting of a man named Leroy Williams. Williams had been killed on January 9, 1971, during a holdup attempt outside the 101 Ranch Bar in Detroit. Mosley had not been arrested on this charge or interrogated about it by Detective Cowie. Before questioning Mosley about this homicide, Detective Hill carefully advised him of his "*Miranda* rights." Mosley read the notification form both silently and aloud, and Detective Hill then read and explained the warnings to him and had him sign the form. Mosley at first denied any involvement in the Williams murder, but after the officer told him that Anthony Smith had confessed to participating in the slaying and had named him as the "shooter," Mosley made a statement implicating himself in the homicide. The interrogation by Detective Hill lasted approximately 15 minutes, and at no time during its course did Mosley ask to consult with a lawyer or indicate that he did not want to discuss the homicide. In short, there is no claim that the procedures followed during Detective Hill's interrogation of Mosley, standing alone, did not fully comply with the strictures of the *Miranda* opinion.

Mosley was subsequently charged in a one-count information with first-degree murder. Before the trial he moved to suppress his incriminating statement on a number of grounds, among them the claim that under the doctrine of the *Miranda* case it was constitutionally impermissible for Detective Hill to question him about the Williams murder after he had told Detective Cowie that he did not want to answer any questions about the robberies. The trial court denied the motion to suppress after an evidentiary hearing, and the incriminating statement was subsequently introduced in evidence against Mosley at his trial. The jury convicted Mosley of first-degree murder, and the court imposed a mandatory sentence of life imprisonment.

. . . We granted the writ because of the important constitutional question presented.

In the *Miranda* case this Court promulgated a set of safeguards to protect the there-delineated constitutional rights of persons subjected to custodial police interrogation. In sum, the Court held in that case that unless law enforcement officers give certain specified warnings before questioning a person in custody, and follow certain specified procedures during the course of any subsequent interrogation, any statement made by the person in custody cannot over his objection be admitted in evidence against him as a defendant at trial, even though the statement may in fact be wholly voluntary. See *Michigan v. Tucker*, 417 U.S. 433, 443.

Neither party in the present case challenges the continuing validity of the *Miranda* decision, or of any of the so-called guidelines it established to protect what the Court there said was a person's constitutional privilege against compulsory self-incrimination. The issue in this case, rather, is whether the conduct of the Detroit police that led to Mosley's incriminating statement did in fact violate the *Miranda* "guidelines," so as to render the statement inadmissible in evidence against Mosley at his trial. Resolution of the question turns almost entirely on the interpretation of a single passage in the *Miranda* opinion, upon which the Michigan appellate court relied in finding a per se violation of *Miranda*:

> "Once warnings have been given, the subsequent procedure is clear. If the individual indicates in any manner, at any time prior to or during questioning, that he wishes to remain silent, the interrogation must cease. At this point, he has shown that he intends to exercise his Fifth Amendment privilege; any statement taken after the person invokes his privilege cannot be other than the product of compulsion, subtle or otherwise. Without the right to cut off questioning, the setting of in-custody interrogation operates on the individual to overcome free choice in producing a statement after the privilege has been once invoked." 384 U.S., at 473–474.

This passage states that "the interrogation must cease" when the person in custody indicates that "he wishes to remain silent." It does not state under what circumstances, if any, a resumption of questioning is permissible. The passage could be literally read to mean that a person who has invoked his "right to silence" can never again be subjected to custodial interrogation by any police officer at any time or place on any subject. Another possible construction of the passage would characterize "any statement taken after the person invokes his privilege" as "the product of compulsion" and would therefore mandate its exclusion from evidence, even if it were volunteered by the person in custody without any further interrogation whatever. Or the passage could be interpreted to require only the immediate cessation of questioning, and to permit a resumption of interrogation after a momentary respite.

It is evident that any of these possible literal interpretations would lead to absurd and unintended results. To permit the continuation of custodial interrogation after a momentary cessation would clearly frustrate the purposes of *Miranda* by allowing repeated rounds of questioning to undermine the will of the person being questioned. At the other extreme, a blanket prohibition against the taking of voluntary statements or a permanent immunity from further interrogation, regardless of the circumstances, would transform the *Miranda* safeguards into wholly irrational obstacles to legitimate police investigative activity, and deprive suspects of an opportunity to make informed and intelligent assessments of their interests. Clearly, therefore, neither this passage nor any other passage in the *Miranda* opinion can sensibly be read to create a per se proscription of indefinite duration upon any further questioning by any police officer on any subject, once the person in custody has indicated a desire to remain silent.

A reasonable and faithful interpretation of the *Miranda* opinion must rest on the intention of the Court in that case to adopt "fully effective means . . . to notify the person of his right of silence and to assure that the exercise of the right will be scrupulously honored. . . ." 384 U.S., at 479. The critical safeguard identified in the passage at issue is a person's "right to cut off questioning." Through the exercise of his option to terminate questioning he can control the time at which questioning occurs, the subjects discussed, and the duration of the interrogation. The requirement that law enforcement authorities must respect a person's exercise of that option counteracts the coercive pressures of the custodial setting. We therefore conclude that the admissibility of statements obtained after the person in custody has decided to remain silent depends under *Miranda* on whether his "right to cut off questioning" was "scrupulously honored."

A review of the circumstances leading to Mosley's confession reveals that his "right to cut off questioning" was fully respected in this case. Before his initial interrogation, Mosley was carefully advised that he was under no obligation to answer any questions and could remain silent if he wished. He orally acknowledged that he understood the *Miranda* warnings and then signed a printed notification-of-rights form. When Mosley stated that he did not want to discuss the robberies, Detective Cowie immediately ceased the interrogation and did not try either to resume the questioning or in any way to persuade Mosley to reconsider his position. After an interval of more than two hours, Mosley was questioned by another police officer at another location about an unrelated holdup murder. He was given full and complete *Miranda* warnings at the outset of the second interrogation. He was thus reminded again that he could remain silent and could consult with a lawyer, and was carefully given a full and fair opportunity to exercise these options. The subsequent questioning did not undercut Mosley's previous decision not to answer Detective Cowie's inquiries. Detective Hill did not resume the interrogation about the White Tower

Restaurant robbery or inquire about the Blue Goose Bar robbery, but instead focused exclusively on the Leroy Williams homicide, a crime different in nature and in time and place of occurrence from the robberies for which Mosley had been arrested and interrogated by Detective Cowie. Although it is not clear from the record how much Detective Hill knew about the earlier interrogation, his questioning of Mosley about an unrelated homicide was quite consistent with a reasonable interpretation of Mosley's earlier refusal to answer any questions about the robberies.

This is not a case, therefore, where the police failed to honor a decision of a person in custody to cut off questioning, either by refusing to discontinue the interrogation upon request or by persisting in repeated efforts to wear down his resistance and make him change his mind. In contrast to such practices, the police here immediately ceased the interrogation, resumed questioning only after the passage of a significant period of time and the provision of a fresh set of warnings, and restricted the second interrogation to a crime that had not been a subject of the earlier interrogation.

. . .

For these reasons, we conclude that the admission in evidence of Mosley's incriminating statements did not violate the principles of *Miranda v. Arizona*. Accordingly, the judgment of the Michigan Court of Appeals is vacated, and the case is remanded to that court for further proceedings not inconsistent with this opinion.

It is so ordered.

Noncustodial Interrogation:
Oregon v. Mathiason, *429 U.S. 492 (1977)*

PER CURIAM.

Respondent Carl Mathiason was convicted of first-degree burglary after a bench trial in which his confession was critical to the State's case. At trial he moved to suppress the confession as the fruit of questioning by the police not preceded by the warnings required in *Miranda v. Arizona*, 384 U.S. 436 (1966). The trial court refused to exclude the confession because it found that Mathiason was not in custody at the time of the confession.

The Oregon Court of Appeals affirmed respondent's conviction, but on his petition for review in the Supreme Court of Oregon that court by a divided vote reversed the conviction. It found that although Mathiason had not been arrested or otherwise formally detained, "the interrogation took place in a 'coercive environment'" of the sort to which *Miranda* was intended to apply. . . . The State of Oregon has petitioned for certiorari to review the judgment of the Supreme Court of Oregon. We think that court has read *Miranda* too broadly, and we therefore reverse its judgment.

The Supreme Court of Oregon described the factual situation surrounding the confession as follows:

> "An officer of the State Police investigated a theft at a residence near Pendleton. He asked the lady of the house which had been burglarized if she suspected anyone. She replied that the defendant was the only one she could think of. The defendant was a parolee and a 'close associate' of her son. The officer tried to contact defendant on three or four occasions with no success. Finally, about 25 days after the burglary,

the officer left his card at defendant's apartment with a note asking him to call because 'I'd like to discuss something with you.' The next afternoon the defendant did call. The officer asked where it would be convenient to meet. The defendant had no preference; so the officer asked if the defendant could meet him at the state patrol office in about an hour and a half, about 5:00 p.m. The patrol office was about two blocks from defendant's apartment. The building housed several state agencies.

"The officer met defendant in the hallway, shook hands and took him into an office. The defendant was told he was not under arrest. The door was closed. The two sat across a desk. The police radio in another room could be heard. The officer told defendant he wanted to talk to him about a burglary and that his truthfulness would possibly be considered by the district attorney or judge. The officer further advised that the police believed defendant was involved in the burglary and [falsely stated that] defendant's fingerprints were found at the scene. The defendant sat for a few minutes and then said he had taken the property. This occurred within five minutes after defendant had come to the office. The officer then advised defendant of his *Miranda* rights and took a taped confession.

"At the end of the taped conversation the officer told defendant he was not arresting him at this time; he was released to go about his job and return to his family. The officer said he was referring the case to the district attorney for him to determine whether criminal charges would be brought. It was 5:30 p.m. when the defendant left the office.

"The officer gave all the testimony relevant to this issue. The defendant did not take the stand either at the hearing on the motion to suppress or at the trial."

. . .

Our decision in *Miranda* set forth rules of police procedure applicable to "custodial interrogation." "By custodial interrogation, we mean questioning initiated by law enforcement officers after a person has been taken into custody or otherwise deprived of his freedom of action in any significant way." 384 U.S., at 444. Subsequently we have found the *Miranda* principle applicable to questioning which takes place in a prison setting during a suspect's term of imprisonment on a separate offense, *Mathis v. United States,* 391 U.S. 1 (1968), and to questioning taking place in a suspect's home, after he has been arrested and is no longer free to go where he pleases. *Orozco v. Texas,* 394 U.S. 324 (1969).

In the present case, however, there is no indication that the questioning took place in a context where respondent's freedom to depart was restricted in any way. He came voluntarily to the police station, where he was immediately informed that he was not under arrest. At the close of a one half-hour interview respondent did in fact leave the police station without hindrance. It is clear from these facts that Mathiason was not in custody "or otherwise deprived of his freedom of action in any significant way."

Such a noncustodial situation is not converted to one in which *Miranda* applies simply because a reviewing court concludes that, even in the absence of any formal arrest or restraint on freedom of movement, the questioning took place in a "coercive environment." Any interview of one suspected of a crime by a police officer will have coercive aspects to it, simply by virtue of the fact that the police officer is part of a law enforcement system which may ultimately cause the suspect to be charged with a crime. But police officers are not required to administer *Miranda* warnings to everyone whom they question. Nor is the requirement of warnings to be imposed simply because the questioning takes place in the station house, or because the questioned person is one whom the police suspect. *Miranda* warnings are required only where there has been such a restriction on a person's freedom as to render him "in custody." It was that sort of coercive environment to which *Miranda* by its terms was made applicable, and to which it is limited.

The officer's false statement about having discovered Mathiason's fingerprints at the scene was found by the Supreme Court of Oregon to be another circumstance contributing to the coercive environment which makes the *Miranda* rationale applicable. Whatever relevance this fact may have to other issues in the case, it has nothing to do with whether respondent was in custody for purposes of the *Miranda* rule.

The petition for certiorari is granted, the judgment of the Oregon Supreme Court is reversed, and the case is remanded for proceedings not inconsistent with this opinion.

The Use of Confession for Impeachment: Harris v. New York, *401 U.S. 222 (1971)*

Mr. Chief Justice BURGER delivered the opinion of the Court.

We granted the writ in this case to consider petitioner's claim that a statement made by him to police under circumstances rendering it inadmissible to establish the prosecution's case in chief under *Miranda v. Arizona* may not be used to impeach his credibility.

The State of New York charged petitioner in a two-count indictment with twice selling heroin to an undercover police officer. At a subsequent jury trial the officer was the State's chief witness, and he testified as to details of the two sales. A second officer verified collateral details of the sales, and a third offered testimony about the chemical analysis of the heroin.

Petitioner took the stand in his own defense. He admitted knowing the undercover police officer but denied a sale on January 4, 1966. He admitted making a sale of contents of a glassine bag to the officer on January 6 but claimed it was baking powder and part of a scheme to defraud the purchaser.

On cross-examination petitioner was asked seriatim whether he had made specified statements to the police immediately following his arrest on January 7—statements that partially contradicted petitioner's direct testimony at trial. In response to the cross-examination, petitioner testified that he could not remember virtually any of the questions or answers recited by the prosecutor. At the request of petitioner's counsel the written statement from which the prosecutor had read questions and answers in his impeaching process was placed in the record for possible use on appeal; the statement was not shown to the jury.

The trial judge instructed the jury that the statements attributed to petitioner by the prosecution could be considered only in passing on petitioner's credibility and not as evidence of guilt. In closing summations both counsel argued the substance of the impeaching statements. The jury then found petitioner guilty on the second count of the indictment. . . .

At trial the prosecution made no effort in its case in chief to use the statements allegedly made by petitioner, conceding that they were inadmissible under *Miranda v. Arizona.* The transcript of the interrogation used in the impeachment, but not given to the jury, shows that no warning of a right to appointed counsel was given before questions were put to petitioner when he was taken into custody. Petitioner makes no claim that the statements made to the police were coerced or involuntary.

Some comments in the *Miranda* opinion can indeed by read as indicating a bar to use of an uncounseled statement for any purpose, but discussion of that issue was not at all necessary to the Court's holding and cannot be regarded as controlling. *Miranda* barred the prosecution from making its case with statements of an accused made while in custody prior to having or effectively waiving counsel. It does not follow from *Miranda* that evidence inadmissible against an accused in the prosecution's case in chief is barred for all purposes, provided of course that the trustworthiness of the evidence satisfies legal standards.

In *Walder v. United States,* 347 U.S. 62 (1954), the Court permitted physical evidence, inadmissible in the case in chief, to be used for impeachment purposes.
. . .

It is true that Walder was impeached as to collateral matters included in his direct examination, whereas petitioner here was impeached as to testimony bearing more directly on the crimes charged. We are not persuaded that there is a difference in principle that warrants a result different from that reached by the Court in *Walder.* Petitioner's testimony in his own behalf concerning the events of January 7 contrasted sharply with what he told the police shortly after his arrest. The impeachment process here undoubtedly provided valuable aid to the jury in assessing petitioner's credibility, and the benefits of this process should not be lost, in our view, because of the speculative possibility that impermissible police conduct will be encouraged thereby. Assuming that the exclusionary rule has a deterrent effect on proscribed police conduct, sufficient deterrence flows when the evidence in question is made unavailable to the prosecution in its case in chief.

Every criminal defendant is privileged to testify in his own defense, or to refuse to do so. But that privilege cannot be construed to include the right to commit perjury. Having voluntarily taken the stand, petitioner was under an obligation to speak truthfully and accurately, and the prosecution here did no more than utilize the traditional truth-testing devices of the adversary process. Had inconsistent statements been made by the accused to some third person, it could hardly be contended that the conflict could not be laid before the jury by way of cross-examination and impeachment.

The shield provided by *Miranda* cannot be perverted into a license to use perjury by way of a defense, free from the risk of confrontation with prior inconsistent utterances. We hold, therefore, that petitioner's credibility was appropriately impeached by use of his earlier conflicting statements.

Affirmed.

Compulsory Disclosure:
California v. Byers, *402 U.S. 424 (1971)*

Mr. Chief Justice BURGER announced the judgment of the Court and an opinion in which Mr. Justice STEWART, Mr. Justice WHITE, and Mr. Justice BLACKMUN join.

This case presents the narrow but important question of whether the constitutional privilege against compulsory self-incrimination is infringed by California's so-called "hit and run" statute which requires the driver of a motor vehicle involved in an accident to stop at the scene and give his name and address. Similar "hit and run" or "stop and report" statutes are in effect in all 50 States and the District of Columbia.

On August 22, 1966, respondent Byers was charged in a two-count criminal complaint with two misdemeanor violations of the California Vehicle Code. Count 1 charged that on August 20 Byers passed another vehicle without maintaining the "safe distance" required by § 21750 (Supp. 1971). The second count charged that Byers had been involved in án accident but had failed to stop and identify himself as required by § 20002(a)(1) (Supp. 1971).

This statute provides:

> "The driver of any vehicle involved in an accident resulting in damage to any property including vehicles shall immediately stop the vehicle at the scene of the accident and shall then and there . . . locate and notify the owner or person in charge of such property of the name and address of the driver and owner of the vehicle involved. . . ."

It is stipulated that both charges arose out of the same accident.

Byers demurred to Count 2 on the ground that it violated his privilege against compulsory self-incrimination. His position was ultimately sustained by the California Supreme Court. That court held that the privilege protected a driver who "reasonably believes that in self-incrimination." Here the court found that Byers' apprehensions were reasonable because compliance with § 20002(a)(1) confronted him with "substantial hazards of self-incrimination." Nevertheless the court upheld the validity of the statute by inserting a judicially created use restriction on the disclosures that it required. The court concluded, however, that it would be "unfair" to punish Byers for his failure to comply with the statute because he could not reasonably have anticipated the judicial promulgation of the use restriction. We granted certiorari to assess the validity of the California Supreme Court's premise that without a use restriction § 20002(a)(1) would violate the privilege against compulsory self-incrimination. We conclude that there is no conflict between the statute and the privilege.

(1)

Whenever the Court is confronted with the question of a compelled disclosure that has an incriminating potential, the judicial scrutiny is invariably a close one. Tension between the State's demand for disclosures and the protection of the right against self-incrimination is likely to give rise to serious questions. Inevitably these must be resolved in terms of balancing the public need on the one hand, and the individual claim to constitutional protections on the other; neither interest can be treated lightly.

An organized society imposes many burdens on its constituents. It commands the filing of tax returns for income; it requires producers and distributors of consumer goods to file informational reports on the manufacturing process and the content of products, on the wages, hours, and working conditions of employees. Those who borrow money on the public market or issue securities for sale to the public must file various information reports; industries must report periodically the volume and content of pollutants discharged into our waters and atmosphere. Comparable examples are legion.

In each of these situations there is some possibility of prosecution—often a very real one—for criminal offenses disclosed by or deriving from the information that the law compels a person to supply. Information revealed by these reports could well be "a link in the chain" of evidence leading to prosecution and conviction. But under our holdings the mere possibility of incrimination is insufficient to defeat the strong policies in favor of a disclosure called for by statutes like the one challenged here.
. . .

Although the California Vehicle Code defines some criminal offenses, the statute is essentially regulatory, not criminal. The California Supreme Court noted that § 20002(a)(1) was not intended to facilitate criminal convictions but to promote the satisfaction of civil liabilities arising from automobile accidents. In *Marchetti* the Court rested on the reality that almost everything connected with gambling is illegal under "comprehensive" state and federal statutory schemes. The Court noted that in almost every conceivable situation compliance with the statutory gambling requirements would have been incriminating. Largely because of these pervasive criminal prohibitions, gamblers were considered by the Court to be "a highly selective group inherently suspect of criminal activities."

In contrast, § 20002(a)(1), like income tax laws, is directed at all persons—here all persons who drive automobiles in California. This group, numbering as it does in the millions, is so large as to render § 20002(a)(1) a statute "directed at the public at large." It is difficult to consider this group as either "highly selective" or "inherently suspect of criminal activities." Driving an automobile, unlike gambling, is a lawful activity. Moreover, it is not a criminal offense under California law to be a driver "involved in an accident." An accident may be the fault of others; it may occur without any driver having been at fault. No empirical data are suggested in support of the conclusion that there is a relevant correlation between being a driver and criminal prosecution of drivers. So far as any available information instructs us, most accidents occur without creating criminal liability even if one or both of the drivers are guilty of negligence as a matter of tort law.

The disclosure of inherently illegal activity is inherently risky. Our decisions in *Albertson* and the cases following illustrate that truism. But disclosures with respect to automobile accidents simply do not entail the kind of substantial risk of self-incrimination involved in *Marchetti, Grosso,* and *Haynes.* Furthermore, the statutory purpose is noncriminal and self-reporting is indispensable to its fulfillment.

(2)

Even if we were to view the statutory reporting requirement as incriminating in the traditional sense, in our view it would be the "extravagant" extension of the privilege Justice Holmes warned against to hold that it is testimonial in the Fifth Amendment sense. Compliance with § 20002(a)(1) requires two things: first, a driver involved in an accident is required to stop at the scene; second, he is required to give his name and address. The act of stopping is no more testimonial—indeed less so in some respects—than requiring a person in custody to stand or walk in a police lineup, to speak prescribed words, or to give samples of handwriting, fingerprints, or blood. Disclosure of name and address is an essentially neutral act. Whatever the collateral consequences of disclosing name and address, the statutory purpose is to implement the state police power to regulate use of motor vehicles.

. . .

Stopping in compliance with § 20002(a)(1) therefore does not provide the State with "evidence of a testimonial or communicative nature" within the meaning of the Constitution. It merely provides the State and private parties with the driver's identity for, among other valid state needs, the study of causes of vehicle accidents and related purposes, always subject to the driver's right to assert a Fifth Amendment privilege concerning specific inquiries.

Respondent argues that since the statutory duty to stop is imposed only on the "driver of any vehicle involved in an accident," a driver's compliance is testimonial because his action gives rise to an inference that he believes that he was the "driver of [a] vehicle involved in an accident." From this, the respondent tells us, it can be further inferred that he was indeed the operator of an "accident involved" vehicle.

. . .

After having stopped, a driver involved in an accident is required by § 20002(a) (1) to notify the driver of the other vehicle of his name and address. A name, linked with a motor vehicle, is no more incriminating than the tax return, linked with the disclosure of income, in *United States v. Sullivan,* supra. It identifies but does not by itself implicate anyone in criminal conduct.

Although identity, when made known, may lead to inquiry that in turn leads to arrest and charge, those developments depend on different factors and independent evidence. Here the compelled disclosure of identity could have led to a charge that might not have been made had the driver fled the scene; but this is true only in the same sense that a taxpayer can be charged on the basis of the contents of a tax return or failure to file an income tax form. There is no constitutional right to refuse to file an income tax return or to flee the scene of an accident in order to avoid the possibility of legal involvement.

The judgment of the California Supreme Court is vacated and the case is remanded for further proceedings not inconsistent with this opinion.

Vacated and remanded.

ᵉ⸲ 5 ᵉ⸲

Indictment
by
Grand Jury

> No person shall be held to an-
> swer for a capital, or otherwise infamous crime, unless on a
> presentment or indictment of a Grand Jury, except in cases
> arising in the land or naval forces, or in the Militia, when in
> actual service in time of War or public danger.
>
> —Fifth Amendment

THE ORIGINS OF THE GRAND JURY

It would be difficult to find an institution in criminal justice that has suffered
a fate similar to the grand jury. What other institution has been so lavishly
extolled as a defense against tyranny only to be dismissed by reformers from
Jeremy Bentham to Roscoe Pound as a piece of useless antiquarian baggage?
Although the movement to abolish the grand jury appears to have at least
temporarily subsided, it has left in its wake considerable doubts about this
old and venerable institution.

The grand jury is Carlovingian in its origins and was brought to England
by the Normans. As a formal method of public accusation, it gradually replaced
the judicial committee of the sheriff's town[1] and came into widespread use
during the reign of Henry II. In the Assize of Clarendon,[2] 1166, Henry II
and his barons legislated that

> for the preservation of peace and the maintenance of justice enquiries be
> made throughout each county and hundred by twelve legal men of the hun-

191

dred and four legal men from each township upon their oath to tell the truth if in their hundred or their township there be any man who is accused of or generally suspected of being a robber or murderer or thief, or any man who is a receiver of robbers, murderers or thieves since our lord the king was king.[3]

From the time of the Assize of Clarendon and the Assize or Northampton (1176), the grand jury has been a remarkably stable institution. It was closely associated with the rise of itinerant crown justice and as such was a part of the centralizing movement begun by the Norman kings. Henry II undoubtedly viewed the grand jury not only as a method for enforcing order in an unruly kingdom, but as a means of answering questions about land tenure, thereby ensuring that the crown would receive its just royal revenues.[4] Like the sheriff's inquest, the grand jury was a sworn body of local citizens with inquisitional powers. As an accusatorial body, the grand jury did not determine guilt or innocence, although for some time an accusation had the practical effect of declaring guilt.[5] At least after the establishment of the petit jury, the grand jury's formal function was to determine whether sufficient probable cause existed to merit endorsing the Crown's request for an indictment or to issue on its own initiative a presentment. It was never an adversary body, and those accused by grand juries were never accorded the right either to appear or to present counterclaims. And so it has remained, a Norman vestige of the continental system of inquisitorial procedure.

When the English settled in America, they brought with them the grand jury. It became intimately associated with local government, often acting as an overseer of the government and as an instrument of protection against royal and absentee control.[6] By the time of the Revolution, the grand jury was firmly established as a common-law institution, and at least two of the new states incorporated a grand jury provision in their new constitutions. Although no provision was made for the grand jury in the original federal Constitution, in 1789 it was incorporated into the Bill of Rights, and, in the Judiciary Act of 1789, Congress provided that grand juries attend the newly created federal circuit and district courts.[7]

Although the grand jury has survived for over eight hundred years,[8] it is not surprising that it has come under heavy attack. First, the grand jury, although widely used, has never been the sole means of criminal accusation. "Appeal," or accusation by a private party, was widely used for a variety of crimes and only gradually merged into tort law or came into disuse.[9] Furthermore, by 1494, criminal information by the Crown existed as a third method of accusation, becoming increasingly common after 1689.[10] Originally limited to misdemeanors, criminal informations enabled the prosecution to seek trial solely on its own motion without an independent determination of probable cause. The administrative ease of informations reflected adversely on the more cumbersome and time-consuming grand jury system.

Finally, the attack on the grand jury is in part an outgrowth of the contradictory forces that have propelled the institution from the outset. The grand jury has always been both a popular instrument of local control and an instrument of the Crown or the prosecution. Support of the institution was largely a result of the former. Particularly during the reign of the Stuarts, the grand jury came to be viewed as a bulwark against royal oppression. For example, the refusal of the grand jury to indict the Earl of Shaftsbury for treason against Charles II in 1681 was the cause of popular rejoicing.[11] And as late as the middle of the nineteenth century, Chief Justice Shaw of the Massachusetts Supreme Court praised the grand jury in these words:

> The right of individual citizens to be secure from an open and public accusation of crime, and from the trouble, expense and anxiety of a public trial before a probable cause is established by the presentment and indictment of a grand jury, in case of high offenses, is justly regarded as one of the securities to the innocent against hasty, malicious and oppressive public prosecutions, and as one of the ancient immunities and privileges of English liberty.[12]

But the other aspect of the grand jury has been its long association with the prosecution. Whatever may have been the case in a more rural and legally less complicated era, the fact is that today grand juries rarely act independently of the prosecutor. The growing anonymity of urban life coupled with the increasing complexity of the criminal law have contributed to the decline of the grand jury as a cohesive group of local townspeople and to its inability to function independently as an agency for the determination of probable cause. The result has been charges of costliness and inefficient rubber-stamping.[13]

This prosecutorial domination[14] raises a question: Is the grand jury an appropriate instrument for the protection of individual liberty against executive abuses of discretion? Former U.S. Senator Charles Goodell has argued that during the Nixon administration, federal grand juries under the domination of federal prosecutors became the latter-day equivalent of the now moribund congressional committees that once hunted witches and spies. Indeed, Goodell charged that "grand juries have always served the interests of whichever political element could control them. . . . The problem is not that the grand jury has ceased to be what it never actually was. It is that prosecutors who have repressive purposes in mind are virtually unchecked in abusing the panel's compulsory process and its role of secrecy."[15]

We might challenge the scope of this charge by pointing to the work of the federal grand juries in the Watergate affair. However, it is far from clear just what inferences can be made from the proceedings of all of the Watergate-related grand juries. The federal prosecutor's original submission to the grand jury in the first Watergate indictments failed to go to the heart of the conspiracy, and it was largely through the probing efforts of the trial judge, John Sirica, that the greater conspiracy was uncovered. In any event, a concern about prosecutorial abuse of power has led some to advocate grand jury reform, especially at the federal level.

APPLICATION FOR THE STATES

Given the controversy surrounding the institution, it is not surprising that the Supreme Court has repeatedly refused to impose a grand jury requirement on the states. In *Hurtado v. California* (1884), where the Court was asked to hold that a bill of information did not satisfy the requirements of due process and that settled usage and custom demanded indictment, the Court replied:

> But to hold that such a characteristic is essentially due process of law, would be to deny every quality of the law but its age, and to render it incapable of progress or improvement. It would be to stamp upon our jurisprudence the unchangeableness attributed to the laws of the Medes and Persians.
>
> This would be all the more singular and surprising, in this quick and active age, when we consider that, owing to the progressive development of legal ideas and institutions in England, the words of the Magna Charta stood for very different things at the time of the separation of the American Colonies from what they represented originally.[16]

In *Hurtado*, the Court endorsed a broad definition of due process, holding that legislatures were free to devise criminal procedures so long as the legislation was not arbitrary. Any legislation that preserved the principles of liberty and justice would meet the standards of due process. Judged by this broad ruling, California's system of informations, accompanied by a preliminary examination and the surrounding rights of counsel and cross-examination, satisfied due process.[17] Since 1884, the decision has been reaffirmed on at least seven occasions,[18] and as recently as 1972 the Court indicated by dictum that *Hurtado* would not soon be reexamined.[19]

However strong the case against the grand jury may be, it is not likely that the constitutional requirement will be dropped at the federal level, if for no other reason than not to set a fearful precedent of amending the Bill of Rights. Of course, federal criminal cases constitute only a small percentage of the criminal cases filed annually in the United States. Thus the application of the constitutional requirement to the federal arena is of relatively minor importance. On the other hand, half of the states, mainly those east of the Mississippi River, still make extensive use of the grand jury. Although the law governing grand juries varies from state to state, many of the major features of state grand juries are similar to the following features of the federal grand jury:

1. *Capital and infamous crimes.* The Fifth Amendment requirement of indictment applies only to capital and infamous crimes. An *infamous crime* is defined not by the character of the crime, but rather by the potential punish-

ment that could be imposed. The general rule is that when the accused could be subjected to punishment of imprisonment in excess of one year, or imprisonment at hard labor, indictment by grand jury rather than by information is required, unless indictment is waived.[20] For the calendar year 1973, there were 29,152 criminal cases commenced in federal district courts by indictment, and 10,375 by information.[21]

2. *Size.* The federal grand jury may range from sixteen to twenty-three members, and a true bill may be reported only with the concurrence of at least twelve members of the panel.[22]

3. *Selection and voting.* Under provisions of the Jury Selection and Service Act of 1968,[23] grand jury panels must be selected on a random basis from a list of registered voters in a given federal judicial district. To achieve a cross-section, a voter list may be supplemented in a given district by sources of names other than those on the list. The methods for selecting members of state grand juries are, of course, not generally controlled by federal legislation. However, if a state elects to use a grand jury in criminal proceedings, then the state may not systematically or arbitrarily exclude identifiable groups from the grand jury. Indeed, since 1875, it has been a federal criminal offense to exclude from grand or petit jury service, in *any* court of the United States or any state, an otherwise qualified individual because of race, color, or previous condition of servitude.[24] Furthermore, the Supreme Court has long held that racial or ethnic bias in grand jury selection implicates the constitutional values of due process and equal protection.[25]

4. *Powers and duties.* A grand jury is an inquisitorial agency with plenary powers to investigate, charge, and report on criminal offenses. The breadth of the grand jury's power is captured in the following lines of Justice Brown's opinion in *Hale v. Henkel* (1906):

> The oath of a grand juryman—and his oath is the commission under which he acts—assigns no limits, except those marked by diligence itself, to the course of his inquiries: Why, then, should it be circumscribed by more contracted boundaries? Shall diligent inquiry be enjoined? And shall the means and opportunities of inquiry be prohibited or restrained? . . .
>
> We deem it entirely clear that under the practice in this country, at least, the examination of witnesses need not be preceded by a presentment or indictment formally drawn up, but that the grand jury may proceed, either upon their own knowledge or upon the examination of witnesses, to inquire for themselves whether a crime cognizable by the court has been committed; that the result of their investigations may be subsequently embodied in an indictment, and that, in summoning witnesses, it is quite sufficient to apprise them of the names of the parties with respect to whom they will be called to testify, without indicating the nature of the charge against them.[26]

The proceedings of a grand jury are secret and present only the prosecutor's position. No one under investigation by a grand jury is entitled to know the nature of the investigation or to be present. And no one who is present is entitled to have counsel or to cross-examine other witnesses. Because the grand jury's function is not to determine guilt or innocence, but rather to determine whether there is probable cause that a crime has been committed by an individual named by the prosecution or by the panel, the constitutional rights of witnesses are limited by the nonadversary nature of the proceedings. As the Supreme Court noted over half a century ago:

> The witness is bound not only to attend, but to tell what he knows in answer to questions framed for the purpose of bringing out the truth of the matter under inquiry.
>
> He is not entitled to urge objections of incompetency or irrelevancy, such as a party might raise, for this is no concern of his. . . .
>
> On familiar principles, he is not entitled to challenge the authority of the court or of the grand jury, provided they have a de facto existence and organization.
>
> He is not entitled to set limits to the investigation that the grand jury may conduct. . . . It is a grand inquest, a body with powers of investigation and inquisition, the scope of whose inquiries is not to be limited narrowly by questions of propriety or forecasts of the probable result of the investigation, or by doubts whether any particular individual will be found properly subject to an accusation of crime. As has been said before, the identity of the offender, and the precise nature of the offense, if there be one, normally are developed at the conclusion of the grand jury's labors, not at the beginning.[27]

A witness may have the protection of the right against self-incrimination and may, on occasion, be entitled to assert the privilege of confidential matters.[28] Also, one charged in an indictment is entitled to a copy of the indictment, which must contain the essential facts of the offense charged, but an individual cannot attack the indictment on the basis of the competence or legality of the evidence used in support of the indictment. The Supreme Court has held that the indictment may be based entirely on hearsay evidence, or on illegally obtained evidence, or on legally incompetent evidence.[29] In short, the grand jury is not bound by the technical procedures and evidentiary rules that govern an adversary proceeding. In fact, we might question whether an indictment may be challenged on the basis of a total lack of any evidence sufficient to warrant a true bill.[30]

DUE PROCESS AND THE CHARGING SYSTEM

The failure of the grand jury to work as an effective check against hasty and unwarranted prosecutions has left a curious void in criminal due process. *Hurtado* and its progeny have left the states free to devise their own systems for initiating criminal prosecutions.[31] States are free to use indictments, informations, or, as many jurisdictions do, preliminary examinations coupled with informations. Yet the methods used for initiating criminal prosecutions and detaining an individual for trial have important implications for due process.

Presumably, one function of due process is to prevent erroneous and arbitrary determinations of personal rights. Thus, the Supreme Court has held that due process requires a hearing for the revocation of probation,[32] for the termination of welfare benefits,[33] and for the revocation of a driver's license.[34] Yet the Court has been reluctant to establish any minimal due process standard in the charging area. Surely the decision by the state to file a formal criminal accusation against an individual is at least as serious as the revocation of a driver's license. The mere filing of a criminal accusation carries with it a certain social stigma and additionally implies that the accused and his or her family will face a number of burdens in defending against the charges. Unless we assume that all persons formally accused are guilty in fact and law, then due process would appear to require some minimal protections against hasty and unwarranted accusations.

Although it is true that a preliminary examination or hearing is necessary, in some form or other, for felony cases in every state,[35] still the variations are enormous. Many have been characterized as "backward models,"[36] emphasizing the legality of the detention first and focusing backward to the crime and the arrest. Their standard for binding over for trial is probable cause for arrest. These proceedings are generally nonadversary, with magistrates exercising a limited role and with defendants exercising few trial-like rights. The only federally protected constitutional right of defendants is to counsel.[37]

These preliminary hearings approximate the present statutorily mandated federal preliminary hearing and have been implicitly endorsed by the Supreme Court.[38] In *Gerstein v. Pugh*[39] (1975), the Supreme Court struck down a Florida procedure whereby one arrested without a warrant and charged by information might be detained for trial without any judicial determination of *probable cause for detention*. Although ruling that an accused was entitled under the Fourth Amendment to a nonadversary judicial determination of probable cause, the majority held that the determination was not critical within the meaning of prior decisions[40] and that the standard to be applied was the same as in probable cause for arrest. The majority then observed:

> In holding that the prosecutor's assessment of probable cause is not sufficient alone to justify restraint on liberty pending trial, we do not imply that the accused is entitled to judicial oversight or review of the decision to prosecute. Instead, we adhere to the Court's prior holding that a judicial hearing is not prerequisite to prosecution by information.[41]

The opinion seems to close the door, for the present, to any due process requirement of a preliminary hearing. There may come a time, however, when the Court will listen to arguments that favor an adversary-type preliminary hearing (similar to that which now obtains in California), which offers numerous advantages to both prosecution and defense.[42]

CONCLUSION

The decision to charge a suspect with a crime carries with it immense implications, and this decision is almost entirely at the discretion of the prosecutor.[43] If the grand jury is as much a tool of the executive as commentators have suggested, then the absence of a constitutionally mandated requirement of a preliminary hearing raises a serious question about the need for an appropriate set of controls on prosecutorial discretion. Given the widespread entries of guilty pleas and the minimal judicial role in the acceptance of such pleas, pretrial procedure becomes de facto the only procedure for most defendants. Although most jurisdictions statutorily provide for a degree of judicial oversight of the prosecutor's decision to charge, the quality of the oversight, particularly as to the sufficiency, competence, and credibility of the evidence, varies. To dismiss this issue, as a majority of the Supreme Court did in *Gerstein*, implies that the system of criminal justice in America has more discretion than would appear to be healthy in a constitutional society.[44]

NOTES

1. James Fitzjames Stephen, *A History of the Criminal Law in England* (London: Macmillan, 1883), vol. 1, pp. 68, 244–272.

2. Although an assize is normally a court, the Assize of Clarendon was simply a meeting of Henry II and his chief barons, at which they agreed to certain criminal procedures.

3. Quoted in William Holdsworth, *A History of English Law* (London: Methuen, 1938), vol. 1, p. 77.

4. Ibid. at 313.

5. Stephen, *History of the Criminal Law*, vol. 1, pp. 250–254. See below, pp 331.

6. See Richard A. Youngner, *The People's Panel* (Providence, R.I.: Brown University Press, 1963), chap. 2.

7. Ibid., at 45–46.

8. The grand jury was abolished in England in 1933.

9. Stephen, *History of the Criminal Law*, vol. 1, pp. 244–250.

10. Ibid. at 294–296.

11. *Proceedings Against the Earl of Shaftsbury*, 8 How. St. Tr. 759 (1681).

12. *Jones v. Robbins*, 74 Mass. Rep. 329 (1857).

13. E.g., Wayne Morse, "A Survey of the Grand Jury System," 10 *Ore. L. Rev.* 101, 363 (1931); and Raymond Molley, "Initiation of Criminal Prosecutions by Indictment or Information," 29 *Mich. L. Rev.* 403 (1931). Cf. George Dession, "From Indictment to Information: Implications of the Shift," 42 *Yale L.J.* 163 (1932).

14. E.g., see Roger Brice, "Grand Jury Proceedings: The Prosecutor, the Trial Judge, and Undue Influence," 39 *U. Chi. L. Rev.* 761 (1972).

15. Charles E. Goodell, "Where Did the Grand Jury Go?" *Harper's*, vol. 246 (May 1973), p. 23. Copyright © 1973 by Charles Goodell.

16. *Hurtado v. California*, 110 U.S. 516, 529 (1884).

17. Ibid. at 538.

18. *McNulty v. California*, 149 U.S. 645 (1893); *Hodgson v. Vermont*, 168 U.S. 262 (1897) *Bollen v. Nebraska*, 176 U.S. 83 (1900); *Maxwell v. Dow*, 176 U.S. 581 (1900); *Graham v. West Virginia*, 224 U.S. 616 (1912); *Lem Woon v. Oregon*, 229 U.S. 586 (1913); and *Gaines v. Washington*, 277 U.S. 81 (1928).

19. *Alexander v. Louisiana*, 405 U.S. 625, 633 (1972).

20. Title 18, Fed. Rules Crim. Proc., rule 7; *Ex parte Wilson*, 114 U.S. 417 (1885); *Wong Wing v. United States*, 163 U.S. 228 (1896); and *United States v. Moreland*, 258 U.S. 433 (1922). Cf. *Green v. United States*, 356 U.S. 165 (1958).

21. See Director for the Administrative Office of the United States Courts, *Annual Report, 1973* (Washington, D.C.: GPO, 1974), p. 394, table D-2.

22. Fed. Rules Crim. Proc., rule 6.

23. Pub. L. 90-274.

24. 18 U.S.C. 243, Act of March 1, 1875. See *Ex parte Virginia*, 100 U.S. 339 (1880).

25. *Strauder v. West Virginia*, 100 U.S. 303 (1880); *Hernandez v. Texas*, 347 U.S. 475 (1954); *Eubanks v. Louisiana*, 356 U.S. 584 (1958); *Alexander v. Louisiana;* and *Peters v. Kiff*, 407 U.S. 493 (1972). This last case, by plurality opinion, held that the exclusion of blacks from a grand jury could be raised by a white defendant. Cf. *United States v. McDaniels*, 370 F. Supp. 298 (1973).

26. *Hale v. Henkel*, 201 U.S. 43, 61–66 (1906).

27. *Blair v. United States*, 250 U.S. 273, 282 (1919).

28. Cf. *Branzburg v. Hayes*, 408 U.S. 665 (1972), holding that a journalist is not entitled to refuse to testify before a grand jury on grounds of freedom of the press; and *Nixon v. Sirica*, 487 F.2d 700 (1973), and *United States v. Nixon*, 418 U.S. 683 (1974), regarding the limits on executive privilege in the failure to respond to a request for materials.

29. *Holt v. United States*, 218 U.S. 245 (1910); *Costello v. United States*, 350 U.S. 359 (1956); and *United States v. Calandra*, 414 U.S. 338, 613 (1974).

30. *Brady v. United States*, 24 F.2d 405 (1928). Cf. *United States v. Farrington*, 5 Fed. 343 (1881), and *Czarlinsky v. United States*, 59 F.2d 889 (1931).

31. For a compilation of state laws on the initiation of prosecutions, see note, "Initiation of Prosecution by Information—Leave of the Court or Preliminary Examination?" 25 *Mont. L. Rev.* 135 (1963).

32. *Gagnon v. Scarpelli*, 411 U.S. 778 (1973); parole, *Morrissey v. Brewer*, 408 U.S. 471 (1972).

33. *Goldberg v. Kelly*, 397 U.S. 254, 267 (1970).

34. *Bell v. Burson*, 402 U.S. 535 (1971).

35. See note, "The Function of the Preliminary Hearing in Federal Pretrial Procedure," 83 *Yale L.J.* 771, 773 (1974).

36. Id.

37. The Supreme Court declared in *Coleman v. Alabama*, 399 U.S. 1 (1970), that when a preliminary hearing is a critical stage in the prosecution—that is, when substantial rights of the defendant are at stake—then counsel for defense is required. See also *Hamilton v. Alabama*, 368 U.S. 52 (1961).

38. Federal preliminary examinations, although a statutory right in all nonpetty offenses, Fed. Rules Crim. Proc., rule 5(c), and 18 U.S.C. 3060 (1970), are easily defeated by the prosecution seeking a continuance. The indictment obviates the requirement of a preliminary hearing; see *United States v. Quinn*, 357 F. Supp. 1348 (1973).

39. *Gerstein v. Pugh*, 420 U.S. 103 (1975).

40. Ibid. at 125, n. 26.

41. Ibid at 118–119.

42. See note, "Function of the Preliminary Hearing"; Richard P. Alexander and Sheldon Portman, "Grand Jury Indictment Versus Prosecution by Information—An Equal Protection and Due Process Issue," 25 *Hast. L.J.* 997 (1974); and note, "A Constitutional Right to Preliminary Hearings," 48 *So. Calif. L. Rev.* 158 (1974).

43. See Frank W. Miller, *Prosecution: The Decision to Charge a Suspect with a Crime* (Boston: Little, Brown, 1969), chaps. 8 and 20.

44. On checking prosecutorial discretion, see Kenneth Culp Davis, *Discretionary Justice: A Preliminary Inquiry* (Baton Rouge: Louisiana State University Press, 1969), chap. 7.

JUDICIAL DECISION

Application to the States:
Hurtado v. California, *110 U.S. 516 (1884)*

Mr. Justice MATTHEWS delivered the opinion of the court:

The Constitution of the State of California adopted in 1879, in article I., section 8, provides as follows:

> "Offenses heretofore required to be prosecuted by indictment shall be prosecuted by information after examination and commitment by a magistrate, or by indictment, with or without such examination and commitment, as may be prescribed by law. A grand jury shall be drawn and summoned at least once a year in each county."

. . .

In pursuance of the foregoing provision of the Constitution, and of the several sections of the Penal Code of California, the District Attorney of Sacramento County, on the 20th day of February, 1882, made and filed an information against the plaintiff in error, charging him with the crime of murder in the killing of one José Antonio Stuardo. Upon this information and without any previous investigation of the cause by any grand jury, the plaintiff in error was arraigned on the 22d day of March, 1882, and pleaded not guilty. A trial of the issue was thereafter had, and on May 7, 1882, the jury rendered its verdict, in which it found the plaintiff in error guilty of murder in the first degree.

On the fifth day of June, 1882, the Superior Court of Sacramento County, in which the plaintiff in error had been tried, rendered its judgment upon said verdict, that the said Joseph Hurtado, plaintiff in error, be punished by the infliction of death, and the day of his execution was fixed for the 20th day of July, 1882.

From this judgment an appeal was taken, and the Supreme Court of the State of California affirmed the judgment.

. . .

Thereupon the plaintiff in error, by his counsel, objected to the execution of said judgment and to any order which the court might make fixing a day for the execution of the same, upon the grounds:

. . .

> 9. That the said plaintiff in error had been held to answer for the said crime of murder by the district attorney of the said County of Sacramento, upon an information filed by him, and had been tried and illegally found guilty of the said crime, without any presentment or indictment of any grand or other jury, and that the judgment rendered upon the alleged verdict of the jury in such case was and is void, and if executed would deprive the plaintiff in error of his life or liberty without due process of law.

. . .

It is claimed on behalf of the prisoner that the conviction and sentence are void, on the ground that they are repugnant to that clause of the 14th article of Amendment to the Constitution of the United States which is in these words:

> "Nor shall any State deprive any person of life, liberty or property without due process of law."

The proposition of law we are asked to affirm is, that an indictment or presentment by a grand jury, as known to the common law of England, is essential to that "due process of law," when applied to prosecutions for felonies, which is secured and guarantied by this provision of the Constitution of the United States, and which accordingly it is forbidden to the States respectively to dispense with in the administration of criminal law.

The question is one of grave and serious import, affecting both private and public rights and interests of great magnitude, and involves a consideration of what additional restrictions upon the legislative policy of the States have been imposed by the 14th Amendment to the Constitution of the United States.

. . . It is maintained on behalf of the plaintiff in error that the phrase "due process of law" is equivalent to "law of the land," as found in the 29th chapter of Magna Charta; that, by immemorial usage, it has acquired a fixed, definite and technical meaning; that it refers to and includes, not only the general principles of public liberty and private right, which lie at the foundation of all free government, but the very institutions which, venerable by time and custom, have been tried by experience and found fit and necessary for the preservation of those principles, and which, having been the birthright and inheritance of every English subject, crossed the Atlantic with the colonists and were transplanted and established in the fundamental laws of the State; that, having been originally introduced into the Constitution of the United States as a limitation upon the powers of the government, brought into being by that instrument, it has now been added as an additional security to the individual against oppression by the States themselves; that one of these institutions is that of the grand jury, an indictment or presentment by which against the accused in cases of alleged felonies is an essential part of due process of law, in order that he may not be harassed and destroyed by prosecutions founded only upon private malice or popular fury.

. . .

The Constitution of the United States was ordained, it is true, by descendants of Englishmen, who inherited the traditions of English law and history; but it was made for an undefined and expanding future, and for a people gathered and to be gathered from many Nations and of many tongues. And while we take just pride in the principles and institutions of the common law, we are not to forget that in lands where other systems of jurisprudence prevail, the ideas and processes of civil justice are also not unknown. Due process of law, in spite of the absolutism of continental governments, is not alien to that Code which survived the Roman Empire as the foundation of modern civilization in Europe, and which has given us that fundamental maxim of distributive justice, *Suum cuique tribuere*. There is nothing in Magna Charta, rightly construed as a broad charter of public right and law, which ought to exclude the best ideas of all systems and of every age; and as it was the characteristic principle of the common law to draw its inspiration from every fountain of justice, we are not to assume that the sources of its supply have been exhausted. On the contrary, we should expect that the new and various experiences of our own situation and system will mold and shape it into new and not less useful forms.

The concessions of Magna Charta were wrung from the King as guaranties against the oppressions and usurpations of his prerogative. It did not enter into the minds of the barons to provide security against their own body or in favor of the commons by limiting the power of Parliament; so that bills of attainder, ex post facto laws, laws declaring forfeitures of estates, and other arbitrary Acts of legislation which occur so frequently in English history, were never regarded as inconsistent with the law of the land; for notwithstanding what was attributed to Lord Coke in *Bonham's Case*, 8 Coke, 115, 118 a, the omnipotence of Parliament over the common law was absolute, even against common right and reason. The actual and practical security for English liberty against legislative tyranny was the power of a free public opinion represented by the Commons.

In this country written constitutions were deemed essential to protect the rights and liberties of the people against the encroachments of power delegated to their governments, and the provisions of Magna Charta were incorporated into bills of rights. They were limitations upon all the powers of government, legislative as well as executive and judicial.

It necessarily happened, therefore, that as these broad and general maxims of liberty and justice held in our system a different place and performed a different function from their position and office in English constitutional history and law, they would receive and justify a corresponding and more comprehensive interpretation. Applied in England only as guards against executive usurpation and tyranny, here they have become bulwarks also against arbitrary legislation; but, in that application, as it would be incongruous to measure and restrict them by the ancient customary English law, they must be held to guaranty not particular forms of procedure, but the very substance of individual rights to life, liberty and property.

Restraints that could be fastened upon executive authority with precision and detail, might prove obstructive and injurious when imposed on the just and necessary discretion of legislative power; and, while in every instance, laws, that violated express and specific injunctions and prohibitions, might, without embarrassment, be judicially declared to be void, yet, any general principle or maxim, founded on the essential nature of law, as a just and reasonable expression of the public will and of government, as instituted by popular consent and for the general good, can only be applied to cases coming clearly within the scope of its spirit and purpose, and not to legislative provisions merely establishing forms and modes of government. . . .

We are to construe this phrase in the 14th Amendment by the *usus loquendi* of the Constitution itself. The same words are contained in the 5th Amendment. That article makes specific and express provision for perpetuating the institution of the grand jury, so far as relates to prosecutions, for the more aggravated crimes under the laws of the United States. It declares that "no person shall be held to answer for a capital or otherwise infamous crime, unless on a presentment or indictment of a grand jury, except in cases arising in the land or naval forces, or in the militia when in actual service in time of war or public danger; nor shall any person be subject for the same offense to be twice put in jeopardy of life or limb; nor shall he be compelled in any criminal case to be a witness against himself." It then immediately adds: "nor be deprived of life, liberty or property, without due process of law." According to a recognized canon of interpretation, especially applicable to formal and solemn instruments of constitutional law, we are forbidden to assume, without clear reason to the contrary, that any part of this most important Amendment is superfluous. The natural and obvious inference is, that in the sense of the Constitution, "due process of law" was not meant or intended to include, *ex vi termini*, the institution and procedure of a grand jury in any case. The conclusion is equally irresistible, that when the same phrase was employed in the 14th Amendment to restrain the action of the States, it was used in the same sense and with no greater extent; and that if in the adoption of that Amendment it had been part of its purpose to perpetuate in the institution of the grand jury in all the States, it would have embodied, as did the 5th Amendment, express declarations to that effect. Due process of law in the latter refers to that law of the land, which derives its authority from the legislative powers conferred upon Congress by the Constitution of the United States, exercised within the limits therein prescribed, and interpreted according to the principles of the common law. In the 14th Amendment by parity of reason, it refers to that law of the land in each State, which derives its authority from the inherent and reserved powers of the State, exerted within the limits of those fundamental principles of liberty and justice which lie at the base of all our civil and political institutions, and the greatest security for which resides in the right of the people to make their own laws, and alter them at their pleasure. "The 14th Amendment," as was said by Mr. Justice Bradley in *Mo. v. Lewis* [supra], "does not profess to secure to all persons in the United States the benefit of the same laws and the same remedies. Great diversities in these respects may exist in two States separated only by an imaginary line. On one side of this line there may be a right of trial by jury, and on the other side no such right. Each State prescribes its own modes of judicial proceeding."

But it is not to be supposed that these legislative powers are absolute and despotic, and that the Amendment prescribing due process of law is too vague and indefinite to operate as a practical restraint. It is not every Act, legislative in form, that is law. Law is something more than mere will exerted as an act of power. It must not be a special rule for a particular person or a particular case, but in the language of Mr. Webster, in his familiar definition, "The general law, a law which hears before it condemns, which proceeds upon inquiry, and renders judgment only after trial," so "that every citizen shall hold his life, liberty, property and immunities under the protection of the general rules which govern society," and thus excluding as not due process of law, Acts of attainder, Bills of pains and penalties, Acts of confiscation, Acts reversing judgments and Acts directly transferring one man's estate to another, legislative judgments and decrees, and other similar special, partial and arbitrary exertions of power under the forms of legislation. Arbitrary power, enforcing its edicts to the injury of the persons and property of its subjects, is not law, whether manifested as the decree of a personal monarch or of an impersonal multitude. And the limitations imposed by our constitutional law upon the action of the governments, both state and national, are essential to the preservation of public and private rights, notwithstanding the representative character of our political insitutions. The enforcement of these limitations by judicial process is the device of self-governing communities to protect the rights of individuals and minorities, as well against the power of numbers, as against the violence of public agents transcending the limits of lawful authority, even when acting in the name and wielding the force of the government.
. . .

It follows that any legal proceeding enforced by public authority, whether sanctioned by age and custom, or newly devised in the discretion of the legislative power, in furtherance of the general public good, which regards and preserves these principles of liberty and justice, must be held to be due process of law.
. . .

Tried by these principles, we are unable to say that the substitution for a present-ment or indictment by a grand jury of the proceeding by information, after examina-tion and commitment by a magistrate, certifying to the probable guilt of the defen-dant, with the right on his part to the aid of counsel, and to the cross-examination of the witnesses produced for the prosecution, is not due process of law. It is, as we have seen, an ancient proceeding at common law, which might include every case of an offense of less grade than a felony, except misprision of treason; and in every circumstance of its administration, as authorized by the Statute of California, it carefully considers and guards the substantial interest of the prisoner. It is merely a preliminary proceeding, and can result in no final judgment, except as the conse-quence of a regular judicial trial, conducted precisely as in cases of indictments.

In reference to this mode of proceeding at the common law, and which he says "is as ancient as the common law itself," Blackstone adds, 4 Com., 305: "And as to those offenses in which informations were allowed as well as indictments, so long as they were confined to this high and respectable jurisdiction, and were carried on in a legal and regular course in His Majesty's Court of King's Bench, the subject had no reason to complain. The same notice was given, the same process was issued, the same pleas were allowed, the same trial by jury was had, the same judgment was given by the same judges, as if the prosecution had originally been by indictment."

For these reasons, finding no error therein, the judgment of the Supreme Court of California is

Affirmed.

6

Bail

Excessive bail shall not be required.

—Eighth Amendment

Some criminal procedures are rooted in practices so ancient that their origins remain obscure. Bail is one such procedure. The idea of someone acting as surety for another may have its origin in the Anglo-Saxon use of the *wergeld* (peace money) contract or the system of suretyship may have evolved out of the frankpledge.[1] Whatever its origin there is little dispute that after the Norman Conquest bail became a widely accepted and used procedure. Both Glanvill[2] and Bracton,[3] medieval legal commentators, discussed bail in their writings.

Originally, bail was set by a sheriff. It was a secured pledge by a friend or relative or local notable to produce the accused for trial at some future date. This was a sensible arrangement in medieval England, where circumstances required that most prisoners be released. With a system of itinerant justice, trials might be delayed months or even years, creating both personal hardship for prisoners and excessive costs for sheriffs. Furthermore, prisons were neither secure, safe, nor healthy. Finally, because the criminal process was frequently invoked by private criminal actions, called *appeals*, the chance of a vindictive action based on no good cause was always present. Bail provided a reasonable arrangement shifting the burden of custody to local citizens of importance or to the friends of the accused.[4]

Although bail was a normal and expected procedure, it was limited by the kind of offense. Homicide, for example, was from the outset considered a non-bailable offense, except at the pleasure of the king. Another limitation was the degree of discretion that appears to have been vested in sheriffs. Bracton, for example, cautioned sheriffs before granting bail to have regard for the importance of the charge, the character of the prisoner, and the gravity of the evidence.[5] But this discretion was ill-defined, subject at an early date to three chancery writs that had the effect of countermanding a sheriff's decision not to allow bail.[6] Abuse of the procedure was also common, and in 1275 the Statute of Westminster I was enacted to reform and codify the bail procedure.[7] Westminster I noted that sheriffs and others "have taken and kept in prison persons detected of felony, and incontinent have let out by replevin such as were not replevisable, and have kept in prison such as were replevisable because they would gain of the one party and grieve the other."[8] The statute then listed some sixteen nonbailable offenses, including the broad category of "manifest offenses." But the implied evidentiary discretion of "manifest offenses" was balanced by inclusion in the list of bailable offenses of persons held on "light suspicion."

Westminster I is of more than antiquarian interest because it casts some light on the question of whether bail is a right or a matter of grace. Although the statute provides no conclusive answers, it at least suggests that bail was a common and expected procedure, subject at times to ill-defined discretion and occasional legislative limitations. Its standing in the hierarchy of criminal procedures is attested to by the inclusion in the English Bill of Rights (1688) of a provision against no excessive bail—a provision later incorporated in the American Bill of Rights.[9]

Almost from the outset, American experience with bail departed somewhat from English traditions.[10] The Judiciary Act of 1789, governing federal bail procedure, provided that "upon all arrests in criminal cases, bail shall be admitted, except where punishment may be death." In capital cases bail was made discretionary, depending on the circumstances surrounding the offense, the evidence, and usages of the law.[11]

The liberal bail provision of the act provides some insight into the curious ambiguity of the Eighth Amendment's provision against excessive bail. A strict, literal interpretation of the amendment suggests that bail is not a constitutional right, but rather that when, by law, the right to bail exists it cannot be excessive. A conflicting interpretation suggests that bail is a constitutional right and that the language of the provision simply addresses the problem of excessive bail, ensuring that it will not undermine the constitutional right.[12] Neither interpretation, however, forecloses the exercise of legislative limitations nor the exercise of reasonable judicial discretion.

THE PURPOSES OF BAIL

As early as 1935, the Supreme Court noted that bail, in a criminal case, "is taken to secure the due attendance of the party accused to answer the indictment and to submit to a trial, and the judgment of the court thereon."[13] More recently, the Court observed:

> The right to release before trial is conditioned upon the accused's giving adequate assurance that he will stand trial and submit to sentence if found guilty. . . . Like the ancient practice of securing the oaths of responsible persons to stand as sureties for the accused, the modern practice of requiring a bail bond or the deposit of a sum of money subject to forfeiture serves as additional assurance of the presence of an accused. . . .
>
> Since the function of bail is limited, the fixing of bail for any individual defendant must be based upon standards relevant to the purpose of assuring the presence of that defendant.[14]

PREVENTIVE DETENTION

Realistically, we must recognize that high bail, or the denial of bail, is used in some situations not merely to prevent flight, but also to prevent the accused from committing further offenses. Preventive detention, although never sanctioned directly by the Supreme Court, has long been recognized and permitted by lower federal courts. Justice Douglas, while sitting as a circuit judge, noted that it would be "irresponsible judicial action" to grant bail in instances where community safety is in question.[15] Similarly, a federal appellate court has stated that "bail should not be granted where the offense of which the defendant has been convicted is an atrocious one, and there is danger that if he is given his freedom he will commit another of like character."[16]

Although courts rarely acknowledge that bail is set high to prevent an accused from committing additional crimes, most scholars quickly acknowledge the fact.[17] Is recidivism, then, a major problem? Based on various studies, the answer appears to be no. If we use conviction rates rather than re-arrest rates, and if we eliminate nondangerous or nonviolent crimes, then bail recidivism rates appear to be low. A study of bail recidivism in Boston found that only 4.1 percent of the people studied were re-arrested and convicted of a dangerous or violent crime.[18] Studies in the 1960s in the District of Columbia reported bail recidivism ranging from 7.5 percent to 9.4 percent;[19] other studies report much lower rates of bail arrests.[20] Offsetting the reported rates of re-arrests is the considerable amount of unreported crime, some of which may be attributed to those who have been released pending trial. On the other hand, it is impossible to determine how many individuals have been unnecessarily detained for fear that they might commit crimes if granted release.

In response to public concern about crime and bail recidivism, Congress included a provision in a 1970 act to allow preventive detention in the District of Columbia.[21] Under the terms of this legislation, a judge may order pretrial detention for a person charged with a dangerous or violent crime.[22] Although this legislation does make explicit what has heretofore been hidden under the guise of high monetary bail, the legislation nonetheless raises serious questions, first among these, numerous constitutional problems. Even assuming that there is no conditional constitutional right to bail in noncapital cases, the legislation may violate the presumption of innocence and effectively punish those who have not been convicted, and this by a standard that is far short of that required for conviction.[23] Further, the category "dangerous offense" may be both unconstitutionally vague and of little predictive value. In fact, one study has found little correlation between the initial offense charged and bail recidivism,[24] and concluded that the criteria of the legislation, when applied to the sample study, were unable to provide a means of isolating even a small group of defendants more of whom were recidivists than were not.[25]

Bailed felons do commit crimes, and society is justifiably concerned when this occurs. However, in the absence of any demonstrated ability to predict recidivism in individual cases, pretrial detention raises at least as many problems as it attempts to solve. To detain large numbers of persons who would not commit serious offenses in order to protect the community from those who would implies that we are willing to reduce serious crime by a small amount through the large-scale denial of what has been customarily thought of as a right to bail.

EXCESSIVE BAIL

The prohibition against excessive bail implies a standard of reasonableness but cannot be reduced to a formula. The beginning point in any determination of what is excessive bail is to recall that the purpose of bail is to give adequate assurance that a defendant will stand trial and submit to any adverse judgment. Although the Supreme Court has never directly ruled on excessive bail, the Court did observe in *Stack v. Boyle* (1951) that "bail set at a figure higher than an amount reasonably calculated to fulfill this purpose is 'excessive' under the Eighth Amendment."[26]

Bail is often set in a routine manner, frequently by recourse to a bail schedule,[27] and the defendant has little opportunity to present information that would be relevant to the determination of bail.[28] In many jurisdictions, bail is considered at the time of the initial appearance or arraignment, with little or no input from defense counsel, and almost invariably the bail recommendation of the prosecutor is accepted.[29] On the other hand, the Supreme Court has indicated that bail should be fixed individually, in accordance with standards relevant to the purpose of assuring the presence of the particular defendant.[30] Many of the common-law standards have now been incorporated

into statutory provisions. In 1966, Congress passed the first major bail legislation since the Judiciary Act of 1789. Among the provisions of the Bail Reform Act are the following:

(a) Any person charged with an offense, other than an offense punishable
by death, shall, at his appearance before a judicial officer, be ordered released
pending trial on his personal recognizance or upon the execution of an unse-
cured appearance bond in an amount specified by the judicial officer unless
the officer determines, in the exercise of his discretion, that such a release will
not reasonably assure the appearance of the person as required. . . .

(b) In determining which conditions of release will reasonably assure appearance, the judicial officer shall, on the basis of available information, take
into account the nature and circumstances of the offense charged, the weight
of the evidence against the accused, the accused's family ties, employment,
financial resources, character and mental condition, the length of his residence
in the community, his record of convictions, and his record of appearance at
court proceedings or of flight to avoid prosecution or failure to appear at court
proceedings.[31]

Whether bail in a particular case is excessive is determined, then, by a
compound consideration of factors such as those set forth in paragraph (b)
above.[32] If courts had this kind of information available, they would be able
to individualize bail determinations, thereby reducing defaults in court appearances. In a study conducted by the Vera Institute in conjunction with the
Manhattan Bail Project, there was evidence to suggest that the lower bail
"jump rate" among those released on personal recognizance was related to the
defendants' roots in the community,[33] a factor that was determined in advance
of bail hearings.[34]

Even though ROR (Release on Own Recognizance) programs and other
alternatives to money bail have received wide-spread endorsement,[35] large
numbers of defendants are still detained because of their inability to post a
cash bail or a bond. Indeed, over half of the prison population in the United
States is composed of pretrial defendants who either have been denied bail or
could not meet bail requirements.[36] Courts have generally held that although
the financial ability of a defendant to meet the monetary requirements of bail
should be considered, the defendant's financial inability to post bail does not
as such mean that the amount of bail is excessive.[37]

Because the criminal courts are generally populated by the poor, even a
small bond premium is frequently beyond the financial means of many defendants. Studies have indicated that somewhere between 50 and 75 percent
of defendants cannot make their money bonds.[38] The financial inability of the
indigent to meet bond requirements raises a serious question under the equal
protection clause. Society is not protected by money bail from rich-but-danger-
ous defendants, especially those in organized crime,[39] whereas poor defendants must languish in overcrowded county and city jails[40] at considerable

cost to taxpayers.[41] Indeed, money bail is economically self-defeating to all but the insurance companies and bonding agents.[42] To make pretrial freedom dependent in no small measure on the financial means of defendants would appear to be inconsistent with the evolving standards of equal protection of the law.[43]

Although the equal protection argument has never been directly ruled on by the Supreme Court, the Court in 1972 did endorse the Illinois cash deposit bail system. The Illinois legislation was introduced as a reform measure to eliminate bail bonds. Under the legislation, an accused who is not released on personal recognizance and is eligible for bail may deposit 10 percent of the required bail with the court; 90 percent of the sum deposited is refundable and the balance is retained as a charge. There is no 10 percent charge to those who deposit the full bail by cash, securities, or real estate, nor do those who are released on personal recognizance pay a charge. In upholding the measure against an attack under the equal-protection clause, a majority of the Court held in *Schilb v. Kuebel* that the defendant had failed to demonstrate that the legislation set up a poor-versus-affluent bail system, and therefore the Court could not assume that the legislation worked "to deny relief to the poor man merely because of his poverty."[44]

However correct the majority may have been in regard to the particular set of facts in *Schilb*, few commentators deny that money bail works an invidious discrimination against the poor.[45] The discrimination is probably not new and may well have worked in a similar manner at the time the Eighth Amendment was written. The changes that have occurred in the intervening years are twofold: The attitude toward the poor is quite different today than it was in 1789 and the Constitution now includes a proscription against denials of equal protection of the laws.

Finally, a system of money bail arises a substantial question under the due process clause. There is evidence to suggest that those who are detained prior to trial are prejudiced thereby. Not only are they hampered in preparing for trial, but, more significantly, the mere fact of pretrial detention may prejudice trial results. A study conducted by the New York Legal Aid Society revealed that defendants free on personal recognizance or bail were less likely to plead guilty and more likely to have their cases dismissed than were defendants held in pretrial detention. Similarly, released defendants whose cases were not dismissed were less likely to receive a prison sentence or, if a prison sentence was imposed, more likely to receive a shorter sentence than were detained defendants.[46]

CONCLUSION

For well over thirty years, the system of money bail has been under serious attack. As a result of this criticism, numerous reforms have been introduced, largely through the legislative process. For the judiciary, particularly the Supreme Court, the bail clause has remained an almost forgotten constitutional provision. The Court has neither provided guidelines for excessive bail nor confronted the more fundamental issue of the indigent in the context of a bond system. This lack of judicial participation in the bail system has left the nation ill-prepared to resolve not only the issue of indigency and bail, but the troubling problem of preventive detention.

Although there is a strong presumption favoring pretrial freedom, unquestionably society must have some assurance that a defendant will submit to trial and to the judgment of the court, and that it will not be plagued by the wholesale recidivism of those already accused of crimes. What is remarkable is that after almost two hundred years, we have not adopted alternatives that would give society the necessary minimum assurances without at the same time raising serious questions about due process and equal protection of the laws. It is equally remarkable that society has continued to use extensively a money bail system that is an enormous financial drain on local government as well as a contributory factor in a good deal of unnecessary human misery.

NOTES

1. See Elsa De Haas, *Antiquities of Bail* (New York: AMS Press, 1966). Cf. William Holdsworth, *A History of English Law* (London: Methuen, 1938), vol. 2, p. 104.

2. Ranulf De Glanvill, d. 1190.

3. Henry De Bracton, d. 1268.

4. James Fitzjames Stephen, *A History of the Criminal Law in England* (London: Macmillan, 1883), vol. 1, pp. 233–243.

5. Ibid. at 234.

6. The writs were *de homine replegiando, de odiv et atia,* and *de ponendo* (mainprise). For a discussion of these early writs see De Haas, *Antiquities,* chaps. 3–4. The writs subsequently fell into disuse and were replaced by habeas corpus.

7. 3 Edw. 1, chap. 12.

8. Stephen, *History of Criminal Law,* vol. 1, p. 234.

9. 1 W. & M. 2, chap. 2, § 1(10).

10. For an account of the Colonial American experience with bail, see Caleb Foote, "The Coming Crisis in Bail," 113 *U. Penn. L. Rev.* 959 (1965).

11. 1 Stat. 73, 91 (1789). Thirty-nine states have adopted similar bail provisions; see Daniel Freed and Patricia Wald, *Bail in the United States: 1964* (Washington, D.C.: National Conference on Bail and Criminal Justice, 1964), pp. 2–3, n. 8.

12. See Foote, *Coming Crisis,* p. 970.

13. *Ex parte Milburn,* 9 Peters 704, 710 (1835).

14. *Stack v. Boyle,* 342 U.S. 1, 5 (1951).

15. *Carbo v. United States,* 82 S. Ct. 662 (1962).

16. *United States ex rel. Estabrook v. Otis,* 18 F.2d 689, 690 (1927).

17. E.g., see *Proceedings* (Washington, D.C.: National Conference on Bail and Criminal Justice, 1965), pp. 151–179.

18. "Preventive Detention," 6 *Harv. C. R.-C. L. Rev.* 291, 382 (1971).

19. "An Answer to the Problem of Bail," 9 *Colum. J. L. Soc. Prob.* 394, 432 (1973).

20. See *Proceedings*, pp. 172–173, 182–183.

21. District of Columbia Court Reform and Criminal Procedure Act of 1970, Pub. L. 91-358, 84 Stat. 473.

22. § 23-1322 and § 23-1331. *Dangerous crime* is the commission or attempted commission of robbery, burglary, or arson, or of certain serious drug violations; *violent crime* is murder, rape, mayhem, kidnapping, robbery, burglary, voluntary manslaughter, extortion, arson, assault with a dangerous weapon, blackmail accompanied by threats of violence, and improper, immoral, or indecent behavior with a child, or the attempt or conspiracy to commit any of the above crimes.

23. Sam Ervin, Jr., "Foreword: Preventive Detention—A Step Backward for Criminal Justice," 6 *Harv. CR.-C.L. Rev.* 291, 298 (1971).

24. Ibid. at 384, table 16.

25. Ibid. at 369.

26. *Stack v. Boyle*, 342 U.S. at 5.

27. E.g., see the landmark study by Arthur Beeley, *The Bail System in Chicago* (Chicago: University of Chicago Press, 1927), p. 155.

28. See note, "Administration of Pretrial Release and Detention," 83 *Yale L.J.* 153, 155 (1973).

29. Freed and Wald, *Bail*, pp. 18–19.

30. *Stack v. Boyle*, 342 U.S. at 5.

31. Pub. L. 89-465, 80 Stat. 214. It is unclear whether any of the standards set forth in paragraph (b) have constitutional status. Of course, the legislation applies directly only to federal bail proceedings; whether state bail proceedings must use similar standards is unclear because the Supreme Court has never ruled directly on whether the excessive-bail provision applies to the states. In *Schilb v. Kuebel*, the Court noted: "Bail, of course, is basic to our system of law and the Eighth Amendment's proscription of excessive bail has been assumed to have application to the States through the Fourteenth Amendment," 404 U.S. 357, 365 (1972). Both the fifth and eighth federal courts of appeals have indicated that the proscription against excessive bail applies to the states; see *Henderson v. Dutton*, 397 F.2d 375 (1968), and *Pilkinton v. Circuit Court*, 324 F.2d 45 (1963). However, a federal habeas corpus petition questioning excessive bail by states is limited to the question of whether bail was set in an arbitrary manner; *Mastrian v. Hedman*, 326 F.2d 708 (1964), and *Simon v. Woodson*, 454 F.2d 161 (1972).

32. E.g., see the opinion of New Jersey Supreme Court in *State v. Johnson*, 294 A.2d 245 (1972).

33. Mitchell Pines, "An Answer to the Problem of Bail," 9 *Colum. J. L. Soc. Prob.* 394, 420–424 (1973).

34. The same study, however, also revealed that the jump vote for release on recognizance was higher than when a bail bond had been required, ibid. at 418.

35. Freed and Wald, *Bail*, pp. 56–77.

36. Note, "Administration of Pretrial Release and Detention, 83 *Yale L.J.* 153, 154 (1973).

37. E.g., *Simon v. Woodson*.

38. Pines, "Answer to the Problem of Bail," p. 409. For an analysis of bond practices, see Freed and Wald, *Bail*, chap. 3.

39. Ibid. at 49–50.

40. On the deplorable conditions of pretrial detention, see note, "Constitutional Limitations on Conditions of Pretrial Detention," 79 *Yale L.J.* 941 (1970).

41. On the social and economic costs of pretrial detention, see note, "The Costs of Preventive Detention," 79 *Yale L.J.* 926 (1970); and Freed and Wald, *Bail*, chap. 4.

42. On the beneficiaries of the bail system, see Ronald Goldfarb, *Ransom: A Critique of the American Bail System* (New York; Harper & Row, 1965), chap. 3; and Paul Wice, *Freedom for All* (Lexington, Mass.: Lexington Books, 1974).

43. E.g., *Griffin v. Illinois,* 351 U.S. 12 (1956).

44. *Schilb v. Kuebel,* 404 U.S. at 370.

45. See Foote, *Coming Crisis.*

46. Pines, "Answer to the Problem of Bail," pp. 401–403. The study also confirmed that, as between those released and those detained prior to trial, there was no correlation between the conviction rates and harsh sentences, and such factors as the weight of evidence, prior criminal records, and the type of crime.

JUDICIAL DECISION

The Functions of Bail:
Stack v. Boyle, *342 U.S. 1 (1951)*

Mr. Chief Justice VINSON delivered the opinion of the Court.

Indictments have been returned in the Southern District of California charging the twelve petitioners with conspiring to violate the Smith Act, 18 USC (Supp. IV) §§ 371, 2385. Upon their arrest, bail was fixed for each petitioner in the widely varying amounts of $2,500, $7,500, $75,000 and $100,000. On motion of petitioner Schneiderman following arrest in the Southern District of New York, his bail was reduced to $50,000 before his removal to California. On motion of the Government to increase bail in the case of other petitioners, and after several intermediate procedural steps not material to the issues presented here, bail was fixed in the District Court for the Southern District of California in the uniform amount of $50,000 for each petitioner.

Petitioners moved to reduce bail on the ground that bail as fixed was excessive under the Eighth Amendment. In support of their motion, petitioners submitted statements as to their financial resources, family relationships, health, prior criminal records, and other information. The only evidence offered by the Government was a certified record showing that four persons previously convicted under the Smith Act in the Southern District of New York had forfeited bail. No evidence was produced relating those four persons to the petitioners in this case. At a hearing on the motion petitioners were examined by the District Judge and cross-examined by an attorney for the Government. Petitioners' factual statements stand uncontroverted.

After their motion to reduce bail was denied, petitioners filed applications for habeas corpus in same District Court. Upon consideration of the record on the motion to reduce bail, the writs were denied. The Court of Appeals for the Ninth Circuit affirmed. 192 F.2d 56. . . .

Relief in this type of case must be speedy if it is to be effective. The petition for certiorari and the full record are now before the Court and, since the questions presented by the petition have been fully briefed and argued, we consider it appropriate to dispose of the petition for certiorari at this time. Accordingly, the petition for certiorari is granted for review of questions important to the administration of criminal justice.

First. From the passage of the Judiciary Act of 1789, 1 Stat. 73, 91, to the present Federal Rules of Criminal Procedure, Rule 46(a)(1), federal law has unequivocally provided that a person arrested for a non-capital offense *shall* be admitted to bail. This traditional right to freedom before conviction permits the unhampered preparation of a defense, and serves to prevent the infliction of punishment prior to conviction. See *Hudson v. Parker,* 156 U.S. 277, 285 (1895). Unless this right to bail before trial is preserved, the presumption of innocence, secured only after centuries of struggle, would lose its meaning.

The right to release before trial is conditioned upon the accused's giving adequate assurance that he will stand trial and submit to sentence if found guilty. *Ex parte Milburn* (U.S.) 9 Pet. 704 (1835). Like the ancient practice of securing the oaths of responsible persons to stand as sureties for the accused, the modern practice of requiring a bail bond or the deposit of a sum of money subject to forfeiture serves as additional assurance of the presence of an accused. Bail set at a figure higher than an amount reasonably calculated to fulfill this purpose is "excessive" under the Eighth Amendment.

Since the function of bail is limited, the fixing of bail for any individual defendant must be based upon standards relevant to the purpose of assuring the presence of that defendant. The traditional standards as expressed in the Federal Rules of Criminal Procedure are to be applied in each case to each defendant. In this case petitioners are charged with offenses under the Smith Act and, if found guilty, their convictions are subject to review with the scrupulous care demanded by our Constitution. Upon final judgment of conviction, petitioners face imprisonment of not more than five years and a fine of not more than $10,000. It is not denied that bail for each petitioner has been fixed in a sum much higher than that usually imposed for offenses with like penalties and yet there has been no factual showing to justify such action in this case. The Government asks the courts to depart from the norm by assuming, without the introduction of evidence, that each petitioner is a pawn in a conspiracy and will, in obedience to a superior, flee the jurisdiction. To infer from the fact of indictment alone a need for bail in an unusually high amount is an arbitrary act. Such conduct would inject into our own system of government the very principles of totalitarianism which Congress was seeking to guard against in passing the statute under which petitioners have been indicted.

If bail in an amount greater than that usually fixed for serious charges of crimes is required in the case of any of the petitioners, that is a matter to which evidence should be directed in a hearing so that the constitutional rights of each petitioner may be preserved. In the absence of such a showing, we are of the opinion that the fixing of bail before trial in these cases cannot be squared with the statutory and constitutional standards for admission to bail.

. . .

The Court concludes that bail has not been fixed by proper methods in this case and that petitioners' remedy is by motion to reduce bail, with right of appeal to the Court of Appeals. Accordingly, the judgment of the Court of Appeals is vacated and the case is remanded to the District Court with directions to vacate its order denying petitioners' applications for writs of habeas corpus and to dismiss the applications without prejudice. Petitioners may move for reduction of bail in the criminal proceeding so that a hearing may be held for the purpose of fixing reasonable bail for each petitioner.

It is so ordered.

⋑ 7 ⋐

Pleas
of Guilty
and
Plea Bargaining

Given the attention that the Constitution devotes to the trial rights of criminal defendants, it comes as something of a shock to realize that relatively few defendants exercise their right to a trial. The majority of federal and state criminal cases are disposed of by pleas of guilty. For example, of the criminal cases in federal district courts from July 1972 through June 1973, 75 percent were disposed of by pleas of guilty.[1] The fact that the vast majority of all convictions in the United States are obtained by pleas of guilty reflects a certain calculus: To exercise one's trial rights is a risky business. Not only are the odds in favor of conviction, but, more significantly, a defendant convicted at trial is more likely to receive a harsher sentence than is one who pleads guilty.[2] For many defendants, the decision to plead guilty is often the result of plea bargaining.

Plea bargaining is generally a pretrial negotiation between the defense and the prosecution in which the prosecution agrees to certain concessions in exchange for a plea of guilty.[3] The concessions are varied but usually consist of some combination of the following:

1. An agreement to reduce the number of charges, dropping certain offenses (particularly those that carry longer sentences)
2. An agreement to recommend to the sentencing judge a lighter sentence, or to make no sentencing recommendation, or to allow the defense to set the recommended minimum sentence with the prosecution setting the recommended maximum sentence

Widespread plea bargaining is a product of the twentieth century.[4] However, there is evidence to suggest that it was used extensively in both rural and urban America during the nineteenth century.[5] In any event, the historical roots of the process go deep into English history. Before the Norman Conquest, and long before the system of Crown or public justice was fully established, a remedial system for controlling blood feuds was practiced in Anglo-Saxon England. The system involved bargaining between parties over compensation.[6] Frequently, the alternative to compensatory bargaining was private vengeance. However, after the conquest, this system of private justice declined, giving way to royal authority—an authority that often considered it an affront to bargain with malefactors. As the system of royal justice spread, the state became increasingly opposed to agreements that interfered with criminal prosecutions, particularly for grave public offenses.[7] Still, the process of bargaining continued, at least for misdemeanors. On the eve of the American Revolution, Blackstone noted:

> It is not uncommon, when a person is convicted of a misdemeanor, which principally and more immediately affects some individual, as a battery, imprisonment or the like, for the Court to permit the defendant to speak with the prosecutor, before any judgment is pronounced; and if the prosecutor declares himself satisfied, to inflict but a trivial punishment. . . . But it surely is a dangerous practice. . . . Nay even a voluntary forgiveness by the party injured ought not, in true policy, to intercept the stroke of justice.[8]

In nineteenth-century America, the conflict between the practice of bargaining and the broader considerations of public policy continued. Some jurisdictions were opposed to plea bargaining largely out of fear that pleas might be involuntary;[9] other jurisdictions, either tacitly[10] or directly, approved voluntary plea bargaining.[11] The legal profession publicly opposed the procedure,[12] and it was not until recently that the practice was endorsed by the American Bar Association (ABA) and the President's Commission on Law Enforcement and Administration of Justice. This changed position presumably reflects the growing dependence of courts and prosecutors on plea bargaining.

There are probably numerous reasons why plea bargaining is used widely in America. From the perspective of both the prosecution and the defense, there are tactical considerations involving the strength or weakness of the state's case. The greater the uncertainty of the state's evidence, the greater the likelihood of a trial acquittal; hence, the prosecution is prepared to make certain concessions. The most basic consideration, however, is administrative efficiency: Plea bargaining is quick and relatively inexpensive; it does not consume the time of judges, prosecutors, public defenders, and jurors that most trials would consume. In a system of scarce resources, plea bargaining is a kind of assembly line justice that enables the system to continue to function. To these justifications, we can add that a negotiated or bargained plea of guilty spares defendants and their families the further embarrassment and expense attendant to a public trial. Finally, as one study cautioned,

> confining trials to cases involving substantial issues may also help to preserve the significance of the presumption of innocence and the requirement of proof beyond a reasonable doubt. If trial were to become routine even in cases in which there is no substantial issue of guilt, the overwhelming statistical probability of guilt might incline judges and jurors to be more skeptical of the defense than at present.[13]

Yet despite all the arguments in favor of plea bargaining, the process still generates suspicion. It could be argued that some defendants are not dealt with as severely as the facts merit, and in consequence this leniency may reduce the deterrent impact of the law. Recently, the National Advisory Commission on Criminal Justice Standards and Goals, in recommending the gradual abolition of the practice, argued that plea bargaining may have a negative impact on correctional goals. By reducing charges, a prosecutor could limit judicial sentencing discretion to options that are inconsistent with correctional goals.[14] Indeed, plea bargaining could undermine the correctional system by leaving the impression with the guilty that justice can be manipulated or by encouraging some to conclude that they are the victims of a corrupt and mindless system.

Perhaps the strongest argument against the practice is its low visibility. Plea bargaining is generally a private affair—an off-the-record event attended by only the prosecutor, the defense, and occasionally the trial judge. The prosecutor operates almost totally without legislative guidance and with few judicial controls. Furthermore, it is not uncommon for a prosecutor to overcharge in order to gain bargaining leverage,[15] thereby introducing an element of sham into the process. It has also been argued that low visibility coupled with differential sentencing allow the prosecutor to exert improper pressure on those defendants who may be innocent. In the dubious case, where there is evidential doubt, many prosecutors bargain simply to avoid the trial forum and the resolution of evidentiary conflicts. Thus the fact-finding process, protected during trial by rules of evidence, is thwarted by plea bargaining. As one commentator noted, "If trials ever serve a purpose, their utility is presumably greatest when the outcome is in doubt."[16] A just system of criminal law requires a degree of discretion at almost every level of administration. On the other hand, the high degree of prosecutorial discretion in plea bargaining and the low visibility of the process itself run counter to the rule of law.

The uneasiness that some scholars share about the prospect of an innocent defendant's pleading guilty would probably be greatly diminished if differential sentencing were not a reality of the context of plea bargaining. In almost all jurisdictions, a defendant who pleads guilty is more likely to receive a lighter sentence than is a convicted defendant who exercised the right to a trial. For example, in 1970, federal defendants who pleaded guilty at arraignment received an average sentence that was 33 percent lighter than those who pleaded not guilty and later changed their plea to guilty. And even more astonishing was the fact that defendants who pleaded not guilty and were convicted after a trial by jury received an average sentence that was 180 percent greater than the average sentence received by those who pleaded guilty at arraignment.[17]

Differential sentencing raises several serious questions. It is debatable whether sentence leniency should be distributed unevenly among offenders. Assuming that all convicted defendants, whether convicted by a trial or by a plea of guilty, are in fact guilty, why should one group receive preferential sentencing? The ABA's Project on Minimum Standards for Criminal Justice justifies the discrepancy on the following bases:

(i) that the defendant by his plea has aided in ensuring prompt and certain application of correctional measures to him;

(ii) that the defendant has acknowledged his guilt and shown a willingness to assume responsibility for his conduct;

(iii) that the concessions will make possible alternative correctional measures which are better adapted to achieving rehabilitative, protective, deterrent or other purposes of correctional treatment, or will prevent undue harm to the defendant from the form of conviction;

(iv) that the defendant has made public trial unnecessary when there are good reasons for not having the case dealt with in a public trial;

(v) that the defendant has given or offered cooperation when such cooperation has resulted or may result in the successful prosecution of other offenders engaged in equally serious or more serious criminal conduct;

(vi) that the defendant by his plea has aided in avoiding delay (including delay due to crowded dockets) in the disposition of the case and thereby has increased the probability of prompt and certain application of correctional measures to other offenders.[18]

Still, the ABA's defense of plea bargaining does not address itself to the troublesome problem of covert coercion that may be inherent in differential sentencing. Although the coercion may not be blatant, still "the pleader's freedom of choice is seriously inhibited when he is aware of such differentials in punishment."[19] To exact a penalty, albeit an indirect one, on the exercise of the constitutional rights to silence and trial, raises a due process question that cannot be easily dismissed by answers of administrative efficiency. And the flexibility of plea bargaining itself suggests a system unconstrained by legislative standards and guidelines and judicial oversight.[20]

CONSTITUTIONAL DIMENSIONS

For a defendant to enter a plea of guilty is a momentous decision. Not only is the plea an acknowledgment of guilt, but it is also a waiver of important constitutional rights. As the Supreme Court noted, some years ago:

> A plea of guilty differs in purpose and effect from a mere admission or an extrajudicial confession; it is itself a conviction. Like a verdict of a jury it is conclusive. More is not required; the court has nothing to do but give judgment and sentence. Out of just consideration for persons accused of crime, courts are careful that a plea of guilty shall not be accepted unless made voluntarily after proper advice and with full understanding of the consequences.[21]

The Voluntary Plea

The most basic constitutional requirement of a plea of guilty is that it be voluntary. The voluntary plea of guilty is an expression of a defendant's free choice, unconstrained by coercion, terror, improper inducements, or threats. Whether a particular plea is voluntary, however, depends somewhat on the circumstances of the individual case. It has been suggested that deception, threats,[22] physical or mental coercion, or *improper* promises[23] may invalidate a guilty plea.

Because a plea of guilty is a waiver of the right against self-incrimination as well as all trial rights, the plea must be an intelligent act, based on an awareness of the direct legal consequences of the waiver. In the context of the guilty plea, a waiver is an intentional relinquishment of a defendant's rights.[24] The minimum constitutional requirement is that the record of the trial court reveal that before accepting a plea of guilty, the judge inquired as to the voluntariness of the plea and ensured that the defendant fully understood the true nature or substance of the charge.[25]

Additionally, it now seems that due process requires that no plea of guilty be accepted from a defendant charged with any offense carrying a prison sentence unless the defendant has been represented by competent counsel or that counsel has been freely and intelligently waived.[26] Finally, before accepting a bargained plea, the court must be informed of any promises made by the prosecution;[27] if the plea rests in any significant degree on a promise or agreement by the prosecutor, then such promises or agreements must be fulfilled by the prosecutor's office.[28] Of course, in those situations where the sentencing judge has not been involved in arranging the plea agreement,[29] the judge is not bound to accept the plea agreement. Although judges normally follow a prosecutor's sentencing recommendation, rejection is not uncommon, particularly in those situations where a presentence report is thought by a judge not to support the plea agreement.

If a plea of guilty rests in any significant degree on a plea agreement and the agreement is rejected, then due process would seem to require that a defendant be allowed to withdraw a plea by a timely presentence motion. Indeed, in federal cases, a defendant is given the unqualified right in such situations to withdraw a plea.[30] In the absence of a judicially rejected plea agreement, however, a defendant does not have an absolute right to withdraw a plea of guilty, even by a timely presentence motion. In general, the federal courts have held that withdrawal of a plea of guilty is left to the sound discretion of the trial court,[31] subject to the broad standard that a withdrawal should be granted where the circumstances indicate that it would be "fair and just."[32] It is settled law, however, that once a court has allowed a plea of guilty to be withdrawn, the guilty plea may not subsequently be introduced against the defendant in refutation of a plea of not guilty.[33]

Until recently, the courts in many jurisdictions accepted pleas of guilty without inquiry. This was probably due to judicial concern that a prosecutorial promise or concession might later, in a postconviction proceeding, be used to attack the voluntariness of a plea. Since the Supreme Court's endorsement of plea bargaining in *Brady v. United States* (1970), the need for this charade has been eliminated. In *Brady,* the defendant was charged with kidnapping; if he had elected a trial by jury, he would have been subject to the maximum penalty of death. Under a provision of the statute,[34] the death penalty could be imposed only on the recommendation of a jury. Thus, in a trial without a jury or in a plea of guilty, a defendant would not face the death penalty. Originally, Brady pleaded not guilty and then changed his plea to guilty after learning that his codefendant pleaded guilty and was thus available to testify against him. Brady attacked the plea as involuntary, maintaining that the provision effectively coerced his plea and that the plea was based on representations of a reduced sentence. In rejecting both contentions, the Supreme Court placed its imprimatur on plea bargaining:

> We decline to hold, however, that a guilty plea is compelled and invalid under the Fifth Amendment whenever motivated by the defendant's desire to accept the certainty or probability of a lesser penalty rather than face a wider range of possibilities extending from acquittal to conviction and a higher penalty authorized by law for the crime charged.
>   . . . We cannot hold that it is unconstitutional for the State to extend a benefit to a defendant who in turn extends a substantial benefit to the State and who demonstrates by his plea that he is ready and willing to admit his crime and to enter the correctional system in a frame of mind that affords hope

for success in rehabilitation over a shorter period of time than might otherwise be necessary.[35]

The *Brady* opinion fails to give a satisfactory answer to the issue of whether the particular death penalty provision effectively coerced Brady's plea. Justice White's majority opinion responded to this issue by noting that "even if we assume that Brady would not have pleaded guilty except for the death penalty provision . . . this assumption merely identifies the penalty provision as a 'but for' cause of his plea. That the statute caused the plea in this sense does not necessarily prove that the plea was coerced and invalid as an involuntary act."[36]

An even more troublesome problem with *Brady* is the manner in which the majority treated the issue of the possible correlation between promises of leniency and innocent defendants' guilty pleas. The opinion noted:

> We would have serious doubts about this case if the encouragement of guilty pleas by offers of leniency substantially increased the likelihood that defendants, advised by competent counsel, would falsely condemn themselves. But our view is to the contrary and is based on our expectations that courts will satisfy themselves that pleas of guilty are voluntarily and intelligently made by competent defendants with adequate advice of counsel and that there is nothing to question the accuracy and reliability of the defendants' admissions that they committed the crimes with which they are charged.[37]

Contrary to the Court's reasoning, the mere presence of competent counsel does not foreclose the issue of whether an innocent defendant can be induced to plead guilty. Defense counsel may urge acceptance of a bargain, even though convinced of a client's innocence, in order to obtain optimal disposition of the case.[38] The opinion also ignores the reality of the routine relationship between defense counsel, often a public defender, and defendant—a relationship that frequently casts counsel in the role of agent-mediator rather than defense advocate.[39]

Collateral Attacks on Other Grounds

Although defendants can challenge the voluntariness of their plea of guilty in a postconviction hearing, defendants are generally precluded from attacking the plea on grounds other than voluntariness. In *McMann v. Richardson* (1970), decided on the same day as *Brady*, the Supreme Court ruled that state prisoners are not entitled to attack their pleas of guilty on the antecedent grounds that an alleged coerced confession induced the plea of guilty. Although the Court held open the possibility that a coerced confession could have an abiding impact on a plea, and thus taint the plea,[40] still the majority ruled that, absent other factors, a coerced confession alone does not justify a collateral attack on the plea. The Court reasoned that it was improbable that a defendant who thought the state's case weak, in the absence of an admissible confession, would plead guilty. It concluded that a defendant in such a situation would contest the charge, because a plea of guilty "is nothing less than a refusal to present his federal claims to the state court in the first instance—a choice by the defendant to take the benefits, if any, of a plea of guilty and then pursue his coerced confession claim in collateral proceedings."[41] Indeed, the only avenue left open by *McMann* was the possibility of an attack on the competency of legal counsel. But here, the Court made it evident that federal courts should take a broad view of the range of legal advice that could be considered competent. Thus the Court noted that even if counsel erroneously advised a client that a confession was admissible, and such advice became a part of defendant's calculus in deciding to plead guilty, the plea would not necessarily become an unintelligent and voidable act.[42] Erroneous advice, the Court reasoned, may be reasonably competent; that is, within the range of competence demanded of an attorney working in any area that is inherently uncertain.

Three years after *McMann*, the Court reiterated its policy against postconviction attacks on pleas of guilty. In *Tollett v. Henderson* (1973), respondent Henderson had pleaded guilty to a charge of first-degree murder in 1948, having been previously indicted by a grand jury. He was sentenced to ninety-nine years in prison. Over twenty years later, Henderson sought a federal writ of habeas corpus, asserting that blacks had been systematically excluded from the grand jury that had indicted him. The state of Tennessee, in effect, conceded that such exclusion had occurred. However, Henderson had been represented by counsel in 1948, and the plea of guilty was made after counsel had obtained an agreement that the sentence recommendation would be ninety-nine years rather than death. The majority of the justices rejected Henderson's immediate release and ruled that, in order to obtain a federal writ of habeas corpus, Henderson would be required to establish not only that the grand jury was unconstitutionally selected, but that his attorney's advice to plead guilty without challenging the composition of the grand jury was advice outside the range of competence demanded of attorneys in criminal cases.[43] In reaffirming *Brady*, the *Henderson* majority observed:

A guilty plea, voluntarily and intelligently entered, may not be vacated because the defendant was not advised of every conceivable constitutional plea in abatement he might have to the charge, no matter how peripheral such a plea might be to the normal focus of counsel's inquiry. And just as it is not sufficient for the criminal defendant seeking to set aside such a plea to show that his counsel in retrospect may not have correctly appraised the constitutional significance of certain historical facts . . . it is likewise not sufficient that he show if counsel had pursued a certain factual inquiry such a pursuit would have uncovered a possible constitutional infirmity in the proceedings.[44]

Brady and *McMann* not only attempted to foreclose a reexamination of antecedent constitutional infirmities in pleas of guilty; the majority opinions in these cases made it clear that a defendant who pleaded guilty has waived the constitutional rights as then defined and also has waived the right to attack a guilty plea based on *subsequently defined rights*. In effect, the waiver of undefined rights—rights that might be subsequently declared by the courts—would preclude any retroactive application of newly defined constitutional rights to the vast majority of prisoners.[45] This abrupt attempt to insulate guilty pleas from subsequent constitutional attack was met with sharp dissent by Justices Brennan, Marshall, and Douglas, and subsequent decisions have revealed some cracks in this aspect of the cases.

In *Blackledge v. Perry* (1974), respondent Perry was initially charged and convicted of a misdemeanor.[46] When Perry pursued his statutory right of a trial de novo, or retrial, the prosecutor obtained a felony indictment covering the same conduct. Perry pleaded guilty to the felony charge and then sought review by a habeas corpus petition. The Supreme Court ruled that because Perry had a statutory right to a trial de novo, the state could not retaliate by substituting a felony charge for the original misdemeanor charge, subjecting Perry to a stiffer sentence. Furthermore, the majority ruled that Perry's right to challenge his felony conviction was not waived by his plea of guilty. Although it accepted the *Brady* rationale that normally antecedent constitutional violations do not survive a plea of guilty, Justice Stewart's majority opinion limited the open-ended waiver of *Brady* and *McMann*. This opinion in *Blackledge* is narrow, but it does suggest that a defendant who pleads guilty does not waive the right to subsequently challenge the power of the state to initiate or proceed with a prosecution, at least where a violation cannot be "cured." Thus, a claim of prior jeopardy would survive a plea of guilty, as would a claim that the state was without power to initiate and proceed with a prosecution because the state lacked statutory authority or the statutory authority was unconstitutional on its face.[47] On the other hand, *Blackledge* accepts the waiver of those rights that deal with establishing the fact of criminal conduct: confrontation and cross-examination, the state's burden of proof, per se evidentiary rules (such as those that apply to coerced confessions), and illegally seized evidence.

In 1975, a five-justice majority, again led by Justice Stewart, went a step beyond *Blackledge*. In *Lefkowitz v. Newsome*, respondent Newsome was arrested on a charge of loitering. An incidental search of respondent revealed a small quantity of heroin. He was first tried on the loitering charge and was convicted. When his motion to suppress the heroin was denied, he then pleaded guilty to a reduced charge of attempted possession of a dangerous drug. New York law, however, allows a defendant who has been convicted by a plea of guilty to continue to pursue on appeal an order denying a motion to suppress evidence. In short, New York law did not require a defendant to waive judicial review of constitutional claims made antecedent to the guilty plea. Therefore, the majority ruled that "when state law permits a defendant to plead guilty without forfeiting his right to judicial review of specified constitutional issues, the defendant is not foreclosed from pursuing those constitutional claims in a federal habeas corpus proceeding."[48] Thus, even though Newsome had lost his appeal in the state courts, he was granted the right to pursue his claim through a federal habeas corpus proceeding. Of course, under *Newsome,* a state would be free to alter the statutory scheme and foreclose judicial review of certain antecedent constitutional violations. On the other hand, the New York scheme is aimed at those defendants who conclude that they could not prevail at trial unless they could exclude an allegedly coerced confession or suppress evidence seized by the police. By providing post–guilty plea appellate review of pretrial motions to suppress, the statute encourages some defendants to plead guilty who would otherwise go to trial in order to preserve their constitutional claims.

Bargaining Threats

Although *Blackledge* involved the possibility of prosecutorial vindictiveness in subsequently charging the defendant with a more serious offense than was originally charged, the original context of the case was not a plea bargain. In *Blackledge,* the prosecution reindicted the convicted misdemeanant on a felony charge after the defendant had invoked an appellate remedy. The Court ruled that it was not constitutionally proper for a prosecutor to respond to a defendant's invocation of a statutory right of appeal by bringing a more serious charge. This, of course, left open the question of whether a prosecutor, in the context of plea bargaining, may threaten a defendant with a more serious charge if the defendant refuses to plead guilty to a lesser offense. This issue was answered in 1978, in *Bordenkircher v. Hayes.*[49]

In *Hayes,* the defendant was indicted for issuing a forged eighty-eight-dollar check. The prosecutor met with Hayes and his attorney to discuss a possible plea arrangement. The prosecutor offered to recommend a five-year sentence on the forging charge and pointedly stated that if Hayes did not accept this arrangement, he would seek an additional indictment of Hayes as an habitual criminal, an offense conveying a mandatory life sentence.[50] Hayes refused the bargain, and the prosecution obtained the additional indictment. At trial, Hayes was convicted of the forgery offense; in a separate proceeding, he was found to have been twice convicted of felony offenses and was sentenced to life imprisonment.

In upholding Hayes's conviction, the Court rejected the contention that he was punished with a more severe charge in retaliation for refusing to plead guilty. The five-justice majority noted that Hayes was made aware at the outset of negotiations of the prosecutor's intentions and that the threat of the added indictment did not come after the negotiations on the recommended five-year sentence had failed. For all practical purposes, Hayes was in the same position as if the grand jury had originally indicted him as a recidivist and the prosecutor had offered to drop that charge. The Court concluded that there is no such thing as punishment or retaliation so long as the accused is free to accept or reject an offer by a prosecutor.

One of the dissents agreed that to reverse Hayes's conviction might induce aggressive prosecutors to overcharge and then bargain. The dissent concluded, however, that the procedure—the prosecutor having been content to make visible to the public only one charge and thereafter introducing the prospect of a more serious charge in the bargaining session—gives the appearance of prosecutorial vindictiveness.[51] Indeed, as Justice Powell noted in a separate dissent, the prosecutor's purpose was to discourage and then to penalize with unique severity the exercise of the constitutional right to enter a plea of not guilty.[52]

CONCLUSION

The Supreme Court's endorsement of plea bargaining would seem to preclude its abolition, at least in the near future. In the absence of conclusive evidence that plea bargaining results in countless numbers of innocent defendants pleading guilty and given the specter of the criminal justice system grinding to a halt without plea bargaining, critics of the practice might be well advised to attempt reforms rather than abolition. Considering the low visibility of the bargaining process and the range of prosecutorial discretion in charging, one reform would be to require the prosecution to disclose, unless the defense objects, the evidence on which proof of the charge is based.[53] Because the purpose of prosecutorial plea bargaining is to obtain the consent of a defendant to a conviction without trial, disclosure would at least obviate the charge that the defendant is forced to bargain in the dark.[54]

Beyond this issue, plea bargaining in its present state will remain a largely invisible and unreviewable form of justice and, as Justice Cardozo said in another context, "irrational in its mercies as in its rigors."[55] For all of its claimed efficiency and flexibility, doubts remain about the compatibility of the practice and a constitutional system of criminal justice. The element of the rule of law in criminal justice elevates the system from mere coercion and naked power to a system clothed with moral authority. Procedural regularity and reliability in the determination of guilt and punishment are not niceties that are expendable; they give a degree of assurance to the public that the criminal sanction is imposed in an evenhanded manner, free of arbitrariness however masked. To the extent that plea bargaining has about it elements of coercion and arbitrariness, it will remain a suspected, albeit efficient, process.

NOTES

1. Director of the Administrative Office, United States Courts, *Annual Report, 1973* (Washington, D.C.: GPO, 1974), p. 402, table D-4.

2. Throughout this section, the use of "guilty plea" includes the plea of *nolo contendere* (no contest). For a discussion of nolo contendere pleas, see *Hudson v. United States,* 272 U.S. 451 (1926); and *North Carolina v. Alford,* 400 U.S. 25 (1970). The issue of differential sentencing is treated below, pp. 220–221.

3. The standard reference work in plea bargaining is Donald J. Newman, *Conviction: The Determination of Guilt or Innocence Without Trial* (Boston: Little, Brown, 1966).

4. Raymond Moley, "The Vanishing Jury," 2 *So. Calif. L. Rev.* 96 (1928).

5. Ibid. at 107, 109.

6. See note, "The Plea Bargain in Historical Perspective," 23 *Buff. L. Rev.* 499 (1974).

7. Ibid. at 508–509.

8. William Blackstone, *Commentaries on the Laws of England,* Cooley ed. (Chicago: Callaghan, 1884), vol. 2, bk. 4, pp. 364–365.

9. E.g., *Commonwealth v. Bottis,* 1 Mass. 94 (1804); and *Edwards v. People,* 39 Mich. 760 (1878).

10. E.g., *State v. Reinghous,* 43 Iowa 149 (1876).

11. E.g., *Monahan v. State,* 135 Ind. 216 (1893).

12. See Albert Alschuler, "The Prosecutor's Role in Plea Bargaining," 36 *U. Chi. L. Rev.* 50, 51 (1968).

13. President's Commission on Law Enforcement and the Administration of Justice, *Task Force Report: The Courts* (Washington, D.C.: GPO, 1967), p. 10.

14. National Advisory Commission on Criminal Justice Standards and Goals, *The Courts* (Washington, D.C.: GPO, 1973), p. 44.

15. See Alschuler, "Prosecutor's Role," pp. 85–105.

16. Ibid. at 64.

17. U.S. Department of Justice, *Sourcebook of Criminal Justice Statistics, 1973* (Washington, D.C.: GPO, 1974), p. 329, table 5.36. Comparisons here are hazardous because a "harsher" sentence may reflect a variety of factors, among them the prior criminal record of the defendant.

18. Quoted in note, "The Unconstitutionality of Plea Bargaining," 83 *Harv. L. Rev.* 1387, 1388 (1970).

19. Note, "The Influence of the Defendant's Plea on Judicial Determination of Sentence," 66 *Yale L.J.* 205, 221 (1956).

20. For a more supportive view of differential sentencing, see Newman, *Conviction,* pp. 62–66.

21. *Kercheval v. United States,* 274 U.S. 220, 223 (1927).

22. *Von Moltke v. Gillies,* 332 U.S. 708 (1948), deception; and *Wally v. Johnson,* 316 U.S. 101 (1942), threats.

23. *Brady v. United States,* 397 U.S. 742, 755 (1970).

24. *Brookhurst v. Janis,* 384 U.S. 1, 4 (1966).

25. *Boykin v. Alabama,* 395 U.S. 238, 244 (1969); and *Henderson v. Morgan,* 426 U.S. 637 (1976).

26. *Moore v. Michigan,* 355 U.S. 155 (1957); and *Brady v. United States,* 397 U.S. at 748, n. 6.

27. *Santobello v. New York,* 404 U.S. 257, 261 (1971). Rule 11 of the Federal Rules of Criminal Procedure, as amended in 1975, requires in federal cases that if a plea agreement has been reached, the agreement must be disclosed, normally in open court and on the record (rule 11-1-[2]).

28. *Santobello v. New York,* 404 U.S. at 262.

29. Rule 11-(e)-(1), Fed. Rules Crim. Proc., prohibits a federal judge from partici-pating in plea bargaining. See also Kathleen Gallagher, "Judicial Participation in Plea Bargaining," 9 *Harv. C.R.-C.L. Rev.* 29 (1974).

30. Fed. Rules Crim. Proc., rule 11-(e)-(4).

31. E.g., *United States v. Marshall,* 410 F.2d 792, 795 (1975).

32. *Kercheval v. United States,* 274 U.S. at 224; and *United States v. Banker,* 414 F.2d 208 (1975).

33. *Kercheval v. United States.*

34. *United States v. Jackson,* 390 U.S. 470 (1968). Previously held unconstitutional.

35. *Brady v. United States,* 397 U.S. at 750–753.

36. Ibid. at 750.

37. Ibid. at 758.

38. Welsh White, "A Proposal for Reform of the Plea Bargaining Process," 119 *U. Penn. L. Rev.* 438, 452 (1971).

39. See Abraham S. Blumberg, "The Practice of Law as a Confidence Game," *Warner Modular Publications,* no. 148 (1973).

40. *McMann v. Richardson,* 397 U.S. 759, 767 (1970). See also *Pennsylvania ex rel. Herman v. Claudy,* 350 U.S. 116 (1959); and *Fontaine v. United States,* 411 U.S. 213 (1973).

41. *McMann v. Richardson,* 397 U.S. at 768.

42. Ibid. at 769.

43. *Tollett v. Henderson,* 411 U.S. 258, 268 (1973).

44. Ibid. at 267–268.

45. See Robert Schwartz, "The Guilty Plea as a Waiver of 'Present but Unknowable' Constitutional Rights," 74 *Colum. L. Rev.* 1435 (1974).

46. *Blackledge v. Perry,* 417 U.S. 21 (1974).

47. See *Menna v. New York,* 423 U.S. 61 (1975).

48. *Lefkowitz v. Newsome,* 420 U.S. 283, 293 (1975).

49. *Bordenkircher v. Hayes,* 434 U.S. 357 (1978).

50. Hayes had previously been convicted of robbery, and he had previously pled guilty to the offense of detaining a female.

51. See dissent of Justice Blackmun, joined by Justices Brennan and Marshall, *Bordenkircher v. Hayes,* 434 U.S. at 365.

52. Ibid. at 372–373. See *Corbitt v. New Jersey,* _____ U.S. _____ (1978), upholding a statute that may penalize certain defendants who refuse to plead *non vult* to a general indictment of murder.

53. Joseph Goldstein, "For Harold Lasswell," 84 *Yale L.J.* 683, 699 (1975).

54. For a discussion of the effect of discovery limitations on the bargaining process, see Alschuler, "Prosecutor's Role," pp. 64–70.

55. Quoted ibid. at 122.

JUDICIAL DECISIONS

The Constitutionality of Plea Bargaining:
Brady v. United States, 397 U.S. 742 (1970)

Mr. Justice WHITE delivered the opinion of the Court.

In 1959, petitioner was charged with kidnaping in violation of 18 U.S.C. § 1201 (a). Since the indictment charged that the victim of the kidnaping was not liberated unharmed, petitioner faced a maximum penalty of death if the verdict of the jury should so recommend. Petitioner, represented by competent counsel throughout, first elected to plead not guilty. Apparently because the trial judge was unwilling to try the case without a jury, petitioner made no serious attempt to reduce the possibility of a death penalty by waiving a jury trial. Upon learning that his codefendant, who had confessed to the authorities, would plead guilty and be available to testify against him, petitioner changed his plea to guilty. His plea was accepted after the trial judge twice questioned him as to the voluntariness of his plea. Petitioner was sentenced to 50 years imprisonment, later reduced to 30.

In 1967, petitioner sought relief under 28 U.S.C. § 2255, claiming that his plea of guilty was not voluntarily given because § 1201(a) operated to coerce his plea, because his counsel exerted impermissible pressure upon him, and because his plea was induced by representations with respect to reduction of sentence and clemency. It was also alleged that the trial judge had not fully complied with Rule 11 of the Federal Rules of Criminal Procedure.

After a hearing, the District Court for the District of New Mexico denied relief. According to the District Court's findings, petitioner's counsel did not put impermissible pressure on petitioner to plead guilty and no representations were made with respect to a reduced sentence or clemency. The court held that § 1201(a) was constitutional and found that petitioner decided to plead guilty when he learned that his codefendant was going to plead guilty: petitioner pleaded guilty "by reason of other matters and not by reason of the statute" or because of any acts of the trial judge. The court concluded that "the plea was voluntarily and knowingly made."

The Court of Appeals for the Tenth Circuit affirmed, determining that the District Court's findings were supported by substantial evidence and specifically approving the finding that petitioner's plea of guilty was voluntary. We granted certiorari to consider the claim that the Court of Appeals was in error in not reaching a contrary result on the authority of this Court's decision in *United States v. Jackson*, 390 U.S. 570 (1968). We affirm.

I

. . .

That a guilty plea is a grave and solemn act to be accepted only with care and discernment has long been recognized. Central to the plea and the foundation for entering judgment against the defendant is the defendant's admission in open court that he committed the acts charged in the indictment. He thus stands as a witness against himself and he is shielded by the Fifth Amendment from being compelled to do so—hence the minimum requirement that his plea be the voluntary expression of his own choice. But the plea is more than an admission of past conduct; it is the defendant's consent that judgment of conviction may be entered without a trial—a waiver of his right to trial before a jury or a judge. Waivers of constitutional rights not only must be voluntary but must be knowing, intelligent acts done with sufficient awareness of the relevant circumstances and likely consequences. On neither score was Brady's plea of guilty invalid.

<h2 style="text-align:center">II</h2>

The trial judge in 1959 found the plea voluntary before accepting it; the District Court in 1968, after an evidentiary hearing, found that the plea was voluntarily made; the Court of Appeals specifically approved the finding of voluntariness. We see no reason on this record to disturb the judgment of those courts. Petitioner, advised by competent counsel, tendered his plea after his codefendant, who had already given a confession, determined to plead guilty and became available to testify against petitioner. It was this development that the District Court found to have triggered Brady's guilty plea.

The voluntariness of Brady's plea can be determined only by considering all of the relevant circumstances surrounding it. One of these circumstances was the possibility of a heavier sentence following a guilty verdict after a trial. It may be that Brady, faced with a strong case against him and recognizing that his chances for acquittal were slight, preferred to plead guilty and thus limit the penalty to life imprisonment rather than to elect a jury trial which could result in a death penalty. But even if we assume that Brady would not have pleaded guilty except for the death penalty provision of § 1201(a), this assumption merely identifies the penalty provision as a "but for" cause of his plea. That the statute caused the plea in this sense does not necessarily prove that the plea was coerced and invalid as an involuntary act.

The State to some degree encourages pleas of guilty at every important step in the criminal process. For some people, their breach of a State's law is alone sufficient reason for surrendering themselves and accepting punishment. For others, apprehension and charge, both threatening acts by the Government, jar them into admitting their guilt. In still other cases, the post-indictment accumulation of evidence may convince the defendant and his counsel that a trial is not worth the agony and expense to the defendant and his family. All these pleas of guilty are valid in spite of the State's responsibility for some of the factors motivating the pleas; the pleas are no more improperly compelled than is the decision by a defendant at the close of the State's evidence at trial that he must take the stand or face certain conviction.

Of course, the agents of the State may not produce a plea by actual or threatened physical harm or by mental coercion overbearing the will of the defendant. But nothing of the sort is claimed in this case; nor is there evidence that Brady was so gripped by fear of the death penalty or hope of leniency that he did not or could not, with the help of counsel, rationally weigh the advantages of going to trial against the advantages of pleading guilty. Brady's claim is of a different sort: that it violates the Fifth Amendment to influence or encourage a guilty plea by opportunity or promise of leniency and that a guilty plea is coerced and invalid if influenced by the fear of a possibly higher penalty for the crime charged if a conviction is obtained after the State is put to its proof.

Insofar as the voluntariness of his plea is concerned, there is little to differentiate Brady from (1) the defendant, in a jurisdiction where the judge and jury have the same range of sentencing power, who pleads guilty because his lawyer advises him that the judge will very probably be more lenient than the jury; (2) the defendant, in a jurisdiction where the judge alone has sentencing power, who is advised by counsel that the judge is normally more lenient with defendants who plead guilty than with those who go to trial; (3) the defendant who is permitted by prosecutor and judge to plead guilty to a lesser offense included in the offense charged; and (4) the defendant who pleads guilty to certain counts with the understanding that other charges will be dropped. In each of these situations, as in Brady's case, the defendant might never plead guilty absent the possibility or certainty that the plea will result in a lesser penalty than the sentence that could be imposed after a trial and a verdict of guilty. We decline to hold, however, that a guilty plea is compelled and invalid under the Fifth Amendment whenever motivated by the defendant's desire to accept the certainty or probability of a lesser penalty rather than face a wider range of possibilities extending from acquittal to conviction and a higher penalty authorized by law for the crime charged.

The issued we deal with is inherent in the criminal law and its administration because guilty pleas are not constitutionally forbidden, because the criminal law characteristically extends to judge or jury a range of choice in setting the sentence in individual cases, and because both the State and the defendant often find it advantageous to preclude the possibility of the maximum penalty authorized by law. For a defendant who sees slight possibility of acquittal, the advantages of pleading guilty and limiting the probable penalty are obvious—his exposure is reduced, the correctional process can begin immediately, and the practical burdens of a trial are eliminated. For the State there are also advantages—the more promptly imposed punishment after an admission of guilt may more effectively attain the objectives of punishment; and with the avoidance of trial, scarce judicial and prosecutorial resources are conserved for those cases in which there is a substantial issue of the defendant's guilt or in which there is substantial doubt that the State can sustain its burden of proof. It is this mutuality of advantage that perhaps explains the fact that at present well over three-fourths of the criminal convictions in this country rest on pleas of guilty, a great many of them no doubt motivated at least in part by the hope or assurance of a lesser penalty than might be imposed if there were a guilty verdict after a trial to judge or jury.

Of course, that the prevalence of guilty pleas is explainable does not necessarily validate those pleas or the system which produces them. But we cannot hold that it is unconstitutional for the State to extend a benefit to a defendant who in turn extends a substantial benefit to the State and who demonstrates by his plea that he is ready and willing to admit his crime and to enter the correctional system in a frame of mind that affords hope for success in rehabilitation over a shorter period of time than might otherwise be necessary.

A contrary holding would require the States and Federal Government to forbid guilty pleas altogether, to provide a single invariable penalty for each crime defined by the statutes, or to place the sentencing function in a separate authority having no knowledge of the manner in which the conviction in each case was obtained. In any event, it would be necessary to forbid prosecutors and judges to accept guilty pleas to selected counts, to lesser included offenses, or to reduced charges. The Fifth Amendment does not reach so far.

. . .

III

The record before us also supports the conclusion that Brady's plea was intelligently made. He was advised by competent counsel, he was made aware of the nature of the charge against him, and there was nothing to indicate that he was incompetent or otherwise not in control of his mental faculties; once his confederate had pleaded guilty and became available to testify, he chose to plead guilty, perhaps to ensure that he would face no more than life imprisonment or a term of years. Brady was aware of precisely what he was doing when he admitted that he had kidnaped the victim and had not released her unharmed.

It is true that Brady's counsel advised him that § 1201(a) empowered the jury to impose the death penalty and that nine years later in *United States v. Jackson*, supra, the Court held that the jury had no such power as long as the judge could impose only a lesser penalty if trial was to the court or there was a plea of guilty. But these facts do not require us to set aside Brady's conviction.

Often the decision to plead guilty is heavily influenced by the defendant's appraisal of the prosecution's case against him and by the apparent likelihood of securing leniency should a guilty plea be offered and accepted. Considerations like these frequently present imponderable questions for which there are no certain answers; judgments may be made that in the light of later events seem improvident, although they were perfectly sensible at the time. The rule that a plea must be intelligently made to be valid does not require that a plea be vulnerable to later attack if the defendant did not correctly assess every relevant factor entering into his decision. A defendant is not entitled to withdraw his plea merely because he discovers long after the plea has been accepted that his calculus misapprehended the quality of the State's case or the likely penalties attached to alternative courses of action. More particularly, absent misrepresentation or other impermissible conduct by state agents, cf. *Von Moltke v. Gillies*, 332 U.S. 708 (1948), a voluntary plea of guilty intelligently made in the light of a then applicable law does not become vulnerable because later judicial decisions indicate that the plea rested on a faulty premise. A plea of guilty triggered by the expectations of a competently counseled defendant that the State will have a strong case against him is not subject to later attack because the defendant's lawyer correctly advised him with respect to the then existing law as to possible penalties but later pronouncements of the courts, as in this case, hold that the maximum penalty for the crime in question was less than was reasonably assumed at the time the plea was entered.

. . .

Although Brady's plea of guilty may well have been motivated in part by a desire to avoid a possible death penalty, we are convinced that his plea was voluntarily and intelligently made and we have no reason to doubt that his solemn admission of guilt was truthful.

Affirmed.

Plea Bargaining and Threats:
Bordenkircher v. Hayes, 434 U.S. 357 (1978)

Mr. Justice STEWART delivered the opinion of the Court.

The question in this case is whether the Due Process Clause of the Fourteenth Amendment is violated when a state prosecutor carries out a threat made during plea negotiations to reindict the accused on more serious charges if he does not plead guilty to the offense with which he was originally charged.

I

The respondent, Paul Lewis Hayes, was indicted by a Fayette County, Ky., grand jury on a charge of uttering a forged instrument in the amount of $88.30, an offense then punishable by a term of two to 10 years in prison. Ky. Rev. Stat. § 434.130 (repealed 1974). After arraignment, Hayes, his retained counsel, and the Commonwealth's attorney met in the presence of the clerk of the court to discuss a possible plea agreement. During these conferences the prosecutor offered to recommend a sentence of five years in prison if Hayes would plead guilty to the indictment. He also said that if Hayes did not plead guilty and "save the court the inconvenience of a trial," he would return to the grand jury to seek an indictment under the Kentucky Habitual Criminal Act, then Ky. Rev. Stat. § 431.190 (repealed 1975), which would subject Hayes to a mandatory sentence of life imprisonment by reason of his two prior felony convictions. Hayes chose not to plead guilty, and the prosecutor did obtain an indictment charging him under the Habitual Criminal Act. It is not disputed that the recidivist charge was fully justified by the evidence, that the prosecutor was in possession of this evidence at the time of the original indictment, and that Hayes' refusal to plead guilty to the original charge was what led to his indictment under the habitual criminal statute.

A jury found Hayes guilty on the principal charge of uttering a forged instrument and, in a separate proceeding, further found that he had twice before been convicted of felonies. As required by the habitual offender statute, he was sentenced to a life term in the penitentiary. The Kentucky Court of Appeals rejected Hayes' constitutional objections to the enhanced sentence, holding in an unpublished opinion that imprisonment for life with the possibility of parole was constitutionally permissible in light of the previous felonies of which Hayes had been convicted, and that the prosecutor's decision to indict him as an habitual offender was a legitimate use of available leverage in the plea bargaining process.

On Hayes' petition for a federal writ of habeas corpus, the United States District Court for the Eastern District of Kentucky agreed that there had been no constitutional violation in the sentence or the indictment procedure, and denied the writ. The Court of Appeals for the Sixth Circuit reversed the District Court's judgment. While recognizing "that plea bargaining now plays an important role in our criminal justice system," the appellate court thought that the prosecutor's conduct during the bargaining negotiations had violated the principles of *Blackledge v. Perry,* 417 U.S. 21, which "protect[ed] defendants from the vindictive exercise of a prosecutor's discretion." . . . We granted certiorari to consider a constitutional question of importance in the administration of criminal justice.

II

It may be helpful to clarify at the outset the nature of the issue in this case. While the prosecutor did not actually obtain the recidivist indictment until after the plea conferences had ended, his intention to do so was clearly put forth at the outset of the plea negotiations. Hayes was thus fully informed of the true terms of the offer when he made his decision to plead not guilty. This is not a situation, therefore, where the prosecutor without notice brought an additional and more serious charge after plea negotiations relating only to the original indictment had ended with the defendant's insistence on pleading not guilty. As a practical matter, in short, this case would be no different if the grand jury had indicted Hayes as a recidivist from the outset, and the prosecutor had offered to drop that charge as part of the plea bargain.

. . .

III

We have recently had occasion to observe that "whatever might be the situation in an ideal world, the fact is that the guilty plea and the often concomitant plea bargain are important components of this country's criminal justice system. Properly administered, they can benefit all concerned." *Blackledge v. Allison,* 431 U.S. 63, 71. The open acknowledgment of this previously clandestine practice has led this Court to recognize the importance of counsel during plea negotiations, *Brady v. United States,* 397 U.S. 742, 758, the need for a public record indicating that a plea was knowingly and voluntarily made, *Boykin v. Alabama,* 395 U.S. 238, 242, and the requirement that a prosecutor's plea bargaining promise must be kept, *Santobello v. New York,* 404 U.S. 257, 262. . . .

IV

. . .

To punish a person because he has done what the law plainly allows him to do is a due process violation of the most basic sort, see *North Carolina v. Pearce,* supra, 395 U.S., at 738 (opinion of Black, J.), and for an agent of the State to pursue a course of action whose objective is to penalize a person's reliance on his legal rights is "patently unconstitutional." *Chaffin v. Stynchcombe,* supra, 412 U.S., at 32–33, n. 20. But in the "give-and-take" of plea bargaining, there is no such element of punishment or retaliation so long as the accused is free to accept or reject the prosecution's offer.

Plea bargaining flows from "the mutuality of advantage" to defendants and prosecutors, each with his own reasons for wanting to avoid trial. *Brady v. United States,* supra, 397 U.S., at 752. Defendants advised by competent counsel and protected by other procedural safeguards are presumptively capable of intelligent choice in response to prosecutorial persuasion, and unlikely to be driven to false self-condemnation. Id., at 758. Indeed, acceptance of the basic legitimacy of plea bargaining necessarily implies rejection of any notion that a guilty plea is involuntary in a constitutional sense simply because it is the end result of the bargaining process. By hypothesis, the plea may have been induced by promises of a recommendation of a lenient sentence or a reduction of charges, and thus by fear of the possibility of a greater penalty upon conviction after a trial.

While confronting a defendant with the risk of more severe punishment clearly may have a "discouraging effect on the defendant's assertion of his trial rights, the imposition of these difficult choices [is] an inevitable"—and permissible—"attribute of any legitimate system which tolerates and encourages the negotiation of pleas." *Chaffin v. Stynchcombe,* supra, 412 U.S., at 31. It follows that, by tolerating and encouraging the negotiation of pleas, this Court has necessarily accepted as constitutionally legitimate the simple reality that the prosecutor's interest at the bargaining table is to persuade the defendant to forego his right to plead not guilty.

It is not disputed here that Hayes was properly chargeable under the recidivist statute, since he had in fact been convicted of two previous felonies. In our system, so long as the prosecutor has probable cause to believe that the accused committed an offense defined by statute, the decision whether or not to prosecute, and what charge to file or bring before a grand jury, generally rests entirely in his discretion. Within the limits set by the legislature's constitutionally valid definition of chargeable offenses, "the conscious exercise of some selectivity in enforcement is not in itself a federal constitutional violation" so long as "the selection was [not] deliberately based upon an unjustifiable standard such as race, religion, or other arbitrary classification." *Oyler v. Boyles,* 368 U.S. 448, 456. To hold that the prosecutor's desire to induce a guilty plea is an "unjustifiable standard," which, like race or religion, may play no part in his charging decision, would contradict the very premises that underlie the concept of plea bargaining itself. Moreover, a rigid constitutional rule that would prohibit a prosecutor from acting forthrightly in his dealings with the defense could only invite unhealthy subterfuge that would drive the practice of plea bargaining back into the shadows from which it has so recently emerged.

There is no doubt that the breadth of discretion that our country's legal system vests in prosecuting attorneys carries with it the potential for both individual and institutional abuse. And broad though that discretion may be, there are undoubtedly constitutional limits upon its exercise. We hold only that the course of conduct engaged in by the prosecutor in this case, which no more than openly presented the defendant with the unpleasant alternatives of foregoing trial or facing charges on which he was plainly subject to prosecution, did not violate the Due Process Clause of the Fourteenth Amendment.

Accordingly, the judgment of the Court of Appeals is

Reversed.

8

Double
Jeopardy

> Nor shall any person be sub-
> ject for the same offence to be twice put in jeopardy of life
> or limb.
>
> —Fifth Amendment

HISTORICAL BACKGROUND

The restriction against double jeopardy would seem to be axiomatic to any form of limited government. Indeed, the concept has existed in a variety of forms for hundreds of years. Perhaps the earliest expression of the concept is found in the Book of Nahum, where it is said that the Lord "will not take vengeance twice against his foes."[1] In the Digest of Justinian, compiled in 533 A.D., it is recorded that "the governor should not permit the same person to be again accused of crime of which he has been acquitted."[2] But however ancient the maxim *nemo vis in iclipsum* (no man ought to be punished twice for the same offense) may be, its immediate relevance and acceptance in Anglo-American criminal procedure is a relatively recent development.[3] None of the great medieval legal scholars—Glanvill, Britton, Bracton—even mentions the concept, and indeed there is some speculation that Henry II rejected it in 1176 when Thomas à Becket pressed it in the dispute over the criminal jurisdiction of the clergy.[4] The slow acceptance of double jeopardy is largely the consequence of two factors: The first was the slow evolution in the separation of criminal and civil liabilities, particularly between crimes and torts. English law only gradually came to distinguish between acts and omissions considered sufficiently grave to be called *criminal,* and acts and omissions that were private wrongs, or torts. In the absence of a clear distinction, a plea of former jeopardy would have been difficult to maintain. The second factor was the dual system for prosecuting criminal offenses. In addition to indictment by the Crown, it was possible until 1819 for a private party to bring a criminal suit—the so-called suit of vengeance[5]—by a process called "appeal." Although by the fifteenth century formal pleas of former jeopardy were occasionally noted, by statute the plea of *autrefois acquit* (previous acquittal) under the Crown's indictment was not a bar to a private suit by appeal.

By the first half of the seventeenth century, *autrefois acquit, autrefois attaint,* and pardon—technical bars to additional prosecution—were considered by Sir Edward Coke to be an established part of the common law. In the *Third Institute,* Coke wrote: "*Autrefoit acquite,* must be of the same felony, and albeit he be acquit of the latter felony, yet may he be arraigned of any former felony."[6] Legal commentators after Coke generally recognized the technical pleas. Sir Matthew Hale and later William Hawkins both discussed the pleas in their works.[7] By the second half of the seventeenth century, former jeopardy began to take on some of its modern cast. The Crown was no longer able to appeal an acquittal, but a defendant was, on conviction, permitted to seek a new trial.[8] Furthermore, private appeals following convictions on the Crown's indictments were now barred in certain situations.[9] Blackstone, writing on the eve of the American Revolution, justified the pleas of *autrefois acquit* and *convict* as follows:

> The plea of *autrefoits acquit,* or a former acquittal, is grounded on this universal maxim of the common law of England, that no man is to be brought into jeopardy of his life more than once for the same offence. And hence it is allowed as a consequence, that when a man is once fairly found not guilty upon any indictment, or other prosecution, before any court having competent jurisdiction of the offence he may plead such acquittal in bar of any subsequent accusation for the same crime.
>
> . . . The plea of *autrefoits convict,* or a former conviction for the same identical crime, though no judgment was ever given, or perhaps will be . . . is a good plea in bar to an indictment. And this depends upon the same principle as the former, that no man ought to be twice brought in danger of his life for one and the same crime.[10]

On the other hand, as late as the early eighteenth century, double jeopardy did not command a central position in the rights of the English, either at home or in the colonies. It did not appear in the Magna Charta (1215), nor was it included in the English Bill of Rights (1689). In the colonies, a form of double jeopardy protection was included in the Body of Liberties in Massachusetts in 1641, but the protection was only rarely noted in Colonial case law and only two states, New Hampshire and Pennsylvania, thought the right worthy of recognition in their respective bills of rights.[11] The failure to raise double jeopardy to the level of a constitutional right is probably of little significance because the colonies and the newly formed states did recognize the common law of England. In any event, James Madison included the following provision in his proposed amendments to the federal Constitution in 1789: "No person shall be subject, except in cases of impeachment, to more than one punishment or trial for the same offense."[12] The framers, fearing that Madison's wording might be construed as a limitation on the right of one convicted of a crime to seek a new trial, changed the wording to read: "Nor shall any person be subject for the same offence to be twice put in jeopardy of life or limb."

The modified version, approved and adopted, incorporated certain antique, imprecise wording.[13] But, like other parts of the Fifth Amendment, the double-jeopardy clause was intended, not as a code provision, but rather as a declaration of broad policy and, presumably, an endorsement of the common law as it stood in 1789.[14] The policy was twofold: First, it was intended to preclude, through the plea of *autrefois convict*, multiple punishment for a single act. The constraint was aimed both at the prosecutor seeking new trials after a conviction and at judicial interpretation of substantive criminal offenses. Second, the policy was intended to bar multiple prosecutions for a single act after an acquittal. The bar was intended not only to conserve resources by precluding unnecessary and prolonged litigation, but to serve the additional purposes of allowing a person who had been acquitted to plan ahead without the fear of possible prosecutorial harassment. In the absence of the plea of former jeopardy, a prosecutor who felt that an acquittal was unjustified could continue to prosecute until a judge or a jury willing to convict was found. Not only would such prosecutorial discretion amount to harassment, it would also undermine confidence in judicial decisions.

The reasons for these policy limitations are not entirely clear. It may be that the common law of double jeopardy developed rapidly in the seventeenth and early eighteenth centuries partially in response to the increased power of the state and the harshness of criminal penalties. Certainly in the reign of Henry II (1154–1189), royal justice was both literally and physically limited: There were few criminal offenses, and the methods of proof were subject to so much corruption that the Crown found it difficult to obtain convictions.[15] By the seventeenth century, the situation had altered vastly: The Crown had most of the advantages in a criminal trial and acquittals were relatively uncommon. To have subjected an individual to the Crown's machine of justice more than once for a single act would almost certainly have defied the increasingly popular Whiggish notions of limited government.

Shortly after the adoption of the American Bill of Rights, the law of jeopardy was to undergo considerable change—a change that was in no small way the result of the rapid growth in substantive criminal offenses and the spectacular rise in the number of capital offenses. During the seventeenth century, when the law of former jeopardy was being developed and accepted, there were few criminal offenses—at the beginning of the century there were only twenty-seven felonies.[16] Although the number of offenses was small, their scope was large, and indictments were framed according to factual transactions rather than, as later, according to a legal theory of offenses. Thus, if the facts of the second indictment were the same as had been set forth in the first indictment, a former jeopardy plea was accepted.[17] By the middle of the eighteenth century, the number of offenses had increased and the question of overlapping charges in separate indictments had become a major problem.[18] Indeed, about the time that the protection against double jeopardy was being raised to the constitutional level in America, the stage was being set in the English courts for a long-term judicial erosion of the protection.[19]

In the absence of a precise constitutional guideline, the double-jeopardy clause was to become something of a parchment barrier to multiple prosecution and punishment. The rapid growth of the substantive criminal law in the eighteenth and nineteenth centuries created a dilemma. As society, and particularly the economy, grew more complex, the judiciary tended to defer to the legislature in defining antisocial behavior. Indeed, we could argue that it is within the special competence of the legislature to separately define criminal conduct and to increase or decrease penalties according to its own determination of social harm, deterrence value, and the prospects of rehabilitation. Unfortunately, what tended to happen was that legislatures piled one crime on top of another, with little thought of related offenses. In consequence, the judiciary has often confronted a labyrinth rather than a coherent set of proscriptions and penalties. The judiciary, in turn, has sanctioned the confusion and injustice. Indeed, it compounded the problem by adopting a variety of so-called same-evidence tests that effectively defeated the policy against multiple punishments and prosecutions for the same offense.

THE SAME-EVIDENCE TEST

In eighteenth-century England, the law pertaining to indictments was highly technical, and variances in an indictment could lead to directed verdicts of acquittal, allowing felons to escape legitimate punishment. The courts moved to bridge this gap in 1796, in *Rex v. Vandercomb and Abbott*.[20] In *Vandercomb*, the defendants were indicted on a charge of burglariously breaking and entering a certain house, and stealing property from the house. However, the indictment placed the crime on the wrong day. Because indictments could not be amended, the variance proved fatal, and the court directed a verdict of acquittal. Subsequently the Crown charged the defendants in a new indictment with breaking and entering with intent to steal. The defendants entered a plea of *autrefois acquit,* which Justice Buller denied. He held that, where the offenses are distinct and the proof offered in the second indictment would not have been sufficient to convict under the first indictment, no plea of former jeopardy will be accepted.[21]

The same-evidence test, or Buller's rule, came to be widely accepted in America. It was first used in Massachusetts in 1871 and was subsequently adopted in modified form in other jurisdictions.[22] The test generally asserts that: "a single act may be an offense against two statutes; and if each statute requires proof of an additional fact which the other does not, an acquittal or conviction under either statute does not exempt defendant from prosecution and punishment."[23]

The same-evidence test recognizes that a single act or transaction may have multiple legal consequences (a robbery that also involves a murder, a Sunday sale of liquor to a minor). One major problem with the test is that it fails to consider such overlapping offenses as assault and mayhem, for example. In its most extreme form, the test has allowed a single violation of the same statute to be split into multiple offenses because different evidence was offered for each offense: for instance, where seventy-five hands of poker were dealt in a single game[24] or where in one transaction several mail bags were opened.[25] In fact, the test encourages offense splitting and piecemeal prosecution. The enormous discretion conferred on the prosecution by the test, if fully used, would render the double-jeopardy protections against multiple punishments and multiple trials a constitutional nullity.

The same-evidence test does not, however, allow the prosecution, after an acquittal or a conviction for a greater offense, to subsequently charge one with a lesser offense that would have necessarily been a part of the greater offense. Thus, a person indicted and convicted or acquitted of murder cannot be subsequently prosecuted for manslaughter; nor can a person prosecuted for adultery subsequently be prosecuted for fornication. In both situations, the lesser offenses are merged in the greater offenses.[26]

This does not suggest that the mere overlapping of crimes calls into play the greater-lesser offense limitation. For example, conspiracy does not normally merge with the subsequent commission of the crime, and thus the limitation does not apply.[27] Finally, it is important to recognize that in the greater-lesser offense limitation, the double-jeopardy bar applies regardless of the sequence of the prosecutions. Thus, initial prosecution for the lesser offense of joyriding (taking or operating a car without the owner's consent) precludes a subsequent prosecution for the greater offense of auto theft.[28] As the Supreme Court recently noted, "Whatever the sequence may be, the

Fifth Amendment forbids successive prosecution and cumulative punishment for a greater and lesser included offense."[29]

THE SAME-TRANSACTION TEST

Although federal courts continue to apply some form of the same-evidence test, a few states have adopted the *same-transaction* test[30]—a test aimed primarily at the problem of piecemeal prosecution and the resultant harassment of defendants. The test focuses on the behavior of the defendant rather than on the evidence or the statutes. If a defendant's conduct constituted a single act or transaction, or was the result of a single intent, then the prosecution is barred from splitting the transaction into multiple trials. The same-transaction test, then, precludes a prosecutor from reserving a charge arising out of a single act against a defendant on the contingency that either the verdict or the punishment on the charge pressed is unacceptable. The defendant in *Cicucci v. Illinois* (1958) in a single act committed arson and four murders.[31] The prosecution initially charged the defendant with only two murders, for which he was sentenced to a lengthy prison term. The prosecution continued to prosecute the defendant through two additional trials, each time charging a new murder, until a sentence of death was fixed in the final trial. The same-evidence test would sanction this situation, whereas the same-transaction test would require joinder of all offenses in a single trial, although multiple and even consecutive punishment would not be precluded.[32]

On the surface, the same-transaction test appears to be consonant with the framers' intended policy against harassment. However, defining what constitutes a single transaction is frequently an impossible task. Any sequence of human conduct can be broken into a number of acts, which leaves the test shapeless in many situations. Indeed, some jurisdictions that purport to follow the same-transaction test have embellished it with the same-evidence test![33]

MULTIPLE PUNISHMENTS IN A SINGLE TRIAL

The Same Offense

Perhaps the clearest objective of the double-jeopardy clause is to preclude two punishments for the same offense. The objective is so clear that the problem rarely occurs. In *Ex parte Lange* (1874), the defendant was sentenced to one year in jail and fined $200; the maximum penalty allowed under the statute was either a maximum of one year in jail *or* a fine of not less than $10 nor more than $200. After the fine had been paid and after the defendant had begun serving the jail sentence, the trial judge vacated the original sentence and imposed a new sentence—one year in jail. The Supreme Court, in reversing this double punishment, noted:

> If there is anything settled in the jurisprudence of England and America, it is that no man can be twice lawfully punished for the same offense. And though there have been nice questions in the application of this rule to cases in which the act charged was such as to come within the definition of more than one statutory offense, or to bring the party within the jurisdiction of more than one court, there has never been any doubt of its entire and complete protection of the party when a second punishment is proposed in the same court, on the same facts, for the same statutory offense.[34]

Lange has also been extended to the computation of a sentence of a person who has successfully obtained a new trial and has served some portion of the original sentence. In *Simpson v. Rice* (1969), the defendant obtained a new trial, having served over two years of the original sentence.[35] On retrial and sentencing, no credit was given for the time already spent in prison. Relying on *Lange*, the Court ruled

> that the constitutional guarantee against multiple punishments for the same offense absolutely requires that punishment already exacted must be fully "credited" in imposing sentence upon a new conviction for the same offense. If, upon a new trial, the defendant is acquitted, there is no way the years he spent in prison can be returned to him. But if he is reconvicted, those years can and must be returned—by subtracting them from whatever new sentence is imposed.[36]

Related Offenses and the Unit of Prosecution

In contrast to the problem raised in *Lange,* the issue of multiple punishments in a single trial for related offenses is vexing and recurring. The source of the problem is overlapping statutes, and it is compounded by a lack of clear legislative intent and a reluctance on the part of the judiciary to enter, in the words of Justice Frankfurter, the tantalizing domain of "the proper apportionment of punishment."[37]

The problem is particularly vexing in the area of narcotics control. A quick perusal of the federal code reveals that Congress has separately defined at least forty-five offenses in the area of narcotic and hallucinogenic substances.[38] Thus a single narcotic transaction is likely to result in the commission of several offenses, each separately punishable. For example, in *Gore v. United States* (1958), the defendant was charged with two illegal sales (the sales were separated by forty-eight hours). Instead of a two-count indictment, the defendant was charged with six counts, three parallel counts for each sale. The parallel counts were "sale without a proper written order," "sale not in the original stamped package," and "concealment and sale of an unlawfully imported drug." The defendant was sentenced separately on each count; the sentences for the first three running consecutively, and the sentences for counts four, five, and six to run concurrently with counts one, two, and three. Justice Frankfurter, writing for the majority, upheld the separate punishments by relying on the *Gavieres-Blockburger,* same offense-same evidence tests. Considering an attack on *Blockburger* as an attack on the legislative power in the area of penology, Justice Frankfurter argued:

> Suppose Congress, instead of enacting the three provisions before us, had passed an enactment substantially in this form: "Anyone who sells drugs except from the original stamped package and who sells such drugs not in pursuance of a written order of the person to whom the drug is sold, and who does so by way of facilitating the concealment and sale of drugs knowing the same to have been unlawfully imported, shall be sentenced to not less than fifteen years' imprisonment: *Provided, however,* That if he makes such sale in pursuance of a written order of the person to whom the drug is sold he shall be sentenced to only ten years' imprisonment: *Provided further,* That if he sells such drugs in the original stamped package he shall also be sentenced to only ten years' imprisonment: *And provided further,* That if he sells such drugs in pursuance of a written order and from a stamped package, he shall be sentenced to only five years' imprisonment." Is it conceivable that such a statute would not be within the power of Congress? And is it rational to find such a statute constitutional but to strike down the Blockburger doctrine as violative of the double jeopardy clause?[39]

As one commentator pointed out, however, the fallacy of the argument is that the hypothetical statute of Justice Frankfurter is not the equivalent of the statutes under which Gore was convicted. The hypothetical statute is definite and precise, leaving no room for arbitrary administration.[40]

Frequently, it is possible to break down into separate offense units the conduct a legislature has concluded merits the criminal sanction. In conduct that is especially complex or difficult to detect, the legislature may well be correct in conferring on the prosecutor a choice as to the unit of prosecution, and double jeopardy stands as no barrier to turning a single act into plural offenses. Yet normally the prosecution's choice should be limited to one unit, not to all or several possible units. To have punished Gore three times for a single act cannot be justified under the ban against multiple punishments for the same offense, unless, of course, we conclude that the protection against double jeopardy can never limit the legislature's power to split criminal conduct into offenses ad infinitum[41]—a conclusion that the Supreme Court has long accepted. As Justice Brandeis stated, "There is nothing in the Constitution which prevents Congress from punishing separately each step leading to the consummation of a transaction which it has power to prohibit and punishing also the completed transaction."[42] Indeed, on at least two recent occasions the Court has suggested that the double-jeopardy clause does not apply to the risk of double punishment but rather to the risk of double prosecution.[43]

MULTIPLE PROSECUTION

Appeals by the Defendant

Ordinarily when a defendant appeals a conviction, he or she waives the protection against double jeopardy, and on winning a reversal of the conviction may be tried again on the same charge.[44] There are, however, exceptions to the implicit waiver. For example, a defendant who appeals a conviction that was based on insufficient evidence does not waive the protection against double jeopardy. In *Burks v. United States* (1978), the petitioner's conviction was reversed on grounds that the conviction lacked sufficient evidence; the Supreme Court ruled that merely because Burks had sought a new trial as a remedy against a wrongful conviction did not mean that he had waived his right against double jeopardy.[45] The Court concluded that when an appellate court reverses a conviction for lack of sufficient evidence, the only appropriate remedy is to instruct that the trial court enter a judgment of acquittal, precluding a second trial. However, the *Burks* opinion distinguished between appellate reversals based on insufficient evidence and those based on trial error. In the latter situation, there is no implication that the government has failed to prove its case, and thus retrial is appropriate. On the other hand, a reversal based on lack of sufficient evidence carries with it the implicit assumption that the government failed to prove its case; to allow a retrial then would be directly contrary to the double-jeopardy policy of allowing the government to have only one opportunity to assemble and offer its proof of guilt.

A second exception to a defense waiver on appeal applies to situations where the defendant appeals a jury conviction based on the lesser of two charges. In these situations, the Court has ruled that the defendant does not, by an appeal, lose all protection against double jeopardy. In *Green v. United States* (1957), the trial judge charged the jury that it could find the defendant guilty of either first-degree or second-degree murder. The jury found Green guilty of second-degree murder but was silent on the first-degree charge. Green appealed the second-degree conviction and won a reversal. He was subsequently charged again with the same first-degree murder. The Supreme Court, in upholding his claim of double jeopardy, reasoned that

> Green was in direct peril of being convicted and punished for first degree murder at his first trial. He was forced to run the gantlet once on that charge

and the jury refused to convict him. When given the choice between finding him guilty of either first or second degree murder it chose the latter. In this situation the great majority of cases in this country have regarded the jury's verdict as an implicit acquittal on the charge of first degree murder.[46]

In a subsequent decision, the *Green* rationale was carried a step further. In *Price v. Georgia* (1970), the defendant was convicted of voluntary manslaughter and received an implicit acquittal on a charge of murder. On winning a new trial, he was, like Green, retried on both charges. Unlike Green's second trial, however, Price was again convicted in the second trial of only the lesser offense. In reversing Price's second conviction, the Supreme Court rejected the argument that because Price suffered no greater conviction or punishment at the second trial, the second jeopardy was therefore harmless error. To the contrary, the Court reasoned:

> The Double Jeopardy Clause, as we have noted, is cast in terms of the risk or hazard of trial and conviction, not of the ultimate legal consequences of the verdict. To be charged and to be subjected to a second trial for first-degree murder is an ordeal not to be viewed lightly. Further, and perhaps of more importance, we cannot determine whether or not the murder charge against petitioner induced the jury to find him guilty of the less serious offense of voluntary manslaughter rather than to continue to debate his innocence.[47]

The protection against double jeopardy does not per se control the length of sentence of one convicted on a retrial of the same charge. In *North Carolina v. Pearce* (1969), the Court noted:

> Long-established constitutional doctrine makes clear that . . . the guarantee against double jeopardy imposes no restrictions upon the length of a sentence imposed upon reconviction. At least since 1896 . . . it has been settled that this constitutional guarantee imposes no limitations whatever upon the power to *retry* a defendant who has succeeded in getting his first conviction set aside.
> . . . And at least since 1919 . . . it has been settled that a corollary of the power to retry a defendant is the power, upon the defendant's reconviction, to impose whatever sentence may be legally authorized, whether or not it is greater than the sentence imposed after the first conviction.[48]

However, *Pearce* did hold that a judge, consistent with due process, may not impose a greater sentence on retrial for the purpose of punishing a defendant who was able to have the original conviction set aside:

> In order to assure the absence of such a motivation, we have concluded that whenever a judge imposes a more severe sentence upon a defendant after a new trial, the reasons for his doing so must affirmatively appear. Those reasons must be based upon objective information concerning identifiable conduct on the part of the defendant occurring after the time of the original sentencing

proceeding. And the factual data upon which the increased sentence is based must be made part of the record, so that the constitutional legitimacy of the increased sentence may be fully reviewed on appeal.[49]

New Indictments and Appeals by the Government

A defendant is able to appeal a conviction, but there is no parallel right for the state to appeal an acquittal. Although under English common law the Crown was generally precluded from appealing acquittals,[50] throughout the nineteenth century some American states provided by statute for the government to seek writs of error in acquittals in criminal cases. However, during that time, federal appellate courts refused to hear appeals by the government after a defendant had been acquitted. Apparently the federal courts followed this policy not only out of consideration for the protection against double jeopardy, but more particularly because Congress had not authorized jurisdiction in such cases. As the Supreme Court said in *United States v. Sanges* (1892):

> Under the common law, as generally understood and administered in the United States, and in the absence of any statute expressly giving the right to the State, a writ of error cannot be sued out in a criminal case after a final judgment in favor of the defendant, whether that judgment has been rendered upon a verdict of acquittal, or upon a determination by the court of an issue of law. In either case, the defendant, having been once put upon his trial and discharged by the court, is not to be again vexed for the same cause, unless the Legislature, acting within its constitutional authority, has made express provision for a review of the judgment at the instance of the government.[51]

Four years after *Sanges,* the Court ruled that after a general verdict of not guilty, the government could not charge a defendant in a new indictment with the same offense, even though the defendant had been tried originally under a fatally defective indictment. Quoting from an earlier state case, Justice Gray, writing for the Court, observed:

> This case, in short, presents the novel and unheard of spectacle of a public officer, whose business it was to frame a correct bill, openly alleging his own inaccuracy or neglect, as a reason for a second trial, when it is not pretended that the merits were not fairly in issue on the first. That a party shall be deprived of the benefit of an acquittal by a jury, on a suggestion of this kind, coming, too, from the officer who drew the indictment, seems not to comport with that universal and humane principle of criminal law, "that no man shall be brought into danger more than once for the same offense." It is very like permitting a party to take advantage of his own wrong. If this practice be tolerated, when are trials of the accused to end?[52]

Neither of these cases settled conclusively the matter of government appeals in criminal cases. Finally, in *Kepner v. United States* (1904), the Supreme Court, in a 5-to-4 decision, concluded:

Undoubtedly in those jurisdictions where a trial of one accused of crime can only be to a jury, and a verdict of acquittal or conviction must be by a jury, no legal jeopardy can attach until a jury has been called and charged with the deliverance of the accused. But, protection being against a second trial for the same offense, it is obvious that where one has been tried before a competent tribunal having jurisdiction he has been in jeopardy as much as he could have been in those tribunals where a jury is alone competent to convict or acquit.[53]

Although *Kepner* precludes an appeal by the government in instances of acquittal by courts having jurisdiction to try a case, there are limited situations in which the government may appeal trial court rulings, among them erroneous decisions of law.[54]

In 1970, Congress amended the Criminal Appeals Act in order to provide federal prosecutors with greater latitude to appeal erroneous rulings of law made by federal trial judges. The new provision reads:

In a criminal case an appeal by the United States shall lie to a court of appeals from a decision, judgment, or order of a district court dismissing an indictment or information as to any one or more counts, except that no appeal shall lie where the double jeopardy clause of the United States Constitution prohibits further prosecution.

An appeal by the United States shall lie to a court of appeals from a decision or order of a district court suppressing or excluding evidence or requiring the return of seized property in a criminal proceeding, not made after the defendant has been put in jeopardy and before the verdict or finding on an indictment or information, if the United States attorney certifies to the district court that the appeal is not taken for purpose of delay and that the evidence is a substantial proof of a fact material in the proceeding.[55]

This new provision was first reviewed by the Supreme Court in 1975, in two separate cases. In *United States v. Wilson,* the defendant was tried before a jury and found guilty; *after* the verdict, the trial judge dismissed the indictment. The government appealed the dismissal. The Court upheld the government's right to appeal because, if the government prevailed, no new trial would be granted, merely the reinstatement of the jury's verdict of guilty.[56] However, the majority opinion made it clear that a system of appeals by the government is constrained by the double-jeopardy clause. Speaking for the majority, Justice Marshall wrote:

A system permitting review of all claimed legal errors would have symmetry to recommend it and would avoid the release of some defendants who have benefited from instructions or evidentiary rulings that are unduly favorable to them. But we have rejected this position in the past, and we continue to be of the view that the policies underlying the Double Jeopardy Clause militate against permitting the Government to appeal after a verdict of acquittal. Granting the Government such broad appeal rights would allow the prosecutor to seek to persuade a second trier of fact of the defendant's guilt after having failed with the first; it would permit him to re-examine the weaknesses in his first presentation in order to strengthen it in the second; and it would disserve the defendant's legitimate interest in the finality of a verdict of acquittal.[57]

In the second case, *United States v. Jenkins*, an indictment was dismissed by the trial judge after a bench trial. Because it was unclear whether the dismissal was based on a resolution of factual issues and/or conclusions of law by the trial judge, the Court applied the *Wilson* rule and upheld the dismissal. The Court reasoned that, because further proceedings of some sort devoted to resolving factual issues would have been necessary, a reversal of the dismissal would have exposed the defendant to a second trial.[58] Of course, consistent with the *Wilson* rule, if the dismissal had been based only on conclusions of law after a verdict of guilty, then an appeal by the government would presumably have been permitted.

Neither *Jenkins* nor *Wilson* appeared to disturb the rule that the government could not appeal an acquittal, even one based on an egregiously erroneous foundation.[59] The *Jenkins* rationale, however, was short-lived. By 1978 a narrow majority of five, led by Justice Rehnquist, overruled *Jenkins*. In *United States v. Scott*, the defendant moved to dismiss two of the three counts of his indictment on grounds that the defense to these counts had been prejudiced by the government's preindictment delay. At the close of all evidence, the trial judge granted the defense motion.[60] Scott was later found not guilty on the third count. When the government sought to appeal the dismissals, it was barred under the *Jenkins* rationale. The Supreme Court reversed, concluding that "in a case such as this the defendant, by deliberately choosing to seek termination of the proceedings against him on a basis unrelated to factual guilt or innocence of the offense of which he is accused, suffers no injury cognizable under the Double Jeopardy Clause if the Government is permitted to appeal such a ruling of the trial court in favor of the defendant."[61] In short, the majority argued that there is a constitutional difference between formal acquittals and midtrial dismissals.

The majority's strained definition of *acquittal* is neither logical nor practical. The majority apparently concluded that a "true" acquittal is one based on a determination by the trier of fact that the defendant is innocent. Yet the majority recognized that there are affirmative defenses, such as insanity and entrapment, that can lead to an acquittal that bars retrial. Surely no one would maintain that such defenses necessarily mean that the defendant did not commit a criminal act. As Justice Brennan noted in his dissent, determinations of insanity or entrapment by a trial court are no more "factual" than the determination, based on evidence presented at the trial, that the defense has been prejudiced by preindictment delay. Insofar as double jeopardy is concerned, why should the policy favoring entrapment or insanity defenses be preferred to the policy regarding prejudice to the defense in preindictment delay? Entrapment, insanity, and preindictment delay are all equally subject to evaluation at trial on the basis of the factual evidence presented. None is bound to the definition of a particular crime and each is equally subject to erroneous evidentiary rulings. Retrial should be barred after an acquittal, whether the acquittal is based on a verdict of the fact finder or entered by the trial judge after the presentation of evidence. In the absence of such a bar, the government is allowed to have a second chance at conviction and, in the process, to strengthen its case and to subject the defendant to the expense and anxiety attendant to a criminal trial. Presumably there will be acquittals based on error, even egregious error,[62] but that is only to recognize the human limits to trials of disputes. *Jenkins* allowed errors to escape review, but the simplicity of *Jenkins* was a source of strength. The *Jenkins* rule treated all acquittals equally, but the *Scott* decision now requires the lower state and federal courts to differentiate the double-jeopardy consequences of all affirmative defenses.

Splitting a Case: Joinder and Collateral Estoppel

A single criminal episode may have multiple consequences, either in the form of multiple violations of a single criminal law (multiple murder) or in the form of simultaneous violation of several related or unrelated criminal laws. The principal problem, insofar as double jeopardy is concerned, is whether the prosecutor should be allowed to split the course of action into two or more prosecutions. Two policy considerations are at issue here: one is whether the prosecution should be allowed the discretion to engage in prolonged and unnecessary litigation; the other is whether the discretion to split a case subjects the individual to harassment. The short answer to the problem is that there is no general, federal constitutional bar to multiple prosecutions for violations arising out of a single episode, act, or transaction. The Supreme Court has stated that the underlying idea of double jeopardy is that the state "with all its resources and power should not be allowed to make repeated attempts to convict an individual for an alleged offense, thereby subjecting him to embarrassment, expense and ordeal and compelling him to live in a continuing state of anxiety and insecurity, as well as enhancing the possibility that even though innocent he may be found guilty."[63] Still, the *Gavieres-Blockburger*, same evidence–same offense, test allows the prosecution almost total freedom to proceed in a single prosecution or to split the case.[64]

Two related developments have somewhat reduced the possibility of prosecutorial abuse of discretion. The first is the statutory movement in favor of joinder; that is, the requirement that the prosecution combine into a single prosecution the several related charges that emerge from a single criminal episode. But, "while it would be desirable to have a definite rule . . . by which to determine the precise scope of what should be brought within a single criminal trial, the possibility seems illusory in view of the futile attempts in civil suits to define a 'cause of action.' The best solution may be to enact a general rule, to make plain its objectives, and to exhort the courts to construe the rule broadly in the light of its objectives."[65]

Although joinder in criminal cases is permitted in many jurisdictions, including the federal courts,[66] it has not been held by the Supreme Court to be constitutionally required. Justice Brennan, however, has indicated that not only should the same evidence–same offense test be abandoned, but that joinder should be constitutionally mandated in most cases. In his concurring opinion in *Ashe v. Swenson* (1970), he wrote:

> In my view, the Double Jeopardy Clause requires the prosecution, except in most limited circumstances, to join at one trial all the charges against a defendant that grow out of a single criminal act, occurrence, episode, or transaction. This "same transaction" test of "same offense" not only enforces the ancient prohibition against vexatious multiple prosecutions embodied in the Double Jeopardy Clause, but responds as well to the increasingly widespread recognition that the consolidation in one lawsuit of all issues arising out of a single transaction or occurrence best promotes justice, economy, and convenience. Modern rules of criminal and civil procedure reflect this recognition.[67]

The primary drawback of offense splitting is that it allows a prosecutor to reserve one or more related charges and to make a subsequent determination of whether to accept either an acquittal or a light sentence.[68] In short, although a prosecutor may not appeal an acquittal, by reserving charges he or she may accomplish the same end. There are both conceptual and technical problems associated with compulsory joinder,[69] but it has proved workable in several jurisdictions.[70] Furthermore, joinder has the great advantage of reducing the possibility of harassment without undermining legislative discretion in the areas of penology and sentencing.

The second development that has somewhat reduced multiple prosecutions is the recent imposition of the doctrine of collateral estoppel in criminal cases. Estoppel and its twin, res judicata,[71] were accepted by English common law long before the technical plea of double jeopardy was considered binding law.[72] Res judicata and collateral estoppel are legal bars, or impediments, to raising issues that have been conclusively determined by prior actions; they overlap with the common-law policy against being twice vexed—*bis vexari*— for the same cause.[73] Long accepted in civil actions as a means of protecting defendants from the burdens of relitigation, res judicata, or more specifically collateral estoppel, has been an accepted part of federal criminal procedure at least since the 1916 decision in *United States v. Oppenheimer*.[74] In *Oppenheimer*, Justice Holmes held that res judicata existed alongside double jeopardy as a complementary protection against a second prosecution following an acquittal on the merits.[75]

It was not until 1970 that collateral estoppel was incorporated into the constitutional protection against double jeopardy. In *Ashe v. Swenson,* the defendant was originally charged with robbing one of several men in the course of a poker game. The defense offered no testimony, instead attacking the state's identification of Ashe.[76] In the first trial the defendant was acquitted. The state subsequently charged the defendant with robbing another poker player, one not named in the original charge. This time the defendant was judged guilty. Thus far, the facts were almost identical to those in a 1958 case, but here the Supreme Court ruled that collateral estoppel barred the second prosecution.[77]

For the eight-justice majority, Justice Stewart wrote:

> "Collateral estoppel" is an awkward phrase, but it stands for an extremely important principle in our adversary system of justice. It means simply that when a(n) issue of ultimate fact has once been determined by a valid and final judgment, that issue cannot again be litigated between the same parties in any future lawsuit.
>
> Where a previous judgment of acquittal was based upon a general verdict, as is usually the case, this approach requires a court to "examine the record of a prior proceeding, taking into account the pleadings, evidence, charge, and other relevant matter, and conclude whether a rational jury could have grounded its verdict upon an issue other than that which the defendant seeks to foreclose from consideration." The inquiry "must be set in a practical frame and viewed with an eye to all the circumstances of the proceedings."
>
> Straightforward application of the federal rule to the present case can lead to but one conclusion. For the record is utterly devoid of any indication that the first jury could rationally have found that an armed robbery had not occurred. . . . The single rationally conceivable issue in dispute before the jury was whether the petitioner had been one of the robbers. And the jury by its verdict found that he had not.[78]

Although *Ashe* does not totally preclude "dry run" prosecutions, it does reduce the possibility of such harassment. *Ashe* applies only to those new prosecutions in which the defendant was previously acquitted by a general verdict for an offense arising out of the same episode.[79] It is not binding on other parties[80] and is a bar only to the relitigation of an issue that a jury *must* have decided when it held a defendant not guilty. The potential problem with the *Ashe* rule is that it requires a post hoc determination of what the jury decided. But, because in most criminal cases the defendant offers only a single defense, post hoc reconstruction of the jury's reasoning is in fact possible.[81]

There remains the possibility, however, that an acquitted defendant who testified in his or her own behalf could subsequently be charged with perjury. The danger here is that the prosecution can be given a second chance to relitigate the issue, even though the charge is distinct.[82] If a perjury trial is nothing more than a reconsideration of the veracity of the acquitted defendant's original testimony—a relitigation of the defendant's credibility—it can be stopped.[83]

Mistrials

One of the most common problems in double jeopardy is whether a defendant may be prosecuted again after a mistrial. To expose a defendant to the hazard of conviction and punishment, to terminate the trial without a verdict, and then to subject the defendant a second time to the same hazard would appear to be at the heart of double jeopardy. Yet until quite recently, few defendants have successfully raised a plea of double jeopardy in cases of mistrials. For well over a hundred years, mistrials and double jeopardy were controlled by *United States v. Perez* (1824).[84] *Perez* involved a jury that was discharged because it was unable to agree on a verdict, a so-called hung jury.[85] Justice Story upheld the second prosecution, and his opinion suggested that trial judges have wide discretion in declaring mistrials:

> In all cases of this nature, the law has invested courts of justice with the authority to discharge a jury from giving any verdict, whenever, in their opinion, taking all the circumstances into consideration, there is a manifest necessity for the act, or the ends of public justice would otherwise be defeated. They are to exercise a sound discretion on the subject; and it is impossible to define all the circumstances which would render it proper to interfere. To be sure, the power ought to be used with the greatest caution, under urgent circumstances, and for very plain and obvious causes; and, in capital cases especially, courts should be extremely careful how they interfere with any of the chances of life, in favor of the prisoner. But, after all, they have the right to order the discharge; and the security which the public have for the faithful, sound and conscientious exercise of this discretion, rests, in this, as in other cases, upon the responsibility of the judges, under their oaths of office.[86]

The problem with mistrials and, indeed, with Justice Story's opinion, is that we are confronted with conflicting policy goals. First, there is the fundamental constitutional policy that in mistrials the defendant has already been once placed in jeopardy. Although mechanical rules in this area should probably be avoided, still jeopardy is said to attach at the time a defendant is first placed in jeopardy: In a jury trial, jeopardy attaches when the jury is impaneled and sworn;[87] in a bench trial, when the trial judge has begun to receive evidence.[88] Once jeopardy attaches, a defendant has a valued right to have the trial completed before the same tribunal or jury. To place no limitations on mistrials would afford to the prosecution the enormous advantage of seeking a more favorable opportunity for convicting a defendant, and thus contradicting the double-jeopardy policy that the state "with all its resources and power should not be allowed to make repeated attempts to convict an individual for an alleged offense, thereby subjecting him to embarrassment, expense and ordeal and compelling him to live in a continuing state of anxiety and insecurity, as well as enhancing the possibility that even though innocent he may be found guilty."[89]

On the other hand, a declaration of mistrial may well ensure that those guilty of crimes do not escape just conviction and punishment. The "manifest necessity" spoken of by Justice Story is apparent in those rare situations where a trial has been disrupted by natural disasters, such as floods or earthquakes. In such extraordinary circumstances, justice does not require that a defendant receive absolution merely because nature has prevented a trial from ending in a just verdict. Similarly, we could argue that the "ends of public justice" are served by mistrials where a trial is interrupted by the death or prolonged illness of the judge, the prosecutor, or defense counsel.

Manifest necessity is less apparent in those situations where a sworn jury is dismissed because of a procedural irregularity, particularly if the prosecutor contributed to the irregularity. In *Lovato v. New Mexico* (1916), the Supreme Court upheld the temporary dismissal of a sworn jury after the prosecutor realized that the defendant had not pleaded to the indictment. Once the irregularity was corrected, the same jury was sworn again and the trial was resumed.[90] More recently, *Lovato* was extended in *Illinois v. Somerville* (1973) to a situation where the prosecutor realized that the indictment was defective and could not be amended. After the jury had been sworn, but before any evidence was taken, a mistrial was declared. Defendant Somerville was reindicted within two days of the mistrial, and within approximately two weeks was tried and convicted. In disallowing a plea of former jeopardy the Supreme Court, Justice Rehnquist writing for the majority, said: "Where the declaration of a mistrial implements a reasonable state policy and aborts a proceeding that at best would have produced a verdict that could have been upset at will by one of the parties, the defendant's interest in proceeding to verdict is outweighed by the competing and equally legitimate demand for public justice."[91]

Lovato and *Somerville* do not offer a satisfactory solution to the problem of determining when a trial court has abused its discretion. The almost unlimited discretion of the *Perez* line of cases could lend itself to prosecutorial manipulation and judicial overreaching. For example, in *Downum v. United States* (1963), a sworn jury was discharged at the request of the prosecution and over the objection of the defendant because a key prosecution witness had not been served with a summons and was not present.[92] However, the five-justice majority, in reversing Downum's conviction, only hinted at a policy resolution of the abuse-of-discretion principle. Speaking for the majority, Justice Douglas chose to rely largely on a 1931 appellate court decision that had upheld the plea in a similar situation. There, Judge Wilbur said:

An examination of the cases cited will disclose the fact that no court has gone to the extent of holding that, after the impanelment of the jury for the trial of a criminal case, the failure of the district attorney to have present sufficient witnesses, or evidence to prove the offense charged, is an exception to the rule that the discharge of a jury after its impanelment for the trial of a criminal case operates as a protection against a retrial of the same case.[93]

The failure of the Supreme Court in *Downum* to give any clear policy directives may have been an indication of the numerical weakness of the majority. In fact, then-recent changes in judicial personnel may alone have accounted for even the slim majority.[94] Indeed, in *Gori v. United States* (1961), just two years before *Downum*, a five-justice majority had turned down a similar plea where the trial judge had declared a mistrial *sua sponte* (on his own volition) in the interests of the defendant but without the defendant's approval or objection.[95] In *Gori,* Justice Frankfurter, writing for the majority, cautioned against categorical rules for resolving the issue of discretion and observed:

> We are unwilling, where it clearly appears that a mistrial has been granted in the sole interest of the defendant, to hold that its necessary consequence is to bar all retrial. It would hark back to the formalistic artificialities of seventeenth century criminal procedure so to confine our federal trial courts by compelling them to navigate a narrow compass between Scylla and Charybdis. We would not thus make them unduly hesitant conscientiously to exercise their most sensitive judgment—according to their own lights in the immediate exigencies of trial—for the more effective protection of the criminal accused.[96]

In 1971, in *United States v. Jorn,* the Court again considered a mistrial declared *sua sponte* by a judge, this time in the interests of the witnesses.[97] Again the Court was narrowly divided, with only a plurality joining the opinion of Justice Harlan. Although the majority supported the plea, the plurality opinion does not appear to undercut the wide latitude accorded the trial judge since the days of *Perez*. Much as the *Gori* opinion had rejected categorical rules, the *Jorn* opinion suggests that the problem is too elusive to enable the Court to present "bright-line" rules. Noting that the defendant has a valued right to have his trial completed by a particular tribunal, Justice Harlan reasoned:

> If that right to go to a particular tribunal is valued, it is because, independent of the threat of bad faith conduct by judge or prosecutor, the defendant has a significant interest in the decision whether or not to take the case from the jury when circumstances occur which might be thought to warrant a declaration of mistrial. Thus, where circumstances develop not attributable to prosecutorial or judicial overreaching, a motion by the defendant for mistrial is ordinarily assumed to remove any barrier to reprosecution, even if the defendant's motion is necessitated by prosecutorial or judicial error. In the absence of such a motion, the *Perez* doctrine of manifest necessity stands as a command to trial

judges not to foreclose the defendant's option until a scrupulous exercise of judicial discretion leads to the conclusion that the ends of public justice would not be served by a continuation of the proceedings.[98]

The dictum in *Jorn*—absent judicial or prosecutorial overreaching, a defense request for a mistrial removes any barrier to a second prosecution—was accepted in 1976 as a rule. In *United States v. Dinitz*, the trial judge impaneled, ordered defense counsel excluded from the trial, and thereafter told the defendant he had the following three options: (1) a stay or recess pending an appeal of his order, (2) a continuation of the trial with co-counsel of record, or (3) a declaration of a mistrial.[99] Dinitz chose to request a mistrial and the request was granted. The Court ruled that a second trial was not barred by the double-jeopardy provision, even though the request may have been occasioned by a judicial error. Relying on the plurality opinion in *Jorn,* the Court ruled that in the absence of judicial or prosecutorial actions intended to provoke a mistrial request, a defense motion for a mistrial does not bar a second trial. The majority reasoned that even when the defense motion is prompted by serious prosecutorial or judicial error, the mistrial request serves interests not unlike those served by the double-jeopardy provision. The error may be reversible error, but if the defense continues with the first trial rather than seeks an immediate mistrial, the defense must then undergo the anxiety, expense, and delay that would be occasioned by an appeal, a reversal, and a subsequent prosecution.

The elusive standards of "manifest" or "imperious" necessity and "the ends of public justice" give the trial judge almost unbounded discretion to declare a mistrial with or without the defendant's or prosecutor's approval. On the whole, the Court's reluctance to adopt rigid rules in this area is understandable. In the easy cases where jeopardy has attached and where the prosecution has sought a *nolle prosequi* or a mistrial largely in order to shore up a weak case,[100] a second prosecution should be barred by the plea. But the typical case is a good deal more complex and bright-line rules would be almost impossible to formulate. Having said that, we should hasten to add that given the underlying constitutional policy against double jeopardy the Court should do more than simply caution trial courts against mistrials except in urgent circumstances. Mistrials sometimes do serve the ends of justice, but before a mistrial is declared, the trial court ought to be convinced that there are no reasonable alternatives. What the Supreme Court has failed to do is insist that the record make clear that alternatives (dropping one or more counts, a continuance) would not have been reasonable in the circumstances of a given case. This would seem to be especially important in those cases in which alternatives do exist and the mistrial is based on prosecutorial negligence.[101] However, it is equally true, where a mistrial is declared over defense objection on the basis of improper conduct by defense counsel, that the trial record should make clear that there were no meaningful and practical alternatives to a mistrial.

Normally the trial judge would be required, on the record, to make findings of the manifest necessity for the mistrial. Yet the decision in *Arizona v. Washington* (1978) held that an explicit finding of manifest necessity was not required nor was the mistrial defective by reason of the failure of the trial judge either to explain the ruling or to indicate what alternatives had been explored.[102] The record in *Washington* appears to support the trial judge's conclusion that defense counsel had made improper and potentially prejudicial opening comments to the jury. The Supreme Court agreed that a trial judge, in declaring a mistrial, may not act precipitately, irrationally, or irresponsibly, but the majority concluded that where the basis for a mistrial is adequately disclosed in the record, no specific finding of necessity nor indication of alternatives explored and rejected is required in the record. In short, the *Washington* majority concluded that appellate courts must give special respect and deference to a trial judge's evaluations.

APPLICATION TO THE STATES
AND THE DUAL-SOVEREIGNTY DOCTRINE

In line with the steady movement toward incorporating major provisions of the Bill of Rights into the due process clause of the Fourteenth Amendment, the Supreme Court in 1969, in *Benton v. Maryland,* held that the double-jeopardy clause now applied to the states as well as to the federal government. Asserting that the protection was a fundamental ideal in American constitutional heritage, the Court overruled the earlier decision in *Palko v. Connecticut* and declared that the same constitutional standards in double jeopardy apply equally to state and federal governments.

Prior to *Benton,* forty-five of the states had constitutional provisions covering the protection against double jeopardy, and the remaining states had common-law coverage.[103] Thus, the importance of *Benton* is not that it imposed on the states an entirely foreign concept, but rather that the federal clause is now a minimum standard below which an individual state cannot go.

One year after *Benton,* the Court carried its decision a step further, holding that a state could not prosecute an individual for the same acts that had been involved in an earlier municipal prosecution in the same state.[104] *Waller v. Florida,* combined with *Benton,* raises the interesting question of whether the dual-sovereignty doctrine in double jeopardy has been overturned *sub silentio.*

One of the peculiar anomalies of the American federal system has been the constitutional possibility that a single act could violate the laws of both a state and the federal government and, in consequence, that an individual could be tried and punished twice for the same offense. The anomaly is part of the constitutional legacy of dual sovereignty and dual federalism.[105]

Throughout the nineteenth century, the doctrine of dual sovereignty did not pose a particular problem in criminal justice. During an era when the

national government did not feel compelled to backstop the states in the exercise of general police powers, the likelihood of overlapping criminal offenses
was remote. Although the problem was occasionally and indirectly noted in
nineteenth-century cases,[106] it was not until 1922 that the Supreme Court
directly endorsed dual sovereignty as a limitation on the protection against
double jeopardy. In *United States v. Lanza,* the Court upheld the federal prosecution of the defendant for violation of the National Prohibition Act, even
though the defendant had been previously tried and convicted by the state of
Washington for the exact and same transaction. Chief Justice Taft, speaking
for a unanimous Court, reasoned:

> We have here two sovereignties, deriving power from different sources, cap-
> able of dealing with the same subject-matter within the same territory. Each
> may, without interference by the other, enact laws to secure prohibition, with
> the limitation that no legislation can give validity to acts prohibited by the
> Amendment. Each government, in determining what shall be an offense against
> its peace and dignity, is exercising its own sovereignty, not that of the other.[107]

Although *Lanza* has been the subject of considerable scholarly criticism,[108]
it has been reaffirmed by the Court on at least seven occasions, most recently
in 1959.[109] In *Bartkus v. Illinois* and *Abbate v. United States,*[110] the majority
justified retention of the *Lanza* rule largely on grounds of precedent but also
because of what appeared to be practical considerations. Justice Brennan,
writing for the majority in *Abbate,* reasoned:

> If the States are free to prosecute criminal acts violating their laws, and the
> resultant state prosecutions bar federal prosecutions based on the same acts,
> federal law enforcement must necessarily be hindered. For example, the
> petitioners in this case insist that their Illinois convictions resulting in three
> months' prison sentences should bar this federal prosecution which could result
> in a sentence of up to five years. Such a disparity will very often arise when,
> as in this case, the defendants' acts impinge more seriously on a federal interest
> than on a state interest.
>   . . . Thus, unless the federal authorities could somehow insure that there
> would be no state prosecutions for particular acts that also constitute federal
> offenses, the efficiency of federal law enforcement must suffer if the Double
> Jeopardy Clause prevents successive state and federal prosecutions. Needless
> to say, it would be highly impractical for the federal authorities to attempt to
> keep informed of all state prosecutions which might bear on federal offenses.[111]

Justice Black's dissent in *Abbate* made the pointed observation that it appeared strange that the dual-sovereignty doctrine would allow a state and the
federal government to do together what neither could do separately.[112] He
continued his dissent in *Bartkus,* attacking both the ethical foundations of the
Lanza rule and the supposed practical reasons for its continuation. Justice
Black observed that the subtlety of dual sovereignty must surely escape one

who is prosecuted twice for the same offense. Furthermore, he pointed out that the argument that federal criminal laws could be undermined by potentially weak state laws simply cannot be maintained. Under the supremacy clause, Congress could preempt any area of concurrent jurisdiction and thereby ensure that federal criminal penalties would prevail.

It is possible to argue that the issue of successive prosecutions is a relatively minor problem, tempered by statutes in twenty states and by a federal administrative policy that bar successive prosecutions.[113] The issue may well be minor in terms of the number of cases, but within certain areas, particularly in the overlapping areas of gun control and bank robbery,[114] the problem is widespread. To continue the *Lanza-Abbate-Bartkus* rule in face of *Benton* and *Waller* promotes none of the virtues of federalism and serves only to harass individuals and to undermine confidence in a national system of justice. As federal district Judge Kellan observed, "It seems clear that *Benton* overrules *Bartkus*. But does it overrule *Abbate?* By logic, it would seem so. What is sauce for the goose ought to be sauce for the gander."[115] Unfortunately, Judge Kellan spoke with neither the authority of the Supreme Court nor even that of the federal appellate courts, which continue to adhere to *Lanza*.[116]

CONCLUSION

A discussion of double jeopardy reveals the immense complexity of criminal procedure, and thereby stands as a warning against the easy adoption of rigid and mechanical rules. At the outset, devising rules to implement the constitutional protection is made difficult because the language adopted in the Fifth Amendment is both antique and imprecise. However, the historical consensus surrounding the adoption of double jeopardy in America suggests that the protection is intended to fulfill three goals: (1) to conserve legal-judicial resources, (2) to protect the innocent by maintaining confidence in judicial decisions, and (3) to prevent harassment of the acquitted. The protection against harassment acts as a rule of finality, protecting against the continuing distress of the defendant and allowing a defendant at some point to close a chapter in life and plan ahead. As the Court said in *Green:*

> The underlying idea, one that is deeply ingrained in at least the Anglo-American system of jurisprudence, is that the State with all its resources and power should not be allowed to make repeated attempts to convict an individual for an alleged offense, thereby subjecting him to embarrassment, expense and ordeal and compelling him to live in a continuing state of anxiety and insecurity, as well as enhancing the possibility that even though innocent he may be found guilty.[117]

Perhaps because of the complexity of the problems involved in double jeopardy, the Supreme Court has been generally cautious and indeed skeptical about pleas of double jeopardy. This approach is particularly evident in the *Gavieres-Blockburger* line of cases. The same-evidence test encourages offense splitting and piecemeal prosecution and should be abandoned in favor of compulsory joinder. However, overturning the same-evidence test, while it would assist in resolving the problem of multiple prosecutions, would not per se resolve the problem of multiple punishments.

Because the double-jeopardy clause does not limit the legislative power to define appropriate punishment, the problem of multiple punishments for what is, in effect, a single act may well require a variety of solutions. The issue really boils down to one of cumulating convictions and punishments in a single trial. One solution then would be a clearer declaration by the legislature in support of concurrent sentencing. In the absence of such clear legislative intent, the Supreme Court should expand the rule of lenity—a rule that makes a presumption against legislative harshness in punishment.[118]

Finally, the broad policy objectives of double jeopardy cannot be realized when trial judges continue to exercise wide discretion in mistrials and when the courts continue to recognize the doctrine of dual sovereignty. Discretion in criminal trials is a necessity and drawing lines is always difficult, yet establishing rules and drawing lines, however difficult, are fundamental to the constitutional order. Similarly, to justify successive prosecutions under the fiction of dual sovereignty, because to abandon the fiction might undermine law enforcement, is to say that law enforcement is *the* paramount policy of the Constitution.

Living with a limited government is never an easy task, particularly when it means extending the protections of the Constitution to those whom we strongly suspect of violating the criminal laws. Of course, as a people we will probably survive, and some even flourish, with practice in discord with constitutional provisions. But the cynics will then say that the Bill of Rights is parchment law.

NOTES

1. Nah. 1:9.
2. Quoted in Justice Black's dissent in *Bartkus v. Illinois*, 359 U.S. 121, 152, n. 3 (1959).
3. See Marion S. Kirk, "Jeopardy During the Period of the Year Books," 82 *U. Penn. L. Rev.* 602 (1934); and Jay A. Sigler, "A History of Double Jeopardy," 7 *Am. J. Legal Hist.* 283 (1963).
4. See Martin Friedland, *Double Jeopardy* (Oxford: Clarendon Press, 1969), p. 5.
5. Abolished by 59 Geo. 3, chap. 46 (1819).
6. Edward Coke, *The Third Part of the Institutes of the Laws of England* (London: E. & R. Brooke, 1797), chap. 101, p. 213.
7. E.g., William Hawkins, *A Treatise of the Pleas of the Crown* (London: J. Walthoe, 1724), bk. 2, chaps. 35–37.
8. *Rex v. Read*, 83 Eng. Rep. 27 (1660).

9. *Armstrong v. Lisle*, 84 Eng. Rep. 1095 (1690).

10. William Blackstone, *Commentaries on the Laws of England*, Cooley ed. (Chicago: Callaghan, 1884), vol. 2, bk. 4, p. 335.

11. Sigler, "History of Double Jeopardy," pp. 299–300.

12. Ibid. at 304.

13. The imprecision of the phrase "life or limb" was recently recognized in *Breed v. Jones*, 421 U.S. 519 (1975), where the Supreme Court unanimously extended the protection against double jeopardy to juvenile proceedings and in the process noted that "although the constitutional language, 'jeopardy of life or limb' suggests proceedings in which only the most serious penalties can be imposed, the clause has long been construed to mean something far broader than its literal language."

14. Sigler, "History of Double Jeopardy," pp. 306–307.

15. William Holdsworth, *A History of English Law* (London: Methuen, 1938), vol. 1, pp. 310–311.

16. Note, "Statutory Implementation of Double Jeopardy Clauses," 65 *Yale L.J.* 340, 342 (1956).

17. E.g., *Rex v. Segar*, 90 Eng. Rep. 554 (1696).

18. Blackstone counted 160 capital offenses in the 1760s; Blackstone, *Commentaries*, bk. 4, p. 18. Cf. Leon Radzinowicz, *A History of English Criminal Law* (New York: Macmillan, 1948), vol. 15, pp. 3–4.

19. See *Rex v. Vandercomb and Abbott*, 168 Eng. Rep. 455 (1796).

20. Ibid.

21. Ibid. at 461.

22. See *Morey v. Commonwealth*, 108 Mass. 433 (1871); and note, "Twice in Jeopardy," 75 *Yale L.J.* 262, 269–276 (1965).

23. *Gavieres v. United States*, 220 U.S. 338, 342 (1911). The *Gavieres* formulation of the same-evidence test is also known as the *Blockburger* test; see *Blockburger v. United States*, 284 U.S. 299, 304 (1932).

24. *Johnson v. Commonwealth*, 256 S.W. 388 (1923).

25. *Ebeling v. Morgan*, 237 U.S. 625 (1915).

26. See *Ex parte Nielsen*, 131 U.S. 176, 188 (1889).

27. See *Iunnelli v. United States*, 420 U.S. 770 (1975).

28. See *Brown v. Ohio*, 432 U.S. 161 (1977).

29. Ibid. at 167. For exceptions to the rule announced in *Brown v. Ohio*, see *Jeffers v. United States*, 97 S. Ct. 2207 (1977).

30. See "Statutory Implementation," p. 348.

31. *Cicucci v. Illinois*, 356 U.S. 571 (1958).

32. In *Cicucci*, the Supreme Court upheld the multiple prosecution because at that time the double-jeopardy clause had not been applied to the states.

33. See "Statutory Implementation," p. 349.

34. *Ex parte Lange*, 85 U.S. 163, 168 (1874). However, where a defendant has not yet suffered a lawful punishment, errors in sentencing may be corrected; *In re Bonner*, 151 U.S. 242 (1894), and accord *Bozza v. United States*, 330 U.S. 160, 166 (1947), and *Pollard v. United States*, 352 U.S. 354 (1957). Sentence may be amended by the Court at the term in which it was imposed providing the punishment is not augmented; *United States v. Benz*, 282 U.S. 304 (1931).

35. *Simpson v. Rice*, 395 U.S. 711 (1969).

36. Ibid. at 718–719.

37. *Gore v. United States*, 357 U.S. 386, 393 (1958).

38. See 21 U.S.C. 812–848, and 21 U.S.C. 951–963.

39. *Gore v. United States*, 357 U.S. at 392–393.

40. "Twice in Jeopardy," 75 *Yale L.J.* 263, 304 (1965).

41. Cf. *Bell v. United States*, 349 U.S. 81 (1955), where the Mann Act was statu-

torily construed not to allow the prosecution to multiply the offense units by the number of women transported in any single act.

42. *Albrecht v. United States*, 273 U.S. 1, 11 (1927). Cf. *Prince v. United States*, 352 U.S. 322 (1957), and *Ladner v. United States*, 358 U.S. 169 (1958).

43. See *Price v. Georgia*, 398 U.S. 323, 329 (1970), and *Breed v. Jones*, 421 U.S. 519, 1787 (1975). See also dictum in *Holiday v Johnston*, 313 U.S. 342, 349 (1940), to the effect that the imposition of two sentences for a single offense does not constitute double jeopardy.

44. *Ball v. United States*, 163 U.S. 662, 672 (1896).

45. *Burks v. United States*, 437 U.S. 1 (1978).

46. *Green v. United States*, 355 U.S. 184, 190–191 (1957), reaff'd, *Benton v. Maryland*, 395 U.S. 784 (1969).

47. *Price v. Georgia*, 398 U.S. at 331.

48. *North Carolina v. Pearce*, 395 U.S. 711, 719–723 (1969).

49. Ibid. at 725–726. The *Pearce* decision was modified in *Chaffin v. Stynchombe*, 412 U.S. 17 (1973), where it was held that in a retrial a *jury* can impose a greater sentence so long as the jury is not informed of the prior sentence, and the second sentence is not otherwise shown to be the product of vindictiveness. And see *Blackledge v. Perry*, 417 U.S. 21 (1974), and *Colton v. Kentucky*, 407 U.S. 1953 (1972).

50. See *The Duchess of Kingston's Case*, 20 How. St. Tr. 355, 528 (1776).

51. *United States v. Sanges*, 144 U.S. 311, 318 (1892).

52. *Ball v. United States*, 163 U.S. at 667–670.

53. *Kepner v. United States*, 195 U.S. 100, 128 (1904).

54. See Jack Friedenthal, "Government Appeals in Federal Criminal Cases," 12 *Stan. L. Rev.* 71 (1959); and *Di Bella v. United States*, 389 U.S. 90 (1967). In *Palko v. Connecticut*, 302 U.S. 319 (1937), the Supreme Court did uphold a state statute permitting government appeal from an acquittal, but *Benton v. Maryland*, 395 U.S. 784 (1969), must be presumed to have overruled *Palko* on that point.

55. 18 U.S.C. 3731; Omnibus Crime Control Act of 1970, title III, Pub. L. 91–644.

56. *United States v. Wilson*, 420 U.S. 332 (1975).

57. Ibid. at 352.

58. *United States v. Jenkins*, 420 U.S. 358 (1975).

59. *Fong Foo v. United States*, 369 U.S. 141 (1962). See *United States v. Martin Linen Supply Co.*, 430 U.S. 564 (1977), where the Court held that an appeal by the government is barred even though the acquittal was entered by the trial judge four months after the jury had been unable to agree on a decision. See also *Sanabria v. United States*, 437 U.S. 54 (1978), where the Court ruled that the government could not appeal a judgment of acquittal entered prior to the end of trial, even though the judgment was based on an erroneous evidentiary ruling.

60. *United States v. Scott*, 437 U.S. 82 (1978).

61. Ibid. at 87.

62. Thus in *Sanabria v. United States*, 437 U.S. 54 (1978), the Court ruled that an acquittal based on an erroneous evidentiary ruling bars further prosecution.

63. *Green v. United States*, 355 US. 184, 187–188 (1957).

64. *Hoag v. New Jersey*, 356 U.S. 464 (1958).

65. "Statutory Implementation," pp. 359–361.

66. See rules 8(b) and 13 of the Federal Rules of Criminal Procedure.

67. *Ashe v. Swenson*, 397 U.S. 436, 452–456 (1970).

68. E.g., *Cicucci v. Illinois*.

69. See Justice Brennan's opinion in *Ashe v. Swenson*, 397 U.S. at 454, n. 8; and "Twice in Jeopardy," pp. 292–294.

70. Any legislation would have to provide for limited exceptions, at the discretion of

the trial judge, to joinder taken either by the state or the defense where prejudice to legitimate interests could be demonstrated; Ibid. at 294–295.

71. In civil law, *res judicata* is a rule that a matter finally adjudicated is conclusive on the parties in subsequent suits.

72. See Friedland, *Double Jeopardy*, p. 6.

73. See Daniel Mayers and Fletcher Yarbrough, *"Bis Vexari*: New Trials and Successive Prosecutions," 74 *Harv. L. Rev.* 1 (1960).

74. *United States v. Oppenheimer*, 242 U.S. 85. (1916).

75. Ibid. at 88. And see *Sealfon v. United States*, 332 U.S. 575 (1948).

76. *Ashe v. Swenson*, 397 U.S. at 438.

77. See *Hoag v. New Jersey*. The conclusion in *Ashe* was influenced by the Court's decision to apply the double-jeopardy protection to the states in *Benton v. Maryland*.

78. *Ashe v. Swenson*, 397 U.S. at 443–446 (1970); accord, *Harris v. Washington*, 404 U.S. 55 (1971).

79. Cf. *United States v. Addington*, 471 F.2d 560 (1973).

80. E.g., *California v. Seltzer*, 101 Cal. Rptr. 260 (1974).

81. E.g., *United States v. Nash*, 447 F.2d 1382 (1971), and *Johnson v. Estelle*, 506 F.2d 347 (1975). It should also be noted that *Ashe* may encourage a one-defense strategy, and thereby foreclose defense options.

82. E.g., *United States v. Nash*.

83. Cf. *United States v. Williams*, 341 U.S. 58 (1951). And see note, "Perjury by Defendants: The Uses of Double Jeopardy and Collateral Estoppel," 74 *Harv. L. Rev.* 752 (1961).

84. *United States v. Perez*, 22 U.S. 579 (1824). And see *Simmons v. United States*, 142 U.S. 148 (1891); *Logan v. United States*, 144 U.S. 263 (1892); and *Kierl v. Montana*, 213 U.S. 1358 (1909).

85. Of course, whether a jury is indeed "hung" may not be left to the arbitrary discretion of the trial judge; presumably, a judge must allow a reasonable amount of time for the jury to reach agreement. See *Kierl v. Montana* (jury unable to reach agreement after two days of deliberations) and *Logan v. United States* (jury unable to reach agreement after forty hours). In addition to the amount of time expended by the jury in deliberations, other factors affecting a determination of whether a declaration of a mistrial was an abuse of discretion are (1) the length of the trial and the complexity of the issues facing the jury, *United States v. Goldstein*, 479 F.2d 1061, 1068 (1973); (2) a statement from the jury that it is hopelessly deadlocked, *United States v. Lansdown*, 460 F.2d 164, 170 (1972); and (3) a follow-up inquiry of the jury by the judge to determine whether agreement can be reached within a reasonable time, *United States v. See*, 505 F.2d 845, 851 (1974), although the judge may not know how the jury is numerically divided, *Brasfield v. United States*, 272 U.S. 448 (1926).

86. *United States v. Perez*, 22 U.S. at 580.

87. E.g., *Green v. United States*, 355 U.S. at 188. In 1978, in *Crist v. Bretz*, 437 U.S. 28, the Court ruled that the federal rule of attachment of jeopardy in jury trials (that is, jeopardy attaches when the jury is impaneled and sworn) applies equally to the states.

88. E.g., *Serfass v. United States*, 420 U.S. 377, 388 (1975). In 1975, in *Breed v. Jones*, the Court unanimously ruled that jeopardy attaches in a juvenile proceeding whose object is to determine if a criminal violation has occurred, barring a subsequent prosecution as an adult in a superior court.

89. *Green v. United States*, 355 U.S. at 188–189.

90. *Lovato v. New Mexico*, 242 U.S. 199 (1916).

91. *Illinois v. Somerville*, 410 U.S. 458, 471 (1973). In *Lee v. United States*, 432 U.S. 23 (1977), the Court again upheld a second prosecution after a dismissal of indictment even though jeopardy had attached. Defense, in opening statement, requested dismissal

based on a faulty indictment, but the dismissal did not occur until after both the government and defense had presented their cases. In these particular circumstances, the Court ruled that dismissal was the functional equivalent of a mistrial.

92. *Downum v. United States*, 372 U.S. 734 (1963).

93. *Cornero v. United States*, 48 F.2d 69, 71 (1931).

94. Justices Goldberg and White had been appointed to the Court in 1962.

95. *Gori v. United States*, 367 U.S. 364 (1961).

96. Ibid. at 369–370.

97. *United States v. Jorn*, 400 U.S. 470 (1971).

98. Ibid. at 485–486.

99. *United States v. Dinitz*, 424 U.S. 600 (1976).

100. E.g., *McNeal v. Hollowell*, 481 F.2d 1145 (1973).

101. See the dissenting opinion of Justice Marshall in *Illinois v. Somerville*, 410 U.S. at 477.

102. *Arizona v. Washington*, 434 U.S. 497 (1978).

103. See Leonard G. Miller, *Double Jeopardy and the Federal System* (Chicago: University of Chicago Press, 1968), p. 102.

104. *Waller v. Florida*, 397 U.S. 387 (1970).

105. For a discussion of the demise of the doctrine of dual federalism, see Edward S. Corwin, *The Twilight of the Supreme Court* (New Haven, Conn.: Yale University Press, 1934).

106. E.g., *Houston v. Moore*, 18 U.S. 1 (1820); *Fox v. Ohio*, 46 U.S. 410 (1847); and *United States v. Criukshank*, 92 U.S. 542 (1876).

107. *United States v. Lanza*, 260 U.S. 377, 382 (1922).

108. E.g., J. A. C. Grant, "The *Lanza* Rule of Successive Prosecutions," 34 *Colum. L. Rev.* 1309 (1932); and Walter Fisher, "Double Jeopardy and Federalism," 50 *Minn. L. Rev.* 607 (1966).

109. E.g., *Hebert v. Louisiana*, 272 U.S. 312 (1926); *Westfall v. United States*, 274 U.S. 256 (1927); *People v. Shell Co.*, 302 U.S. 253 (1937); *Jerome v. United States*, 318 U.S. 101 (1943); and *Screws v. United States*, 325 U.S. 91 (1944).

110. *Bartkus v. Illinois*, 359 U.S. 121 (1959); and *Abbate v. United States*, 359 U.S. 187 (1959).

111. Ibid. at 195. And see a similar argument by Justice Frankfurter in *Bartkus*, 359 U.S. at 137.

112. *Abbate v. United States*, 359 U.S. at 203.

113. See Miller, *Double Jeopardy*, pp. 102–103. The federal policy against multiple prosecutions, known as the *Petite policy*, see *Petite v. United States*, 361 U.S. 529 (1960), evidently does not protect against a federal prosecution where the Department of Justice wishes to ensure against a state conviction being reversed on appeal; see *Rinaldi v. United States*, 434 U.S. 22 (1977).

114. E.g., *United States v. Hayles*, 492 F. 2d 125 (1974); and *United States v. Vaughan*, 491 F.2d 1096 (1974).

115. *United States v. Treadway*, 321 F. Supp. 307, 308 (1970).

116. E.g., *United States v. Delay*, 500 F.2d 1360 (1974); and *United States v. Vaughan*, 491 F.2d 1096 (1974).

117. *Green v. United States*, 355 U.S. at 187.

118. See *Ladner v. United States*, 358 U.S. at 178.

JUDICIAL DECISIONS

The Same-offense Limitation:
Blockburger v. United States, *284 U.S. 299 (1932)*

Mr. Justice SUTHERLAND delivered the opinion of the Court.

The petitioner was charged with violating provisions of the Harrison Narcotic Act. The indictment contained five counts. The jury returned a verdict against petitioner upon the second, third and fifth counts only. Each of these counts charged a sale of morphine hydrochloride to the same purchaser. The second count charged a sale on a specified day of ten grains of the drug not in or from the original stamped package; the third count charged a sale on the following day of eight grains of the drug not in or from the original stamped package; the fifth count charged the latter sale also as having been made not in pursuance of a written order of the purchaser as required by the statute. The court sentenced petitioner to five years' imprisonment and a fine of $2,000 upon each count, the terms of imprisonment to run consecutively; and this judgment was affirmed on appeal.

The principal contentions here made by petitioner are as follows: (1) that, upon the facts, the two sales charged in the second and third counts as having been made to the same person, constitute a single offense; and (2) that the sale charged in the third count as having been made not from the original stamped package, and the same sale charged in the fifth count as having been made not in pursuance of a written order of the purchaser, constitute but one offense for which only a single penalty lawfully may be imposed.

One. The sales charged in the second and third counts, although made to the same person, were distinct and separate sales made at different times. It appears from the evidence that shortly after delivery of the drug which was the subject of the first sale, the purchaser paid for an additional quantity, which was delivered the next day. But the first sale had been consummated, and the payment for the additional drug, however closely following, was the initiation of a separate and distinct sale completed by its delivery.

The contention on behalf of petitioner is that these two sales, having been made to the same purchaser and following each other with no substantial interval of time between the delivery of the drug in the first transaction and the payment for the second quantity sold, constitute a single continuing offense. The contention is unsound. The distinction between the transactions here involved and an offense continuous in its character is well settled, as was pointed out by this court in the case of *Re Snow,* 120 U.S. 274. There it was held that the offense of cohabiting with more than one woman was a continuous offense, and was committed, in the sense of the statute, where there was a living or dwelling together as husband and wife. The court said

> "It is, inherently, a continuous offence, having duration; and not an offence consisting of an isolated act."
>
> . . .

The Narcotic Act does not create the offense of engaging in the business of selling the forbidden drugs, but penalizes any sale made in the absence of either of the qualifying requirements set forth. Each of several successive sales constitutes a distinct offense, however closely they may follow each other. The distinction stated by Mr. Wharton is that "when the impulse is single, but one indictment lies, no matter how long the action may continue. If successive impulses are separately given, even though all unite in swelling a common stream of action, separate indictments lie." Whart. Crim. Law, 11th ed. § 34. Or, as stated in note 3 to that section, "The test is whether the individual acts are prohibited, or the course of action which they constitute. If the former, then each act is punishable separately. . . . If the latter, there can be but one penalty."

In the present case, the first transaction, resulting in a sale, had come to an end. The next sale was not the result of the original impulse, but of a fresh one—that is to say, of a new bargain. The question is controlled, not by the *Snow* Case, but by such cases as that of *Ebeling v. Morgan*, 237 U.S. 625. There the accused was convicted under several counts of a wilful tearing, etc., of mail bags with intent to rob. The court (p. 628) stated the question to be, "whether one who, in the same transaction, tears or cuts successively mail bags of the United States used in conveyance of the mails, with intent to rob or steal any such mail, is guilty of a single offense or of additional offenses because of each successive cutting with the criminal intent charged." Answering this question, the court, after quoting the statute, § 189, Criminal Code, (U.S.C. title 18, § 312) said (p. 629):

> "These words plainly indicate that it was the intention of the lawmakers to protect each and every mail bag from felonious injury and mutilation. Whenever any one mail bag is thus torn, cut or injured, the offense is complete. Although the transaction of cutting the mail bags was in a sense continuous, the complete statutory offense was committed every time a mail bag was cut in the manner described, with the intent charged. The offense as to each separate bag was complete when that bag was cut, irrespective of any attack upon, or mutilation of, any other bag."

Two. Section 1 of the Narcotic Act creates the offense of selling any of the forbidden drugs except in or from the original stamped package; and § 2 creates the offense of selling any of such drugs not in pursuance of a written order of the person to whom the drug is sold. Thus, upon the face of the statute, two distinct offenses are created. Here there was but one sale, and the question is whether, both sections being violated by the same act, the accused committed two offenses or only one.

The statute is not aimed at sales of the forbidden drugs qua sales, a matter entirely beyond the authority of Congress, but at sales of such drugs in violation of the requirements set forth in §§ 1 and 2, enacted as aids to the enforcement of the stamp tax imposed by the act.

Each of the offenses created requires proof of a different element. The applicable rule is that where the same act or transaction constitutes a violation of two distinct statutory provisions, the test to be applied to determine whether there are two offenses or only one, is whether each provision requires proof of an additional fact which the other does not. *Gavieres v. United States*, 220 U.S. 338, 342, and authorities cited. In that case this court quoted from and adopted the language of the Supreme Court of Massachusetts in *Morey v. Comm.* 108 Mass. 433: "A single act may be an offense against two statutes; and if each statute requires proof of an additional fact which the other does not, an acquittal or conviction under either statute does not exempt the defendant from prosecution and punishment under the other." Applying the test, we must conclude that here, although both sections were violated by the one sale, two offenses were committed.

. . .

Judgment affirmed.

Greater and Lesser Included Offenses:
Brown v. Ohio, 432 U.S. 161 (1977)

Mr. Justice POWELL delivered the opinion of the Court.

The question in this case is whether the Double Jeopardy Clause of the Fifth Amendment bars prosecution and punishment for the crime of stealing an automobile following prosecution and punishment for the lesser included offense of operating the same vehicle without the owner's consent.

I

On November 29, 1973, the petitioner, Nathaniel Brown, stole a 1965 Chevrolet from a parking lot in East Cleveland, Ohio. Nine days later, on December 8, 1973, Brown was caught driving the car in Wickliffe, Ohio. The Wickliffe police charged him with "joyriding"—taking or operating the car without the owner's consent—in violation of Ohio Rev. Code § 4549.04(D). The complaint charged that "on or about December 8, 1973 . . . Nathaniel H. Brown did unlawfully and purposely take, drive or operate a certain motor vehicle to wit; a 1965 Chevrolet . . . without the consent of the owner one Gloria Ingram. . . ." App. 3. Brown pled guilty to this charge and was sentenced to 30 days in jail and a $100 fine.

Upon his release from jail on January 8, 1974, Brown was returned to East Cleveland to face further charges, and on February 5 he was indicted by the Cuyahoga County grand jury. The indictment was in two counts, the first charging the theft of the car "on or about the 29th day of November 1973," in violation of Ohio Rev. Code § 4549.04(A), and the second charging joyriding on the same date in violation of § 4549.04(D). A bill of particulars filed by the prosecuting attorney specified that

"on or about the 29th day of November, 1973 . . . Nathaniel Brown unlawfully did steal a Chevrolet motor vehicle, and take, drive or operate such vehicle without the consent of the owner, Gloria Ingram. . . ." App. 10.

Brown objected to both counts of the indictment on the basis of former jeopardy.

On March 18, 1974, at a pretrial hearing in the Cuyahoga County Court of Common Pleas, Brown pled guilty to the auto theft charge on the understanding that the court would consider his claim of former jeopardy on a motion to withdraw the plea. Upon submission of the motion, the court overruled Brown's double jeopardy objections. The court sentenced Brown to six months in jail but suspended the sentence and placed Brown on probation for one year.

The Ohio Court of Appeals affirmed. It held that under Ohio law the misdemeanor of joyriding was included in the felony of auto theft:

"Every element of the crime of operating a motor vehicle without the consent of the owner is also an element of the crime of auto theft. 'The difference between the crime of stealing a motor vehicle, and operating a motor vehicle without the consent of the owner is that conviction for stealing requires proof of an intent on the part of the thief to *permanently* deprive the owner of possession.' . . . The crime of operating a motor vehicle without the consent of the owner is a lesser included offense of auto theft. . . ." App. 22.

Although this analysis led the court to agree with Brown that "for purposes of double jeopardy the two prosecutions involve the same statutory offense," id., at 23, it nonetheless held the second prosecution permissible:

"The two prosecutions are based on two separate acts of the appellant, one which occurred on November 29th and one which occurred on December 8th. Since appellant has not shown that both prosecutions are based on the same act or transaction, the second prosecution is not barred by the double jeopardy clause." Ibid.

The Ohio Supreme Court denied leave to appeal.

. . .

II

The Double Jeopardy Clause of the Fifth Amendment, applicable to the States through the Fourteenth, provides that no person shall "be subject for the same offence to be twice put in jeopardy of life or limb." It has long been understood that separate statutory crimes need not be identical—either in constituent elements or in actual proof—in order to be the same within the meaning of the constitutional prohibition. 1 Bishop's New Criminal Law § 1051 (1892); Comment, Twice in Jeopardy, 75 Yale L.J. 262, 268–269 (1965). The principal question in this case is whether auto theft and joyriding, a greater and lesser included offense under Ohio law, constitute the "same offense" under the Double Jeopardy Clause.

Because it was designed originally to embody the protection of the common law pleas of former jeopardy, the Fifth Amendment double jeopardy guarantee serves principally as a restraint on courts and prosecutors. The legislature remains free under the Double Jeopardy Clause to define crimes and fix punishments; but once the legislature has acted courts may not impose more than one punishment for the same offense and prosecutors ordinarily may not attempt to secure that punishment in more than one trial.

The Double Jeopardy Clause "protects against a second prosecution for the same offense after acquittal. It protects against a second prosecution for the same offense after conviction. And it protects against multiple punishments for the same offense." *North Carolina v. Pearce*, 395 U.S. 711, 717 (1969). Where consecutive sentences are imposed at a single criminal trial, the role of the constitutional guarantee is limited to assuring that the court does not exceed its legislative authorization by imposing multiple punishments for the same offense. Where successive prosecutions are at stake, the guarantee serves "a constitutional policy of finality for the defendant's benefit." *United States v. Jorn*, 400 U.S. 470, 479 (1971) (plurality opinion). That policy protects the accused from attempts to relitigate the facts underlying a prior acquittal and from attempts to secure additional punishment after a prior conviction and sentence.

The established test for determining whether two offenses are sufficiently distinguishable to permit the imposition of cumulative punishment was stated in *Blockburger v. United States*, 284 U.S. 299, 304 (1932):

> "The applicable rule is that where the same act or transaction constitutes a violation of two distinct statutory provisions, the test to be applied to determine whether there are two offenses or only one, is whether each provision requires proof of an additional fact which the other does not. . . ."

This test emphasizes the elements of the two crimes. . . .

If two offenses are the same under this test for purposes of barring consecutive sentences at a single trial, they necessarily will be the same for purposes of barring successive prosecutions. Where the judge is forbidden to impose cumulative punishment for two crimes at the end of a single proceeding, the prosecutor is forbidden to strive for the same result in successive proceedings. Unless "each statute requires proof of an additional fact which the other does not," *Morey v. Commonwealth*, 108 Mass. 433, 434 (1871), the Double Jeopardy Clause prohibits successive prosecutions as well as cumulative punishment.

We are mindful that the Ohio courts "have the final authority to interpret . . . that State's legislation." *Garner v. Louisiana*, 368 U.S. 157, 169 (1961). Here the Ohio Court of Appeals has authoritatively defined the elements of the two Ohio crimes: joyriding consists of taking or operating a vehicle without the owner's consent, and auto theft consists of joyriding with the intent permanently to deprive the owner of possession. App. 22. Joyriding is the lesser included offense. The prosecutor who has established joyriding need only prove the requisite intent in order to establish auto theft; the prosecutor who has established auto theft necessarily has established joyriding as well.

Applying the *Blockburger* test, we agree with the Ohio Court of Appeals that joyriding and auto theft, as defined by the court, constitute "the same statutory offense" within the meaning of the Double Jeopardy Clause. App. 23. For it is clearly *not* the case that "each statute requires proof of an additional fact which the other does not." 284 U.S., at 304. As is invariably true of a greater and lesser included offense, the lesser offense—joyriding—requires no proof beyond that which is required for conviction of the greater—auto theft. The greater offense is therefore by definition the "same" for purposes of double jeopardy as any lesser offense included in it.

This conclusion merely restates what has been this Court's understanding of the Double Jeopardy Clause at least since *In re Nielsen* was decided in 1889. In that case the Court endorsed the rule that

> "where . . . a person has been tried and convicted for a crime which has various incidents included in it, he cannot be a second time tried for one of those incidents without being twice put in jeopardy for the same offense." 131 U.S., at 188.

Although in this formulation the conviction of the greater precedes the conviction of the lesser, the opinion makes it clear that the sequence is immaterial. Thus the Court treated the formulation as just one application of the rule that two offenses are the same unless each requires proof that the other does not. . . .

III

After correctly holding that joyriding and auto theft are the same offense under the Double Jeopardy Clause, the Ohio Court of Appeals nevertheless concluded that Nathaniel Brown could be convicted of both crimes because the charges against him focused on different parts of his 9-day joyride. App. 23. We hold a different view. The Double Jeopardy Clause is not such a fragile guarantee that prosecutors can avoid its limitations by the simple expedient of dividing a single crime into a series of temporal or spatial units. The applicable Ohio statutes, as written and as construed in this case, make the theft and operation of a single car a single offense. Although the Wickliffe and East Cleveland authorities may have had different perspectives on Brown's offense, it was still only one offense under Ohio law. Accordingly, the specification of different dates in the two charges on which Brown was convicted cannot alter the fact that he was placed twice in jeopardy for the same offense in violation of the Fifth and Fourteenth Amendments.

Reversed.

Collateral Estoppel:
Ashe v. Swenson, 397 U.S. 436 (1970)

Mr. Justice STEWART delivered the opinion of the Court.

In *Benton v. Maryland*, 395 U.S. 784, the Court held that the Fifth Amendment guarantee against double jeopardy is enforceable against the States through the Fourteenth Amendment. The question in this case is whether the State of Missouri violated that guarantee when it prosecuted the petitioner a second time for armed robbery in the circumstances here presented.

Sometime in the early hours of the morning of January 10, 1960, six men were engaged in a poker game in the basement of the home of John Gladson at Lee's Summit, Missouri. Suddenly three or four masked men, armed with a shotgun and pistols, broke into the basement and robbed each of the poker players of money and various articles of personal property. The robbers—and it has never been clear whether there were three or four of them—then fled in a car belonging to one of the victims of the robbery. Shortly thereafter the stolen car was discovered in a field, and later that morning three men were arrested by a state trooper while they were walking on a highway not far from where the abandoned car had been found. The petitioner was arrested by another officer some distance away.

The four were subsequently charged with seven separate offenses—the armed robbery of each of the six poker players and the theft of the car. In May 1960 the petitioner went to trial on the charge of robbing Donald Knight, one of the participants in the poker game. At the trial the State called Knight and three of his fellow poker players as prosecution witnesses. Each of them described the circumstances of the holdup and itemized his own individual losses. The proof that an armed robbery had occurred and that personal property had been taken from Knight as well as from each of the others was unassailable. The testimony of the four victims in this regard was consistent both internally and with that of the others. But the State's evidence that the petitioner had been one of the robbers was weak. Two of the witnesses thought that there had been only three robbers altogether, and could not identify the petitioner as one of them. Another of the victims, who was the petitioner's uncle by marriage, said that at the "patrol station" he had positively identified each of the other three men accused of the holdup, but could say only that the petitioner's voice "sounded very much like" that of one of the robbers. The fourth participant in the poker game did identify the petitioner, but only by his "size and height, and his actions."

The cross-examination of these witnesses was brief, and it was aimed primarily at exposing the weakness of their identification testimony. Defense counsel made no attempt to question their testimony regarding the holdup itself or their claims as to their losses. Knight testified without contradiction that the robbers had stolen from him his watch, $250 in cash, and about $500 in checks. His billfold, which had been found by the police in the possession of one of the three other men accused of the robbery, was admitted in evidence. The defense offered no testimony and waived final argument.

The trial judge instructed the jury that if it found that the petitioner was one of the participants in the armed robbery, the theft of "any money" from Knight would sustain a conviction. He also instructed the jury that if the petitioner was one of the robbers, he was guilty under the law even if he had not personally robbed Knight. The jury—though not instructed to elaborate upon its verdict—found the petitioner "not guilty due to insufficient evidence."

Six weeks later the petitioner was brought to trial again, this time for the robbery of another participant in the poker game, a man named Roberts. The petitioner filed a motion to dismiss, based on his previous acquittal. The motion was overruled, and the second trial began. The witnesses were for the most part the same, though this time their testimony was substantially stronger on the issue of the petitioner's identity. For example, two witnesses who at the first trial had been wholly unable to identify the petitioner as one of the robbers, now testified that his features, size, and mannerisms matched those of one of their assailants. Another witness who before had identified the petitioner only by his size and actions now also remembered him by the unusual sound of his voice. The State further refined its case at the second trial by declining to call one of the participants in the poker game whose identification testimony at the first trial had been conspicuously negative. The case went to the jury on instructions virtually identical to those given at the first trial. This time the jury found the petitioner guilty, and he was sentenced to a 35-year term in the state penitentiary.

The Supreme Court of Missouri affirmed the conviction. . . . The petitioner then brought the present habeas corpus proceeding in the United States District Court. . . . Considering itself bound by this court's decision in *Hoag v. New Jersey*, 356 U.S. 464, the District Court denied the writ. . . .

As the District Court and the Court of Appeals correctly noted, the operative facts here are virtually identical to those of *Hoag v. New Jersey*, supra. In that case the defendant was tried for the armed robbery of three men who, along with others, had been held up in a tavern. The proof of the robbery was clear, but the evidence identifying the defendant as one of the robbers was weak, and the defendant interposed an alibi defense. The jury brought in a verdict of not guilty. The defendant was then brought to trial again, on an indictment charging the robbery of a fourth victim of the tavern holdup. This time the jury found him guilty. After appeals in the state courts proved unsuccessful, Hoag brought his case here.

Viewing the question presented solely in terms of Fourteenth Amendment due process—whether the course that New Jersey had pursued had "led to fundamental unfairness," 356 U.S., at 467, this Court declined to reverse the judgment of conviction, because "in the circumstances shown by this record, we cannot say that petitioner's later prosecution and conviction violated due process." 356 U.S., at 466. The Court found it unnecessary to decide whether "collateral estoppel"—the principle that bars relitigation between the same parties of issues actually determined at a previous trial—is a due process requirement in a state criminal trial. . . .

The doctrine of *Benton v. Maryland,* 395 U.S. 784, puts the issues in the present case in a perspective quite different from that in which the issues were perceived in *Hoag v. New Jersey,* supra. The question is no longer whether collateral estoppel is a requirement of due process, but whether it is a part of the Fifth Amendment's guarantee against double jeopardy. And if collateral estoppel is embodied in that guarantee, then its applicability in a particular case is no longer a matter to be left for state court determination within the broad bounds of "fundamental fairness," but a matter of constitutional fact we must decide through an examination of the entire record.

"Collateral estoppel" is an awkward phrase, but it stands for an extremely important principle in our adversary system of justice. It means simply that when an issue of ultimate fact has once been determined by a valid and final judgment, that issue cannot again be litigated between the same parties in any future lawsuit. Although first developed in civil litigation, collateral estoppel has been an established rule of federal criminal law at least since this Court's decision more than 50 years ago in *United States v. Oppenheimer,* 242 U.S. 85. As Mr. Justice Holmes put the matter in that case, "It cannot be that the safeguards of the person, so often and so rightly mentioned with solemn reverence, are less than those that protect from a liability in debt." 242 U.S., at 87. As a rule of federal law, therefore, "it is much too late to suggest that this principle is not fully applicable to a former judgment in a criminal case, either because of lack of 'mutuality' or because the judgment may reflect only a belief that the Government had not met the higher burden of proof exacted in such cases for the Government's evidence as a whole although not necessarily as to every link in the chain." *United States v. Kramer,* 289 F.2d 909, 913.

The federal decisions have made clear that the rule of collateral estoppel in criminal cases is not to be applied with the hypertechnical and archaic approach of a 19th century pleading book, but with realism and rationality. Where a previous judgment of acquittal was based upon a general verdict, as is usually the case, this approach requires a court to "examine the record of a prior proceeding, taking into account the pleadings, evidence, charge, and other relevant matter, and conclude whether a rational jury could have grounded its verdict upon an issue other than that which the defendant seeks to foreclose from consideration." The inquiry "must be set in a practical frame and viewed with an eye to all the circumstances of the proceedings." *Sealfon v. United States,* 332 U.S. 575, 579. Any test more technically restrictive would, of course, simply amount to a rejection of the rule of collateral estoppel in criminal proceedings, at least in every case where the first judgment was based upon a general verdict of acquittal.

Straightforward application of the federal rule to the present case can lead to but one conclusion. For the record is utterly devoid of any indication that the first jury could rationally have found that an armed robbery had not occurred, or that Knight had not been a victim of that robbery. The single rationally conceivable issue in dispute before the jury was whether the petitioner had been one of the robbers. And the jury by its verdict found that he had not. The federal rule of law, therefore, would make a second prosecution for the robbery of Roberts wholly impermissible.

The ultimate question to be determined, then, in the light of *Benton v. Maryland,* supra, is whether this established rule of federal law is embodied in the Fifth Amendment guarantee against double jeopardy. We do not hesitate to hold that it is. For whatever else that constitutional guarantee may embrace, it surely protects a man who has been acquitted from having to "run the gantlet" a second time.

The question is not whether Missouri could validly charge the petitioner with six separate offenses for the robbery of the six poker players. It is not whether he could have received a total of six punishments if he had been convicted in a single trial of robbing the six victims. It is simply whether, after a jury determined by its verdict that the petitioner was not one of the robbers, the State could constitutionally hale him before a new jury to litigate that issue again.

After the first jury had acquitted the petitioner of robbing Knight, Missouri could certainly not have brought him to trial again upon that charge. Once a jury had determined upon conflicting testimony that there was at least a reasonable doubt that the petitioner was one of the robbers, the State could not present the same or different identification evidence in a second prosecution for the robbery of Knight in the hope that a different jury might find that evidence more convincing. The situation is constitutionally no different here, even though the second trial related to another victim of the same robbery. For the name of the victim, in the circumstances of this case, had no bearing whatever upon the issue of whether the petitioner was one of the robbers.

In this case the State in its brief has frankly conceded that following the petitioner's acquittal, it treated the first trial as no more than a dry run for the second prosecution: "No doubt the prosecutor felt the state had a provable case on the first charge and, when he lost, he did what every good attorney would do—he refined his presentation in light of the turn of events at the first trial." But this is precisely what the constitutional guarantee forbids.

The judgment is reversed. . . .

It is so ordered.

Reversed and remanded.

Mr. Justice BRENNAN, whom Mr. Justice DOUGLAS and Mr. Justice MARSHALL join, concurring.

I agree that the Double Jeopardy Clause incorporates collateral estoppel as a constitutional requirement and therefore join the Court's opinion. However, even if the rule of collateral estoppel had been inapplicable to the facts of this case, it is my view that the Double Jeopardy Clause nevertheless bars the prosecution of petitioner a second time for armed robbery. . . .

In my view, the Double Jeopardy Clause requires the prosecution, except in most limited circumstances, to join at one trial all the charges against a defendant that grow out of a single criminal act, occurrence, episode, or transaction. This "same transaction" test of "same offence" not only enforces the ancient prohibition against vexatious multiple prosecutions embodied in the Double Jeopardy Clause, but responds as well to the increasingly widespread recognition that the consolidation in one lawsuit of all issues arising out of a single transaction or occurrence best promotes justice, economy, and convenience. Modern rules of criminal and civil procedure reflect this recognition. . . .

Mistrials—The Hung Jury:
United States v. Perez, 9 Wheat. 579 (1824)

Mr. Justice STORY delivered the opinion of the court:

This cause comes up from the Circuit Court for the southern District of New York, upon a certificate of division in the opinions of the judges of that court. The prisoner, Josef Perez, was put upon trial for a capital offense, and the jury, being unable to agree, were discharged by the court from giving any verdict upon the indictment, without the consent of the prisoner, or of the attorney for the United States. The prisoner's counsel, thereupon, claimed his discharge as of right, under these circumstances; and this forms the point upon which the judges were divided. The question, therefore, arises, whether the discharge of the jury by the court from giving any verdict upon the indictment, with which they were charged, without the consent of the prisoner, is a bar to any future trial for the same offense. If it be, then he is entitled to be discharged from custody; if not, then he ought to be held in imprisonment until such trial can be had. We are of opinion that the facts constitute no legal bar to a future trial. The prisoner has not been convicted or acquitted, and may again be put upon his defense. We think, that in all cases of this nature, the law has invested courts of justice with the authority to discharge a jury from giving any verdict, whenever, in their opinion, taking all the circumstances into consideration, there is a manifest necessity for the act, or the ends of public justice would otherwise be defeated. They are to exercise a sound discretion on the subject; and it is impossible to define all the circumstances which would render it proper to interfere. To be sure, the power ought to be used with the greatest caution, under urgent circumstances, and for very plain and obvious causes; and, in capital cases especially, courts should be extremely careful how they interfere with any of the chances of life, in favor of the prisoner. But, after all, they have the right to order the discharge; and the security which the public have for the faithful, sound and conscientious exercise of this discretion, rests, in this, as in other cases, upon the responsibility of the judges, under their oaths of office. We are aware that there is some diversity of opinion and practice on this subject, in the American courts; but, after weighing the question with due deliberation, we are of opinion that such a discharge constitutes no bar to further proceedings, and gives no right of exemption to the prisoner from being again put upon trial. A certificate is to be directed to the Circuit Court, in conformity to this opinion.

. . .

Mistrials—Defense Motion:
United States v. Dinitz, 424 U.S. 600 (1976)

Mr. Justice STEWART delivered the opinion of the Court.

The question in this case is whether the Double Jeopardy Clause of the Fifth Amendment was violated by the retrial of the respondent after his original trial had ended in a mistrial granted at his request.

I

The respondent, Nathan Dinitz, was arrested on December 8, 1972, following the return of an indictment charging him with conspiracy to distribute LSD and with distribution of that controlled substance in violation of 21 U.S.C. §§ 841(a)(1), 846. On the day of his arrest, the respondent retained a lawyer named Meldon to represent him. Meldon appeared with the respondent at his arraignment, filed numerous pretrial motions on his behalf, and was completely responsible for the preparation of the case until shortly before trial. Some five days before the trial was scheduled to begin, the respondent retained another lawyer, Maurice Wagner, to conduct his defense. Wagner had not been admitted to practice before the United States District Court for the Northern District of Florida, but on the first day of the trial the court permitted him to appear *pro hac vice*. In addition to Meldon and Wagner, Fletcher Baldwin, a professor of law at the University of Florida, also appeared on the respondent's behalf.

The jury was selected and sworn on February 14, 1973, and opening statements by counsel began on the following afternoon. The prosecutor's opening statement briefly outlined the testimony that he expected an undercover agent named Steve Cox to give regarding his purchase of LSD from the respondent. Wagner then began his opening statement for the defense. After introducing himself and his cocounsel, Wagner turned to the case against the respondent:

> "Mr. Wagner: After working on this case over a period of time it appeared to me that if we would have given nomenclature, if we would have named this case so there could be no question about identifying it in the future, I would have called it The Case—
>
> "Mr. Reed [Asst. U.S. Attorney]: Your Honor, we object to personal opinions.
>
> "The Court: Objection sustained. The purpose of the opening statement is to summarize the facts the evidence will show, state the issues, not to give personal opinions. Proceed, Mr. Wagner.
>
> "Mr. Wagner: Thank you, Your Honor. I call this the Case of the Incredible Witness."

The prosecutor again objected and the judge excused the jury. The judge then warned Wagner that he did not approve of his behavior and cautioned Wagner that he did not want to have to remind him again about the purpose of the opening statement.

Following this initial incident, the trial judge found it necessary twice again to remind Wagner of the purpose of the opening statement and to instruct him to relate "the facts that you expect the evidence to show, the admissible evidence." Later on in his statement, Wagner started to discuss an attempt to extort money from the respondent that had occurred shortly after his arrest. The prosecutor objected and the jury was again excused. Wagner informed the trial judge of some of the details of the extortion attempt and assured the court that he would connect it with the prospective government witness Cox. But it soon became apparent that Wagner had no information linking Cox to the extortion attempt, and the trial judge then excluded Wagner from the trial and ordered him to leave the courthouse.

The judge then asked Meldon if he was prepared to proceed with the trial. Upon learning that Meldon had not discussed the case with the witnesses, the judge gave Meldon until 9:00 the following morning to prepare. Meldon informed the judge that the respondent was "in a quandary because he hired Mr. Wagner to argue the case and he feels he needs more time to obtain outside counsel to argue the case for him. The judge responded that "you are his counsel and have been" but stated that he would consider the matter "between now and 9:00 o'clock tomorrow morning."

The next morning, Meldon told the judge that the respondent wanted Wagner and not himself or Baldwin to try the case. The judge then set forth three alternative courses that might be followed—(1) a stay or recess pending application to the Court of Appeals to review the propriety of expelling Wagner, (2) continuation of the trial with Meldon and Baldwin as counsel, or (3) a declaration of a mistrial which would permit the respondent to obtain other counsel. Following a short recess, Meldon moved for a mistrial, stating that, after "full consideration of the situation and an explanation of the alternatives before him, [the respondent] feels that he would move for a mistrial and that this would be in his best interest." The government prosecutor did not oppose the motion. The judge thereupon declared a mistrial, expressing his belief that such a course would serve the interest of justice.

Before his second trial, the respondent moved to dismiss the indictment on the ground that a retrial would violate the Double Jeopardy Clause of the Constitution. This motion was denied. The respondent represented himself at the new trial, and he was convicted by the jury on both the conspiracy and distribution counts. A divided panel of the Court of Appeals for the Fifth Circuit reversed the conviction, holding that the retrial violated the respondent's constitutional right not to be twice put in jeopardy. . . .

II

The Double Jeopardy Clause of the Fifth Amendment protects a defendant in a criminal proceeding against multiple punishments or repeated prosecutions for the same offense. Underlying this constitutional safeguard is the belief that "the State with all its resources and power should not be allowed to make repeated attempts to convict an individual for an alleged offense, thereby subjecting him to embarrassment, expense and ordeal and compelling him to live in a continuing state of anxiety and insecurity, as well as enhancing the possibility that even though innocent he may be found guilty." *Green v. United States*, 355 U.S. 184, 187–188. Where, as here, a mistrial has been declared, the defendant's "valued right to have his trial completed by a particular tribunal" is also implicated. *Wade v. Hunter*, 336 U.S. 684, 689.

Since Justice Story's 1824 opinion for the Court in *United States v. Perez*, 9 Wheat. 579, 580, this Court has held that the question whether under the Double Jeopardy Clause there can be a new trial after a mistrial has been declared without the defendant's request or consent depends on whether "there is a manifest necessity for the [mistrial], or the ends of public justice would otherwise be defeated." Different considerations obtain, however, when the mistrial has been declared at the defendant's request. The reasons for the distinction were discussed in the plurality opinion in the *Jorn* case:

> "If that right to go to a particular tribunal is valued, it is because, independent of the threat of bad-faith conduct by judge or prosecutor, the defendant has a significant interest in the decision whether or not to take the case from the jury when circumstances occur which might be thought to warrant a declaration of mistrial. Thus,

where circumstances develop not attributable to prosecutorial or judicial overreaching, a motion by the defendant for mistrial is ordinarily assumed to remove any barrier to reprosecution, even if the defendant's motion is necessitated by prosecutorial or judicial error. In the absence of such a motion, the *Perez* doctrine of manifest necessity stands as a command to trial judges not to foreclose the defendant's option until a scrupulous exercise of judicial discretion leads to the conclusion that the ends of public justice would not be served by a continuation of the proceedings. See *United States v. Perez*, 9 Wheat., at 580, 400 U.S., at 485."

The distinction between mistrials declared by the court *sua sponte* and mistrials granted at the defendant's request or with his consent is wholly consistent with the protections of the Double Jeopardy Clause. Even when judicial or prosecutorial error prejudices a defendant's prospects of securing an acquittal, he may nonetheless desire "to go to the first jury and, perhaps, end the dispute then and there with an acquittal." *United States v. Jorn*, supra, at 484. Our prior decisions recognize the defendant's right to pursue this course in the absence of circumstances of manifest necessity requiring a *sua sponte* judicial declaration of mistrial. But it is evident that when judicial or prosecutorial error seriously prejudices a defendant, he may have little interest in completing the trial and obtaining a verdict from the first jury. The defendant may reasonably conclude that a continuation of the tainted proceeding would result in a conviction followed by a lengthy appeal and, if a reversal is secured, by a second prosecution. In such circumstances, a defendant's mistrial request has objectives not unlike the interests served by the Double Jeopardy Clause—the avoidance of the anxiety, expense, and delay occasioned by multiple prosecutions.

The Court of Appeals viewed the doctrine that permits a retrial following a mistrial sought by the defendant as resting on a waiver theory. The court concluded, therefore, that "something more substantial than a Hobson's choice" is required before a defendant can "be said to have relinquished voluntarily his right to proceed before the first jury." See 492 F.2d, at 59. The court thus held that no waiver could be imputed to the respondent because the trial judge's action in excluding Wagner left the respondent with "no choice but to move for or accept a mistrial." Ibid. But traditional waiver concepts have little relevance where the defendant must determine whether or not to request or consent to a mistrial in response to judicial or prosecutorial error. In such circumstances, the defendant generally does face a "Hobson's choice" between giving up his first jury and continuing a trial tainted by prejudicial judicial or prosecutorial error. The important consideration, for purposes of the Double Jeopardy Clause, is that the defendant retains primary control over the course to be followed in the event of such error.

The Court of Appeals' determination that the manifest necessity standard should be applied to a mistrial motion when the defendant has "no choice" but to request a mistrial undermines rather than furthers the protections of the Double Jeopardy Clause. In the event of severely prejudicial error a defendant might well consider an immediate new trial a preferable alternative to the prospect of a probable conviction followed by an appeal, a reversal of the conviction, and a later retrial. Yet the Court of Appeals' decision, in effect, instructs trial judges to reject the most meritorious mistrial motion in the absence of manifest necessity and to require, instead, that the trial proceed to its conclusion despite a legitimate claim of seriously prejudicial error. For if a trial judge follows that course, the Double Jeopardy Clause will present no obstacle to a retrial if the conviction is set aside by the trial judge or reversed on appeal.

The Double Jeopardy Clause does protect a defendant against governmental actions intended to provoke mistrial requests and thereby subject defendants to the substantial burdens imposed by multiple prosecutions. It bars retrials where "bad-faith conduct by the judge or prosecutor" threatens the "harassment of an accused by successive prosecutions or declaration of a mistrial so as to afford the prosecution a more favorable opportunity to convict" the defendant. *United States v. Jorn,* supra, 400 U.S. at 485.

But here the trial judge's banishment of Wagner from the proceedings was not done in bad faith in order to goad the respondent into requesting a mistrial or to prejudice his prospects for an acquittal. As the Court of Appeals noted, Wagner "was guilty of improper conduct" during his opening statement which "may have justified disciplinary action," 492 F.2d, at 60–61. Even accepting the appellate court's conclusion that the trial judge overreacted in expelling Wagner from the courtroom, ibid., the court did not suggest, the respondent has not contended, and the record does not show that the judge's action was motivated by bad faith or undertaken to harass or prejudice the respondent.

Under these circumstances we hold that the Court of Appeals erred in finding that the retrial violated the respondent's constitutional right not to be twice put in jeopardy. Accordingly, the judgment before us is reversed, and the case is remanded to the Court of Appeals for further proceedings consistent with this opinion.

It is so ordered.

Judgment reversed.

Mr. Justice BRENNAN, with whom Mr. Justice MARSHALL concurs, dissenting.

The Court's premise is that the mistrial was directed at respondent's request or with his consent. I agree with the Court of Appeals that, for purposes of double jeopardy analysis, it was not, but rather that, ". . . the trial judge's response to the conduct of defense counsel deprived Dinitz's motion for a mistrial of its necessary consensual character." 492 F.2d 53, 59 n. 9. Therefore the rule that "a motion by the defendant for mistrial is ordinarily assumed to remove any barrier to reprosecution," *United States v. Jorn,* 400 U.S. 485, is inapplicable. Accordingly, I agree that respondent's motion, for the reasons expressed in the panel and en banc opinions of the Court of Appeals, did not remove the bar of double jeopardy to reprosecution in "the extraordinary circumstances of the present case, in which judicial error alone, rather than [respondent's] exercise of any option to stop or go forward, took away his 'valued right to have his trial completed by a particular tribunal.'" 504 F.2d, at 854–855. I also agree with the holding in the panel opinion that "in view of . . . [the] alternatives which would not affect the ability to continue the trial, we cannot say that there was manifest necessity for the trial judge's actions." 492 F.2d, at 61. I would affirm.

Dual Sovereignty:
Waller v. Florida, 397 U.S. 387 (1970)

Mr. Chief Justice BURGER delivered the opinion of the Court.

We granted the writ in this case to review a narrow question which can best be treated on the basis of the facts as stated by the District Court of Appeal of Florida, Second District, and the holding of that court. Petitioner was one of a number of persons who removed a canvas mural which was affixed to a wall inside the City Hall of St. Petersburg, Florida. After the mural was removed, the petitioner and others carried it through the streets of St. Petersburg until they were confronted by police officers. After a scuffle, the officers recovered the mural, but in a damaged condition.

The petitioner was charged by the City of St. Petersburg with the violation of two ordinances: first, destruction of city property; and second, disorderly breach of the peace. He was found guilty in the municipal court on both counts, and a sentence of 180 days in the county jail was imposed.

Thereafter an information was filed against the petitioner by the State of Florida charging him with grand larceny. It is conceded that this information was based on the same acts of the petitioner as were involved in the violation of the two city ordinances.

Before his trial in the Circuit Court on the felony charge, petitioner moved in the Supreme Court of Florida for a writ of prohibition to prevent the second trial, asserting the claim of double jeopardy as a bar. Relief was denied without opinion. *State ex rel. Waller v. Circuit Court for the Sixth Judicial Circuit in and for Pinellas County*, 201 So.2d 554 (1967). Thereafter petitioner was tried in the Circuit Court of Florida by a jury and was found guilty of the felony of grand larceny. After verdict in the state court, he was sentenced to six months to five years less 170 days of the 180-day sentence previously imposed by the municipal court of St. Petersburg, Florida.

On appeal, the District Court of Appeal of Florida considered and rejected petitioner's claim that he had twice been put in jeopardy because prior to his conviction of grand larceny, he had been convicted by the municipal court of an included offense of the crime of grand larceny. *Waller v. State*, 213 So.2d 623 (1968). The opinion of the District Court of Appeal first explicitly acknowledged that the charge on which the state court action rested "was based on the same acts of the appellant as were involved in the violation of the two city ordinances." Then in rejecting Waller's claim of double jeopardy, the court said:

> "Assuming but not holding that the violations of the municipal ordinances were included offenses of the crime of grand larceny, the appellant nevertheless has not twice been put in jeopardy, because *even if a person has been tried in a municipal court for the identical offense with which he is charged in a state court, this would not be a bar to the prosecution of such person in the proper state court.* This has been the law of this state since 1894. . . ." (Emphasis added.)

. . .

Whether in fact and law petitioner committed separate offenses which could support separate charges was not decided by the Florida courts, nor do we reach that question. What is before us is the asserted power of the two courts within one State to place petitioner on trial for the same alleged crime.

In *Benton v. Maryland*, 395 U.S. 784 (1969), this Court declared the double jeopardy provisions of the Fifth Amendment applicable to the States, overruling

Palko v. Connecticut, 302 U.S. 319 (1937). Here, as in *North Carolina v. Pearce,* 395 U.S. 711 (1969), *Benton* should be applied to test petitioner's conviction, although we need not and do not decide whether each of the several aspects of the constitutional guarantee against double jeopardy requires such application in similar procedural circumstances.

Florida does not stand alone in treating municipalities and the State as separate sovereign entities, each capable of imposing punishment for the same alleged crime. Here, respondent State of Florida seeks to justify this separate sovereignty theory by asserting that the relationship between a municipality and the State is analogous to the relationship between a State and the Federal Government. Florida's chief reliance is placed upon this Court's holdings in *Bartkus v. Illinois,* 359 U.S. 121 (1959), and *Abbate v. United States,* 359 U.S. 187 (1959), which permitted successive prosecutions by the Federal and State Governments as separate sovereigns. Any such reading of *Abbate* is foreclosed. In another context, but relevant here, this Court noted—

> "Political subdivisions of States—counties, cities, or whatever—never were and never have been considered as sovereign entities. Rather, they have been traditionally regarded as subordinate governmental instrumentalities created by the State to assist in the carrying out of state governmental functions." *Reynolds v. Sims,* 377 U.S. 533, 575 (1964).

Florida has recognized this unity in its Constitution. . . . Moreover, Art. V, § 1, of the Florida Constitution (1885), which does not appear to have been changed in the 1968 Constitutional revision, declares:

> "The judicial power of the *State of Florida* is vested in a supreme court . . . and such other courts, *including municipal courts* . . . as the legislature may from time to time ordain and establish." (Emphasis added.)

These provisions of the Florida Constitution demonstrate that the judicial power to try petitioner on the first charges in municipal court springs from the same organic law that created the state court of general jurisdiction in which petitioner was tried and convicted for a felony. Accordingly, the apt analogy to the relationship between municipal and state governments is to be found in the relationship between the government of a Territory and the Government of the United States. The legal consequence of that relationship was settled in *Grafton v. United States,* 206 U.S. 333 (1907), where this Court held that a prosecution in a court of the United States is a bar to a subsequent prosecution in a territorial court, since both are arms of the same sovereign. In *Grafton* a soldier in the United States Army had been acquitted by a general court-martial convened in the Philippine Islands of the alleged crime of feloniously killing two men. Subsequently, a criminal information in the name of the United States was filed in a Philippine court while those islands were a federal territory, charging the soldier with the same offense committed in violation of local law. When Philippine courts upheld a conviction against a double jeopardy challenge, this Court reversed, resting upon the single-sovereign rationale and distinguishing cases like *Fox v. Ohio,* 5 How. 410 (1847), which sanctioned successive prosecutions by State and Federal Governments for the same acts. . . .

Thus *Grafton,* not *Fox v. Ohio,* supra, or its progeny, *Bartkus v. Illinois,* supra, or *Abbate v. United States,* supra, controls, and we hold that on the basis of the facts upon which the Florida District Court of Appeal relied petitioner could not lawfully be tried both by the municipal government and by the State of Florida. In this context a "dual sovereignty" theory is an anachronism, and the second trial constituted double jeopardy violative of the Fifth and Fourteenth Amendments to the United States Constitution.

. . .

The second trial of petitioner which resulted in a judgment of conviction in the state court for a felony having no valid basis, that judgment is vacated and the case remanded. . . .

It is so ordered.

Attachment of Jeopardy:
Crist v. Bretz, 437 U.S. 28 (1978)

Mr. Justice STEWART delivered the opinion of the Court.

This case involves an aspect of the constitutional guarantee against being twice put in jeopardy. The precise issue is whether the federal rule governing the time when jeopardy attaches in a jury trial is binding on Montana through the Fourteenth Amendment. The federal rule is that jeopardy attaches when the jury is empaneled and sworn; a Montana statute provides that jeopardy does not attach until the first witness is sworn.

I

The appellees, Merrel Cline and L. R. Bretz, were brought to trial in a Montana court on charges of grand larceny, obtaining money and property by false pretenses, and several counts of preparing or offering false evidence. A jury was empaneled and sworn following a three-day selection process. Before the first witness was sworn, however, the appellees filed a motion drawing attention to the allegation in the false pretenses charge that the defendants' illegal conduct began on January 13, 1974. Effective January 1, 1974, the particular statute relied on in that count of the information, Mont. Rev. Codes Ann. § 94–1805 (1947), had been repealed. The prosecutor moved to amend the information, claiming that "1974" was a typographical error, and that the date on which the defendants' alleged violation of the statute had commenced was actually January 13, 1973, the same date alleged in the grand larceny count. The trial judge denied the prosecutor's motion to amend the information and dismissed the false pretenses count. The State promptly but unsuccessfully asked the Montana Supreme Court for a writ of supervisory control ordering the trial judge to allow the amendment.

Returning to the trial court, the prosecution then asked the trial judge to dismiss the entire information so that a new one could be filed. That motion was granted, and the jury was dismissed. A new information was then filed, charging the appellees with grand larceny and obtaining money and property by false pretenses. Both charges were based on conduct commencing January 13, 1973. Other than the change in dates, the new false pretenses charge described essentially the same offense charged in the earlier defective count.

After a second jury had been selected and sworn, the appellees moved to dismiss the new information, claiming that the Double Jeopardy Clauses of the United States and Montana Constitutions barred a second prosecution. The motion was denied, and the trial began. The appellees were found guilty on the false pretenses count, and sentenced to terms of imprisonment. The Montana Supreme Court affirmed the judgment as to Bretz and also denied habeas corpus relief on the ground that under state law jeopardy had not attached in the first trial.

The appellees then brought a habeas corpus proceeding in a federal district court, again alleging that their convictions had been unconstitutionally obtained because the second trial violated the Fifth and Fourteenth Amendment guarantee against double jeopardy. The federal court denied the petition, holding that the Montana statute providing that jeopardy does not attach until the first witness is sworn does not violate the United States Constitution. The court held in the alternative that even if jeopardy had attached, a second prosecution was justified, as manifest necessity supported the first dismissal.

The Court of Appeals for the Ninth Circuit reversed. . . .

The State appealed pursuant to 28 U.S.C. § 1254(2), seeking review only of the holding of the Court of Appeals that Montana is constitutionally required to recognize that, for purposes of the constitutional guarantee against double jeopardy, jeopardy attaches in a criminal trial when the jury is impaneled and sworn. We noted probable jurisdiction of the appeal and the case was argued orally. Thereafter the case was set for reargument, and the parties were asked to address the following two questions:

"1. Is the rule heretofore applied in the federal courts—that jeopardy attaches in jury trials when the jury is sworn—constitutionally mandated?"
"2. Should this Court hold that the Constitution does not require jeopardy to attach in any trial—state or federal, jury or nonjury—until the first witness is sworn?"

II

A

The unstated premise of the questions posed on reargument is that if the rule "that jeopardy attaches in jury trials when the jury is sworn" is "constitutionally mandated," then that rule is binding on Montana, since "the double jeopardy prohibition of the Fifth Amendment . . . [applies] to the States through the Fourteenth Amendment," and "the same constitutional standards" must apply equally in federal and state courts. *Benton v. Maryland*, 395 U.S. 784, 794–795. The single dispositive question, therefore, is whether the federal rule is an integral part of the constitutional guarantee.

The Double Jeopardy Clause of the Fifth Amendment is stated in brief compass: "Nor shall any person be subject for the same offence to be twice put in jeopardy of life or limb." But this deceptively plain language has given rise to problems both subtle and complex, problems illustrated by no less than eight cases argued here this very Term. This case, however, presents a single straightforward issue concerning the point during a jury trial when a defendant is deemed to have been put in jeopardy, for only if that point has once been reached does any subsequent prosecution of the defendant bring the guarantee against double jeopardy even potentially into play.

The Fifth Amendment guarantee against double jeopardy derived from English common law, which followed then, as it does now, the relatively simple rule that a defendant has been put in jeopardy only when there has been a conviction or an acquittal—after a complete trial. A primary purpose served by such a rule is akin to that served by the doctrines of res judicata and collateral estoppel—to preserve the finality of judgments. And it is clear that in the early years of our national history the constitutional guarantee against double jeopardy was considered to be equally limited in scope. . . .

But this constitutional understanding was not destined to endure. Beginning with this Court's decision in *United States v. Perez*, 9 Wheat. 579, it became firmly established by the end of the 19th Century that a defendant could be put in jeopardy even in a prosecution that did not culminate in a conviction or an acquittal, and this concept has been long established as an integral part of double jeopardy jurisprudence. . . .

Although it has thus long been established that jeopardy may attach in a criminal trial that ends inconclusively, the precise point at which jeopardy does attach in a jury trial might have been open to argument before this Court's decision in *Downum v. United States*, 372 U.S. 734. There the Court held that the Double Jeopardy Clause prevented a second prosecution of a defendant whose first trial had ended just after the jury had been sworn and before any testimony had been taken. The Court thus necessarily pinpointed the stage in a jury trial that jeopardy attaches, and the *Downum* case has since been understood as explicit authority for the proposition that jeopardy attaches when the jury is empaneled and sworn.

The reason for holding that jeopardy attaches when the jury is empaneled and sworn lies in the need to protect the interest of an accused in retaining a chosen jury. That interest was described in *Wade v. Hunter*, supra, as a defendant's "valued right to have his trial completed by a particular tribunal." 336 U.S. at 689. It is an interest with roots deep in the historic development of trial by jury in the Anglo-American system of criminal   justice. Throughout that history there ran a strong tradition that once banded together a jury should not be discharged until it had completed its solemn task of announcing a verdict.

Regardless of its historic origin, however, the defendant's "valued right to have his trial completed by a particular tribunal" is now within the protection of the constitutional guarantee against double jeopardy, since it is that "right" that lies at the foundation of the federal rule that jeopardy attaches when the jury is empaneled and sworn.

B

It follows that Montana's view as to when jeopardy attaches is impermissible under the Fourteenth Amendment unless it can be said that the federal rule is not "at the core" of the Double Jeopardy Clause. In asking us to hold that it is not, Montana argues that the federal standard is no more than an arbitrarily chosen rule of convenience, similar in its lack of constitutional status to the federal requirement of a unanimous verdict by 12 jurors, which has been held not to bind the States.

If the rule that jeopardy attaches when the jury is sworn were simply an arbitrary exercise of line-drawing, this argument might well be persuasive, and it might reasonably be concluded that jeopardy does not constitutionally attach until the first witness is sworn, to provide consistency in jury and nonjury trials. Indeed, it might then be concluded that the point of the attachment of jeopardy could be moved a few steps forward or backward without constitutional significance.

But the federal rule as to when jeopardy attaches in a jury trial is not only a settled part of federal constitutional law. It is a rule that both reflects and protects the defendant's interest in retaining a chosen jury. We cannot hold that this rule, so grounded, is only at the periphery of double jeopardy concerns. Those concerns—the finality of judgments, the minimization of harassing exposure to the harrowing experience of a criminal trial, and the valued right to continue with the chosen jury—have combined to produce the federal law that in a jury trial jeopardy attached when the jury is empaneled and sworn.

We agree with the Court of Appeals that the time when jeopardy attaches in a jury trial "serves as the lynchpin for all double jeopardy jurisprudence." In *Illinois v. Somerville,* 410 U.S. 458, 467, a case involving the application of the Double Jeopardy Clause through the Fourteenth Amendment, the Court said that "jeopardy 'attached' when the first jury was selected and sworn." Today we explicitly hold what *Somerville* assumed: the federal rule that jeopardy attaches when the jury is empaneled and sworn is an integral part of the constitutional guarantee against double jeopardy.

The judgment is affirmed.

Mr. Chief Justice BURGER, dissenting.

As a "rulemaking" matter, the result reached by the Court is a reasonable one; it is the Court's decision to constitutionalize the rule that jeopardy attaches at the point when the jury is sworn—so as to bind the States—that I reject. This is but another example of how constitutional guarantees are trivialized by the insistence on mechanical uniformity between state and federal practice. There is, course, no reason why the state and federal rules must be the same. In the period between the swearing of the jury and the swearing of the first witness, the concerns underlying the constitutional guarantee against double jeopardy are simply not threatened in any meaningful sense even on the least sanguine of assumptions about prosecutorial behavior. We should be cautious about constitutionalizing every procedural device found useful in federal courts, thereby foreclosing the States from experimentation with different approaches which are equally compatible with constitutional principles. All things "good" or "desirable" are not mandated by the Constitution. States should remain free to have procedures attuned to the special problems of the criminal justice system at the state and local levels. Principles of federalism should not so readily be compromised for the sake of a uniformity finding sustenance perhaps in considerations of convenience but certainly not in the Constitution. Countless times in the past 50 years this court has extolled the virtues of allowing the States to serve as "laboratories" to experiment with procedures which differ from those followed in the federal courts. Yet we continue to press the States into a procrustean federal mold. The Court's holding will produce no great mischief, but it continues, I repeat, the business of trivializing the Constitution on matters better left to the States.

Accordingly, I join Mr. Justice Powell's dissent.

⟡ 9 ⟡

Counsel
for
the
Defense

HISTORICAL BACKGROUND

On the morning of August 18, 1681, Lord Chief Justice North pronounced the following sentence on Stephen Colledge:

> There is nothing now remaining, but to pronounce the sentence, which the law provides for such an offence, which is this, and the court does award, "That you Stephen Colledge shall be carried from hence to the place from whence you came, and from thence you shall be drawn on an hurdle to the place of execution, where you shall be hanged up by the neck, and be cut down alive, your privy members shall be cut off, and your bowels taken out and burnt before your face, your head shall be cut off from your body, your body be divided into four quarters, which are to be at the king's dispose, and the Lord have mercy upon your soul."[1]

On the previous day, Colledge had been tried and convicted of high treason. Within two weeks, he was executed before the castle gate in Oxford. At the gallows, Colledge gave the traditional pardon to his executioner and ended his life with these simple words: "Let my blood speak to the justness of my cause I have done. May God have mercy upon you all."[2]

Three hundred years after his death, Colledge is all but forgotten. In truth, there is little to remember about the life of this man except the force of his courage during the month of August 1681, when he stood trial before a hostile court and without benefit of counsel. Colledge, by trade a joiner (carpenter) and by passion a religious dissenter, was known as the Protestant Joiner. He was described by contemporaries as an active and hot man with a great temper.[3] At his trial, the Crown attempted to prove, among other things, that Colledge was in Oxford during the mutiny of the Oxford Parliament, and that he went about the coffee houses and inns of the town singing ballads that defamed Charles II, accusing the king of arbitrary government and popery. Given the volatile circumstances of the time, particularly in regard to the question of religion and royal succession, it appears that Colledge was indeed a most injudicious man. Presumably, the Crown wanted to make an example of him—an object lesson of what happens to those in the lower orders who meddle in politics.

After his arrest, Colledge was able to obtain some written legal advice. These documents were seized, and when he requested their return, the court denied the request as well as his request for counsel. Both denials were in keeping with the criminal procedure at that time in England. In felony cases, counsel was only allowed a defendant on debatable questions of law, and only at the discretion of the trial court. At the outset of Colledge's trial, the following exchange took place:

> CLERK OF THE COURT: How sayest thou, Stephen Colledge, art thou Guilty of this high treason, whereof thou standest indicted, and hast now been arraigned, or Not Guilty?

> COLLEDGE: My lord, I do desire, if it please your lordship, to be heard a few words. . . . My lord, I am wholly ignorant of the law, I may ruin myself by mistaking the law; I desire counsel, not to delay my trial, but only to advise me, whether there is not something in law proper for me to plead to this Indictment, and those things I alledged were not at all to delay the trial, but only that I may not be wanting to myself in what I may by law have. . . . I only plead, that I may have my birthright; and that which the law gives me; if I may have justice, I desire no more.

> LORD CHIEF JUSTICE: That which you demand, justice, you shall have by the grace of God to the best of our skill, without any partiality in the world. But you must trust the public justice of the kingdom. We are to be of counsel for you, so far as to see that all things proceed fairly on all sides. And when things come before us that are fit for you to have counsel upon, you shall have counsel assigned you; for we are tender of the life of a man, as well as the life of the king, and of the public justice of the kingdom.[4]

At the time of Colledge's trial, English law narrowly restricted the benefit of counsel in criminal trials: Misdemeanants were allowed counsel at trial; felons were not.[5] The justification for the lack of counsel was the belief that to admit the need for defense counsel would be tantamount to admitting that the Crown might be biased—an admission that would affront the dignity if not the sovereignty of the monarch. Instead, as in *Colledge*, the judges acted as counsel for accused felons, and only on occasion would appoint defense counsel if a disputed point of law arose. (The role of appointed counsel was limited to arguing the disputed point of law.)

Although Parliament did enact legislation in 1695 allowing those indicted for treason to be represented by counsel,[6] the basic law in felony cases remained unchanged in England until 1836. Indeed, writing during the first quarter of the eighteenth century, William Hawkins noted:

> I take it to be a settled Rule at Common Law, that no Counsel shall be allowed a Prisoner, whether he be a Peer or Commoner, upon the General Issue, on an Indictment of Treason or Felony, unless some Point of Law arise, proper to be debated.
>
> This indeed many have complained of as very unreasonable, yet if it be considered, that generally every one of Common Understanding may as properly speak to a Matter of Fact, as if he were the best Lawyer; and that it requires no manner of Skill to make a plain and honest defence, which in Cases of this Kind is always the best, the Simplicity and Innocence, artless and ingenuous Behaviour of one whose Conscience acquits him, having something in it more moving and convincing than the highest Eloquence of Persons speaking in a Cause not their own. And if it be farther considered that it is the Duty of the Court to be indifferent between the King and Prisoner, and to see that the Indictment be good in Law, and the Proceedings regular, and the Evidence legal, and such as fully proves the Point in Issue, there seems no great Reason to fear but that, generally speaking, the Innocent, for whose Safety alone the Law is concerned, have rather an Advantage than Prejudice in having the Court their only Counsel.[7]

Beginning around 1750, however, English judicial practice gradually allowed defense counsel to perform an increasing number of trial functions, including the examination of witnesses.[8] Finally, in 1836, Parliament enacted legislation allowing full trial representation by counsel for all criminal defendants.[9]

THE COLONIAL AMERICAN BACKGROUND

In England, at least until the nineteenth century, the right to counsel in criminal cases was a matter of common law, and thus was largely shaped by the judiciary. In contrast, many Colonial legislatures showed an early interest in the issue. Although there was diversity in declared Colonial policy, the fact

that at least five of the colonies had either statutory or charter provisions according defendants limited rights to counsel is evidence that there was an
awareness of the marked disadvantage of the unrepresented defendant.[10] Of
course, given the shortage of trained lawyers in Colonial America, the declared
policy could not be immediately realized. In any event, during the revolutionary period a majority of the new states incorporated some form of right
to counsel in their new constitutions. When the issue of ratification of the federal Constitution arose in 1787–1788, at least three states suggested that the
document include a provision protecting the right to counsel. These suggestions were adopted by James Madison in 1789, when he drafted the package
of individual rights. The Sixth Amendment of the Bill of Rights provides: "In
all criminal prosecutions, the accused shall enjoy the right . . . to have the
Assistance of Counsel for his defence."

Of course this right originally applied only to criminal defendants in federal cases, and even in this limited context the intent was not entirely clear.
The Judiciary Act of 1789 and legislation passed in 1790 cast some additional
light on the scope of the right. The Judiciary Act of 1789 provided: "In all
courts of the United States, the parties may plead and manage their own
causes personally or by the assistance of . . . counsel or attorneys at law."[11]
The legislation of 1790 went a step further, providing that persons accused of
treason and other capital offenses had a right not only to be defended by
counsel, but, on request of the defendant, to be assigned counsel and to be
allowed reasonable access to that counsel.[12]

Thus the First Congress, the Congress that proposed the Sixth Amendment,
fully endorsed the right of a defendant to retain privately employed counsel,
and, in a limited way, endorsed court-appointed counsel. The issue of the
broad right of the indigent to counsel in criminal cases had to wait subsequent
court decisions.

INDIGENCY

Because most criminal defendants are poor, the right to retain privately employed counsel would be, without funds, an empty right. It should come as no
particular surprise that the issue of poverty and due process is relatively
modern. Indeed, the surprise is that as early as 1790 Congress even obliquely
concerned itself with the defense of the poor in federal criminal cases.[13] It
was not until 1932, in *Powell v. Alabama,* that the Supreme Court addressed
itself to the issue.[14]

The case developed out of the famous Scottsboro trial of 1931. In late
March 1931, a number of black teenage boys were riding in an open freight
car through Alabama. With them were a number of white teenagers, including
two girls. A fight broke out, and all but one of the white boys were thrown off
the train. When word of the incident reached the sheriff of Jackson County,

he went with a posse to meet the train at some point before Scottsboro. The defendants were arrested and taken to Scottsboro, where they were apparently met by a large and hostile crowd of whites. They were then taken, in company with soldiers, to a nearby town for safekeeping. They were charged with the rape of the two white girls and were arraigned on March 31, 1931. When the defendants appeared at the arraignment without counsel, the presiding judge casually appointed all of the members of the local bar to represent the defendants. When the first of the seven defendants' cases was called for trial, on April 6, the same judge again indicated that all of the members of the local bar would help the defendants; he appointed no counsel of record. An out-of-state lawyer did appear and volunteer to help any court-appointed local attorney, and a local attorney, not previously nor subsequently appointed as defense counsel, did agree to help the unappointed, out-of-state attorney. The trial judge simply left the counsel issue in this muddled state, and the trials proceeded. Each lasted one day, and all of the defendants were convicted and sentenced to death. As the majority of the Supreme Court was later to say, the trial judge's action in respect to the appointment of counsel was "little more than an expansive gesture, imposing no substantial or definite obligation upon any one."[15] In what was considered to be a landmark case, the Court reversed the convictions. The majority opinion in *Powell*, however, did not make the basis for reversing entirely clear. The opinion stressed both the ineffective nature of the counsel and the insufficient opportunity to obtain counsel, as well as the factors of indigency, illiteracy, and ignorance within the context of a capital case. The most pertinent passages of the decision are as follows:

> We are of opinion that, under the circumstances just stated, the necessity of counsel was so vital and imperative that the failure of the trial court to make an effective appointment of counsel was likewise a denial of due process within the meaning of the Fourteenth Amendment. Whether this would be so in other criminal prosecutions, or under other circumstances, we need not determine. All that it is necessary now to decide, as we do decide, is that in a capital case, where the defendant is unable to employ counsel, and is incapable adequately of making his own defense because of ignorance, feeblemindedness, illiteracy, or the like, it is the duty of the court, whether requested or not, to assign counsel for him as a necessary requisite of due process of law; and that duty is not discharged by an assignment at such a time or under such circumstances as to preclude the giving of effective aid in the preparation and trial of the case. . . . In a case such as this, whatever may be the rule in other cases, the right to have counsel appointed, when necessary, is a logical corollary from the constitutional right to be heard by counsel.[16]

Although *Powell* did not establish a per se rule, it was a clear warning to the states that in capital cases most indigent defendants were entitled to appointed counsel. Six years after *Powell*, the Supreme Court again had an opportunity to rule on the issue of indigency and counsel, this time in the context of a noncapital federal case. In *Johnson v. Zerbst,* the petitioner had been convicted in a federal court on charges of counterfeiting and was sentenced to four and a half years in the penitentiary. Although Johnson was indigent he did, after arrest, ask the jailer to call a lawyer for him; the request was denied. Subsequently Johnson was tried even though the trial judge was aware that Johnson had no counsel nor the funds to obtain counsel.[17] In reversing the denial of habeas corpus, the majority opinion noted that the Sixth Amendment

> embodies a realistic recognition of the obvious truth that the average defendant does not have the professional legal skill to protect himself when brought before a tribunal with power to take his life or liberty, wherein the prosecution is presented by experienced and learned Counsel. That which is simple, orderly and necessary to the lawyer—to the untrained layman—may appear intricate, complex and mysterious. Consistently with the wise policy of the Sixth Amendment and other parts of our fundamental charter, this Court has pointed to ". . . the humane policy of the modern criminal law . . ." which now provides that a defendant ". . . if he be poor . . . may have counsel furnished him by the state . . . not infrequently . . . more able than the attorney for the state."[18]

The *Johnson* decision was clear and to the point: A federal court is without jurisdiction to proceed in a felony case unless the defendant has a lawyer or has intelligently and competently waived the right to counsel. In other words, a federal court's jurisdiction "at the beginning of a trial may be lost in the course of the proceedings due to failure to complete the court—as the Sixth Amendment requires—by providing counsel for an accused who is unable to obtain counsel, who has not intelligently waived this constitutional guaranty, and whose life or liberty is at stake."[19]

Johnson did establish a per se rule in federal criminal cases, but the Supreme Court continued a somewhat meandering path in the areas of indigency and state criminal defendants. In 1940, just two years after *Johnson,* the Court handed down its unanimous opinion in *Avery v. Alabama.*[20] Avery was charged with the murder of his estranged wife. Unlike Osie Powell, Lonnie Avery had specific counsel appointed by the trial court at the time of his arraignment, but the trial in this capital case was scheduled only three days after the arraignment and both appointed lawyers were engaged in other business until the day before the trial. At the trial, counsel requested a continuance in order to prepare an adequate defense; the continuance was denied. Justice Black, speaking for the Court, affirmed the denial, concluding in a brief opinion that the trial had been fairly conducted and that a continuance would not have produced additional defenses that were not explored and exhausted by counsel prior to trial.

In 1941, the Court again handed down a state counsel case, and again

Justice Black wrote the unanimous opinion. In *Smith v. O'Grady*,[21] petitioner Albert Smith was arrested by Nebraska authorities presumably on a charge of simple burglary. Petitioner, shortly after arrest, agreed to plead guilty in exchange for a three-year sentence. Without receiving, as he requested, a copy of the charge, he was, without counsel, summarily arraigned. He pleaded guilty. To his amazement and consternation, he was sentenced to twenty years' imprisonment. He again requested a copy of the charge and permission to withdraw his plea. Both requests were immediately denied, and within the hour he was on his way to the state penitentiary. He later discovered that he had been duped into pleading guilty to burglary with explosives, an offense that carried a minimum twenty-year sentence. In reversing his conviction, the Court observed:

> The circumstances under which petitioner asserts he was entrapped and imprisoned in the penitentiary are wholly irreconcilable with the constitutional safeguards of due process. For his petition presents a picture of a defendant, without counsel, bewildered by court processes strange and unfamiliar to him, and inveigled by false statements of state law enforcement officers into entering a plea of guilty.[22]

Because *Smith* involved several constitutional issues, the import of the decision in the area of counsel was far from clear. Shortly after *Smith*, the Supreme Court handed down still another state right-to-counsel case. This time the majority appeared to be in full retreat from *Powell*. In *Betts v. Brady* (1942), the petitioner had been arraigned on a charge of robbery in a Maryland court. When he informed the court that he was without funds and requested the appointment of counsel, his request was denied. In upholding the denial, the majority noted:

> To deduce from the due process clause a rule binding upon the states in this matter would be to impose upon them . . . a requirement without distinction between criminal charges of different magnitude or in respect of courts of varying jurisdiction. . . .
> As we have said, the Fourteenth Amendment prohibits the conviction and incarceration of one whose trial is offensive to the common and fundamental ideas of fairness and right, and while want of counsel in a particular case may result in a conviction lacking in such fundamental fairness, we cannot say that the amendment embodies an inexorable command that no trial for any offense, or in any court can be fairly conducted and justice accorded a defendant who is not represented by counsel.[23]

Not only did *Betts* have the appearance of a retreat, it was also out of line with the law in a majority of the states. In 1942, twenty-six states provided by statute for counsel for indigents in capital and noncapital cases. Another thirteen states offered similar assistance either by constitutional provisions or through judicial decisions.[24] Justice Black, writing in dissent for himself and Justices Douglas and Murphy, pointed out that defense of the poor had long been considered a judicial duty in civilized societies, and that "a practice cannot be reconciled with 'common and fundamental ideas of fairness and right,' which subjects innocent men to increased dangers of conviction merely because of their poverty."[25]

Betts was not to stand as the final word on the issue. By 1945 the Court began to reverse denials of writs of habeas corpus sought by state prisoners in cases where indigents claimed a denial of counsel.[26] These reversals did not always command the unanimous support of the justices. Indeed, as recently as 1957, four justices dissented when the majority granted a defense motion for a new trial where the defendant had pleaded guilty to a first-degree murder charge without benefit of counsel.[27] Still, the basic thrust of the Court's decisions was directed toward increasing the right. By 1961 it was clear that the entire membership of the Court had concluded that a right to counsel did exist in all state cases involving capital offenses;[28] all that remained was to drop the distinction between capital and noncapital cases. In fact, Nathan Lewin, former law clerk to Justice Harlan, indicated that even before 1961 the Court was determined to find just the right case in which to overturn *Betts*.[29]

The "right" case was filed in a Florida pauper's petition in 1962. Clarence Gideon, a Florida prisoner, had been charged with breaking and entering a poolroom with intent to commit a misdemeanor, a felony charge under Florida law. At trial he requested and was denied counsel, the trial judge noting that counsel could be appointed only in a capital-offense case. After conviction, he petitioned the Supreme Court for a hearing, and he had the good luck to have his petition accepted as the vehicle for overturning *Betts*,[30] and the added good fortune to be asigned a future Supreme Court justice, Abe Fortas, as his advocate before the Court.

Justice Black, writing for a unanimous Court, quickly buried *Betts* in a short opinion that not only overruled *Betts* but held that the right to counsel was now made applicable to the states under the due process clause of the Fourteenth Amendment. In regard to the matter of indigency, he observed:

> Reason and reflection require us to recognize that in our adversary system of criminal justice, any person haled into court, who is too poor to hire a lawyer, cannot be assured a fair trial unless counsel is provided for him. This seems to us to be an obvious truth. Governments, both state and federal, quite properly spend vast sums of money to establish machinery to try defendants accused of crime. Lawyers to prosecute are everywhere deemed essential to protect the public's interest in an orderly society. Similarly, there are few defendants charged with crime, few indeed, who fail to hire the best lawyers they can get to prepare and present their defenses. That government hires lawyers to prosecute and defendants who have the money hire lawyers to defend are the

strongest indications of the widespread belief that lawyers in criminal courts are necessities, not luxuries.[3]

Although Justice Harlan's concurring opinion called for a more respectful burial of *Betts,* the fact was that time had not treated *Betts* kindly. Indeed, twenty-two states filed amicus curiae briefs in support of Gideon, with only the states of Florida and Alabama filing opposing briefs. At the time that *Gideon* was decided, the holding was already the declared law in forty-five states.[32]

Gideon did determine that indigent defendants in felony cases are entitled to free legal counsel, but the case did not address the issue of how indigency should be determined. Some post-*Gideon* studies have suggested that the judicial determination of indigency is at best arbitrary and capricious.[33] Although commonly a judge determines the eligibility for free counsel, apparently many jurisdictions have no guidelines or systematic method for making such determinations. If tests are employed, they vary widely and often include features of dubious constitutionality. For example, one study reported that the release of a defendant on bail was commonly used as a factor precluding counsel, the assumption being that if a defendant could afford bail, then he or she could afford to pay for counsel.[34] On the other hand, the absence of guidelines could result in free counsel for some defendants who can afford to pay all or part of the costs of their defense. (Although, given the general poverty of most criminal defendants, leniency would probably not be a problem of major proportion.) At the national level, the Criminal Justice Act of 1964 simply provides that a federal criminal defendant is entitled to an adequate defense, and that the judge or U.S. magistrate shall determine whether the defendant is financially unable to obtain counsel.[35]

Assuming that adequate and competent legal representation is required in criminal cases by due process, the mere fact that a defendant requests appointment of counsel should create a presumption that the defendant is indigent unless, after careful consideration, the presumption is overcome. The determination should measure the total cost of a defense, including the use of investigatory services and expert witnesses where appropriate, as against the total financial assets of the defendant, discounted by immediate financial obligations to a family.

Recoupment

Since the *Gideon* decision, a number of states[36] and the federal government have passed legislation that entitles the government to recoup all or part of the public expense in defending an indigent. Although there is considerable variation in recoupment legislation, most statutes provide for repayment only if, at the time of sentencing, it appears likely that a defendant will at some future date be able to repay, in whole or part, the costs incurred in his or her defense. Initially the Supreme Court rejected recoupment statutes, claiming they violated the equal-protection clause.[37] However, in 1974 a divided Court upheld an Oregon recoupment statute against claims of equal protection and the right to counsel.[38] Although we might agree with the majority in the Oregon case—that a carefully drafted recoupment statute need not fall prey to constitutional limitations, particularly where recoupment is sought only from convicted defendants[39]—still we might question the social utility of any expenditure of bureaucratic resources aimed at recoupment.

Delivery Systems

Because the national rate of indigency among defendants charged with felony offenses is estimated to be 65 percent,[40] the methods of delivering legal counsel to indigent criminal defendants are important. At the time of *Gideon*, most of the jurisdictions that offered free counsel used a variety of assigned-counsel systems. Under these systems, judges appoint attorneys from private practice to represent defendants on a case-by-case basis. After *Gideon*, public-defender systems became the major method of delivery, particularly in metropolitan areas. (Assigned counsel predominate in rural areas.) By 1975, it was estimated that over 5,000 full- and part-time attorneys were employed by defender agencies.[41] Given the case load recommendations of the National Advisory Commission, however, a considerable staff expansion in defender offices would appear to be necessary.[42] Indeed, a 1973 study indicated that an additional 14,400 full-time defenders would be needed.[43]

THE SCOPE OF THE RIGHT

Although *Gideon* nationalized the right to counsel in criminal cases, it did not address the issue of whether the indigent defendant is entitled to counsel in each and every criminal prosecution, regardless of the seriousness of the offense. The Sixth Amendment provides that "in all criminal prosecutions, the accused shall . . . have the Assistance of Counsel for his defence." A literal interpretation of the amendment would require that all indigent defendants in *any* criminal prosecution, whether a misdemeanor or a felony, be accorded counsel. Certainly *Gideon* extends the requirements to felony cases, but does the ruling apply to misdemeanors as well? Annually, there are several million traffic offenses and infractions of municipal ordinances that carry the misdemeanor label and that do not provide for a prison sentence. Should a per se rule be adopted for misdemeanor offenses with inconsequential results?

Some years after *Gideon*, the Supreme Court confronted this problem in *Argersinger v. Hamlin*.[44] Argersinger, an indigent, was charged with carrying a concealed weapon, an offense punishable by imprisonment up to six months and/or a $1,000 fine. Argersinger, unrepresented by counsel, pleaded guilty and was sentenced to ninety days in jail or a $500 fine. The Court, rejecting the petty-offense distinction applied in trial-by-jury cases,[45] concluded that the requirement of counsel may be necessary for a fair trial even in a petty-offense prosecution. Justice Douglas, writing for the Court, noted: "We are by no means convinced that legal and constitutional questions involved in a case that actually leads to imprisonment even for a brief period are any less complex than when a person can be sent off for six months or more."[46] The Court rejected the legislative label "misdemeanor," but it did not make clear what it was substituting in lieu of traditional labels. The somewhat narrow ruling of the case is "that absent a knowing and intelligent waiver, no person may be imprisoned for any offense, whether classified as petty, misdemeanor, or felony, unless he was represented by counsel at his trial."[47]

The *Argersinger* opinion did not rule that all indigent criminal defendants have a right to counsel; the touchstone of *Argersinger* is imprisonment, although it is unclear whether actual imprisonment includes suspended jail sentences and probation. In practice what the rule requires is that a judge anticipate, before a trial, whether there is a strong probability that on conviction a defendant will receive a jail sentence. As Justice Douglas noted in his opinion for the Court:

> Under the rule we announce today, every judge will know when the trial of a misdemeanor starts that no imprisonment may be imposed, even though local law permits it, unless the accused is represented by counsel. He will have a measure of the seriousness and gravity of the offense and therefore know when to name a lawyer to represent the accused before the trial starts.
>
> The run of misdemeanors will not be affected by today's ruling. But in those that end up in the actual deprivation of a person's liberty, the accused will receive the benefit of "the guiding hand of counsel" so necessary when one's liberty is in jeopardy.[48]

One objection to this pretrial prediction is that it could undermine the ability of a trial judge to render an impartial verdict based on the evidence presented. Indeed, in the case of a bench trial, it is questionable whether a judge may properly be given the kind of pretrial information necessary to make the requisite prediction. Furthermore, given the volume of misdemeanor cases, it does not seem likely that judges and prosecutors would have the time to make the individualized predictions anticipated by *Argersinger*. It seems far more likely that a judge must adopt a routine procedure for disposing of counsel for indigents in misdemeanor cases, and indeed that appears to be what has happened. One national study of defender systems reported that 36 percent of the reporting defenders indicated that all indigent misdemeanor defendants were provided with counsel; another 39 percent that counsel was provided only when the offense was punishable by a jail sentence; and only

24 percent reported that some kind of pretrial, judge-prosecutor prediction regarding the probability of a jail sentence was determinative. The same post-*Argersinger* study reported that in those areas that used an assigned-counsel system, 55 percent of the respondents reported that counsel was routinely assigned either for all indigent misdemeanor defendants or at least in any case in which an offense was punishable by a jail sentence. On the other hand, 33 percent reported that counsel was assigned only on a prediction that a guilty defendant would receive a jail sentence.[49]

Defining the Baseline

Assuming that a defendant is entitled to counsel, at what time does the right attach? There is no disagreement that the right to counsel covers the actual trial, but there is some confusion concerning pretrial representation. It is generally recognized that a trial right to counsel can be rendered meaningless by failure to provide or allow a defendant adequate pretrial representation. In *Powell v. Alabama,* the Court observed "that during the most critical period of the proceedings against these defendants, that is to say, from the time of their arraignment until the beginning of their trial, when consultation, thorough-going investigation and preparation were vitally important, the defendants did not have the aid of counsel, in any real sense, although they were as much entitled to such aid during that period as at the trial itself."[50] Almost thirty years later, the Court reaffirmed in *Hamilton v. Alabama* (1961) that in a jurisdiction where arraignment is a critical stage—critical to the preservation of trial rights—a defendant is entitled to be represented by counsel at the arraignment. Similarly, in *White v. Maryland* (1963) the Court has held that a defendant is entitled to counsel in jurisdictions where the preliminary hearing is a critical stage.[51] In *Coleman v. Alabama* (1970), the Court reaffirmed *White,* holding that under Alabama law the preliminary hearing was a critical stage that required the guiding hand of counsel. In language that would apply to preliminary hearings in many jurisdictions in the United States, the Court reasoned:

> Plainly the guiding hand of counsel at the preliminary hearing is essential to protect the indigent accused against an erroneous or improper prosecution. First, the lawyer's skilled examination and cross-examination of witnesses may expose fatal weaknesses in the State's case that may lead the magistrate to refuse to bind the accused over. Second, in any event, the skilled interrogation of witnesses by an experienced lawyer can fashion a vital impeachment tool for use in cross-examination of the State's witnesses at the trial, or preserve testimony favorable to the accused of a witness who does not appear at the trial. Third, trained counsel can more effectively discover the case the State has against his client and make possible the preparation of a proper defense to meet that case at the trial. Fourth, counsel can also be influential at the

preliminary hearing in making effective arguments for the accused on such matters as the necessity for an early psychiatric examination or bail.[52]

Additionally, the Court ruled in *Coleman* that if a defendant is unrepresented at a critical stage, assuming no waiver, the defendant need not demonstrate that the lack of counsel resulted in actual prejudice to the preservation of trial rights.[53] In short, a defendant is entitled to counsel as early as the time of arraignment or preliminary hearing if either stage is critical to preserving a trial right.[54]

In *Powell, Hamilton, White,* and *Coleman,* the key to the time element was the beginning of formal adversary proceedings. Yet anyone familiar with the criminal justice system would be quick to point out that the stage of formal accusation may, in some situations, come too late for the effective appointment of counsel. In 1964, in *Escobedo v. Illinois,* a five-justice majority ruled that incriminating statements made by a defendant during a preindictment police interrogation were inadmissible at trial where the defendant had been denied counsel at the interrogation.[55] Noting that the interrogation was as critical as an arraignment or preliminary hearing and that police interrogation could affect the whole trial, the majority concluded that the right to counsel would be a hollow thing if, for all practical purposes, a conviction is assumed by pretrial interrogation.[56]

In *Escobedo,* the majority argued that a defendant's right to silence at any pretrial stage could be rendered meaningless if a defendant did not have the guiding hand of counsel. Yet the right to counsel, rather than the protection against self-incrimination, was central to the thrust of the Court's argument.[57] Two years later, however, in *Miranda v. Arizona,* the Sixth Amendment argument gave way to the centrality of the Fifth Amendment right against compulsory self-incrimination. Still, the majority opinion in *Miranda* did include the notice of right to counsel as a part of the specific warnings that must be given to one held in custody by the police. Chief Justice Warren, writing for the majority, justified the requirement as a means of protecting an individual's right against self-incrimination, but added:

> The presence of counsel at the interrogation may serve several significant subsidiary functions as well. If the accused decides to talk to his interrogators, the assistance of counsel can mitigate the dangers of untrustworthiness. With a lawyer present the likelihood that the police will practice coercion is reduced, and if coercion is nevertheless exercised the lawyer can testify to it in court. The presence of a lawyer can also help to guarantee that the accused gives a fully accurate statement to the police and that the statement is rightly reported by the prosecution at trial.[58]

Not only does *Miranda* require that an individual be given notice of the right to an attorney and the right to have the attorney present during interrogation, but the notice must also clearly indicate that an indigent may have an attorney appointed prior to interrogation. The Chief Justice went on to provide certain guidelines:

> An individual need not make a pre-interrogation request for a lawyer. While such request affirmatively secures his right to have one, his failure to ask for a lawyer does not constitute a waiver. No effective waiver of the right to counsel during interrogation can be recognized unless specifically made after the warnings we here delineate have been given. The accused who does not know his rights and therefore does not make a request may be the person who most needs counsel.
>
> If an individual indicates that he wishes the assistance of counsel before any interrogation occurs, the authorities cannot rationally ignore or deny his request on the basis that the individual does not have or cannot afford a retained attorney. . . .
>
> This does not mean, as some have suggested, that each police station must have a "station house lawyer" present at all times to advise prisoners. It does mean, however, that if police propose to interrogate a person they must make known to him that he is entitled to a lawyer and that if he cannot afford one, a lawyer will be provided for him prior to any interrogation. . . .
>
> If the interrogation continues without the presence of an attorney and a statement is taken, a heavy burden rests on the government to demonstrate that the defendant knowingly and intelligently waived his privilege against self-incrimination and his right to retained or appointed counsel. . . .
>
> An express statement that the individual is willing to make a statement and does not want an attorney followed closely by a statement could constitute a waiver. But a valid waiver will not be presumed simply from the silence of the accused after warnings are given or simply from the fact that a confession was in fact eventually obtained.[59]

Although the *Miranda* opinion attempted to spell out in some detail the right of a suspect to an attorney during interrogation, still no opinion could anticipate the myriad conditions and responses possible in a police-suspect confrontation. It does not seem improbable that some individuals who are entitled to the presence of an attorney and who have received the required notices and warnings will in fact waive the right. The post-interrogation issue then becomes, not whether the waiver was wise, but whether the waiver was intelligently and knowingly made. Furthermore, if a suspect-defendant wants an attorney present during interrogation, that will have to be made clear in unequivocal terms and with some persistence.[60] Indeed, a number of federal courts have indicated that even though an attorney has been appointed or retained, interrogation in the absence of the attorney does not necessarily violate *Miranda* standards.[61] However, the Supreme Court has indicated that once adversary proceedings have commenced, an individual has a right to legal representation when interrogation occurs. In *Brewer v. Williams* (1977), Williams was arrested and arraigned on a murder charge in Davenport, Iowa,[62] and then was transported to Des Moines for trial. Both his Davenport and

Des Moines attorneys had an agreement with the police that he was not to be questioned during the trip. Contrary to this agreement, Williams was induced during the trip to give the police incriminating information. In upholding Williams's petition for a writ of habeas corpus, the five-justice majority relied on the right to counsel rather than on the *Miranda* rule. Furthermore, the majority limited its rule to those situations where judicial proceedings against a defendant have commenced. As Justice Stewart, writing for the majority, noted: "Whatever else it may mean, the right to counsel . . . means at least that a person is entitled to the help of a lawyer at or after the time that judicial proceedings have been initiated against him."[63]

Given the necessarily limited obligations of the police-prosecutor under *Miranda,* it seems likely that some suspect-defendants will forego, perhaps unwisely, the right to the presence of an attorney during interrogation. Although the state should not be allowed to defeat a suspect's request for an attorney, still *Miranda* does not require that the suspect be told that a waiver of the right to the presence of an attorney could be detrimental to his or her rights. Early impact studies of *Miranda* suggested that few suspect-defendants in fact have counsel present during interrogations.[64] Whether in fact the absence of counsel is the result of large-scale voluntary waivers or simply the product of police disregard of requests for counsel is an open question.

In any event, the Court has ruled that *Miranda* does not require an express waiver of counsel by a defendant. In *North Carolina v. Butler* (1979), the defendant was arrested and given a copy of the FBI's "Advice of Rights" form to read.[65] It was claimed that he both read it and acknowledged that he understood his rights. He refused, however, to sign the waiver form, but said he would talk to the agents. Thereupon, he made incriminating statements that were admitted at his trial over his objection that he had not waived his right to counsel during interrogation. In upholding Butler's conviction, the majority refused to adopt a per se rule requiring express waiver of the right to counsel. Instead, it held that the issue of waiver is to be determined by all the facts and circumstances surrounding a case, including the background and conduct of the accused. The majority failed, however, to make clear what background facts or circumstances supported Butler's waiver. *Butler* is yet another indication that the Burger Court has lost sight of the *Miranda* rationale, which maintains that isolated police interrogations will give rise to needless disputes about what actually occurred at the interrogations.

Pretrial Identifications

In 1967, one year after the *Miranda* decision, the Warren Court took yet another step in expanding the critical-stage baseline in right-to-counsel cases. In *United States v. Wade,* a six-justice majority held that a post-indictment, pretrial lineup at which an accused is exhibited to identifying witnesses is a critical stage of the criminal prosecution. In the absence of intelligent waiver, the presence of counsel is a requisite to the use of the lineup.[66] Because of the vagaries of eyewitness identification, the impediments to objective observations, and the possibility of intentionally or unintentionally suggestive lineups, the Court concluded that the presence of a defense attorney was the most appropriate means of lessening the hazards of the procedure. In the absence of counsel at the lineup,

> the trial which might determine the accused's fate may well not be that in the courtroom but that at the pretrial confrontation, with the State aligned against the accused, the witness the sole jury, and the accused unprotected against the overreaching, intentional or unintentional, and with little or no effective appeal from the judgment there rendered by the witness—"that's the man."[67]

The dissenters in *Wade* not only disputed the majority's implication that improper police suggestion during lineups was widespread, but also questioned whether such a broad prophylactic rule was necessary. Justice White, joined by Justice Harlan and Stewart, argued:

> The Court goes beyond assuming that a great majority of the country's police departments are following improper practices at pretrial identifications. To find the lineup a "critical" stage of the proceeding and to exclude identifications made in the absence of counsel, the Court must also assume that police "suggestion," if it occurs at all, leads to erroneous rather than accurate identifications and that reprehensible police conduct will have an unavoidable and largely undiscoverable impact on the trial. . . . I am unable to share the Court's view of the willingness of the police and the ordinary citizen-witness to dissemble, either with respect to the identification of the defendant or with respect to the circumstances surrounding a pretrial identification.[68]

The language of the majority opinion was broad and suggested that counsel was guaranteed at any stage, formal or informal, where counsel's absence might derogate from a defendant's right to a fair trial.[69] Indeed, throughout the majority opinion, the focus of the discussion was *any* compelled pretrial confrontation between the state and the accused at which the presence of counsel is necessary in order to preserve a defendant's right to a fair trial. Still, the opinion did not make clear the precise chronological baseline, and this lack of clarity was later to be used as the basis for limiting the *Wade* rule to postindictment lineups.

By 1972, the six-justice majority in *Wade* had disappeared. Three of the six justices had resigned (Justices Warren, Fortas, and Clark), and Justice Black was dead. President Nixon's four new appointees joined Justice Stewart, in *Kirby v. Illinois*, to limit *Wade* to postindictment lineups.[70] *Kirby* involved a postarrest, preindictment, station house identification. The facts, as reported by the Court, were as follows:

On February 21, 1968, a man named Willie Shard reported to the Chicago police that the previous day two men had robbed him on a Chicago street of a wallet containing, among other things, traveler's checks and a Social Security card. On February 22, two police officers stopped the petitioner and companion, Ralph Bean, on West Madison Street in Chicago. When asked for identification, the petitioner produced a wallet that contained three traveler's checks and a Social Security card, all bearing the name of Willie Shard. Papers with Shard's name on them were also found in Bean's possession. When asked to explain his possession of Shard's property, the petitioner first said that the traveler's checks were "play money," and then told the officers that he had won them in a crap game. The officers then arrested the petitioner and Bean and took them to a police station.

Only after arriving at the police station, and checking the records there, did the arresting officers learn of the Shard robbery. A police car was then dispatched to Shard's place of employment, where it picked up Shard and brought him to the police station. Immediately upon entering the room in the police station where the petitioner and Bean were seated at a table, Shard positively identified them as the men who had robbed him two days earlier. No lawyer was present in the room, and neither the petitioner nor Bean had asked for legal assistance, or been advised of any right to the presence of counsel. . . . At the trial Shard testified as a witness for the prosecution. In his testimony he described his identification of the two men at the police station on February 22, and identified them again in the courtroom as the two men who had robbed him on February 20. He was cross-examined at length regarding the circumstances of his identification of the two defendants.[71]

A plurality of the justices agreed not to extend the *Wade* per se exclusionary rule to a preindictment show-up, concluding that the right to counsel attaches only with the beginning of formal adversary proceedings. Justice Stewart, writing for the plurality, argued:

The initiation of judicial criminal proceedings is far from a mere formalism. It is the starting point of our whole system of adversary criminal justice. For it is only then that the government has committed itself to prosecute, and only then that the adverse positions of government and defendant have solidified. It is then that a defendant finds himself faced with the prosecutorial forces of organized society, and immersed in the intricacies of substantive and procedural criminal law. It is this point, therefore, that marks the commencement of the "criminal prosecutions" to which alone the explicit guarantees of the Sixth Amendment are applicable.[72]

Recognizing, however, that an identification procedure may be abused, Justice Stewart noted that due process forbids any lineup that is unnecessarily suggestive and conducive to irreparable mistaken identification.[73]

We cannot help but be struck by the narrow and somewhat arbitrary baseline arrived at in *Kirby*. Pretrial identifications can pose grave dangers to a suspect; in the absence of counsel they can place a defendant at a distinct disadvantage in reconstructing at trial the identification procedure, limiting the defense's ability to meaningfully cross-examine witnesses for the prosecution. If this is true, then it is difficult to comprehend why the same reasoning would not hold true even before the legal formalism of indictment. Indeed, this was the conclusion of the vast majority of state and lower federal courts that considered the issue of preindictment identifications after the *Wade* decision.[74]

In 1973, the Court again dealt with the issue of pretrial identification. *United States v. Ash* involved a postindictment, pretrial photographic display.[75] Witnesses to a bank robbery were shown five color photographs; three of the four witnesses selected the photograph of defendant Ash. Ash later objected to the procedure, claiming that because the display took place after the indictment, at a critical stage, his attorney should have been present. The Court, in a 6-to-3 decision, rejected this claim, holding that the Sixth Amendment did not grant the accused the right to counsel at a photographic display by the government for the purpose of identifying an offender. Of course, because the display took place after the indictment, there would have been some logic in extending *Wade* to the *Ash* setting, but the *Ash* majority was concerned that doing so would open the door to extending the right to counsel to a host of pretrial, prosecutorial interview situations. Justice Blackmun, writing for the majority, reasoned:

> Even if we were willing to view the counsel guarantee in broad terms as a generalized protection of the adversary process, we would be unwilling to go so far as to extend the right to a portion of the prosecutor's trial-preparation interviews with witnesses. Although photography is relatively new, the interviewing of witnesses before trial is a procedure that predates the Sixth Amendment. In England in the 16th and 17th centuries counsel regularly interviewed witnesses before trial. . . . The traditional counterbalance in the American adversary system for these interviews arises from the equal ability of defense counsel to seek and interview witnesses himself.
>
> That adversary mechanism remains as effective for a photographic display as for other parts of pretrial interviews. No greater limitations are placed on defense counsel in constructing displays, seeking witnesses, and conducting photographic identifications than those applicable to the prosecution. Selection of the picture of a person other than the accused, or the inability of a witness to make any selection, will be useful to the defense in precisely the same manner that the selection of a picture of the defendant would be useful to the prosecution.[76]

The decisions in *Kirby* and *Ash* appear to be an attempt by the Burger Court to draw a line in right-to-counsel cases involving pretrial procedures, halting the expansion of per se exclusionary rules. Further support for this contention can be seen in *Gerstein v. Pugh* (1975).[77] In *Gerstein*, a unanimous Court struck down a Florida procedure that allowed an individual to be jailed for an extended period solely on the probable-cause determination of the state's attorney. Although that was the only issue that needed to be resolved, a majority of the justices anticipated a further constitutional issue. By way of dictum, they concluded that because a probable-cause determination under Florida law is not an adversary proceeding, it is not a "critical stage" that requires the appointment of counsel.[78]

Unquestionably, lines must be drawn, but to reject the critical stage as a basis for drawing the line, as the Court did in *Kirby*, exalts formalism over the reality of the criminal process. The line drawn in *Ash* may arguably be justified because of the absence of physical confrontation between the accused and the witnesses, yet the argument in *Kirby* is strained. Its real justification may be the one suggested in the last line of Justice Stewart's plurality opinion: "It serves the interest of society in the prompt and purposeful investigation of an unsolved crime."[79]

Waiver

Although neither the requirements of due process nor those of the Sixth Amendment demand that a defendant accept the guiding hand of counsel,[80] the Court has consistently held that a waiver of the right to counsel should not lightly be presumed. Indeed, the Supreme Court has urged trial judges to indulge every reasonable presumption against waiver and to determine whether a waiver of counsel is an intentional, voluntary, and intelligent relinquishment of a known right.[81] The judicial determination must appear on the record and at a minimum must include an explicit offer of counsel;[82] that is, the trial judge must fully inform the defendant of the right to counsel, inquire into the particular facts and circumstances of the case, and advise the defendant of the consequences of a waiver. As Justice Black remarked, to be valid a waiver

> must be made with an apprehension of the nature of the charges, the statutory offenses included within them, the range of allowable punishments thereunder, possible defenses to the charges and circumstances in mitigation thereof, and all other facts essential to a broad understanding of the whole matter. A judge can make certain that an accused's professed waiver of counsel is understandingly and wisely made only from a penetrating and comprehensive examination of all the circumstances under which such a plea is tendered.[83]

A waiver of the right to counsel in any case involving a serious offense, either at trial or at a plea of guilty, is at best hazardous for the defendant, and consequently judges are under a particular obligation to ensure that a waiver is voluntarily and intelligently made. It need not, contrary to Justice Black's suggestion, be a wise decision, but it must be a free choice based on knowledge. It can never be the product of coercion, duress, or fear.[84] If, however, after appropriate notices and warnings by the trial judge, a defendant expressly declines counsel and the record so indicates, then the burden is on the defendant to prove, in any subsequent proceedings for relief, that the choice was involuntary. No such burden exists, however, if the record shows no express declination of counsel.[85]

Given the ignorance of the average person about the complexities of the criminal law and the consequent recognized need for the guidance of counsel, the cautious position of appellate courts in matters of waiver is justified. Most of the waiver cases decided by the Supreme Court were written at a time when the right to counsel was not fully accepted in all state jurisdictions, and waiver cases of the 1940s and 1950s can be viewed as an indirect attack on *Betts v. Brady,* preparatory to its eventual overturning. In a post-*Gideon* era, it does not seem likely that judges or even prosecutors would lightly sanction the absence of counsel at trial or in a plea of guilty. Indeed, the problem today is the voluntary but sometimes unwise decision made by a defendant to waive counsel and to present a *pro se* defense.

The Right to Self-Representation

A long line of cases, beginning at least as early as *Powell,* has stressed that even an educated and intelligent layman is generally without the skill or knowledge to prepare and present an adequate defense to a criminal charge. Yet in the rush to provide counsel, we have forgotten that the original rule and practice in both England and Colonial America was self-representation. As criminal procedure grew more complex and the substantive criminal law more harsh, the movement was in the direction of enlarging the right to self-representation to include the *assistance* of counsel. Although the right to assistance of counsel may have become in practice the right to be represented only through counsel,[86] still a majority of the states and the federal government have retained early statutory or constitutional provisions that allow a defendant the right to self-representation.[87]

It was not until 1975 that the Supreme Court directly confronted the issue of self-representation. In *Faretta v. California,* a six-justice majority concluded that both English and Colonial jurisprudence strongly supported the right of self-representation and that the Sixth Amendment was intended only to supplement this primary right.[88] Faretta had been charged with grand theft and was assigned counsel. He petitioned the trial court that he be permitted to represent himself, observing that the public defender's office had a heavy case load. Although his request was originally granted, sometime prior to trial the judge ruled that Faretta had not made an intelligent and knowing waiver of the right to counsel and that he had no constitutional right to self-representation. Subsequently, a public defender was appointed to represent him.

In upholding Faretta's claim, the majority reasoned:

The language and spirit of the Sixth Amendment contemplate that counsel, like the other defense tools guaranteed by the Amendment, shall be an aid to a willing defendant—not an organ of the State interposed between an unwilling defendant and his right to defend himself personally. To thrust counsel upon the accused, against his considered wish, thus violates the logic of the Amendment. In such a case, counsel is not an assistant, but a master; and the right to make a defense is stripped of the personal character upon which the Amendment insists. . . . An unwanted counsel "represents" the defendant only through a tenuous and unacceptable legal fiction. Unless the accused has acquiesced in such representation, the defense presented is not the defense guaranteed him by the Constitution, for, in a very real sense, it is not *his* defense.[89]

The majority recognized that in most situations defendants could better defend themselves through counsel than by their own unskilled efforts. Because waiver of counsel carries with it the surrender of valuable benefits, the majority noted that the record must substantiate that a defendant's choice was made knowingly and intelligently; thus a strong judicial warning presumably must accompany any waiver. If the record demonstrates, as the majority concluded it did in *Faretta*, that a defendant is literate, competent, and understanding, and that the choice was the product of an informed free will, then the defendant will have to bear the personal consequences of the choice, including, presumably, any subsequent claim to an incompetent defense.

The *Faretta* dissenters denied that the historical evidence presented in the majority opinion had any conclusive quality.[90] They further argued that the majority not only ignored the possible negative impact that such a precedent could have on the already burdened resources of trial courts, but that it failed to justify how incompetent self-representation that results in an unjust conviction could ever be socially desirable.

The fear that *Faretta* would contribute further to trial-court congestion by allowing inexperienced defendants to add to trial delay was probably unfounded. If we assume that the vast majority of defendants want to make a wise and rational choice, and if we further assume that the quality of defender systems will not substantially decline, then it seems likely that *pro se* defenses will be extremely rare. On the other hand, we might argue that, in the absence of the right of self-representation, the indigent "political" defendant would be vulnerable to a sham defense imposed by the state, and perhaps that was the unstated fear of the *Faretta* majority. Certainly political criminal trials are not beyond possibility in the United States, but the real problem would surely not be the absence of trusted, competent, and experienced trial advocates. Neither the treason trials of seventeenth-century England nor the post–World War II conspiracy trials in the United States indicate that the right of self-representation would have measurably strengthened individual liberty.

We need not anticipate a sudden rash of *pro se* defenses; still, given the probability of conviction in any criminal trial, it is questionable whether appellate courts will require *pro se* defendants to live with their choice. Can appellate courts uphold an unjust conviction where the record indicates that the conviction is the result of an incompetent *pro se* defense, however voluntary it may have been? If defendants choose a *pro se* defense because they fear that appointed counsel is either incompetent or not to be trusted, then surely the answer is not an equally incompetent *pro se* defense. If *Faretta* addresses a real problem, then both the majority and the minority opinions lost sight of it. Anthony Faretta rejected the appointment of a public defender and three times requested the appointment of private counsel because he thought the public defender's office was "loaded down with . . . a heavy case load."[91] Assuming that Faretta was contending that he would not receive an effective defense from the overburdened defender's office, then perhaps his request for private counsel was closer to an appropriate solution than was the push to the constitutional right of self-representation. This is not to suggest that a trial judge is bound to accept an indigent defendant's conclusions about the effectiveness of the local public defender's office; rather, *Faretta* ignored what may well have been the real problem—the adequacy of resources available to public defenders.

THE RIGHT TO EFFECTIVE COUNSEL

All convicted defendants have probably, at one time or another, concluded that their attorney was at best ineffective and at worst their enemy.[92] Of course, the right to counsel does not mean the right to be acquitted, but it does mean the right to effective counsel. At least since *Powell v. Alabama*,[93] it has been generally recognized that the Sixth Amendment and due process guarantee the right to *effective* counsel.[94] For example, the Supreme Court has held that defendants are entitled to the assistance of counsel untrammeled and unimpaired by conflicting interests,[95] and that defendants have a right to an attorney who will consult with them and subpoena witnesses on their behalf.[96] More recently, the Court has noted that "defendants facing felony charges are entitled to the effective assistance of competent counsel. . . . If the right to counsel guaranteed by the Constitution is to serve its purpose, defendants cannot be left to the mercies of incompetent counsel and . . . judges should strive to maintain proper standards of performance by attorneys who are representing defendants in criminal cases in their courts."[97]

Although claims of ineffective counsel are commonplace, the Supreme Court has never enunciated a clear standard for passing on such claims. Consequently, the states and lower federal courts have been left free to develop their own standards. A claim of ineffective counsel involves a degree of second-guessing, which is why the lower courts have been reluctant to adopt excessively rigid standards of performance. Even competent attorneys often disagree about the value or propriety of a particular strategy or tactic. As a result, the most common standard of ineffectiveness is that a defense must not be so inadequate "as to make . . . a trial a farce, sham or mocking of justice."[98]

A minority of the U.S. courts of appeals even rejected the "farce and mocking of justice" standard in favor of a not-too-different rule requiring that effective counsel is counsel that is "reasonably likely to render and rendering reasonably effective assistance."[99]

Under both standards, counsel is presumed to be effective, placing the burden on the defendant to establish a claim of ineffectiveness by reference to particular details.[100] Neither standard provides an objective and prospectively usable set of rules but rather a series of judicial admonitions. The admonitions frequently begin with the observation that effective counsel does not mean error-free counsel or counsel judged ineffective by hindsight.[101] Certain minimum requirements of a general nature do, however, appear to be widely accepted. These include prompt appointment of counsel, consultation with the defendant, and investigation of facts and applicable law.[102]

Many appellate courts continue to rely on the generalized requirement of "normal competence demanded of attorneys in criminal cases,"[103] but some have adopted specific guidelines, such as the following one, which was adopted by the U.S. Fourth Circuit:

Counsel for an indigent defendant should be appointed promptly. Counsel should be afforded a reasonable opportunity to prepare to defend an accused. Counsel must confer with his client without undue delay and as often as necessary, to advise him of his rights and to elicit matters of defense or to ascertain that potential defenses are unavailable. Counsel must conduct appropriate investigations, both factual and legal, to determine if matters of defense can be developed, and to allow himself enough time for reflection and preparation for trial.[104]

Although the outcome of a particular claim of ineffective counsel depends on the total circumstances of a case, it is possible to catalog some of the typical claims.[105]

1. Advising the defendant to plead guilty even though the state's case is weak
2. The attorney's ignorance of the law
3. The failure of the attorney to consult with the defendant
4. The failure of the attorney to investigate the facts
5. Insufficient time to prepare for trial
6. The attorney's inexperience
7. Specific derelictions:
   a. Failure to challenge the composition of the grand or petit jury
   b. Failure to advance a particular defense
   c. Failure to subpoena particular witnesses
   d. Failure to make objections to certain evidence
   e. Failure to cross-examine witnesses
   f. Failure to make opening or closing statements
   g. Failure to request instructions

In addition to the requirement that a petitioner must overcome the presumption of effective counsel,[106] a petitioner must prove that the failure by counsel to perform some essential duty resulted in prejudice to the defendant.[107] Thus an error by defense counsel may not have prejudiced a defendant's right to a fair trial, and is covered by the harmless-error rule.[108]

Finally, as a practical matter, many defendants may be effectively precluded from successfully proving a claim of ineffective counsel. The vast majority of defendants plead guilty, and claims of ineffective counsel in such cases are especially difficult to establish. So long as a plea was voluntarily entered and meets the plea-taking requirements,[109] it seems unlikely that, at least in federal habeas corpus proceedings, many claims of ineffective counsel would be sustained. In *McMann v. Richardson* (1970), the defendant pleaded guilty on the advice of counsel. He subsequently claimed that his counsel was ineffective because the attorney wrongly concluded that the defendant's confession was admissible. In disallowing the claim, the Supreme Court noted that the requirement of an intelligent plea of guilty does not demand that all advice offered by an attorney withstand retrospective examination. "Whether a plea of guilty is unintelligent and therefore vulnerable when motivated by a confession erroneously thought admissible in evidence depends . . . on whether the advice was within the range of competence demanded of attorneys in criminal cases."[110] Effective counsel in pleas of guilty appears, then, to consist primarily of three facets: consultation with the defendant, adequate knowledge of the relevant law, and conscientious evaluation of the facts.

If we face a problem in the quality of defense counsel, the problem is not likely to be resolved by the generalized requirements listed above. In practical terms, the issue boils down to seeing that public defenders and appointed counsel are adequately compensated; that they are given a reasonable case load; that they have adequate training, knowledge, and experience in criminal law and procedure; and, finally, that they are given expert and investigational assistance.

Ancillary Services for the Indigent

Even if an indigent defendant is provided with counsel, justice may be denied if counsel does not have the resources to effectively challenge the state's case— a case generally founded on the full range of scientific and technological counsel available to its greater resources.

> Furnishing him with a lawyer is not enough: The best lawyer in the world can not competently defend an accused person if the lawyer cannot obtain existing evidence crucial to the defense, e.g., if the defendant cannot pay the fee of an investigator to find a pivotal missing witness or a necessary document, or that of an expert accountant or mining engineer or chemist. It might indeed be argued that for the government to defray such expenses, which the indigent

> accused cannot meet, is essential to that assistance by counsel which the Sixth Amendment guarantees. . . . In such circumstances, if the government does not supply the funds, justice is denied the poor—and represents but an upper-bracket privilege.[111]

Strong constitutional arguments can be made that due process and the rights to counsel and to summon witnesses demand that the poor be given a means in the adversary system to exercise these protections. The Supreme Court, however, has never recognized any constitutional obligation on the part of the government to provide ancillary services to indigent defendants.[112]

The Court's failure to address this problem may reflect the conclusion of some of the justices that the problem is being successfully handled by other agencies of the government. It is true that a number of groups have considered the issue and that some advances have occurred. In 1961, Attorney General Robert Kennedy appointed a special committee to investigate poverty and the administration of criminal justice. The report of this committee, which appeared in 1963, recommended that federal legislation be enacted to provide counsel for indigent defendants with services essential to the proper conduct of the defense, including investigatory services and the assistance of expert witnesses. As the committee noted, the consequences of not providing essential ancillary services can be devastating to a defendant and may well induce assigned counsel to advise a plea of guilty.[113]

In 1964, Congress passed the Criminal Justice Act, which incorporated a provision allowing federal district judges to authorize counsel appointed for indigents in federal cases to expend, when necessary, the sum of $300 for investigative and expert services.[114] Some states have followed the example of Congress, passing similar legislation but often with excessively rigid restrictions.[115] Although federal judges have been liberal in providing indigents in federal cases with the services authorized by the 1964 legislation,[116] there is some indication that the problem remains unresolved in many states, particularly in those areas using appointed counsel rather than a public-defender system. For example, the Report of the National Defender Survey in 1973 indicated that investigative assistance is not available in the vast majority of assigned-counsel areas, and in consequence judges report that indigents' cases are less adequately investigated than are those of the prosecution.[117]

If the interests of justice demand that the poor receive an adequate defense in criminal prosecutions, it seems to follow that this would include any expert and investigatory services necessary to preserve a defendant's right to a fair trial. When, for example, the defense of insanity can be successfully maintained only by recourse to the expert testimony of a psychiatrist, then to deny that testimony to a poor defendant is to make a mockery of equal justice. Where indigent defendants have not received adequate ancillary services, it may be necessary for higher courts to reverse these convictions. This, of course, is not a satisfactory solution, but it is the way the judiciary has of alerting legislative bodies to the need for remedial legislation.

CONCLUSION

Given the political conditions in England in 1681, it may well be that Stephen Colledge would have suffered the same fate even if he had a dozen attorneys to represent him. Conditions have altered greatly since the reign of Charles II; the state no longer stands in the same relationship to the individual as it did at that time. Evidence of this altered status is scattered in countless documents and judicial decisions, from the English Petition of Right, to the American Bill of Rights, and on to such landmark decisions as *Gideon v. Wainwright* and *Argersinger v. Hamlin.* The abuses of state power created a healthy distrust of the state and a recognition of the need to tether the instruments of power. Even in the area of criminal law, where popular sentiment frequently supports the exercise of state power, the United States has repeatedly reaffirmed, at least on paper, its commitment to an adversary system of criminal justice in which the accused is afforded numerous protections against a potentially overzealous or careless state.

In an urban and often remote society, the preservation of a vital adversary system is dependent in large measure on the availability and quality of counsel for the defense. If the state is to be held to account for the exercise of the power of the criminal law, then we must have a vigorous and competent system of defense counsel available at all critical stages of the criminal process. Thus the *Gideon, Argersinger,* and *Miranda* decisions should be viewed, not as compassion for criminals, but as practical steps in carrying out the design of the Sixth Amendment—checking the exercise of state power. When, however, the Supreme Court retreats to formalism, as it did in *Kirby,* it lowers the constitutional pressure on the states and erodes the adversary system.

Perhaps even more counterproductive to the goal of preserving a vital adversary system than the formalism of *Kirby* is the failure of the Court to address the issues of effective counsel and ancillary services. One excuse for this failure could be the resource problem that would necessarily be involved. Certainly, some jurisdictions would face a new financial burden should the Court insist on effective counsel coupled with adequate ancillary services. On the other hand, if indigent defendants are provided with ineffective counsel and inadequate or no ancillary services, then the right to counsel becomes, for most defendants, a paper right.

NOTES

1. *Trial of Stephen Colledge,* 8 How. St. Tr. 550, 715 (1681).
2. Ibid. at 723.
3. Ibid. at 552.
4. Ibid. at 569–571.
5. Although apparently counsel was allowed in those private criminal accusations

called *appeals;* see James Fitzjames Stephen, *A History of the Criminal Law in England* (London: Macmillan, 1883), vol. 1, pp. 247–250.

6. 7 & 8 Will. 3, chap. 13. See William Holdsworth, *A History of English Law* (London: Methuen, 1938), vol. 6, pp. 233–234.

7. William Hawkins, *A Treatise of The Pleas of The Crown* (London: E. Dayer, 1724), bk. 2, p. 400.

8. See Stephen, *Criminal Law in England,* vol. 1, p. 424.

9. 6 & 7 Will. 4, chap. 114, § 1. It was not, however, until 1903 in the Poor Prisoners' Defence Act, 3 Edw. 7, chap. 38, § 1, that indigents were accorded full rights to appointed counsel.

10. See generally William Beaney, *The Right to Counsel in American Courts* (Ann Arbor: University of Michigan Press, 1955), chap. 1–2.

11. 1 Stat. 73, § 35 (1789).

12. 1 Stat. 118, § 29 (1790).

13. Ibid.

14. *Powell v. Alabama,* 287 U.S. 45 (1932).

15. Ibid. at 56.

16. Ibid. at 71–72.

17. *Johnson v. Zerbst,* 304 U.S. 458 (1938).

18. Ibid. at 462–463.

19. Ibid. at 468.

20. *Avery v. Alabama,* 308 U.S. 444 (1940).

21. *Smith v. O'Grady,* 312 U.S. 329 (1941).

22. Ibid. at 334.

23. *Betts v. Brady,* 316 U.S. 455, 464–473 (1942).

24. See ibid. at 477–480. The listings in this appendix are open to question because Florida was included as a state offering indigents the right to counsel in noncapital cases— a listing that is certainly questionable in view of *Gideon v. Wainwright,* 372 U.S. 335 (1963).

25. *Betts v. Brady,* 316 U.S. at 476.

26. E.g., *Williams v. Kaiser,* 323 U.S. 471 (1945); *Pennsylvania v. Claudy,* 350 U.S. 116 (1956); *Moore v. Michigan,* 355 U.S. 155 (1957); and *Hudson v. North Carolina,* 363 U.S. 697 (1960).

27. *Moore v. Michigan.*

28. *Hamilton v. Alabama,* 368 U.S. 52 (1961).

29. Nathan Lewin, "Helping the Court with Its Work," *New Republic,* March 3, 1973, pp. 15–19.

30. For a popular treatment of *Gideon,* see Anthony Lewis, *Gideon's Trumpet* (New York: Knopf, 1964).

31. *Gideon v. Wainwright,* 372 U.S. at 344.

32. Note "The Indigent's Expanding Right to Appointed Counsel," 37 *Alb. L. Rev.* 383, 398 (1973).

33. See Lee Silverstein, *Defense of the Poor in Criminal Cases* (Chicago: American Bar Foundation, 1965), vol. 1, chap. 7; and Steven Duke, "The Right to Appointed Counsel: *Argersinger* and Beyond," 12 *Am. Crim. L. Rev.* 601, 625–630 (1975).

34. Silverstein, *Defense of the Poor,* vol. 2, pp. 107–108.

35. 18 U.S.C. 3006, A-9(a)-(b).

36. For a partial listing of state recoupment statutes, see *James v. Strange,* 407 U.S. 128, 133 (1972); and 18 U.S.C. 3006, A-(e).

37. See *Rinaldi v. Yeager,* 384 U.S. 305 (1966); and *James v. Strange.*

38. *Fuller v. Oregon,* 417 U.S. 40 (1974).

39. The federal provision makes no distinction between acquitted and convicted defendants, 18 U.S.C. 3006; A-(f).

40. Lawrence Benner, "Tokenism and the American Indigent," 12 *Amer. Crim. L. Rev.* 667, 668 (1975). The indigency rate among misdemeanants is estimated to be 47 percent, ibid.

41. Ibid. at 671.

42. National Advisory Commission on Criminal Justice Standards and Goals, *The Courts* (Washington, D.C.: GPO, 1973), standard 13.12.

43. The National Defender Survey, *The Other Face of Justice,* 1973, p. 77.

44. *Argersinger v. Hamlin,* 407 U.S. 25 (1972).

45. See below, pp. 333–336.

46. *Argersinger v. Hamlin,* 407 U.S. at 33.

47. Ibid. at 37; see *Scott v. Illinois,* ___ U.S. ___ (1979), where the Supreme Court ruled that the Sixth Amendment does not require an indigent defendant to be represented by counsel when he is tried under a statute that allows a maximum fine of $500 and a year in prison or both, but is given only a fine.

48. Ibid. at 40. Whether, in the absence of a jail sentence, counsel may be denied to indigents remains something of an open question; see *Wood v. Superintendent, Carolina Correctional Unit,* 355 F. Supp. 338 (1973). Cf. *Mosby v. Superintendent, Virginia State Penitentiary,* 381 F. Supp. 5 (1974).

49. The National Defender Survey, *Other Face of Justice,* pp. 22, 38.

50. *Powell v Alabama,* 287 U.S. at 57.

51. *White v. Maryland,* 373 U.S. 59 (1963).

52. *Coleman v. Alabama,* 399 U.S. 1, 9 (1970).

53. Ibid. at 60.

54. At the federal level, the Rules of Criminal Procedure provide that representation by counsel begins from the time of a defendant's initial appearance before a federal magistrate or court, Fed. Rules Crim. Proc., rule 44(a).

55. *Escobedo v. Illinois,* 378 U.S. 478 (1964).

56. Ibid. at 487.

57. As it had been a few months earlier in *Massiah v. United States,* 377 U.S. 201 (1964).

58. *Miranda v. Arizona,* 384 U.S. 436, 470 (1966).

59. Ibid. at 470–475.

60. See *United States v. Manchildon,* 519 F.2d 337 (1975).

61. See *Coughlin v. United States,* 391 F.2d 371 (1968); *United States v. Cobbs,* 481 F.2d 196 (1973), where the court allowed the testimony to be admitted but noted its disapproval; and see *United States v. Thomas,* 474 F.2d 110 (1973), where the court stated that a retained or appointed attorney must be given notice of any intention to interrogate but that a violation of this requirement amounted only to a violation of the court's canon of ethics and not to a violation of *Miranda.*

62. *Brewer v. Williams,* 430 U.S. 387.

63. Ibid. at 398.

64. E.g., R. J. Medalil, "Custodial Police Interrogation in Our Nation's Capital," 66 *Mich. L. Rev.* 1347 (1968).

65. *North Carolina v. Butler,* ___ U.S. ___ (1979); see also *Fare v. Michael C.,* ___ U.S. ___ (1979), where the Court ruled that a juvenile's request before interrogation to see his probation officer was not equivalent to a request to see an attorney, and subsequent incriminating statements were admissible on the basis of normal standards of waiver; on the issue of police ignoring requests for an attorney, see A. Leiken, "Police Interrogation in Colorado," 47 *Den. L.J.* 1 (1970).

66. *United States v. Wade,* 388 U.S. 218 (1967); and see *Gilbert v. California,* 388 U.S. 263 (1967), decided the same day.

67. *United States v. Wade,* 388 U.S. at 235–236.

68. Ibid. at 252–253.

69. Ibid. at 226–227.

70. *Kirby v. Illinois,* 406 U.S. 682 (1972). One of the dissenters in *Wade,* Justice White, felt bound by *Wade* and therefore dissented in *Kirby;* the third *Wade* dissenter, Justice Harlan, died before the *Kirby* decision.

71. Ibid. at 684–686.

72. Ibid. at 689–690.

73. Id. In 1977, in *Moore v. Illinois,* 434 U.S. 220, the Court relaxed its *Kirby* ruling, holding that the right to presence of counsel in corporeal identification begins at or after the initiation of adversary judicial proceedings, including, as in *Moore, a* preliminary hearing.

74. See Justice Brennan's dissenting opinion in *Kirby,* 406 U.S. at 704, n. 14.

75. *United States v. Ash,* 413 U.S. 300 (1973).

76. Ibid. at 317–320.

77. *Gerstein v. Pugh,* 420 U.S. 103 (1975).

78. Ibid. at 122. Four justices in a concurring opinion noted that they did not join in the dictum.

79. *Kirby v. Illinois,* 406 U.S. at 691.

80. *Carter v. Illinois,* 329 U.S. 173, 174 (1946).

81. *Johnson v. Zerbst,* 304 U.S. 458, 464 (1938).

82. *Carnley v. Cochran,* 369 U.S. 506 (1962).

83. *Von Moltke v. Gillies,* 332 U.S. 708, 724 (1948).

84. *Moore v. Michigan,* 355 U.S. at 164.

85. *Carnley v. Cochran,* 369 U.S. at 516.

86. However, *pro se* representation was a common practice in the trial of minor offenses in justice-of-the-peace courts.

87. See 28 U.S.C. 1654; and *Faretta v. California,* 422 U.S. 806, 813 at n. 10 (1975).

88. Ibid. at 832.

89. Ibid. at 820–821.

90. See the dissent by Justice Blackmun, joined by Chief Justice Burger and Justice Rehnquist, ibid. at 836.

91. Ibid. at 807.

92. See Jonathan Casper, *American Criminal Justice: The Defendant's Perspective* (Englewood Cliffs, N.J.: Prentice-Hall, 1972), chap. 4.

93. *Powell v. Alabama,* 287 U.S. at 57.

94. Prior to *Gideon,* the right to effective counsel was covered only by due process; see *Hawk v. Olson,* 326 U.S. 271, 274 (1945).

95. *Glasser v. United States,* 315 U.S. 60, 70 (1942).

96. *White v. Regan,* 324 U.S. 760 (1945).

97. *McMann v. Richardson,* 397 U.S. 759, 771 (1970).

98. *United States v. Stern,* 519 F.2d 521 (9th Cir. 1975).

99. *Maglaya v. Buchkol,* 515 F.2d 265, 269 (6th Cir. 1975).

100. E.g., *Gilpin v. United States,* 252 F.2d 685, 687 (1958).

101. *MacKenna v. Ellis,* 280 F.2d 592, 599 (1960).

102. See generally Joel J. Finer, "Ineffective Assistance of Counsel," 58 *Cornell L. Rev.* 1077 (1973).

103. E.g., *Tollett v. Henderson,* 411 U.S. 258, 268 (1973); and *Moore v. United States,* 432 F.2d 730 (3d Cir. 1970).

104. *Coles v. Peyton,* 389 F.2d 224, 226 (1968). The District of Columbia Court of Appeals adopted guidelines in *United States v. De Coster,* 487 F.2d 1197 (1973).

105. For a detailed statement, see Jon Waltz, "Inadequacy of Trial Defense Representation," 59 *Nw. U. L. Rev.* 289 (1964).

106. *McQueen v. Swenson,* 489 F.2d 207, 216 (1974).

107. There is a division among the federal circuits as to whether the initial burden is

on the defense or the government to establish prejudice or the lack of prejudice; see *Coles v. Peyton,* 389 F.2d 224, 226 (4th Cir. 1968). Cf. *Green v. Rundle,* 434 F.2d 1112, 1115 (3d Cir. 1970).

108. *Chapman v. California,* 386 U.S. 18 (1967); and *McQueen v. Swenson,* 498 F.2d 207, 218 (1974).

109. See *Boykin v. Alabama,* 395 U.S. 238, 242–243 (1969).

110. *McMann v. Richardson,* 397 U.S. 770–771.

111. Judge Jerome Frank dissenting in *United States v. Johnson,* 238 F.2d 565, 572 (1956).

112. See generally Dennis Alexander, "Assistance in Addition to Counsel for Indigent Defendants," 16 *Vill. L. Rev.* 323 (1970); and Craig Bowman, "The Indigent's Right to an Adequate Defense: Expert and Investigational Assistance," 6 *Crim. L. Bull.* 491 (1970).

113. The Attorney General's Committee on Poverty and the Administration of Criminal Justice, *Poverty and the Administration of Federal Criminal Justice* (Washington, D.C.: GPO, 1964), p. 26.

114. 18 U.S.C. §3006 A (e). In 1970 Congress amended this provision to allow a federal judge to waive the $300 maximum when necessary to provide for adequate compensation, Pub. L. 91-447.

115. For a listing of state legislation, see Bowman, "Right to an Adequate Defense," p. 495, n. 26.

116. E.g., *United States v. Tate,* 419 F.2d 131 (1969); and *United States v. Pope,* 251 F. Supp. 234 (1966).

117. The National Defender Survey, *Other Face of Justice,* p. 68.

JUDICIAL DECISIONS

Application to the States:
Gideon v. Wainwright, 372 U.S. 335 (1963)

Mr. Justice BLACK delivered the opinion of the Court.

Petitioner was charged in a Florida state court with having broken and entered a poolroom with intent to commit a misdemeanor. This offense is a felony under Florida law. Appearing in court without funds and without a lawyer, petitioner asked the court to appoint counsel for him, whereupon the following colloquy took place:

> "THE COURT: Mr. Gideon, I am sorry, but I cannot appoint Counsel to represent you in this case. Under the laws of the State of Florida, the only time the Court can appoint Counsel to represent a Defendant is when that person is charged with a capital offense. I am sorry, but I will have to deny your request to appoint Counsel to defend you in this case.
>
> "THE DEFENDANT: The United States Supreme Court says I am entitled to be represented by Counsel."

Put to trial before a jury, Gideon conducted his defense about as well as could be expected from a layman. He made an opening statement to the jury, cross-examined the State's witnesses, presented witnesses in his own defense, declined to testify himself, and made a short argument "emphasizing his innocence to the charge contained in the Information filed in this case." The jury returned a verdict of guilty, and petitioner was sentenced to five years in the state prison. Later, petitioner filed in the Florida Supreme Court this habeas corpus petition attacking his conviction and sentence on the ground that the trial court's refusal to appoint counsel for him denied him rights "guaranteed by the Constitution and the Bill of Rights by the United States Government." Treating the petition for habeas corpus as properly before it, the State Supreme Court, "upon consideration thereof" but without an opinion, denied all relief. Since 1942, when *Betts v. Brady*, 316 U.S. 455, was decided by a divided Court, the problem of a defendant's federal constitutional right to counsel in a state court has been a continuing source of controversy and litigation in both state and federal courts. To give this problem another review here, we granted certiorari. Since Gideon was proceeding *in forma pauperis*, we appointed counsel to represent him and requested both sides to discuss in their briefs and oral arguments the following: "Should this Court's holding in *Betts v. Brady* be reconsidered.

I.

The facts upon which Betts claimed that he had been unconstitutionally denied the right to have counsel appointed to assist him are strikingly like the facts upon which Gideon here bases his federal constitutional claim. Betts was indicted for robbery in a Maryland state court. On arraignment, he told the trial judge of his lack of funds to hire a lawyer and asked the court to appoint one for him. Betts was advised that it was not the practice in that county to appoint counsel for indigent defendants except in murder and rape cases. He then pleaded not guilty, had witnesses summoned, cross-examined the State's witnesses, examined his own, and chose not to testify himself. He was found guilty by the judge, sitting without a jury, and sentenced to eight years in prison. Like Gideon, Betts sought release by habeas corpus, alleging that he had been denied the right to assistance of counsel in violation of the Fourteenth Amendment. Betts was denied any relief, and on review this Court affirmed. It was held that a refusal to appoint counsel for an indigent defendant charged with a felony did not necessarily violate the Due Process Clause of the Fourteenth Amendment, which for reasons given the Court deemed to be the only applicable federal constitutional provision. The Court said:

> "Asserted denial [of due process] is to be tested by an appraisal of the totality of facts in a given case. That which may, in one setting, constitute a denial of fundamental fairness, shocking to the universal sense of justice, may, in other circumstances, and in the light of other considerations, fall short of such denial."

Treating due process as "a concept less rigid and more fluid than those envisaged in other specific and particular provisions of the Bill of Rights," the Court held that refusal to appoint counsel under the particular facts and circumstances in the *Betts* case was not so "offensive to the common and fundamental ideas of fairness" as to amount to a denial of due process. Since the facts and circumstances of the two cases are so nearly indistinguishable, we think the *Betts v. Brady* holding if left standing would require us to reject Gideon's claim that the Constitution guarantees him the assistance of counsel. Upon full reconsideration we conclude that *Betts v. Brady* should be overruled.

II.

The Sixth Amendment provides, "In all criminal prosecutions, the accused shall enjoy the right . . . to have the Assistance of Counsel for his defence." We have construed this to mean that in federal courts counsel must be provided for defendants unable to employ counsel unless the right is competently and intelligently waived. Betts argued that this right is extended to indigent defendants in state courts by the Fourteenth Amendment. In response the Court stated that, while the Sixth Amendment laid down "no rule for the conduct of the states, the question recurs whether the constraint laid by the amendment upon the national courts expresses a rule so fundamental and essential to a fair trial, and so, to due process of law, that it is made obligatory upon the states by the Fourteenth Amendment." 316 U.S., at 465. In order to decide whether the Sixth Amendment's guarantee of counsel is of this fundamental nature, the Court in *Betts* set out and considered "relevant data on the subject . . . afforded by constitutional and statutory provisions subsisting in the colonies and the states prior to the inclusion of the Bill of Rights in the national Constitution, and in the constitutional, legislative, and judicial history of the states to the present date." 316 U.S., at 465. On the basis of this historical data the Court concluded that "appointment of counsel is not a fundamental right, essential to a fair trial." 316 U.S. at 471. It was for this reason the *Betts* Court refused to accept the contention that the Sixth Amendment's guarantee of counsel for indigent federal defendants was extended to or, in the words of that Court, "made obligatory upon the states by the Fourteenth Amendment." Plainly, had the Court concluded that appointment of counsel for an indigent criminal defendant was "a fundamental right, essential to a fair trial," it would have held that the Fourteenth Amendment requires appointment of counsel in a state court, just as the Sixth Amendment requires in a federal court.

We think the Court in *Betts* had ample precedent for acknowledging that those guarantees of the Bill of Rights which are fundamental safeguards of liberty immune from federal abridgment are equally protected against state invasion by the Due Process Clause of the Fourteenth Amendment. This same principle was recognized, explained, and applied in *Powell v. Alabama*, 287 U.S. 45 (1932), a case upholding the right of counsel, where the Court held that despite sweeping language to the contrary in *Hurtado v. California*, 110 U.S. 516 (1884), the Fourteenth Amendment "embraced" those " 'fundamental principles of liberty and justice which lie at the base of all our civil and political institutions,' " even though they had been "specifically dealt with in another part of the Federal Constitution." 287 U.S., at 67. In many cases other than *Powell* and *Betts*, this Court has looked to the fundamental nature of original Bill of Rights guarantees to decide whether the Fourteenth Amendment makes them obligatory on the States. Explicitly recognized to be of this "fundamental nature" and therefore made immune from state invasion by the Fourteenth, or some part of it, are the First Amendment's freedoms of speech, press, religion, assembly, association, and petition for redress of grievances. For the same reason, though not always in precisely the same terminology, the Court has made obligatory on the States the Fifth Amendment's command that private property shall not be taken for public use without just compensation, the Fourth Amendment's prohibition of un-reasonable searches and seizures, and the Eighth's ban on cruel and unusual pun-ishment. On the other hand, this Court in *Palko v. Connecticut*, 302 U.S. 319 (1937), refused to hold that the Fourteenth Amendment made the double jeopardy provision of the Fifth Amendment obligatory on the States. In so refusing, however, the Court, speaking through Mr. Justice Cardozo, was careful to emphasize that "immunities that are valid as against the federal government by force of the specific pledges of particular amendments have been found to be implicit in the concept of ordered liberty, and thus, through the Fourteenth Amendment, become valid as against the states" and that guarantees "in their origin . . . effective against the federal govern-ment alone" had by prior cases "been taken over from the earlier articles of the Federal Bill of Rights and brought within the Fourteenth Amendment by a process of absorption." 302 U.S., at 324–325, 326.

We accept *Betts v. Brady*'s assumption, based as it was on our prior cases, that a provision of the Bill of Rights which is "fundamental and essential to a fair trial" is made obligatory upon the States by the Fourteenth Amendment. We think the Court in *Betts* was wrong, however, in concluding that the Sixth Amendment's guarantee of counsel is not one of these fundamental rights. . . . The fact is that in deciding as it did—that "appointment of counsel is not a fundamental right, essential to a fair trial"—the Court in *Betts v. Brady* made an abrupt break with its own well-considered precedents, sounder we believe than the new, we but restore constitutional prin-ciples established to achieve a fair system of justice. Not only these precedents but also reason and reflection require us to recognize that in our adversary system of criminal justice, any person haled into court, who is too poor to hire a lawyer, can-not be assured a fair trial unless counsel is provided for him. This seems to us to be an obvious truth. Governments, both state and federal, quite properly spend vast sums of money to establish machinery to try defendants accused of crime. Lawyers to prosecute are everywhere deemed essential to protect the public's interest in an orderly society. Similarly, there are few defendants charged with crime, few indeed, who fail to hire the best lawyers they can get to prepare and present their defenses. That government hires lawyers to prosecute and defendants who have the money hire lawyers to defend are the strongest indications of the widespread belief that lawyers in criminal courts are necessities, not luxuries. The right of one charged with crime to counsel may not be deemed fundamental and essential to fair trials in some countries, but it is in ours. From the very beginning, our state and national constitutions and laws have laid great emphasis on procedural and substantive safeguards designed to assure fair trials before impartial tribunals in which every defendant stands equal before the law. This noble ideal cannot be realized if the poor man charged with crime has to face his accusers without a lawyer to assist him. A defendant's need for a lawyer is nowhere better stated than in the moving words of Mr. Justice Sutherland in *Powell v. Alabama*:

> "The right to be heard would be, in many cases, of little avail if it did not comprehend the right to be heard by counsel. Even the intelligent and educated layman has small and sometimes no skill in the science of law. If charged with crime, he is incapable, generally, of determining for himself whether the indictment is good or bad. He is unfamiliar with the rules of evidence. Left without the aid of counsel he may be put on trial without a proper charge, and convicted upon incompetent evidence, or evidence irrelevant to the issue or otherwise inadmissible. He lacks both the skill and knowledge adequately to prepare his defense, even though he have a perfect one. He requires the guiding hand of counsel at every step in the proceedings against him. Without it, though he be not guilty, he faces the danger of conviction because he does not know how to establish his innocence." 287 U.S., at 68–69.

The Court in *Betts v. Brady* departed from the sound wisdom upon which the Court's holding in *Powell v. Alabama* rested. Florida, supported by two other States, has asked that *Betts v. Brady* be left intact. Twenty-two States, as friends of the Court, argue that *Betts* was "an anachronism when handed down" and that it should now be overruled. We agree.

The judgment is reversed and the cause is remanded to the Supreme Court of Florida for further action not inconsistent with this opinion.

Reversed.

Mr. Justice DOUGLAS.

. . .

In agreeing with the Court that the right to counsel in a case such as this should now be expressly recognized as a fundamental right embraced in the Fourteenth Amendment, I wish to make a further observation. When we hold a right or immunity, valid against the Federal Government, to be "implicit in the concept of ordered liberty" and thus valid against the States, I do not read our past decisions to suggest that by so holding, we automatically carry over an entire body of federal law and apply it in full sweep to the States. Any such concept would disregard the frequently wide disparity between the legitimate interests of the States and of the Federal Government, the divergent problems that they face, and the significantly different consequences of their actions. In what is done today I do not understand the Court to depart from the principles laid down in *Palko v. Connecticut*, 302 U.S. 319, or to embrace the concept that the Fourteenth Amendment "incorporates" the Sixth Amendment as such.

On these premises I join in the judgment of the Court.

The Scope of the Right:
Argersinger v. Hamlin, 407 U.S. 25 (1972)

Mr. Justice DOUGLAS delivered the opinion of the Court.

Petitioner, an indigent, was charged in Florida with carrying a concealed weapon, an offense punishable by imprisonment up to six months, a $1,000 fine, or both. The trial was to a judge, and petitioner was unrepresented by counsel. He was sentenced to serve 90 days in jail, and brought this habeas corpus action in the Florida Supreme Court, alleging that, being deprived of his right to counsel, he was unable as an indigent layman properly to raise and present to the trial court good and sufficient defenses to the charge for which he stands convicted. The Florida Supreme Court . . . held that the right to court-appointed counsel extends only to trials "for non-petty offenses punishable by more than six months imprisonment." 236 So.2d 442, 443.

. . . We reverse.

The Sixth Amendment, which in enumerated situations has been made applicable to the States by reason of the Fourteenth Amendment provides specified standards for "all criminal prosecutions."

One is the requirement of a "public trial." *In re Oliver*, supra, held that the right to a "public trial" was applicable to a state proceeding even though only a 60-day sentence was involved. 333 U.S., at 272.

Another guarantee is the right to be informed of the nature and cause of the accusation. Still another, the right of confrontation. And another, compulsory process for obtaining witnesses in one's favor. We have never limited these rights to felonies or to lesser but serious offenses.

. . .

The right to trial by jury, also guaranteed by the Sixth Amendment by reason of the Fourteenth, was limited by *Duncan v. Louisiana* to trials where the potential punishment was imprisonment for six months or more. But, as the various opinions . . . make plain, the right to trial by jury has a different genealogy and is brigaded with a system of trial to a judge alone.

. . .

While there is historical support for limiting the "deep commitment" to trial by jury to "serious criminal cases," there is no such support for a similar limitation on the right to assistance of counsel. . . .

The Sixth Amendment thus extended the right to counsel beyond its common-law dimensions. But there is nothing in the language of the Amendment, its history, or in the decisions of this Court, to indicate that it was intended to embody a retraction of the right in petty offenses wherein the common law previously did require that counsel be provided.

We reject, therefore, the premise that since prosecutions for crimes punishable by imprisonment for less than six months may be tried without a jury, they may also be tried without a lawyer.

. . .

The requirement of counsel may well be necessary for a fair trial even in a petty-offense prosecution. We are by no means convinced that legal and constitutional questions involved in a case that actually leads to imprisonment even for a brief period are any less complex than when a person can be sent off for six months or more.

The trial of vagrancy cases is illustrative. While only brief sentences of imprisonment may be imposed, the cases often bristle with thorny constitutional questions.

In re Gault, 387 U.S. 1, dealt with juvenile delinquency and an offense which, if committed by an adult, would have carried a fine of $5 to $50 or imprisonment in jail for not more than two months, but which when committed by a juvenile might lead to his detention in a state institution until he reached the age of 21. We said that "the juvenile needs the assistance of counsel to cope with problems of law, to make skilled inquiry into the facts, to insist upon regularity of the proceedings, and to ascertain whether he has a defense and to prepare and submit it. . . . The premise of *Gault* is that even in prosecutions for offenses less serious than felonies, a fair trial may require the presence of a lawyer.

Beyond the problem of trials and appeals is that of the guilty plea, a problem which looms large in misdemeanor as well as in felony cases. Counsel is needed so that the accused may know precisely what he is doing, so that he is fully aware of the prospect of going to jail or prison, and so that he is treated fairly by the prosecution.

In addition, the volume of misdemeanor cases, far greater in number than felony prosecutions, may create an obsession for speedy dispositions, regardless of the fairness of the result. . . .

We must conclude, therefore, that the problems associated with misdemeanor and petty offenses often require the presence of counsel to insure the accused a fair trial. Mr. Justice Powell suggests that these problems are raised even in situations where there is no prospect of imprisonment. We need not consider the requirements of the Sixth Amendment as regards the right to counsel where loss of liberty is not involved, however, for here petitioner was in fact sentenced to jail. And, as we said in *Baldwin v. New York*, 399 U.S., at 73, "the prospect of imprisonment for however short a time will seldom be viewed by the accused as a trivial or 'petty' matter and may well result in quite serious repercussions affecting his career and his reputation."

We hold, therefore, that absent a knowing and intelligent waiver, no person may be imprisoned for any offense, whether classified as petty, misdemeanor, or felony, unless he was represented by counsel at his trial.

. . .

We do not sit as an ombudsman to direct state courts how to manage their affairs but only to make clear the federal constitutional requirement. How crimes should be classified is largely a state matter. The fact that traffic charges technically fall within the category of "criminal prosecutions" does not necessarily mean that many of them will be brought into the class where imprisonment actually occurs.

. . .

Under the rule we announce today, every judge will know when the trial of a misdemeanor starts that no imprisonment may be imposed, even though local law permits it, unless the accused is represented by counsel. He will have a measure of the seriousness and gravity of the offense and therefore know when to name a lawyer to represent the accused before the trial starts.

The run of misdemeanors will not be affected by today's ruling. But in those that end up in the actual deprivation of a person's liberty, the accused will receive the benefit of "the guiding hand of counsel" so necessary when one's liberty is in jeopardy

Reversed

Mr. Justice POWELL, with whom Mr. Justice REHNQUIST joins, concurring in the result.

. . .

If I were satisfied that the guarantee of due process required the assistance of counsel in every case in which a jail sentence is imposed or that the only workable method of insuring justice is to adopt the majority's rule, I would not hesitate to join the Court's opinion despite my misgivings as to its effect upon the administration of justice. But in addition to the resulting problems of availability of counsel, of costs, and especially of intolerable delay in an already overburdened system, the majority's drawing of a new inflexible rule may raise more Fourteenth Amendment problems than it resolves. Although the Court's opinion does not deal explicitly with any sentence other than deprivation of liberty however brief, the according of special constitutional status to cases where such a sentence is imposed may derogate from the need for counsel in other types of cases, unless the Court embraces an even broader prophylactic rule. Due process requires a fair trial in all cases. Neither the six-month rule approved below nor the rule today enunciated by the Court is likely to achieve this result.

III

I would hold that the right to counsel in petty-offense cases is not absolute but is one to be determined by the trial courts exercising a judicial discretion on a case-by-case basis. . . .

Police Interrogation:
Brewer v. Williams, 430 U.S. 387 (1977)

Mr. Justice STEWART delivered the opinion of the Court.

An Iowa trial jury found the respondent, Robert Williams, guilty of murder. . . .

I

On the afternoon of December 24, 1968, a 10-year-old girl named Pamela Powers went with her family to the YMCA in Des Moines, Iowa, to watch a wrestling tournament in which her brother was participating. When she failed to return from a trip to the washroom, a search for her began. The search was unsuccessful.

Robert Williams, who had recently escaped from a mental hospital, was a resident of the YMCA. Soon after the girl's disappearance Williams was seen in the YMCA lobby carrying some clothing and a large bundle wrapped in a blanket. He obtained help from a 14-year-old boy in opening the street door of the YMCA and the door to his automobile parked outside. When Williams placed the bundle in the front seat of his car the boy "saw two legs in it and they were skinny and white." Before anyone could see what was in the bundle Williams drove away. His abandoned car was found the following day in Davenport, Iowa, roughly 160 miles east of Des Moines. A warrant was then issued in Des Moines for his arrest on a charge of abduction.

On the morning of December 26, a Des Moines lawyer named Henry McKnight went to the Des Moines police station and informed the officers present that he had just received a long distance call from Williams, and that he had advised Williams to turn himself in to the Davenport police. Williams did surrender that morning to the police in Davenport, and they booked him on the charge specified in the arrest warrant and gave him the warnings required by *Miranda v. Arizona*. The Davenport police then telephoned their counterparts in Des Moines to inform them that Williams had surrendered. McKnight, the lawyer, was still at the Des Moines police head-quarters, and Williams conversed with McKnight on the telephone. In the presence of the Des Moines Chief of Police and a Police Detective named Leaming, McKnight advised Williams that Des Moines police officers would be driving to Davenport to pick him up, that the officers would not interrogate him or mistreat him, and that Williams was not to talk to the officers about Pamela Powers until after consulting with McKnight upon his return to Des Moines. As a result of these conversations, it was agreed between McKnight and the Des Moines police officials that Detective Leaming and a fellow officer would drive to Davenport to pick up Williams, that they would bring him directly back to Des Moines, and that they would not question him during the trip.

In the meantime Williams was arraigned before a judge in Davenport on the out-standing arrest warrant. The judge advised him of his *Miranda* rights and committed him to jail. Before leaving the courtroom, Williams conferred with a lawyer named Kelly, who advised him not to make any statements until consulting with McKnight back in Des Moines.

Detective Leaming and his fellow officer arrived in Davenport about noon to pick up Williams and return him to Des Moines. Soon after their arrival they met with Williams and Kelly, who, they understood, was acting as Williams' lawyer. Detective Leaming repeated the *Miranda* warnings, and told Williams:

> ". . . we both know that you're being represented here by Mr. Kelly and you're being represented by Mr. McKnight in Des Moines, and . . . I want you to remember this because we'll be visiting between here and Des Moines."

Williams then conferred again with Kelly alone, and after this conference Kelly reit-erated to Detective Leaming that Williams was not to be questioned about the disap-pearance of Pamela Powers until after he had consulted with McKnight back in Des Moines. When Leaming expressed some reservations, Kelly firmly stated that the agreement with McKnight was to be carried out—that there was to be no interrogation of Williams during the automobile journey to Des Moines. Kelly was denied permis-sion to ride in the police car back to Des Moines with Williams and the two officers.

The two Detectives, with Williams in their charge, then set out on the 160-mile drive. At no time during the trip did Williams express a willingness to be interrogated in the absence of an attorney. Instead, he stated several times that "when I get to Des Moines and see Mr. McKnight, I am going to tell you the whole story." Detective Leaming knew that Williams was a former mental patient, and knew also that he was deeply religious.

The Detective and his prisoner soon embarked on a wide-ranging conversation covering a variety of topics, including the subject of religion. Then, not long after leaving Davenport and reaching the interstate highway, Detective Leaming delivered what has been referred to in the briefs and oral arguments as the "Christian burial speech." Addressing Williams as "Reverend," the Detective said:

> "I want to give you something to think about while we're traveling down the road. . . . Number one, I want you to observe the weather conditions, it's raining, it's sleeting, it's freezing, driving is very treacherous, visibility is poor, it's going to be dark early this evening. They are predicting several inches of snow for tonight, and I feel that you yourself are the only person that knows where this little girl's body is, that you yourself have only been there once, and if you get a snow on top of it you yourself may be unable to find it. And, since we will be going right past the area on the way into Des Moines, I feel that we could stop and locate the body, that the parents of this little girl should be entitled to a Christian burial for the little girl who was snatched away from them on Christmas Eve and murdered. And I feel we should stop and locate it on the way in rather than waiting until morning and trying to come back out after a snow storm and possibly not being able to find it at all.'"

Williams asked Detective Leaming why he thought their route to Des Moines would be taking them past the girl's body, and Leaming responded that he knew the body was in the area of Mitchellville—a town they would be passing on the way to Des Moines. Leaming then stated: "I do not want you to answer me. I don't want to discuss it further. Just think about it as we're riding down the road."

As the car approached Grinnell, a town approximately 100 miles west of Davenport, Williams asked whether the police had found the victim's shoes. When Detective Leaming replied that he was unsure, Williams directed the officers to a service station where he said he had left the shoes; a search for them proved unsuccessful. As they continued towards Des Moines, Williams asked whether the police had found the blanket, and directed the officers to a rest area where he said he had disposed of the blanket. Nothing was found. The car continued towards Des Moines, and as it approached Mitchellville, Williams said that he would show the officers where the body was. He then directed the police to the body of Pamela Powers.

Williams was indicted for first-degree murder. Before trial, his counsel moved to suppress all evidence relating to or resulting from any statements Williams had made during the automobile ride from Davenport to Des Moines. After an evidentiary hearing the trial judge denied the motion. He found that "an agreement was made between defense counsel and the police officials to the effect that the Defendant was not to be questioned on the return trip to Des Moines," and that the evidence in question had been elicited from Williams during "a critical stage in the proceedings requiring the presence of counsel on his request." The judge ruled, however, that Williams had "waived his right to have an attorney present during the giving of such information."

The evidence in question was introduced over counsel's continuing objection at the subsequent trial. The jury found Williams guilty of murder, and the judgment of conviction was affirmed by the Iowa Supreme Court. . . .

Williams then petitioned for a writ of habeas corpus in the United States District Court. . . . The District Court . . . concluded as a matter of law that the evidence in question had been wrongly admitted at Williams' trial. . . .

The Court of Appeals for the Eighth Circuit, with one judge dissenting affirmed this judgment. . . .

II

. . . There is no need to review in this case the doctrine of *Miranda v. Arizona*, supra, a doctrine designed to secure the constitutional privilege against compulsory self-incrimination. It is equally unnecessary to evaluate the ruling of the District Court that Williams' self-incriminating statements were, indeed, involuntarily made. For it is clear that the judgment before us must in any event be affirmed upon the ground that Williams was deprived of a different constitutional right—the right to the assistance of counsel.

This right, guaranteed by the Sixth and Fourteenth Amendments, is indispensable to the fair administration of our adversary system of criminal justice. Its vital need at the pretrial stage has perhaps nowhere been more succinctly explained than in Mr. Justice Sutherland's memorable words for the Court 44 years ago in *Powell v. Alabama*, 287 U.S. 45, 57.

> "During perhaps the most critical period of the proceedings against these defendants, that is to say, from the time of their arraignment until the beginning of their trial, when consultation, thoroughgoing investigation and preparation were vitally important, the defendants did not have the aid of counsel in any real sense, although they were as much entitled to such aid during that period as at the trial itself."

There has occasionally been a difference of opinion within the Court as to the peripheral scope of this constitutional right. But its basic contours, which are identical in state and federal contexts, are too well established to require extensive elaboration here. Whatever else it may mean, the right to counsel granted by the Sixth and Fourteenth Amendments means at least that a person is entitled to the help of a lawyer at or after the time that judicial proceedings have been initiated against him— "whether by way of formal charge, preliminary hearing, indictment, information, or arraignment." *Kirby v. Illinois*, supra, 406 U.S. at 689.

There can be no doubt in the present case that judicial proceedings had been initiated against Williams before the start of the automobile ride from Davenport to Des Moines. A warrant had been issued for his arrest, he had been arraigned on that warrant before a judge in a Davenport courtroom, and he had been committed by the court to confinement in jail. The State does not contend otherwise.

There can be no serious doubt, either, that Detective Leaming deliberately and designedly set out to elicit information from Williams just as surely as—and perhaps more effectively than—if he had formally interrogated him. Detective Leaming was fully aware before departing for Des Moines that Williams was being represented in Davenport by Kelly and in Des Moines by McKnight. Yet he purposely sought during Williams' isolation from his lawyers to obtain as much incriminating information as possible. Indeed, Detective Leaming conceded as much when he testified at Williams' trial. . . .

The state courts clearly proceeded upon the hypothesis that Detective Leaming's "Christian burial speech" had been tantamount to interrogation. Both courts recognized that Williams had been entitled to the assistance of counsel at the time he made the incriminating statements. Yet no such constitutional protection would have come into play if there had been no interrogation.

The circumstances of this case are thus constitutionally indistinguishable from those presented in *Massiah v. United States*. The petitioner in that case was indicted for violating the federal narcotics law. He retained a lawyer, pleaded not guilty, and was released on bail. While he was free on bail a federal agent succeeded by surreptitious means in listening to incriminating statements made by him. Evidence of these statements was introduced against the petitioner at his trial, and he was convicted. This Court reversed the conviction, holding "that the petitioner was denied the basic protections of that guarantee [the right to counsel] when there was used against him at his trial evidence of his own incriminating words, which federal agents had deliberately solicited from him after he had been indicted and in the absence of his counsel." 377 U.S., at 206.

That the incriminating statements were elicited surreptitiously in the *Massiah* case, and otherwise here, is constitutionally irrelevant. Rather, the clear rule of *Massiah* is that once adversary proceedings have commenced against an individual, he has a right to legal representation when the government interrogates him. It thus requires no wooden or technical application of the *Massiah* doctrine to conclude that Williams was entitled to the assistance of counsel guaranteed to him by the Sixth and Fourteenth Amendments.

III

. . .

Despite Williams' express and implicit assertions of his right to counsel, Detective Leaming proceeded to elicit incriminating statements from Williams. Leaming did not preface this effort by telling Williams that he had a right to the presence of a lawyer, and made no effort at all to ascertain whether Williams wished to relinquish that right. The circumstances of record in this case thus provide no reasonable basis for finding that Williams waived his right to the assistance of counsel.

. . .

IV

The crime of which Williams was convicted was senseless and brutal, calling for swift and energetic action by the police to apprehend the perpetrator and gather evidence with which he could be convicted. No mission of law enforcement officials is more important. Yet "disinterested zeal for the public good does not assure either wisdom or right in the methods it pursues." *Haley v. Ohio*, 332 U.S. 596, 605. Although we do not lightly affirm the issuance of a writ of habeas corpus in this case, so clear a violation of the Sixth and Fourteenth Amendments as here occurred cannot be condoned. The pressures on state executive and judicial officers charged with the administration of the criminal law are great, especially when the crime is murder and the victim a small child. But it is precisely the predictability of those pressures that makes imperative a resolute loyalty to the guarantees that the Constitution extends to us all.

The judgment of the Court of Appeals is affirmed.

It is so ordered.

Mr. Chief Justice BURGER, dissenting.

The result in this case ought to be intolerable in any society which purports to call itself an organized society. It continues the Court—by the narrowest margin—on the much-criticized course of punishing the public for the mistakes and misdeeds of law enforcement officers, instead of punishing the officer directly, if in fact he is guilty of wrongdoing. It mechanically and blindly keeps reliable evidence from juries whether the claimed constitutional violation involves gross police misconduct or honest human error.

Williams is guilty of the savage murder of a small child; no member of the Court contends he is not. While in custody, and after no fewer than *five* warnings of his rights to silence and to counsel, he led police to the concealed body of his victim. The Court concedes Williams was not threatened or coerced and that he spoke and acted voluntarily and with full awareness of his constitutional rights. In the face of all this, the Court now holds that because Williams was prompted by the detective's statement—not interrogation but a statement—the jury must not be told how the police found the body.

Today's holding fulfills Justice Cardozo's grim prophecy that someday some court might carry the exclusionary rule to the absurd extent that its operative effect would exclude evidence relating to the body of a murder victim because of the means by which it was found. In so ruling the Court regresses to playing a grisly game of "hide and seek," once more exalting the sporting theory of criminal justice which has been experiencing a decline in our jurisprudence. . . .

Miranda *and Waiver of Counsel:* North Carolina v. Butler, —— U.S. —— (1979)

Mr. Justice STEWART delivered the opinion of the Court.

In evident conflict with the present view of every other court that has considered the issue, the North Carolina Supreme Court has held that *Miranda v. Arizona,* 384 U.S. 436, requires that no statement of a person under custodial interrogation may be admitted in evidence against him unless, at the time the statement was made, he explicitly waived the right to the presence of a lawyer. We granted certiorari to consider whether this per se rule reflects a proper understanding of the *Miranda* decision.

The respondent was convicted in a North Carolina trial court of kidnapping, armed robbery, and felonious assault. The evidence at his trial showed that he and a man named Elmer Lee had robbed a gas station in Goldsboro, N. C., in December 1976, and had shot the station attendant as he was attempting to escape. The attendant was paralyzed, but survived to testify against the respondent.

The prosecution also produced evidence of incriminating statements made by the respondent shortly after his arrest by FBI agents in the Bronx, N. Y., on the basis of a North Carolina fugitive warrant. Outside the presence of the jury, FBI Agent Martinez testified that at the time of the arrest he fully advised the respondent of the rights delineated in the *Miranda* case. According to the uncontroverted testimony of Martinez, the agents then took the respondent to the FBI office in nearby New Rochelle, N. Y. There, after the agents determined that the respondent had an 11th grade education and was literate, he was given the Bureau's "Advice of Rights" form which he read. When asked if he understood his rights, he replied that he did. The respondent refused to sign the waiver at the bottom of the form. He was told that he need neither speak nor sign the form, but that the agents would like him to talk to them. The respondent replied, "I will talk to you but I am not signing any form." He then made inculpatory statements. Agent Martinez testified that the respondent said nothing when advised of his right to the assistance of a lawyer. At no time did the respondent request counsel or attempt to terminate the agents' questioning.

At the conclusion of this testimony the respondent moved to suppress the evidence of his incriminating statements on the ground that he had not waived his right to the assistance of counsel at the time the statements were made. The court denied the motion. . . . The respondent's statements were then admitted into evidence, and the jury ultimately found the respondent guilty of each offense charged.

On appeal, the North Carolina Supreme Court reversed the convictions and ordered a new trial. It found that the statements had been admitted in violation of the requirements of the *Miranda* decision, noting that the respondent had refused to waive in writing his right to have counsel present and that there had not been a *specific* oral waiver. As it had in at least two earlier cases, the court read the *Miranda* opinion as

"provid[ing] in plain language that waiver of the right to counsel during interrogation will not be recognized unless such waiver is 'specifically made' after the *Miranda* warnings have been given."

We conclude that the North Carolina Supreme Court erred in its reading of the *Miranda* opinion. There, this Court said that

"If the interrogation continues without the presence of an attorney and a statement is taken, a heavy burden rests on the government to demonstrate that the defendant knowingly and intelligently waived his privilege against self-incrimination and his right to retained or appointed counsel." 384 U.S., at 475.

The Court's opinion went on to say that

"An express statement that the individual is willing to make a statement and does not want an attorney followed closely by a statement could constitute a waiver. But a valid waiver will not be presumed simply from the silence of the accused after warnings are given or simply from the fact that a confession was in fact eventually obtained." Ibid.

Thus the Court held that an express statement can constitute a waiver, and that silence alone after such warnings cannot do so. But the Court did not hold that such an express statement is indispensable to a finding of waiver.

An express written or oral statement of waiver of the right to remain silent or of the right to counsel is usually strong proof of the validity of that waiver, but is not inevitably either necessary or sufficient to establish waiver. The question is not one of form, but rather whether the defendant in fact knowingly and voluntarily waived the rights delineated in the *Miranda* case. As was unequivocally said in *Miranda*, mere silence is not enough. That does not mean that the defendant's silence, coupled with an understanding of his rights and a course of conduct indicating waiver, may never support a conclusion that a defendant has waived his rights. The courts must presume that a defendant did not waive his rights; the prosecution's burden is great; but in at least some cases waiver can be clearly inferred from the actions and words of the person interrogated.

. . .

There is no doubt that this respondent was adequately and effectively apprised of his rights. The only question is whether he waived the exercise of one of those rights, the right to the presence of a lawyer. Neither the state court, nor the respondent has offered any reason why there must be a negative answer to that question in the absence of an *express* waiver. This is not the first criminal case to question whether a defendant waived his constitutional rights. It is an issue with which courts must repeatedly deal. Even when the right so fundamental as that to counsel at trial is involved, the question of waiver must be determined on "the particular facts and circumstances surrounding that case, including the background, experience, and conduct of the accused." *Johnson v. Zerbst,* 304 U.S. 458, 464.

We see no reason to discard that standard and replace it with an inflexible per se rule in a case such as this. As stated at the outset of this opinion, it appears that every court that has considered this question has now reached the same conclusion. Ten of the 11 United States Courts of Appeals and the courts of at least 17 States have held that an explicit statement of waiver is not invariably necessary to support a finding that the defendant waived the right to remain silent or the right to counsel guaranteed by the *Miranda* case. By creating an inflexible rule that no implicit waiver can ever suffice, the North Carolina Supreme Court has gone beyond the requirements of federal organic law. It follows that its judgment cannot stand, since a state court can neither add to nor subtract from the mandates of the United States Constitution.

Accordingly, the judgment is vacated, and the case is remanded to the North Carolina Supreme Court for further proceedings not inconsistent with this opinion.

Mr. Justice BRENNAN, with whom Mr. Justice MARSHALL and Mr. Justice STEVENS joins, dissenting.

. . .

The rule announced by the Court today allows a finding of waiver based upon "infer[rence] from the actions and words of the person interrogated." The Court thus shrouds in half-light the question of waiver, allowing courts to construct inferences from ambiguous words and gestures. But the very premise of *Miranda* requires that ambiguity be interpreted against the interrogator. That premise is the recognition of the "compulsion inherent in custodial" interrogation, 384 U.S., at 458, and of its purpose "to subjugate the individual to the will of [the] examiner," id., at 457. Under such conditions, only the most explicit waivers of rights can be considered knowingly and freely given.

The instant case presents a clear example of the need for an express waiver requirement. As the Court acknowledges, there is a disagreement over whether respondent was orally advised of his rights at the time he made his statement. A.n. 1. The fact that Butler received a written copy of his rights is deemed by the Court to be sufficient basis to resolve the disagreement. But, unfortunately, there is also a dispute over whether Butler could read. See Tr. of Oral Arg. 22, 23. And, obviously, if Butler did not have his rights read to him, and could not read them himself, there could be no basis upon which to conclude that he knowingly waived them. Indeed, even if Butler could read this is no reason to believe that his oral statements, which followed a refusal to sign a written waiver form, were intended to signify relinquishment of his rights.

Faced with "actions and words" of uncertain meaning, some judges may find waivers where none occurred. Others may fail to find them where they did. In the former case, the defendant's rights will have been violated; in the latter, society's interest in effective law enforcement will have been frustrated. A simple prophylactic rule requiring the police to obtain an express waiver of the right to counsel before proceeding with interrogation eliminates these difficulties. And since the Court agrees that *Miranda* requires the police to obtain some kind of waiver—whether express or implied—the requirement of an express waiver would impose no burden on the police not imposed by the Court's interpretation. It would merely make that burden explicit. Had Agent Martinez simply elicited a clear answer from Willie Butler to the question, "Do you waive your right to a lawyer?," this journey through three courts would not have been necessary.

Trial
by
Jury

By the time of the American Revolution, trial by jury was a respected and highly regarded institution, widely acclaimed as a popular instrument for the protection of liberty. Indeed, Thomas Jefferson mentioned in the Declaration of Independence that the denial of the benefit of trial by jury was one of the injuries suffered by the colonies at the hands of George III. Yet the English origins of the right in criminal cases would not have led one to expect that the institution would come to be regarded as a bulwark of liberty.

In the years after the Norman Conquest (1066), when trial by jury was being gradually introduced into England, the jury was an extension of royal power. Coupled with the system of circuit justices and royal writs, the jury was, in the hands of Henry II, a means of imposing royal order on an unruly kingdom.[1] Thus, it is not surprising that for several hundred years, the Crown enjoyed numerous advantages in the selection and control of criminal juries, including forcing defendants to submit to trial by jury on pain of being pressed to death.[2] Furthermore, there was originally no remedy for a wrongful conviction, and an acquittal by a jury could subject the jurors to fine and imprisonment.[3]

The trial, or petit, jury grew out of the presentment, or grand, jury. At the time the Norman kings introduced the presentment jury as a method of public criminal accusation, the methods of proof—the legal means for deciding which alternative set of facts is to be accepted—were varied. In the civil area, they included compurgation, or law wager, and trial by witnesses;[4] in public criminal matters—that is, indictments by a presentment jury—the methods of proof were trial by ordeal (fire, water) and compurgation. Both ordeal and compurgation were subject to corruption, making it difficult for the Crown to obtain convictions.[5] In 1215, the Lateran Council called for the abolition of ordeal, which effectively left England without a means of proving public criminal accusations. What appears to have happened then is that a presentment jury would sometimes be enlarged to act as a trial jury, which was the practical equivalent of saying that a formal accusation was a conviction. Gradually, a second, smaller jury was convened to try the disputed facts. Because the petit jury was a simple and more rational method of establishing the truth, it gained wide acceptance in both the criminal and civil areas. One great advantage was that the jury was composed of local persons, and thus it involved the community in the settlement of disputes. Indeed, in the early years of the petit jury, the jurors were thought of as witnesses to the fact of dispute, and only gradually became judges of the evidence given by others.[6]

By the middle of the fifteenth century, the major configurations of trial by jury in criminal cases had been established. A jury in a criminal case was to be drawn from a group of local men and was to consist of twelve members. The jury was to listen to the evidence and make a corporate and unanimous decision. The jurors were to be men of good character, and a prospective juror who was biased was subject to challenge. Thus constituted, the petit jury was to be the sole judge of the facts. This is not to suggest that by the fifteenth century the petit jury was a perfect instrument of justice: Juries were the subject of corruption on the one hand, and were often bullied and roughly treated by judges and the Crown on the other. As late as 1670, in the London trial of William Penn for conspiracy to engage in a tumultuous assembly,[7] the judge several times refused to accept the jury's verdict—a verdict that in effect held Penn and his codefendant not guilty. When the jury continued to bring in the unacceptable verdict, the recorder (judge) addressed the following comment to Bushell, the jury foreman, and his fellow jurors:

> RECORDER. Gentlemen, you shall not be dismissed till we have a verdict that the court will accept; and you shall be locked up, without meat, drink, fire, and tobacco; you shall not think thus to abuse the court; we will have a verdict, by the help of God, or you shall starve for it. . . .
>
> OBSER. The court swore several persons, to keep the jury all night without

meat, drink, fire, or any other accommodation; they had not so much as a chamber-pot, though desired.

CRIER. O Yes, &c.

The court adjourns till 7 of the clock next morning.

On the following day, when the jury persisted in its refusal to convict Penn, the recorder again addressed the jury:

REC. I am sorry, gentlemen, you have followed your own judgments and opinions, rather than the good and wholesome advice which was given you; God keep my life out of your hands, but for this the Court fines you 40 marks a man; and imprisonment till paid. At which Penn stept up towards the bench, and said:

PENN. I demand my liberty, being freed by the Jury.[8]

Bushell was imprisoned for his behavior but was subsequently released by Chief Justice Vaughan, who in a famous opinion argued that jurors could not be punished for their decisions.[9]

Perhaps his experience in the London trial in part accounts for Penn's including the following provision in the Pennsylvania Frame of Government (1682):

VIII. That all trials shall be by twelve men, and as near as may be, peers or equals, and of the neighbourhood, and men without just exception; in cases of life, there shall be first twenty-four returned by the Sheriffs, for a grand inquest, of whom twelve, at least, shall find the complaint to be true; and then the twelve men, or peers, to be likewise returned by the sheriff, shall have the final judgment. But reasonable challenges shall be always admitted against the said twelve men, or any of them.[10]

The Pennsylvania provision was similar to other trial-by-jury provisions in Colonial America;[11] in fact, trial by jury in major criminal offenses was an accepted part of the Colonial legal system. The practice did vary somewhat, depending on local traditions and conditions, among them the distance from London and the Inns of Court, the sparse population, and the absence of any substantial number of trained lawyers.[12] But whatever the variations, one thing appears to be certain: the English settlers believed they had a constitutional right under English law to trial by jury. In the years immediately preceding the Revolution, the colonists fought attempts by Parliament to curtail that right. For example, when Parliament gave courts of admiralty the authority to try violations of the Stamp Act of 1765, the colonists resisted because admiralty courts functioned without juries. Not only did the Stamp Act Congress remonstrate against infringements on the protection, so too did the Continental Congress in 1774 and again in 1775. In a declaration passed on July 6, 1775,

Congress listed the infringement on trial by jury as one of the causes for taking up arms.[13] And, of course, in the following year, Jefferson included the denial of the right as one justification for declaring independence. Given the role played by trial by jury in the politics of the American Revolution, it is not surprising that the new state constitutions and bills of rights included provisions securing this right.[14]

Further evidence of the value placed on the right to trial by jury can be seen in the fact that it was one of the few fundamental rights placed in the original constitution drafted in 1787. A jury trial clause was suggested in the New Jersey Plan and was finally incorporated into article III (the judicial article) in the following words: "The trial of all crimes, except in cases of impeachment, shall be by jury; and such trial shall be held in the state where the said crimes shall have been committed." Apparently the only objection raised to the clause was that it did not provide sufficiently precise details about the protection: in particular, the absence of a narrowly drawn vicinage requirement and an explicitly stated right to challenge prospective jurors.[15]

When the first Congress met in 1789 and began discussion of a federal bill of rights, James Madison agreed to correlate the various proposals. He originally suggested deleting the jury trial clause from article III and substituting a more detailed clause. Apparently, some members wanted a vicinage clause that would ensure that jurors would be drawn on a local rather than statewide basis. In the end, article III was left unchanged, and although the Sixth Amendment does specify that one has a right to an impartial jury, otherwise the jury provision is almost identical to that in article III.

THE SCOPE OF THE RIGHT

Whether an individual has a right to a trial by jury in a criminal case depends, not on whether the offense charged is a felony or a misdemeanor, but rather on whether the offense charged is serious or petty. Because the label *felony* carries with it a social presumption of gravity and because felonies generally carry a potential prison sentence in excess of one year, it is assumed that all felony offenses are serious.[16] This does not mean that the right does not attach to misdemeanors. In fact, the right attaches to all offenses except those that come within the so-called petty-offense exception.

The petty-offense exception stems from English common law and American Colonial practice. In seventeenth- and eighteenth-century England and Colonial America, a larger number of offenses, generally called *petty offenses,* were subject to summary trial by a judge without a jury.[17] It was not until 1888, in *Callan v. Wilson,* that the Supreme Court considered the scope of the right to trial by jury in criminal cases. There, the Court observed:

> The third article of the Constitution provides for a jury in the trial of "all crimes, except in cases of impeachment." The word "crime," in its more ex-

tended sense, comprehends every violation of public law; in a limited sense, it embraces offenses of a serious or atrocious character. In our opinion, the provision is to be interpreted in the light of the principles which, at common law, determined whether the accused, in a given class of cases, was entitled to be tried by a jury. It is not to be construed as relating only to felonies, or offenses punishable by confinement in the penitentiary. It embraces as well some classes of misdemeanors, the punishment of which involves or may involve the deprivation of the liberty of the citizen. . . .

According to many adjudged cases, arising under Constitutions which declare, generally, that the right of trial by jury shall remain inviolate, there are certain minor or petty offenses that may be proceeded against summarily, and without a jury; and, in respect to other offenses, the constitutional requirement is satisfied if the right to a trial by jury in an appellate court is accorded to the accused.[18]

Callan was convicted in a District of Columbia police court of labor law conspiracy and was fined $25. In default of payment, he was sentenced to thirty days in jail. Without discussing the insignificant fine and jail sentence, the Court reversed Callan's conviction, holding that he should have been allowed a trial by jury because the crime of conspiracy is not a petty or trivial offense, but rather one of grave character.

Callan seems to suggest that the seriousness of an offense is measured in terms of how society views a crime rather than in terms of the severity of the punishment. Some years later, in *Schick v. United States* (1904), the Court again confirmed that petty offenses are exempt from the jury trial provision.[19] In Schick, the defendant was liable only to a fine of $50 for a single violation of the Oleomargarine Act,[20] and consequently the Court ruled that Schick was not entitled to a jury trial. This time, however, the Court suggested that both the nature of the crime and the punishment determine whether an offense is petty or serious.

The Court did not rule directly on the issue again until 1930, when, in *District of Columbia v. Colts*, the Court appeared to swing back to the *Callan* rationale—that the nature of an offense, rather than the severity of the punishment,[21] is the key to the distinction. Colts had been convicted in a police court of violating a speeding law: driving in excess of 22 miles per hour so as to endanger property or life. He faced a maximum fine of $100 or a jail sentence of not more than thirty days. In upholding his claim to trial by jury, the Court noted that although some traffic offenses are petty, those endangering life and property are such obvious acts of depravity "that to characterize it as a petty offense would be to shock the general moral sense."[22]

Seven years after *Colts*, the Court upheld the conviction of a defendant who had been tried for selling secondhand property without a license.[23] The defendant faced a maximum fine of $300 or imprisonment for not more than ninety days. The Court concluded that the moral quality of the crime was relatively inoffensive and that historically a ninety-day jail sentence for an otherwise petty offense did not require a trial by jury. Finally, in 1968, in *Duncan v. Louisiana,* the Warren Court held that not only are the states bound by the requirements of the jury trial provision of the Sixth Amendment, but that one charged with a misdemeanor violation carrying a maximum penalty of two years' imprisonment is faced with a serious crime and not a petty offense.[24]

Duncan did not settle an exact line separating petty from serious offenses, but in practice the line appears to have been drawn at those offenses carrying a punishment of six months in jail or less. Federal law specifically defines a petty offense as a grade of misdemeanor carrying a prison sentence of six months or less, or a fine of not more than $500.[25] Indeed, at the time of the *Duncan* decision, only three states denied a jury trial for a crime punishable by imprisonment for longer than six months. Two of the states, Louisiana and New Jersey, subsequently altered their laws to bring them into conformity with general practice. In 1970, the Court struck down the relevant statute in New York, the third state, in *Baldwin v. New York.*[26] There, a plurality, in reversing the conviction, observed:

> One who is threatened with the possibility of imprisonment for six months may find little difference between the potential consequences that face him, and the consequences that face appellant here. Indeed, the prospect of imprisonment for however short a time will seldom be viewed by the accused as a trivial or "petty" matter and may well result in quite serious repercussions affecting his career and his reputation. Where the accused cannot possibly face more than six months' imprisonment, we have held that these disadvantages, onerous though they may be, may be outweighed by the benefits that result from speedy and inexpensive non-jury adjudications. We cannot, however, conclude that these administrative conveniences, in light of the practices that now exist in every one of the 50 states as well as in the federal courts, can similarly justify denying an accused the important right to trial by jury where the possible penalty exceeds six months' imprisonment.[27]

One final problem is in the area of criminal contempt of court. Beginning in 1968, the Supreme Court has held that serious criminal contempts are subject to the jury trial provision. In *Bloom v. Illinois,* the Court held that a twenty-four-month contempt sentence was not a petty contempt and thus was subject to the requirements of a jury trial.[28] Since the *Bloom* decision, the Court has had several occasions to reexamine the issue. It has held that a suspended sentence and probation,[29] and concurrent sentences of up to six months[30] do not require a trial by jury, but that a sentence of six months each on several counts of contempt, with the sentences running consecutively, does require a trial by jury.[31] Thus, at least insofar as imprisonment is concerned, the law of contempts follows the general practice: Any imprisonment over six months is considered a serious offense and entitles a defendant to a jury trial. In regard to fines for contempt, the Court's position is less clear. In 1975, in *Muniz v. Hoffman,* the Court held that a $10,000 fine against a labor union did not entitle the union to a jury trial, but the Court made clear that the magnitude of the fine had to be viewed against the size and potential resources of the union.[32]

WAIVER

The right to trial by jury, like other constitutionally protected rights, may be waived. Unlike other waivers, however, the waiver of this particular right may require the consent of the prosecution and the approval of the trial judge. Even though the right is principally for the benefit of the accused, still the Supreme Court has noted that a person does not have an absolute right to a bench trial and that a waiver may be conditioned on consent and approval.

> Trial by jury is the normal and, with occasional exceptions, the preferable mode of disposing of issues of fact in criminal cases above the grade of petty offenses. In such cases the value and appropriateness of jury trial have been established by long experience, and are not now to be denied. Not only must the right of the accused to a trial by a constitutional jury be jealously preserved, but the maintenance of the jury as a fact-finding body in criminal cases is of such importance and has such a place in our traditions, that, before any waiver can become effective, the consent of government counsel and the sanction of the court must be had, in addition to the express and intelligent consent of the defendant.[33]

The requirement that a waiver is conditioned on prosecutorial consent and judicial approval is expressed in rule 23(a) of the Federal Rules of Criminal Procedure. In 1965, for the first time, the Court directly confronted this issue as it pertains to federal trials. In *Singer v. United States*, the defendant had requested a bench trial and, although the judge agreed, the federal prosecutor refused to give the consent of the government. The judge, relying on rule 23(a), proceeded with a jury trial. The Supreme Court upheld this denial of waiver. In a unanimous opinion, Chief Justice Warren argued that under both English common law and Colonial American practice, a criminal defendant does not have the right to a bench trial.

> A defendant's only constitutional right concerning the method of trial is to an impartial trial by jury. We find no constitutional impediment to conditioning a waiver of this right on the consent of the prosecuting attorney and the trial judge when, if either refuses to consent, the result is simply that the defendant is subject to an impartial trial by jury—the very thing that the Constitution guarantees him. The Constitution recognizes an adversary system as the proper method of determining guilt, and the Government, as a litigant, has a legitimate interest in seeing that cases in which it believes a conviction is warranted are tried before the tribunal which the Constitution regards as most likely to produce a fair result.[34]

The Constitution does express a preference for trial by jury in criminal cases, and there is more at stake in considering a waiver than the mere interest and benefit of the accused, but there are practical and logical problems with the *Singer* rationale. On the practical level, if the prosecution is under no obligation to justify its refusal to consent to waiver, as presumably it is not, then there is more than a remote possibility that a denial is not motivated by lofty principles of public policy but by strategic considerations aimed at securing a conviction. Also, the *Singer* rationale failed to explain how an accused can be limited by a right; that is, how an accused who has made an intelligent and knowing choice to waive a right can be restricted by that right simply because the government, for reasons privy only to the prosecution, refuses to consent to the waiver.

Given the somewhat varied practice among the states in matters of waiver and that *Singer* was decided prior to the time the Court extended trial by jury to state criminal cases, it is likely that at some point the Court will have to clarify this issue. The need is particularly urgent in regard to whether state law may forbid waiver under any circumstances short of a plea of guilty and whether a right to waiver may be lost by failure to make a timely request for a bench trial.[35]

THE IMPARTIAL JURY

The Venire List

The key to public trust and confidence in the criminal jury probably lies in the belief that jury decisions represent the common sense of the community. If, as Blackstone believed, the jury is a palladium of liberty, then the key to this protection must be found in how we have come to view the jury as a group of local and impartial members of the community. In theory, at least, the modern jury is made up of reasonable citizens, working under the supervision of a judge, who are sworn to decide a dispute on the basis of the evidence admitted without prejudice or partiality to the defense or the state. The jury, then, acts not only as a buffer between the accused and the state, but as a means of ensuring shared community responsibility in those important decisions that affect life and liberty.

Presumably, the first step in obtaining an impartial jury is to ensure that the panel, or venire list, from which the trial jury is selected is a representative cross section of the community in which the trial will take place. That the venire list must be representative has been a constant theme in jury selection cases. Perhaps the most widely quoted statement on this constitutional requirement is Justice Murphy's opinion in *Thiel v. Southern Pacific Company*

(1946).[36] Thiel, suing the Southern Pacific Company for damages, attempted to strike the entire jury panel as unrepresentative because the jury commissioner had excluded all daily wage earners from it. In upholding Thiel's claim, Justice Murphy argued:

> The American tradition of trial by jury, considered in connection with either criminal or civil proceedings, necessarily contemplates an impartial jury drawn from a cross-section of the community. . . . This does not mean, of course, that every jury must contain representatives of all the economic, social, religious, racial, political and geographical groups of the community; frequently such complete representation would be impossible. But it does mean that prospective jurors shall be selected by court officials without systematic and intentional exclusion of any of these groups. Recognition must be given to the fact that those eligible for jury service are to be found in every stratum of society. Jury competence is an individual rather than a group or class matter. That fact lies at the very heart of the jury system. To disregard it is to open the door to class distinctions and discriminations which are abhorrent to the democratic ideals of trial by jury.[37]

Yet the distance is often great between the ideal—a jury drawn from a cross section of the community—and the reality—the many sworn juries that are unrepresentative of their community. In part, the gap is there because legislatures have been generous, perhaps overly so, in creating statutory exemptions for professions and occupations (doctors, nurses, educators, certain public servants) deemed essential to the ongoing life of the community. In part, the gap exists as the natural consequence of establishing certain minimal qualifications (age, citizenship, residency) and disqualifications (illiteracy, physical and mental infirmities, prior felony convictions, pending criminal charges of a serious nature) for jury service—qualifications and disqualifications aimed at eliminating from the venire list those who might be unable to render impartial service. That judges must be allowed a degree of discretion in excusing potential jurors for reasons of personal or family hardship has also separated the ideal from reality. And, finally, the gap exists because we have no firm idea of what constitutes a community. It may well be that in the early nineteenth century we could speak with some knowledge about the community, but in a mobile and urban society *community* is often an elusive term.

The Supreme Court has never required a specific method for selecting a venire list. Indeed, it has indicated that "some play in the joints of the jury-selection process is necessary in order to accommodate the practical problems of judicial administration."[38] However, the systematic exclusion of some groups from venire lists is constitutionally invalid. For example, the Court has consistently held that race is not a valid qualification for jury service:[39] "For racial exclusion to result in the exclusion from jury service of otherwise qualified groups not only violates our Constitution and the laws enacted under it but is at war with our basic concepts of a democratic society and a representative government."[40] Indeed, racial exclusion from jury service is a violation of both the equal-protection clause of the Fourteenth Amendment and federal statutory law, which makes it a criminal offense to exclude anyone from grand or petit jury service on the basis of race.[41]

Of course, a mere allegation of racial exclusion is not sufficient to invalidate a conviction; a petitioner must prove racial exclusion.[42] Once a prima facie case of invidious discrimination is established, however, the burden shifts to the state to demonstrate that racially neutral standards produced the racially imbalanced result.[43] On the other hand, the Court has held that neither a jury roll nor a venire list need be a perfect mirror of the community, perfectly reflecting the proportionate numbers of an identifiable group.[44]

Racial exclusion has been a primary problem in jury selection, but the Supreme Court has also indicated that the systematic exclusion of any group of persons could violate constitutional guarantees. In *Hernandez v. Texas* (1954), a unanimous Court reversed the conviction of a Mexican-American who had been tried before a jury from which persons of Mexican descent had been systematically excluded.[45] Writing for the Court, Chief Justice Warren noted:

> Throughout our history differences in race and color have defined easily iden-
> tifiable groups which have at times required the aid of the courts in securing
> equal treatment under the laws. But community prejudices are not static, and
> from time to time other differences from the community norm may define other
> groups which need the same protection. Whether such a group exists within a
> community is a question of fact. When the existence of a distinct class is dem-
> onstrated, and it is further shown that the laws, as written or as applied, single
> out that class for different treatment not based on some reasonable classifi-
> cation, the guarantees of the Constitution have been violated.[46]

A careful reading of *Hernandez* suggests that a defendant who seeks to challenge a venire list on the basis of group discrimination must establish not only that the group is a recognizable class in the community, but that it is a class that has been the subject of some community prejudice and thus merits group-based protection. In fact, in a decision in 1965, the Court extended the constitutional prohibition against jury exclusion to any identifiable group in the community that may be the subject of prejudice.[47]

More recently, the Court noted by way of dictum that the young are not an identifiable group entitled to group-based protection.[48] Similarly, a lower federal court ruled that the Federal Jury Selection Act[49] does not require that a venire list constitute a cross section of the various strata of a community classified according to income or economic status.[50] Even if it were possible to establish the outer limits of categories like "young," "middle aged," "old," "poor," and "nonpoor," it does not follow that because a group of people can be identified by a common characteristic, it is entitled to representation on venire lists. On the other hand, should a jury commission deliberately exclude otherwise qualified people because of their economic status or their age, then a constitutional issue would be raised.

Finally, the Supreme Court has held that women may not be exempted or presumably disqualified from jury service. The Court's rationale provides some insight into its current position on the representative requirement:

> We accept the fair cross section requirement as fundamental to the jury trial guaranteed by the Sixth Amendment and are convinced that the requirement has solid foundation. The purpose of a jury is to guard against the exercise of arbitrary power—to make available the commonsense judgement of the community as a hedge against the overzealous or mistaken prosecutor and in preference to the professional or perhaps overconditioned or biased response of a judge. . . . This prophylactic vehicle is not provided if the jury pool is made up of only special segments of the populace or if large, distinctive groups are excluded from the pool. Community participation in the administration of the criminal law, moreover, is not only consistent with our democratic heritage but is also critical to public confidence in the fairness of the criminal justice system. Restricting jury service to only special groups or excluding identifiable segments playing major roles in the community cannot be squared with the constitutional concept of jury trial. . . .
>
> Our holding does not augur or authorize the fashioning of detailed jury selection codes by federal courts. The fair cross section principle must have much leeway in application. The States remain free to prescribe relevant qualifications for their jurors and to provide reasonable exemptions so long as it may be fairly said that the jury lists or panels are representative of the community. . . .
>
> It should also be emphasized that in holding that petit juries must be drawn from a source fairly representative of the community we impose no requirement that petit juries actually chosen must mirror the community and reflect the various distinctive groups in the population. Defendants are not entitled to a jury of any particular composition . . . but the jury wheels, pools of names, panels or venires from which juries are drawn must not systematically exclude distinctive groups in the community and thereby fail to be reasonably representative thereof.[51]

The Voir Dire

Beyond the cross-sectional requirement in developing a venire list, there are additional protections that are designed to ensure an impartial jury. A voir dire, or preliminary oral examination, of prospective members of the petit jury is conducted in order to determine whether those individuals will be able to serve as impartial jurors. Voir dire procedures vary from state to state: In some areas, the judge questions prospective jurors, sometimes in response to specific requests from the defense and prosecution; in other areas, the voir dire is conducted directly by the attorneys. During this oral examination, the attorneys have an opportunity to challenge, either for cause or peremptorily (without any stated legal justification), individual members of the poll of jurors tentatively selected to serve on the petit jury.

The system of challenges is deeply rooted in Anglo-American law. The matter was the subject of legislation as early as 1305,[52] by which time it was established that felony defendants had an unlimited right to challenge for cause as well as the right to make thirty-five peremptory challenges. The Crown was also allowed to challenge for cause, and in lieu of peremptory challenges the Crown was allowed to ask a juror to stand aside without assigning cause and was only later required to assign cause if there were not enough jurors. This system, with some modifications, became part of the settled law of Colonial America. Today all states and the federal government provide for challenges to prospective jurors.

At the federal level, the rules allow each side twenty peremptory challenges in cases involving the death penalty; in cases involving punishment of more than one year, the defense is entitled to ten challenges and the government to six.[53] At the state level, there is considerable variation, but generally the states follow a pattern regulating the number of peremptory challenges according to the gravity of an offense.[54]

The Supreme Court has never made the constitutional status of peremptory challenges entirely clear. On the one hand, the Court has said that there is nothing in the Constitution that requires Congress or the states to grant peremptory challenges.[55] On the other hand, it has indicated that they are a necessary part of trial by jury, and that denial or impairment of the right to challenge constitutes reversible error.[56]

Challenges for Cause

THE DEATH-QUALIFIED JURY.   A challenge for cause is a challenge based on a prospective juror's lack of legal qualification for jury service, or bias, or other legally recognizable impediment to impartial service. For many years in cases of capital punishment, one of the common challenges for cause was the death qualification—against prospective jurors who entertained qualms about the death penalty. However, in 1968, the Supreme Court ruled it a violation of the Sixth Amendment to exclude persons from jury service simply because they have expressed conscientious scruples against the infliction of the death penalty. In *Witherspoon v. Illinois*, the trial judge began the voir dire with the statement: "Let's get these conscientious objectors out of the way without wasting any time on them."[57] The judge was simply following the state's normal procedure in murder cases. As a result, forty-seven veniremen were challenged for cause and excused on the basis of their attitudes toward the death penalty, even though only five of the forty-seven explicitly stated that under no cir-

cumstances would they vote to impose the death penalty. In reversing Witherspoon's *sentence*, the majority called the Illinois jury a "hanging jury," claiming that the state had stacked the deck against him. To allow challenges for
cause for all those who expressed conscientious or religious scruples against
capital punishment and all who opposed it in principle was, in the words of
the majority, to produce "a jury uncommonly willing to condemn a man to
die."[58] Notice that the majority did not reverse Witherspoon's conviction,
merely the sentence. In a narrow, qualified holding, it specifically held only
that the "*sentence* of death cannot be carried out if the jury that imposed or
recommended it was chosen by excluding veniremen for cause simply because
they voiced general objections to the death penalty or expressed conscientious
or religious scruples against its infliction."[59]

Witherspoon did not hold that a hanging jury is an unrepresentative jury or
that such a jury substantially increases the risk of conviction. Indeed, the decision was aimed only at the sentence of death, not at other types of sentences,
and not at the issue of guilt. The failure of the majority to find a hanging jury
unrepresentative was questioned by Justice Douglas in his concurring opinion:

> We can as easily assume that the absence of those opposed to capital punish-
> ment would rob the jury of certain peculiar qualities of human nature as would
> the exclusion of women from juries. . . . I would not require a specific showing
> of a likelihood of prejudice, for I feel that we must proceed on the assumption
> that in many, if not most, cases of class exclusion on the basis of beliefs or
> attitudes some prejudice does result and many times will not be subject to
> precise measurement. Indeed, that prejudice "is so subtle, so intangible, that
> it escapes the ordinary methods of proof."[60]

PRE-TRIAL PUBLICITY.   One of the ironies of trial by jury is that originally jurors
were considered to be witnesses to a dispute and thus were expected to have
knowledge of the facts. Once jurors lost the role of witness, however, they
were expected to be ignorant of the facts. (Only a juror who is ignorant of a
dispute can be "indifferent as he stands unsworne.")[61] Today, in a world of mass
media, the judiciary is under constant pressure to accept challenges for cause
in situations where there have been varying degrees of pretrial publicity that
could arguably impair the impartiality of prospective jurors.

The Supreme Court addressed the issue in *Irvin v. Dowd* (1961). Irvin was
charged with a murder that occurred in a rural area of Indiana. Six murders
had been committed in the area in a period of four months. There was intensive
news coverage, including both newspaper and television stories. The stories
revealed details of Irvin's background, including references to his earlier criminal activity. Furthermore, there was a series of sensational stories about
Irvin's confession to the six murders (and twenty-four burglaries), his offer to
plea-bargain, and the prosecutor and sheriff's demand for the death penalty.
The Court found a pattern of deep and bitter local prejudice against the defendant at the time the jury panel was assembled. The panel consisted of 430

names. Of these the judge excused 268 on challenges for cause (having a fixed opinion of the defendant's guilt); another 103 were excused for having objections to the death penalty; another 30 were peremptorily challenged by the defense and prosecution and 17 were excused on personal grounds. Of the 12 jurors placed in the jury box, 8 indicated during the voir dire that they thought the defendant was guilty. The Supreme Court reversed Irvin's conviction observing:

> Here the "pattern of deep and bitter prejudice" shown to be present throughout the community . . . was clearly reflected in the sum total of the *voir dire* examination of a majority of the jurors finally placed in the jury box. Eight out of the 12 thought petitioner was guilty. With such an opinion permeating their minds, it would be difficult to say that each could exclude this preconception of guilt from his deliberations. The influence that lurks in an opinion once formed is so persistent that it unconsciously fights detachment from the mental processes of human nature—we can only say that in the light of the circumstances here the finding of impartiality does not meet constitutional standards. Two-thirds of the jurors had an opinion that petitioner was guilty and were familiar with the material facts and circumstances involved, including the fact that other murders were attributed to him, some going so far as to say that it would take evidence to overcome their belief. With his life at stake, it is not requiring too much that petitioner be tried in an atmosphere undisturbed by so huge a wave of public passion and by a jury other than one in which two-thirds of the members admit, before hearing any testimony, to possessing a belief in his guilt.[62]

It would be misleading to conclude that *Irvin* creates a constitutional right to challenge jurors for cause solely on the basis of their exposure to pretrial publicity and their impressions or opinions. As the Court noted:

> It is not required, however, that the jurors be totally ignorant of the facts and issues involved. In these days of swift, widespread and diverse methods of communication, an important case can be expected to arouse the interest of the public in the vicinity, and scarcely any of those best qualified to serve as jurors will not have formed some impression or opinion as to the merits of the case. This is particularly true in criminal cases. To hold that the mere existence of any preconceived notion as to the guilt or innocence of an accused, without more, is sufficient to rebut the presumption of a prospective juror's impartiality would be to establish an impossible standard. It is sufficient if the juror can lay aside his impression or opinion and render a verdict based on the evidence presented in court.[63]

In order to demonstrate actual identifiable prejudice that has resulted from adverse pretrial publicity, a defendant must prove that the jury was not free of some dominant and adverse influence of knowledge gained outside the courtroom.[64] In short, there is no presumption of juror partiality merely because individual members of a jury have been exposed to adverse publicity about a defendant, at least in those situations where the voir dire does not indicate that there is an atmosphere in the community or courtroom that is hostile to the defendant.[65]

Peremptory Challenges

In contrast to the challenge for cause, the peremptory challenge, or strike, requires no justification and is exercised with complete freedom.[66] The peremptory challenge enables the state and the defense to eliminate real or imagined partiality or bias that may be based only on a hunch, an impression, a look, or a gesture.[67] To require in such circumstances that counsel prove partiality would be to risk the hostility or resentment of the juror. Furthermore, the peremptory challenge allows counsel to eliminate prospective jurors on the basis of habits, associations, occupations, race, nationality, sex, and even religion.[68] Indeed, the Court, in *Swain v. Alabama* (1965), upheld the conviction of a black defendant against the claim that the prosecution denied him equal protection of the laws when it peremptorily challenged all black jurors from the petit jury venire. In refusing to uphold the defendant's claim, the Court reasoned:

> In the light of the purpose of the peremptory system and the function it serves in a pluralistic society in connection with the institution of jury trial, we cannot hold that the Constitution requires an examination of the prosecutor's reasons for the exercise of his challenges in any given case. The presumption in any particular case must be that the prosecutor is using the State's challenges to obtain a fair and impartial jury to try the case before the court. The presumption is not overcome and the prosecutor therefore subjected to examination by allegations that in the case at hand all Negroes were removed from the jury or that they were removed because they were Negroes. Any other result, we think, would establish a rule wholly at odds with the peremptory challenge system as we know it.[69]

However, the Court went on to warn that a different question, with perhaps a different answer, would arise if blacks otherwise qualified for jury service were, by use of peremptory challenge, eliminated from all trial service in a particular jurisdiction.[70] In short, in a properly documented case, the presumption protecting the prosecutor could be overcome.

In those jurisdictions in which a judge conducts the voir dire, do defendants have a constitutional right to demand that certain questions be asked of prospective jurors? The issue has generally arisen in the context of racial prejudice, particularly where the defendant is of one race and the victim is of another. In *Aldridge v. United States* (1931), the defendant was accused of murdering a white police officer. Defense counsel's request that the judge on voir dire inquire into racial prejudice was denied. In reversing the conviction, the Court noted that although judges have broad discretion in selecting the questions to ask of prospective jurors, that discretion is subject to the essential demands of fairness.[71] The Court concluded that racial prejudice was not so remote a possibility as to preclude the inquiry.

Some forty years later, the issue was again before the Court in *Ham v. South Carolina* (1973). The black defendant, a long-time resident of South Carolina, was convicted of violating a state law that prohibited the possession of marihuana.[72] The defendant had been active locally in the civil rights movement and claimed that the drug charge was a frame. His timely request that on voir dire the judge ask questions relating to racial prejudice was denied. Given the facts of the case, the Court held that due process required that the petitioner's request be honored, although it noted that a judge still retains discretion as to the form and number of questions.

Three years after *Ham*, in *Restaino v. Ross* (1976),[73] the Court retreated from its decisions in *Aldridge* and *Ham*. Ross, a black was convicted in a Massachusetts court of certain violent crimes against a white security guard. Counsel for Ross requested at the voir dire that prospective jurors be questioned about racial prejudice. When the judge inquired if there were any circumstances peculiar to the case that might necessitate the question, counsel replied that there were not other than that the victim was white and the defendant black. The request was denied, and the judge then conducted the voir dire, instructing prospective jurors of the obligations of jurors and the need for impartiality. Eventually eighteen veniremen were excused for cause on grounds of prejudice, including one who admitted racial bias. In denying Ross's claim, the Court held that there is no constitutional requirement that judges accede to a defense request to interrogate prospective jurors about racial prejudice when the accused and the victim are of different racial or ethnic backgrounds. The Court limited *Aldridge* to the exercise of supervisory power over lower federal courts[74] and limited *Ham* to the circumstances of that case (a special showing by the defense of a signicant likelihood of racial prejudice). Thus, under the *Ross* holding, a constitutional claim can be sustained only in those situations where a racial issue is a part of the background of a case.

Ross should be read in light of two other Supreme Court rulings. In another part of *Ham*, the Court sustained the trial judge's refusal to inquire about prejudice against people who wear beards, noting that it was impossible to constitutionally distinguish between possible prejudice against people who wear beards and a host of similar prejudices.[75] In 1974, the year following *Ham*, the Court also refused to sustain a claim in a federal obscenity prosecution that the defense was entitled to have prospective jurors examined about the potential effect of religious, political, and educational biases.[76]

Certainly we can agree that a voir dire should not become a protracted examination aimed at uncovering every possible unconscious antipathy. As

Judge Learned Hand once remarked, "If trial by jury is not to break down by its own weight, it is not feasible to probe more than the upper levels of a juror's mind."[77] But at least as important as saving time is the need for an impartial jury. [78] Impartial juries are not likely to be impaneled if the defense is precluded from asking probing questions aimed at uncovering a predisposition by potential jurors to side with authority.[79] Implied bias should at least be allowed to surface during the voir dire so that the examining judge can determine whether a potential juror could, in the face of implied bias, nonetheless faithfully discharge the duty of an impartial juror.

JURY SIZE

Until 1970 it was settled law that the Sixth Amendment meant a jury of twelve —no more, no less.[80] There is no precise date at which English common law came to require twelve jurors, nor is it certain why that number was finally settled on.[81] But it is certain that by the early fifteenth century, the number had been fixed at twelve; and there is no doubt when article III was written and Amendment Six proposed that a federal jury was thought of as a common-law jury of twelve. Indeed, the Judiciary Act of 1789 so provided, and it is still a requirement in federal criminal trials to this day.[82] In 1970, in *Williams v. Florida*, however, the twelve-juror requirement lost its assumed constitutional status.[83]

Williams had been tried in a felony case by a six-person jury as provided by Florida in all noncapital cases. Because in 1968 the Court had held that the states were bound by the jury requirement of the Sixth Amendment,[84] the question arose whether that requirement meant a jury of twelve persons. In a holding in which only Justice Marshall dissented, the Court ruled that a twelve-juror panel is not a necessary ingredient of trial by jury: "To read the Sixth Amendment as forever codifying a feature so incidental to the real purpose of the Amendment is to ascribe a blind formalism to the Framers which would require considerably more evidence than we have been able to discover in the history and language of the Constitution or in the reasoning of our past decisions."[85]

Aside from this casual dismissal of a five-hundred-year-old practice, *Williams* has several major weaknesses in its rationale. True, the number twelve has no magic about it. What was presumably wanted, as Sir Patrick Devlin has noted, was a number large enough to create a formidable body of opinion in favor of the side that won.[86] Second, although the Court noted in *Williams* that there were no data to indicate any discernible difference between the results reached by different-sized juries, at least one scholar of the American jury has refuted that claim. Professor Hans Zeisel noted that the jury system is predicated on an insight to human behavior—that people see and evaluate things differently. One function of a jury is to bring divergent perceptions and evaluations into the jury room.[87] "It should not be difficult to see that however well or poorly twelve people may represent a widely stratified community, a six-member jury must do less well."[88]

Indeed, it is simple mathematics that six-member juries are less likely to represent a minority group than are twelve-member juries. If, for example, in a given community there is a minority group representing 10 percent of the population, then on randomly selected juries there will be on the average at least one minority representative, or 72 out of every 100 twelve-member juries, whereas only 47 of every 100 six-member juries will have at least one minority representative.[89] Although a given minority group has no constitutional right to representation on a particular jury, should a society that has had minority problems take a step that reduces minority input into the criminal justice system?[90]

Williams did expressly uphold a six-member criminal jury, but the Court reserved ruling on any number smaller than six. The issue came up again in 1978. In *Ballew v. Georgia,* the petitioner had been charged with misdemeanor violations of Georgia's obscenity law, for which conviction carried a possible twelve-month sentence and/or a fine not in excess of $1,000. Ballew was tried, over his objection, before a five-member jury. In reversing Ballew's conviction, the Court concluded that the purpose and function of a jury in a criminal case are constitutionally impaired by a reduction in size below six members.[91]

THE UNANIMOUS-VERDICT REQUIREMENT

Another feature of the jury system in criminal trials that was until recently considered settled is the requirement of a unanimous verdict. Originally, juries decided disputes by a majority verdict; however, in 1367, it was ruled that a verdict must be unanimous.[92] Early Colonial experience was not uniform on this issue; still, by the eighteenth century, the unanimity rule was accepted in America.[93] It is of course true that the rule, like the twelve-member-jury rule, was not specifically provided for in the Sixth Amendment, but it has been the unbroken practice in all federal trials, civil and criminal, since the beginning of the government, and it is specifically required by the Federal Rules of Criminal Procedure.[94] Furthermore, until 1972, the Supreme Court had consistently recognized the constitutionality of the unanimity rule.[95] As recently as 1948, the Court noted that "unanimity in jury verdicts is required where the Sixth and Seventh Amendments apply. In criminal cases this requirement of unanimity extends to all issues—character or degree of the crime, guilt and punishment—which are left to the jury."[96]

In 1972, in *Apodaca v. Oregon* and *Johnson v. Louisiana,* the Court by narrow margins voted not to apply the unanimity rule to state jury cases and concluded that the rule lacks constitutional stature.[97] Rejecting the historical background of the rule as scanty and inconclusive, the majority upheld the verdicts in which the juries had voted 11 to 1, 10 to 2, and 9 to 3 for conviction. The majority and plurality also rejected the argument of the petitioners that a unanimous verdict in criminal cases is a necessary component of the requirement of guilt beyond a reasonable doubt. Justice White's majority opinion in *Johnson* argued:

> Of course, the State's proof could perhaps be regarded as more certain if it had convinced all 12 jurors instead of only nine; it would have been even more compelling if it had been required to convince and had, in fact, convinced 24 or 36 jurors. But the fact remains that nine jurors—a substantial majority of the jury—were convinced by the evidence. In our view disagreement of three jurors does not alone establish reasonable doubt, particularly when such a heavy majority of the jury, after having considered the dissenters' views, remains convinced of guilt. That rational men disagree is not in itself equivalent to a failure of proof by the State, nor does it indicate infidelity to the reasonable-doubt standard. . . . That want of jury unanimity is not to be equated with the existence of a reasonable doubt emerges even more clearly from the fact that when a jury in a federal court, which operates under the unanimity rule and is instructed to acquit a defendant if it has a reasonable doubt about his guilt . . . cannot agree unanimously upon a verdict, the defendant is not acquitted, but is merely given a new trial. . . . If the doubt of a minority of jurors indicates the existence of a reasonable doubt, it would appear that a defendant should receive a directed verdict of acquittal rather than a retrial.[98]

Contrary to Justice White's argument, there is evidence to suggest that eliminating the unanimity rule allows the prosecution to win the bulk of those cases in which heretofore the prosecution had failed to eliminate reasonable doubt and to convince all of the jurors. About 5 percent of all juries are hung; that is, unable to reach the required unanimity. But the final vote of most hung juries favors the prosecution. Professors Kalven and Zeisel in their study of the jury system in America found that 44 percent of hung juries favored conviction by at least a 9-to-3 vote, whereas only 12 percent favored acquittal by at least a vote of 9 to 3.[99] Not only does the elimination of the unanimity rule give the prosecution the bulk of these cases, but it increases the prospects for conviction in still another way. The Kalven-Zeisel study indicated that in split jury votes, where there was an initial majority favoring either acquittal or conviction, the vast majority (105 of 146 cases) favored conviction. The study also indicated that in approximately 10 percent of the cases the initial dissenting minority was able to persuade the proconviction majority to change its mind. Thus, under the unanimity requirement, the prosecution would lose more cases than it could gain by allowing debate to continue.[100]

If we are able to generalize about American juries on the basis of Kalven and Zeisel's data, it is difficult to disagree with Justice Douglas's dissent in *Johnson*—that by abandoning the unanimity requirement, the Court has reduced the reliability of jury verdicts.[101] "The diminution of verdict reliability flows from the fact that nonunanimous juries need not debate and deliberate as fully as must unanimous juries. As soon as the requisite majority is attained, further consideration is not required . . . even though the dissident jurors might, if given the chance, be able to convince the majority."[102]

Whatever the origins of the unanimity requirement, it has long been justified because it supports the requirement of guilt beyond a reasonable doubt.[103] By whatever standard we use to measure doubt, it seems clear that a unanimous verdict reflects less doubt than does a 9-to-3 or an 8-to-4 verdict. Of course, our greater confidence in larger numbers, particularly in unanimity, is at once an affirmation of faith and a statement of principle. Those who continue to believe in the unanimity rule are not living in some historical scrap heap, but are simply reaffirming that a democratic society is not prepared to surrender the liberty of an individual to the state unless the state has been successful in dispelling the reasonable doubts of all of those chosen to decide a factual dispute.

JURY NULLIFICATION

Lord Coke's maxim that judges do not answer questions of fact and juries do not answer questions of law[104] presumably delineates the responsibilities and authority of judges and juries. A jury, operating under the supervision and instructions of a judge, is the sole determiner of the factual questions at issue between the defendant and the state, and enjoys complete freedom to decide the factual dispute without fear of judicial reprisal.[105] But Lord Coke's maxim does not answer the question of whether a jury is bound by the evidence presented and the judge's instructions. Does a jury have the power to nullify the law and to ignore the facts? In the words of Justice Holmes, criminal juries do have "the power to bring in a verdict in the teeth of both law and facts,"[106] and occasionally that is just what a jury does, particularly in a situation where it concludes that equity requires a verdict contrary to law and facts.[107] Does this mean, then, that a jury should be instructed that it is free to disregard the law and the facts? No. The weight of judicial opinion denies a defendant the right to have a jury instructed that it is free to nullify the judge's instructions on the applicable law.

In *Sparf v United States* (1895), Sparf was convicted of murder.[108] At his trial, he requested the judge to instruct the jury that under the indictment the defendant could be convicted of either murder or manslaughter or an attempt to commit either offense. The trial judge rejected Sparf's request and instead instructed the jury that under federal law there were two kinds of felonious homicide—murder and manslaughter. He defined murder for the jury and also briefly defined manslaughter, but then went on to say: "I do not consider it necessary, gentlemen, to explain further, for if a felonious homicide has been committed, of which you are to be the judges from the proof, there is nothing in this case to reduce it below the grade of murder. In other words, it may be in the power of the jury . . . of finding defendant guilty of a less crime than murder, to wit, manslaughter; yet, as I have said . . . if a felonious homicide has been committed at all, of which, I repeat you are the judges, there is nothing to reduce it below the grade of murder."[109] In short, the judge told the jury that because of the absence of any evidence to support manslaughter, it could not consistent with the law return a verdict that Sparf was guilty of manslaughter. In upholding this instruction, the Supreme Court reasoned:

> Public and private safety alike would be in peril, if the principle be established that juries in criminal cases may, of right, disregard the law as expounded to them by the court and become a law unto themselves. Under such a system, the principal function of the judge would be to preside and keep order while jury-men, untrained in the law, would determine questions affecting life, liberty, or property according to such legal principles as in their judgment were applicable to the particular case being tried. If because, generally speaking, it is the function of the jury to determine the guilt or innocence of the accused according to the evidence, of the truth or weight of which they are to judge, the court should be held bound to instruct them upon a point in respect to which there was no evidence whatever, or to forbear stating what the law is upon a given state of facts, the result would be that the enforcement of the law against criminals and the protection of citizens against unjust and groundless prosecutions would depend entirely upon juries uncontrolled by any settled, fixed, legal principles. . . . Upon the court rests the responsibility of declaring the law; upon the jury, the responsibility of applying the law so declared to the facts as they, upon their conscience, believe them to be.[110]

Although there have been notable instances in Anglo-American history where juries have defied instructions and disregarded uncontradicted evidence,[111] the explicit avowal of the right of jury nullification may, in the words of Judge Harold Leventhal, "risk the ultimate logic of anarchy."[112] In a case arising out of an antiwar demonstration in the offices of the Dow Chemical Company, the defendants requested that the trial judge instruct the jury that it could disregard his instructions. The judge refused to instruct the jury that "moral compulsion" or "choice of the lesser evil" constituted a legal defense. In upholding the judge's refusal, Judge Leventhal cautioned:

> What makes for health as an occasional medicine would be disastrous as a daily diet. The fact that there is widespread existence of the jury's prerogative, and approval of its existence as a "necessary counter to case-hardened judges and arbitrary prosecutors," does not establish as an imperative that the jury must be informed by the judge of that power. On the contrary, it is pragmatically useful to structure instructions in such wise that the jury must feel strongly about the values involved in the case, so strongly that it must itself identify the case as establishing a call of high conscience, and must independently initiate and undertake an act in contravention of the established instructions.[113]

We might counter this argument, as did Judge Bazelon's dissent, with the proposition that a positive instruction on nullification is needed in order for a jury, as the embodiment of the conscience of the community, to determine whether a defendant, regardless of his or her conduct, is blameworthy. Although blameworthiness, or mental culpability, ought to be a restraining principle of the criminal law,[114] its elusive character would seem to require certain previously articulated boundaries, among them the law of excuses. To suggest, as Judge Bazelon appears to have done, that blameworthiness is an entirely open-ended question comes close to proposing that every criminal jury become a minilegislature, free to revise the criminal law at will.

CONCLUSION

The widespread attacks on the jury in civil cases may well have had some spillover into the criminal area, with a consequent undermining of legislative and judicial confidence in criminal juries. It is difficult not to conclude that the attacks on the twelve-member jury and the unanimity principle are based on certain negative conclusions about juries and certain positive ones about judges. The jury system has been attacked as wasteful, expensive, slow, and frequently unable or unwilling to follow and comprehend subtle legal arguments. Contrary to being the embodiment of the collective wisdom of the community, the jury is said to be twelve people of average ignorance.[115] Yet juries, by providing popular participation in the criminal process, introduce an important check on the power of the state. Indeed, there are data from Kalven and Zeisel's study that indicate that juries are not unable to comprehend the evidence and are not more gullible than judges.[116] Furthermore, the study found that generally juries are more faithful to the standard of guilt beyond a reasonable doubt than are judges.[117] The bitter irony of this scholarly study— by far the most elaborate and sophisticated study ever undertaken of the jury system—is that it did not renew the confidence of the Supreme Court in the criminal jury.

We need not have blind faith in the jury system simply because it is an institution that has existed for several hundred years. Certainly we can question its deliberative process and the problems inherent in the cross-sectional requirement and the area of pretrial publicity. But encroachments on the criminal jury system should receive skeptical and cautious review. Blackstone's ringing words may be more of an appeal to faith than to reason, but students of constitutional government can still, after two hundred years, benefit by reading his defense of the jury:

> So that the liberties of England cannot but subsist so long as this *palladium* remains sacred and inviolate; not only from all open attacks (which none will be so hardy as to make) but also from all secret machinations, which may sap and undermine it; by introducing new and arbitrary methods of trial, by

justices of the peace, commissioners of the revenue, and courts of conscience. And however *convenient* these may appear at first (as doubtless all arbitrary powers, well executed, are the most *convenient*) yet let it be again remembered, that delays and little inconveniences in the forms of justice, are the price that all free nations must pay for their liberty in more substantial matters; that these inroads upon this sacred bulwark of the nation are fundamentally opposite to the spirit of our constitution; and that though begun in trifles, the precedent may gradually increase and spread, to the utter disuse of juries in questions of the most momentous concern.[118]

NOTES

1. William Holdsworth, *A History of English Law* (London: Methuen, 1938), vol. 1, pp. 312–350.

2. This was the infamous treatment of *peine forte et dure,* forced on one who stood mute and refused to plead—who, in effect, refused to "submit himself to his country"; see ibid. at 326–327.

3. Ibid. at 325–326, 340.

4. *Trial by witnesses* was a method whereby each disputant produced a band of witnesses who swore to the truth of their principal's tale. Similarly, in *compurgation,* a defendant produced a required number of compurgators to swear by a fixed form of words to the truth of their principal's assertions. See ibid. at 302–308.

5. *Trial by battle,* which was introduced by the Normans, was not used when the Crown was a party; its use was limited to "appeals" (private criminal accusations).

6. James Fitzjames Stephen, *A History of the Criminal Law in England* (London: Macmillan, 1883), vol. 1, pp. 259–260.

7. Penn and his religious followers had been excluded from their regular place of worship and thereafter held a street meeting.

8. *The Trial of Penn and Mead,* 6 How. St. Tr. 951, 963–967 (1670).

9. *Bushell's Case,* 6 How. St. Tr. 999 (1670).

10. Richard Perry and John Cooper, eds., *Sources of Our Liberties* (Chicago: American Bar Foundation, 1959), p. 217.

11. E.g., 1641, Massachusetts Body of Liberties, § 29; and 1677, Concessions and Agreements of West New Jersey, chap. 17, quoted in *Sources of Our Liberties,* ed. Perry and Cooper, pp. 146 and 182.

12. See Harold Hyman and Catherine Tarrant, "Aspects of American Trial Jury History," in *The Jury System in America,* ed. Rita Simon (Beverly Hills: Sage, 1975), pp. 23–40.

13. "Declaration of the Causes and Necessity of Taking Up Arms," quoted in *Sources of Our Liberties,* ed. Perry and Cooper, p. 295.

14. See Francis Heller, *The Sixth Amendment to the Constitution* (Lawrence: University of Kansas Press, 1951), pp. 22–24.

15. Ibid. at 25. There was also opposition to the absence of any protection of trial by jury in federal civil cases; see Alexander Hamilton, *Federalist Papers* No. 83.

16. Juvenile proceedings, even though they may result in detention longer than one year, are not considered criminal prosecutions that require trial by jury; *McKeiver v. Pennsylvania,* 403 U.S. 528 (1970).

17. See generally Felix Frankfurter and Thomas Corcoran, "Petty Federal Offenses and the Constitutional Guaranty of Trial by Jury," 39 *Harv. L. Rev.* 917 (1926). Cf. George Kaye, "Petty Offenders Have No Peers," 26 *U. Chi. L. Rev.* 245 (1959).

18. *Callan v. Wilson,* 127 U.S. 540, 549–552 (1888).
19. *Schick v. United States,* 195 U.S. 65 (1904).
20. 24 Stat 209, chap. 840 (1886).
21. *District of Columbia v. Colts,* 282 U.S. 63 (1930).
22. Ibid. at 73.
23. *District of Columbia v. Clawans,* 300 U.S. 617 (1937).
24. *Duncan v. Louisiana,* 391 U.S. 145, 162 (1968).
25. 18 U.S.C. § 1 (3).
26. *Baldwin v. New York,* 399 U.S. 66 (1970).
27. Ibid. at 73–74. It should be noted that in 1970 five states did deny trial by jury in certain misdemeanor cases carrying a potential sentence of up to one year in jail, but that all such trials were subject to trial *de novo* before a common-law jury; see the appendix to the dissent of Justice Harlan, ibid. at 141 (1970).
28. *Bloom v. Illinois,* 391 U.S. 194 (1968). Two years previously, the Court had ruled that a six months' sentence for criminal contempt was not subject to the requirement, *Cheff v. Schnackenberg,* 384 U.S. 373 (1966).
29. *Frank v. United States,* 395 U.S. 147 (1969).
30. *Taylor v. Hayes,* 418 U.S. 488 (1974).
31. *Codispoti v. Pennsylvania,* 418 U.S. 506 (1974).
32. *Muniz v. Hoffman,* 422 U.S. 454, 477 (1975).
33. *Patton v. United States,* 281 U.S. 276, 312 (1930).
34. *Singer v. United States,* 380 U.S. 24, 36 (1965).
35. E.g., *Iowa v. Volk,* 220 N.W.2d 607 (1974).
36. *Thiel v. Southern Pacific Co.,* 328 U.S. 217 (1946).
37. Ibid. at 220. Cf. *Fay v. New York,* 332 U.S. 261 (1947).
38. *Hamling v. United States,* 418 U.S. 87, 138 (1974).
39. *Strauder v. West Virginia,* 100 U.S. 303 (1880). See also *Peters v. Kiff,* 407 U.S. 493 (1972), where the Court held that a white defendant had standing to challenge exclusions of blacks from grand jury lists that indicted him.
40. *Smith v. Texas,* 311 U.S. 128, 130 (1940).
41. 18 Stat. 336 (1875); and 18 U.S.C. 243.
42. *Brownfield v. South Carolina,* 189 U.S. 426 (1903); and *Tarrance v. Florida,* 188 U.S. 519 (1903).
43. *Eubanks v. Louisiana,* 356 U.S. 584 (1958).
44. *Swain v. Alabama,* 380 U.S. 202, 208 (1965).
45. *Hernandez v. Texas,* 347 U.S. 475 (1954).
46. Ibid. at 478.
47. *Swain v. Alabama,* 380 U.S. at 205.
48. *Hamling v. United States,* 418 U.S. at 137. See also *United States v. Ross,* 468 F.2d 1213 (1972), where the Ninth Circuit disallowed a claim of underrepresentation of persons between twenty-one and twenty-four years of age.
49. 28 U.S.C. 1861.
50. *United States v. McDaniels,* 370 F. Supp. 298. (1973).
51. *Taylor v. Louisiana,* 419 U.S. 522; 530–538 (1975); see *Duren v. Missouri,* ___ U.S. ___ (1979), where the Supreme Court extended the *Taylor* ruling to include jury selection procedures that allowed women to request an exemption.
52. 33 Edw. 1, st. 4. See Stephen, *History of Criminal Law,* vol. 1, pp. 301–303.
53. Fed. Rules Crim. Proc., rule 24(a). In offenses involving a punishment of not more than one year in prison, each side has three peremptory challenges.
54. See *Swain v. Alabama,* 380 U.S. at 217, n. 20.
55. *Stilson v. United States,* 250 U.S. 583, 586 (1919).
56. *Lewis v. United States,* 146 U.S. 370, 376 (1892); and see *Swain v. Alabama.*
57. *Witherspoon v. Illinois,* 391 U.S. 510, 514 (1968).

58. Ibid. at 521.

59. Ibid. at 522. For a list of the majority's qualifications, see p. 522, n. 21. For subsequent decisions on death-qualified juries, see *Boulden v. Holman*, 394 U.S. 478 (1969), and *Maxwell v. Bishop*, 398 U.S. 262 (1970).

60. *Witherspoon v. Illinois*, 391 U.S. at 531.

61. Lord Coke quoted in *Irvin v. Dowd*, 366 U.S. 717, 722 (1961).

62. Ibid. at 727–728.

63. Ibid. at 722–723.

64. E.g., *New Hampshire v. Laaman*, 331 A.2d 354 (1974).

65. *Murphy v. Florida*, 421 U.S. 794 (1975). Claims of denial of a fair trial based on an inherently prejudiced trial atmosphere are treated below, pp. 394–397.

66. The system of peremptory strikes is an alternative to the peremptory challenge and is used in a number of jurisdictions; see *Swain v. Alabama* 380 U.S. at 216–218.

67. *Lewis v. United States*, 146 U.S. at 376.

68. E.g., *Miles v. United States*, 103 U.S. 304 (1881), a challenge for actual bias on grounds of religion; and *Aldridge v. United States*, 283 U.S. 308 (1931).

69. *Swain v. Alabama*, 380 U.S. at 222.

70. Ibid. at 223–224.

71. *Aldridge v. United States*, 283 U.S. at 310.

72. *Ham v. South Carolina*, 409 U.S. 524 (1973).

73. *Restaino v. Ross*, 424 U.S. 589 (1976).

74. The majority acknowledged that had Ross been a federal defendant, his request would have been honored under *Aldridge;* ibid. at 1022, n. 9.

75. *Ham v. South Carolina*, 409 U.S. at 528.

76. *Hamling v. United States*, 418 U.S. at 139–140. See also *Connors v. United States*, 158 U.S. 408, 412 (1895), disallowing inquiry as to political affiliations.

77. *United States v. Dennis*, 183 F.2d 201, 206 (1951).

78. See Levit, "Expediting Voir Dire: An Empirical Study," 44 *So. Calif. L. Rev.* 916 (1971).

79. See Michael Fried et al., "Juror Selection: An Analysis of Voir Dire," in *Jury System in America*, ed. Simon, chap. 2.

80. *Thompson v. Utah*, 170 U.S. 343 (1898).

81. Stephen, *History of Criminal Law*, vol. 1, p. 257; and Holdsworth, *History of English Law*, vol. 1, p. 325.

82. Act of September 24, 1789, 1 Stat. 88; and Fed. Rules Crim. Proc., 230(b).

83. *Williams v. Florida*, 399 U.S. 78 (1970).

84. *Duncan v. Louisiana*.

85. *Williams v. Florida*, 399 U.S. at 102–103.

86. Sir Patrick Devlin, *Trial by Jury* (London: Stevens, 1956), p. 8.

87. Hans Zeisel, "The Waning of the American Jury," 58 *A.B.A.J.* 367, 368 (1972); and see Hans Zeisel and S. S. Diamond, "Convincing Empirical Evidence on the Six-Member Jury," 41 *U. Chi. L. Rev.* 281 (1974).

88. Zeisel, "Waning," p. 368.

89. Id.

90. At the time of *Williams*, five states (Florida, Utah, Louisiana, Texas, and South Carolina) used juries of less than twelve in noncapital felony cases, and an additional eight states used six-member panels in misdemeanor cases. See the dissent of Justice Harlan, *Baldwin v. New York*, 399 U.S. at 138 (1970).

91. *Ballew v. Georgia*, 435 U.S. 223 (1978).

92. Holdsworth, *History of English Law*, vol. 1, p. 318.

93. See authorities cited in *Williams v. Florida*, 399 U.S. at 98, n. 45 (1970); and *Apodaca v. Oregon*, 406 U.S. 404, 408, n. 3 (1972).

94. Rule 31(a).

95. E.g., *Maxwell v. Dow.* 176 U.S. 581, 586 (1900); and *Thompson v. Utah*, 170 U.S. at 345.

96. *Andreas v. United States*, 333 U.S. 740, 748 (1948).

97. *Apodaca v. Oregon* and *Johnson v. Louisiana*, 406 U.S. 356 (1972).

98. Ibid. at 362–363.

99. Harry Kalven and Hans Zeisel, *The American Jury* (Chicago: University of Chicago Press, 1966), p. 460.

100. Ibid. at 488, table 139.

101. *Johnson v. Louisiana*, 406 U.S. at 388.

102. Id.

103. Stephen, *History of Criminal Law*, vol. 1, pp. 304–305; in *Burch v. Louisiana*, ___ U.S. ___ (1979), the Court did reject nonunanimous jury decisions in six-member juries, reserving for the future, however, the question of nonunanimous decisions rendered by juries of more than six.

104. *Ad questiones facti non respondent iudices; ad questiones non legis respondent iuratores.* See Holdsworth, *History of English Law*, vol. 1, p. 298.

105. *Bushell's Case*, 6 How. St. Tr. 999 (1670).

106. *Horning v. District of Columbia*, 254 U.S. 135, 138 (1920).

107. For an extensive discussion of jury equity, see "Toward Principles of Jury Equity," 83 *Yale L.J.* 1023 (1974); and Kalven and Zeisel, *American Jury*, chaps. 15–21.

108. *Sparf v. United States*, 156 U.S. 51 (1895).

109. Ibid. at 60.

110. Id.

111. E.g., nineteenth-century acquittals under the federal fugitive-slave laws and English acquittals under harsh laws inflicting capital punishment for well over two hundred offenses.

112. Judge Leventhal in *United States v. Dougherty*, 473 F.2d 1113 (1972).

113. Ibid. at 1136–1137.

114. See Herbert Packer, *The Limits of the Criminal Sanction* (Stanford, Calif.: Stanford University Press, 1968), chap. 5.

115. See Kalven and Ziesel, *American Jury*, chap. 1, for a summary of arguments about the jury system.

116. Ibid. at chaps. 13–15.

117. Ibid. at 181.

118. William Blackstone, *Commentaries on the Laws of England*, Cooley ed. (Chicago: Callaghan, 1884), bk. 4, p. 350.

JUDICIAL DECISIONS

Application to the States:
Duncan v. Louisiana, *391 U.S. 145 (1968)*

Mr. Justice WHITE delivered the opinion of the Court.

Appellant, Gary Duncan, was convicted of simple battery in the Twenty-fifth Judicial District Court of Louisiana. Under Louisiana law simple battery is a misdemeanor, punishable by a maximum of two years' imprisonment and a $300 fine. Appellant sought trial by jury, but because the Louisiana Constitution grants jury trials only in cases in which capital punishment or imprisonment at hard labor may be imposed, the trial judge denied the request. Appellant was convicted and sentenced to serve 60 days in the parish prison and pay a fine of $150. Appellant sought review in the Supreme Court of Louisiana, asserting that the denial of jury trial violated rights guaranteed to him by the United States Constitution. The Supreme Court, finding "no error of law in the ruling complained of," denied appellant a writ of certiorari. . . .

I.

The Fourteenth Amendment denies the States the power to "deprive any person of life, liberty, or property, without due process of law." In resolving conflicting claims concerning the meaning of this spacious language, the Court has looked increasingly to the Bill of Rights for guidance; many of the rights guaranteed by the first eight Amendments to the Constitution have been held to be protected against state action by the Due Process Clause of the Fourteenth Amendment. . . .

The test for determining whether a right extended by the Fifth and Sixth Amendments with respect to federal criminal proceedings is also protected against state action by the Fourteenth Amendment has been phrased in a variety of ways in the opinions of this Court. The question has been asked whether a right is among those " 'fundamental principles of liberty and justice which lie at the base of all our civil and political institutions,' " *Powell v. State of Alabama,* 287 U.S. 45, 67 (1932); whether it is "basic in our system of jurisprudence," *In re Oliver,* 333 U.S. 257, 273 (1948); and whether it is "a fundamental right, essential to a fair trial," *Gideon v. Wainwright,* 372 U.S. 335, 343–344 (1963). The claim before us is that the right to trial by jury guaranteed by the Sixth Amendment meets these tests. The position of Louisiana, on the other hand, is that the Constitution imposes upon the States no duty to give a jury trial in any criminal case, regardless of the seriousness of the crime or the size of the punishment which may be imposed. Because we believe that trial by jury in criminal cases is fundamental to the American scheme of justice, we hold that the Fourteenth Amendment guarantees a right of jury trial in all criminal cases which—were they to be tried in a federal court—would come within the Sixth Amendment's guarantee. Since we consider the appeal before us to be such a case, we hold that the Constitution was violated when appellant's demand for jury trial was refused.

The history of trial by jury in criminal cases has been frequently told. It is sufficient for present purposes to say that by the time our Constitution was written, jury trial in criminal cases had been in existence in England for several centuries and carried impressive credentials traced by many to Magna Carta. Its preservation and proper operation as a protection against arbitrary rule were among the major objectives of the revolutionary settlement which was expressed in the Declaration and Bill of Rights of 1689. . . .

Jury trial came to America with English colonists, and received strong support from them. Royal interference with the jury trial was deeply resented. Among the resolutions adopted by the First Congress of the American Colonies (the Stamp Act Congress) on October 19, 1765—resolutions deemed by their authors to state "the most essential rights and liberties of the colonists"—was the declaration:

> "That trial by jury is the inherent and invaluable right of every British subject in these colonies."

. . . The Declaration of Independence stated solemn objections to the King's making "judges dependent on his will alone, for the tenure of their offices, and the amount and payment of their salaries," to his "depriving us in many cases, of the benefits of Trial by Jury," and to his "transporting us beyond Seas to be tried for pretended offenses." The Constitution itself, in Art. III, § 2, commanded:

> "The Trial of all Crimes, except in Cases of Impeachment, shall be by Jury; and such Trial shall be held in the State where the said Crimes shall have been committed."

. . .

The constitutions adopted by the original States guaranteed jury trial. Also, the constitution of every State entering the Union thereafter in one form or another protected the right to jury trial in criminal cases.

Even such skeletal history is impressive support for considering the right to jury trial in criminal cases to be fundamental to our system of justice, an importance frequently recognized in the opinions of this Court. . . .

Jury trial continues to receive strong support. The laws of every State guarantee a right to jury trial in serious criminal cases; no State has dispensed with it; nor are there significant movements underway to do so. Indeed, the three most recent state constitutional revisions, in Maryland, Michigan, and New York, carefully preserved the right of the accused to have the judgment of a jury when tried for a serious crime.

. . .

The guarantees of jury trial in the Federal and State Constitutions reflect a profound judgment about the way in which law should be enforced and justice administered. A right to jury trial is granted to criminal defendants in order to prevent oppression by the Government. Those who wrote our constitutions knew from history and experience that it was necessary to protect against unfounded criminal charges brought to eliminate enemies and against judges too responsive to the voice of higher authority. The framers of the constitutions strove to create an independent judiciary but insisted upon further protection against arbitrary action. Providing an accused with the right to be tried by a jury of his peers gave him an inestimable safeguard against the corrupt or overzealous prosecutor and against the compliant, biased, or eccentric judge. If the defendant preferred the common-sense judgment of a jury to the more tutored but perhaps less sympathetic reaction of the single judge, he was to have it. Beyond this, the jury trial provisions in the Federal and State Constitutions reflect a fundamental decision about the exercise of official power—a reluctance to entrust plenary powers over the life and liberty of the citizen to one judge or to a group of judges. Fear of unchecked power, so typical of our State and Federal Governments in other respects, found expression in the criminal law in this insistence upon community participation in the determination of guilt or innocence. The deep commitment of the Nation to the right of jury trial in serious criminal cases as a defense against arbitrary law enforcement qualifies for protection under the Due Process Clause of the Fourteenth Amendment, and must therefore be respected by the States.

. . .

II.

Louisiana's final contention is that even if it must grant jury trials in serious criminal cases, the conviction before us is valid and constitutional because here the petitioner was tried for simple battery and was sentenced to only 60 days in the parish prison. We are not persuaded. It is doubtless true that there is a category of petty crimes or offenses which is not subject to the Sixth Amendment jury trial provision and should not be subject to the Fourteenth Amendment jury trial requirement here applied to the States. Crimes carrying possible penalties up to six months do not require a jury trial if they otherwise qualify as petty offenses, *Cheff v. Schnackenberg*, 384 U.S. 373 (1966). But the penalty authorized for a particular crime is of major relevance in determining whether it is serious or not and may in itself, if severe enough, subject the trial to the mandates of the Sixth Amendment. *District of Columbia v. Clawans*, 300 U.S. 617 (1937). The penalty authorized by the law of the locality may be taken "as a gauge of its social and ethical judgments." 300 U.S., at 628, of the crime in question. . . . In the case before us the Legislature of Louisiana has made simple battery a criminal offense punishable by imprisonment for up to two years and a fine. The question, then, is whether a crime carrying such a penalty is an offense which Louisiana may insist on trying without a jury.

We think not. So-called petty offenses were tried without juries both in England and in the Colonies and have always been held to be exempt from the otherwise comprehensive language of the Sixth Amendment's jury trial provisions. There is no substantial evidence that the Framers intended to depart from this established common-law practice, and the possible consequences to defendants from convictions for petty offenses have been thought insufficient to outweigh the benefits to efficient law enforcement and simplified judicial administration resulting from the availability of speedy and inexpensive nonjury adjudications. These same considerations compel the same result under the Fourteenth Amendment. Of course the boundaries of the petty offense category have always been ill-defined, if not ambulatory. In the absence of an explicit constitutional provision, the definitional task necessarily falls on the courts, which must either pass upon the validity of legislative attempts to identify those petty offenses which are exempt from jury trial or, where the legislature has not addressed itself to the problem, themselves face the question in the first instance. In either case it is necessary to draw a line in the spectrum of crime, separating petty from serious infractions. This process, although essential, cannot be wholly satisfactory, for it requires attaching different consequences to events which, when they lie near the line, actually differ very little.

In determining whether the length of the authorized prison term or the seriousness of other punishment is enough in itself to require a jury trial, we are counseled by *District of Columbia v. Clawans*, supra, to refer to objective criteria, chiefly the existing laws and practices in the Nation. In the federal system, petty offenses are defined as those punishable by no more than six months in prison and a $500 fine. In 49 of the 50 States crimes subject to trial without a jury, which occasionally include simple battery, are punishable by no more than one year in jail. Moreover, in the late 18th century in America crimes triable without a jury were for the most part punishable by no more than a six-month prison term, although there appear to have been exceptions to this rule. We need not, however, settle in this case the exact location of the line between petty offenses and serious crimes. It is sufficient for our purposes to hold that a crime punishable by two years in prison is, based on past and contemporary standards in this country, a serious crime and not a petty offense. Consequently, appellant was entitled to a jury trial and it was error to deny it.

The judgment below is reversed and the case is remanded for proceedings not inconsistent with this opinion.

Reversed and remanded.

Serious and Petty Offenses:
Baldwin v. New York, 399 U.S. 66 (1970)

Mr. Justice WHITE announced the judgment of the Court and delivered an opinion in which Mr. Justice BRENNAN and Mr. Justice MARSHALL join.

Appellant was arrested and charged with "jostling"—a Class A misdemeanor in New York, punishable by a maximum term of imprisonment of one year. He was brought to trial in the New York City Criminal Court. Section 40 of the New York City Criminal Court Act declares that all trials in that court shall be without a jury. Appellant's pretrial motion for jury trial was accordingly denied. He was convicted and sentenced to imprisonment for the maximum term. The New York Court of Appeals affirmed the conviction, rejecting appellant's argument that § 40 was unconstitutional insofar as it denied him an opportunity for jury trial. We noted probable jurisdiction. We reverse.

In *Duncan v. Louisiana*, 391 U.S. 145 (1968), we held that the Sixth Amendment, as applied to the States through the Fourteenth, requires that defendants accused of serious crimes be afforded the right to trial by jury. We also reaffirmed the long-established view that so-called "petty offenses" may be tried without a jury. Thus the task before us in this case is the essential if not wholly satisfactory one, see *Duncan,* at 161, of determining the line between "petty" and "serious" for purposes of the Sixth Amendment right to jury trial.

Prior cases in this Court narrow our inquiry and furnish us with the standard to be used in resolving this issue. In deciding whether an offense is "petty," we have sought objective criteria reflecting the seriousness with which society regards the offense, *District of Columbia v. Clawans*, 300 U.S. 617, 628 (1937), and we have found the most relevant such criteria in the severity of the maximum authorized penalty. *Frank v. United States*, 395 U.S. 147, 148 (1969). Applying these guidelines, we have held that a possible six-month penalty is short enough to permit classification of the offense as "petty," *Dyke v. Taylor Implement Mfg. Co.*, 391 U.S.

216, 220 (1968); but that a two-year maximum is sufficiently "serious" to require an opportunity for jury trial, *Duncan v. Louisiana*, supra. The question in this case is whether the possibility of a one-year sentence is enough in itself to require the opportunity for a jury trial. We hold that it is. More specifically, we have concluded that no offense can be deemed "petty" for purposes of the right to trial by jury where imprisonment for more than six months is authorized.

New York has urged us to draw the line between "petty" and "serious" to coincide with the line between misdemeanor and felony. As in most States, the maximum sentence of imprisonment for a misdemeanor in New York is one year, for a felony considerably longer. It is also true that the collateral consequences attaching to a felony conviction are more severe than those attaching to a conviction for a misdemeanor. And, like other States, New York distinguishes between misdemeanors and felonies in determining such things as whether confinement shall be in county or regional jails, rather than state prison, and whether prosecution may proceed by information or complaint, rather than by grand jury indictment. But while these considerations reflect what may readily be admitted—that a felony conviction is more serious than a misdemeanor conviction—they in no way detract from appellant's contention that some misdemeanors are also "serious" offenses. Indeed we long ago declared that the Sixth Amendment right to jury trial "is not to be construed as relating only to felonies, or offences punishable by confinement in the penitentiary. It embraces as well some classes of misdemeanors, the punishment of which involves or may involve the deprivation of the liberty of the citizen." *Callan v. Wilson*, 127 U.S. 540, 549 (1888).

A better guide "in determining whether the length of the authorized prison term or the seriousness of other punishment is enough in itself to require a jury trial" is disclosed by "the existing laws and practices in the Nation." *Duncan v. Louisiana*, supra, 391 U.S. at 161. In the federal system, as we noted in *Duncan*, petty offenses have been defined as those punishable by no more than six months in prison and a $500 fine. And, with a few exceptions, crimes triable without a jury in the American States since the late 18th century were also generally punishable by no more than a six-month prison term. . . . Except for the criminal courts of New York City, every other court in the Nation proceeds under jury trial provisions that reflect this "fundamental decision about the exercise of official power," *Duncan v. Louisiana*, supra, 391 U.S., at 156, when what is at stake is the deprivation of individual liberty for a period exceeding six months. This near-uniform judgment of the Nation furnishes us with the only objective criterion by which a line could ever be drawn—on the basis of the possible penalty alone—between offenses that are and that are not regarded as "serious" for purposes of trial by jury.

Of necessity, the task of drawing a line "requires attaching different consequences to events which, when they lie near the line, actually differ very little." *Duncan v. Louisiana*, supra, at 161. One who is threatened with the possibility of imprisonment for six months may find little difference between the potential consequences that face him, and the consequences that faced appellant here. Indeed, the propect of imprisonment for however short a time will seldom be viewed by the accused as a trivial or "petty" matter and may well result in quite serious repercussions affecting his career and his reputation. Where the accused cannot possibly face more than six months' imprisonment, we have held that these disadvantages, onerous though they may be, may be outweighed by the benefits that result from speedy and inexpensive nonjury adjudications. We cannot, however, conclude that these administrative conveniences, in light of the practices that now exist in every one of the 50 States as well as in the federal courts, can similarly justify denying an accused the important right to trial by jury where the possible penalty exceeds six months' imprisonment. The conviction is

Reversed.

Mr. Chief Justice BURGER, dissenting.

. . .

I find it somewhat disconcerting that with the constant urging to adjust ourselves to being a "pluralistic society"—and I accept this in its broad sense—we find constant pressure to conform to some uniform pattern on the theory that the Constitution commands it. I see no reason why an infinitely complex entity such as New York City should be barred from deciding that misdemeanants can be punished with up to 365 days' confinement without a jury trial while in less urban areas another body politic would fix a six-month maximum for offenses tried without a jury. That the "near-uniform judgment of the Nation" is otherwise than the judgment in some of its parts affords no basis for me to read into the Constitution something not found there. . . .

The Cross-sectional Requirement:
Thiel v. Southern Pacific Company, 328 U.S. 217 (1946)

Mr. Justice MURPHY delivered the opinion of the Court.

Petitioner, a passenger, jumped out of the window of a moving train operated by the respondent, the Southern Pacific Company. He filed a complaint in a California state court to recover damages, alleging that the respondent's agents knew that he was "out of his normal mind" and should not be accepted as a passenger or else should be guarded and that, having accepted him as a passenger, they left him unguarded and failed to stop the train before he finally fell to the ground. . . .

After demanding a jury trial, petitioner moved to strike out the entire jury panel, alleging inter alia that "mostly business executives or those having the employer's viewpoint are purposely selected on said panel, thus giving a majority representation to one class or occupation and discriminating against other occupations and classes, particularly the employees and those in the poorer classes who constitute, by far, the great majority of citizens eligible for jury service." Following a hearing at which testimony was taken, the motion was denied. Petitioner then attempted to withdraw his demand for a jury trial but the respondent refused to consent. A jury of twelve was chosen. Petitioner thereupon challenged these jurors upon the same grounds previously urged in relation to the entire jury panel and upon the further ground that six of the twelve jurors were closely affiliated and connected with the respondent. The court denied this challenge. The trial proceeded and the jury returned a verdict for the respondent.

. . . We brought the case here on certiorari "limited to the question whether petitioner's motion to strike the jury panel was properly denied."

The American tradition of trial by jury, considered in connection with either criminal or civil proceedings, necessarily contemplates an impartial jury drawn from a cross-section of the community. *Smith v. Texas*, 311 US 128, 130. This does not mean, of course, that every jury must contain representatives of all the economic, social, religious, racial, political and geographical groups of the community; frequently such complete representation would be impossible. But it does mean that prospective jurors shall be selected by court officials without systematic and intentional exclusion of any of these groups. Recognition must be given to the fact that those eligible for jury service are to be found in every stratum of society. Jury competence is an individual rather than a group or class matter. That fact lies at the very heart of the jury system. To disregard it is to open the door to class distinctions and discriminations which are abhorrent to the democratic ideals of trial by jury.

The choice of the means by which unlawful distinctions and discriminations are to be avoided rests largely in the sound discretion of the trial courts and their officers. This discretion, of course, must be guided by pertinent statutory provisions. . . .

The undisputed evidence in this case demonstrates a failure to abide by the proper rules and principles of jury selection. Both the clerk of the court and the jury commissioner testified that they deliberately and intentionally excluded from the jury lists all persons who work for a daily wage. They generally used the city directory as the source of names of prospective jurors. In the words of the clerk, "If I see in the directory the name of John Jones and it says he is a longshoreman, I do not put his name in, because I have found by experience that that man will not serve as a juror, and I will not get people who will qualify. The minute that a juror is called into court on a venire and says he is working for $10 a day and cannot afford to work for four, the Judge has never made one of those men serve, and so in order to avoid putting names of people in who I know won't become jurors in the court, won't qualify as jurors in this court, I do leave them out. . . . Where I thought the designation indicated that they were day laborers, I mean they were people who were compensated solely when they were working by the day, I leave them out." The jury commissioner corroborated this testimony, adding that he purposely excluded "all the iron craft, bricklayers, carpenters, and machinists" because in the past "those men came into court and offered that [financial hardship] as an excuse, and the judge usually let them go." The evidence indicated, however, that laborers who were paid weekly or monthly wages were placed on the jury lists, as well as the wives of daily wage earners.

It was further admitted that business men and their wives constituted at least 50% of the jury lists, although both the clerk and the commissioner denied that they consciously chose according to wealth or occupation. Thus the admitted discrimination was limited to those who worked for a daily wage, many of whom might suffer financial loss by serving on juries at the rate of $4 a day and would be excused for that reason.

This exclusion of all those who earn a daily wage cannot be justified by Federal or state law. Certainly nothing in the Federal statutes warrants such an exclusion. And the California statutes are equally devoid of justification for the practice. . . .

Moreover, the general principles underlying proper jury selection clearly outlaw the exclusion practiced in this instance. Jury competence is not limited to those who earn their livelihood on other than a daily basis. One who is paid $3 a day may be as fully competent as one who is paid $30 a week or $300 a month. In other words, the pay period of a particular individual is completely irrelevant to his eligibility and capacity to serve as a juror. Wage earners, including those who are paid by the day, constitute a very substantial portion of the community, a portion that cannot be intentionally and systematically excluded in whole or in part without doing violence to the democratic nature of the jury system. Were we to sanction an exclusion of this nature we would encourage whatever desires those responsible for the selection of jury panels may have to discriminate against persons of low economic and social status. We would breathe life into any latent tendencies to establish the jury as the instrument of the economically and socially privileged. That we refuse to do.

It is clear that a Federal judge would be justified in excusing a daily wage earner for whom jury service would entail an undue financial hardship. But that fact cannot support the complete exclusion of all daily wage earners regardless of whether there is actual hardship involved. Here there was no effort, no intention, to determine in advance which individual members of the daily wage earning class would suffer an undue hardship by serving on a jury at the rate of $4 a day. All were systematically and automatically excluded. In this connection it should be noted that the mere fact that a person earns more than $4 a day would not serve as an excuse. Jury service is a duty as well as a privilege of citizenship; it is a duty that cannot be shirked on a plea of inconvenience or decreased earning power. Only when the financial embarrassment is such as to impose a real burden and hardship does a valid excuse of this nature appear. Thus a blanket exclusion of all daily wage earners, however well-intentioned and however justified by prior actions of trial judges, must be counted among those tendencies which undermine and weaken the institution of jury trial. . . . It is . . . immaterial that the jury which actually decided the factual issue in the case was found to contain at least five members of the laboring class. The evil lies in the admitted wholesale exclusion of a large class of wage earners in disregard of the high standards of jury selection. To reassert those standards, to guard against the subtle undermining of the jury system, requires a new trial by a jury drawn from a panel properly and fairly chosen.

Reversed.

Racial Exclusion:
Alexander v. Louisiana, 405 U.S. 625 (1972)

Mr. Justice WHITE delivered the opinion of the Court.

After a jury trial in the District Court for the Fifteenth Judicial District of Lafayette Parish, Louisiana, petitioner, a Negro, was convicted of rape and sentenced to life imprisonment. His conviction was affirmed on appeal by the Louisiana Supreme Court, and this Court granted certiorari. Prior to trial, petitioner had moved to quash the indictment because (1) Negro citizens were included on the grand jury list and venire in only token numbers, and (2) female citizens were systematically excluded from the grand jury list, venire, and impaneled grand jury. Petitioner therefore argued that the indictment against him was invalid because it was returned by a grand jury impaneled from a venire made up contrary to the requirements of the Equal Protection Clause and the Due Process Clause of the Fourteenth Amendment. Petitioner's motions were denied.

According to 1960 U.S. census figures admitted into evidence below, Lafayette

Parish contained 44,986 persons over 21 years of age and therefore presumptively eligible for grand jury service; of this total, 9,473 persons (21.06%) were Negro. At the hearing on petitioner's motions to quash the indictment, the evidence revealed that the Lafayette Parish jury commission consisted of five members, all of whom were white, who had been appointed by the court. The commission compiled a list of names from various sources (telephone directory, city directory, voter registration rolls, lists prepared by the school board, and by the jury commissioners themselves) and sent questionnaires to the persons on this list to determine those qualified for grand jury service. The questionnaire included a space to indicate the race of the recipient. Through this process, 7,374 questionnaires were returned, 1,015 of which (13.76%) were from Negroes, and the jury commissioners attached to each questionnaire an information card designating, among other things, the race of the person, and a white slip indicating simply the name and address of the person. The commissioners then culled out about 5,000 questionnaires, ostensibly on the ground that these persons were not qualified for grand jury service or were exempted under state law. The remaining 2,000 sets of papers were placed on a table, and the papers of 400 persons were selected, purportedly at random, and placed in a box from which the grand jury panels of 20 for Lafayette Parish were drawn. Twenty-seven of the persons thus selected were Negro (6.75%). On petitioner's grand jury venire, one of the 20 persons drawn was Negro (5%), but none of the 12 persons on the grand jury that indicted him, drawn from this 20, was Negro.

I

For over 90 years, it has been established that a criminal conviction of a Negro cannot stand under the Equal Protection Clause of the Fourteenth Amendment if it is based on an indictment of a grand jury from which Negroes were excluded by reason of their race. *Strauder v. West Virginia,* 100 U.S. 303 (1880). Although a defendant has no right to demand that members of his race be included on the grand jury that indicts him, *Virginia v. Rives,* 100 U.S. 313 (1880), he is entitled to require that the State not deliberately and systematically deny to members of his race the right to participate as jurors in the administration of justice. *Ex parte Virginia,* 100 U.S. 339 (1880). It is only the application of these settled principles that is at issue here.

This is not a case where it is claimed that there have been no Negroes called for service. . . . Rather, petitioner argues that, in his case, there has been a consistent process of progressive and disproportionate reduction of the number of Negroes eligible to serve on the grand jury at each stage of the selection process until ultimately an all-white grand jury was selected to indict him.

In Lafayette Parish, 21% of the population was Negro and 21 or over, therefore presumptively eligible for grand jury service. Use of questionnaires by the jury commissioners created a pool of possible grand jurors which was 14% Negro, a reduction by one-third of possible black grand jurors. The commissioners then twice culled this group to create a list of 400 prospective jurors, 7% of whom were Negro—a further reduction by one-half. The percentage dropped to 5% on petitioner's grand jury venire and to zero on the grand jury that actually indicted him. Against this background, petitioner argues that the substantial disparity between the proportion of blacks chosen for jury duty and the proportion of blacks in the eligible population raises a strong inference that racial discrimination and not chance has produced this result because elementary principles of probability make it extremely unlikely that a random selection process would at each stage, have so consistently reduced the number of Negroes.

This Court has never announced mathematical standards for the demonstration of "systematic" exclusion of blacks but has, rather, emphasized that a factual inquiry is necessary in each case that takes into account all possible explanatory factors. The progressive decimation of potential Negro grand jurors is indeed striking here, but we do not rest our conclusion that petitioner has demonstrated a prima facie case of invidious racial discrimination on statistical improbability alone, for the selection procedures themselves were not racially neutral. The racial designation on both the questionnaire and the information card provided a clear and easy opportunity for racial discrimination. At two crucial steps in the selection process, when the number of returned questionnaires was reduced to 2,000 and when the final selection of the 400 names was made, these racial identifications were visible on the forms used by the jury commissioners, although there is no evidence that the commissioners consciously selected by race. The situation here is thus similar to *Avery v. Georgia*, 345 U.S. 559 (1953), where the Court sustained a challenge to an array of petit jurors in which the names of prospective jurors had been selected from segregated tax lists. Juror cards were prepared from these lists, yellow cards being used for Negro citizens and white cards for whites. Cards were drawn by a judge, and there was no evidence of specific discrimination. The Court held that such evidence was unnecessary, however, given the fact that no Negroes had appeared on the final jury: "Obviously that practice makes it easier for those to discriminate who are of a mind to discriminate." 345 U.S., at 562. . . .

Once a prima facie case of invidious discrimination is established, the burden of proof shifts to the State to rebut the presumption of unconstitutional action by showing that permissible racially neutral selection criteria and procedures have produced the monochomatic result. The State has not carried this burden in this case; it has not adequately explained the elimination of Negroes during the process of selecting the grand jury that indicted petitioner. As in *Whitus v. Georgia*, the clerk of the court, who was also a member of the jury commission, testified that no consideration was given to race during the selection procedure. The Court has squarely held, however, that affirmations of good faith in making individual selections are insufficient to dispel a prima facie case of systematic exclusion. "The result bespeaks discrimination, whether or not it was a conscious decision on the part of any individual jury commissioner." *Hernandez v. Texas*, 347 U.S., at 482. The clerk's testimony that the mailing list for questionnaires was compiled from nonracial sources is not, in itself, adequate to meet the State's burden of proof, for the opportunity to discriminate was presented at later stages in the process. The commissioners, in any event, had a duty "not to pursue a course of conduct in the administration of their office which would operate to discriminate in the selection of jurors on racial grounds." *Hill v. Texas*, 316 U.S. 400, 404 (1942). We conclude, therefore, that "the opportunity for discrimination was present and [that it cannot be said] on this record that it was not resorted to by the commissioners." *Whitus v. Georgia*, supra, 385 U.S., at 552.

. . .

Reversed.

The Exclusion of Women:
Taylor v. Louisiana, *419 U.S. 522 (1975)*

Mr. Justice WHITE delivered the opinion of the Court.

When this case was tried, Art. VII, § 41, of the Louisiana Constitution, and Art. 402 of the Louisiana Code of Criminal Procedure provided that a woman should not be selected for jury service unless she had previously filed a written declaration of her desire to be subject to jury service. The constitutionality of these provisions is the issue in this case.

I

Appellant, Billy J. Taylor, was indicted by the grand jury of St. Tammany Parish, in the Twenty-second Judicial District of Louisiana, for aggravated kidnaping. On April 12, 1972, appellant moved the trial court to quash the petit jury venire drawn for the special criminal term beginning with his trial the following day. Appellant alleged that women were systematically excluded from the venire and that he would therefore be deprived of what he claimed to be his federal constitutional right to "a fair trial by jury of a representative segment of the community. . . ."

The Twenty-second Judicial District comprises the parishes of St. Tammany and Washington. The appellee has stipulated that 53% of the persons eligible for jury service in these parishes were female, and that no more than 10% of the persons on the jury wheel in St. Tammany Parish were women. During the period from December 8, 1971, to November 3, 1972, 12 females were among the 1,800 persons drawn to fill petit jury venires in St. Tammany Parish. It was also stipulated that the discrepancy between females eligible for jury service and those actually included in the venire was the result of the operation of La. Const., Art. VII, § 41, and La. Code Crim. Proc., Art. 402. In the present case, a venire totaling 175 persons was drawn for jury service beginning April 13, 1972. There were no females on the venire.

Appellant's motion to quash the venire was denied that same day. After being tried, convicted, and sentenced to death, appellant sought review in the Supreme Court of Louisiana, where he renewed his claim that the petit jury venire should have been quashed. The Supreme Court of Louisiana, recognizing that this claim drew into question the constitutionality of the provisions of the Louisiana Constitution and Code of Criminal Procedure dealing with the service of women on juries, squarely held, one justice dissenting, that these provisions were valid and not unconstitutional under federal law. 282 So.2d 491, 497 (1973).

Appellant appealed from that decision to this Court. We noted probable jurisdiction, 415 U.S. 911 (1974), to consider whether the Louisiana jury-selection system deprived appellant of his Sixth and Fourteenth Amendment right to an impartial jury trial. We hold that it did and that these Amendments were violated in this case by the operation of La. Const., Art. VII, § 41, and La. Code Crim. Proc., Art. 402. In consequence, appellant's conviction must be reversed.

II

The Louisiana jury-selection system does not disqualify women from jury service, but in operation its conceded systematic impact is that only a very few women, grossly disproportionate to the number of eligible women in the community, are called for jury service. In this case, no women were on the venire from which the petit jury was drawn. The issue we have, therefore, is whether a jury-selection system which operates to exclude from jury service an identifiable class of citizens constituting 53% of eligible jurors in the community comports with the Sixth and Fourteenth Amendments.

. . .

III

. . . Our inquiry is whether the presence of a fair cross section of the community on venires, panels, or lists from which petit juries are drawn is essential to the fulfillment of the Sixth Amendment's guarantee of an impartial jury trial in criminal prosecutions.

. . .

The unmistakable import of this Court's opinions, at least since 1940, *Smith v. Texas*, supra, and not repudiated by intervening decisions, is that the selection of a petit jury from a representative cross section of the community is an essential component of the Sixth Amendment right to a jury trial. . . .

We accept the fair-cross-section requirement as fundamental to the jury trial guaranteed by the Sixth Amendment and are convinced that the requirement has solid foundation. The purpose of a jury is to guard against the exercise of arbitrary power—to make available the commonsense judgment of the community as a hedge against the overzealous or mistaken prosecutor and in preference to the professional or perhaps overconditioned or biased response of a judge. *Duncan v. Louisiana*, 391 U.S., at 155–156. This prophylactic vehicle is not provided if the jury pool is made up of only special segments of the populace or if large, distinctive groups are excluded from the pool. Community participation in the administration of the criminal law, moreover, is not only consistent with our democratic heritage but is also critical to public confidence in the fairness of the criminal justice system. Restricting jury service to only special groups or excluding identifiable segments playing major roles in the community cannot be squared with the constitutional concept of jury trial. . . .

IV

We are also persuaded that the fair-cross-section requirement is violated by the systematic exclusion of women, who in the judicial district involved here amounted to 53% of the citizens eligible for jury service. This conclusion necessarily entails the judgment that women are sufficiently numerous and distinct from men and that if they are systematically eliminated from jury panels, the Sixth Amendment's fair-cross-section requirement cannot be satisfied. This very matter was debated in *Ballard v. United States*, supra. Positing the fair-cross-section rule—there said to be a statutory one—the Court concluded that the systematic exclusion of women was unacceptable. The dissenting view that an all-male panel drawn from various groups in the community would be as truly representative as if women were included, was firmly rejected:

"The thought is that the factors which tend to influence the action of women are the same as those which influence the action of men—personality, background, economic status—and not sex. Yet it is not enough to say that women when sitting as jurors neither act nor tend to act as a class. Men likewise do not act as a class. But, if the shoe were on the other foot, who would claim that a jury was truly representative of the community if all men were intentionally and systematically excluded from the panel? The truth is that the two sexes are not fungible; a community made up exclusively of one is different from a community composed of both; the subtle interplay of influence one on the other is among the imponderables. To insulate the courtroom from either may not in a given case make an iota of difference. Yet a flavor, a distinct quality is lost if either sex is excluded. The exclusion of one may indeed make the jury less representative of the community than would be true if an economic or racial group were excluded." 329 U.S., at 193–194.

In this respect, we agree with the Court in *Ballard*: If the fair-cross-section rule is to govern the selection of juries, as we have concluded it must, women cannot be systematically excluded from jury panels from which petit juries are drawn. This conclusion is consistent with the current judgment of the country, now evidenced by legislative or constitutional provisions in every State and at the federal level qualifying women for jury service.

V

There remains the argument that women as a class serve a distinctive role in society and that jury service would so substantially interfere with that function that the State has ample justification for excluding women from service unless they volunteer, even though the result is that almost all jurors are men. . . .

The States are free to grant exemptions from jury service to individuals in case of special hardship or incapacity and to those engaged in particular occupations the uninterrupted performance of which is critical to the community's welfare. *Rawlins v. Georgia,* 201 U.S. 638 (1906). It would not appear that such exemptions would pose substantial threats that the remaining pool of jurors would not be representative of the community. A system excluding all women, however, is a wholly different matter. It is untenable to suggest these days that it would be a special hardship for each and every woman to perform jury service or that society cannot spare *any* women from their present duties. This may be the case with many, and it may be burdensome to sort out those who should be exempted from those who should serve. But that task is performed in the case of men, and the administrative convenience in dealing with women as a class is insufficient justification for diluting the quality of community judgment represented by the jury in criminal trials.

. . .

Reversed and remanded.

The Six-person Jury:
Williams v. Florida, 399 U.S. 78 (1970)

Mr. Justice WHITE delivered the opinion of the Court.

. . . Petitioner . . . filed a pretrial motion to impanel a 12-man jury instead of the six-man jury provided by Florida law in all but capital cases. That motion . . . was denied. Petitioner was convicted as charged and was sentenced to life imprisonment. The District Court of Appeal affirmed, rejecting petitioner's claims that his Fifth and Sixth Amendment rights had been violated. We granted certiorari.

. . .

II

In *Duncan v. Louisiana,* 391 U.S. 145 (1968), we held that the Fourteenth Amendment guarantees a right to trial by jury in all criminal cases that—were they to be tried in a federal court—would come within the Sixth Amendment's guarantee. Petitioner's trial for robbery on July 3, 1968, clearly falls within the scope of that holding. See *Baldwin v. New York,* 399 U.S. 66 (1968). The question in this case then is whether the constitutional guarantee of a trial by "jury" necessarily requires trial by exactly 12 persons, rather than some lesser number—in this case six. We hold that the 12-man panel is not a necessary ingredient of "trial by jury," and that respondent's refusal to impanel more than the six members provided for by Florida law did not violate petitioner's Sixth Amendment rights as applied to the States through the Fourteenth.

We had occasion in *Duncan v. Louisiana,* supra, to review briefly the oft-told history of the development of trial by jury in criminal cases. That history revealed a long tradition attaching great importance to the concept of relying on a body of one's peers to determine guilt or innocence as a safeguard against arbitrary law enforcement. That same history, however, affords little insight into the considerations that gradually led the size of that body to be generally fixed at 12. Some have suggested that the number 12 was fixed upon simply because that was the number of the presentment jury from the hundred, from which the petit jury developed. Other, less circular but more fanciful reasons for the number 12 have been given, "but they were all brought forward after the number was fixed," and rest on little more than mystical or superstitious insights into the significance of "12." Lord Coke's explanation that the *"number of twelve* is much respected *in holy writ,* as 12 *apostles,* 12 *stones,* 12 *tribes, etc.,"* is typical. In short, while sometime in the 14th century the size of the jury at common law came to be fixed generally at 12, that particular feature of the jury system appears to have been a historical accident, unrelated to the great purposes which gave rise to the jury in the first place. The question before us is whether this accidental feature of the jury has been immutably codified into our Constitution.

. . .

While "the intent of the Framers" is often an elusive quarry, the relevant constitutional history casts considerable doubt on the easy assumption in our past decisions that if a given feature existed in a jury at common law in 1789, then it was necessarily preserved in the Constitution. Provisions for jury trial were first placed in the Constitution in Article III's provision that "the Trial of all Crimes . . . shall be by Jury; and such Trial shall be held in the State where the said Crimes shall have been committed." The "very scanty history [of this provision] in the records of the Constitutional Convention" sheds little light either way on the intended correlation between Article III's "jury" and the features of the jury at common law. . . .

We do not pretend to be able to divine precisely what the word "jury" imported to the Framers, the First Congress, or the States in 1789. It may well be that the usual expectation was that the jury would consist of 12, and that hence, the most likely conclusion to be drawn is simply that little thought was actually given to the specific question we face today. But there is absolutely no indication in "the intent of the Framers" of an explicit decision to equate the constitutional and common-law characteristics of the jury. Nothing in this history suggests, then, that we do violence to the letter of the Constitution by turning to other than purely historical considerations to determine which features of the jury system, as it existed at common law, were preserved in the Constitution. The relevant inquiry, as we see it, must be the function that the particular feature performs and its relation to the purposes of the jury trial. Measured by this standard, the 12-man requirement cannot be regarded as an indispensable component of the Sixth Amendment.

The purpose of the jury trial, as we noted in *Duncan*, is to prevent oppression by the Government. "Providing an accused with the right to be tried by a jury of his peers gave him an inestimable safeguard against the corrupt or overzealous prosecutor and against the compliant, biased, or eccentric judge." *Duncan v. Louisiana,* supra, 391 U.S., at 156. Given this purpose, the essential feature of a jury obviously lies in the interposition between the accused and his accuser of the commonsense judgment of a group of laymen, and in the community participation and shared responsibility that results from that group's determination of guilt or innocence. The performance of this role is not a function of the particular number of the body that makes up the jury. To be sure, the number should probably be large enough to promote group deliberation, free from outside attempts at intimidation, and to provide a fair possibility for obtaining a representative cross-section of the community. But we find little reason to think that these goals are in any meaningful sense less likely to be achieved when the jury numbers six, than when it numbers 12—particularly if the requirement of unanimity is retained. And, certainly the reliability of the jury as a factfinder hardly seems likely to be a function of its size.

It might be suggested that the 12-man jury gives a defendant a greater advantage since he has more "chances" of finding a juror who will insist on acquittal and thus prevent conviction. But the advantage might just as easily belong to the State, which also needs only one juror out of twelve insisting on guilt to prevent acquittal. What few experiments have occurred—usually in the civil area—indicate that there is no discernible difference between the results reached by the two different-sized juries. In short, neither currently available evidence nor theory suggests that the 12-man jury is necessarily more advantageous to the defendant than a jury composed of fewer members.

Similarly, while in theory the number of viewpoints represented on a randomly selected jury ought to increase as the size of the jury increases, in practice the difference between the 12-man and the six-man jury in terms of the cross-section of the community represented seems likely to be negligible. Even the 12-man jury cannot insure representation of every distinct voice in the community, particularly given the use of the peremptory challenge. As long as arbitrary exclusions of a particular class from the jury rolls are forbidden, see, e.g., *Carter v. Jury Commission,* 396 U.S. 320, 329–330 (1970), the concern that the cross-section will be significantly diminished if the jury is decreased in size from 12 to six seems an unrealistic one.

We conclude, in short, as we began: the fact that the jury at common law was composed of precisely 12 is a historical accident, unnecessary to effect the purposes of the jury system and wholly without significance "except to mystics." *Duncan v. Louisiana,* supra, 391 U.S., at 182 (Harlan, J., dissenting). To read the Sixth Amendment as forever codifying a feature so incidental to the real purpose of the Amendment is to ascribe a blind formalism to the Framers which would require considerably more evidence than we have been able to discover in the history and language of the Constitution or in the reasoning of our past decisions. We do not mean to intimate that legislatures can never have good reasons for concluding that the 12-man jury is preferable to the smaller jury, or that such conclusions—reflected in the provisions of most States and in our federal system—are in any sense unwise. Legislatures may well have their own views about the relative value of the larger and smaller juries, and may conclude that, wholly apart from the jury's primary function, it is desirable to spread the collective responsibility for the determination of guilt among the larger group. In capital cases, for example, it appears that no State provides for less than 12 jurors—a fact that suggests implicit recognition of the value of the larger body as a means of legitimating society's decision to impose the death penalty. Our holding does no more than leave these considerations to Congress and the States, unrestrained by an interpretation of the Sixth Amendment that would forever dictate the precise number that can constitute a jury. Consistent with this holding, we conclude that petitioner's Sixth Amendment rights, as applied to the States through the Fourteenth Amendment, were not violated by Florida's decision to provide a six-man rather than a 12-man jury. The judgment of the Florida District Court of Appeal is

Affirmed.

The Five-person Jury:
Ballew v. Georgia, 435 U.S. 323 (1978)

Mr. Justice BLACKMUN announced the judgment of the Court and delivered an opinion in which Mr. Justice STEVENS joined.

This case presents the issue whether a state criminal trial to a jury of only five persons deprives the accused of the right to trial by jury guaranteed by him by the Sixth and Fourteenth Amendments. Our resolution of the issue requires an application of principles enunciated in *Williams v. Florida,* 399 U.S. 78 (1970), where the use of a six-person jury in a state criminal trial was upheld against similar constitutional attack.

I

In November 1973 petitioner Claude Davis Ballew was the manager of the Paris Art Adult Theatre at 293 Peachtree Street, Atlanta, Ga. On November 9 two investigators from the Fulton County Solicitor General's office viewed at the theater a motion picture film entitled "Behind the Green Door." After they had seen the film, they obtained a warrant for its seizure, returned to the theater, viewed the film once again, and seized it. Petitioner and a cashier were arrested. Investigators returned to the theater on November 26, viewed the film in its entirety, secured still another warrant, and on November 27 once again viewed the motion picture and seized a second copy of the film.

On September 14, 1974, petitioner was charged in a two-count misdemeanor accusation with:

> "distributing obscene materials in violation of Georgia Code Section 26-2101 in that the said accused did, knowing the obscene nature thereof, exhibit a motion picture film entitled 'Behind the Green Door' that contained obscene and indecent scenes. . . ."

Petitioner was brought to trial in the Criminal Court of Fulton County. After a jury of five persons had been selected and sworn, petitioner moved that the court impanel a jury of 12 persons. That court, however, tried its misdemeanor cases before juries of five persons pursuant to Ga. Const., Art. 6, § 16, ¶ 1. . . . Petitioner contended that for an obscenity trial, a jury of only five was constitutionally inadequate to assess the contemporary standards of the community. He also argued that the Sixth and Fourteenth Amendments required a jury of at least six members in criminal cases.

The motion for a 12-person jury was overruled, and the trial went on to its conclusion before the five-person jury that had been impaneled. At the conclusion of the trial, the jury deliberated for 38 minutes and returned a verdict of guilty on both counts of the accusation. The court imposed a sentence of one year and a $1,000 fine on each count, the periods of incarceration to run concurrently and to be suspended upon payment of the fines. After a subsequent hearing, the court denied an amended motion for a new trial.

Petitioner took an appeal to the Court of Appeals of the State of Georgia. . . . The Court of Appeals rejected petitioner's contentions. . . . The Supreme Court of Georgia denied certiorari.

. . .

II

The Fourteenth Amendment guarantees the right of trial by jury in all state non-petty criminal cases. *Duncan v. Louisiana*, 391 U.S. 145, 159–162 (1968). The Court in *Duncan* applied this Sixth Amendment right to the States because "trial by jury in criminal cases is fundamental to the American scheme of justice." Id., at 149. The right attaches in the present case because the maximum penalty for violating § 26–2101, as it existed at the time of the alleged offenses, exceeded six months' imprisonment.

. . .

III

When the Court in *Williams* permitted the reduction in jury size—or, to put it another way, when it held that a jury of six was not unconstitutional—it expressly reserved ruling on the issue whether a number smaller than six passed constitutional scrutiny. The Court refused to speculate when this so-called "slippery slope" would become too steep. We face now, however, the twofold question whether a further reduction in the size of the state criminal trial jury does make the grade too dangerous, that is, whether it inhibits the functioning of the jury as an institution to a significant degree, and, if so, whether any state interest counterbalances and justifies the disruption so as to preserve its constitutionality.

Williams v. Florida and *Colgrove v. Battin,* 413 U.S. 149 (1973) (where the Court held that a jury of six members did not violate the Seventh Amendment right to a jury trial in a civil case), generated a quantity of scholarly work on jury size. These writings do not draw or identify a bright line below which the number of jurors would not be able to function as required by the standards enunciated in *Williams.* On the other hand, they raise significant questions about the wisdom and constitutionality of a reduction below six. We examine these concerns:

First, recent empirical data suggest that progressively smaller juries are less likely to foster effective group deliberation. At some point, this decline leads to inaccurate fact-finding and incorrect application of the common sense of the community to the facts. Generally, a positive correlation exists between group size and both the quality of group performance and group productivity. . . . The smaller the group, the less likely are members to make critical contributions necessary for the solution of a given problem. Because most juries are not permitted to take notes memory is important for accurate jury deliberations. As juries decrease in size, then, they are less likely to have members who remember each of the important pieces of evidence or argument. Furthermore, the smaller the group, the less likely it is to overcome the biases of its members to obtain an accurate result. When individual and group decisionmaking were compared, it was seen that groups performed better because prejudices of individuals were frequently counterbalanced, and objectivity resulted. Groups also exhibited increased motivation and self-criticism. All these advantages, except, perhaps, self-motivation, tend to diminish with group size. . . .

Second, the data now raise doubts about the accuracy of the results achieved by smaller and smaller panels. Statistical studies suggest that the risk of convicting an innocent person (Type I error) rises as the size of the jury diminishes. Because the risk of not convicting a guilty person (Type II error) increases with the size of the panel, an optimal jury size can be selected as a function of the interaction between the two risks. Nagel & Neef concluded that the optimal size, for the purpose of minimizing errors, should vary with the importance attached to the two types of mistakes. After weighing Type I error as 10 times more significant than Type II, perhaps not an unreasonable assumption, they concluded that the optimal jury size was between six and eight. As the size diminished to five and below, the weighted sum of errors increased because of the enlarging risk of the conviction of innocent defendants.

Another doubt about progressively smaller juries arises from the increasing inconsistency that results from the decreases. Saks argued that the "more a jury type fosters consistency, the greater will be the proportion of juries which select the correct (i.e., the same) verdict and the fewer 'errors' will be made." . . .

Third, the data suggest that the verdicts of jury deliberation in criminal cases will vary as juries become smaller, and that the variance amounts to an imbalance to the detriment of one side, the defense. Both Lempert and Zeisel found that the number of hung juries would diminish as the panels decreased in size. Zeisel said that the number would be cut in half—from 5% to 2.4% with a decrease from 12 to six members. Both studies emphasized that juries in criminal cases generally hang with only one, or more likely two jurors remaining unconvinced of guilt. Also, group theory suggests that a person in the minority will adhere to his position more frequently when he has at least one person supporting his argument. . . .

Fourth, what has just been said about the presence of minority viewpoint as juries decrease in size foretells problems not only for jury decisionmaking, but also for the representation of minority groups in the community. The Court repeatedly has held that meaningful community participation cannot be attained with the exclusion of minorities or other identifiable groups from jury service. . . . The exclusion of elements of the community from participation "contravenes the very idea of a jury . . . composed of 'the peers or equals of the person whose rights it is selected or summoned to determine.'" *Carter v. Jury Commission*, 396 U.S. 320, 330 (1970). . . . Although the Court in Williams concluded that the six-person jury did not fail to represent adequately a cross-section of the community, the opportunity for meaningful and appropriate representation does decrease with the size of the panels. . . .

Fifth, several authors have identified in jury research methodological problems tending to mask differences in the operation of smaller and larger juries. For example, because the judicial system handles so many clear cases, decisionmakers will reach similar results through similar analyses most of the time. One study concluded that smaller and larger juries could disagree in their verdicts in no more than 14% of the cases. Disparities, therefore, appear in only small percentages. Nationwide, however, these small percentages will represent a large number of cases. And it is with respect to those cases that the jury trial right has its greatest value. When the case is close, and the guilt or innocence of the defendant is not readily apparent, a properly functioning jury system will insure evaluation by the common sense of the community and will also tend to insure accurate factfinding.

. . .

IV

While we adhere to, and reaffirm our holding in *Williams v. Florida*, these studies, most of which have been made since *Williams* was decided in 1979, lead us to conclude that the purpose and functioning of the jury in a criminal trial is seriously impaired, and to a constitutional degree, by a reduction in size to below six members. We readily admit that we do not pretend to discern a clear line between six members and five. But the assembled data raise substantial doubt about the reliability and appropriate representation of panels smaller than six. Because of the fundamental importance of the jury trial to the American system of criminal justice, any further reduction that promotes inaccurate and possibly biased decisionmaking, that causes untoward differences in verdicts, and that prevents juries from truly representing their communities, attains constitutional significance.

. . .

V

With the reduction in the number of jurors below six creating a substantial threat to Sixth and Fourteenth Amendment guarantees, we must consider whether any interest of the State justifies the reduction. We find no significant state advantage in reducing the number of jurors from six to five.

The States utilize juries of less than 12 primarily for administrative reasons. Savings in court time and in financial costs are claimed to justify the reductions. The financial benefits of the reduction from 12 to six are substantial; this is mainly because fewer jurors draw daily allowances as they hear cases. On the other hand, the asserted saving in judicial time is not so clear. Pabst in his study found little reduction in the time for voir dire with the six-person jury because many questions were directed at the veniremen as a group. Total trial time did not diminish, and court delays and backlogs improved very little. The point that is to be made, of course, is that a reduction in size from six to five or four or even three would save the States little. They could reduce slightly the daily allowances, but with a reduction from six to five the saving would be minimal. If little time is gained by the reduction from 12 to six, less will be gained with a reduction from six to five. Perhaps this explains why only three States, Georgia, Louisiana, and Virginia, have reduced the size of juries in certain nonpetty criminal cases to five. Other States appear content with six members or more. In short the State has offered little or no justification for its reduction to five members.

Petitioner, therefore, has established that his trial on criminal charges before a five-member jury deprived him of the right to trial by jury guaranteed by the Sixth and Fourteenth Amendments.

VI

The judgment of the Court of Appeals is reversed, and the case is remanded for further proceedings not inconsistent with this opinion.

It is so ordered.

Mr. Justice POWELL, with whom THE CHIEF JUSTICE and Mr. Justice REHNQUIST join, concurring in the judgment.

I concur in the judgment, as I agree that use of a jury as small as five members, with authority to convict for serious offenses, involves grave questions of fairness. As the opinion of Mr. Justice Blackmun indicates, the line between five- and six-member juries is difficult to justify, but a line has to be drawn somewhere if the substance of jury trial is to be preserved.

I do not agree, however, that every feature of jury trial practice must be the same in both federal and state courts. . . . Also, I have reservations as to the wisdom—as well as the necessity—of Mr. Justice Blackmun's heavy reliance on numerology derived from statistical studies. . . . The studies relied on merely represent unexamined findings of persons interested in the jury system.

For these reasons I concur only in the judgment.

The End of the Unanimity Rule:
Apodaca v. Oregon, *406 U.S. 404 (1972)*

Mr. Justice WHITE announced the judgment of the Court in an opinion in which THE CHIEF JUSTICE, Mr. Justice BLACKMUN, and Mr. Justice REHNQUIST joined.

Robert Apodaca, Henry Morgan Cooper, Jr., and James Arnold Madden were convicted respectively of assault with a deadly weapon, burglary in a dwelling, and grand larceny before separate Oregon juries, all of which returned less-than-unanimous verdicts. The vote in the cases of Apodaca and Madden was 11–1, while the vote in the case of Cooper was 10–2, the minimum requisite vote under Oregon law for sustaining a conviction. After their convictions had been affirmed by the Oregon Court of Appeals, 1 Or. App. 483, 462 P.2d 691 (1969), and review had been denied by the Supreme Court of Oregon, all three sought review in this Court upon a claim that conviction of crime by a less-than-unanimous jury violates the right to trial by jury in criminal cases specified by the Sixth Amendment and made applicable to the States by the Fourteenth. See *Duncan v. Louisiana*, 391 U.S. 145 (1968). . . .

In *Williams v. Florida*, 399 U.S. 78 (1970), we had occasion to consider a related issue: whether the Sixth Amendment's right to trial by jury requires that all juries consist of 12 men. After considering the history of the 12-man requirement and the functions it performs in contemporary society, we concluded that it was not of constitutional stature. We reach the same conclusion today with regard to the requirement of unanimity.

I

Like the requirement that juries consist of 12 men, the requirement of unanimity arose during the Middle Ages and had become an accepted feature of the common-law jury by the 18th century. But, as we observed in *Williams*, "the relevant constitutional history casts considerable doubt on the easy assumption . . . that if a given feature existed in a jury at common law in 1789, then it was necessarily preserved in the Constitution." Id., at 92–93. The most salient fact in the scanty history of the Sixth Amendment, which we reviewed in full in *Williams*, is that, as it was introduced by James Madison in the House of Representatives, the proposed Amendment provided for trial

> "by an impartial jury of freeholders of the vicinage, with the requisite of unanimity for conviction, of the right of challenge, and other accustomed requisites. . . ." 1 Annals of Cong. 435 (1789).

Although it passed the House with little alteration, this proposal ran into considerable opposition in the Senate, particularly with regard to the vicinage requirement of the House version. The draft of the proposed Amendment was returned to the House in considerably altered form, and a conference committee was appointed. That committee refused to accept not only the original House language but also an alternate suggestion by the House conferees that juries be defined as possessing "the accustomed requisites." Letter from James Madison to Edmund Pendleton, Sept. 23, 1789, in 5 Writings of James Madison 424 (G. Hunt ed. 1904). Instead, the Amendment that ultimately emerged from the committee and then from Congress and the States provided only for trial

> "by an impartial jury of the State and district wherein the crime shall have been committed, which district shall have been previously ascertained by law. . . ."

As we observed in *Williams*, one can draw conflicting inferences from this legislative history. One possible inference is that Congress eliminated references to unanimity and to the other "accustomed requisites" of the jury because those requisites were thought already to be implicit in the very concept of jury. A contrary explanation, which we found in *Williams* to be the more plausible, is that the deletion was intended to have some substantive effect. Surely one fact that is absolutely clear from this history is that, after a proposal had been made to specify precisely which of the common-law requisites of the jury were to be preserved by the Constitution, the Framers explicitly rejected the proposal and instead left such specification to the future. As in *Williams*, we must accordingly consider what is meant by the concept "jury" and determine whether a feature commonly associated with it is constitutionally required. And, as in *Williams*, our inability to divine "the intent of the Framers" when they eliminated references to the "accustomed requisites" requires that in determining what is meant by a jury we must turn to other than purely historical considerations.

II

Our inquiry must focus upon the function served by the jury in contemporary society. As we said in *Duncan*, the purpose of trial by jury is to prevent oppression by the Government by providing a "safeguard against the corrupt or overzealous prosecutor and against the compliant, biased, or eccentric judge." *Duncan v. Louisiana*, 391 U.S., at 156. "Given this purpose, the essential feature of a jury obviously lies in the interposition between the accused and his accuser of the commonsense judgment of a group of laymen. . . ." *Williams v. Florida*, supra, 399 U.S., at 100. A requirement of unanimity, however, does not materially contribute to the exercise of this commonsense judgment. As we said in *Williams*, a jury will come to such a judgment as long as it consists of a group of laymen representative of a cross section of the community who have the duty and the opportunity to deliberate, free from outside attempts at intimidation, on the question of a defendant's guilt. In terms of this function we perceive no difference between juries required to act unanimously and those permitted to convict or acquit by votes of 10 to two or 11 to one. Requiring unanimity would obviously produce hung juries in some situations where nonunanimous juries will convict or acquit. But in either case, the interest of the defendant in having the judgment of his peers interposed between himself and the officers of the State who prosecute and judge him is equally well served.

III

Petitioners nevertheless argue that unanimity serves other purposes constitutionally essential to the continued operation of the jury system. Their principal contention is that a Sixth Amendment "jury trial" made mandatory on the States by virtue of the Due Process Clause of the Fourteenth Amendment, *Duncan v. Louisiana*, supra, should be held to require a unanimous jury verdict in order to give substance to the reasonable-doubt standard otherwise mandated by the Due Process Clause. See *In re Winship*, 397 U.S. 358, 363–364 (1970).

We are quite sure, however, that the Sixth Amendment itself has never been held to require proof beyond a reasonable doubt in criminal cases. The reasonable-doubt standard developed separately from both the jury trial and the unanimous verdict. As the Court noted in the *Winship* case, the rule requiring proof of crime beyond a reasonable doubt did not crystallize in this country until after the Constitution was adopted. And in that case, which held such a burden of proof to be constitutionally required, the Court purported to draw no support from the Sixth Amendment.

Petitioners' argument that the Sixth Amendment requires jury unanimity in order to give effect to the reasonable-doubt standard thus founders on the fact that the Sixth Amendment does not require proof beyond a reasonable doubt at all. The reasonable-doubt argument is rooted, in effect, in due process and has been rejected in *Johnson v. Louisiana*, 406 U.S. 356.

IV

Petitioners also cite quite accurately a long line of decisions of this Court upholding the principle that the Fourteenth Amendment requires jury panels to reflect a cross section of the community. See, e.g., *Whitus v. Georgia*, 385 U.S. 545 (1967). They then contend that unanimity is a necessary precondition for effective application of the cross-section requirement, because a rule permitting less than unanimous verdicts will make it possible for convictions to occur without the acquiescence of minority elements within the community.

There are two flaws in this argument. One is petitioners' assumption that every distinct voice in the community has a right to be represented on every jury and a right to prevent conviction of a defendant in any case. All that the Constitution forbids, however, is systematic exclusion of identifiable segments of the community from jury panels and from the juries ultimately drawn from those panels; a defendant may not, for example, challenge the makeup of a jury merely because no members of his race are on the jury, but must prove that his race has been systematically excluded. No group, in short, has the right to block convictions; it has only the right to participate in the overall legal processes by which criminal guilt and innocence are determined.

We also cannot accept petitioners' second assumption—that minority groups, even when they are represented on a jury, will not adequately represent the viewpoint of those groups simply because they may be outvoted in the final result. They will be present during all deliberations, and their views will be heard. We cannot assume that the majority of the jury will refuse to weigh the evidence and reach a decision upon rational grounds, just as it must now do in order to obtain unanimous verdicts, or that a majority will deprive a man of his liberty on the basis of prejudice when a minority is presenting a reasonable argument in favor of acquittal. We simply find no proof for the notion that a majority will disregard its instructions and cast its votes for guilt or innocence based on prejudice rather than the evidence.

We accordingly affirm the judgment of the Court of Appeals of Oregon.

It is so ordered.

Judgment affirmed.

Six-person Juries and the Unanimity Rule:
Burch v. Louisiana, ＿＿ U.S. ＿＿ (1979)

Mr. Justice REHNQUIST delivered the opinion of the Court.

The Louisiana Constitution and Code of Criminal Procedure provide that criminal cases in which the punishment imposed may be confinement for a period in excess of six months "shall be tried before a jury of six persons, five of whom must concur to render a verdict." We granted certiorari to decide whether conviction by a non-unanimous six-person jury in a state criminal trial for a nonpetty offense as contemplated by these provisions of Louisiana law violates the rights of an accused to trial by jury guaranteed by the Sixth and Fourteenth Amendments.

Petitioners, an individual and a Louisiana corporation, were jointly charged in two counts with the exhibition of two obscene motion pictures. Pursuant to Louisiana law, they were tried before a six-person jury, which found both petitioners guilty as charged. A poll of the jury after verdict indicated that the jury had voted unanimously to convict petitioner Wrestle, Inc. and had voted 5–1 to convict petitioner Burch. Burch was sentenced to two consecutive 7-month prison terms, which were suspended, and fined $1,000; Wrestle, Inc. was fined $600 on each count.

. . .

We agree with the Louisiana Supreme Court that the question presented is a "close" one. Nonetheless, we believe that conviction by a nonunanimous six-member jury in a state criminal trial for a nonpetty offense deprives an accused of his constitutional right to trial by jury.

. . .

Last Term in *Ballew v. Georgia,* 435 U.S. 223 (1978), we considered whether a jury of less than six members passes constitutional scrutiny, a question that was explicitly reserved in *Williams v. Florida.* See 399 U.S., at 91 n. 28. The Court, in separate opinions, held that conviction by a unanimous five-person jury in a trial for a nonpetty offense deprives an accused of his right to trial by jury. While readily admitting that the line between six members and five was not altogether easy to justify, at least five Members of the Court believed that reducing a jury to five persons in nonpetty cases raised sufficiently substantial doubts as to the fairness of the proceeding and proper functioning of the jury to warrant drawing the line at six.

We thus have held that the Constitution permits juries of less than 12 members, but that it requires at least six. *Ballew v. Georgia,* supra; *Williams v. Florida,* supra. And we have approved the use of certain nonunanimous verdicts in cases involving 12-person juries. *Apodaca v. Oregon,* supra (10–2); *Johnson v. Louisiana,* 406 U.S. 356 (1972) (9–3). These principles are not questioned here. Rather, this case lies at the intersection of our decisions concerning jury size and unanimity. As in *Ballew,* we do not pretend the ability to discern a priori a bright line below which the number of jurors participating in the trial or in the verdict would not permit the jury to function in the manner required by our prior cases. But having already departed from the strictly historical requirements of jury trial, it is inevitable that lines must be drawn somewhere if the substance of the jury trial right is to be preserved.

This line drawing process, "although essential, cannot be wholly satisfactory, for it requires attaching different consequences to events which, when they lie near the line, actually differ very little." *Duncan v. Louisiana,* supra, at 161. However, much the same reasons that led us in *Ballew* to decide that use of a five-member jury threatened the fairness of the proceeding and the proper role of the jury, lead us to conclude now that conviction for a nonpetty offense by only five members of a six-person jury presents a similar threat to preservation of the substance of the jury trial guarantee and justifies our requiring verdicts rendered by six-person juries to be unanimous. We are buttressed in this view by the current jury practices of the several States. It appears that of those States that utilize six-member juries in trials of nonpetty offenses, only two, including Louisiana, also allow nonunanimous verdicts. We think that this near-uniform judgment of the Nation provides a useful guide in delimiting the line between those jury practices that are constitutionally permissible and those that are not.

The State seeks to justify its use of nonunanimous six-person juries on the basis of the "considerable time" savings that it claims results from trying cases in this manner. It asserts that under its system, juror deliberation time is shortened and the number of hung juries is reduced. Brief of Respondent 14. Undoubtedly, the State has a substantial interest in reducing the time and expense associated with the administration of its system of criminal justice. But that interest cannot prevail here. First, on this record, any benefits that might accrue by allowing five members of a six-person jury to render a verdict, as compared with requiring unanimity of a six-member jury, are speculative, at best. More importantly, we think that when a State has reduced the size of its juries to the minimum number of jurors permitted by the Constitution, the additional authorization of nonunanimous verdicts by such juries sufficiently threatens the constitutional principles that led to the establishment of the size threshold that any countervailing interest of the State should yield.

The judgment of the Louisiana Supreme Court affirming the conviction of petitioner Burch is, therefore, reversed and its judgment affirming the conviction of petitioner Wrestle, Inc. is affirmed. The case is remanded to the Louisiana Supreme Court for proceedings not inconsistent with this opinion.

It is so ordered.

~§ 11 §~

Trial
Rights

THE TRIAL OF LADY ALICE LISLE

In the summer of 1685, shortly after James II became king, an abortive rebellion known as Monmouth's Insurrection was staged in the southwest of England. In the aftermath of the insurrection, Lord Chief Justice James Jefferys conducted a series of treason trials on the western circuit. History knows these trials as the Bloody Assize. One trial was that of Lady Alice Lisle, on August 27, 1685, in Winchester. Lady Alice was a woman over seventy, who was accused by the Crown of harboring a Monmouth traitor by the name of Hicks. The trial was a series of injustices, not the least of which was Lord Jefferys's notorious conduct toward Lady Alice's friend, the witness James Dunne. No evidence was introduced that Lady Alice knew Hicks to be anything more than a nonconformist parson. Indeed, at the time of Lady Alice's trial, Hicks had not been convicted of any act of rebellion. But with nothing more than hearsay, a brutal cross-examination of Dunne, and several threats to the jury, Jefferys made a quick day of the trial.

CLERK. How sayest thou, Alice Lisle, art thou Guilty of the high-treason contained in this indictment or Not Guilty?

LADY ALICE. Not Guilty.

CLERK. Culprit, by whom wilt thou be tried?

LADY ALICE. By God and my country.

CLERK. God send thee a good deliverance.

. . .

MR. JENNINGS. Swear Mr. James Dunne.

. . .

LORD CHIEF JUSTICE JEFFERYS. Then let my honest man, Mr. Dunne, stand forward a little. Come, friend, you have had some time to recollect yourself; let us see whether we can have the truth out of you now. . . . Come now . . . and tell it us so, that a man may understand and believe that thou dost speak truth. What was that business that my lady asked thee, whether the other man knew; and then you answered her, that he did know nothing of it? [Then he paused a while.] . . . He is studying and musing how he shall prevaricate; but thou hadst better tell the truth, friend. . . .

DUNNE. I cannot give an account of it, my lord.

LORD CHIEF JUSTICE JEFFERYS. Oh blessed God! Was there ever such a villain upon the face of the earth; to what times we are reserved! Dost thou believe that there is a God?

DUNNE. Yes, my lord, I do.

. . .

LORD CHIEF JUSTICE JEFFERYS. Prithee tell us the truth then now. . . .

DUNNE. My lord, I do tell the truth, as far as I can remember.

LORD CHIEF JUSTICE JEFFERYS. I hope, gentlemen of the jury, that you can take notice of the strange and horrible carriage of this fellow; and withal, you cannot but observe the spirit of that sort of people, what a villainous and devilish one it is: good God!

. . .

LORD CHIEF JUSTICE JEFFERYS. Thou wretch! all the mountains and hills in the world heaped upon one another, will not cover thee from the vengeance of the great God for this transgression of false witness-bearing. What hopes can there be for so profligate a villain as thou art, that so impudently stands in open defiance of the omnipresence, omniscience, and justice of God, by persisting in so palpable a lye? I therefore require it of you, in his name, to tell me the truth.

DUNNE. I cannot tell what to say, my lord.

LORD CHIEF JUSTICE JEFFERYS.   Good God! Was there ever such an impudent rascal! Well, I will try once more, and tell thee what I mean; you said you told that honest man (for he truly seems so to be) that my lady asked you whether he knew of the business; and you told her, he did not: prithee be so free as to tell us what that business was?

. . .

DUNNE.   My lord, I told her, he knew nothing of our coming there.

LORD CHIEF JUSTICE JEFFERYS.   . . . but what was the business that thou told'st her he did not know?

DUNNE.   She asked me whether I did not know that Hicks was a nonconformist?

LORD CHIEF JUSTICE JEFFERYS.   Did my lady Lisle ask you that question?

DUNNE.   Yes, my lord; I told her I did not.

LORD CHIEF JUSTICE JEFFERYS.   But that is not my question; what was that business that he did not know?

DUNNE.   It was the same thing: whether Mr. Hicks was a nonconformist.

LORD CHIEF JUSTICE JEFFERYS.   That cannot be all; there must be something more in it.

. . .

LORD CHIEF JUSTICE JEFFERYS.   Why, dost thou think, that after all this pains that I have been at to get an answer to my question, that thou can'st banter me with such sham stuff as this. Hold the candle to his face, that we may see his brazen face.

. . .

DUNNE.   I am quite cluttered out of my senses; I do not know what I say. [A candle being held nearer his nose.]

LORD CHIEF JUSTICE JEFFERYS.   But to tell the truth, would rob thee of none of thy senses, if ever thou hadst any. . . .

. . .

MR. JENNINGS.   My lord, we have done, we have no more witnesses.

LORD CHIEF JUSTICE JEFFERYS.   Then you that are for the prisoner at the bar, now is your time to make your defence. . . . What have you to say for yourself?

LADY ALICE.   My lord, that which I have to say it, is this: I knew of nobody's coming to my house but Mr. Hicks, and for him I was informed that he did abscond, by reason of warrants that were out against him for preaching in private meetings, but I never heard that he was in the army. . . . I did not in the least suspect him to have been in the army, being a Presbyterian minister, that used to preach, and not to fight.

LORD CHIEF JUSTICE JEFFERYS.   But I will tell you, there in no one of those lying, sniveling, canting Presbyterian rascals, but one way or other had a hand in the late horrid conspiracy and rebellion; upon my conscience I believe it, and would have been as deep in the actual rebellion, had it had any little success, as that other fellow Hicks; their principles carry them to it; Presbytery has all manner of villainy in it, nothing but Presbytery could lead that fellow Dunne to tell so many lies as he has here told; for shew me a Presbyterian, and I will engage to shew a lying knave.[1]

The result of the trial was a foregone conclusion: Lady Alice was convicted by the jury after Jefferys threatened it with attaint.[2] Sentence was passed by Jefferys the same day, and she was condemned by the Lord Chief Justice "to be drawn on a hurdle to the place of Execution, where your body is to burnt alive till you be dead."[3] The sentence was to be carried out on September 2, 1685, but Lady Alice petitioned King James, who replied:

Whereas the said Alicia Lisle has humbly petitioned us to alter the manner of the said execution, by causing her head to be severed from her body: We, being graciously pleased to condescend to her request, have thought fit hereby to signify our will and pleasure accordingly. And our further will and pleasure is, that you deliver the head and body to her relations to be privately and decently interred: And for so doing this shall be your warrant.—Given at our court at Windsor, the 31st day of August 1685, in the first year of our reign.[4]

We look back to the trial of Lady Alice, not for antiquarian reasons, but because it offers certain insights into the problems of a criminal trial. In the year 1685 there was no body of law called *evidence*, no hearsay rule, no standard of reasonable doubt, no counsel for the defense, and no right of cross-examination. Judicial neutrality was an ideal, not a reality. The English criminal trial in the late seventeenth century was far from a perfect instrument for the discovery of truth in a criminal accusation, with most advantages resting with the crown's representative. What was missing was not just a set of procedural rules to ensure that truth was not simply in the making of the charge, but, more significantly, those political conditions essential to modern due process: an internally secure state and certain democratic ideals about the state and the individual.

CONTEMPORARY TRIAL RIGHTS

In all criminal prosecutions, the accused shall enjoy the right to a speedy and public trial, by an impartial jury of the State and district wherein the crime shall have been committed, which district shall have been previously ascertained by law, and to be informed of the nature and cause of the accusation; to be confronted with the witnesses against him; to have compulsory process for obtaining witnesses in his favor, and to have the Assistance of Counsel for his defence.

—Sixth Amendment

Criminal trials are tied to a host of procedural rights aimed at ensuring that the results of such trials will be fair and just and as close to the truth as the wit of man can divine. Of course, that these rights exist does not guarantee that trials will be anything more than "solemn pageants."[5] On the other hand, without these basic procedural rights trials could not be fair and results just. Many of these rights are specifically mentioned in the Sixth Amendment; others, long a part of the common law, have been incorporated into the requirements of due process by the courts.

Notice and Certainty of the Charge

Perhaps nothing made the administration of justice more farcical than the excessively technical requirements of eighteenth- and nineteenth-century criminal pleading.[6] Blackstone's list of the requirements of indictments, down to the precise and only acceptable adverbs, has long since passed on to the legal scrap heap.[7] But although many of the technicalities are gone, we retain the fundamental and essential essence of Blackstone's indictment: An accused must be notified of the charge with precision and sufficient certainty.[8]

In 1833, in one of the Supreme Court's earliest statements on notice and certainty of a criminal charge, the Court said: "In all cases the offense must be set forth with clearness, and all necessary certainty, to appraise the accused of the crime with which he stands charged."[9] Over the years, the Court has had numerous opportunities to refine the degree of particularity necessary to a charging document. For example, because most offenses consist of more than one element, the Court has held that a charging document is not sufficient unless it accurately and clearly alleges all of the ingredients of which an offense is composed.[10]

Generally, it is sufficient that a charge sets forth an offense in the words of the statute itself, so long as those words fully, directly, and with certainty describe all of the elements that constitute the offense.[11] But sometimes the statutory language must be accompanied by a statement of the specific facts and circumstances of a particular case: The charge must descend to the particulars.[12] For example, when an offense is defined by a statute in generic terms (a conspiracy to threaten a citizen in the enjoyment of any right or privilege secured by the Constitution),[13] then it must detail the how, when, and where of the specific transgression (a particular citizen was threatened in the enjoyment of a specific right or privilege).[14] Failure to descend to the particulars denies an accused the basic protections of the requirement of notice with reasonable certainty. Fundamentally, it denies the accused an opportunity to know and be prepared to meet the charges.[15] Furthermore, without the particulars, an accused is at a loss in any subsequent proceedings to plead former acquittal or conviction.[16] And, finally, a degree of particularity is necessary so that the trial court knows the alleged facts and can decide whether, as a matter of law, they are sufficient to support a conviction.[17]

A charging document must be sufficiently clear so that a defendant is not misled in preparing a defense, but the Supreme Court has upheld slight variations between an indictment and proof so long as they do not substantially affect the rights of the accused.[18] Of course, it would be a substantial denial of the right of notice to try a defendant on a charge not made in the indictment, and to do so is more than harmless error.[19]

The Supreme Court has never ruled directly on whether the notice and certainty of a charge has been incorporated into the due process requirements of the Fourteenth Amendment. However, the Court has on several occasions indicated by way of dictum that the states are bound by the requirement. In *Twining v. New Jersey* (1908),[20] the majority opinion limited the degree to which federal criminal procedures were incorporated into the due process clause of the Fourteenth Amendment, but even there the Court concluded that due process required sufficient notice.[21] A similar narrow analysis was made by Justice Cardozo in 1934, again with the proviso that "what may not be taken away is notice of the charge."[22] Some years later, in 1948, the Court again observed by way of dictum that "no principle of procedural due process is more clearly established than that notice of the specific charge and a chance to be heard in a trial of the issues raised by that charge, if desired, are among the Constitutional rights of every accused in a criminal proceeding in all courts, state and federal."[23]

Venue

The common law recognized a territorial principle in venue; that is, crime is local and should be punishable at the place where it is committed. This territorial principle is still generally recognized in American law. Venue for a criminal offense normally is before a court of appropriate jurisdiction in the county, city, or other political division where the offense is alleged to have been committed. Strictly speaking, however, there are no constitutional limitations or guarantees in terms of venue, except in regard to the locality from which a jury must be selected: Congress and the states are free to fix venue at any place where the acts denounced as crimes occur. But the Supreme Court has indicated that it would not be unmindful of the implications to the fair administration of justice if venue caused needless hardship to an accused or if venue were fixed in a jurisdiction favorable to the prosecution.[24] Although a request for a change in venue based on claims of a local atmosphere prejudicial to a fair trial does raise constitutional issues,[25] normally the Court has treated venue as a federal statutory problem; only rarely has it examined a state venue case. Without detailing the sometimes complex federal venue problems for such offenses as postal crimes or crimes associated with interstate movement,[26] it is sufficient to say that the federal government follows the limited territorial principle expressed in the Sixth Amendment: The trial of an offense must be in the federal judicial district in which the crime was committed.[27] In most situations, this principle satisfies the needs of both the defendant and the witnesses.[28]

The Presence of the Defendant

A corollary of the adversary system of criminal justice is that a defendant has a right to be present at his or her trial. Certainly, before the right of counsel was accepted, the presence of the defendant was necessary to allow him or her an opportunity to meet the charges. Perhaps because the common law had long held that a defendant had the privilege of presence, it was thought unnecessary to mention this right in the Constitution or the Bill of Rights. In any event, on the few occasions in which the Supreme Court has confronted the issue, it has consistently, if occasionally confusedly stated that a defendant has a right to be present at trial.

In one of the earliest cases, *Lewis v. United States* (1892), the trial judge ordered that the jury challenges be made privately and independently, thus excluding the defense from a portion of the impanelment.[29] In reversing Lewis's conviction, the Court noted that "a leading principle that pervades the entire law of criminal procedure is that, after indictment found, nothing shall be done in the absence of the prisoner. While this rule has, at times, and in the cases of misdemeanors, been somewhat relaxed, yet in felonies, it is not in the power of the prisoner, either by himself or his counsel, to waive the right to be personally present during the trial."[30] The *Lewis* decision, if read today, would hold nothing more than that criminal defendants have the right of presence subject to certain exceptions and limitations.

Contrary to the inference we might draw from *Lewis,* there are a number of procedures that can take place in the absence of a defendant, including, in some situations, the continuation of a trial once it has started. In *Diaz v. United States* (1912), the defendant was present in person and represented by counsel at the beginning and during a major portion of the trial. At two points during the trial, however, Diaz voluntarily absented himself, having consented to the continuation of the trial in his absence.[31] When he later claimed that the continuation was illegal, the Supreme Court disallowed his claim, noting that "where the offense is not capital and the accused is not in custody, the prevailing rule has been, that if after the trial has begun in his presence, he voluntarily absents himself, this does not nullify what has been done or prevent the completion of the trial, but, on the contrary, operates as a waiver of his right to be present, and leaves the court free to proceed with the trial in like manner and with like effect as if he were present.[32]

Thus, once a trial has begun with the defendant present and then the defendant is voluntarily absent, the absence is considered a waiver of the right of presence.[33] Obviously, to hold that the presence of a defendant is absolutely required during a trial could defeat the ends of justice. A defendant who is at liberty during a trial and is present when the trial begins should not have the power, thereafter, to cause a mistrial merely by voluntarily relinquishing the right of presence.

Finally, although defendants have the right of presence, this does not mean that a defendant represented by counsel has a right to be personally present at proceedings that do not have a substantial and reasonable relationship to "the fullness of his opportunity to defend against the charge."[34] Thus, although both state and federal defendants have a right in the prosecution of a felony to be present at trial, the right does not extend to situations where the presence "would be useless, or the benefit but a shadow."[35] In *Snyder v. Massachusetts* (1934), the Court ruled that a defendant does not have the right to be present at an out-of-court viewing by a jury of the scene of a crime when the viewing is made in the presence of defense counsel and when no arguments or unnecessary comments are made by the prosecution or judge.[36] On the other hand, a defendant has the right of presence during instructions to the jury and at the time the jury returns its verdict.[37]

It is of some interest that although the Court has on numerous occasions acknowledged the right of presence, both under the Sixth and Fourteenth Amendments, there remains some uncertainty as to whether this constitutional right applies to nonfelony cases. The opinions in both *Lewis* and *Diaz* appear to suggest that the right extends only to felony cases. However, both of these cases were decided long before *Argersinger v. Hamlin* (1972), in which the Court ruled on the right to counsel in misdemeanor cases:[38] "Absent a knowing and intelligent waiver, no person may be imprisoned for any offense, whether classified as petty, misdemeanor or felony, unless he was represented by counsel at his trial."[39] Given the requirements of *Argersinger,* it seems inconceivable that due process would not demand the right of presence in any criminal trial, absent a knowing waiver or the exclusion of the defendant due to misconduct. It would not seem to make any difference to a fair and just hearing whether the maximum sentence is a jail term rather than a prison sentence, or even whether the maximum possible sentence is only a fine.[40] The orderly administration of an adversary system of criminal justice demands that a defendant have the right of presence in order to meet the charges, exempting only those situations in which the defendant waives this right[41] or surrenders it by personal misconduct.

Although in 1934 the Supreme Court noted in *Snyder* that a defendant could lose the right of presence by personal misconduct, it was not until 1970 that the Court directly confronted the issue.[42] In *Illinois v. Allen,* the Court decided a case in which the petitioner had been excluded by the judge from the trial courtroom during a substantial portion of the trial.[43] The petitioner had refused court-appointed counsel and attempted to conduct his own defense. During the voir dire and subsequently at the trial, petitioner made unprovoked remarks to the judge that were abusive, disrespectful, and threatening. After repeated warnings, he was excluded from the courtroom during a portion of the voir dire, at which time the court-appointed attorney acted on his behalf. Allen was allowed to return at the beginning of the trial, but when he continued his abusive and disruptive behavior he was again excluded, and remained excluded throughout the presentation of the state's case-in-chief. After promising to behave properly he was allowed to return to the courtroom during the time his court-appointed attorney conducted the defense.

In rejecting Allen's petition, the Court unanimously held

> that a defendant can lose his right to be present at trial if, after he has been warned by the judge that he will be removed if he continues his disruptive behavior, he nevertheless insists on conducting himself in a manner so disorderly, disruptive, and disrespectful of the court that his trial cannot be carried on with him in the courtroom. Once lost, the right to be present can, of course, be reclaimed as soon as the defendant is willing to conduct himself consistently with the decorum and respect inherent in the concept of courts and judicial proceedings.[44]

The Court reasoned that Allen's flagrant disregard of the elementary standards of proper conduct could not be tolerated and warned that defendants who stubbornly defy the dignity, order, and decorum of a court proceeding face one of three courses of action: (1) The judge can bind and gag the defendant, keeping him or her present in the courtroom; (2) the judge can cite the defendant for contempt; and (3) the judge can have the defendant removed from the courtroom until the defendant promises to conduct himself or herself properly. Because of the inherent disadvantages to the defense in binding and gagging, the opinion indicated that the method should be tried only as a last resort. The opinion also noted that, although threatening to cite or citing an obstreperous defendant might be sufficient to stop disorderly or disrespectful conduct, if a trial judge concluded that such a course of action would dissuade a persistently unruly defendant, then upon proper warning the defendant could be excluded.

The *Allen* rule does not undermine the right of presence. Clearly no defendant has a constitutional right to adopt a course of conduct that abuses the dignity of a court of law and that is calculated to frustrate the orderly progress of a trial. Trials cannot be conducted in a circus atmosphere. There may well be defendants and defense counsel who firmly believe that a criminal trial is an opportunity to stage a public spectacle, where the intended audience is not the jury but the mass media. *Allen* should give such persons ample warning that they run substantial risks in attempting to abuse or misuse a court of law.

A Speedy Trial

Little is known about the origins of the Sixth Amendment requirement of a speedy trial. There is a hint of the requirement in chapter 29 of the Magna Charta (1215), wherein King John promised: "We will sell to no man, we will not deny or defer to any man either justice or right." Several centuries later, Sir Edward Coke seized on this passage and concluded that the Magna Charta meant that every subject had a right to justice "speedily and without delay."[45] What this meant in practice is uncertain, but by the time of the American Revolution the right to a speedy criminal trial was generally recognized in the common law. Six of the original thirteen states made specific constitutional provision for the guarantee.[46] The incorporation of the guarantee into the Sixth Amendment apparently provoked little debate, and consequently little is known about the specific intent of James Madison and others who were instrumental in drafting the Bill of Rights.[47]

The sparse knowledge of the historical background of the requirement and the imprecise wording of the provision makes the requirement something of a slippery rock. Both undue haste in beginning a trial as well as undue delay can contribute equally to denials of justice. From the perspective of the accused, the guarantee is intended as "an important safeguard to prevent undue and oppressive incarceration prior to trial, to minimize anxiety and concern accompanying public accusation and to limit the possibilities that long delay will impair the ability of an accused to defend himself."[48] On the other hand, the courts have long recognized that "the right of a speedy trial is necessarily relative. It is consistent with delays and depends on circumstances."[49] Indeed, in contrast to other constitutional rights of defendants, the Supreme Court has recognized that the speedy-trial provision is designed to protect certain societal interests that may at times be in conflict with the interests of the accused. As the Court noted in *Barker v. Wingo* (1972):

> The inability of courts to provide a prompt trial has contributed to a large backlog of cases in urban courts which, among other things, enables defendants to negotiate more effectively for pleas of guilty to lesser offenses and otherwise manipulate the system. In addition, persons released on bond for lengthy periods awaiting trial have an opportunity to commit other crimes.
>   . . . Moreover, the longer an accused is free awaiting trial, the more tempting becomes his opportunity to jump bail and escape. Finally, delay between arrest and punishment may have a detrimental effect on rehabilitation.
>   If an accused cannot make bail, he is generally confined. . . . to a local jail. This contributes to the overcrowding and generally deplorable state of those institutions. Lengthy exposure to these conditions "has a destructive effect on human character and makes the rehabilitation of the individual offender much more difficult."
>   . . . Finally, lengthy pretrial detention is costly.
>   . . . In addition, society loses wages which might have been earned, and it must often support families of incarcerated breadwinners.[50]

Perhaps of even greater significance is that, in contrast to other procedural guarantees, the deprivation of the right to a speedy trial does not always work to the disadvantage of the accused; indeed, in some situations it may benefit the accused. Long delays can weaken memories and witnesses can disappear. In fact, because the prosecution carries the burden of proof, delay can weaken the state's case.

Because *speedy* is a vague term and because delay does not necessarily prejudice the defense, the Court has refused to endorse rigid approaches to this procedural guarantee. Although the Court has held that the guarantee applies to the states,[51] it has also indicated that the states are free, within certain broad guidelines, to establish their own procedures to effectuate the provision.[52] One such guideline is that the guarantee does not begin to operate until there is "either a formal indictment or information or else the actual restraints imposed by arrest and holding to answer a criminal charge."[53] In rejecting an approach that would quantify the days or months that constitute a denial of a speedy trial, the Court in *Barker* adopted a flexible approach, endorsing a balancing test that

> necessarily compels courts to approach speedy trial cases on an *ad hoc* basis. We can do little more than identify some of the factors which courts should assess in determining whether a particular defendant has been deprived of his right. Though some might express them in different ways, we identify four such factors: length of delay, the reason for the delay, the defendant's assertion of his right, and prejudice to the defendant.[54]

Delay is, of course, the triggering device, and until a delay occurs, there is no necessity to inquire into the other factors. Whether a delay is excessive depends on the nature of the crime because certain crimes require additional trial preparation. Furthermore, not all delays can be charged against the prosecution; some are the result of pretrial motions by the defense, and others may be occasioned by the need of either the prosecution or the defense to secure missing witnesses. The Court also noted in *Barker* that a defendant is under some obligation to assert the right of a speedy trial, and that although the failure to assert does not necessarily imply a waiver, it "will make it difficult for a defendant to prove that he was denied a speedy trial."[55] Finally, the Court noted that in determining whether delay was prejudicial to a defendant, courts should consider the anxiety caused by delay, oppressive pretrial incarceration, and the constraints imposed by delay in limiting the defense, particularly where delay impairs the defense by allowing witnesses to disappear or their recall to fade.

Like other balancing tests, the *Barker* guidelines may prove to be impractical if for no other reason than that their imprecision invites dispute and appeal. At the federal level, the guidelines have been rejected in part in the Speedy Trial Act of 1974.[56] Under the 1974 legislation, federal prosecutions are ultimately governed by a specific timetable, which, with exclusions for certain types of delays, requires that no more than one hundred days elapse from arrest to trial.

Finally, the Court has warned prosecutors that where it is determined that a defendant was denied a speedy trial, the only possible remedies are a dismissal of the indictment or a setting aside of the judgment against the convicted defendant.[57]

As we noted above, prompt, but not hasty, justice serves a host of interests, including those of many defendants. The causes for delays in justice are many, some attributable to the prosecution and some to deliberate defense strategies. To set aside a conviction or to dismiss with prejudice an indictment are of course the only remedies that the judiciary can offer. These remedies mean that there is a likelihood that defendants who are guilty of serious crimes will go free, a far from satisfactory solution. Still, given the limited remedial powers of the judiciary and that a constitutional guarantee is at stake, these are the only remedies that may prompt a more satisfactory solution by legislative bodies; namely, increased resources for public defenders, prosecutors, and the courts.

A Public Trial

> In all criminal prosecutions, the accused shall enjoy the right to a . . . public trial.
>
> —Sixth Amendment

Closed or secret trials seem so antithetical to a system of public justice that we seldom pause to consider the important constitutional right of a public trial. Like other English trial procedures, both the origins of and justifications for the public-trial requirement are somewhat uncertain. Open criminal trials were customary at least by the sixteenth century, and by the eighteenth century the right to a public trial was considered a common-law right.[58] Presumably, the intent of this right is to protect the accused from arbitrary conviction, the assumption being that in those trials subject to public scrutiny judges will be less likely to bend to the prosecution or to their own private prejudices. Although the right is personal to the accused and may be waived, it has also been justified for the beneficial effect it may have in maintaining public confidence in the integrity of the judicial process. Public trials do not preclude judicial favoritism or prejudice, but it is reasonable to assume that the light of a public trial *with a public record* lessens the prospects of corruption and injustice. As Justice Holmes once remarked, trials should take place under the eye of the public because "it is of the highest moment that those who administer justice should always act under the sense of public responsibility and that every citizen should be able to satisfy himself with his own eyes as to the mode in which a public duty is performed."[59]

Whether, on a routine basis, public trials do help maintain public confidence in the integrity of the judicial process is an open question. The public's knowledge of the judicial process in the criminal area is generally obtained from the mass media, not from personal courtroom experience. If the mass media tend to focus largely on sensational trials and lurid details, then is the public actually monitoring the judicial process? Still, there is little objection today to open public trials, and indeed the question has been the subject of only two Supreme Court decisions. In *In re Oliver* (1948), the Court ruled that a judge may not, consistent with due process,[60] try and convict an individual in a closed and secret trial. The Court noted that, with the exception of the instant case, there was no known instance of a federal, state, or municipal criminal trial being held *in camera*, and that without exception all courts have recognized that an accused is, at the very least, entitled to have friends, relatives, and counsel present, regardless of the charge.[61]

Oliver should not be read, however, to hold that the right to a public trial is an absolute right without qualification. Although the Supreme Court has never provided a set of guidelines, the lower federal courts and the state courts have long recognized that the right must on occasion be balanced against other interests that justify limiting or excluding some or all spectators from a criminal proceeding. Clearly, the normal seating capacity of a courtroom is an administrative limitation on the number of spectators that can be admitted. Furthermore, it is generally recognized that a court may exclude spectators who behave improperly or who pose a threat to witnesses.[62]

There are two common exceptions to the right of public trial. The first is in trials of sex crimes where the victim and/or the complaining witness is a minor. The states have generally recognized the right of courts to temporarily bar the public from such a trial. The acknowledged justification for such exclusions is to protect a minor from possible embarrassment. On the other hand, it is questionable whether a court should be permitted to bar the public from any and all trials for sex crimes merely in order to spare the public the lurid details.[63] It is one thing to temporarily bar spectators during the testimony of a minor witness; it is quite another to bar the public entirely.[64] The second commonly recognized exception to a public trial is the temporary exclusion of spectators during the testimony of an undercover agent in narcotics cases. Here the courts have justified the exclusion during an agent's testimony in order to protect the agent's safety and to ensure his or her continued usefulness.[65]

The right to a public trial should never include the presence of a clamorous or hostile crowd. Criminal trials are for the resolution of factual disputes; they are not the occasion for the mass viewing of high theatrical performances. Having said this, we must quickly add that judicial authority to limit spectators in criminal trials should not be exercised routinely. Criminal courts exercise a public power, even if this means that the doors of the criminal courts are open not only to those who are serious spectators, but to those who may come out of morbid curiosity. In short, what must be recognized is a societal interest in public trials. Unfortunately, the Supreme Court may be moving in an opposite direction. In *Gannett v. DePasquale* (1979), a narrow majority held that where all parties agree to a closed pretrial suppression in the interest of a defendant's fair-trial rights, then a trial judge may bar the public, including the press. However, the majority went beyond the facts of the case (a closed suppression hearing) and ruled that members of the public have no constitutional right under the Sixth or Fourteenth Amendments to attend criminal trials.[66] Hopefully, subsequent decisions of the Court will limit the *Gannett* decision.

Free Press and Fair Trial

All criminal defendants are entitled to have their guilt or innocence determined in a calm, dispassionate manner. Although defendants are entitled to a public trial, they are free of any obligation to provide a public spectacle. Because most criminal trials do not involve great drama—sex, murder, society, and suspense—we are not often confronted with trials that risk becoming Roman holidays. Occasionally, however, there are trials that begin in an atmosphere of passion and excitement, which without restraint threaten the right to a fair trial.

The problem is essentially a conflict between two important constitutional values—free press and fair trial. "A trial is a public event. What transpires in the courtroom is public property. . . . Those who see and hear what transpired can report it with impunity."[67] A problem arises, however, when a given criminal event has so inflamed the community, particularly through extensive pretrial publicity, that the chances of securing an unbiased jury are reduced. The solution to this is a carefully conducted and searching voir dire or, in unusual circumstances, a change of venue.[68]

Overlapping with the issue of pretrial publicity is the issue of the general atmosphere of a criminal trial, particularly as it relates to the media's coverage of a trial. The two leading cases pertaining to this problem are *Estes v. Texas* (1965)[69] and *Sheppard v. Maxwell* (1966).[70] *Estes* was the notorious, heavily publicized, highly sensational trial of Billie Sol Estes on the charge of swindling. After a change of venue, the trial judge allowed live television and radio coverage of the initial hearings, during which at least twelve cameramen, with full equipment, were present in the courtroom. When the trial began, the judge, over defense objections, allowed the media to continue in-court television coverage, although under somewhat greater restriction than had obtained during the initial hearings. When Estes petitioned the Supreme Court, he did not claim that televising his trial resulted in specific and demonstrable prejudice to his right to a fair trial. Rather, he claimed that he was denied due process when, over his objection, the trial court allowed the courtroom proceedings to be televised. Five justices voted to reverse the conviction, with four of the five justices concluding that any use of television in the courtroom during the proceedings of a criminal trial inherently violates due process.[71] Justice Clark, writing for the majority, concluded: "A defendant on trial for a specific crime is entitled to his day in court, not in a stadium, or a city or nationwide arena. The heightened public clamor resulting from radio and television coverage will inevitably result in prejudice. Trial by television is, therefore, foreign to our system."[72]

The major significance of *Estes* does not lie in its ban on the televising of criminal proceedings. After all, at the time of *Estes*, forty-eight states and the rules of the federal judiciary prohibited television in courtrooms.[73] The importance of the case lies in its warning to trial judges that a criminal trial should be conducted with "solemn decorum." The opinion is a reminder that it is the responsibility of trial judges to make certain that defendants receive a fair trial, and to that end judges must control the proceedings so as to minimize extraneous influences that could intrude on the quality of a trial. They must guard against distractions (television cameras, crews) that interfere with the jury's concentration, with the quality of witnesses' testimony, and with the ability of all officers of the court—counsel and judges alike—to direct their attention and energies to "the sober search for the truth."

Estes came too late to warn Judge Blythin of his responsibilities in the 1954 trial of Dr. Samuel Sheppard for the murder of his wife. Marilyn Sheppard was bludgeoned to death on the night of July 4, 1954. The case was immediately sensationalized by the mass media, involving as it did the almost perfect formula of sex, murder, society, and suspense. Sheppard became the subject of extensive and prejudicial publicity, and the coverage continued throughout the summer and during the nine-week trial that began in the fall. The prejudicial publicity alone would have created a problem in securing an unbiased jury and conducting a fair trial, but *Sheppard* involved more than extensive and unfavorable publicity. First, the judge made no attempt to set a reasonable limit on the number of media representatives; consequently, the small courtroom remained so packed with reporters that their presence often interfered with counsel and witnesses. Indeed, the judge allowed the media unlimited access to the corridors outside the courtroom, and broadcast facilities were even installed next to the jury room. Second, there was constant photographing of the defendant, witnesses, and jury, as they entered and left the courtroom and during recesses. Third, the jurors were not sequestered until after the case was submitted to them, so they were constantly exposed to the media coverage, including many unfavorable stories about the defendant. Even when the jury was finally sequestered, its members were allowed to make phone calls. Fourth, the police released unfavorable statements about the defendant and about alleged evidence that was never introduced at trial, although it was reported in the media. Finally, the judge allowed himself to be the subject of press interviews.

In reversing the denial of a writ of habeas corpus, the Supreme Court characterized the trial atmosphere as carnivallike and noted: "The fact is that bedlam reigned at the courthouse during the trial and newsmen took over practically the entire courtroom, hounding most of the participants in the trial, especially Sheppard."[74] The Court concluded that the fundamental error of the trial judge was his holding that he had no power to control publicity about the trial. On the contrary, the Court noted that a trial judge does have the powers to reduce the appearance of prejudicial material and to protect the jury from outside influence. A judge certainly can control the courtroom and courthouse premises, including therein the use and conduct of media representatives. Also, a judge has the power to insulate witnesses from the press and press reports of courtroom proceedings. And, a judge has the power in appropriate circumstances to impose controls over the out-of-court statements made by counsel, the police, witnesses, and court officials. Finally, where publicity threatens to prevent a fair trial, a judge should consider a change of venue or a postponement or, once the trial begins, the sequestration of the jury. If none of these measures produces the judicial serenity and calm to which a defendant is entitled, then the trial judge has the powers to declare a mistrial and to take disciplinary actions against officers of the court.

The one element of the *Sheppard* opinion that was to cause controversy was the Court's apparent endorsement of restraining, or gag, orders. However, at no point, in the opinion did the Court endorse prior restraint on the press. It did indicate that a trial judge might proscribe extrajudicial statements by "any lawyer, party, witness, or court official which divulged prejudicial matters."[75] And it went on to suggest that a judge could warn the press to check the accuracy of its accounts, inferring that there might be sanctions available against a recalcitrant press.[76] Still, the opinion stopped short of endorsing a gag order that would impose prior restraints on the press, particularly from reporting matters of public record.

Unfortunately, *Sheppard* was read by many trial courts to support press gag orders. By 1975, there were at least 174 cases involving restrictive orders, and eighty of the ninety-four federal district courts had adopted rules under which restrictive orders could be issued.[77]

Because the state and federal courts were divided on the issue,[78] the Supreme Court in *Nebraska Press Association v. Stuart* (1976) accepted jurisdiction in a gag order case.[79] In this case, the trial judge, in anticipation of the trial for the murder of an entire family, entered a gag order that restrained newspapers, journalists, news media associations, broadcasters, and wire services from disclosing the accounts of confessions or admissions made by the accused to the police, prosecutors, or third parties, except members of the press, and further prohibited the reporting of other facts "strongly implicative" of the accused.[80] In reversing the order, the Court started with the proposition that there is a "heavy presumption against the . . . constitutional validity" of prior restraints on the press.[81] Given the alternatives to prior restraint suggested in *Sheppard* and that the trial judge had not attempted to use these less severe measures, the Court concluded that the state had not met the burden of supporting prior restraint. Chief Justice Burger's opinion, however, left in doubt those circumstances that would justify a press gag order, although it did note that "we need not rule out the possibility of showing the kind of threat to fair trial rights that would possess the requisite degree of certainty to justify restraint."[82]

The problems of free press and fair trial have yet to be resolved. *Estes* and *Sheppard* probably had a healthy and desirable impact. First, these decisions cautioned the police, prosecutors, and defense counsel that trial by press release is inconsistent with our system of justice. Second, the decisions reminded trial judges of their basic responsibility to exercise reasonable and even firm control of criminal trials, including the use of remedies designed to ensure fairness. It is possible, however, that these decisions encouraged a fairly widespread use of gag orders aimed at the press; and therefore *Nebraska Press* was a necessary clarification. Undoubtedly there have been situations in which a free, but arrogant and irresponsible, press has operated so as to make a fair trial more difficult. Press gag orders correctly assume that pretrial publicity can jeopardize a fair trial, but they incorrectly assume that other corrective measures could not fully protect the constitutional rights of defendants.

The Disqualification of Judges and General Conduct of a Trial

A fair tribunal is a basic requirement to due process.[83] At the outset, in order to reduce the probability of an unfair tribunal, no judge may try a case in which he or she has an interest, either prejudicially or economically, in the outcome. For example, in *Tumey v. Ohio* (1927), the judge who presided at Tumey's trial had an interest in the $100 fine he imposed;[84] under procedures then used in parts of Ohio, judges retained a certain portion of the fines they levied. Noting that judges are disqualified from trying cases by their interest in the controversy to be decided, the Supreme Court held that it "violates the 14th Amendment and deprives a defendant in a criminal case of due process of law to subject his liberty or his property to the judgment of a court, the judge of which has a direct, personal, substantial pecuniary interest in reaching a conclusion against him in a case."[85]

No one doubts that the principle of disqualification for direct interest has constitutional status.[86] The principle of disqualification has been a part of English common law at least since the early seventeenth century,[87] and *Tumey* settled the issue in American law. On the other hand, *Tumey* left open the question of other traditional areas of disqualification, among them the personal bias of judges.[88] Lower federal courts have not hesitated to rule that disqualification for bias is a part of due process.[89] The fact that the Supreme Court has not ruled on this constitutional issue is probably not an indication of its lack of concern. Because the states generally follow the pattern of the federal government in providing statutorily for the filing of affidavits of personal bias or prejudice against a judge designated to try a case, the constitutional question is largely academic.

An issue that is far from academic, however, and that has been raised frequently is that of bias on the part of judges in the conduct of trials. Trial judges walk a difficult path. Their behavior must not preclude "that atmosphere of austerity which should especially dominate a criminal trial and which is indispensable for an appropriate sense of responsibility on the part of the court, counsel and jury."[90] In short, judges must maintain the appearance and substance of impartiality and judicious detachment. On the other hand, trial judges are something more than courtroom ornaments or even moderators. Judges are participants in trials, albeit disinterested and objective participants, and it often is necessary for them to interpose themselves in a trial. In particular, judges who preside over jury trials have the responsibility to see that the evidence and testimony are presented to the jury in a clear and straightforward manner.[91] On occasion, this may require a judge to direct additional questions to witnesses, but such participation must not reveal a bias against the defense or an attempt to rescue the state's faltering case.[92]

As federal judge Irving Kaufman has noted, we must recognize that criminal trials are "not conducted in the cool and calm conditions of a quiet sanctuary or an ivory tower, and that enormous pressures are placed upon . . . judges."[93] Wasteful and excessive interrogation of witnesses by inept counsel or even the deliberate baiting of a judge by a provocative counsel may result in "a show of evanescent irritation—a modicum of quick temper that must be allowed even judges."[94] But gratuitous implications of ineptness directed at the defense or an antagonistic or deprecatory attitude toward the defense, especially in front of a jury, suggests that a judge has concluded that the defense's case lacks merit.[95] For a judge to display a negative attitude toward the defense in front of the jury is especially damaging because "the influence of the trial judge on the jury is necessarily and properly of great weight and . . . his lightest word of intimation is received with deference and may prove controlling."[96]

The line between judicial bias and detachment is never easy to draw, and this is particularly true in regard to a judge's instructions to a jury.

> In charging the jury, the trial judge is not limited to instructions of an abstract sort. It is within his province, whenever he thinks necessary, to assist the jury in arriving at a just conclusion by explaining and commenting upon the evidence, by drawing their attention to the parts of it which he thinks important, and he may express his opinion upon the facts, provided he makes it clear to the jury that all matters of fact are submitted to their determination.[97]

But the instructions may not be hostile or calculated to excite a prejudice against the defense. The instructions must leave the jury free to exercise its own judgment.[98]

Not only does due process limit the conduct of a trial judge, it also limits the conduct of the prosecution. The function of the trial is the accurate resolution of disputed facts, and the prosecutor has a responsibility to ensure that the government's case is presented honestly. It would be a denial of due process for the prosecution (1) to solicit false testimony, (2) to use testimony known to be perjured and allow it to go uncorrected, (3) to withhold exculpatory evidence, or (4) to withhold information bearing adversely on the credibility of a prosecution witness.[99] In short, the government may not contrive a conviction "through the pretense of a trial which in truth is but used as a means of depriving a defendant of liberty through a deliberate deception of court and jury."[100] Thus due process is violated when the reliability of a witness may be a determinant of guilt and the prosecutor fails to disclose evidence that affects the witness's credibility, such as a government promise of leniency.[101]

A courtroom is not a sports arena, and a defendant is entitled to a neutral atmosphere free of judicial and prosecutorial bias. Repeated prosecutorial sarcasm directed at the defense, particularly in front of a jury, or unprovoked personal attacks on the defense must be firmly rebuked by the trial judge, or there is a risk that the jury will be affected.[102] A vigorous prosecution must still conform to the standards of fair trial. Intemperate and undignified conduct by the prosecutor, misleading assertions, and improper insinuations can have a cumulative effect on a jury, and thus deny a fair trial to a defendant.[103]

The Standard of Proof: Guilt Beyond a Reasonable Doubt

A criminal defendant stands in far greater jeopardy than does a defendant in a civil action. A criminal defendant risks liberty, reputation, perhaps even life, whereas a civil defendant's risk usually does not exceed money damages. Furthermore, generally society has no stake in the outcome of a private civil action, and consequently an erroneous judgment there is not considered as serious as an erroneous criminal judgment. Of course, all litigation has a margin of error, but because we recognize that in criminal cases one party "has at stake an interest of transcending value—as a criminal defendant his liberty— this margin of error is reduced as to him by the process of placing on the other party the burden of . . . persuading the factfinder at the conclusion of the trial of his guilt beyond a reasonable doubt."[104]

In effect, the higher standard of proof required in criminal cases[105] reflects not only society's concern for individual liberty, but something of the equities of a criminal prosecution. The standard assumes that the state must carry the burden of proof and persuasion, and it also recognizes that its requirements will allow certain guilty persons to go free. On the other hand, the standard also is a "flat rejection of the doctrine that it is better that all guilty men should go unpunished than any innocent men . . . should be punished."[106]

The origins of the requirement of proof beyond a reasonable doubt are somewhat obscure.[107] The standard appears to have come into general use sometime in the late eighteenth century, at first only in capital cases. It was not, however, until 1970 that the Supreme Court expressly ruled that the standard is required by due process in criminal cases. In *In re Winship,* a juvenile proceeding in New York, Winship had been accused of stealing a sum of money—an act that had it been committed by an adult would constitute a felony. In adjudging Winship a delinquent, the family-court judge acknowledged that the proof of guilt might not have been established beyond a reasonable doubt. In reversing the determination, the Supreme Court ruled: "Lest there remain any doubt about the Constitutional stature of the reasonable doubt standard, we explicitly hold that the Due Process Clause protects the accused against conviction except upon proof beyond a reasonable doubt of every fact necessary to constitute the crime with which he is charged."[108]

As a matter of due process, then, all juries in criminal cases must be instructed regarding the reasonable-doubt standard. As a practical matter, the instruction must caution jurors to place aside any inferences of guilt that they may have assumed from the defendant's arrest and indictment. The precise requirements of the charge, however, have not been made clear. Often the charge begins with a statement of the presumption of innocence, although the presumption of innocence neither is technically a presumption nor does it have evidentiary significance.[109] But the presumption of innocence does serve as a convenient way to inform the jury that the burden is on the government to produce evidence and the persuasion of guilt, and that the defendant is under no legal obligation to produce any evidence. Indeed, in 1978, the Court reversed a conviction where the trial judge had refused a defense request to give a jury instruction on the presumption of innocence. The Court indicated that such instruction is intended to have a salutary effect on a lay jury and complements the required instruction on the burden of proof.[110]

Beyond the notice of the government's burden, a charge must make clear to the jury that the government must prove guilt beyond a reasonable doubt as to every essential element of the crime charged.[111] Finally, a charge may attempt to define reasonable doubt. Definitions abound, and the Supreme Court has never endorsed any specific one nor has the Court directly stated whether a definition is even required in instructing a jury.

Some commentators and judges are critical of attempts to define *reasonable doubt* in instructions.[112] They conclude that the standard defines itself because it is composed of common words that jurors are fully capable of understanding. The attempt to define the phrase can become a trap, producing confusion in the minds of jurors. Finally, attempts at definition often list what the standard does not demand, in the process inducing the jury to accept a lesser standard of guilt.[113]

At the present time, there is wide variation in judicial responses to the definition requirement. Most federal courts follow the so-called federal rule, which provides for a definition in instructions to the jury.[114] On the other hand, many state courts have held that a definition is either not required or not required unless it is requested.[115]

Perhaps the most widely cited definition of reasonable doubt is the one contained in the Court's opinion in *Dunbar v. United States* (1895):

> Repeated attempts have been made by judges to make clear to the minds of the jury what is meant by the words "reasonable doubt," but, as said by *Mr. Justice* Woods, speaking for this court, in *Miles v. United States* . . . "attempts to explain the term 'reasonable doubt' do not usually result in making it any clearer to the minds of the jury." And so, when the court in this case said to the jury, "I will not undertake to define a reasonable doubt further than to say that a reasonable doubt is not an unreasonable doubt—that is to say, by a reasonable doubt you are not to understand that all doubt is to be excluded; it is impossible in the determination of these questions to be absolutely certain. You are required to decide the question submitted to you upon the strong probabilities of the case, and the probabilities must be so strong as not to exclude reasonable doubt," it gave all the definition of reasonable doubt which a court can be required to give, and one which probably made the meaning as intelligible to the jury as any elaborate discussion of the subject would have done. While it is true that it used the words "probabilities" and "strong probabilities," yet it emphasized the fact that those probabilities must be so strong as to exclude any reasonable doubt, and that is unquestionably the law.[116]

It seems doubtful that a particular definition should be required or even that a definition should be attempted. What due process requires is that the jury understand that the standard of proof is guilt beyond a reasonable doubt; that the standard is a commonsense standard based, not on suspicion or conjecture, but on reason; that reasonable doubt may arise on the basis of the admitted evidence or the lack of evidence; and that the burden of proof and persuasion is on the state.[117]

Shifting the Burden of Proof: Presumptions and Inferences

Although the burden of proof and persuasion rests on the state, the courts have long recognized certain common-law and statutory presumptions and inferences that shift the burden of proof to defendants.[118] One of the most commonly recognized inferences is the common-law inference that deals with the possession of recently stolen property: An inference of guilty knowledge is accepted on proof of the unexplained possession of recently stolen goods.[119] Thus, if the state is able to prove that a defendant possessed recently stolen goods, the proof creates an inference of guilty knowledge, even though the state has offered no direct evidence of guilt on the part of the defendant. The inference effectively shifts the burden to the defendant to offer evidence of innocent possession. This shift may undermine a defendant's right not to testify, but the Supreme Court has upheld both statutory and common-law presumptions and inferences so long as they meet the standard of rational connection.[120]

Presumptions and inferences deal, or should deal, in commonsense probabilities; that is, if the accuser can prove fact A, then fact B is inferred or presumed because of a sensible and probable connection. The common law has long held a high probability between possession of recently stolen goods and guilty knowledge: Experience suggests that individuals who possess recently stolen property either had some part in the theft or were the knowing receivers of such property. But the connection must be rational and not strained. Thus, the Court has held that there is no rational connection between the fact of possession of a firearm and the statutory presumption that the firearm had been shipped or received in violation of interstate, rather than intrastate, laws.[121] Similarly, the Court has held that a statute that allowed a jury to infer from a defendant's possession of marihuana that the marihuana was illegally imported into the United States was not supportable. The Court held that under the rational-connection test, the knowledge of illegal importation could be presumed only if it could be determined that at least a majority of marihuana possessors have knowledge of its foreign origin. The Court concluded no such determination could be made and therefore struck down the presumption.[122]

On the other hand, the Court has often upheld statutory presumptions and inferences. For example, it upheld a statutory inference between an unexplained presence at an illegal still and carrying on the business of distiller without having the required bond.[123] In upholding this statutory inference, the Court noted: "Congress was undoubtedly aware that manufacturers of illegal liquor are notorious for the deftness with which they locate arcane spots for plying their trade. Legislative recognition of the implications of seclusion only confirms what the folklore teaches—that strangers to the illegal business rarely penetrate the curtain of secrecy."[124] Similarly, in *Barnes v. United States* (1973), the Court upheld the permissive inference that one who has unexplained possession of recently stolen mail knows that the mail was stolen.

Until recently the Court had not made clear the exact standard of proof necessary before a jury is permitted to infer a fact. There are two general standards against which a trier of fact must judge an inference: One is the arguably lower standard that the inference is "more likely than not" true; the other is the more stringent standard that a rational juror finds the inferred fact to be true beyond a reasonable doubt. The Court had stated that if a judge submits an inference to the jury under the reasonable-doubt standard, then the inference, assuming a rational connection, was in accord with due process.[125] In *County Court of Ulster v. Allen* (1979), the Court seized upon a distinction between permissive and mandatory presumptions and concluded that the reasonable-doubt standard applied only to mandatory presumptions. In the case of permissive presumptions, the fact inferred by the presumption is held only to the more-likely-than-not standard as long as it is clear that "the presumption is not the sole and sufficient basis for a finding of guilt."[126]

Inferences and presumptions raise serious constitutional questions. Certainly they allow a defendant to be convicted in the absence of the prosecution's producing evidence of all elements of the crime. Thus, in *Barnes,* the defendant was convicted of possessing U.S. treasury checks stolen from the mails, knowing them to be stolen, even though the government produced no evidence that Barnes knew the checks were stolen from the mails. In the trial, the government offered evidence to prove (a) that the mail was stolen and (b) that the recently stolen *contents* of the mail, the treasury checks, were in Barnes's possession. The final element of the crime—knowledge that the checks were stolen from the mails—was allowed to be inferred from the other evidence introduced by the government. As Justice Black remarked in another context, "Undoubtedly a presumption which can be used to produce convictions without the necessity of proving a crucial element of the crime charged—and a sometimes difficult-to-prove element at that—is a boon to prosecutors and an incongruous snare to defendants in a country that claims to require proof of guilt beyond a reasonable doubt."[127]

Presumptions and inferences also raise a serious question in regard to a defendant's right to trial by jury and the role of the jury as trier of the facts. A presumption takes away a jury's right to be the sole fact finder by predetermining a factual element of the crime without allowing the jury to discharge the role of weighing the sufficiency of the admitted evidence of all elements of the crime. Finally, presumptions and inferences can undermine a defendant's right to silence. When element *C* of a crime is automatically presumed on proof and persuasion of elements *A* and *B*, the burden shifts to the defendant to introduce evidence disproving *C*, forcing the defendant to testify or to remain quiet at his or her peril.[128]

In analyzing the due process problems of presumptions and inferences, it should be made clear that the issue does not involve the right of the fact finder to make reasonable inferences based on the admitted evidence. Rather the problems revolve around such issues as shifting the burden of proof and allowing the prosecutor to secure convictions without offering proof or persuasion of an essential element of a crime. Clearly, as between presumptions and inferences, the former raises the more serious constitutional problem. Presumptions of a mandatory character often make inferences that a fact finder would not ordinarily make. For example, a jury would not ordinarily assume that one who is present at the site of an illegal still was in fact the operator of the still. Although presence is probative, it would not necessarily be dispositive of guilt. The mandatory presumption of proof of presence makes presence dispositive, at least in the absence of convincing evidence to the contrary. Yet convincing evidence to the contrary may, in some situations, place an impossible burden on the defense.

One solution to the problem would be to disallow presumptions and inferences that shift the burden of proof. However, such a development seems neither likely nor necessarily desirable, particularly so long as courts subject presumptions and inferences to the rational-connection test and the reasonable-doubt standard. Still, many defendants do face an added evidentiary burden, the crux of which is the lack of defense resources to produce the favorable evidence that is necessary to rebut presumptions and inferences.[129] Christie and Pye suggested three steps that could be taken to relieve the defense problem. The first would be to expand the rules of discovery in criminal cases, so that defendants are assured in advance of trial that they have received from the prosecution all evidence favorable to the defendant. Second, the defense should be provided with adequate funds for investigation and to secure expert witnesses. Finally, the defense should have some assurance that government witnesses will cooperate with defense counsel prior to trial,[130] at least in the absence of any suggestion that a witness will be harassed if he or she cooperates. Because presumptions create the obligation for the defense to come forward with evidence, these proposals would go a long way toward reducing the possibility of a miscarriage of justice.

Sufficient Evidence

That a conviction must rest on substantial proof of guilt beyond a reasonable doubt would appear to be essential to an adversary system and an elemental concept of due process. However, even though it is now recognized that proof beyond a reasonable doubt is a requirement of due process, it is far from clear whether that standard applies only as an admonition in instructions to juries. Indeed, it was not until 1960, in *Thompson v. Louisville*, that the Supreme Court ruled that a state cannot convict and punish a defendant without evidence of guilt.[131] But the *Thompson* rule is essentially a rule governing appellate review: Where a defendant has properly raised and preserved the issue of the sufficiency of the state's evidence, an appellate court may not sustain a conviction based on a record lacking any relevant evidence as to a crucial element of the offense charged.[132]

In most criminal trials, the defense's first opportunity to raise the issue of sufficient evidence is at the end of the presentation of the government's case-in-chief. At this point, the defense may request a directed verdict or motion of acquittal. As one federal court has stated, "One of the greatest safeguards for the individual under our system of criminal justice is the requirement that the prosecution must establish a prima facie case by its own evidence before the defendant may be put to his defense."[133] At least insofar as federal criminal trials are concerned, a trial court is required on its own or by motion of the defense to enter a judgment of acquittal on one or more of the offenses charged if the government has failed to offer evidence sufficient to sustain a conviction.[134] But does this mean that a defendant may be put to his or her defense or a case submitted to a jury in the face of serious questions about the sufficiency of evidence against the defendant? In particular, does due process require that a trial judge, responding to a motion for a directed verdict or a motion for a judgment of acquittal, must apply the reasonable-doubt standard? Or may the judge apply the preponderance-of-evidence rule that obtains in civil cases?[135] For the present at least, the Supreme Court has not indicated that due process requires a trial judge to apply the reasonable-doubt standard in responding to defense motions that raise the issue of sufficient evidence.

Two arguments support the use of the reasonable-doubt standard as a requirement of due process in judicial screening of cases prior to their submission to the jury. The first argument is twofold: Because due process requires that guilt be determined by the reasonable-doubt standard and because the very existence of motions for directed verdicts rests on the proposition that the state must establish a prima facie case, logic seems to require that a judge apply the reasonable-doubt standard in responding to a motion for a directed verdict. Another, perhaps more powerful argument has been suggested: By applying the reasonable-doubt test to the question of the sufficiency of evidence, a judge keeps the pressure on the "prosecutor, and police to act as reasonably as possible in screening out cases not fit for trial. Placing the prestige of the judiciary directly on the scales in favor of strict standards of proof, it announces that the sufficiency of evidence will be ruled upon, deliberately, by a judge and will not simply pass into the anonymity of the general verdict."[136]

In 1972, the U.S. Court of Appeals for the Second Circuit rejected an earlier rule that allowed trial judges to apply the civil-trial standard of preponderance of evidence to motions for directed verdicts. The court ruled that a motion for a directed verdict of acquittal must be granted when the trial judge concludes that the evidence necessarily leaves a reasonable doubt as to the defendant's guilt.[137] Given the serious consequences of a criminal conviction, this rule appears to be an appropriate development in due process.

The due process question of the sufficiency of evidence, particularly in state prosecutions, ought not to rest on the rather weak protection of the decision in *Thompson v. Louisville*. In effect, *Thompson* provides a guideline only for appellate review, and in practice it is useful only to correct those convictions that are totally devoid of evidentiary support.[138] If the reasonable-doubt standard is to be something more than a passing admonition of a trial judge to the jury, then the standard must be incorporated at an earlier stage, and the appropriate point is in response to a motion for a directed verdict.

Given that a substantial percentage of criminal defendants are regularly acquitted, we could conclude that pretrial administrative procedures for screening out the factually innocent are not without error. In this context, the maintenance of the reasonable-doubt standard becomes central to a just system of criminal law, helping to ensure community confidence in the system and, it is hoped, measurably increasing the reliability of verdicts.

Compulsory Process

> In all criminal prosecutions, the accused shall enjoy the right
> . . . to have compulsory process for obtaining witnesses in his
> favor.
>
> —Sixth Amendment

Perhaps no trial right is more important to a criminal defendant than the right to make a defense of the charges; that is, to obtain witnesses and documentary evidence and to have these presented to the trier of the disputed facts. Yet the right of compulsory process is one of the most neglected areas of constitutional law. The Supreme Court has only rarely examined the numerous problems associated with it, and, indeed, there is really only one major Supreme Court opinion in this area, that of *Washington v. Texas* (1967).[139]

Although this Anglo-American trial right is of relatively recent origin, it was initially addressed to a problem that dates back earlier than the late seventeenth century. Before that time, a criminal defendant did not have the right to present witnesses, sworn or unsworn.[140] Royal abuses of power, which were particularly evident in seventeenth-century treason trials, gave rise to the recognition that the inquisitorial procedures of criminal trials did not protect defendants against the considerable advantages enjoyed by the Crown. By the end of the seventeenth century, it was widely recognized that defendants should be able to present sworn witnesses in treason and felony trials.[141] By 1702, Parliament passed legislation authorizing sworn defense witnesses in treason and felony trials,[142] and the courts construed this legislation to authorize compulsory process.

In the American colonies, there were parallel developments. By 1750, the rights of the defense to present sworn testimony and to compulsory process were recognized in Pennsylvania, New York, Virginia, Maryland, and Massachusetts. By the end of the American Revolution, the right of compulsory process was incorporated into the constitutions or bills of rights of nine states.[143] When the federal Constitution failed to provide such a right, several states specifically requested that the new Congress include a provision for defense witnesses in a bill of rights. The compulsory-process clause, which was proposed by James Madison in 1789, was adopted as part of the Sixth Amendment. The wording is narrow, appearing to provide only for a defense power of subpoena. However, it seems likely that Madison did not intend to formulate a narrow right of subpoena, as evidenced by Chief Justice Marshall's opinion as circuit judge in the trial of Aaron Burr.[144] Still, a broad, constitutionally protected defense right to prepare and present a defense is largely a product of the past decade. Furthermore, it is largely a product of federal appellate court interpretations of one Supreme Court opinion, that in 1967 in *Washington v. Texas*. The opinion held that the compulsory-process clause applied to the states and without dissent gave the following sweeping definition of the clause:

> The right to offer the testimony of witnesses, and to compel their attendance, if necessary, is in plain terms the right to present a defense, the right to present the defendant's version of the facts as well as the prosecution's to the jury so it may decide where the truth lies. Just as an accused has the right to confront the prosecution's witnesses for the purpose of challenging their testimony, he has the right to present his own witnesses to establish a defense. This right is a fundamental element of due process of law.[145]

Evidently, the decision did not reflect any long-term commitment by the Court to provide guidelines for the lower courts in resolving the numerous problems that surround this right. For example, in *Washington* the Court overturned a Texas law that excluded whole categories of defense witnesses (accomplices, accessories, principals) from testifying on the presumption that such witnesses are not worthy of belief. Presumably, the *Washington* rule disallows arbitrary exclusion of whole categories of defense witnesses and encourages trial courts to determine the competence of witnesses on an individual basis. Although *Washington* does not indicate a precise standard for the determination of competence, it appears to suggest that a witness is competent if he or she is physically and mentally capable of testifying to events personally observed and if the testimony is relevant and material to the defense.[146] Still, the Court has not suggested any constitutional guidelines to assist trial courts in determining whether proffered evidence is material or relevant.[147] This can be an important issue in those jurisdictions that set statutory limits on the number of defense subpoenas.

Finally, the Court has not addressed itself to the constitutional issue of discovery. If the right of compulsory process is, as the Court indicated in *Washington,* the right to present a defense, then an argument can be made that this includes the right to discover exculpatory evidence in the possession of the government. The Federal Rules of Criminal Procedure already provide for a limited nonconstitutional right in federal trials.[148] Although the Court has never imposed a similar requirement on the states, it has indicated that suppression by a state of favorable evidence requested by an accused violates due process.[149] But to come forth with material exculpatory evidence is no more than a prosecutorial-police duty, corresponding to the duty not to knowingly present or let stand false evidence.[150] The due process requirement of disclosure is related to, but not a substitute for, discovery.

The closest the Court has come to embracing a discovery requirement came in 1973 in *Wardius v. Oregon,* a case arising out of a state notice-of-alibi rule. The state rule required that a defendant file, in advance of trial, a notice of alibi. The Court held that such rules must be reciprocal; that is, that the state must grant a reciprocal right of discovery to the defendant: "The ends of justice will best be served by a system of liberal discovery which gives both parties the maximum possible amount of information with which to prepare their cases and thereby reduces the possiblity of a surprise at trial."[151]

Given the state's considerable advantage in information gathering and that a criminal trial is a search for truth, then the exaggerated fears of perjury and intimidation of witnesses that might result from defense discovery would appear to be "an old hobgoblin."[152] If a defendant is to be allowed to present a defense under the compulsory-process clause, then a degree of defense discovery must be required. Of course the amount of discovery, both by the defense and the state, is subject to debate. There are defense considerations of no compulsory self-incrimination and the burden of proof, and there are prosecutorial considerations, among them interference with ongoing investigation. But these considerations will never be resolved until the Court effectively mandates that the right of compulsory process includes a measure of defense discovery. If the state is to have the powers of the grand jury, of search and seizure, of arrest of material witnesses, of pretrial identification procedures, including fingerprinting, lineups, and voice exemplars, it seems reasonable and fair to allow the defense to discover the names and addresses of state witnesses, and to see copies of defendant's statements and reports of scientific analyses of evidence. Indeed, the defense, as a practical matter, already has a degree of discovery in those state jurisdictions that use a preliminary hearing as a substitute for a grand jury. The preliminary hearing generally requires the prosecution to reveal sufficient evidence to warrant holding a defendant for trial. Yet the preliminary hearing is not constitutionally mandated, and in many jurisdictions the prosecution may protect its evidence by using the secret grand jury rather than the preliminary-hearing procedure.[153]

The Confrontation and Cross-examination of Witnesses

Again it is appropriate to look back to the formative years in Anglo-American criminal procedure, and again the setting is seventeenth-century England. The time is November 17, 1603, and the place the Bishop's Palace in the city of Winchester, a safe sixty miles from London's then-raging plague. The occasion was the treason trial of Sir Walter Raleigh, who had been accused by Lord Cobham of a conspiracy against the recently crowned James I. Cobham was Raleigh's co-conspirator and sole accuser, and in conformity with established procedure did not appear at the trial. The injustice and harshness of this procedure is revealed in the following excerpts from Raleigh's trial:

> RALEIGH.   The Proof of the Common Law is by witness and jury: let Cobham be here, let him speak it. Call my accuser before my face, and I have done.
>
>   . . .
>
> LORD CECIL.   Sir Walter Raleigh presseth, that my Lord Cobham should be brought face to face. If he asks things of favour and grace, they must only

come from him that can give them. If we sit here as commissioners, how shall we be satisfied whether he ought to be brought, unless we hear the Judges speak?

LORD CHIEF JUSTICE. This thing cannot be granted, for then a number of Treasons should flourish. . . .

. . .

RALEIGH. The Common Trial of England is by Jury and Witnesses.

LORD CHIEF JUSTICE. No, by examination: if three conspire a Treason, and they all confess it; here is never a Witness, yet they are condemned.

. . .

RALEIGH. I know not how you conceive the Law.

LORD CHIEF JUSTICE. Nay, we do not conceive the Law, but we know the law.

RALEIGH. The wisdom of the Law of God is absolute and perfect *Haec fac et vives, &c.* But now by the Wisdom of the State, the Wisdom of the Law is uncertain. Indeed, where the Accuser is not to be had conveniently, I agree with you; but here my Accuser may; he is alive and in the house.

. . .

RALEIGH. My lords, vouchsafe me this grace: let him be brought, being alive, and in this house; let him avouch any of these things, I will confess the whole Indictment, and renounce the king's mercy.

. . .

RALEIGH. The lord Cobham hath accused me, you see in what manner he hath forsworn it. Were it not for his Accusation all this were nothing. Let him be asked, if I knew of the letter which Lawrency brought to him from Aremberg. Let me speak for my life, it can be no hurt for him to be brought; he dares not accuse me. If you grant me not this favour, I an strangely used.

ATTORNEY GENERAL COKE. He is a party, and may not come; the law is against it.

RALEIGH. It is a toy to tell me of law; I defy such law, I stand on the fact.

. . .

RALEIGH. If truth be constant, and constancy be in truth, why hath he forsworn that that he hath said? You have not proved any one thing against me by direct Proofs, but all by circumstances.

ATTORNEY GENERAL COKE. Have you done? The king must have the last.

RALEIGH. Nay, Mr. Attorney, he which speaketh for his life, must speak last. False repetitions and mistakings must not mar my cause.

ATTORNEY GENERAL COKE. Thou art the most vile and execrable Traitor that ever lived.

RALEIGH. You speak indiscreetly, barbarously, and uncivilly.

ATTORNEY GENERAL COKE. I want words sufficient to express thy viperous Treasons.

RALEIGH. I think you want words indeed, for you have spoken one thing half a dozen times.[154]

It took the jury only fifteen minutes to find Raleigh guilty, but it was nearly fifteen years later before James I sent Raleigh to the scaffold. Raleigh's wit was with him to the end. As he approached the headsman, he asked to see the ax. Feeling the edge of it, he was reported to have said, "This is sharp medicine, but it is a physician that will cure all diseases."[155]

Raleigh's trial is but one example in the development of criminal procedure where the state was not yet strong enough to be generous.[156] But the trial did mark a turning point. Paper depositions in criminal trials came under increasing attack in the common-law courts of seventeenth-century England,[157] and by the end of the century the common-law courts had accepted a general hearsay rule against paper depositions in criminal trials and in favor of confrontation, or *viva voce*, and cross-examination.[158]

The essence of the right of criminal defendants to confrontation and cross-examination of witnesses against them is the allocation of the trial burden on the prosecution: It requires the prosecution to produce its witnesses for a face-to-face examination. As the Supreme Court stated in *Mattox v. United States* (1895):

> The primary object of the constitutional provision in question was to prevent depositions or ex parte affidavits, such as were sometimes admitted in civil cases, being used against the prisoner in lieu of a personal examination and cross-examination of the witness, in which the accused has an opportunity, not only of testing the recollection and sifting the conscience of the witness, but of compelling him to stand face to face with the jury in order that they may look at him, and judge by his demeanor upon the stand and the manner in which he gives his testimony whether he is worthy of belief.[159]

Although the right of confrontation and cross-examination applies in equal manner to both federal and state criminal trials,[160] there are exceptions to its absolute application. One of the oldest exceptions, commonly thought of as an exception to the hearsay rule, is for dying declarations. The arguable assumption of this exception is that the approach of death frees one of any motive to deceive or misstate; in fact, it is contended that one is induced by powerful considerations to tell the truth.[161] Although originally the exception was general in both civil and criminal cases, today it is limited to homicide prosecutions and by the following requirements:

1. The witness must be unavailable by reason of death.
2. The death statement must be made by the victim of the pending homicide prosecution.

3. The death statement must be limited to events immediately surrounding the death.
4. The declarant must have been aware of impending death.

If a death declaration meets these requirements, it may be admitted on behalf of either the state or the defense.[162] In *Mattox,* the victim's declaration was made after he had been shot three times, had asked a physician about his chances, and was told they were all against him. The declarant died within a few hours. Before his death, he said he did not know who shot him, and this was admitted without objection. But when Mattox's attorney attempted to refresh the memory of the interrogator of the victim by asking whether the victim had also said that he knew he was not shot by Clyde Mattox, the trial judge sustained a prosecution objection. On appeal the Supreme Court reversed, holding that the rule on dying declarations should be no more rigorous when applied in favor of an accused than when it is applied against an accused.[163]

Mattox did not end with the reversal. Mattox was tried a second time, and his second trial and appeal provide occasion to note another major exception to the right of confrontation and cross-examination, one that is far more likely to occur than a dying declaration exception. This exception concerns the prior sworn testimony of unavailable witnesses, and was occasioned in the second trial by the death of two of the government's previous witnesses. A transcribed copy of their prior testimony, which had been subjected to cross-examination, was admitted as evidence in the second trial. In upholding the admission of the testimony, the Court argued that necessity demanded the exception and noted:

> To say that a criminal, after having once been convicted by the testimony of a certain witness, should go scot free simply because death has closed the mouth of the witness, would be carrying his constitutional protection to an unwarrantable extent. The law in its wisdom declares that the rights of the public shall not be wholly sacrificed in order that an incidental benefit may be preserved to the accused.
> . . . The substance of the constitutional protection is preserved to the prisoner in the advantage he has once had of seeing the witness face to face, and of subjecting him to the ordeal of a cross-examination.[164]

Recently, the Court has made clear that prior testimony must be testimony of a witness who in fact is not available. In 1968, it reversed the conviction in *Barber v. Page,* where the state had been allowed to introduce the prior testimony (at the preliminary hearing) of a witness who at the time of the trial was in a federal prison in another state. No effort was made to obtain the presence of the missing witness. Furthermore, defense counsel had not cross-examined the missing witness during the hearing.[165] The Court noted that the testimony of federal prisoners is commonly obtained by writs of *habeas corpus ad testificandum.*[166]

The threshold question of whether the prior testimony was subject to or in fact subjected to cross-examination is yet to be resolved. The issue was raised in 1965, in the landmark case *Pointer v. Texas*. In *Pointer*, the Court objected to the use of the missing witness's testimony because the statement "had not been taken at a time and under circumstances affording petitioner through counsel an adequate opportunity to cross-examine."[167]

Whatever ambiguities may be found in *Barber* and *Pointer*, they are pale in comparison to those that emerged in two cases heard by the court in 1970. The first, *California v. Green*, might have been a clear rule but for the fact that it presented a situation in which it was virtually impossible to cross-examine the witness about his prior testimony.[168] The witness had testified in a preliminary hearing and had been subjected to extensive cross-examination by defense counsel. However, at the trial, the witness proved to be remarkably evasive and uncooperative, and the state was allowed to "refresh" his memory by reading parts of his prior testimony under a California prior–inconsistent statement rule. The Supreme Court, rejecting contentions that the confrontation rule incorporates the common-law rule against hearsay evidence,[169] upheld the admission of the prior statements. The Court based its ruling on two points: First, it held that where a declarant testifies at the trial and is subject to full and effective cross-examination, the confrontation requirement has been met. Second, the Court indicated that even if the witness had not been available at trial, his prior testimony could have been admitted because it was taken under circumstances closely approximating those that surround a typical trial.

The problem with the *Green* rationale is that it makes a shambles of the defense right of cross-examination. Insofar as defense cross-examination is concerned, it makes little difference whether a witness is either unable or unwilling to testify about the events contained in a prior statement. Defense cannot cross-examine silence.[170] It may be that the witness is lying or it may be an honest failure of memory, but the result is the same: The defense is precluded from qualifying or discrediting the witness's prior statement because the witness has not affirmed the prior statement.

The second decision is further evidence of the Court's retreat from *Pointer*. In *Dutton v. Evans*, a plurality of the Court again indicated that the right of confrontation and cross-examination does not incorporate rules against hearsay evidence.[171] At Evans's trial, a witness was allowed to testify as to a remark made to him by an alleged accomplice of the defendant. The accomplice was not produced at trial, even though the admitted remark attributed to him implied that Evans had been the perpetrator of the crime. The plurality's rationale for allowing this hearsay testimony to stand was threefold: First, it noted that the right of confrontation does not place an absolute bar on hearsay evidence. Further, it noted that a witness under oath and subject to cross-examination is a reliable informant as to what he or she has seen *and* also as to what he or she has heard. Finally, the plurality suggested that the particular hearsay admitted had indicia of reliability—the hearsay was spontaneous and against the penal interest of the alleged accomplice.

The dissenters in *Dutton* properly asked why the state was not forced to confront Evans with the person who allegedly gave witness against him.[172] Indeed, there would seem to be little meaning to a confrontation right where the demeanor purpose is dismissed under such vague and questionable indicia as "spontaneous utterance" and "against the penal interest."[173]

CONCLUSION

Over the past three hundred years, Anglo-American law has evolved procedures to ensure that criminal trials are something more than solemn pageants. The rights range from speedy and public trial to compulsory process. Like other criminal procedures, they tether the state and consequently are burdensome and even irksome to prosecutors and not a few trial judges. But democracy has yet to perfect a better instrument for the discovery of truth than a public trial in which the accused is allowed to face his or her accusers and to present a defense, with the full benefit of guilt beyond a reasonable doubt.

All of the Sixth Amendment rights have been nationalized, applying equally to state and federal criminal trials. There are, of course, many pitfalls in the nationalization of these rules of criminal procedure. Yet all of the caveats about moving too far and too fast, about the constraints of federalism and the wisdom of preserving room for growth,[174] hardly make an argument for no movement and no growth. The troublesome problems of presumptions, discovery, and hearsay cannot obscure the need to ensure criminal defendants that their trials are just and fair. The Supreme Court's recent retreats from providing the criminal courts with adequate guidelines in areas that are central to fair trial (compulsory process, confrontation) are difficult to support. To retreat into an argument that a fair criminal trial does not demand reasonably precise rules is to ignore the rationale that stands in back of the rise of rules of criminal procedure in Anglo-American history: The truth of a criminal charge is not in its making. Of course, when we move from a broad constitutional principle, such as that of fair trial, and descend to rules, we lose a degree of flexibility. But constitutional principles without operative meaning—that is, without rules—remain hollow.

NOTES

1. *Trial of Lady Alice Lisle,* 2 How. St. Tr. 342–359 (1685).

2. *Attaint* was a Crown action against jurors for corrupt or perverse verdicts. See James Fitzjames Stephen, *A History of the Criminal Law in England* (London: Macmillan, 1883), vol. 1, pp. 306–307.

3. *Trial* at 375.

4. Ibid. at 379.

5. Joseph Story, *Commentaries on the Constitution* (Boston: Little, Brown, 1851), bk. 3, § 1791.

6. Stephen, *History of Criminal Law*, vol. 1, p. 284.

7. William Blackstone, *Commentaries on the Laws of England*, Cooley ed. (Chicago: Callaghan, 1884), bk. 4, § 307.

8. Ibid. at § 306.

9. *United States v. Mills*, 7 Pet. 138 (1833).

10. *United States v. Cook*, 17 Wall. 168 (1872).

11. *Hamling v. United States*, 418 U.S. 87, 117 (1974); and *United States v. Simmons*, 96 U.S. 360, 362 (1878).

12. *United States v. Hess*, 124 U.S. 483, 487 (1888).

13. Enforcement Act of May, 1870, 16 Stat 141, § 6.

14. *United States v. Cruikshank*, 92 U.S. 542, 558 (1876).

15. Id.

16. *Cochran v. United States*, 157 U.S. 286, 290 (1895).

17. *United States v. Cruikshank*, 92 U.S. at 548.

18. *Berger v. United States*, 295 U.S. 78 (1935). However, the charges in a grand jury indictment may not be broadened by amendment except by the grand jury, *Ex parte Bain*, 121 U.S. 1 (1887).

19. *Stirone v. United States*, 361 U.S. 212 (1960).

20. *Twining v. New Jersey*, 211 U.S. 78 (1908).

21. Ibid. at 112.

22. *Snyder v. Massachusetts*, 291 U.S. 97, 105 (1934).

23. *Cole v. Arkansas*, 333 U.S. 196, 201 (1948); and see *In re Oliver*, 333 U.S. 257, 275 (1948). State courts assume that the requirement is binding on them, e.g., *Vermont v. Hartman*, 349 A.2d 223 (1975), and *Michigan v. Jones*, 236 N.W.2d 461 (1975). For the notice requirement for federal indictments, see Fed. Rules of Crim. Proc., rule 7-C, 18 U.S.C.

24. *United States v. Johnson*, 323 U.S. 273, 275–276 (1944); and see the dissent of Justice Douglas in *Johnson v. United States*, 351 U.S. 215, 223 (1956).

25. See below, p. 396.

26. See *Hyde v. United States*, 225 U.S. 347, 363 (1912); *Palliser v. United States*, 136 U.S. 357 (1890); and *Travis v. United States*, 364 U.S. 631 (1961).

27. See Fed. Rules Crim. Proc., rule 18, 18 U.S.C.

28. Rule 18 and rule 21 of the Federal Rules of Criminal Procedure both mention the convenience of parties and witnesses in fixing the place of a federal trial.

29. *Lewis v. United States*, 146 U.S. 370 (1892).

30. Ibid. at 372.

31. *Diaz v. United States*, 223 U.S. 442 (1912).

32. Ibid. at 455.

33. Accord, *Taylor v. United States*, 414 U.S. 19 (1973).

34. *Snyder v. Massachusetts*, 291 U.S. at 106.

35. Ibid. at 107.

36. Id.

37. *Shields v. United States*, 273 U.S. 583 (1927); accord, *Rogers v. United States*, 422 U.S. 35 (1975). See also rule 43, Fed. Rules Crim. Proc., which provides that defendants in federal trials shall also be present at the imposition of sentence, 18 U.S.C. Federal courts also generally require the presence of defendants for any subsequent increases in the sentence, e.g., *United States v. Marquez*, 506 F.2d 620 (1974), but not for a reduction in the sentence, e.g., *United States v. McCray*, 468 F.2d 446 (1962). There is also some variation in federal courts on whether a represented defendant has a right of

presence in chamber conferences, e.g., *McKissick v. United States,* 379 F.2d 754 (1967); cf. *United States v. Sinclair,* 430 F.2d 50 (1971).

38. *Argersinger v. Hamlin,* 407 U.S. 25 (1972).

39. Ibid. at 37.

40. Excluding, however, parking offenses.

41. It is uncertain whether a defendant in a capital offense even has a right of waiver; see *Diaz v. United States,* 223 U.S. at 455, and *Near v. Cunningham,* 313 F.2d 929, 931 (1963).

42. *Snyder v. Massachusetts,* 291 U.S. at 106.

43. *Illinois v. Allen,* 397 U.S. 337 (1970).

44. Ibid. at 343.

45. Quoted in *Klopfer v. North Carolina,* 386 U.S. 213, 224 (1967).

46. Ibid. at 225, n. 21.

47. See note, "The Right to a Speedy Trial," 20 *Stan. L. Rev.* 476, 482 (1968).

48. *United States v. Ewell,* 383 U.S. 116, 120 (1966).

49. *Beavers v. Haubert,* 198 U.S. 77, 87 (1905).

50. *Barker v. Wingo,* 407 U.S. 514, 519–521 (1972).

51. *Klopfer v. North Carolina.*

52. *Barker v. Wingo,* 407 U.S. at 523.

53. *United States v. Marion,* 404 U.S. 308, 320 (1971).

54. *Barker v. Wingo,* 407 U.S. at 530.

55. Ibid. at 532.

56. Pub. L. 93-619, 88 Stat. 2076. It is problematical whether the more restricted time limits of the legislation of 1974 will be implemented. Federal prosecutors, defenders, and judges have urged Congress to amend the act.

57. *Strunk v. United States,* 412 U.S. 434, 440 (1973).

58. See Max Radin, "The Right to a Public Trial," 6 *Temple L.Q.* 381 (1932).

59. *Cowley v. Pulsifer,* 137 Mass. 392, 394 (1884).

60. As a requirement of due process, the right to a public trial is presumably binding on the states.

61. *In re Oliver,* 333 U.S. at 271–272.

62. E.g., *United States ex rel. Orlando v. Jay,* 350 F.2d 967 (1965).

63. E.g., *Pennsylvania v. Stevens,* 352 A.2d 509 (1975); and *Illinois v. Latimore,* 342 N.E.2d 209 (1975).

64. E.g., *Marshall v. Indiana,* 258 N.E.2d 169 (1969).

65. E.g., *United States ex rel. Maisonet v. La Vallee,* 405 F. Supp. 925 (1975); and *New York v. Rickenbacker,* 374 N.Y. Supp. 2d 672 (1975).

66. *Gannett v. DePasquale,* ___ U.S. ___ (1979).

67. *Craig v. Harvey,* 331 U.S. 367, 374 (1947); in *Gannett v. DePasquale,* the majority indicated that the press as well as the public has no First Amendment right to be present at a trial.

68. For a discussion of pretrial publicity and the voir dire, see Chapter 10, p. 342–344. On the issue of fair trial and pretrial publicity occurring outside of the courtroom, see *Rideau v. Louisiana,* 373 U.S. 723 (1963).

69. *Estes v. Texas,* 381 U.S. 532 (1965).

70. *Sheppard v. Maxwell,* 384 U.S. 333 (1966).

71. Justice Harlan's concurring opinion limited his agreement to prohibiting television coverage in the courtroom of a highly publicized and sensational criminal trial, *Estes v. Texas,* 381 U.S. at 590.

72. Ibid. at 549.

73. Additionally, canon 35 of the Judicial Canons of the American Bar Association opposed broadcasting, televising, and photographing in the courtroom.

74. *Sheppard v. Maxwell*, 384 U.S. at 355.

75. Ibid. at 361.

76. Ibid. at 358.

77. Jack C. Landau, "Fair Trial and Free Press: A Due Process Proposal," 62 *A.B.A.J.* 55 (1976).

78. E.g., *United States v. CBS*, 497 F.2d 102 (1974). Cf. *State of Florida ex rel. Miami Herald v. Rose*, 271 So.2d 483 (1972); and cases cited in *New York v. Marino*, 383 N.Y. Supp. 2d 147, 149 (1976).

79. *Nebraska Press Ass'n. v. Stuart*, 427 U.S. 539 (1976).

80. Ibid. at 543.

81. Relying on *New York Times v. United States*, 403 U.S. 713 (1971).

82. *Nebraska Press Ass'n. v. Stuart*, 427 U.S. at 556. Four of the justices in concurring opinions indicated doubts about the validity of any form of prior restraint on the press; see the concurring opinion of Justice Brennan, joined by Justices Stewart and Marshall, at 556–557.

83. *In re Muchison*, 349 U.S. 133, 136 (1955).

84. *Tumey v. Ohio*, 273 U.S. 510 (1927).

85. Ibid. at 523.

86. See generally John P. Frank, "Disqualification of Judges," 35 *Law & Contemp. Prob.* 43 (1970).

87. See Sir Edward Coke's opinion in *The Dr. Bonham Case*, 77 Eng. Rep. 633 (1608).

88. *Tumey v. Ohio*, 273 U.S. at 523. Federal statutory law does, however, provide for disqualification of federal judges based on bias or prejudice; see 28 U.S.C. 144, and *Berger v. United States*, 255 U.S. 22 (1921).

89. E.g., *United States v. Sciuto*, 531 F.2d 842, 845 (1976).

90. *Offutt v. United States*, 348 U.S. 11, 17 (1954).

91. *United States v. Nozzaro*, 472 F.2d 302, 313 (1973).

92. Id.

93. Id.

94. *Offutt v. United States*, 348 U.S. at 17.

95. *United States v. Dellinger*, 472 F.2d 340, 387 (1972).

96. *Starr v. United States*, 153 U.S. 614, 626 (1894).

97. *Quercia v. United States*, 289 U.S. 466, 469 (1933).

98. *Starr v. United States*, 153 U.S. at 625.

99. *Brady v. Maryland*, 373 U.S. 83, 87 (1963); *Napue v. Illinois*, 360 U.S. 264, 269 (1959); and *Alcorta v. Texas*, 355 U.S. 28 (1957).

100. *Mooney v. Holohan*, 294 U.S. 103, 110 (1935).

101. *Giglio v. United States*, 405 U.S. 150, 153 (1972).

102. *United States v. Dellinger*, 472 F.2d at 386.

103. See *Berger v. United States* (1935); and *Miller v Pate*, 386 U.S. 1 (1967). Cf. *Donnelly v. DeChristoforo*, 416 U.S. 637 (1974).

104. *Speiser v. Randall*, 357 U.S. 513, 525 (1958).

105. The standard of proof in civil cases is the preponderance-of-evidence rule, Wigmore, *On Evidence*, vol. 5, § 2498, 1923 ed. A clear and convincing rule is sometimes applied, see note, "Does Due Process Require Clear and Convincing Proof . . .?" 24 *Emory L.J.* 105 (1975).

106. George Christie and A. K. Pye, "Presumptions and Assumptions in the Criminal Law," 1970 *Duke L.J.* 919, 927 (1970).

107. See Wigmore, *On Evidence,* § 2497, n. 2.

108. *In re Winship*, 397 U.S. 358, 364 (1970). *Winship* also held that juvenile proceedings are bound by the reasonable-doubt standard.

109. See Wigmore, *On Evidence,* vol. 5, § 2511; and Charles T. McCormick, *Handbook of the Law on Evidence* (St. Paul, Minn.: West, 1954), § 309.

110. *Taylor v. Kentucky,* ___ U.S. ___ (1978). *Taylor* extends to the states a rule that has long obtained in federal criminal trials; see *Coffin v. United States,* 156 U.S. 432, 453 (1895). Cf. *Kentucky v. Whorton,* ___ U.S. ___ (1979), where the Court retreated from *Taylor* and held that failure to give a requested instruction on the presumption of innocence, does not per se violate the Constitution.

111. *Holland v. United States,* 348 U.S. 121, 139 (1954).

112. E.g., McCormick, *On Evidence,* § 321; and Wigmore, *On Evidence,* § 2497.

113. See *West Virginia v. Starr,* 216 S.E. 2d 242 (1975).

114. *Holland v. United States,* 209 F.2d 516, 522–523 (1954), aff'd, 348 U.S. at 139 (1954). Cf. *United States v. Lawsen,* 507 F.2d 433 (1974).

115. E.g., *Kansas v. Sully,* 547 P.2d 344 (1974); and *North Carolina v. Sheppard,* 218 S.E.2d 176 (1975).

116. *Dunbar v. United States,* 156 U.S. 185, 199 (1895).

117. See, e.g., William Mathes, "Jury Instructions," 27 F.R.D. 48, § 2.01 (1960).

118. This section does not treat the issue of assumptions and affirmative defenses. See *Mullaney v. Wilbur,* 421 U.S. 684 (1975); Harold Ashford and Michael Risinger, "Presumptions, Assumptions and Due Process in Criminal Cases," 79 *Yale L.J.* 165, 173–174 (1969). In 1977, in a 5-to-3 decision, the Court handed down its opinion in *Patterson v. New York,* 432 U.S. 197 (1977), involving an affirmative defense of acting under the influence of extreme emotional disturbance to a second-degree-murder charge. The opinion comes close to overturning the *Mullaney* decision and substantially undermines part of the *Winship* decision. Under the particular New York affirmative-defense rule involved in *Patterson,* a defendant could reduce a second-degree-murder charge to a first-degree-manslaughter charge by assuming the burdens of proof *and* persuasion that he or she acted under the influence of extreme emotional disturbance. In upholding this shift in the burden of persuasion, the Court endorsed the possibility that a state may define a criminal offense in extremely narrow terms, deleting from the crime elements that had heretofore been considered essential, among them *mens rea,* or intent. By deleting culpability and treating culpability separately in various forms of affirmative defenses, including acting in the heat of passion on extreme provocation, the burden on the prosecution is reduced. As the dissent noted in *Patterson:*

> The test the Court today established allows a legislature to shift, virtually at will, the burden of persuasion with respect to any factor in a criminal case, so long as it is careful not to mention the nonexistence of that factor in the statutory language that defines the crime. The sole requirement is that any references to the factor be confined to those sections that provide for an affirmative defense.

119. Commentators distinguish between inferences and presumptions, the latter being a legal conclusion presumably binding on the trier of fact, whereas an *inference* is nothing more than a permissible deduction from the evidence. The difference in nomenclature is important only in regard to the permissive and mandatory impact on a jury's freedom to weigh the evidence. See Wigmore, *On Evidence,* vol. 5, § 2490; *Mullaney v. Wilbur,* 421 U.S. at 702–703, n. 31; and McCormick, *On Evidence,* § 308.

120. *Barnes v. United States,* 412 U.S. 837, 843 (1973); and *United States v. Gainey,* 380 U.S. 63 (1965).

121. *Tot v. United States,* 319 U.S. 463, 468 (1943).

122. *Leary v. United States,* 395 U.S. 6 (1969). Cf. *County Court of Ulster v. Allen,* ___ U.S. ___ (1979), where the Court upheld a New York law that allows a permissive presumption that the presence of any firearm in an automobile is presumptive evidence of its possession by all occupants.

123. *United States v. Gainey.* Cf. *United States v. Romano,* 382 U.S. 136 (1965).

124. *United States v. Gainey,* 380 U.S. at 67.

125. *Barnes v. United States,* 412 U.S. at 844–845.

126. *County Court of Ulster v. Allen,* ___ U.S. ___ (1979).

127. Dissenting in *United States v. Gainey,* 380 U.S. at 83.

128. See a discussion of this in Ashford and Risinger, "Presumptions." See also *Sandstrom v. Virginia,* __ U.S. __ (1979), where the Court disallowed a judge's instruction that, in a deliberate homicide case, the law presumes a person intends the ordinary consequences of his or her voluntary acts. Since the defendant acknowledged he had killed the victim, the instruction could have had the effect of conclusively presuming intent without the state's offering any proof of intent.

129. Christie and Pye, "Presumptions and Assumptions."

130. Ibid. at 939.

131. *Thompson v. Louisville,* 362 U.S. 199, 206 (1960), reaff'd, *Vachon v. New Hampshire,* 414 U.S. 478, 480 (1974).

132. *Harris v. United States,* 404 U.S. 1206, 1233 (1971).

133. *Cephus v. United States,* 325 F.2d 893 (1963).

134. Fed. Rules Crim. Proc., rule 29(a).

135. For a general discussion of the relevant cases, see A. Goldstein, "The State and the Accused: Balance of Advantage in Criminal Procedure," 69 *Yale L.J.* 1149, 1155–1163 (1960).

136. Ibid. at 1161.

137. *United States v. Taylor,* 464 F.2d 240, 245 (1972).

138. E.g., *Johnson v. Turner,* 429 F.2d 1152, 1155 (1970). Cf. *Jackson v. Virginia,* __ U.S. __ (1979), where the Court recognized that the *Thompson* no-evidence rule was inadequate and indicated that reviewing courts should examine the evidence in a light most favorable to the prosecution and determine whether *any* rational trier of fact could have found the essential elements of the crime beyond a reasonable doubt.

139. *Washington v. Texas,* 388 U.S. 14 (1967).

140. Nor, of course, did defendants have a right to testify in their own behalf.

141. See generally Peter Westin, "The Compulsory Process Clause," 73 *Mich. L. Rev.* 73 (1974).

142. 1 Anne 2, chap. 9, § 3 (1701).

143. Westin, "Compulsory Process," pp. 93–95.

144. *United States v. Burr,* 25 F. Cas. 30 (no. 14, 692d) (1807), and 25 (no. 14, 694th) F. Cas. 187 (no. 14, 694th) (1807).

145. *Washington v. Texas,* 388 U.S. at 19.

146. Ibid. at 23.

147. See generally Westin, "Compulsory Process," pt. 2, pp. 205–231.

148. Fed. Rules Crim. Proc., rule 16. See also *Jenks v. United States,* 353 U.S. 657 (1957); 18 U.S.C. 3500; and *United States v. Nixon,* 418 U.S. 683, 698–702 (1974).

149. *Brady v. Maryland.*

150. E.g., *Napue v. Illinois* and *Alcorta v. Texas.*

151. *Wardius v. Oregon,* 412 U.S. 470, 473 (1973).

152. Justice Brennan dissenting in *New Jersey v. Tune,* 98 A.2d 881, 901 (1953).

153. See generally Barry Nakell, "Criminal Discovery for the Defense and Prosecution," 50 *N.C. L. Rev.* 437 (1972).

154. *The Trial of Sir Walter Raleigh,* 2 How St. Tr. 1, 1–31 (1603).

155. Ibid. at 44.

156. Stephen, *History of Criminal Law,* vol. 1, p. 355.

157. E.g., *Fitzpatrick's Trial,* 3 How. St. Tr. 419, 421 (1631).

158. E.g., *Fenwick's Trial,* 13 How. St. Tr. 537, 591–607 (1696). See generally Wigmore, *On Evidence,* § 1364.

159. *Mattox v. United States II,* 156 U.S. 237, 242–243 (1895).

160. *Pointer v. Texas,* 380 U.S. 400 (1965).

161. See *Wright v. Littler,* 3 Burr. 1244 (1761); and *Woodcock's Case,* Leach Cr. P. 500 (1789).

162. Subject, however, to general principles of testimonial qualification for the deceased, among them rules on infancy, and subject to impeachment in an area such as the bad testimonial character of the deceased. See generally Wigmore, *On Evidence*, §§1430–1445.

163. *Mattox v. United States I*, 146 U.S. 140, 152 (1892).

164. *Mattox v. United States II*, 156 U.S. at 243–244.

165. *Barber v. Page*, 390 U.S. 719 (1968).

166. The Uniform Act to Secure Attendance of Witnesses is available to secure the testimony of witnesses not in prison.

167. *Pointer v. Texas*, 380 U.S. at 407.

168. *California v. Green*, 399 U.S. 149 (1970).

169. Ibid. at 155–156.

170. E.g., see *Douglas v. Alabama*, 380 U.S. 415, 419–420 (1965).

171. *Dutton v. Evans*, 400 U.S. 74 (1970).

172. Ibid. at 100.

173. For further insight into the Burger Court's treatment of confrontation and cross-examination, see *Nelson v. O'Neill*, 402 U.S. 622 (1971), limiting the *Bruton* rule on admission of a codefendant's confession in a joint trial, *Bruton v. United States*, 391 U.S. 123 (1968), and *Roberts v. Russell*, 392 U.S. 293 (1968).

174. See Henry J. Friendly, "The Bill of Rights as a Code of Criminal Procedure," 53 *Calif. L. Rev.* 929 (1965).

JUDICIAL DECISIONS

The Presence of the Defendant:
Taylor v. United States, *414 U.S. 19 (1973)*

PER CURIAM.

On the first day of his trial on four counts of selling cocaine in violation of 26 U.S.C. § 4705(a) (1964 ed.), petitioner failed to return for the afternoon session. He had been present at the expiration of the morning session when the court announced that the lunch recess would last until 2 p.m., and he had been told by his attorney to return to the courtroom at that time. The judge recessed the trial until the following morning, but petitioner still did not appear. His wife testified that she had left the courtroom the previous day with petitioner after the morning session; that they had separated after sharing a taxicab to Roxbury; that he had not appeared ill; and, finally, that she had not heard from him since. The trial judge then denied a motion for mistrial by defense counsel, who asserted that the jurors' minds would be tainted by petitioner's absence and that continuation of the trial in his absence deprived him of his Sixth Amendment right to confront witnesses against him. Relying upon Fed. Rules Crim. Proc. 43, which expressly provides that a defendant's voluntary absence "shall not prevent continuing the trial," the court found that petitioner had absented himself voluntarily from the proceedings.

Throughout the remainder of the trial, the court admonished the jury that no inference of guilt could be drawn from petitioner's absence. Petitioner was found guilty on all four counts. Following his subsequent arrest, he was sentenced to the statutory five-year minimum. The Court of Appeals affirmed the conviction, 478 F.2d 689 (C.A.1 1973), and we now grant the motion for leave to proceed *in forma pauperis* and the petition for certiorari and affirmed the judgment of the Court of Appeals.

There is no challenge to the trial court's conclusion that petitioner's absence from the trial was voluntary and no claim that the continuation of the trial was not authorized by Rule 43. Nor are we persuaded that Rule 43 is unconstitutional or that petitioner was deprived of any constitutional rights in the circumstances before us. Rule 43 has remained unchanged since the adoption of the Federal Rules of Criminal Procedure in 1945; and with respect to the consequences of the defendant's voluntary absence from trial, it reflects the long-standing rule recognized by this Court in *Diaz v. United States,* 223 U.S. 442, 455 (1912). . . . Under this rule, the District Court and the Court of Appeals correctly rejected petitioner's claims.

Petitioner, however, insists that his mere voluntary absence from his trial cannot be construed as an effective waiver, that is, "an intentional relinquishment or abandonment of a known right or privilege," *Johnson v. Zerbst,* 304 U.S. 458, 464 (1938), unless it is demonstrated that he knew or had been expressly warned by the trial court not only that he had a right to be present but also that the trial would continue in his absence and thereby effectively foreclose his right to testify and to confront personally the witnesses against him.

Like the Court of Appeals, we cannot accept this position. Petitioner had no right to interrupt the trial by his voluntary absence, as he implicitly concedes by urging only that he should have been warned that no such right existed and that the trial would proceed in his absence. The right at issue is the right to be present, and the question becomes whether that right was effectively waived by his voluntary absence. Consistent with Rule 43 and *Diaz,* we conclude that it was.

It is wholly incredible to suggest that petitioner, who was at liberty on bail, had attended the opening session of his trial, and had a duty to be present at the trial, entertained any doubts about his right to be present at every stage of his trial. It seems equally incredible to us, as it did to the Court of Appeals, "that a defendant who flees from a courtroom in the midst of a trial—where judge, jury, witnesses and lawyers are present and ready to continue—would not know that as a consequence the trial could continue in his absence." Here the Court of Appeals noted that when petitioner was questioned at sentencing regarding his flight, he never contended that he was unaware that a consequence of his flight would be a continuation of the trial without him. Moreover, no issue of the voluntariness of his disappearance was ever raised. . . .

Affirmed.

Speedy Trial:
Barker v. Wingo, 407 U.S. 514 (1972)

Mr. Justice POWELL delivered the opinion of the Court.

Although a speedy trial is guaranteed the accused by the Sixth Amendment to the Constitution, this Court has dealt with that right on infrequent occasions. The Court's opinion in *Klopfer v. North Carolina,* 386 U.S. 213 (1967), established that the right to a speedy trial is "fundamental" and is imposed by the Due Process Clause of the Fourteenth Amendment on the States. As Mr. Justice Brennan pointed out . . . in none of these cases have we attempted to set out the criteria by which the speedy trial right is to be judged. This case compels us to make such an attempt.

I

On July 20, 1958, in Christian County, Kentucky, an elderly couple was beaten to death by intruders wielding an iron tire tool. Two suspects, Silas Manning and Willie Barker, the petitioner, were arrested shortly thereafter. The grand jury indicted them on September 15. Counsel was appointed on Septembr 17, and Barker's trial was set for October 21. The Commonwealth had a stronger case against Manning, and it believed that Barker could not be convicted unless Manning testified against him. Manning was naturally unwilling to incriminate himself. Accordingly, on October 23, the day Silas Manning was brought to trial, the Commonwealth sought and obtained the first of what was to be a series of 16 continuances of Barker's trial. Barker made no objection. By first convicting Manning, the Commonwealth would remove possible problems of self-incrimination and would be able to assure his testimony against Barker.

The Commonwealth encountered more than a few difficulties in its prosecution of Manning. The first trial ended in a hung jury. A second trial resulted in a conviction, but the Kentucky Court of Appeals reversed because of the admission of evidence obtained by an illegal search. *Manning v. Commonwealth,* 328 S.W.2d 421 (1959). At his third trial, Manning was again convicted, and the Court of Appeals again reversed because the trial court had not granted a change of venue. *Manning v. Commonwealth,* 346 S.W.2d 755 (1961). A fourth trial resulted in a hung jury. Finally, after five trials, Manning was convicted, in March 1962, of murdering one victim, and after a sixth trial, in December 1962, he was convicted of murdering the other.

The Christian County Circuit Court holds three terms each year—in February, June, and September. Barker's initial trial was to take place in the September term of 1958. The first continuance postponed it until the February 1959 term. The second continuance was granted for one month only. Every term thereafter for as long as the *Manning* prosecutions were in process, the Commonwealth routinely moved to continue Barker's case to the next term. When the case was continued from the June 1959 term until the following September, Barker, having spent 10 months in jail, obtained his release by posting a $5,000 bond. He thereafter remained free in the community until his trial. Barker made no objection, through his counsel, to the first 11 continuances.

When on February 12, 1962, the Commonwealth moved for the twelfth time to continue the case until the following term, Barker's counsel filed a motion to dismiss the indictment. The motion to dismiss was denied two weeks later, and the Commonwealth's motion for a continuance was granted. The Commonwealth was granted further continuances in June 1962 and September 1962, to which Barker did not object.

In February 1963, the first term of court following Manning's final conviction, the Commonwealth moved to set Barker's trial for March 19. But on the day scheduled for trial, it again moved for a continuance until the June term. It gave as its reason the illness of the ex-sheriff who was the chief investigating officer in the case. To this continuance, Barker objected unsuccessfully.

The witness was still unable to testify in June, and the trial, which had been set for June 19, was continued again until the September term over Barker's objection. This time the court announced that the case would be dismissed for lack of prosecution if it were not tried during the next term. The final trial date was set for October 9, 1963. On that date, Barker again moved to dismiss the indictment, and this time specified that his right to a speedy trial had been violated. The motion was denied; the trial commenced with Manning as the chief prosecution witness; Barker was convicted and given a life sentence.

. . .

II

The right to a speedy trial is generically different from any of the other rights enshrined in the Constitution for the protection of the accused. In addition to the general concern that all accused persons be treated according to decent and fair procedures, there is a societal interest in providing a speedy trial which exists separate from, and at times in opposition to, the interests of the accused. The inability of courts to provide a prompt trial has contributed to a large backlog of cases in urban courts which, among other things, enables defendants to negotiate more effectively for pleas of guilty to lesser offenses and otherwise manipulate the system. In addition, persons released on bond for lengthy periods awaiting trial have an opportunity to commit other crimes. It must be of little comfort to the residents of Christian County, Kentucky, to know that Barker was at large on bail for over four years while accused of a vicious and brutal murder of which he was ultimately convicted. Moreover, the longer an accused is free awaiting trial, the more tempting becomes his opportunity to jump bail and escape. Finally, delay between arrest and punishment may have a detrimental effect on rehabilitation.

If an accused cannot make bail, he is generally confined, as was Barker for 10 months, in a local jail. This contributes to the overcrowding and generally deplorable state of those institutions. Lengthy exposure to these conditions "has a destructive effect on human character and makes the rehabilitation of the individual offender much more difficult." At times the result may even be violent rioting. Finally, lengthy pretrial detention is costly. The cost of maintaining a prisoner in jail varies from $3 to $9 per day, and this amounts to millions across the Nation. In addition, society loses wages which might have been earned, and it must often support families of incarcerated breadwinners.

A second difference between the right to speedy trial and the accused's other constitutional rights is that deprivation of the right may work to the accused's advantage. Delay is not an uncommon defense tactic. As the time between the commission of the crime and trial lengthens, witnesses may become unavailable or their memories may fade. If the witnesses support the prosecution, its case will be weakened, sometimes seriously so. And it is the prosecution which carries the burden of proof. Thus, unlike the right to counsel or the right to be free from compelled self-incrimination, deprivation of the right to speedy trial does not per se prejudice the accused's ability to defend himself.

Finally, and perhaps most importantly, the right to speedy trial is a more vague concept than other procedural rights. It is, for example, impossible to determine with precision when the right has been denied. We cannot definitely say how long is too long in a system where justice is supposed to be swift but deliberate. As a consequence, there is no fixed point in the criminal process when the State can put the defendant to the choice of either exercising or waiving the right to a speedy trial. If, for example, the State moves for a 60-day continuance, granting that continuance is not a violation of the right to speedy trial unless the circumstances of the case are such that further delay would endanger the values the right protects. It is impossible to do more than generalize about when those circumstances exist. There is nothing comparable to the point in the process when a defendant exercises or waives his right to counsel or his right to a jury trial. . . .

The amorphous quality of the right also leads to the unsatisfactorily severe remedy of dismissal of the indictment when the right has been deprived. This is indeed a serious consequence because it means that a defendant who may be guilty of a serious crime will go free, without having been tried. Such a remedy is more serious than an exclusionary rule or a reversal for a new trial, but it is the only possible remedy.

III

Perhaps because the speedy trial right is so slippery, two rigid approaches are urged upon us as ways of eliminating some of the uncertainty which courts experience in protecting the right. The first suggestion is that we hold that the Constitution requires a criminal defendant to be offered a trial within a specified time period. The result of such a ruling would have the virtue of clarifying when the right is infringed and of simplifying courts' application of it. Recognizing this, some legislatures have enacted laws, and some courts have adopted procedural rules which more narrowly define the right. The United States Court of Appeals for the Second Circuit has promulgated rules for the district courts in that Circuit establishing that the government must be ready for trial within six months of the date of arrest, except in unusual circumstances, or the charge will be dismissed. This type of rule is also recommended by the American Bar Association.

But such a result would require this Court to engage in legislative or rulemaking activity, rather than in the adjudicative process to which we should confine our efforts. We do not establish procedural rules for the States, except when mandated by the Constitution. We find no constitutional basis for holding that the speedy trial right can be quantified into a specified number of days or months. The States, of course, are free to prescribe a reasonable period consistent with constitutional standards, but our approach must be less precise.

The second suggested alternative would restrict consideration of the right to those cases in which the accused has demanded a speedy trial. Most States have recognized what is loosely referred to as the "demand rule," although eight States reject it. It is not clear, however, precisely what is meant by that term. Although every federal court of appeals that has considered the question has endorsed some kind of demand rule, some have regarded the rule within the concept of waiver, whereas others have viewed it as a factor to be weighed in assessing whether there has been a deprivation of the speedy trial right. We shall refer to the former approach as the demand-waiver doctrine. The demand-waiver doctrine provides that a defendant waives any consideration of his right to speedy trial for any period prior to which he has not demanded a trial. Under this rigid approach, a prior demand is a necessary condition to the consideration of the speedy trial right. This essentially was the approach the Sixth Circuit took below.

Such an approach, by presuming waiver of a fundamental right from inaction, is inconsistent with this Court's pronouncements on waiver of constitutional rights. The Court has defined waiver as "an intentional relinquishment or abandonment of a known right or privilege." *Johnson v. Zerbst*, 304 U.S. 458, 464 (1938). Courts should "indulge every reasonable presumption against waiver," *Aetna Ins. Co. v. Kennedy*, 301 U.S. 389, 393 (1937), and they should "not presume acquiescence in the loss of fundamental rights," *Ohio Bell Tel. Co. v. Public Utilities Comm'n*, 301 U.S. 292, 307 (1937). . . .

In excepting the right to speedy trial from the rule of waiver we have applied to other fundamental rights, courts that have applied the demand-waiver rule have relied on the assumption that delay usually works for the benefit of the accused and on the absence of any readily ascertainable time in the criminal process for a defendant to be given the choice of exercising or waiving his right. But it is not necessarily true that delay benefits the defendant. There are cases in which delay appreciably harms the defendant's ability to defend himself. Moreover, a defendant confined to jail prior to trial is obviously disadvantaged by delay as is a defendant released on bail but unable to lead a normal life because of community suspicion and his own anxiety.

The nature of the speedy trial right does make it impossible to pinpoint a precise time in the process when the right must be asserted or waived, but that fact does not argue for placing the burden of protecting the right solely on defendants. A defendant has no duty to bring himself to trial; the State has that duty as well as the duty of insuring that the trial is consistent with due process. Moreover, for the reasons earlier expressed, society has a particular interest in bringing swift prosecutions, and society's representatives are the ones who should protect that interest.

It is also noteworthy that such a rigid view of the demand-waiver rule places defense counsel in an awkward position. Unless he demands a trial early and often, he is in danger of frustrating his client's right. If counsel is willing to tolerate some delay because he finds it reasonable and helpful in preparing his own case, he may be unable to obtain a speedy trial for his client at the end of that time. Since under the demand-waiver rule no time runs until the demand is made, the government will have whatever time is otherwise reasonable to bring the defendant to trial after a demand has been made. Thus, if the first demand is made three months after arrest in a jurisdiction which prescribes a six-month rule, the prosecution will have a total of nine months—which may be wholly unreasonable under the circumstances. The result in practice is likely to be either an automatic pro forma demand made immediately after appointment of counsel or delays which, but for the demand-waiver rule, would not be tolerated. Such a result is not consistent with the interests of defendants, society, or the Constitution.

We reject, therefore, the rule that a defendant who fails to demand a speedy trial forever waives his right. This does not mean, however, that the defendant has no responsibility to assert his right. We think the better rule is that the defendant's assertion of or failure to assert his right to a speedy trial is one of the factors to be considered in an inquiry into the deprivation of the right. Such a formulation avoids the rigidities of the demand-waiver rule and the resulting possible unfairness in its application. It allows the trial court to exercise a judicial discretion based on the circumstances, including due consideration of any applicable formal procedural rule. It would permit, for example, a court to attach a different weight to a situation in which the defendant knowingly fails to object from a situation in which his attorney acquiesces in long delay without adequately informing his client, or from a situation in which no counsel is appointed. It would also allow a court to weigh the frequency and force of the objections as opposed to attaching significant weight to a purely pro forma objection.

In ruling that a defendant has some responsibility to assert a speedy trial claim, we do not depart from our holdings in other cases concerning the waiver of fundamental rights, in which we have placed the entire responsibility on the prosecution to show that the claimed waiver was knowingly and voluntarily made. Such cases have involved rights which must be exercised or waived at a specific time or under clearly identifiable circumstances, such as the rights to plead not guilty, to demand a jury trial, to exercise the privilege against self-incrimination, and to have the assistance of counsel. We have shown above that the right to a speedy trial is unique in its uncertainty as to when and under what circumstances it must be asserted or may be deemed waived. But the rule we announce today, which comports with constitutional principles, places the primary burden on the courts and the prosecutors to assure that cases are brought to trial. We hardly need add that if delay is attributable to the defendant, then his waiver may be given effect under standard waiver doctrine, the demand rule aside.

We, therefore, reject both of the inflexible approaches—the fixed-time period because it goes further than the Constitution requires; the demand-waiver rule because it is insensitive to a right which we have deemed fundamental. The approach we accept is a balancing test, in which the conduct of both the prosecution and the defendant are weighed.

IV

A balancing test necessarily compels courts to approach speedy trial cases on an ad hoc basis. We can do little more than identify some of the factors which courts should assess in determining whether a particular defendant has been deprived of his right. Though some might express them in different ways, we identify four such factors: Length of delay, the reason for the delay, the defendant's assertion of his right, and prejudice to the defendant.

The length of the delay is to some extent a triggering mechanism. Until there is some delay which is presumptively prejudicial, there is no necessity for inquiry into the other factors that go into the balance. Nevertheless, because of the imprecision of the right to speedy trial, the length of delay that will provoke such an inquiry is necessarily dependent upon the peculiar circumstances of the case. To take but one example, the delay that can be tolerated for an ordinary street crime is considerably less than for a serious, complex conspiracy charge.

Closely related to length of delay is the reason the government assigns to justify the delay. Here, too, different weights should be assigned to different reasons. A deliberate attempt to delay the trial in order to hamper the defense should be weighted heavily against the government. A more neutral reason such as negligence or overcrowded courts should be weighted less heavily but nevertheless should be considered since the ultimate responsibility for such circumstances must rest with the government rather than with the defendant. Finally, a valid reason, such as a missing witness, should serve to justify appropriate delay.

We have already discussed the third factor, the defendant's responsibility to assert his right. Whether and how a defendant asserts his right is closely related to the other factors we have mentioned. The strength of his efforts will be affected by the length of the delay, to some extent by the reason for the delay, and most particularly by the personal prejudice, which is not always readily identifiable, that he experiences. The more serious the deprivation, the more likely a defendant is to complain. The defendant's assertion of his speedy trial right, then, is entitled to strong evidentiary weight in determining whether the defendant is being deprived of the right. We emphasize that failure to assert the right will make it difficult for a defendant to prove that he was denied a speedy trial.

A fourth factor is prejudice to the defendant. Prejudice, of course, should be assessed in the light of the interests of defendants which the speedy trial right was designed to protect. This Court has identified three such interests: (i) to prevent oppressive pretrial incarceration; (ii) to minimize anxiety and concern of the accused; and (iii) to limit the possibility that the defense will be impaired. Of these, the most serious is the last, because the inability of a defendant adequately to prepare his case skews the fairness of the entire system. If witnesses die or disappear during a delay, the prejudice is obvious. There is also prejudice if defense witnesses are unable to recall accurately events of the distant past. Loss of memory, however, is not always reflected in the record because what has been forgotten can rarely be shown.

. . .

We regard none of the four factors identified above as either a necessary or sufficient condition to the finding of a deprivation of the right of speedy trial. Rather, they are related factors and must be considered together with such other circumstances as may be relevant. In sum, these factors have no talismanic qualities; courts must still engage in a difficult and sensitive balancing process. But, because we are dealing with a fundamental right of the accused, this process must be carried out with full recognition that the accused's interest in a speedy trial is specifically affirmed in the Constitution.

V

The difficulty of the task of balancing these factors is illustrated by this case, which we consider to be close. It is clear that the length of delay between arrest and trial—well over five years—was extraordinary. Only seven months of that period can be attributed to a strong excuse, the illness of the ex-sheriff who was in charge of the investigation. Perhaps some delay would have been permissible under ordinary circumstances, so that Manning could be utilized as a witness in Barker's trial, but more than four years was too long a period, particularly since a good part of that period was attributable to the Commonwealth's failure or inability to try Manning under circumstances that comported with due process.

Two counterbalancing factors, however, outweigh these deficiencies. The first is that prejudice was minimal. Of course, Barker was prejudiced to some extent by living for over four years under a cloud of suspicion and anxiety. Moreover, although he was released on bond for most of the period, he did spend 10 months in jail before trial. But there is no claim that any of Barker's witnesses died or otherwise became unavailable owing to the delay. The trial transcript indicates only two very minor lapses of memory—one on the part of a prosecution witness—which were in no way significant to the outcome.

More important than the absence of serious prejudice, is the fact that Barker did not want a speedy trial. Counsel was appointed for Barker immediately after his indictment and represented him throughout the period. No question is raised as to the competency of such counsel. Despite the fact that counsel had notice of the motions for continuances, the record shows no action whatever taken between October 21, 1958, and February 12, 1962, that could be construed as the assertion of the speedy trial right. On the latter date, in response to another motion for continuance, Barker moved to dismiss the indictment. The record does not show on what ground this motion was based, although it is clear that no alternative motion was made for an immediate trial. Instead the record strongly suggests that while he hoped to take advantage of the delay in which he had acquiesced, and thereby obtain a dismissal of the charges, he definitely did not want to be tried. Counsel conceded as much at oral argument. . . . The probable reason for Barker's attitude was that he was gambling on Manning's acquittal. The evidence was not very strong against Manning, as the reversals and hung juries suggest, and Barker undoubtedly thought that if Manning were acquitted, he would never be tried. . . .

That Barker was gambling on Manning's acquittal is also suggested by his failure, following the pro forma motion to dismiss filed in February 1962, to object to the Commonwealth's next two motions for continuances. Indeed, it was not until March 1963, after Manning's convictions were final, that Barker, having lost his gamble, began to object to further continuances. At that time, the Commonwealth's excuse was the illness of the ex-sheriff, which Barker has conceded justified the further delay.

We do not hold that there may never be a situation in which an indictment may be dismissed on speedy trial grounds where the defendant has failed to object to continuances. There may be a situation in which the defendant was represented by incompetent counsel, was severely prejudiced, or even cases in which the continuances were granted ex parte. But barring extraordinary circumstances, we would be reluctant indeed to rule that a defendant was denied this constitutional right on a record that strongly indicates, as does this one, that the defendant did not want a speedy trial. We hold, therefore, that Barker was not deprived of his due process right to a speedy trial.

The judgment of the Court of Appeals is affirmed.

Affirmed.

Free Press and Fair Trial:
Nebraska Press Association v. Stuart, *427 U.S. 539 (1976)*

Mr. Chief Justice BURGER delivered the opinion of the Court.

The respondent State District Judge entered an order restraining the petitioners from publishing or broadcasting accounts of confessions or admission made by the accused or facts "strongly implicative" of the accused in a widely reported murder of six persons. We granted certiorari to decide whether the entry of such an order on the showing made before the state court violated the constitutional guarantee of freedom of the press.

I

On the evening of October 18, 1975, local police found the six members of the Henry Kellie family murdered in their home in Sutherland, Neb., a town of about 850 people. Police released the description of a suspect, Erwin Charles Simants, to the reporters who had hastened to the scene of the crime. Simants was arrested and arraigned in Lincoln County Court the following morning, ending a tense night for this small rural community.

The crime immediately attracted widespread news coverage, by local, regional, and national newspapers, radio and television stations. Three days after the crime, the County Attorney and Simants' attorney joined in asking the County Court to enter a restrictive order relating to "matters that may or may not be publicly reported or disclosed to the public," because of the "mass coverage by news media" and the "reasonable likelihood of prejudicial news which would make difficult, if not impossible, the impaneling of an impartial jury and tend to prevent a fair trial." The County Court heard oral argument but took no evidence; no attorney for members of the press appeared at this stage. The County Court granted the prosecutor's motion for a restrictive order and entered it the next day, October 22. The order prohibited everyone in attendance from "releas[ing] or authoriz[ing] for public dissemination in any form or manner whatsoever any testimony given or evidence adduced"; the order also required members of the press to observe the Nebraska Bar-Press Guidelines.

Simants' preliminary hearing was held the same day, open to the public but subject to the order. The County Court bound over the defendant for trial to the State District Court. The charges, as amended to reflect the autopsy findings, were that Simants had committed the murders in the course of a sexual assault.

Petitioners—several press and broadcast associations, publishers, and individual reporters—moved on October 23 for leave to intervene in the District Court, asking that the restrictive order imposed by the County Court be vacated. The District Court conducted a hearing, at which the County Judge testified and newspaper articles about the Simants case were admitted in evidence. The District Judge granted petitioners' motion to intervene and, on October 27, entered his own restrictive order. The judge found "because of the nature of the crimes charged in the complaint that there is a clear and present danger that pre-trial publicity could impinge upon the defendant's right to a fair trial." The order applied only until the jury was impaneled, and specifically prohibited petitioners from reporting five subjects: (1) the existence or contents of a confession Simants had made to law enforcement officers, which had been introduced in open court at arraignment; (2) the fact or nature of statements Simants had made to other persons; (3) the contents of a note he had written the night of the crime; (4) certain aspects of the medical testimony at the preliminary hearing; (5) the identity of the victims of the alleged sexual assault and the nature of the assault. It also prohibited reporting the exact nature of the restrictive order itself. Like the County Court's order, this order incorporated the Nebraska Bar-Press Guidelines. Finally, the order set out a plan for attendance, seating and courthouse traffic control during the trial.

Four days later, on October 31, petitioners asked the District Court to stay its order. At the same time, they applied to the Nebraska Supreme Court for a writ of mandamus, a stay, and an expedited appeal from the order. . . .

The Nebraska Supreme Court . . . modified the District Court's order to accommodate the defendant's right to a fair trial and the petitioners' interest in reporting pretrial events. The order as modified prohibited reporting of only three matters: (a) the existence and nature of any confessions or admissions made by the defendant to law enforcement officers, (b) any confessions or admissions made to any third parties, except members of the press, and (c) other facts "strongly implicative" of the accused. The Nebraska Supreme Court did not rely on the Nebraska Bar-Press Guidelines. After construing Nebraska law to permit closure in certain circumstances, the court remanded the case to the District Judge for reconsideration of the issue whether pretrial hearings should be closed to the press and public.

We granted certiorari to address the important issues raised by the District Court. . . .

IV

The Sixth Amendment in terms guarantees "trial by an impartial jury . . ." in federal criminal prosecutions. Because "trial by jury in criminal cases is fundamental to the American scheme of justice," the Due Process Clause of the Fourteenth Amendment guarantees the same right in state criminal prosecutions. *Duncan v. Louisiana,* 391 U.S. 145, 149 (1968). . . .

In the overwhelming majority of criminal trials, pretrial publicity presents few unmanageable threats to this important right. But when the case is a "sensational" one tensions develop between the right of the accused to trial by an impartial jury and the rights guaranteed others by the First Amendment. The relevant decisions of this Court, even if not dispositive, are instructive by way of background.

In *Irvin v. Dowd,* 366 U.S. at 726 (1961), for example, the defendant was convicted of murder following intensive and hostile news coverage. The trial judge had granted a defense motion for a change of venue, but only to an adjacent county, which had been exposed to essentially the same news coverage. At trial, 430 persons were called for jury service; 268 were excused because they had fixed opinions as to guilt. Eight of the 12 who served as jurors thought the defendant guilty, but said they could nevertheless render an impartial verdict. On review the Court vacated the conviction and death sentence and remanded to allow a new trial for, "with his life at stake, it is not requiring too much that petitioner be tried in an atmosphere undisturbed by so huge a wave of public passion. . . ." Id., at 728.

Similarly, in *Rideau v. Louisiana,* 373 U.S. 723 (1963), the Court reversed the conviction of a defendant whose staged, highly emotional confession had been filmed with the cooperation of local police and later broadcast on television for three days while he was awaiting trial, saying "any subsequent court proceedings in a community so pervasively exposed to such a spectacle could be but a hollow formality." Id., at 726. And in *Estes v. Texas,* 381 U.S. 532 (1965), the Court held that the defendant had not been afforded due process where the volume of trial publicity, the judge's failure to control the proceedings, and the telecast of a hearing and of the trial itself "inherently prevented a sober search for the truth." Id., at 551.

In *Sheppard v. Maxwell,* 384 U.S. 333 (1966), the Court focused sharply on the impact of pretrial publicity and a trial court's duty to protect the defendant's constitutional right to a fair trial. With only Justice Black dissenting, and he without opinion, the Court ordered a new trial for the petitioner, even though the first trial had occurred 12 years before. Beyond doubt the press had shown no responsible concern for the constitutional guarantee of a fair trial; the community from which the jury was drawn had been inundated by publicity hostile to the defendant. But the trial judge "did not fulfill his duty to protect [the defendant] from the inherently prejudicial publicity which saturated the community and to control disruptive influences in the courtroom." Id., at 363. The Court noted that "unfair and prejudicial news comment on pending trials has become increasingly prevalent," id., at 362, and issued a strong warning:

"Due process requires that the accused receive a trial by an impartial jury free from outside influences. Given the pervasiveness of modern communications and the difficulty of effacing prejudicial publicity from the minds of the jurors, *the trial courts must take strong measures to ensure that the balance is never weighed against the accused.* . . . Of course, there is nothing that proscribes the press from reporting events that transpire in the courtroom. But where there is a reasonable likelihood that prejudicial news prior to trial will prevent a fair trial, the judge should *continue the case* until the threat abates, or *transfer it* to another county not so permeated with publicity. In addition, *sequestration of the jury* was something the judge should have raised *sua sponte* with counsel. If publicity during the proceedings threatens the fairness of the trial, a new trial should be ordered. But we must remember that reversals are but palliatives; the cure lies in those remedial measures that will prevent the prejudice at its inception. The courts must take such steps by rule and regulation that will protect their processes from prejudicial outside interferences. *Neither prosecutors, counsel for defense, the accused, witnesses, court staff nor enforcement officers coming under the jurisdiction of the court should be permitted to frustrate its function.* Collaboration between counsel and the press as to information affecting the fairness of a criminal trial is not only subject to regulation, but is highly censurable and worthy of disciplinary measures." Id., at 362–363 (emphasis added).

Because the trial court had failed to use even minimal efforts to insulate the trial and the jurors from the "deluge of publicity," id., at 357, the Court vacated the judgment of conviction and a new trial followed, in which the accused was acquitted.

Cases such as these are relatively rare, and we have held in other cases that trials have been fair in spite of widespread publicity. In *Stroble v. California*, 343 U.S. 181 (1951), for example, the Court affirmed a conviction and death sentence challenged on the ground that pretrial news accounts, including the prosecutor's release of the defendant's recorded confession, were allegedly so inflammatory as to amount to a denial of due process. The Court disapproved of the prosecutor's conduct, but noted that the publicity had receded some six weeks before trial, that the defendant had not moved for a change of venue, and that the confession had been found voluntary and admitted in evidence at trial. The Court also noted the thorough examination of jurors on voir dire and the careful review of the facts by the state courts, and held that petitioner had failed to demonstrate a denial of due process.

Taken together, these cases demonstrate that pretrial publicity—even pervasive, adverse publicity—does not inevitably lead to an unfair trial. The capacity of the jury eventually impaneled to decide the case fairly is influenced by the tone and extent of the publicity, which is in part, and often in large part, shaped by what attorneys, police, and other officials do to precipitate news coverage. The trial judge has a major responsibility. What the judge says about a case, in or out of the courtroom, is likely to appear in newspapers and broadcasts. More important, the measures a judge takes or fails to take to mitigate the effects of pretrial publicity—the measures described in *Sheppard*—may well determine whether the defendant receives a trial consistent with the requirements of due process. That this responsibility has not always been properly discharged is apparent from the decisions just reviewed.

The costs of failure to afford a fair trial are high. In the most extreme cases, like *Sheppard* and *Estes*, the risk of injustice was avoided when the convictions were reversed. But a reversal means that justice has been delayed for both the defendant and the State; in some cases, because of lapse of time retrial is impossible or further prosecution is gravely handicapped. Moreover, in borderline cases in which the conviction is not reversed, there is some possibility of an injustice unredressed. The "strong measures" outlined in *Sheppard v. Maxwell* are means by which a trial judge can try to avoid exacting these costs from society or from the accused.

The state trial judge in the case before us acted responsibly, out of a legitimate concern, in an effort to protect the defendant's right to a fair trial. What we must decide is not simply whether the Nebraska courts erred in seeing the possibility of real danger to the defendant's rights, but whether in the circumstances of this case the means employed were foreclosed by another provision of the Constitution.

V

The First Amendment provides that "Congress shall make no law . . . abridging the freedom . . . of the press," and it is "no longer open to doubt that the liberty of the press and of speech, is within the liberty safeguarded by the due process clause of the Fourteenth Amendment from invasion by state action." *Near v. Minnesota,* 283 U.S. 697, 707. The Court has interpreted these guarantees to afford special protection against orders that prohibit the publication or broadcast of particular information or commentary—orders that impose a "previous" or "prior" restraint on speech. None of our decided cases on prior restraint involved restrictive orders entered to protect a defendant's right to a fair and impartial jury, but the opinions on prior restraint have a common thread relevant to this case.

. . .

The thread running through all these cases is that prior restraints on speech and publication are the most serious and the least tolerable infringement on First Amendment rights. A criminal penalty or a judgment in a defamation case is subject to the whole panoply of protections afforded by deferring the impact of the judgment until all avenues of appellate review have been exhausted. Only after judgment has become final, correct or otherwise, does the law's sanction become fully operative.

A prior restraint, by contrast and by definition, has an immediate and irreversible sanction. If it can be said that a threat of criminal or civil sanctions after publication "chills" speech, prior restraint "freezes" it at least for the time.

. . .

A

In assessing the probable extent of publicity, the trial judge had before him newspapers demonstrating that the crime had already drawn intensive news coverage, and the testimony of the County Judge, who had entered the initial restraining order based on the local and national attention the case had attracted. The District Judge was required to assess the probable publicity that would be given these shocking crimes prior to the time a jury was selected and sequestered. He then had to examine the probable nature of the publicity and determine how it would affect prospective jurors.

Our review of the pretrial record persuades us that the trial judge was justified in concluding that there would be intense and pervasive pretrial publicity concerning this case. He could also reasonably conclude, based on common human experience, that publicity might impair the defendant's right to a fair trial. He did not purport to say more, for he found only "a clear and present danger that pretrial publicity *could* impinge upon the defendant's right to a fair trial." (Emphasis added.) His conclusion as to the impact of such publicity on prospective jurors was of necessity speculative, dealing as he was with factors unknown and unknowable.

B

We find little in the record that goes to another aspect of our task, determining whether measures short of an order restraining all publication would have insured the defendant a fair trial. Although the entry of the order might be read as a judicial determination that other measures would not suffice, the trial court made no express findings to that effect. . . .

Most of the alternatives to prior restraint of publication in these circumstances were discussed with obvious approval in *Sheppard v. Maxwell*, 384 U.S., at 357–362: (a) change of trial venue to a place less exposed to the intense publicity that seemed imminent in Lincoln County; (b) postponement of the trial to allow public attention to subside; (c) use of searching questioning of prospective jurors, as Chief Justice Marshall did in the *Burr* case, to screen out those with fixed opinions as to guilt or innocence; (d) the use of emphatic and clear instructions on the sworn duty of each juror to decide the issues only on evidence presented in open court. Sequestration of jurors is, of course, always available. Although that measure insulates jurors only after they are sworn, it also enhances the likelihood of dissipating the impact of pretrial publicity and emphasizes the elements of the jurors' oaths.

This Court has outlined other measures short of prior restraints on publication tending to blunt the impact of pretrial publicity. See *Sheppard v. Maxwell*, 384 U.S., at 361–362. Professional studies have filled out these suggestions, recommending that trial courts in appropriate cases limit what the contending lawyers, the police, and witnesses may say to anyone. See American Bar Association, Standards for Criminal Justice, Fair Trial and Free Press 2–15 (Approved Draft, 1968).

We have noted earlier that pretrial publicity, even if pervasive and concentrated, cannot be regarded as leading automatically and in every kind of criminal case to an unfair trial. The decided cases "cannot be made to stand for the proposition that juror exposure to information about a state defendant's prior convictions or to news accounts of the crime with which he is charged alone presumptively deprives the defendant of due process." *Murphy v. Florida*, 421 U.S. 794, 799 (1975). Appellate evaluations as to the impact of publicity take into account what other measures were used to mitigate the adverse effects of publicity. The more difficult prospective or predictive assessment that a trial judge must make also calls for a judgment as to whether other precautionary steps will suffice.

We have therefore examined this record to determine the probable efficacy of the measures short of prior restraint on the press and speech. There is no finding that alternative measures would not have protected Simants' rights, and the Nebraska Supreme Court did no more than imply that such measures might not be adequate. Moreover, the record is lacking in evidence to support such a finding.

C

We must also assess the probable efficacy of prior restraint on publication as a workable method of protecting Simants' right to a fair trial, and we cannot ignore the reality of the problems of managing and enforcing pretrial restraining orders. The territorial jurisdiction of the issuing court is limited by concepts of sovereignty. The need for *in personam* jurisdiction also presents an obstacle to a restraining order that applies to publication at-large as distinguished from restraining publication within a given jurisdiction.

The Nebraska Supreme Court narrowed the scope of the restrictive order, and its opinion reflects awareness of the tensions between the need to protect the accused as fully as possible and the need to restrict publication as little as possible. The dilemma posed underscores how difficult it is for trial judges to predict what information will in fact undermine the impartiality of jurors, and the difficulty of drafting an order that will effectively keep prejudicial information from prospective jurors. When a restrictive order is sought, a court can anticipate only part of what will develop that may injure the accused. But information not so obviously prejudicial may emerge, and what may properly be published in these "gray zone" circumstances may not violate the restrictive order and yet be prejudicial.

Finally, we note that the events disclosed by the record took place in a community of 850 people. It is reasonable to assume that, without any news accounts being printed or broadcast, rumors would travel swiftly by word of mouth. One can only speculate on the accuracy of such reports, given the generative propensities of rumors; they could well be more damaging than reasonably accurate news accounts. But plainly a whole community cannot be restrained from discussing a subject intimately affecting life within it.

Given these practical problems, it is far from clear that prior restraint on publication would have protected Simants' rights.

D

Finally, another feature of this case leads us to conclude that the restrictive order entered here is not supportable. At the outset the County Court entered a very broad restrictive order, the terms of which are not before us; it then held a preliminary hearing open to the public and the press. There was testimony concerning at least two incriminating statements made by Simants to private persons; the statement—evidently a confession—that he gave to law enforcement officials was also introduced. The State District Court's later order was entered after this public hearing and, as modified by the Nebraska Supreme Court, enjoined reporting of (1) "confessions or admissions against interests made by the accused to law enforcement officials"; (2) "confessions or admissions against interest, oral or written, if any, made by the accused to third parties, excepting any statements, if any, made by the accused to representatives of the news media"; and (3) all "other information strongly implicative of the accused as the perpetrator of the slayings."

To the extent that this order prohibited the reporting of evidence adduced at the open preliminary hearing, it plainly violated settled principles: "there is nothing that proscribes the press from reporting events that transpire in the courtroom." *Sheppard v. Maxwell*, supra, 384 U.S., at 362–363. The County Court could not know that closure of the preliminary hearing was an alternative open to it until the Nebraska Supreme Court so construed state law; but once a public hearing had been held, what transpired there could not be subject to prior restraint.

. . .

E

The record demonstrates, as the Nebraska courts held, that there was indeed a risk that pretrial news accounts, true or false, would have some adverse impact on the attitudes of those who might be called as jurors. But on the record now before us it is not clear that further publicity, unchecked, would so distort the views of potential jurors that 12 could not be found who would, under proper instructions, fulfill their sworn duty to render a just verdict exclusively on the evidence presented in open court. We cannot say on this record that alternatives to a prior restraint on petitioners would not have sufficiently mitigated the adverse effects of pretrial publicity so as to make prior restraint unnecessary. Nor can we conclude that the restraining order actually entered would serve its intended purpose. Reasonable minds can have few doubts about the gravity of the evil pretrial publicity can work, but the probability that it would do so here was not demonstrated with the degree of certainty our cases on prior restraint require.

. . .

Our analysis ends as it began, with a confrontation between prior restraint imposed to protect one vital constitutional guarantee and the explicit command of another that the freedom to speak and publish shall not be abridged. We reaffirm that the guarantees of freedom of expression are not an absolute prohibition under all circumstances, but the barriers to prior restraint remain high and the presumption against its use continues intact. We hold that, with respect to the order entered in this case prohibiting reporting or commentary on judicial proceedings held in public, the barriers have not been overcome; to the extent that this order restrained publication of such material, it is clearly invalid. To the extent that it prohibited publication based on information gained from other sources, we conclude that the heavy burden imposed as a condition to securing a prior restraint was not met and the judgment of the Nebraska Supreme Court is therefore

Reversed.

Guilt Beyond a Reasonable Doubt: In re Winship, 397 U.S. 358 (1970)

Mr. Justice BRENNAN delivered the opinion of the Court.

Constitutional questions decided by this Court concerning the juvenile process have centered on the adjudicatory stage at "which a determination is made as to whether a juvenile is a 'delinquent' as a result of alleged misconduct on his part, with the consequence that he may be committed to a state institution." *In re Gault*, 387 U.S. 1, 13 (1967). *Gault* decided that, although the Fourteenth Amendment does not require that the hearing at this stage conform with all the requirements of a criminal trial or even of the usual administrative proceeding, the Due Process Clause does require application during the adjudicatory hearing of " 'the essentials of due process and fair treatment.' " Id., at 30. This case presents the single, narrow question whether proof beyond a reasonable doubt is among the "essentials of due process and fair treatment" required during the adjudicatory stage when a juvenile is charged with an act which would constitute a crime if committed by an adult.

Section 712 of the New York Family Court Act defines a juvenile delinquent as "a person over seven and less than sixteen years of age who does any act which, if done by an adult, would constitute a crime." During a 1967 adjudicatory hearing, conducted pursuant to § 742 of the Act, a judge in New York Family Court found that appellant, then a 12-year-old boy, had entered a locker and stolen $112 from a woman's pocketbook. The petition which charged appellant with delinquency alleged that his act, "if done by an adult, would constitute the crime or crimes of Larceny." The judge acknowledged that the proof might not establish guilt beyond a reasonable doubt, but rejected appellant's contention that such proof was required by the Fourteenth Amendment. The judge relied instead on § 744(b) of the New York Family Court Act which provides that "any determination at the conclusion of [an adjudicatory] hearing that a [juvenile] did an act or acts must be based on a preponderance of the evidence." During a subsequent dispositional hearing, appellant was ordered placed in a training school for an initial period of 18 months, subject to annual extensions of his commitment until his 18th birthday—six years in appellant's case. . . . We noted probable jurisdiction. We reverse.

I

The requirement that guilt of a criminal charge be established by proof beyond a reasonable doubt dates at least from our early years as a Nation. The "demand for a higher degree of persuasion in criminal cases was recurrently expressed from ancient times, [though] its crystallization into the formula 'beyond a reasonable doubt' seems to have occurred as late as 1798. It is now accepted in common-law jurisdictions as the measure of persuasion by which the prosecution must convince the trier of all the essential elements of guilt." C. McCormick, Evidence § 321, pp. 681–682 (1954); see also 9 J. Wigmore, Evidence, § 2497 (3d ed. 1940). Although virtually unanimous adherence to the reasonable-doubt standard in common-law jurisdictions may not conclusively establish it as a requirement of due process, such adherence does "reflect a profound judgment about the way in which law should be enforced and justice administered." *Duncan v. Louisiana*, 391 U.S. 145, 155 (1968).

Expressions in many opinions of this Court indicate that it has long been assumed that proof of a criminal charge beyond a reasonable doubt is constitutionally required. . . .

The reasonable-doubt standard plays a vital role in the American scheme of criminal procedure. It is a prime instrument for reducing the risk of convictions resting on factual error. The standard provides concrete substance for the presumption of innocence—that bedrock "axiomatic and elementary" principle whose "enforcement lies at the foundation of the administration of our criminal law." *Coffin v. United States,* supra, 156 U.S., at 453. As the dissenters in the New York Court of Appeals observed, and we agree, "a person accused of a crime . . . would be at a severe disadvantage, a disadvantage amounting to a lack of fundamental fairness, if he could be adjudged guilty and imprisoned for years on the strength of the same evidence as would suffice in a civil case."

The requirement of proof beyond a reasonable doubt has this vital role in our criminal procedure for cogent reasons. The accused during a criminal prosecution has at stake interest of immense importance, both because of the possibility that he may lose his liberty upon conviction and because of the certainty that he would be stigmatized by the conviction. Accordingly, a society that values the good name and freedom of every individual should not condemn a man for commission of a crime when there is reasonable doubt about his guilt. As we said in *Speiser v. Randall,* supra, 357 U.S., at 525–526: "There is always in litigation a margin of error, representing error in factfinding, which both parties must take into account. Where one party has at stake an interest of transcending value—as a criminal defendant his liberty—this margin of error is reduced as to him by the process of placing on the other party the burden of . . . persuading the factfinder at the conclusion of the trial of his guilt beyond a reasonable doubt. Due process commands that no man shall lose his liberty unless the Government has borne the burden of . . . convincing the factfinder of his guilt." To this end, the reasonable-doubt standard is indispensable, for it "impresses on the trier of fact the necessity of reaching a subjective state of certitude of the facts in issue." Dorsen & Rezneck, *In re Gault* and the Future of Juvenile Law, 1 Family Law Quarterly, No. 4, pp. 1, 26 (1967).

Moreover, use of the reasonable-doubt standard is indispensable to command the respect and confidence of the community in applications of the criminal law. It is critical that the moral force of the criminal law not be diluted by a standard of proof that leaves people in doubt whether innocent men are being condemned. It is also important in our free society that every individual going about his ordinary affairs have confidence that his government cannot adjudge him guilty of a criminal offense without convincing a proper factfinder of his guilt with utmost certainty.

Lest there remain any doubt about the constitutional stature of the reasonable-doubt standard, we explicitly hold that the Due Process Clause protects the accused against conviction except upon proof beyond a reasonable doubt of every fact necessary to constitute the crime with which he is charged.

. . .

III

In sum, the constitutional safeguard of proof beyond a reasonable doubt is as much required during the adjudicatory stage of a delinquency proceeding as are those constitutional safeguards applied in *Gault*—notice of charges, right to counsel, the rights of confrontation and examination, and the privilege against self-incrimination. We therefore hold, in agreement with Chief Judge Fuld in dissent in the Court of Appeals, "that, where a 12-year-old child is charged with an act of stealing which renders him liable to confinement for as long as six years, then, as a matter of due process . . . the case against him must be proved beyond a reasonable doubt." 24 N.Y.2d, at 207.

Reversed.

Inferences and the Reasonable-doubt Standard: Barnes v. United States, 412 U.S. 837 (1973)

Mr. Justice POWELL delivered the opinion of the Court.

Petitioner Barnes was convicted in United States District Court on two counts of possessing United States Treasury checks stolen from the mails, knowing them to be stolen, two counts of forging the checks, and two counts of uttering the checks, knowing the endorsements to be forged. The trial court instructed the jury that ordinarily it would be justified in inferring from unexplained possession of recently stolen mail that the defendant possessed the mail with knowledge that it was stolen. We granted certiorari to consider whether this instruction comports with due process. 409 U.S. 1037 (1972).

The evidence at petitioner's trial established that on June 2, 1971, he opened a checking account using the pseudonym "Clarence Smith." On July 1, and July 3,

1971, the United States Disbursing Office at San Francisco mailed four Government checks in the amounts of $269.02, $154.70, $184, and $268.80 to Nettie Lewis, Albert Young, Arthur Salazar, and Mary Hernandez, respectively. On July 8, 1971, petitioner deposited these four checks into the "Smith" account. Each check bore the apparent endorsement of the payee and a second endorsement by "Clarence Smith."

At petitioner's trial the four payees testified that they had never received, endorsed, or authorized endorsement of the checks. A Government handwriting expert testified that petitioner had made the "Clarence Smith" endorsement on all four checks and that he had signed the payees' names on the Lewis and Hernandez checks. Although petitioner did not take the stand, a postal inspector testified to certain statements made by petitioner at a post-arrest interview. Petitioner explained to the inspector that he received the checks in question from people who sold furniture for him door to door and that the checks had been signed in the payees' names when he received them. Petitioner further stated that he could not name or identify any of the salespeople. Nor could he substantiate the existence of any furniture orders because the salespeople allegedly wrote their orders on scratch paper that had not been retained. Petitioner admitted that he executed the Clarence Smith endorsements and deposited the checks but denied making the payees' endorsements.

The District Court instructed the jury that "possession of recently stolen property, if not satisfactorily explained, is ordinarily a circumstance from which you may reasonably draw the inference and find, in the light of the surrounding circumstances shown by the evidence in the case, that the person in possession knew the property had been stolen."

The jury brought in guilty verdicts on all six counts, and the District Court sentenced petitioner to concurrent three-year prison terms. The Court of Appeals for the Ninth Circuit affirmed, finding no lack of "rational connection" between unexplained possession of recently stolen property and knowledge that the property was stolen. 466 F.2d 1361 (1972). . . . We affirm.

I

We begin our consideration of the challenged jury instruction with a review of four recent decisions which have considered the validity under the Due Process Clause of criminal law presumptions and inferences. *Turner v. United States,* 396 U.S. 398 (1970); *Leary v. United States,* 395 U.S. 6 (1969); *United States v. Romano,* 382 U.S. 136 (1965); *United States v. Gainey,* 380 U.S. 63 (1965).

In *United States v. Gainey,* supra, the Court sustained the constitutionality of an instruction tracking a statute which authorized the jury to infer from defendant's unexplained presence at an illegal still that he was carrying on "the business of a distiller or rectifier without having given bond as required by law." Relying on the holding of *Tot v. United States,* 319 U.S. 463, 467 (1943), that there must be "a rational connection between the fact proved and the ultimate fact presumed," the Court upheld the inference on the basis of the comprehensive nature of the "carrying on" offense and the common knowledge that illegal stills are secluded, secret operations. The following Term the Court determined, however, that presence at an illegal still could not support the inference that the defendant was in possession, custody, or control of the still, a narrower offense. "Presence is relevant and admissible evidence in a trial on a possession charge; but absent some showing of the defendant's function at the still, its connection with possession is too tenuous to permit a reasonable inference of guilt—"the inference of the one from proof of the other is arbitrary. . . .' *Tot v. United States*, 319 U.S. 463, 467." *United States v. Romano*, supra, at 141.

Three and one-half years after *Romano*, the Court in *Leary v. United States*, supra, considered a challenge to a statutory inference that possession of marihuana, unless satisfactorily explained, was sufficient to prove that the defendant knew that the marihuana had been illegally imported into the United States. The Court concluded that in view of the significant possibility that any given marihuana was domestically grown and the improbability that a marihuana user would know whether his marihuana was of domestic or imported origin, the inference did not meet the standards set by *Tot, Gainey,* and *Romano.* Referring to these three cases, the *Leary* Court stated that an inference is " 'irrational' or 'arbitrary,' and hence unconstitutional, unless it can at least be said with substantial assurance that the presumed fact is more likely than not to flow from the proved fact on which it is made to depend." 395 U.S., at 36. In a footnote the Court stated that since the challenged inference failed to satisfy the more-likely-than-not standard, it did not have to "reach the question whether a criminal presumption which passes muster when so judged must also satisfy the criminal 'reasonable doubt' standard if proof of the crime charged or an essential element thereof depends upon its use." Id., at n. 64.

Finally, in *Turner v. United States*, supra, decided the year following *Leary*, the Court considered the constitutionality of instructing the jury that it may infer from possession of heroin and cocaine that the defendant knew these drugs had been illegally imported. The Court noted that *Leary* reserved the question of whether the more-likely-than-not or the reasonable-doubt standard controlled in criminal cases, but it likewise found no need to resolve that question. It held that the inference with regard to heroin was valid judged by either standard. 396 U.S., at 416. With regard to cocaine, the inference failed to satisfy even the more-likely-than-not standard. Id., at 419.

The teaching of the foregoing cases is not altogether clear. To the extent that the "rational connection," "more likely than not," and "reasonable doubt" standards bear ambiguous relationships to one another, the ambiguity is traceable in large part to variations in language and focus rather than to differences of substance. What has been established by the cases, however, is at least this: that if a statutory inference submitted to the jury as sufficient to support conviction satisfies the reasonable-doubt standard (that is, the evidence necessary to invoke the inference is sufficient for a rational juror to find the inferred fact beyond a reasonable doubt) as well as the more-likely-than-not standard, then it clearly accords with due process.

In the present case we deal with a traditional common-law inference deeply rooted in our law. For centuries courts have instructed juries that an inference of guilty knowledge may be drawn from the fact of unexplained possession of stolen goods. James Thayer, writing in his Preliminary Treatise on Evidence (1898), cited this inference as the descendant of a presumption "running through a dozen centuries." Id., at 327. Early American cases consistently upheld instructions permitting conviction upon such an inference, and the courts of appeals on numerous occasions have approved instructions essentially identical to the instruction given in this case. This long-standing and consistent judicial approval of the instruction, reflecting accumulated common experience, provides strong indication that the instruction comports with due process.

This impressive historical basis, however, is not in itself sufficient to establish the instruction's constitutionality. Common-law inferences, like their statutory counter-parts, must satisfy due process standards in light of present-day experience. In the present case the challenged instruction only permitted the inference of guilt from *unexplained* possession of recently stolen property. The evidence established that petitioner possessed recently stolen Treasury checks payable to persons he did not know, and it provided no plausible explanation for such possession consistent with innocence. On the basis of this evidence alone common sense and experience tell us that petitioner must have known or been aware of the high probability that the checks were stolen. Cf. *Turner v. United States*, 396 U.S., at 417; *Leary v. United States*, 395 U.S., at 46. Such evidence was clearly sufficient to enable the jury to find beyond a reasonable doubt that petitioner knew the checks were stolen. Since the inference thus satisfies the reasonable-doubt standard, the most stringent standard the Court has applied in judging permissive criminal law inferences, we conclude that it satisfies the requirements of due process.

II

Petitioner also argues that the permissive inference in question infringes his privilege against self-incrimination. The Court has twice rejected this argument, *Turner v. United States*, supra, 396 U.S., at 417–418; *Yee Hem v. United States*, 268 U.S. 178, 185 (1925), and we find no reason to re-examine the issue at length. The trial court specifically instructed the jury that petitioner had a constitutional right not to take the witness stand and that possession could be satisfactorily explained by evidence independent of petitioner's testimony. Introduction of any evidence, direct or circumstantial, tending to implicate the defendant in the alleged crime increases the pressure on him to testify. The mere massing of evidence against a defendant cannot be regarded as a violation of his privilege against self-incrimination. *Yee Hem v. United States*, supra, 268 U.S., at 185.

. . .

Affirmed.

Mr. Justice BRENNAN, with whom Mr. Justice MARSHALL joins, dissenting.

. . .

We held in *In re Winship*, 397 U.S. 358, 364 (1970), that the Due Process Clause requires "proof beyond a reasonable doubt of every fact necessary to constitute the crime. . . ." Thus, in *Turner v. United States*, 396 U.S. 398, 417 (1970), we approved the inference of "knowledge" from the fact of possessing smuggled heroin because " 'common sense' . . . tells us that those who traffic in heroin will *inevitably* become aware that the product they deal in is smuggled. . . ." (Emphasis added.) The basis of that "common sense" judgment was, of course, the indisputable fact that all or virtually all heroin in this country is necessarily smuggled. Here, however, it cannot be said that all or virtually all endorsed United States Treasury checks have been stolen. Indeed, it is neither unlawful nor unusual for people to use such checks as direct payment for goods and services. Thus, unlike *Turner*, "common sense" simply will not permit the inference that the possessor of stolen Treasury checks "*inevitably*" knew that the checks were stolen.

In short, the practical effect of the challenged instruction was to permit the jury to convict petitioner even if it found insufficient or disbelieved all of the Government's evidence bearing directly on the issue of "knowledge." By authorizing the jury to rely exclusively on the inference in determining the element of "knowledge," the instruction relieved the Government of the burden of proving that element beyond a reasonable doubt. The instruction thereby violated the principle of *Winship* that every essential element of the crime must be proved beyond a reasonable doubt.

Compulsory Process:
Washington v. Texas, 388 U.S. 14 (1967)

Mr. Chief Justice WARREN delivered the opinion of the Court.

We granted certiorari in this case to determine whether the right of a defendant in a criminal case under the Sixth Amendment to have compulsory process for obtaining witnesses in his favor is applicable to the States through the Fourteenth Amendment, and whether that right was violated by a state procedural statute providing that persons charged as principals, accomplices, or accessories in the same crime cannot be introduced as witnesses for each other.

Petitioner, Jackie Washington, was convicted in Dallas County, Texas, of murder with malice and was sentenced by a jury to 50 years in prison. The prosecution's evidence showed that petitioner, an 18-year-old youth, had dated a girl named Jean Carter until her mother had forbidden her to see him. The girl thereafter began dating another boy, the deceased. Evidently motivated by jealousy, petitioner with several other boys began driving around the City of Dallas on the night of August 29, 1964, looking for a gun. The search eventually led to one Charles Fuller, who joined the group with his shotgun. After obtaining some shells from another source, the group of boys proceeded to Jean Carter's home, where Jean, her family and the deceased were having supper. Some of the boys threw bricks at the house and then ran back to the car, leaving petitioner and Fuller alone in front of the house with the shotgun. At the sound of the bricks the deceased and Jean Carter's mother rushed out on the porch to investigate. The shotgun was fired by either petitioner or Fuller, and the deceased was fatally wounded. Shortly afterward petitioner and Fuller came running back to the car where the other boys waited, with Fuller carrying the shotgun.

Petitioner testified in his own behalf. He claimed that Fuller, who was intoxicated, had taken the gun from him, and that he had unsuccessfully tried to persuade Fuller to leave before the shooting. Fuller had insisted that he was going to shoot someone, and petitioner had run back to the automobile. He saw the girl's mother come out of the door as he began running, and he subsequently heard the shot. At the time, he had thought that Fuller had shot the woman. In support of his version of the facts, petitioner offered the testimony of Fuller. The record indicates that Fuller would have testified that petitioner pulled at him and tried to persuade him to leave, and that petitioner ran before Fuller fired the fatal shot.

It is undisputed that Fuller's testimony would have been relevant and material, and that it was vital to the defense. Fuller was the only person other than petitioner who knew exactly who had fired the shotgun and whether petitioner had at the last minute attempted to prevent the shooting. Fuller, however, had been previously convicted of the same murder and sentenced to 50 years in prison, and he was confined in the Dallas County jail. Two Texas statutes provided at the time of the trial in this case that persons charged or convicted as coparticipants in the same crime could not testify for one another, although there was no bar to their testifying for the State. On the basis of these statutes the trial judge sustained the State's objection and refused to allow Fuller to testify. Petitioner's conviction followed, and it was upheld on appeal by the Texas Court of Criminal Appeals. We granted certiorari

I.

We have not previously been called upon to decide whether the right of an accused to have compulsory process for obtaining witnesses in his favor, guaranteed in federal trials by the Sixth Amendment, is so fundamental and essential to a fair trial that it is incorporated in the Due Process Clause of the Fourteenth Amendment. At one time, it was thought that the Sixth Amendment had no application to state criminal trials. That view no longer prevails, and in recent years we have increasingly looked to the specific guarantees of the Sixth Amendment to determine whether a state criminal trial was conducted with due process of law. We have held that due process requires that the accused have the assistance of counsel for his defense, that he be confronted with the witnesses against him, and that he have the right to a speedy and public trial.

The right of an accused to have compulsory process for obtaining witnesses in his favor stands on no lesser footing than the other Sixth Amendment rights that we have previously held applicable to the States. This Court had occasion in *In re Oliver*, 333 U.S. 257 (1948), to describe what it regarded as the most basic ingredients of due process of law. It observed that:

> "A person's right to reasonable notice of a charge against him, and an opportunity to be heard in his defense—a right to his day in court—are basic in our system of jurisprudence; and these rights include, as a minimum, a right to examine the witnesses against him, to offer testimony, and to be represented by counsel." 333 U.S., at 273 (footnote omitted).

The right to offer the testimony of witnesses, and to compel their attendance, if necessary, is in plain terms the right to present a defense, the right to present the defendant's version of the facts as well as the prosecution's to the jury so it may decide where the truth lies. Just as an accused has the right to confront the prosecution's witnesses for the purpose of challenging their testimony, he has the right to present his own witnesses to establish a defense. This right is a fundamental element of due process of law.

II.

Since the right to compulsory process is applicable in this state proceeding, the question remains whether it was violated in the circumstances of this case. The testimony of Charles Fuller was denied to the defense not because the State refused to compel his attendance, but because a state statute made his testimony inadmissible whether he was present in the courtroom or not. We are thus called upon to decide whether the Sixth Amendment guarantees a defendant the right under any circumstances to put his witnesses on the stand, as well as the right to compel their attendance in court. The resolution of this question requires some discussion of the common-law context in which the Sixth Amendment was adopted.

Joseph Story, in his famous Commentaries on the Constitution of the United States, observed that the right to compulsory process was included in the Bill of Rights in reaction to the notorious common-law rule that in cases of treason or felony the accused was not allowed to introduce witnesses in his defense at all. Although the absolute prohibition of witnesses for the defense had been abolished in England by statute before 1787, the Framers of the Constitution felt it necessary specifically to provide that defendants in criminal cases should be provided the means of obtaining witnesses so that their own evidence, as well as the prosecution's, might be evaluated by the jury.

Despite the abolition of the rule generally disqualifying defense witnesses, the common law retained a number of restrictions on witnesses who were physically and mentally capable of testifying. To the extent that they were applicable, they had the same effect of suppressing the truth that the general proscription had had. Defendants and codefendants were among the large class of witnesses disqualified from testifying on the ground of interest. A party to a civil or criminal case was not allowed to testify on his own behalf for fear that he might be tempted to lie. Although originally the disqualification of a codefendant appears to have been based only on his status as a party to the action, and in some jurisdictions co-indictees were allowed to testify for or against each other if granted separate trials, other jurisdictions came to the view that accomplices or co-indictees were incompetent·to testify at least in favor of each other even at separate trials, and in spite of statutes making a defendant competent to testify in his own behalf. It was thought that if two persons charged with the same crime were allowed to testify on behalf of each other, "each would try to swear the other out of the charge." This rule, as well as the other disqualifications for interest, rested on the unstated premises that the right to present witnesses was subordinate to the court's interest in preventing perjury, and that erroneous decisions were best avoided by preventing the jury from hearing any testimony that might be perjured, even if it were the only testimony available on a crucial issue.

The federal courts followed the common-law restrictions for a time, despite the Sixth Amendment. In *United States v. Reid*, 12 How. 361 (1852), the question was whether one of two defendants jointly indicted for murder on the high seas could call the other as a witness. Although this Court expressly recognized that the Sixth Amendment was designed to abolish some of the harsh rules of the common law, particularly including the refusal to allow the defendant in a serious criminal case to present witnesses in his defense, it held that the rules of evidence in the federal courts were those in force in the various States at the time of the passage of the Judiciary Act of 1789, including the disqualification of defendants indicted together. The holding in *United States v. Reid* was not satisfactory to later generations, however, and in 1918 this Court expressly overruled it, refusing to be bound by "the dead hand of the common-law rule of 1789," and taking note of "the conviction of our time that the truth is more likely to be arrived at by hearing the testimony of all persons of competent understanding who may seem to have knowledge of the facts involved in a case, leaving the credit and weight of such testimony to be determined by the jury or by the court. . . ." *Rosen v. United States*, 245 U.S. 467, 471.

Although *Rosen v. United States* rested on nonconstitutional grounds, we believe that its reasoning was required by the Sixth Amendment. In light of the common-law history, and in view of the recognition in the *Reid* case that the Sixth Amendment was designed in part to make the testimony of a defendant's witnesses admissible on his behalf in court, it could hardly be argued that a State would not violate the clause if it made all defense testimony inadmissible as a matter of procedural law. It is difficult to see how the Constitution is any less violated by arbitrary rules that prevent whole categories of defense witnesses from testifying on the basis of a priori categories that presume them unworthy of belief.

The rule disqualifying an alleged accomplice from testifying on behalf of the defendant cannot even be defended on the ground that it rationally sets apart a group of persons who are particularly likely to commit perjury. The absurdity of the rule is amply demonstrated by the exceptions that have been made to it. For example, the accused accomplice may be called by the prosecution to testify against the defendant. Common sense would suggest that he often has a greater interest in lying in favor of the prosecution rather than against it, especially if he is still awaiting his own trial or sentencing. To think that criminals will lie to save their fellows but not to obtain favors from the prosecution for themselves is indeed to clothe the criminal class with more nobility than one might expect to find in the public at large. Moreover, under the Texas statutes, the accused accomplice is no longer disqualified if he is acquitted at his own trial. Presumably, he would then be free to testify on behalf of his comrade, secure in the knowledge that he could incriminate himself as freely as he liked in his testimony, since he could not again be prosecuted for the same offense. The Texas law leaves him free to testify when he has a great incentive to perjury, and bars his testimony in situations where he has a lesser motive to lie.

We hold that the petitioner in this case was denied his right to have compulsory process for obtaining witnesses in favor because the State arbitrarily denied him the right to put on the stand a witness who was physically and mentally capable of testifying to events that he had personally observed, and whose testimony would have been relevant and material to the defense. The Framers of the Constitution did not intend to commit the futile act of giving to a defendant the right to secure the attendance of witnesses whose testimony he had no right to use. The judgment of conviction must be reversed. It is so ordered.

Reversed.

The Cross-examination of Witnesses:
Pointer v. Texas, 380 U.S. 400 (1965)

Mr. Justice BLACK delivered the opinion of the Court.

The Sixth Amendment provides in part that:

> "In all criminal prosecutions, the accused shall enjoy the right . . . to be confronted with the witnesses against him . . . and to have the Assistance of Counsel for his defence."

Two years ago in *Gideon v. Wainwright*, 372 U.S. 335, we held that the Fourteenth

Amendment makes the Sixth Amendment's guarantee of right to counsel obligatory upon the States. The question we find necessary to decide in this case is whether the Amendment's guarantee of a defendant's right "to be confronted with the witnesses against him," which has been held to include the right to cross-examine those witnesses, is also made applicable to the States by the Fourteenth Amendment.

The petitioner Pointer and one Dillard were arrested in Texas and taken before a state judge for a preliminary hearing (in Texas called the "examining trial") on a charge of having robbed Kenneth W. Phillips of $375 "by assault, or violence, or by putting in fear of life or bodily injury," in violation of Texas Penal Code Art. 1408. At this hearing an Assistant District Attorney conducted the prosecution and examined witnesses, but neither of the defendants, both of whom were laymen, had a lawyer. Phillips as chief witness for the State gave his version of the alleged robbery in detail, identifying petitioner as the man who had robbed him at gunpoint. Apparently Dillard tried to cross-examine Phillips but Pointer did not, although Pointer was said to have tried to cross-examine some other witnesses at the hearing. Petitioner was subsequently indicted on a charge of having committed the robbery. Some time before the trial was held, Phillips moved to California. After putting in evidence to show that Phillips had moved and did not intend to return to Texas, the State at the trial offered the transcript of Phillips' testimony given at the preliminary hearing as evidence against petitioner. Petitioner's counsel immediately objected to introduction of the transcript, stating, "Your Honor, we will object to that, as it is a denial of the confrontation of the witness against the Defendant." Similar objections were repeatedly made by petitioner's counsel but were overruled by the trial judge, apparently in part because, as the judge viewed it, petitioner had been present at the preliminary hearing and therefore had been "accorded the opportunity of cross examining the witnesses there against him." The Texas Court of Criminal Appeals, the highest state court to which the case could be taken, affirmed petitioner's conviction, rejecting his contention that use of the transcript to convict him denied him rights guaranteed by the Sixth and Fourteenth Amendments. We granted certiorari to consider the important constitutional question the case involves.

. . .

I.

The Sixth Amendment is a part of what is called our Bill of Rights. In *Gideon v. Wainwright*, supra, in which this Court held that the Sixth Amendment's right to the assistance of counsel is obligatory upon the States, we did so on the ground that "a provision of the Bill of Rights which is 'fundamental and essential to a fair trial' is made obligatory upon the States by the Fourteenth Amendment." 372 U.S., at 342. And last Term in *Malloy v. Hogan*, 378 U.S. 1, in holding that the Fifth Amendment's guarantee against self-incrimination was made applicable to the States by the Fourteenth, we reiterated the holding of *Gideon* that the Sixth Amendment's right-to-counsel guarantee is "'a fundamental right, essential to a fair trial,'" and "thus was made obligatory on the States by the Fourteenth Amendment." 378 U.S., at 6. See also *Murphy v. Waterfront Comm'n*, 378 U.S. 52. We hold today that the Sixth Amendment's right of an accused to confront the witnesses against him is likewise a fundamental right and is made obligatory on the States by the Fourteenth Amendment.

It cannot seriously be doubted at this late date that the right of cross-examination is included in the right of an accused in a criminal case to confront the witnesses against him. And probably no one, certainly no one experienced in the trial of lawsuits, would deny the value of cross-examination in exposing falsehood and bringing out the truth in the trial of a criminal case. See, e.g., 5 Wigmore, Evidence § 1367 (3d ed. 1940). The fact that this right appears in the Sixth Amendment of our Bill of Rights reflects the belief of the Framers of those liberties and safeguards that confrontation was a fundamental right essential to a fair trial in a criminal prosecution. Moreover, the decisions of this Court and other courts throughout the years have constantly emphasized the necessity for cross-examination as a protection for defendants in criminal cases. This Court in *Kirby v. United States*, 174 U.S. 47, 55, 56, referred to the right of confrontation as "one of the fundamental guaranties of life and liberty," and "a right long deemed so essential for the due protection of life and liberty that it is guarded against legislative and judicial action by provisions in the constitution of the United States and in the constitutions of most, if not of all, the states composing the Union." Mr. Justice Stone, writing for the Court in *Alford v. United States*, 282 U.S. 687, 692, declared that the right of cross-examination is "one of the safeguards essential to a fair trial." And in speaking of confrontation and cross-examination this Court said in *Greene v. McElroy*, 360 U.S. 474:

"They have ancient roots. They find expression in the Sixth Amendment which provides that in all criminal cases the accused shall enjoy the right 'to be confronted with the witnesses against him.' This Court has been zealous to protect these rights from erosion." 360 U.S., at 496–497 (footnote omitted).

There are few subjects, perhaps, upon which this Court and other courts have been more nearly unanimous than in their expressions of belief that the right of confrontation and cross-examination is an essential and fundamental requirement for the kind of fair trial which is this country's constitutional goal. Indeed, we have expressly declared that to deprive an accused of the right to cross-examine the witnesses against him is a denial of the Fourteenth Amendment's guarantee of due process of law. In *In re Oliver*, 333 U.S. 257, this Court said:

"A person's right to reasonable notice of a charge against him, and an opportunity to be heard in his defense—a right to his day in court—are basic in our system of jurisprudence; and these rights include, as a minimum, a right to examine the witnesses against him, to offer testimony, and to be represented by counsel." 333 U.S., at 273 (footnote omitted).

And earlier this Term in *Turner v. State of Louisiana*, 379 U.S. 466, 472–473, we held:

"In the constitutional sense, trial by jury in a criminal case necessarily implies at the very least that the 'evidence developed' against a defendant shall come from the witness stand in a public courtroom where there is full judicial protection of the defendant's right of confrontation, of cross-examination, and of counsel."

. . . We hold that petitioner was entitled to be tried in accordance with the protection of the confrontation guarantee of the Sixth Amendment, and that that guarantee, like the right against compelled self-incrimination, is "to be enforced against the States under the Fourteenth Amendment according to the same standards that protect those personal rights against federal encroachment." *Malloy v. Hogan,* supra, 378 U.S., at 10.

II.

Under this Court's prior decisions, the Sixth Amendment's guarantee of confrontation and cross-examination was unquestionably denied petitioner in this case. As has been pointed out, a major reason underlying the constitutional confrontation rule is to give a defendant charged with crime an opportunity to cross-examine the witnesses against him. This Court has recognized the admissibility against an accused of dying declarations, *Mattox v. United States,* 146 U.S. 140, 151, and of testimony of a deceased witness who has testified at a former trial, *Mattox v. United States,* 156 U.S. 237, 240–244. See also *Dowdell v. United States,* supra, 221 U.S., at 330; *Kirby v. United States,* supra, 174 U.S., at 61. Nothing we hold here is to the contrary. The case before us would be quite a different one had Phillips' statement been taken at a full-fledged hearing at which petitioner had been represented by counsel who had been given a complete and adequate opportunity to cross-examine. Compare *Motes v. United States,* supra, 178 U.S., at 474. There are other analogous situations which might not fall within the scope of the constitutional rule requiring confrontation of witnesses. The case before us, however, does not present any situation like those mentioned above or others analogous to them. Because the transcript of Phillips' statement offered against petitioner at his trial had not been taken at a time and under circumstances affording petitioner through counsel an adequate opportunity to cross-examine Phillips, its introduction in a federal court in a criminal case against Pointer would have amounted to denial of the privilege of confrontation guaranteed by the Sixth Amendment. Since we hold that the right of an accused to be confronted with the witnesses against him must be determined by the same standards whether the right is denied in a federal or state proceeding, it follows that use of the transcript to convict petitioner denied him a constitutional right, and that his conviction must be reversed.

Reversed and remanded.

Mr. Justice HARLAN, concurring in the result.

I agree that in the circumstances the admission of the statement in question deprived the petitioner of a right of "confrontation" assured by the Fourteenth Amendment. I cannot subscribe, however, to the constitutional reasoning of the Court.

The Court holds that the right of confrontation guaranteed by the Sixth Amendment in federal criminal trials is carried into state criminal cases by the Fourteenth Amendment. This is another step in the onward march of the long-since discredited "incorporation" doctrine (see, e.g., Fairman, Does the Fourteenth Amendment Incorporate the Bill of Rights? The Original Understanding, 2 Stan. L. Rev. 5 (1949), which for some reason that I have not yet been able to fathom has come into the sunlight in recent years.

For me this state judgment must be reversed because a right of confrontation is "implicit in the concept of ordered liberty," *Palko v. State of Connecticut,* 302 U.S.

319, 325, reflected in the Due Process Clause of the Fourteenth Amendment independently of the Sixth.

While either of these constitutional approaches brings one to the same end result in this particular case, there is a basic difference between the two in the kind of future constitutional development they portend. The concept of Fourteenth Amendment due process embodied in *Palko* and a host of other thoughtful past decisions now rapidly falling into discard, recognizes that our Constitution tolerates, indeed encourages, differences between the methods used to effectuate legitimate federal and state concerns, subject to the requirements of fundamental fairness "implicit in the concept of ordered liberty." The philosophy of "incorporation," on the other hand, subordinates all such state differences to the particular requirements of the Federal Bill of Rights (but see *Ker v. State of California,* supra, 374 U.S., at 34) and increasingly subjects state legal processes to enveloping federal judicial authority. "Selective" incorporation or "absorption" amounts to little more than a diluted form of the full incorporation theory. Whereas it rejects full incorporation because of recognition that not all of the guarantees of the Bill of Rights should be deemed "fundamental," it at the same time ignores the possibility that not all phases of any given guaranty described in the Bill of Rights are necessarily fundamental.

It is too often forgotten in these times that the American federal system is itself constitutionally ordained, that it embodies values profoundly making for lasting liberties in this country, and that its legitimate requirements demand continuing solid recognition in all phases of the work of this Court. The "incorporation" doctrines, whether full blown or selective, are both historically and constitutionally unsound and incompatible with the maintenance of our federal system on even course.

12

Sentencing, Punishment, and Postconviction Relief

SENTENCING

Sentencing, whether viewed as the end of the trial or the beginning of the correctional process, should be central to the system of criminal justice. The facts belie this proposition. Indeed, sentencing has been characterized as a national scandal, as a bizarre practice, and as a wasteland of the law.[1]

There are a number of reasons why the imposition of punishment in the United States has an almost accidental quality about it. Certainly, one major contributing factor is the wide latitude that legislatures have given sentencing authorities. This latitude, which includes ranges in possible prison sentences, stems partly from a sincere commitment to individualize sentencing, to make the punishment fit the crime and the criminal. The misuse of discretion in this area would not be so serious were it not for a second element of the American sentencing procedure: It is generally nonreviewable. Of all the democratic nations in the world, the United States is the only one that does not provide for appellate review and correction of grossly excessive sentences.[2] The general rule here is that the merits of a particular sentence are not subject to appellate review so long as the sentence is within the statutory limits.[3]

The Supreme Court has yet to question its early rulings that appellate review of sentencing is not a necessary part of due process.[4] There simply is no body of appellate law to provide guidelines to sentencing authorities. Thus, we face an anomaly—"that a judicial system which has developed so scrupulous a concern for the protection of a criminal defendant throughout every other stage of the proceedings against him should have so neglected this most important dimension of fundamental justice."[5]

Finally, because the Constitution addresses sentencing only in the Eighth Amendment, and there speaks only to cruel and unusual punishments and excessive fines, the courts would have to build sentencing law out of due process. The omission in the Bill of Rights provides a convenient excuse for not undertaking what could become an unreasonable burden on strained judicial resources. Yet even the strongest critics of appellate review of sentencing probably would not suggest that our system of criminal justice can tolerate unjust sentences, and therefore probably would accept a minimum of due process protection in sentencing. Indeed, the courts, including the Supreme Court, have slowly developed a few due process protections in this area.[6]

Due Process Requirements

The most widely recognized due process protection in the area of sentencing is that a defendant must be present and represented by counsel.[7] Counsel is required not only to ensure the defendant that no legal right is lost, but additionally to marshall facts in mitigation of punishment. The general recognition of the constitutional right of counsel to be present at sentencing presumably carries with it the right of counsel to speak in mitigation of punishment. Apparently there is no corresponding constitutional right of a defendant to speak.[8] The common law recognized as early as 1689[9] the right of allocution; that is, the obligation of sentencing judges, prior to the imposition of sentence, to allow defendants to speak in their own behalf. The Federal Rules of Criminal Procedure provide for the right,[10] and it is reversible error for a sentencing judge to disregard the requirement.[11] The presentation of counsel at sentencing generally is an effective substitute for allocution, but there may be instances where "the most persuasive counsel may not be able to speak for a defendant as the defendant might, with halting eloquence, speak for himself."[12]

Perhaps the most fundamental right of a convicted defendant is the right to be sentenced only on the charge or charges for which the defendant was tried and found guilty,[13] and only within the limits of the applicable statute. An erroneous sentence is subject to appellate review and to correction on remand to the trial court.[14]

Legal accidents or technical errors in the original sentence generally do not result in an otherwise properly convicted felon's escaping punishment. As the Court noted in 1974, "The Constitution does not require that sentencing should be a game in which a wrong move by the judge means immunity for the prisoner."[15] In short, where an attack is not on the conviction but rather on the grounds that the punishment, or mode or place of punishment, transcends the statutory limits, then the erroneous sentence may be corrected.[16] Thus, an erroneous sentence is normally voidable, rather than void, and may be set aside and a new sentence entered.

There are rare occasions, however, where an erroneous sentence is void. For example, a sentence would be void where a sentencing court had no jurisdiction, or where a defendant was sentenced under the wrong statute and the appropriate statute had been subsequently repealed without a saving clause. Similarly, an erroneous sentence is void where it has been complied with, or completed; any attempt to resentence raises the issue of double jeopardy.[17] On the other hand, if an original erroneous sentence has not been fully satisfied, then it may be set aside and a new sentence imposed, always assuming that the new sentence would deduct for any prison time served.[18]

In addition to questions of due process and double jeopardy, sentencing can raise a problem of equal protection of the laws. Equal-protection questions usually do not involve the judicial imposition of a sentence but rather some aspect of classification adopted by the legislature in the penal code. Thus, in *Skinner v. Oklahoma* (1942), the Supreme Court struck down the Oklahoma Habitual Criminal Sterilization statute because it exempted those convicted of embezzlement but included those convicted of larceny.[19] Statutory classifications based on age and sex, particularly where the classifications allow for more severe penalties for women and youthful offenders, are coming under increasing attack as forms of invidious discrimination.[20]

Sentence Disparity

The problem of the erroneous sentence is relatively minor in comparison to the issue of unjustified sentence disparity. Sentence disparity—unequal sentences—is a long-standing problem in almost all jurisdictions in the United States, including the federal level. Certainly, a degree of sentence disparity is to be expected in a system that attempts to individualize sentencing. In fact, disparity, is a necessary by-product of the adjustments that must be made to meet the facts (even mitigating ones) of particular cases. However, it is difficult to imagine what reasonable factors would account for the unusual sentence disparity that regularly occurs in the United States. For example, at the federal level in 1975, the national average sentence for a narcotics violation was just over 65 months; in the federal district for Alaska, the average narcotics sentence in 1975 was 309 months. Similar disparities can be noted for other offenses: The national average sentence for a federal robbery conviction in 1975 was approximately 141 months; the average robbery sentence in the federal district court for the Eastern District of Kentucky in 1975 was 270 months, and the same conviction in the Middle District of Alabama yielded an average sentence of only 50 months![21]

The causes of unreasonable sentence disparity are many. The piecemeal development of penal codes is one contributing factor. A variety of possible sentencing distinctions for separate offenses has been allowed to grow, often without regard to the relative seriousness of groups of offenses. For example, in a single jurisdiction, destruction of a house by fire carries a maximum sentence of twenty years; destruction of a house by explosives carries only a ten-year maximum.[22]

Yet disparity in sentencing cannot be explained merely by reference to disparity in penal codes. Perhaps a more fundamental explanation is the lack of consensus about the purpose or purposes of sentencing. Given the multiple justifications for the imposition of the criminal sanction—deterrence, rehabilitation, incapacitation, and retribution—it is not surprising that there is wide variation in the approach to sentencing by judges and other sentencing authorities. Consensus about sentencing is not likely to be achieved quickly, if at all. Yet the disparity that results from this lack of consensus could be reduced by the development of sentencing guidelines. Judicial discretion in sentencing must be tethered by principled jurisprudence, much as judicial discretion in the law of torts is bound by principles that channel it. Simply because nonmechanical sentencing necessarily involves a high degree of discretion does not mean that discretion can never be subject to a jurisprudence of sentencing. Under judicial tests of equal protection, is a judge precluded from imposing a stiffer sentence on a convicted defendant who continues to maintain his or her innocence? Or, is due process violated when a more severe sentence is imposed on a convicted defendant who continues to maintain his or her innocence, even though to admit guilt might jeopardize appellate review of the conviction?[23] Similarly, may a sentencing judge impose a stiffer sentence because he or she concluded that a defendant's trial testimony was false? The Supreme Court has ruled that such a practice does not violate due process, even though this unreviewable practice would appear to inhibit a defendant's right to testify truthfully.[24]

The kind of judicial discretion in sentencing that Justice Black supported in the late 1940s in *Williams v. New York* (1949) still has much to commend it.[25] Yet to argue that a sentence hearing should not be constrained by the same procedural protections as the trial itself simply is not justification for unreasonable sentence disparity. Something must be done to reduce the problem. Administratively, sentencing councils hold some promise.[26] A sentencing council, which is used in some federal districts, enables a sentencing judge to meet with other judges in order to learn what sentence they would impose in a pending case. Beyond such administrative devices as sentencing councils and periodic sentencing institutes, other steps are also necessary. One would be to require that sentencing judges give a written explanation or rationale for a felony sentence, something that judges rarely do and are nowhere required to do.[27] The development of sentencing standards and the appellate review of sentencing cannot take place in the current sentencing void. Finally, the appellate and legislative development of sentencing standards should give appropriate recognition to the issues of due process and equal protection in sentencing.

PUNISHMENTS

Fines

The Eighth Amendment ban on excessive fines reflects a long-standing concern in Anglo-American law. At least as early as 1215, in the Magna Charta (chapter 20), there was express concern that monetary penalties should be proportionate to the magnitude of an offense and that no penalty should strip either a free man or a serf of the basic necessities of life. In the English Bill of Rights (1689), the issue of monetary penalties was raised again, this time in the language that was to be adopted in various American state bills of rights and in the Eighth Amendment. The act of Parliament in 1689 reads: "That excessive bail ought not to be required, nor excessive fines imposed, nor cruel and unusual punishment inflicted";[28] the language of the Eighth Amendment is almost identical.

Although concern about excessive fines occupied an important niche in Anglo-American law until the adoption of the federal Bill of Rights, since that time the ban has had little practical effect. As a part of our legal culture, the ban may well remind legislatures against authorizing confiscatory fines, and to that end it may continue to have an indirect and beneficial effect. However, there is no body of federal case law on excessive fines. In 1883, the Supreme Court declared: "The eighth amendment is addressed to courts of the United States exercising criminal jurisdiction, and is doubtless mandatory to them and a limitation upon their discretion. But this court has no appellate jurisdiction to revise the sentences of inferior courts in criminal cases; and cannot, even if the excess of the fine were apparent on the record, reverse the sentence."[29] To this day, federal courts continue to disavow any right to review a fine if it is within statutory limits.[30]

The major constitutional issue in the area of fines is not whether they are excessive in terms of the Eighth Amendment but rather whether they deny the poor the equal protection of the laws. In 1970 and again in 1971, the Supreme Court addressed the issue of fines and indigent defendants. In *Williams v. Illinois* (1970), the defendant had been sentenced to one year imprisonment, a $500 fine, and $5 costs. As provided by the state statute, if a defendant was in default of payment at the end of the prison sentence, he or she would remain in jail to work off the fine at the rate of $5 per day. In vacating the judgment, the Court held: "Once the State has defined the outer limits of incarceration necessity (sic) to satisfy its penological interests and policies, it may not then subject a certain class of convicted defendants to a period of imprisonment beyond the statutory maximum solely by reasons of their indigency."[31]

In the following year, the Court had before it a case in which the defendant had accumulated traffic fines of $425. In default of payment, the indigent defendant was committed to a municipal prison farm, again to work off the fines at a rate of $5 per day. Here too the Court reversed on grounds of a denial of equal protection of the laws.[32] The Court noted that it was inconsistent with that protection for the state to legislate a fines-only policy for traffic offenses, and then to convert a fine into a prison sentence for indigent defendants. In both cases, the Court observed that a state has other alternatives, includes installment payments, to serve the valid interest in enforcing the payment of fines.[33] Finally, the Court noted that imprisonment is not precluded for one who voluntarily refuses or neglects to pay a fine,[34] but it reserved to another time any ruling on whether indigent defendants could be imprisoned when alternative means of collecting a fine are unsuccessful.[35]

Other Punishments

Our liberties have not always been secured for us by men and women of the highest character; sometimes rogues have played a part. One rogue in the history of the protection against cruel and unusual punishments was Titus Oates. Before 1678, Oates's life had been a series of sordid intrigues and minor scandals. Apparently he was a man who would do and say almost anything to advance himself. Of course, seventeenth-century England was a time of wild talk and wild schemes by political and religious desperadoes, and Oates stands at the top of the list. In June 1678, he hatched the so-called Popish Plot, claiming that a group of Jesuits known to Oates had conspired to assassinate Charles II. Oates took his fabrication to an advisor of the King, but the King dismissed the plot for the clumsy lie it was. Oates was not dissuaded and made public the plot charges. In the process, he stirred up considerable public fear and passion, to the extent that the Crown was powerless to ignore his charges. Indictments were returned, and for the next year and a half Oates was a busy man, falsely testifying in six treason trials. As a result, at least fourteen people were executed, largely on the basis of his perjured testimony.[36] Time and political circumstances finally caught up with Oates, and in 1685 he was tried and convicted for perjury. There was certainly little about Oates that would have commended him to the mercy of the justices of the King's Bench, and indeed they showed no mercy. For the court, Justice Withins pronounced the following judgment:

"First, The Court does order for a fine, that you pay 1000 marks upon each Indictment.

"Secondly, That you be stript of all your Canonical Habits.

"Thirdly, The Court does award, That you do stand upon the Pillory, and in the Pillory, here before Westminster-hall gate, upon Monday next, for an hour's time, between the hours of 10 and 12; with a paper over your head (which you must first walk with round about to all the Courts in Westminster-hall) declaring your crime." And that is upon the first Indictment.

"Fourthly, (on the Second Indictment), upon Tuesday, you shall stand upon, and in the Pillory, at the Royal Exchange in London, for the space of an hour, between the hours of twelve and two; with the same inscription.

"You shall upon the next Wednesday be whipped from Aldgate to Newgate.

"Upon Friday, you shall be whipped from Newgate to Tyburn, by the hands of the common hangman."

But, Mr. Oates, we cannot but remember, there were several particular times you swore false about and therefore, as annual commemorations, that it may be known to all people as long as you live, we have taken special care of you for an annual punishment.

"Upon the 24th of April every year, as long as you live, you are to stand upon the Pillory, and in the Pillory, at Tyburn, just opposite to the gallows, for the space of an hour, between the hours of ten and twelve.

"You are to stand upon, and in the Pillory, here at Westminster-hall gate, every 9th of August, in every year, so long as you live. And that it may be known what we mean by it, 'tis to remember, what he swore about Mr. Ireland's being in town between the 8th and 12th of August.

"You are to stand upon, and in the Pillory, at Charingcross, on the 10th of August, every year, during your life, for an hour, between ten and twelve.

"The like over-against the Temple gate, upon the 11th.

"And upon the 2d of September, (which is another notorious time, which you cannot but be remember'd of) you are to stand upon, and in the Pillory, for the space of one hour, between twelve and two, at the Royal Exchange: and all this you are to do every year, during your life; and to be committed close prisoner, as long as you live."[37]

It remains an open question whether Oates, a Crown witness, could be subsequently charged by the Crown with perjury in a common-law court.[38] Assuming that Oates did commit an indictable offense at common law and further assuming the wide discretion of the courts in pronouncing sentence in perjury cases, still his punishment was considered cruel and unusual. In fact, it has been suggested that Oates's sentence was what Parliament had in mind when it included the ban on cruel and unusual punishments in the English Bill of Rights.[39] Moreover, the sentence was without judicial precedent. It is possible that the intent of the sentence was to kill Oates, a punishment that the courts did not extend in perjury cases.[40] Certainly, the floggings may have been intended to accomplish the same end, but Oates lived through the floggings and went on in 1689 to obtain a royal pardon and a partial restoration of his royal pension.[41]

It is difficult at this distance to say precisely what there was about the judgments in *Oates* that made them cruel and unusual. Perhaps because parts of the judgments did not conform to standard practice in perjury cases, the judgments were erroneous and subject to reversal. Also objectionable was the physical cruelty of the long floggings coupled with the horror of close confinement for life in a seventeenth-century prison. And beyond the cruelty was the issue of proportion: The judgments, even by seventeenth-century standards, were not commensurate with the crime of perjury, particularly given the uncertain state of seventeenth-century perjury law. Finally, it seems clear that Oates's contemporaries objected to the judgments by reference to what they considered to be the current standard of a society that purported to be civilized and Christian. In short, as the Supreme Court was to note, the words *cruel* and *unusual* are not static; they draw "from the evolving standards of decency that mark the progress of a maturing society."[42]

The principles that appear to have been significant in the contemporary reaction to Oates's judgments have been somewhat sharpened by recent decisions of the Supreme Court in the death penalty cases, but they remain essentially the same. Punishments must be neither physically cruel nor excessive in relationship to an offense. Thus, in *Weems v. United States* (1910), the Court reversed a judgment against Weems for falsifying a public document because of what the court called the "coercive cruelty" of the sentence.[43] Weems had been sentenced to a fine, fifteen years at hard and painful labor during which he was to wear shackles, the loss of his civil rights, and life surveillance. As the Court observed, the Philippine code under which Weems had been sentenced was draconian. However, until the death penalty cases of the 1970s, the Court considered the cruel-and-unusual-punishment clause only infrequently, and, when it did, it was generally supportive of legislative judgments about penalties.[44]

The Death Penalty

No issue in the area of cruel and unusual punishment has captured as much public and judicial attention as that of the death penalty. The death penalty as the common punishment for felonies antedates the Norman Conquest (1066). But however ancient the penalty is, it has long been the subject of passionate controversy.[45] Since 1900, there have been over 5,500 capital executions in the United States.[46] (The highest number of executions in any single year in the twentieth century was 200 in 1933.)[47] But, in the past quarter of a century, the death penalty has been infrequently imposed and, in recent years, rarely executed. In 1977, there were approximately four hundred persons on death row, but from 1966 up to January 1977 there were only two persons executed in the United States.[48] Surprisingly, this decline in the number of executions does not mirror any public dissatisfaction with capital punishment. In 1966, only 42 percent of the population favored capital punishment, but since that time there has been a steady increase in public support for the penalty. By 1976, 65 percent of the population favored capital punishment.[49]

The death penalty cases of the 1970s have divided the Court, often marshalling only plurality opinions. Still, a number of issues have been resolved by a majority of the Court's members:

1. The death penalty is not necessarily cruel and unusual, and it may be imposed for the crime of murder provided that certain procedural safeguards are observed.[50]
2. Where the death penalty is authorized, it must either (a) involve the unnecessary or wanton infliction of pain nor (b) be grossly out of proportion to the severity of the crime, and it must serve some penological purpose, as for example, retribution or deterrence.[51] Thus, the Court has concluded that the sentence is grossly disproportionate and excessive punishment for the crime of raping an adult woman.[52]
3. Where the death penalty is imposed, there must be sufficient procedures to regularize its use and to make it rationally reviewable by appellate courts.[53]
4. The death penalty cannot be mandatory.[54]
5. Although sentencing authorities must be allowed discretion in imposing the death penalty, their discretion cannot be unbridled.[55] Therefore, they must be provided with standards that direct a process of individualized sentencing in which consideration of both the "character and record of the individual offender and the circumstances of the particular offense" are constitutionally indispensable.[56] To meet the constitutional standard, then, "a death penalty statute must not preclude consideration of relevant mitigating factors."[57]
6. Due process requires that when the death penalty is imposed the sentence cannot be based on confidential information contained in a presentence report that is not disclosed to the defendant or to defense counsel.[58]

Although one may disagree with capital punishment, and thus with the Court's refusal to upset legislative judgment, the death penalty cases *are* judicious attempts to ensure that capital punishment is not imposed in a capricious or freakish manner. The safeguards that now surround the imposition of the penalty are considerable. Furthermore, the Court not only has required new procedural safeguards, but it also appears to be moving in the direction of limiting the use of the penalty. The decision in *Coker v. Georgia* (1977), holding that death is a disproportionate penalty for the crime of raping an adult woman, suggests that a majority of the justices entertain doubts about the death penalty in nonmurder cases. Of course, even this move toward limiting capital punishment does not satisfy those who believe that the penalty is not morally justified or who have concluded that the penalty has no greater deterrent effect than does a sentence of life imprisonment.[59]

It may well be that the death penalty conflicts with the standard of decency that ought to obtain in a modern society, and doubtless that belief will continue to propel a constitutional argument. On the other hand, it is difficult to fault the leadership the Supreme Court has assumed in this troubled area. Although the Court has not substituted its judgment, as it is entitled to do under judicial review, for the considered judgments of legislative chambers, still it has forced the legislatures to adopt measures that should reduce caprice in the imposition of this irrevocable penalty.

POSTCONVICTION RELIEF

Once a defendant has been convicted and a final judgment entered, it is still possible for the defendant to attack the judgment on the basis of either an error in law or an error in fact. The precise procedures for postconviction relief vary from jurisdiction to jurisdiction, but they generally range from direct appeal from the trial court to an appellate court, to various forms of collateral attack on the conviction. Many of these procedures are beyond the scope of this book. However, the vindication of the constitutionally protected rights of criminal defendants is well within our inquiry.

The Supreme Court has never overturned the late-nineteenth-century ruling that due process does not require a review by an appellate court of a final judgment in a criminal case;[60] still both state and federal prisoners have limited federal statutory rights to seek redress in federal district courts against wrongful convictions. Federal prisoners can obtain postconviction relief either by direct appeal of the judgment or by separate collateral attack under section 2255 of the Criminal Code.[61] Section 2255 is, for most cases, the functional equivalent of habeas corpus. Generally, the states allow at least one right of direct appeal and beyond that, under federal law, certain state prisoners may collaterally attack their convictions under federal habeas corpus.[62] The major policy issue today is the collateral attack of a conviction under habeas corpus.

Federal Habeas Corpus Relief

For a number of years, controversy has raged about collateral attacks on criminal convictions, particularly by state prisoners under federal habeas corpus. Any prisoner who is held in violation of a federally secured constitutional right may ultimately be allowed to raise the constitutional question in a habeas corpus proceeding, or its functional equivalent.[63] This means that only those errors or trial infirmities that are secured against violation by the federal Constitution may be raised;[64] technical errors may not. The practical effect of this rule is to allow federal district courts a measure of supervision over state criminal trials.

Originally, habeas corpus was not thought of as a writ to challenge a judicial conviction but rather as an extraordinary means of determining the legality of executive detention prior to trial.[65] But Blackstone's great writ of liberty has undergone considerable refashioning over the past twenty-five years. Particularly during the Warren years, the Supreme Court adopted an expansive view of habeas corpus, perhaps, in part, as a means of relieving the Court of the direct appeals stemming from its expansion of defendants' rights. In a trilogy of cases in 1963, the Court ruled:

1. A federal district court must hold an evidentiary hearing on disputed facts in a petition for habeas corpus if the state's fact-finding proceedings are found to be inadequate under specific criteria (the merits of the factual dispute were not resolved in the state hearing, the state's factual determination is not fairly supported by the record).[66]
2. A state procedural ground that is adequate to bar direct review of a state conviction by the Supreme Court is not necessarily a bar to habeas corpus. The habeas judge must determine whether a petitioner, by not presenting a claim in a state court, has deliberately bypassed orderly state procedure.[67] In short, a state petitioner must exhaust available state remedies for postconviction relief before presenting a claim under federal habeas corpus.[68] And, a petitioner cannot reserve one or more constitutional claims for subsequent litigation.[69]
3. A petitioner whose previous application or applications for habeas corpus have been denied may still be granted relief if a new application raises grounds not previously decided on the merits against the petitioner or raises grounds for relief not known at the time of the previous application.[70]

Not only did the Warren Court take an expansive view of postconviction relief; it attempted to ensure that relief would be available to indigent prisoners by requiring that where relief is allowed, it must be available on a meaningful basis to the destitute. Thus, where direct appeal or collateral attack is allowed, the indigent must be provided with a free transcript of the trial[71] and with free counsel.[72]

Collateral attack on a conviction raises a number of serious issues, not the least of which is whether the rulings in 1963 opened the floodgates for frivolous claims, thereby necessitating wasteful federal hearings. There is no question that there has been a dramatic increase in the number of habeas petitions, rising from a few hundred in the early 1960s to several thousand by the late 1970s. Undoubtedly, this has created a greater work load, but whether the actual increase in work load is as large as the increase in the number of petitions is an open question. One study indicated that as many as 90 percent of the petitions were without merit[73] but also noted that hearings associated with the petitions tended to be short.[74] Given the low percentage of meritorious petitions and that federal habeas judges often reach the same conclusion about claims as did the state court, there is a serious question whether a state prisoner should be entitled to a federal court review of a state determination as a matter of right.

Collateral attacks on criminal convictions may also help to undermine the

value of finality of judgment. At some point a case must end. Needless, wasteful petitions may undermine whatever value swift and certain justice affords
society, and they may also have a negative impact on rehabilitation. Furthermore, collateral attacks by state prisoners through federal habeas corpus may
run contrary to principles of federalism, especially to the extent that a habeas
proceeding places a federal judge in a supervisory capacity over state judicial
proceedings. Finally, why should a defendant, whose claim has had a full
hearing in a state court, be allowed to relitigate the same issue in a different
forum, particularly where the petitioner is not required to present a colorable
claim that casts reasonable doubt on the guilt of the petitioner?[75]

The strong arguments that have been raised against collateral attacks may
have influenced the Burger Court to adopt some rather drastic measures to
reduce the number of these proceedings. Perhaps the most drastic limit on
postconviction relief was the decision in *Stone v. Powell* (1976).[76] *Stone* bars
federal habeas relief for a state prisoner on claims arising under the Fourth
Amendment where the state has previously afforded the prisoner a full and
fair opportunity to litigate the issue. In short, a defendant whose Fourth
Amendment claim has been rejected in a state proceeding may not subsequently collaterally attack the conviction in a federal proceeding.[77]

In addition to *Stone*, the Burger Court has also ruled that federal collateral
relief is not available in cases involving pleas of guilty where the pleas were
voluntary.[78] Thus, in guilty-plea cases, constitutional claims that antedate the
guilty plea may not be raised in a federal habeas proceeding. This decision
combined with that in *Stone* will probably close the doors of the federal district
courts to many state prisoners. But the Burger Court's attack on postconviction
relief is by no means limited to these two decisions. The Court has also limited
Fay v. Noia (1963) by ruling that a defendant must show cause as to why he
or she failed to previously raise a federal claim. The defendant must also indicate some measure of prejudice arising out of the claimed denial of a right.[79]
Thus, in *Wainwright v. Sykes* (1977), the defendant, having failed to make
timely objection to the introduction of his confession at his trial, was barred
on procedural grounds from raising the claim in a federal habeas proceeding.[80]

The argument against these decisions stands or falls on the current need for
federal judicial supervision of state criminal proceedings. The trilogy of cases
in 1963 may be viewed as the Warren Court's means of inducing state courts
to apply federal constitutional standards in state criminal proceedings and to
grant adequate postconviction remedies, including, where necessary, evidentiary hearings. Whether the separate forum of a federal habeas proceeding
actually affords a state prisoner a setting more impartially committed to federal
constitutional goals than are the state criminal courts is an open question.
Similarly, it is an open question whether a federal habeas proceeding is a better
means of ensuring uniformity in the application of federal constitutional standards than is a state court determination of applicable federal law.[81]

Finally, we should note that the Burger Court's decisions in the area of habeas corpus very nearly close the door to further development and clarification of those defendants' procedural rights that were expanded during the years of the Warren Court. The Warren Court did not, as it could not, leave a fully developed body of law in this area. To some extent, the resolution of the problems arising out of the expansion of defendants' rights under the Fourth, Fifth, and Sixth Amendments must wait further litigation. And whether the state criminal courts and state appellate courts are the best forum for this resolution remains to be determined.

CONCLUSION

We can agree that finality in criminal procedure is necessary. At some point, criminal trials must end and the correctional process must begin. Yet, however necessary finality may be, it cannot obscure the need to continue basic reforms in sentencing and punishments. A full jurisprudence at sentencing remains a basic need in criminal procedure, as does resolving the problem of sentence disparity. A parsimonious stance in habeas corpus will necessarily preclude the federal judiciary from assuming a leadership role in these areas and from completing its tasks with respect to the death penalty. A somewhat expansive view of federal habeas corpus has been a necessary adjunct of criminal-procedure reform in the United States. It should continue to serve as a means of alerting the public and the legal community to the unresolved problems in this area.

NOTES

1. E.g., Marvin Frankel, "Lawlessness in Sentencing," 41 *Cin. L. Rev.* 1 (1972); and remarks by Alvin Rubin, Pound Conference (1976), reported in 70 F.R.D. 194.
2. President's Commission on Law Enforcement and Administration of Justice, *Task Force Report; The Courts* (Washington, D.C.: GPO, 1967), p. 25.
3. Some states do *permit* appellate review of the merits of a sentence; the federal government does so only for military sentences, id.
4. E.g., *Murphy v. Massachusetts,* 177 U.S. 155, 158 (1900).
5. The observation was made by Justice Stewart while he was a federal appellate judge, in *Shepard v. United States,* 257 F.2d 293, 294 (1958).
6. *Gardner v. Florida,* 430 U.S. 349, 358–360 (1977).
7. *Lewis v. United States,* 146 U.S. 370 (1892); *Mempa v. Rhay,* 389 U.S. 128 (1967); and *Townsend v. Burke,* 334 U.S. 736 (1948).
8. See dictum in *Farrow v. United States,* 373 F. Supp. 113, 120 (1974).
9. *Anonymous Case,* 87 Eng. Rep. 175 (1689).
10. Rule 32(a).
11. *Green v. United States,* 365 U.S. 301 (1961).
12. Ibid. at 304.
13. *Specht v. Patterson,* 386 U.S. 605, 608–609 (1967).
14. The erroneous, or illegal, sentence is one that is not authorized by a particular judgment of conviction, but it presupposes a valid conviction.

15. *Bozza v. United States,* 330 U.S. 160, 166–167 (1947).

16. *In re Bonner,* 151 U.S. 242, 259 (1894).

17. *Murphy v. Massachusetts,* 177 U.S. at 160; and *Ex parte Lange,* 18 Wall. 163 (1874).

18. *In re Bonner,* 151 U.S. at 258. The issue of credit for prison time served prior to sentencing is a separable issue; see *Gremillion v. Henderson,* 425 F.2d 1293, 1294 (1970), and *McGinnis v. Royster,* 410 U.S. 263 (1973).

19. *Skinner v Oklahoma,* 316 U.S. 535 (1942). See also *Marshall v. United States,* 414 U.S. 417 (1974).

20. See generally Mark Berger, "Equal Protection and Criminal Sentencing," 71 *Nw. U. L. Rev.* 29, 48–52 (1976).

21. See Federal Bureau of Prisons, *Statistical Report, Fiscal Year 1975* (Washington, D.C.: GPO, 1976), table B-9. See also Keith Harris and Russell Lura, "The Geography of Justice," 57 *Judicature* 392 (1974).

22. *Task Force Report: The Courts,* p. 15.

23. E.g., *Williams v. United States,* 273 F.2d 469 (1959).

24. *United States v. Grayson,* 438 U.S. 41 (1978).

25. *Williams v. New York,* 337 U.S. 241 (1949).

26. See Shari Diamond and Hans Zeisel, "Sentencing Councils: A Study of Sentence Disparity and Its Reduction," 43 *U. Chi. L. Rev.* 109 (1975).

27. Frankel, "Lawlessness," pp. 9–15.

28. 1 W. & M. 2, chap. 2.

29. *Ex parte Watkins,* 7 Pet. 568, 574 (1833).

30. E.g., *United States v. Glazer,* 532 F.2d 224 (1976).

31. *Williams v. Illinois,* 399 U.S. 235, 242 (1970).

32. *Tate v. Short,* 401 U.S. 395 (1971).

33. Ibid. at 399.

34. Ibid. at 401.

35. On the local impact of *Tate* and *Williams* cases, see Ralph Rossum, "Judicial Administration in Tennessee," *Public Affairs Forum,* vol. 4 (October 1974).

36. James Fitzjames Stephen, *A History of the Criminal Law in England* (London: Macmillan, 1883), vol. 1, p. 392.

37. *The Trial of Titus Oates for Perjury,* 10 How. St. Tr. 1079, 1316–1317 (1685).

38. Stephen, *History of Criminal Law,* vol. 3, p. 246.

39. Ibid. at vol. 1, p. 490.

40. The remarks of Lord Chief Justice Jefferys at the sentencing of Titus Oates, 10 How. St. Tr. 1315 (1685).

41. Ibid. at 1325–1326.

42. *Trop v. Dulles,* 356 U.S. 86, 101 (1958).

43. *Weems v. United States,* 217 U.S. 349 (1910).

44. E.g., *Howard v. Fleming,* 191 U.S. 126 (1903). Cf. *Trop v. Dulles,* declaring unconstitutional a portion of a statute that expatriated citizens convicted by military courts of wartime desertion. The Court has applied the ban to the states; see *Robinson v. California,* 370 U.S. 660 (1962). The Court has also indicated that the ban on cruel and unusual punishments applies to conditions of confinement; see *Estelle v. Gamble,* 429 U.S. 97 (1976), and *Hutto v. Finney,* 437 U.S. 678 (1978).

45. For a general review of the death penalty, see Ugo Bedau, *The Death Penalty in America* (Chicago: Aldine, 1964).

46. William Bowers, *Executions in America* (Lexington, Mass.: Lexington Books, 1974), app. A.

47. *Task Force Report: The Courts,* p. 27.

48. During the early 1970s moratoriums on the death penalty were generally declared by the thirty-three states (1976) that had the penalty.

49. *The Gallup Opinion Index,* no. 132 (July 1976), p. 24.

50. *Gregg v. Georgia*, 428 U.S. 153 (1976).

51. Ibid. at 172–185.

52. *Coker v. Georgia*, 438 U.S. 586, 608 (1977). Mississippi and Florida authorize the death penalty for the adult rape of a child.

53. *Furman v. Georgia*, 408 U.S. 238 (1972), the opinions of Justices Stewart and White; and *Roberts v. Louisiana*, 431 U.S. 633 (1976).

54. *Jurek v. Texas*, 428 U.S. 262 (1976).

55. *Woodson v. North Carolina*, 428 U.S. 280 (1976).

56. Ibid. at 304.

57. *Lockett v. Ohio*, 438 U.S. 586, 608 (1978); and see *Gregg v. Georgia*.

58. *Gardner v. Florida*, 430 U.S. 349 (1977).

59. See Hans Zeisel, "The Deterrent Effect of the Death Penalty: Facts v. Faith," in *1976 Supreme Court Review* (Chicago: University of Chicago Press, 1977), pp. 317–343.

60. *McKane v. Durston*, 153 U.S. 684 (1894); and see *United States v. MacCollom*, 426 U.S. 317 (1976).

61. 28 U.S.C. 2255. For reduction or correction of a sentence, a federal prisoner may make a motion under rule 35 of the Federal Rules of Criminal Procedure.

62. 28 U.S.C. 2254 (a).

63. 28 U.S.C. 2255.

64. *Donnelly v. DeChristoforo*, 416 U.S. 637, 642 (1974).

65. See Dallin Oaks, "Legal History in the High Court: Habeas Corpus," 64 *Mich. L. Rev.* 451 (1966).

66. *Townsend v. Sain*, 372 U.S. 391 (1963). The criteria are now codified in 28 U.S.C. 2254 (a).

67. *Fay v. Noia*, 372 U.S. 391 (1963).

68. See also *Preiser v. Rodriguez*, 411 U.S. 475 (1973).

69. *Murch v. Mottram*, 409 U.S. 41 (1973).

70. *Sanders v. United States*, 373 U.S. 1 (1963).

71. *Griffin v. Illinois*, 351 U.S. 12 (1956), and *Lane v. Brown*, 372 U.S. 477 (1963).

72. *Douglas v. California*, 372 U.S. 353 (1963).

73. David Shapiro, "Federal Habeas Corpus: A Study in Massachusetts," 87 *Harv. L. Rev.* 321 (1973).

74. Ibid. at 337.

75. See Henry Friendly, "Is Innocence Irrelevant: Collateral Attacks on Criminal Judgments," 38 *U. Chi. L. Rev.* 142 (1970).

76. *Stone v. Powell*, 482 U.S. 465 (1976).

77. The *Stone* decision does not preclude direct review of a Fourth Amendment claim by the Supreme Court, but, of course, the number of state prisoners who would be granted such review would be quite small unless a majority of the Court decided to use the per curiam decision as a means of correcting a state's misconstruction of the Fourth Amendment.

78. *Tollett v. Henderson*, 411 U.S. 258 (1973).

79. *Davis v. United States*, 411 U.S. 233 (1973), and *Francis v. Henderson*, 425 U.S. 536 (1976).

80. *Wainwright v. Sykes*, 433 U.S. 72 (1977).

81. For a contrary view, see note, "Recent Developments in the Law: Federal Habeas Corpus," 83 *Harv. L. Rev.* 1038, 1058–1062 (1970).

JUDICIAL DECISIONS

The Validity of the Death Penalty:
Gregg v. Georgia, *428 U.S. 204 (1976)*

Mr. Justice STEWART, Mr. Justice POWELL, and Mr. Justice STEVENS announced the judgment of the Court and filed an opinion delivered by Mr. Justice STEWART.

The issue in this case is whether the imposition of the sentence of death for the crime of murder under the law of Georgia violates the Eighth and Fourteenth Amendments.

I

The petitioner, Troy Gregg, was charged with committing armed robbery and murder. In accordance with Georgia procedure in capital cases, the trial was in two stages, a guilt stage and a sentencing stage. The evidence at the guilt trial established that on November 21, 1973, the petitioner and a traveling companion, Floyd Allen, while hitchhiking north in Florida were picked up by Fred Simmons and Bob Moore. Their car broke down, but they continued north after Simmons purchased another vehicle with some of the cash he was carrying. While still in Florida, they picked up another hitchhiker, Dennis Weaver, who rode with them to Atlanta, where he was let out about 11 p.m. A short time later the four men interrupted their journey for a rest stop along the highway. The next morning the bodies of Simmons and Moore were discovered in a ditch nearby.

On November 23, after reading about the shootings in an Atlanta newspaper, Weaver communicated with the Gwinnett County police and related information concerning the journey with the victims, including a description of their car. The next afternoon, the petitioner and Allen, while in Simmons' car, were arrested in Asheville, N.C. In the search incident to the arrest a .25-caliber pistol later shown to be that used to kill Simmons and Moore, was found in the petitioner's pocket. After receiving the warnings required by *Miranda v. United States,* 384 U.S. 436 (1966), and signing a written waiver of his rights, the petitioner signed a statement in which he admitted shooting, then robbing Simmons and Moore. He justified the slayings on grounds of self-defense. The next day, while being transferred to Lawrenceville, Ga., the petitioner and Allen were taken to the scene of the shootings. Upon arriving there, Allen recounted the events leading to the slayings. His version of these events was as follows: After Simmons and Moore left the car, the petitioner stated that he intended to rob them. The petitioner then took his pistol in hand and positioned himself on the car to improve his aim. As Simmons and Moore came up an embankment towards the car, the petitioner fired three shots and the two men fell near a ditch. The petitioner, at close range, then fired a shot into the head of each. He robbed them of valuables and drove away with Allen.

A medical examiner testified that Simmons died from a bullet wound in the eye and that Moore died from bullet wounds in the cheek and in the back of the head. He further testified that both men had several bruises and abrasions about the face and head which probably were sustained either from the fall into the ditch or from being dragged or pushed along the embankment. Although Allen did not testify, a police detective recounted the substance of Allen's statements about the slayings and indicated that directly after Allen had made these statements the petitioner had admitted that Allen's account was accurate. The petitioner testified in his own defense. He confirmed that Allen had made the statements described by the detective, but denied their truth or ever having admitted to their accuracy. He indicated that he had shot Simmons and Moore because of fear and in self-defense, testifying they had attacked Allen and him, one wielding a pipe and the other a knife.

The trial judge submitted the murder charges to the jury on both felony-murder and nonfelony-murder theories. He also instructed on the issue of self-defense but declined to instruct on manslaughter. He submitted the robbery case to the jury on both an armed-robbery theory and on the lesser included offense of robbery by intimidation. The jury found the petitioner guilty of two counts of armed robbery and two counts of murder.

At the penalty stage, which took place before the same jury, neither the prosecutor nor the petitioner's lawyer offered any additional evidence. Both counsel, however, made lengthy arguments dealing generally with the propriety of capital punishment under the circumstances and with the weight of the evidence of guilt. The trial judge instructed the jury that it could recommend either a death sentence or a life prison sentence on each count. The judge further charged the jury that in determining what sentence was appropriate the jury was free to consider the facts and circumstances presented by the parties, if any, in mitigation or aggravation.

Finally, the judge instructed the jury that it "would not be authorized to consider [imposing] the sentence of death" unless it first found beyond a reasonable doubt one of these aggravating circumstances:

> "One—That the offense of murder was committed while the offender was engaged in the commission o[f] two other capit[a]l felonies, to-wit the armed ro[b]bery of [Simmons and Moore].
> "Two—That the offender committed the offense of murder for the purpose of receiving money and the automobile described in the indictment.
> "Three—The offense of murder was outrageously and wantonly vile, horrible and inhuman, in that they [sic] involved the depravity of the mind of the defendant."

Finding the first and second of these circumstances, the jury returned verdicts of death on each count.

The Supreme Court of Georgia affirmed the convictions and the imposition of the death sentences for murder. 233 Ga. 117, 210 S.E.2d 659 (1974). After reviewing the trial transcript and the record, including the evidence, and comparing the evidence and sentence in similar cases in accordance with the requirements of Georgia law, the court concluded that, considering the nature of the crime and the defendant, the sentences of death had not resulted from prejudice or any other arbitrary factor and were not excessive or disproportionate to the penalty applied in similar cases. The death sentences imposed for armed robbery, however, were vacated on the grounds that the death penalty had rarely been imposed in Georgia for that offense and that the jury improperly considered the murders as aggravating circumstances for the robberies after having considered the armed robberies as aggravating circumstances for the murders.

We granted the petitioner's application for a writ of certiorari challenging the imposition of the death sentences in this case as "cruel and unusual" punishment in violation of the Eighth and the Fourteenth Amendments.

II

Before considering the issues presented it is necessary to understand the Georgia statutory scheme for the imposition of the death penalty. The Georgia statute, as amended after our decision in *Furman v. Georgia,* 408 U.S. 238 (1972), retains the death penalty for six categories of crime: murder, kidnapping for ransom or where the victim is harmed, armed robbery, rape, treason, and aircraft hijacking. The capital defendant's guilt or innocence is determined in the traditional manner, either by a trial judge or a jury, in the first stage of a bifurcated trial.

If trial is by jury, the trial judge is required to charge lesser included offenses when they are supported by any view of the evidence. After a verdict, finding, or plea of guilty to a capital crime, a presentence hearing is conducted before whomever made the determination of guilt. The sentencing procedures are essentially the same in both bench and jury trials. At the hearing,

> "the judge [or jury] shall hear additional evidence in extenuation, mitigation, and aggravation of punishment, including the record of any prior criminal convictions and pleas of guilty or pleas of nolo contendere of the defendant, or the absence of any prior conviction and pleas: Provided, however, that only such evidence in aggravation as the State has made known to the defendant prior to his trial shall be admissible. The judge [or jury] shall also hear argument by defendant or his counsel and the prosecuting attorney . . . regarding the punishment to be imposed." § 27-2503. (Supp. 1975).

The defendant is accorded substantial latitude as to the types of evidence that he may introduce. Evidence considered during the guilt stage may be considered during the sentencing stage without being resubmitted.

In the assessment of the appropriate sentence to be imposed the judge is also required to consider or to include in his instructions to the jury "any mitigating circumstances or aggravating circumstances otherwise authorized by law and any of [10] statutory aggravating circumstances which may be supported by the evidence. . . ." § 27-2534.1(b) (Supp. 1975). The scope of the nonstatutory aggravating or mitigating circumstances is not delineated in the statute. Before a convicted defendant may be sentenced to death, however, except in cases of treason or aircraft hijacking, the jury, or the trial judge in cases tried without a jury, must find beyond a reasonable doubt one of the 10 aggravating circumstances specified in the statute. The sentence of death may be imposed only if the jury (or judge) finds one of the statutory aggravating circumstances and then elects to impose that sentence. If the verdict is death the jury or judge must specify the aggravating circumstance(s) found. In jury cases, the trial judge is bound by the jury's recommended sentence.

In addition to the conventional appellate process available in all criminal cases, provision is made for special expedited direct review by the Supreme Court of Georgia of the appropriateness of imposing the sentence of death in the particular case. The court is directed to consider "the punishment as well as any errors enumerated by way of appeal," and to determine:

"(1) Whether the sentence of death was imposed under the influence of passion, prejudice, or any other arbitrary factor, and

"(2) Whether, in cases other than treason or aircraft hijacking, the evidence supports the jury's or judge's finding of a statutory aggravating circumstance as enumerated in section 27.2534.1(b), and

"(3) Whether the sentence of death is excessive or disproportionate to the penalty imposed in similar cases, considering both the crime and the defendant." § 27-2537 (Supp. 1975).

If the court affirms a death sentence, it is required to include in its decision reference to similar cases that it has taken into consideration. § 27-2537(e).

A transcript and complete record of the trial, as well as a separate report by the trial judge, are transmitted to the court for its use in reviewing the sentence. § 27-2537(a)(1972). The report is in the form of a six and one-half page questionnaire, designed to elicit information about the defendant, the crime, and the circumstances of the trial. It requires the trial judge to characterize the trial in several ways designed to test for arbitrariness and disproportionality of sentence. Included in the report are responses to detailed questions concerning the quality of the defendant's representation, whether race played a role in the trial, and, whether, in the trial court's judgment, there was any doubt about the defendant's guilt or the appropriateness of the sentence. A copy of the report is served upon defense counsel. Under its special review authority, the court may either affirm the death sentence or remand the case for resentencing. In cases in which the death sentence is affirmed there remains the possibility of executive clemency.

III

We address initially the basic contention that the punishment of death for the crime of murder is, under all circumstances, "cruel and unusual" in violation of the Eighth and Fourteenth Amendments of the Constitution. In Part IV of this opinion, we will consider the sentence of death imposed under the Georgia statutes at issue in this case.

The Court on a number of occasions has both assumed and asserted the constitutionality of capital punishment. In several cases that assumption provided a necessary foundation for the decision, as the Court was asked to decide whether a particular method of carrying out a capital sentence would be allowed to stand under the Eighth Amendment. But until *Furman v. Georgia*, 408 U.S. 238 (1972), the Court never confronted squarely the fundamental claim that the punishment of death always, regardless of the enormity of the offense or the procedure followed in imposing the sentence, is cruel and unusual punishment in violation of the Constitution. Although this issue was presented and addressed in *Furman*, it was not resolved by the Court. . . . We now hold that the punishment of death does not invariably violate the Constitution.

A

The history of the prohibition of "cruel and unusual" punishment already has been reviewed by this Court at length. The phrase first appeared in the English Bill of Rights of 1689, which was drafted by Parliament at the accession of William and

Mary. The English version appears to have been directed against punishments unauthorized by statute and beyond the jurisdiction of the sentencing court, as well as those disproportionate to the offense involved. The American draftsmen, who adopted the English phrasing in drafting the Eighth Amendment, were primarily concerned, however, with proscribing "tortures" and other "barbarous" methods of punishment.

In the earliest cases raising Eighth Amendment claims, the Court focused on particular methods of execution to determine whether they were too cruel to pass constitutional muster. The constitutionality of the sentence of death itself was not at issue, and the criterion used to evaluate the mode of execution was its similarity to "torture" and other "barbarous" methods.

But the Court has not confined the prohibition embodied in the Eighth Amendment to "barbarous" methods that were generally outlawed in the 18th century. Instead, the Amendment has been interpreted in a flexible and dynamic manner. The Court early recognized that "a principle to be vital, must be capable of wider application than the mischief which gave it birth." *Weems v. United States*, 217 U.S. 349, 373 (1910). Thus the clause forbidding "cruel and unusual" punishments "is not fastened to the obsolete but may acquire meaning as public opinion becomes enlightened by a humane justice." Id., at 378.

. . .

The substantive limits imposed by the Eighth Amendment on what can be made criminal and punished were discussed in *Robinson v. California*, 370 U.S. 660 (1962). The Court found unconstitutional a state statute that made the status of being addicted to a narcotic drug a criminal offense. It held, in effect, that it is "cruel and unusual" to impose any punishment at all for the mere status of addiction. . . .

It is clear from the foregoing precedents that the Eighth Amendment has not been regarded as a static concept. As Chief Justice Warren said, in an oft-quoted phrase, "the Amendment must draw its meaning from the evolving standards of decency that mark the progress of a maturing society." *Trop v. Dulles, supra*, 356 U.S. at 101. Thus, an assessment of contemporary values concerning the infliction of a challenged sanction is relevant to the application of the Eighth Amendment. As we develop below more fully, this assessment does not call for a subjective judgment. It requires, rather, that we look to objective indicia that reflect the public attitude toward a given sanction.

But our cases also make clear that public perceptions of standards of decency with respect to criminal sanctions are not conclusive. A penalty also must accord with "the dignity of man," which is the "basic concept underlying the Eighth Amendment." *Trop v. Dulles, supra*, 356 U.S., at 100 (plurality opinion). This means, at least, that the punishment not be "excessive." When a form of punishment in the abstract (in this case, whether capital punishment may ever be imposed as a sanction for murder) rather than in the particular (the propriety of death as a penalty to be applied to a specific defendant for a specific crime) is under consideration, the inquiry into "excessiveness" has two aspects. First, the punishment must not involve the unnecessary and wanton infliction of pain. *Furman v. Georgia, supra*, 408 U.S., at 392–393 (Burger, C. J., dissenting). Second, the punishment must not be grossly out of proportion to the severity of the crime. *Trop v. Dulles, supra*, 356 U.S., at 100 (plurality opinion) (dictum).

B

Of course, the requirements of the Eighth Amendment must be applied with an awareness of the limited role to be played by the courts. This does not mean that judges have no role to play, for the Eighth Amendment is a restraint upon the exercise of legislative power. . . .

But, while we have an obligation to insure that constitutional bounds are not over-reached, we may not act as judges as we might as legislators. . . .

Therefore, in assessing a punishment selected by a democratically elected legislature against the constitutional measure, we presume its validity. We may not require the legislature to select the least severe penalty possible so long as the penalty selected is not cruelly inhumane or disproportionate to the crime involved. And a heavy burden rests on those who would attack the judgment of the representatives of the people.

. . . We now consider specifically whether the sentence of death for the crime of murder is a per se violation of the Eighth and Fourteenth Amendments to the Constitution. We note first that history and precedent strongly support a negative answer to this question.

I

The imposition of the death penalty for the crime of murder has a long history of acceptance both in the United States and in England. The common-law rule imposed a mandatory death sentence on all convicted murderers. And the penalty continued to be used into the 20th century by most American States, although the breadth of the common-law rule was diminished, initially by narrowing the class of murders to be punished by death and subsequently by widespread adoption of laws expressly granting juries the discretion to recommend mercy.

It is apparent from the text of the Constitution itself that the existence of capital punishment was accepted by the Framers. At the time the Eighth Amendment was ratified, capital punishment was a common sanction in every State. Indeed, the First Congress of the United States enacted legislation providing death as the penalty for specified crimes. 1 Stat. 112 (1790). The Fifth Amendment, adopted at the same time as the Eighth, contemplated the continued existence of the capital sanction by imposing certain limits on the prosecution of capital cases:

"No person shall be held to answer for a capital, or otherwise infamous crime, unless on a presentment or indictment of a Grand Jury . . . nor shall any person be subject for the same offense to be twice put in jeopardy of life or limb . . . nor be deprived of life, liberty, or property, without due process of law. . . ."

And the Fourteenth Amendment, adopted over three-quarters of a century later, similarly contemplates the existence of the capital sanction in providing that no State shall deprive any person of "life, liberty, or property" without due process of law.
. . .

Four years ago, the petitioners in *Furman* and its companion cases predicated their argument primarily upon the asserted proposition that standards of decency had evolved to the point where capital punishment no longer could be tolerated. The petitioners in those cases said, in effect, that the evolutionary process had come to an end, and that standards of decency required that the Eighth Amendment be construed finally as prohibiting capital punishment for any crime regardless of its depravity and impact on society. This view was accepted by two Justices. . . .

The petitioners in the capital cases before the Court today renew the "standards of decency" argument, but developments during the four years since *Furman* have undercut substantially the assumptions upon which their argument rested. Despite the continuing debate, dating back to the 19th century, over the morality and utility of capital punishment, it is now evident that a large proportion of American society continues to regard it as an appropriate and necessary criminal sanction.

The most marked indication of society's endorsement of the death penalty for murder is the legislative response to *Furman*. The legislatures of at least 35 States have enacted new statutes that provide for the death penalty for at least some crimes that result in the death of another person. And the Congress of the United States, in 1974, enacted a statute providing the death penalty for aircraft piracy that results in death. These recently adopted statutes have attempted to address the concerns expressed by the Court in *Furman* primarily (i) by specifying the factors to be weighed and the procedures to be followed in deciding when to impose a capital sentence, or (ii) by making the death penalty mandatory for specified crimes. But all of the post-*Furman* statutes make clear that capital punishment itself has not been rejected by the elected representatives of the people.
. . .

The jury also is a significant and reliable objective index of contemporary values because it is so directly involved. . . . It may be true that evolving standards have influenced juries in recent decades to be more discriminating in imposing the sentence of death. But the relative infrequency of jury verdicts imposing the death sentence does not indicate rejection of capital punishment per se. Rather, the reluctance of juries in many cases to impose the sentence may well reflect the humane feeling that this most irrevocable of sanctions should be reserved for a small number of extreme cases. Indeed, the actions of juries in many States since *Furman* are fully compatible with the legislative judgments, reflected in the new statutes, as to the continued utility and necessity of capital punishment in appropriate cases. At the close of 1974 at least 254 persons had been sentenced to death since *Furman*, and by the end of March 1976, more than 460 persons were subject to death sentences.

As we have seen, however, the Eighth Amendment demands more than that a challenged punishment be acceptable to contemporary society. The Court also must ask whether it comports with the basic concept of human dignity at the core of the Amendment. Although we cannot "invalidate a category of penalties because we deem less severe penalties adequate to serve the ends of penology," *Furman v. Georgia*, supra, 408 U.S., at 451 (Powell, J., dissenting), the sanction imposed cannot be so totally without penological justification that it results in the gratuitous infliction of suffering.

The death penalty is said to serve two principal social purposes: retribution and deterrence of capital crimes by prospective offenders.

In part, capital punishment is an expression of society's moral outrage at particularly offensive conduct. This function may be unappealing to many, but it is essential in an ordered society that asks its citizens to rely on legal processes rather than self-help to vindicate their wrongs. . . . "Retribution is no longer the dominant objective of the criminal law," *Williams v. New York*, 337 U.S. 241, 248 (1949), but neither is it a forbidden objective nor one inconsistent with our respect for the dignity of men. *Furman v. Georgia*, supra, 408 U.S., at 394–395 (Burger, C. J., dissenting). Indeed, the decision that capital punishment may be the appropriate sanction in extreme cases is an expression of the community's belief that certain crimes are themselves so grievous an affront to humanity that the only adequate response may be the penalty of death.

Statistical attempts to evaluate the worth of the death penalty as a deterrent to crimes by potential offenders have occasioned a great deal of debate. The results simply have been inconclusive. . . .

Although some of the studies suggest that the death penalty may not function as a significantly greater deterrent than lesser penalties, there is no convincing empirical evidence either supporting or refuting this view. We may nevertheless assume safely that there are murderers, such as those who act in passion, for whom the threat of death has little or no deterrent effect. But for many others, the death penalty undoubtedly is a significant deterrent. There are carefully contemplated murders, such as murder for hire, where the possible penalty of death may well enter into the cold calculus that precedes the decision to act. And there are some categories of murder, such as murder by a life prisoner, where other sanctions may not be adequate.

. . .

In sum, we cannot say that the judgment of the Georgia legislature that capital punishment may be necessary in some cases is clearly wrong. Considerations of federalism, as well as respect for the ability of a legislature to evaluate, in terms of its particular state the moral consensus concerning the death penalty and its social utility as a sanction, require us to conclude, in the absence of more convincing evidence, that the infliction of death as a punishment for murder is not without justification and thus is not unconstitutionally severe.

Finally, we must consider whether the punishment of death is disproportionate in relation to the crime for which it is imposed. There is no question that death as a punishment is unique in its severity and irrevocability. When a defendant's life is at stake, the Court has been particularly sensitive to insure that every safeguard is observed. But we are concerned here only with the imposition of capital punishment for the crime of murder, and when a life has been taken deliberately by the offender, we cannot say that the punishment is invariably disproportionate to the crime. It is an extreme sanction, suitable to the most extreme of crimes.

We hold that the death penalty is not a form of punishment that may never be imposed, regardless of the circumstances of the offense, regardless of the character of the offender, and regardless of the procedure followed in reaching the decision to impose it.

We now consider whether Georgia may impose the death penalty on the petitioner in this case.

. . .

V

The basic concern of *Furman* centered on those defendants who were being condemned to death capriciously and arbitrarily. Under the procedures before the Court in that case, sentencing authorities were not directed to give attention to the nature or circumstances of the crime committed or to the character or record of the defendant. Left unguided, juries imposed the death sentence in a way that could only be called freakish. The new Georgia sentencing procedures, by contrast, focus the jury's attention on the particularized nature of the crime and the particularized characteristics of the individual defendant. While the jury is permitted to consider any aggravating or mitigating circumstances, it must find and identify at least one statutory aggravating factor before it may impose a penalty of death. In this way the jury's discretion is channeled. No longer can a jury wantonly and freakishly impose the death sentence; it is always circumscribed by the legislative guidelines. In addition, the review function of the Supreme Court of Georgia affords additional assurance that the concerns that prompted our decision in *Furman* are not present to any significant degree in the Georgia procedure applied here.

For the reasons expressed in this opinion, we hold that the statutory system under which Gregg was sentenced to death does not violate the Constitution. Accordingly, the judgment of the Georgia Supreme Court is affirmed.

It is so ordered.

The Invalidity of the Mandatory Death Penalty: Woodson v. North Carolina, 428 U.S. 280 (1976)

Mr. Justice STEWART, Mr. Justice POWELL, and Mr. Justice STEVENS announced the judgment of the Court and filed an opinion delivered by Mr. Justice STEWART.

The question in this case is whether the imposition of a death sentence for the crime of first-degree murder under the law of North Carolina violates the Eighth and Fourteenth Amendments.

I

The petitioners were convicted of first-degree murder as the result of their participation in an armed robbery of a convenience food store, in the course of which the cashier was killed and a customer was seriously wounded. There were four participants in the robbery: the petitioners Tyrone Woodson and Luby Waxton and two others, Leonard Tucker and Johnnie Lee Carroll. At the petitioners' trial Tucker and Carroll testified for the prosecution after having been permitted to plead guilty to lesser offenses; the petitioners testified in their own defense.

The evidence for the prosecution established that the four men had been discussing a possible robbery for some time. On the fatal day Woodson had been drinking heavily. About 9:30 p.m., Waxton and Tucker came to the trailer where Woodson was staying. When Woodson came out of the trailer, Waxton struck him in the face and threatened to kill him in an effort to make him sober up and come along on the robbery. The three proceeded to Waxton's trailer where they met Carroll. Waxton armed himself with a nickel-plated derringer, and Tucker handed Woodson a rifle. The four then set out by automobile to rob the store. Upon arriving at their destination Tucker and Waxton went into the store while Carroll and Woodson remained in the car as lookouts. Once inside the store, Tucker purchased a package of cigarettes from the woman cashier. Waxton then also asked for a package of cigarettes, but as the cashier approached him he pulled the derringer out of his hip pocket and fatally shot her at point-blank range. Waxton then took the money tray from the cash register and gave it to Tucker, who carried it out of the store, pushing past an entering customer as he reached the door. After he was outside, Tucker heard a second shot from inside the store, and shortly thereafter Waxton emerged, carrying a handful of paper money. Tucker and Waxton got in the car and the four drove away.

The petitioners' testimony agreed in large part with this version of the circumstances of the robbery. It differed diametrically in one important respect: Waxton claimed he never had a gun, and that Tucker had shot both the cashier and the customer.

During the trial Waxton asked to be allowed to plead guilty to the same lesser offenses to which Tucker had pleaded guilty, but the solicitor refused to accept the pleas. Woodson, by contrast, maintained throughout the trial that he had been coerced by Waxton, that he was therefore innocent, and that he would not consider pleading guilty to any offense.

The petitioners were found guilty on all charges, and, as was required by statute, sentenced to death. The Supreme Court of North Carolina affirmed. We granted certiorari to consider whether the imposition of the death penalties in this case comports with the Eighth and Fourteenth Amendments to the United States Constitution.

II

The petitioners argue that the imposition of the death penalty under any circumstances is cruel and unusual punishment in violation of the Eighth and Fourteenth Amendments. We reject this argument for the reasons stated today in *Gregg v. Georgia.*

III

At the time of this Court's decision in *Furman v. Georgia,* 408 U.S. 238 (1972), North Carolina law provided that in cases of first-degree murder, the jury in its unbridled discretion could choose whether the convicted defendant should be sentenced to death or to life imprisonment. After the *Furman* decision the Supreme Court of North Carolina in *State v. Waddell,* 282 N.C. 431 (1973), held unconstitutional the provision of the death penalty statute that gave the jury the option of returning a verdict of guilty without capital punishment, but held further that this provision was severable so that the statute survived as a mandatory death penalty law.

The North Carolina General Assembly in 1974 followed the court's lead and enacted a new statute that was essentially unchanged from the old one except that it made the death penalty mandatory. The statute now reads as follows:

> "*Murder in the first and second degree defined; punishment.*—A murder which shall be perpetrated by means of poison, lying in wait, imprisonment, starving, torture, or by any other kind of willful, deliberate and premeditated killing, or which shall be committed in the perpetration or attempt to perpetrate any arson, rape, robbery, kidnapping, burglary or other felony, shall be deemed to be murder in the first degree and shall be punished with death. All other kinds of murder shall be deemed murder in the second degree, and shall be punished by imprisonment for a term of not less

than two years nor more than life imprisonment in the State's prison." N.C.Gen.Stat. § 14–17 (Cum. Supp. 1975).

It was under this statute that the petitioners, who committed their crime on June 3, 1974, were tried, convicted, and sentenced to death.

North Carolina, unlike Florida, Georgia, and Texas, has thus responded to the *Furman* decision by making death the mandatory sentence for all persons convicted of first-degree murder. In ruling on the constitutionality of the sentences imposed on the petitioners under this North Carolina statute, the Court now addresses for the first time the question whether a death sentence returned pursuant to a law imposing a mandatory death penalty for a broad category of homicidal offenses constitutes cruel and unusual punishment within the meaning of the Eighth and Fourteenth Amendments. The issue, like that explored in *Furman*, involves the procedure employed by the State to select persons for the unique and irreversible penalty of death.

A

The Eighth Amendment stands to assure that the State's power to punish is "exercised within the limits of civilized standards." *Trop v. Dulles*, 356 U.S. 86, 100 (1958) (plurality opinion). Central to the application of the Amendment is a determination of contemporary standards regarding the infliction of punishment. As discussed in *Gregg v. Georgia*, indicia of societal values identified in prior opinions include history and traditional usage, legislative enactments, and jury determinations.

In order to provide a frame for assessing the relevancy of these factors in this case we begin by sketching the history of mandatory death penalty statutes in the United States. At the time the Eighth Amendment was adopted in 1791, the States uniformly followed the common-law practice of making death the exclusive and mandatory sentence for certain specified offenses. Although the range of capital offenses in the American colonies was quite limited in comparison to the more than 200 offenses then punishable by death in England, the colonies at the time of the Revolution imposed death sentences on all persons convicted of any of a considerable number of crimes, typically including at a minimum murder, treason, piracy, arson, rape, robbery, burglary, and sodomy. As at common law, all homicides that were not involuntary, provoked, justified, or excused constituted murder and were automatically punished by death. Almost from the outset jurors reacted unfavorably to the harshness of mandatory death sentences. The States initially responded to this expression of public dissatisfaction with mandatory statutes by limiting the classes of capital offenses.

This reform, however, left unresolved the problem posed by the not infrequent refusal of juries to convict murderers rather than subject them to automatic death sentences. In 1794, Pennsylvania attempted to alleviate the undue severity of the law by confining the mandatory death penalty to "murder of the first degree," encompassing all "willful, deliberate and premeditated" killings. Pa. Laws 1794, c. 1777. Other jurisdictions, including Virginia and Ohio, soon enacted similar measures, and within a generation the practice spread to most of the States.

Despite the broad acceptance of the division of murder into degrees, the reform proved to be an unsatisfactory means of identifying persons appropriately punishable by death. Although its failure was due in part to the amorphous nature of the controlling concepts of willfulness, deliberateness, and premeditation, a more fundamental weakness of the reform soon became apparent. Juries continued to find the death penalty inappropriate in a significant number of first-degree murder cases and refused to return guilty verdicts for that crime.

The inadequacy of distinguishing between murderers solely on the basis of legislative criteria narrowing the definition of the capital offense led the States to grant juries sentencing discretion in capital cases. Tennessee in 1838, followed by Alabama in 1841, and Louisiana in 1846, were the first States to abandon mandatory death sentences in favor of discretionary death penalty statutes. This flexibility remedied the harshness of mandatory statutes by permitting the jury to respond to mitigating factors by withholding the death penalty. By the turn of the century, 23 States and the Federal Government had made death sentences discretionary for first-degree murder and other capital offenses. During the next two decades 14 additional States replaced their mandatory death penalty statutes. Thus, by the end of World War I, all but eight States, Hawaii, and the District of Columbia either had adopted discretionary death penalty schemes or abolished the death penalty altogether. By 1963, all of these remaining jurisdictions had replaced their automatic death penalty statutes with discretionary jury sentencing.

The history of mandatory death penalty statutes in the United States thus reveals that the practice of sentencing to death all persons convicted of a particular offense has been rejected as unduly harsh and unworkably rigid. The two crucial indicators of evolving standards of decency respecting the imposition of punishment in our society—jury determinations and legislative enactments—both point conclusively to the repudiation of automatic death sentences. At least since the Revolution, American jurors have, with some regularity, disregarded their oaths and refused to convict defendants where a death sentence was the automatic consequence of a guilty verdict. As we have seen, the initial movement to reduce the number of capital offenses and to separate murder into degrees was prompted in part by the reaction of jurors as well as by reformers who objected to the imposition of death as the penalty for any crime. Nineteenth century journalists, statesmen, and jurists repeatedly observed that jurors were often deterred from convicting palpably guilty men of first-degree murder under mandatory statutes. Thereafter, continuing evidence of jury reluctance to convict persons of capital offenses in mandatory death penalty jurisdictions resulted in legislative authorization of discretionary jury sentencing—by Congress for federal crimes in 1897, by North Carolina in 1949, and by Congress for the District of Columbia in 1962.

As we have noted today in *Gregg v. Georgia*, legislative measures adopted by the people's chosen representatives weigh heavily in ascertaining contemporary standards of decency. The consistent course charted by the state legislatures and by Congress since the middle of the past century demonstrates that the aversion of jurors to mandatory death penalty statutes is shared by society at large.

. . .

Although it seems beyond dispute that, at the time of the *Furman* decision in 1972, mandatory death penalty statutes had been renounced by American juries and legislatures, there remains the question whether the mandatory statutes adopted by North Carolina and a number of other States following *Furman* evince a sudden reversal of societal values regarding the imposition of capital punishment. In view of the persistent and unswerving legislative rejection of mandatory death penalty statutes beginning in 1838 and continuing for more than 130 years until *Furman,* it seems evident that the post-*Furman* enactments reflect attempts by the States to retain the death penalty in a form consistent with the Constitution, rather than a renewed societal acceptance of mandatory death sentencing. The fact that some States have adopted mandatory measures following *Furman* while others have legislated standards to guide jury discretion appears attributable to diverse readings of this Court's multi-opinioned decision in that case.

. . .

It is now well established that the Eighth Amendment draws much of its meaning from "the evolving standards of decency that mark the progress of a maturing society." *Trop v. Dulles,* 356 U.S., at 101 (plurality opinion). As the above discussion makes clear, one of the most significant developments in our society's treatment of capital punishment has been the rejection of the common-law practice of inexorably imposing a death sentence upon every person convicted of a specified offense. North Carolina's mandatory death penalty statute for first-degree murder departs markedly from contemporary standards respecting the imposition of the punishment of death and thus cannot be applied consistently with the Eighth and Fourteenth Amendments' requirement that the State's power to punish "be exercised within the limits of civilized standards." Id., at 100.

B

A separate deficiency of North Carolina's mandatory death sentence statute is its failure to provide a constitutionally tolerable response to *Furman's* rejection of unbridled jury discretion in the imposition of capital sentences. Central to the limited holding in *Furman* was the conviction that the vesting of standardless sentencing power in the jury violated the Eighth and Fourteenth Amendments. It is argued that North Carolina has remedied the inadequacies of the death penalty statutes held unconstitutional in *Furman* by withdrawing all sentencing discretion from juries in capital cases. But when one considers the long and consistent American experience with the death penalty in first-degree murder cases, it becomes evident that mandatory statutes enacted in response to *Furman* have simply papered over the problem of unguided and unchecked jury discretion.

As we have noted in Part III-A, supra, there is general agreement that American juries have persistently refused to convict a significant portion of persons charged with first-degree murder of that offense under mandatory death penalty statutes. The North Carolina study commission reported that juries in that state "quite frequently" were deterred from rendering guilty verdicts of first-degree murder because of the enormity of the sentence automatically imposed. Moreover, as a matter of historic fact, juries operating under discretionary sentencing statutes have consistently returned death sentences in only a minority of first-degree murder cases. In view of the historic record, it is only reasonable to assume that many juries under mandatory statutes will continue to consider the grave consequences of a conviction in reaching a verdict. North Carolina's mandatory death penalty statute provides no standards to guide the jury in its inevitable exercise of the power to determine which first-degree murderers shall live and which shall die. And there is no way under the North Carolina law for the judiciary to check arbitrary and capricious exercise of that power through a review of death sentences. Instead of rationalizing the sentencing process, a mandatory scheme may well exacerbate the problem identified in *Furman* by resting the penalty determination on the particular jury's willingness to act lawlessly. While a mandatory death penalty statute may reasonably be expected to increase the number of persons sentenced to death, it does not fulfill *Furman's* basic requirement by replacing arbitrary and wanton jury discretion with objective standards to guide, regularize, and make rationally reviewable the process for imposing a sentence of death.

C

A third constitutional shortcoming of the North Carolina statute is its failure to allow the particularized consideration of relevant aspects of the character and record of each convicted defendant before the imposition upon him of a sentence of death. In *Furman*, members of the Court acknowledge what cannot fairly be denied—that death is a punishment different from all other sanctions in kind rather than degree. A process that accords no significance to relevant facets of the character and record of the individual offender or the circumstances of the particular offense excludes from consideration in fixing the ultimate punishment of death the possibility of compassionate or mitigating factors stemming from the diverse frailties of humankind. It treats all persons convicted of a designated offense not as uniquely individual human beings, but as members of a faceless, undifferentiated mass to be subjected to the blind infliction of the penalty of death.

This Court has previously recognized that "for the determination of sentences, justice generally requires consideration of more than the particular acts by which the crime was committed and that there be taken into account the circumstances of the offense together with the character and propensities of the offender." *Pennsylvania v. Ashe*, 302 U.S. 51 (1937). Consideration of both the offender and the offense in order to arrive at a just and appropriate sentence has been viewed as a progressive and humanizing development. See *Williams v. New York*, 337 U.S. 241, 247–249 (1949). While the prevailing practice of individualizing sentencing determinations generally reflects simply enlightened policy rather than a constitutional imperative, we believe that in capital cases the fundamental respect for humanity underlying the Eighth Amendment requires consideration of the character and record of the individual offender and the circumstances of the particular offense as a constitutionally indispensable part of the process of inflicting the penalty of death.

This conclusion rests squarely on the predicate that the penalty of death is qualitatively different from a sentence of imprisonment, however long. Death, in its finality, differs more from life imprisonment than a 100-year prison term differs from one of only a year or two. Because of that qualitative difference, there is a corresponding difference in the need for reliability in the determination that death is the appropriate punishment in a specific case.

For the reasons stated, we conclude that the death sentences imposed upon the petitioners under North Carolina's mandatory death sentence statute violated the Eighth and Fourteenth Amendments and therefore must be set aside. The judgment of the Supreme Court of North Carolina is reversed insofar as it upheld the death sentences imposed upon the petitioners, and the case is remanded for further proceedings not inconsistent with this opinion.

It is so ordered.

Limiting Federal Habeas Corpus:
Stone v. Powell, 482 U.S. 465 (1976)

Mr. Justice POWELL delivered the opinion of the Court.

Respondents in these cases were convicted of criminal offenses in state courts, and their convictions were affirmed on appeal. The prosecution in each case relied upon evidence obtained by searches and seizures alleged by respondents to have been unlawful. Each respondent subsequently sought relief in a federal district court by filing a petition for a writ of federal habeas corpus under 28 U.S.C. § 2254. The question presented is whether a federal court should consider, in ruling on a petition for habeas corpus relief filed by a state prisoner, a claim that evidence obtained by an unconstitutional search or seizure was introduced at his trial, when he has previously been afforded an opportunity for full and fair litigation of his claim in the state courts. The issue is of considerable importance to the administration of criminal justice.

I

We summarize first the relevant facts and procedural history of these cases.

Respondent Lloyd Powell was convicted of murder in June 1968 after trial in a California state court. At about midnight on February 17, 1968, he and three companions entered the Bonanza Liquor Store in San Bernardino, Cal., where Powell became involved in an altercation with Gerald Parsons, the store manager, over the theft of a bottle of wine. In the scuffling that followed Powell shot and killed Parsons' wife. Ten hours later an officer of the Henderson, Nev., Police Department arrested Powell for violation of the Henderson vagrancy ordinance, and in the search incident to the arrest discovered a .38 caliber revolver with six expended cartridges in the cylinder.

Powell was extradited to California and convicted of second-degree murder in the Superior Court of San Bernardino County. Parsons and Powell's accomplices at the liquor store testified against him. A criminologist testified that the revolver found on Powell was the gun that killed Persons' wife. The trial court rejected Powell's contention that testimony by the Henderson police officer as to the search and the discovery of the revolver should have been excluded because the vagrancy ordinance was unconstitutional. In October 1969, the conviction was affirmed by a California District Court of Appeal. Although the issued was duly presented, that court found it unnecessary to pass upon the legality of the arrest and search because it concluded that the error, if any, in admitting the testimony of the Henderson officer was harmless beyond a reasonable doubt under *Chapman v. California*, 386 U.S. 18 (1967). The Supreme Court of California denied Powell's petition for habeas corpus relief.

In August 1971 Powell filed an amended petition for a writ of federal habeas corpus under 28 U.S.C. § 2254 in the United States District Court for the Northern District of California, contending that the testimony concerning the .38 caliber revolver should have been excluded as the fruit of an illegal search. He argued that his arrest had been unlawful because the Henderson vagrancy ordinance was unconstitutionally vague, and that the arresting officer lacked probable cause to believe that he was violating it. The District Court concluded that the arresting officer had probable cause and held that even if the vagrancy ordinance was unconstitutional, the deterrent purpose of the exclusionary rule does not require that it be applied to bar admission of the fruits of a search incident to an otherwise valid arrest. In the alternative, that court agreed with the California District Court of Appeal that the admission of the evidence concerning Powell's arrest, if error, was harmless beyond a reasonable doubt.

In December 1974, the Court of Appeals for the Ninth Circuit reversed. 507 F.2d 93. The Court concluded that the vagrancy ordinance was unconstitutionally vague, that Powell's arrest was therefore illegal, and that although exclusion of the evidence would serve no deterrent purpose with regard to police officers who were enforcing statutes in good faith, exclusion would serve the public interest by deterring legislators from enacting unconstitutional statutes. Id., at 98. After an independent review of the evidence the court concluded that the admission of the evidence was not harmless error since it supported the testimony of Parsons and Powell's accomplices. Id., at 99. . . . We granted their petitions for certiorari. We now reverse.

II

The authority of federal courts to issue the writ of *habeas corpus ad subjiciendum* was included in the first grant of federal court jurisdiction, made by the Judiciary Act of 1789, c. 20 § 14, 1 Stat. 81, with the limitation that the writ extend only to prisoners held in custody by the United States. The original statutory authorization did not define the substantive reach of the writ. It merely stated that the courts of the United States "shall have power to issue writs of . . . habeas corpus. . . ." Ibid. The courts defined the scope of the writ in accordance with the common law and limited it to an inquiry as to the jurisdiction of the sentencing tribunal. See, e.g., *Ex parte Watkins*, 28 U.S. (3 Pet.) 193, (1830) (Marshall, C. J.).

In 1867 the writ was extended to state prisoners. Act of Feb. 5, 1867, c. 28, § 1, 14 Stat. 385. Under the 1867 Act federal courts were authorized to give relief in "all cases where any person may be restrained of his or her liberty in violation of the constitution, or of any treaty or law of the United States. . . ." But the limitation of federal habeas corpus jurisdiction to consideration of the jurisdiction of the sentencing court persisted. See, e.g., *In re Wood*, 140 U.S. 278 (1891). And, although the concept of "jurisdiction" was subjected to considerable strain as the substantive scope of the writ was expanded, this expansion was limited to only a few classes of cases. . . .

In the landmark decisions in *Brown v. Allen*, 344 U.S. 443 (1953), and *Daniels v. Allen*, 344 U.S. 443, the scope of the writ was expanded. . . . In these cases state prisoners applied for federal habeas corpus relief claiming that the trial courts had erred in failing to quash their indictments due to alleged discrimination in the selection of grand jurors and in ruling certain confessions admissible. In *Brown*, the highest court of the State had rejected these claims on direct appeal, *State v. Brown*, 233 N.C. 202, and this Court had denied certiorari, 341 U.S. 943 (1951). Despite the apparent adequacy of the state corrective process, the Court reviewed the denial of the writ of habeas corpus and held that Brown was entitled to a full reconsideration of these constitutional claims, including, if appropriate, a hearing in the Federal District Court. In *Daniels*, however, the state supreme court on direct review had refused to consider the appeal because the papers were filed out of time. This Court held that since the state court judgment rested on a reasonable application of the State's legitimate procedural rules, a ground that would have barred direct review of his federal claims by this Court, the District Court lacked authority to grant habeas corpus relief. See 344 U.S., at 458, 486.

This final barrier to broad collateral re-examination of state criminal convictions in federal habeas corpus proceedings was removed in *Fay v. Noia*, 372 U.S. 391 (1963). Noia and two codefendants had been convicted of felony murder. The sole evidence against each defendant was a signed confession. Noia's codefendants, but not Noia himself, appealed their convictions. Although their appeals were unsuccessful, in subsequent state proceedings they were able to establish that their confessions had been coerced and their convictions therefore procured in violation of the Constitution. In a subsequent federal habeas corpus proceeding, it was stipulated that Noia's confession also had been coerced, but the District Court followed *Daniels* in holding that Noia's failure to appeal barred habeas corpus review. See 183 F. Supp. 222, 225 (1960). The Court of Appeals reversed, ordering that Noia's conviction be set aside and that he be released from custody or a new trial be granted. This Court affirmed the grant of the writ, narrowly restricting the circumstances in which a federal court may refuse to consider the merits of federal constitutional claims.

During the period in which the substantive scope of the writ was expanded, the Court did not consider whether exceptions to full review might exist with respect to particular categories of constitutional claims. Prior to the Court's decision in *Kaufman v. United States*, 394 U.S. 217 (1969), however, a substantial majority of the federal courts of appeals had concluded that collateral review of search-and-seizure claims was inappropriate on motions filed by federal prisoners under 28 U.S.C. § 2255, the modern post-conviction procedure available to federal prisoners in lieu of habeas corpus. The primary rationale advanced in support of those decisions was that Fourth Amendment violations are different in kind from denials of Fifth or Sixth Amendment rights in that claims of illegal search and seizure do not "impugn the integrity of the factfinding process or challenge evidence as inherently unreliable; rather, the exclusion of illegally seized evidence is simply a prophylactic device intended generally to deter Fourth Amendment violations by law enforcement officers." Id., at 224.

Kaufman rejected this rationale and held that search-and-seizure claims are cognizable in § 2255 proceedings. The Court noted that "the federal habeas remedy extends to state prisoners alleging that unconstitutionally obtained evidence was admitted against them at trial," 394 U.S., at 225, citing, e.g., *Mancusi v. DeForte*, 392 U.S. 364 (1968), and concluded, as a matter of statutory construction, that there was no basis for restricting "access by federal prisoners with illegal search-and-seizure claims to federal collateral remedies, while placing no similar restriction on access by state prisoners," 394 U.S., at 226. . . .

The discussion in *Kaufman* of the scope of federal habeas corpus vests on the view that the effectuation of the Fourth Amendment, as applied to the States through the Fourteenth Amendment, requires the granting of habeas corpus relief when a prisoner has been convicted in state court on the basis of evidence obtained in an illegal search or seizure since those Amendments were held in *Mapp v. Ohio*, 367 U.S. 643 (1961), to require exclusion of such evidence at trial and reversal of conviction upon direct review. Until this case we have not had occasion fully to consider the validity of this view. Upon examination, we conclude, in light of the nature and purpose of the Fourth Amendment exclusionary rule, that this view is unjustified. We hold, therefore, that where the State has provided an opportunity for full and fair litigation of a Fourth Amendment claim, the Constitution does not require that a state prisoner be granted federal habeas corpus relief on the ground that evidence obtained in an unconstitutional search or seizure was introduced at his trial.

III

The Fourth Amendment assures the "right of the people to be secure in their persons, houses, papers, and effects, against unreasonable searches and seizures." The Amendment was primarily a reaction to the evils associated with the use of the general warrant in England and the writs of assistance in the Colonies, and was intended to protect the "sanctity of a man's home and the privacies of life," *Boyd v. United States*, 116 U.S. 616, 630 (1886), from searches under unchecked general authority.

The exclusionary rule was a judicially created means of effectuating the rights secured by the Fourth Amendment. Prior to the Court's decisions in *Weeks v. United States*, 232 U.S. 383 (1914), and *Gouled v. United States*, 255 U.S. 298 (1921), there existed no barrier to the introduction in criminal trials of evidence obtained in violation of the Amendment. In *Weeks* the Court held that the defendant could petition before trial for the return of property secured through an illegal search or seizure conducted by federal authorities. In *Gouled* the Court held broadly that such evidence could not be introduced in a federal prosecution. Thirty-five years after *Weeks* the Court held in *Wolf v. Colorado*, 338 U.S. 25 (1949), that the right to be free from arbitrary intrusion by the police that is protected by the Fourth Amendment is "implicit in 'the concept of ordered liberty' and as such enforceable against the States through the [Fourteenth Amendment] Due Process Clause." Id., at 27–28. The Court concluded, however, that the *Weeks* exclusionary rule would not be imposed upon the States as "an essential ingredient of that right." Id., at 29. The full force of *Wolf* was eroded in subsequent decisions, and a little more than a decade later the exclusionary rule was held applicable to the States in *Mapp v. Ohio*, 367 U.S. 643 (1961).

. . . The *Mapp* majority justified the application of the rule to the States on several grounds, but relied principally upon the belief that exclusion would deter future unlawful police conduct. 367 U.S., at 658.

Although our decisions often have alluded to the "imperative of judicial integrity," e.g., *United States v. Peltier*, 422 U.S. 531, 536–539 (1975), they demonstrate the limited role of this justification in the determination whether to apply the rule in a particular context. Logically extended this justification would require that courts exclude unconstitutionally seized evidence despite lack of objection by the defendant, or even over his assent. It also would require abandonment of the standing limitations on who may object to the introduction of unconstitutionally seized evidence and retreat from the proposition that judicial proceedings need not abate when the defendant's person is unconstitutionally seized. Similarly, the interest in promoting judicial integrity does not prevent the use of illegally seized evidence in grand jury proceedings. Nor does it require that the trial court exclude such evidence from use for impeachment of a defendant, even though its introduction is certain to result in convictions in some cases. The teaching of these cases is clear. While courts, of course, must ever be concerned with preserving the integrity of the judicial process, this concern has limited force as a justification for the exclusion of highly probative evidence. The force of this justification becomes minimal where federal habeas corpus relief is sought by a prisoner who previously has been afforded the opportunity for full and fair consideration of his search-and-seizure claim at trial and on direct review.

The primary justification for the exclusionary rule then is the deterrence of police conduct that violates Fourth Amendment rights. Post-*Mapp* decisions have established that the rule is not a personal constitutional right. It is not calculated to redress the injury to the privacy of the victim of the search or seizure, for any "reparation comes too late." *Linkletter v. Walker,* 381 U.S. 618, 637 (1965). Instead,

> "the rule is a judicially created remedy designed to safeguard Fourth Amendment rights generally through its deterrent effect. . . ." *United States v. Calandra,* 414 U.S. at 348.

Mapp involved the enforcement of the exclusionary rule at state trials and on direct review. The decision in *Kaufman,* as noted above, is premised on the view that implementation of the Fourth Amendment also requires the consideration of search-and-seizure claims upon collateral review of state convictions. But despite the broad deterrent purpose of the exclusionary rule, it has never been interpreted to proscribe the introduction of illegally seized evidence in all proceedings or against all persons. As in the case of any remedial device, "the application of the rule has been restricted to those areas where its remedial objectives are thought most efficaciously served." *United States v. Calandra,* 414 U.S. at 348. Thus, our refusal to extend the exclusionary rule to grant jury proceedings was based on a balancing of the potential injury to the historic role and function of the grand jury by such extension against the potential contribution to the effectuation of the Fourth Amendment through deterrence of police misconduct. . . .

IV

We turn now to the specific question presented by these cases. Respondents allege violations of Fourth Amendment rights guaranteed them through the Fourteenth Amendment. The question is whether state prisoners—who have been afforded the opportunity for full and fair consideration of their reliance upon the exclusionary rule with respect to seized evidence by the state courts at trial and on direct review—may invoke their claim again on federal habeas corpus review. The answer is to be found by weighing the utility of the exclusionary rule against the costs of extending it to collateral review of Fourth Amendment claims.

The costs of applying the exclusionary rule even at trial and on direct review are well known: the focus of the trial, and the attention of the participants therein, is diverted from the ultimate question of guilt or innocence that should be the central concern in a criminal proceeding. Moreover, the physical evidence sought to be excluded is typically reliable and often the most probative information bearing on the guilt or innocence of the defendant. . . . Application of the rule thus deflects the truthfinding process and often frees the guilty. The disparity in particular cases between the error committed by the police officer and the windfall afforded a guilty defendant by application of the rule is contrary to the idea of proportionality that is essential to the concept of justice. Thus, although the rule is thought to deter unlawful police activity in part through the nurturing of respect for Fourth Amendment values, if applied indiscriminately it may well have the opposite effect of generating disrespect for the law and administration of justice. These long-recognized costs of the rule persist when a criminal conviction is sought to be overturned on collateral review on the ground that a search-and-seizure claim was erroneously rejected by two or more tiers of state courts.

Evidence obtained by police officers in violation of the Fourth Amendment is excluded at trial in the hope that the frequency of future violations will decrease. Despite the absence of supportive empirical evidence, we have assumed that the immediate effect of exclusion will be to discourage law enforcement officials from violating the Fourth Amendment by removing the incentive to disregard it. More importantly, over the long term, this demonstration that our society attaches serious consequences to violation of constitutional rights is thought to encourage those who formulate law enforcement policies, and the officers who implement them, to incorporate Fourth Amendment ideals into their value system.

We adhere to the view that these considerations support the implementation of the exclusionary rule at trial and its enforcement on direct appeal of state court convictions. But the additional contribution, if any, of the consideration of search-and-seizure claims of state prisoners on collateral review is small in relation to the costs. To be sure, each case in which such claim is considered may add marginally to an awareness of the values protected by the Fourth Amendment. There is no reason to believe, however, that the overall educative effect of the exclusionary rule would be appreciably diminished if search-and-seizure claims could not be raised in federal habeas corpus review of state convictions. Nor is there reason to assume that any specific disincentive already created by the risk of exclusion of evidence at trial or the reversal of convictions on direct review would be enhanced if there were the further risk that a conviction obtained in state court and affirmed on direct review might be overturned in collateral proceedings often occurring years after the incarceration of the defendant. The view that the deterrence of Fourth Amendment violations would be furthered rests on the dubious assumption that law enforcement authorities would fear that federal habeas review might reveal flaws in a search or seizure that went undetected at trial and on appeal. Even if one rationally could assume that some additional incremental deterrent effect would be presented in isolated cases, the resulting advance of the legitimate goal of furthering Fourth Amendment rights would be outweighed by the acknowledged costs to other values vital to a rational system of criminal justice.

In sum, we conclude that where the State has provided an opportunity for full and fair litigation of a Fourth Amendment claim, a state prisoner may not be granted federal habeas corpus relief on the ground that evidence obtained in an unconstitutional search or seizure was introduced at his trial. In this context the contribution of the exclusionary rule, if any, to the effectuation of the Fourth Amendment is minimal, and the substantial societal costs of application of the rule persist with special force.

Accordingly, the judgments of the Courts of Appeals are

Reversed.

13

The Legal Rights of Prisoners

REX V. ACTON

CLERK. William Acton, hold up your hand. (Which he did.) You stand indicted by the name of William Acton, of the parish of St. George the Martyr, &c. for the murder of Thomas Bliss, &c. How say you, William Acton, are you guilty of the murder whereof you stand indicted, or not guilty?

ACTON. Not Guilty.

CLERK. How wilt thou be tried?

ACTON. By God and my country.

CLERK. God send you a good deliverance.

Crier, make proclamation to keep silence upon pain of imprisonment. This is a trial for life and death, and I shall commit any one that don't hold their peace.

MR. HARDING. William Acton stands indicted for the murder of Thomas Bliss.

The indictment sets forth, That John Darby was keeper of the King's Palace-court at Westminster, and had the custody of the prisoners there.

That William Acton, during the time he was servant of the said John Darby, was employed in about the care and custody of the prisoners there.

That the said William Acton, being a person of an inhuman and cruel disposition, did on the 21st of October, in the 13th year of the late king, cruelly, barbarously, and feloniously beat, assault, and wound the said Thomas Bliss, then being a prisoner under the custody of the said Darby; and of malice aforethought did carry the said Bliss into the strong room, and put on irons and fetters of great weight upon his legs; and the said Bliss was exposed to the damp, and wet, and cold of the said room; which is a dangerous, damp, noisome, filthy, and an unwholesome place.

The indictment further sets forth, that he put on an iron instrument, and engine of torture, upon the head of the said Thomas Bliss, called the scull-cap; and also thumbscrews upon this thumbs; and that he remained there three hours under all this torture and torment.

That during the detention of the said Thomas Bliss in the said room, by duress of the imprisonment, contracted such an indisposition, and ill habit of body, that he languished; and, by reason of this duress, died.

Mrs. Anne Bliss sworn.

Mr. Marsh.   Did you know Thomas Bliss?

Mrs. Bliss.   Yes.

Mr. Marsh.   Who was he?

Mrs. Bliss.   My husband.

Mr. Marsh.   Do you remember the time when he was put into the strong room?

Mrs. Bliss.   He was a prisoner in the Marshalsea for a small debt.

Mr. Marsh.   I confine my question only to your husband. What room was he in?

Mrs. Bliss.   The strong room.

Mr. Foster.   Were the irons heavy he had on?

Mrs. Bliss.   Yes, they were.

Mr. Ward.   Do you know this of your own knowledge?

Mrs. Bliss.   When I came the next day to the prison, Nichols said, there is the bitch, his wife, and Acton ordered me to be called into the lodge; and said, Damn you, madam, I will have you before justice Ladd, for bringing the rope to your husband: Damn you, I will confine you; and he put me into the place where they put the irons in, adjoining to the lodge, and kept me there an hour. Whilst I was there, he sent for my husband into the lodge, and put on the scull-cap, collar, thumbscrews, and fetters.

MR. RICHARDSON. When he was in this place, (the Strong Room) did you see any blood about him?

MRS. BLISS. He bled at the mouth, and he told me, that it was caused by having the iron instrument on his head: and the blood flowed from under the nails of his thumbs.

MR. RICHARDSON. Did you see your husband beat?

MRS. BLISS. He was black as any thing with the marks of the bull's pizzle Acton kept.

Susanna Dodd sworn.

MR. WARD. What condition did you see him in?

MRS. DODD. I went to the strong room to carry him some victuals, and he had thumbscrews on his thumbs, irons on his legs, an iron cap on his head.

MR. WARD. Had he fetters on his legs?

MRS. DODD. He had very large fetters on his legs, and iron cross his legs too. I spoke to him through the hole.

The said Irons being produced and viewed by the Witness.

MR. WARD. Are those the same you saw upon Bliss?

MRS. DODD. They are.

The Irons called Sheers being shewn her particularly.

MR. WARD. Look on them, had he any other irons on his legs than those?

MRS. DODD. He had the sheers cross his legs, and fetters on besides. The deceased asked me to give him relief, and desired me to chew his victuals, for his mouth was sore; and I pulled it to pieces, and fed him.

MR. WARD. Did you see him bleed at the mouth, or any where else?

MRS. DODD. There is a great hole on the side of the door, and I saw him screwed, and saw him bleeding at his thumb nails.

Being again shewn the Iron instrument called the Sheers.

MR. WARD. How was it used?

MRS. DODD. It goes between the legs.

Then one was sworn to keep the Jury, and they withdrew, and Baron Carter went to dinner; and when he returned, they gave their Verdict.

CL. OF ARRAIGNS. Gentlemen, are you all agreed in your Verdict?

OMNES. Yes.

CL. OF ARR. Who shall say for you?

OMNES. Foreman.

CL. OF ARR.   William Acton, hold up thy hand. (Which he did.) Look upon the prisoner; how say you; Is he Guilty of the felony and murder whereof he stands indicted, or Not Guilty?

FOREMAN.   Not Guilty.[1]

The trial in 1729 of William Acton for the murder of Thomas Bliss has long since passed into obscurity, yet it offers some insight into the historic problem of the rights of prisoners. Acton's trial and the contemporaneous trial of several other London prison officials was the result of a parliamentary investigation into the conditions of debtor prisons.[2] Although the parliamentary committee found ample evidence of abusive and illegal practices committed against prisoners by the prison wardens and their subordinates, nonetheless no convictions were obtained, and little in the way of lasting reform was accomplished. Major reforms in the treatment of prisoners were at least one hundred years away. In one sense, Acton's trial is nothing more than a sad reminder that prisoners are abandoned to their keepers and to a fate that generally remains a well-guarded secret. On the other hand, the fact that prison officials were prosecuted in 1729 is indicative of a basic proposition that too often has escaped notice: Prisoners are not chattels to be treated by their keepers without regard to their rights. In the Fleet and Marshalsea prison scandals, the issue was the inhumane, even barbarous, treatment of prisoners. Today, the issues are wide-ranging. Certainly, the treatment of prisoners remains a concern, but treatment is only one of a host of issues that has come into the forefront in recent litigation. Indeed, in the last fifteen years, a substantial body of case law has emerged in the area of prisoners' rights.

Before we turn our attention to the case law in this area, we should explore briefly a few fundamental propositions about prisoners and prisons. A basic fact of prison life, especially life in a maximum-security prison, is that the keepers exercise enormous discretion over the lives of prisoners. The daily regulating and ordering of the lives of inmates has often been justified as a necessary means not only of maintaining security, but also of correcting behavior.

Although it may be true that our prisons hold many offenders who should have received other forms of treatment, the fact remains that some prisoners have been appropriately directed. They are in prison because they pose a threat to the lives and property of others. Ideally, these inmates are rehabilitated, but the fallen goals of rehabilitation serve to remind us that prison life is not intended to be pleasant or enjoyable. We are not concerned here with whether the American prison system is a costly and inhumane failure, or with whether prisons, substituting one brutal environment for another, in fact breed crime. Clearly, prisons may be a failure, at least insofar as the goals of deterrence and rehabilitation are concerned, yet they are reasonably effective warehouses for those who menace society. (Of course, we must recognize that the idea of prisons as warehouses is potentially insidious, at least to the extent that it sets the stage for an animal-and-keeper atmosphere.) Today, few defend the prison system; nonetheless, we have not yet reached that utopian state where prisons—*any prisons*—are wholly without merit. Prisons for punishment, for retribution, and for rehabilitation may be socially impossible or morally wrong, but prisons for incapacitating those who threaten our lives, our safety, and our property remain a necessary adjunct of our society.

If prisons must exist, then it seems to follow that prisoners must forfeit a measure of freedom. Although they do not forfeit their humanity, or even all of their legal rights, they necessarily surrender to their correctional officers many of the ordinary liberties associated with life in the world outside prison walls. Inmates are subject to the authority of prison officials, who decide for the prison population a wide range of matters—everything from food, shelter, clothing, work, and recreation to access to other prisoners and the outside world. Beyond this, prison officials are generally conceded to have the power to impose appropriate disciplinary sanctions for those who violate prison rules.

THE COLLATERAL CONSEQUENCES OF CONVICTION

Quite apart from the loss of liberty that attends imprisonment, there are, depending on the state jurisdiction involved, a number of collateral consequences of criminal conviction. Some states consider that convicted offenders are dead to the civil law, and impose harsh disabilities and disqualifications on those convicted of felony offenses. (In fact, this was the historical practice.)[3] In those states, the collateral consequences of conviction can be permanent or can obtain only during the period of confinement and parole.[4] In a few states, convicted felons lose their "civil rights"—a blanket designation that can include the rights to vote, to hold public office, to sue, to serve on a jury, to testify, and to transfer or inherit property.[5] Generally, however, the loss of a right results from a particular statutory enactment. The most common statutory disability is the temporary or permanent loss of the rights to vote and to hold public office. As recently as 1974, the Supreme Court ruled that states are not precluded under the equal-protection clause from disenfranchising felons.[6] The majority noted that section 2 of the Fourteenth Amendment specifically exempts states from any loss of representatives due to their failure to enfranchise those who "participated in rebellion, or *other crime.*" (The italics are mine.) It is difficult to understand why released felons, other than those convicted of violations of election laws, should suffer this permanent disability. The loss of the right to vote or to serve on a jury is clearly not consistent with the goals of rehabilitation. An even greater inconsistency arises from legislative disabilities that bar felons from engaging in the practice of an occupation or profession that is regulated by the state, for example, obtaining a barber's license. It may be that certain kinds of violations would justify the denial of the right to practice a given profession or occupation; however, blanket disqualification can be justified only on the thinnest rationale of administrative convenience.

THE LEGAL RIGHTS OF THE INCARCERATED

Even in the eras of great public indifference to the rights of prisoners, few would have maintained that prisons operate outside of the Constitution. Yet the Constitution itself gives a colorable argument to the proposition that prisoners are souls dead to its protections. The Thirteenth Amendment prohibits slavery or involuntary servitude, "except as punishment for a crime." Although the exception would appear to be a historical curiosity, it is indicative of the public attitude about prisoners that obtained in the United States until recently. When the prison doors slammed shut on an offender, he or she was presumed to have lost any claim to the protections of the Constitution. Indeed, for the greater part of our history, the judiciary followed a hands-off policy in the area of corrections. Even the fabled Warren Court was largely indifferent to the constitutional rights of prisoners.

This judicial neglect was probably a conscious deference to the administrative expertise of correctional officers, as well as a recognition of the need for wide discretion in the administration of penal institutions. The hands-off policy also may have been a by-product of a political system that tends to oil the squeaky wheel. As a class, prisoners have little political clout, and even less in the way of other characteristics that might commend them to the care of the bar and bench.

Yet today the picture has altered substantially. Beginning in the 1960s, the lower federal courts have become increasingly receptive to the claims of both state and federal prisoners.[7] Finally, in the early 1970s, the Burger Court began a brief foray into the area.[8]

Access to the Courts

Without reasonable access to the courts, it would be difficult if not impossible for a prisoner either to challenge a conviction or to seek relief in the conditions of his or her confinement. Beginning as early as 1941, the Supreme Court ruled that correctional officials may not set unreasonable restraints on prisoners' access to the courts,[9] nor presumably may they penalize prisoners for seeking any form of judicial relief.[10] On the other hand, it is still uncertain whether prisoners have the legal right to file civil suits that are unrelated to conviction, the conditions of confinement, or their status as prisoners.

Legal Services

If a state provides for a right of first appeal to attack a conviction, it is well established that the state must afford the indigent the assistance of counsel for this appeal.[11] The indigent must also be afforded free transcripts to prepare for an appeal.[12] However, in *Ross v. Moffitt* (1974), noting that a state need not provide for any appeal of a conviction, the Court ruled that the requirement of counsel for the indigent on appeal is limited to the first appeal as of right, and does not extend to discretionary appeals beyond the first appellate review.[13]

Apart from the issue of counsel for postconviction relief, there remains the issue of counsel for the indigent who want to challenge the conditions of their confinement, any change in their classification, or their status within the correctional system. Certainly, prisoners' challenges to prison conditions have helped to focus judicial as well as public attention on the sometimes deplorable conditions of American prisons, and, certainly, many of the successful challenges have required the assistance of counsel. However, given the size of the prison population and the strong probability that a large percentage of that population is dissatisfied with prison life, we would hesitate to accept that there is a general right for prisoners to have the assistance of counsel.[14] Indeed, the Supreme Court has indicated that there must be a degree of flexibility in this area. In *Gagnon v. Scarpelli* (1973), a case involving a revocation of probation, the Court noted that in like cases the presence and participation of counsel would be unnecessary and perhaps unwise, and therefore in questions of revoking probation no right per se to counsel exists.[15] The Court did note, however, that due process may require that counsel be provided at state expense in other types of cases, but gave no indication of what the broad contours of such cases would be.

Shortly after *Gagnon*, the Court concluded that prisoners are not entitled to counsel, either retained or appointed, in a prison disciplinary proceeding. The Court observed that "the insertion of counsel into the disciplinary process would inevitably give the proceedings a more adversary cast and tend to reduce their utility as a means to further correctional goals."[16]

Short of the services of an attorney, there are alternative forms of legal services that may be made available to prisoners. So-called jailhouse lawyers and writ writers are in long supply in most institutions. These inmates are often available to assist other prisoners, and the Court has indicated that, in the absence of professional legal assistance, the state may not unduly hamper or prohibit inmates from assisting one another in the preparation of petitions for postconviction relief.[17]

The thread that has held most of these cases together is the ruling in 1941 that prisoners may not be denied access to federal courts in order to file petitions of habeas corpus.[18] The thread has grown to include the requirement of a reasonably adequate law library for prisoners[19] and adequate legal assistance in the preparation of civil rights actions by inmates,[20] thereby enabling prisoners not only to seek postconviction relief, but also to challenge the conditions or terms of their confinement. Finally, in 1977, the Court ruled that the access doctrine now includes a requirement that prison authorities assist prisoners in the preparation and filing "of meaningful legal papers by providing prisoners with adequate law libraries or adequate assistance from persons trained in the law."[21] Presumably this decision has now expanded the access doctrine to include legal assistance in pursuing any legal claim that a prisoner may have under either state or federal law, among them attacks on the conviction, and the conditions and terms of confinement, and a host of normal civil problems (divorce, debtor problems) that are unrelated to an offender's status as a prisoner.

Due Process and the Revocation
of Probation and Parole

Although parolees and probationers are not confined, they are subject to restraints. Their liberty to remain outside of prison is subject to revocation if a breach of the conditions of their probation or parole has occurred. However, in *Morrissey v. Brewer* (1972), the Supreme Court ruled that revocation cannot be by summary process. The termination of parole or probation is a "grievous loss" of a valuable liberty, and therefore certain minimum requirements of due process must be observed. The Court did not spell out these requirements in detail, but it did indicate that a parolee-probationer is entitled to notice of an informal preliminary hearing and has the right to be heard and to present information before an impartial officer at a final hearing. Furthermore, the Court has ruled that fundamental fairness may require that counsel be allowed to a parolee-probationer.[22]

Due Process and Prison Disciplinary Proceedings

It is one thing to hold that parolees and probationers are entitled to due process; it is quite another matter to extend due process to those confined in prisons. Yet the Burger Court has attempted to make a reasonable accommodation between institutional needs and the protection of prisoners against arbitrary conduct. For example, in *Wolff v. McDonnell* (1974), the Court ruled that if the state creates a substantial right for prisoners (in *Wolff*, good-time credit), then due process requires that certain minimum requirements be met before the right is taken away. In disciplinary proceedings to deny good-time credit, this means advance written notice of the disciplinary charges, a hearing with a written record, the right to present documentary evidence, and the limited right to call witnesses. The requirements do not include the right to confrontation and cross-examination.

Subsequent to the decision in *Wolff*, a majority of the members of the Court indicated that they were not inclined to expand due process indefinitely within prison walls. In *Meachum v. Fano* (1976), the Court denied relief to a prisoner who claimed that his transfer to a less desirable prison should have been preceded by a hearing. In denying relief, the majority noted that "to hold as we are urged to do that *any* substantial deprivation imposed by prison authorities triggers the procedural protections of the Due Process Clause would subject to judicial review a wide spectrum of discretionary actions that traditionally have been the business of prison administrators rather than of federal courts."[23] Similarly, in *Baxter v. Palmigiano,* also decided in 1976, the Court reiterated that prisoners have neither the right to retained or appointed counsel in disciplinary proceedings nor the right to confrontation and cross-examination.

On their own initiative and in the interests of sound prison administration, many prisons have instituted substantial protections against unfair disciplinary treatment.[24] It is questionable, however, whether these various administrative protections should become matters of constitutional entitlement. The range and character of prison discipline is wide, and to attempt to subject every aspect of discipline to an inflexible constitutional standard may be beyond the competence and resources of the judiciary.[25]

Of course, there are prison disciplinary practices and conditions that could not be sanctioned by any amount of due process. Due process can never turn an inhumane practice into an acceptable one. Prisoners have the protection of the Eighth Amendment ban on cruel and unusual punishment, and they have been successful in seeking relief in federal courts from particular forms of discipline, such as the use of the strap[26] or strip confinement cells.[27] In one particularly egregious case, a federal district court declared the entire penitentiary system to be in violation of the ban on cruel and unusual punishment.[28] This case was subsequently affirmed by the Supreme Court in an opinion that gave particular attention to the practice of isolation confinement.[29]

The First Amendment and Prisoners

In the early 1970s, the National Commission on Criminal Justice Standards advocated that "each correctional agency should immediately develop policies and procedures to assure that individual offenders are able to exercise their constitutional rights of free expression and association to the same extent and subject to the same limitations as the public at large."[30] This may be a matter of sound penology, but it is an arguable constitutional proposition. Indeed, the proposition may be at odds with a host of First Amendment assumptions about people and the physical environment—assumptions that are critical to the amendment. Prisons closely confine a large number of people in a setting that demands a higher degree of order than could be tolerated in the exercise of freedom of expression. Furthermore, and without slipping into a fascist mentality, we must remember that prisons, particularly maximum-security prisons, do hold at least some individuals who are unable to cope with freedom. It is not intended here to suggest that prisons should be or must be authoritarian regimes that break the human spirit; all that we suggest is that the extant body of law governing freedom of speech, press, assembly, and association cannot be lifted from its natural setting and applied without qualification to prisons. A prisoner retains only those First Amendment freedoms "that are not inconsistent with his status as a prisoner or with the legitimate penological objectives of the corrections system."[31] However, the extent to which a prisoner's right to free expression survives incarceration remains problematic.

The lower federal courts have handed down a number of decisions involving First Amendment claims by prisoners, but the Supreme Court has taken jurisdiction in only a few cases, and its decisions have been cautious and its rulings narrow. In *Cruz v. Beto* (1972), the Court ruled it a violation of the freedom of religious exercise for a state to deny a Buddhist prisoner a reasonable opportunity to pursue his or her religion if at the same time it allows major religious groups such an opportunity.[32] The Court left open the question whether a state is obliged actually to provide religious facilities and chaplains; rather the opinion appears to rest on the discrimination against a nonconventional religion.

The Court was equally cautious in its decision in *Procunier v. Martinez* (1974).[33] In *Procunier,* prison regulations allowed officials to censor inmates' mail, both incoming and outgoing. The Court refused to be drawn into an argument about whether mail is a privilege or a matter of constitutional right. Instead, it rested its decision on the First Amendment rights of *both* the addressee and the sender of personal correspondence. Furthermore, the opinion indicated that there was no legal distinction between the nonprisoner as correspondent or recipient. However, although the Court struck down the particular regulations involved, it did hold that censorship of prisoners' mail is permissible if the measures taken are no greater than necessary to accomplish the legitimate goals of prison security and prisoner rehabilitation. In short, the opinion denied to prison officials any extraordinary power to censor personal mail. Given the availability of mail communication with the outside world, the Court has also ruled that it is not a violation of the First Amendment for a state to prohibit face-to-face interviews between press representatives and individual inmates.[34]

Finally, in *Jones v. North Carolina Prisoners' Labor Union, Inc.* (1977), it was apparent that the Burger Court was unwilling to give unlimited support to prison reform at the constitutional level.[35] In *Jones,* the Court refused to extend the protection of the First Amendment to a right of prisoners to organize and solicit membership within prison confines. The majority supported the prison officials' conclusion that a prisoners' labor union would be detrimental to prison order and security. Justice Marshall, writing in dissent, noted that the weight of professional opinion apparently supports recognizing such unions.[36] His interpretation of professional opinion may be accurate, and correctional authorities may be shortsighted in denying prisoners an opportunity to organize. Yet sound penology is not necessarily sound constitutional law.

CONCLUSION

It now seems clear that the long-standing judicial policy of hands off the correctional system is dead. The Civil Rights Act of 1964 combined with a reform-minded correctional community and activist federal appellate courts help to ensure that the legal rights of prisoners will continue to receive attention. It seems unlikely, however, that the direction of this movement will proceed at the constitutional level. Although the Burger Court initially took a surprisingly broad view of the rights of prisoners, it has now expressed reservations about the further constitutional elevation of their legal rights. These reservations are explicit in disciplinary cases and implicit in the Court's cautious approach to First Amendment issues. Certainly, the door to judicially imposed prison reform ought not to be closed, but constitutional litigation is one of the least effective methods to balance social priorities and the claims of prisoners.

NOTES

1. *Rex v. Acton, Turnkey of Marshalsea Prison,* 17 How. St. Tr. 461 (1729).
2. Of passing interest to Americans is that the investigation was led by James Oglethorpe, who shortly after the trials founded the colony of Georgia as a haven for those freed from debtor prisons.
3. See the President's Commission on Law Enforcement and Administration of Justice, *Task Force Report: Corrections* (Washington, D.C.: GPO, 1967), p. 89.
4. For a useful compendium of statutory disabilities, see "The Collateral Consequences of Criminal Conviction," 23 *Vand. L. Rev.* 929 (1970).
5. *Task Force Report: Corrections,* p. 89.
6. *Richardson v. Ramirez,* 418 U.S. 24 (1974).
7. Relief or release may be sought under habeas corpus or under the Civil Rights Act, 42 U.S.C. 1983 and 42 U.S.C. 1343.
8. E.g., *Morrissey v. Brewer,* 408 U.S. 471 (1972). Cf. *Meachum v. Fano,* 427 U.S. 215 (1976).
9. *Ex parte Hull,* 312 U.S. 546 (1941).
10. E.g., *Smartt v. Avery,* 370 F.2d 788 (1967).
11. *Douglas v. California,* 372 U.S. 353 (1963).
12. *Griffin v. Illinois,* 351 U.S. 12 (1956).
13. *Ross v. Moffitt,* 417 U.S. 600 (1974).

14. See *Barker v. Ohio*, 330 F.2d 594 (1964).

15. *Gagnon v. Scarpelli*, 411 U.S. 778 (1973).

16. *Wolff v. McDonnell*, 418 U.S. 539 (1974). In 1976, in *Baxter v. Palmigiano*, 425 U.S. 308, the Court again held against the right to counsel in disciplinary proceedings.

17. *Johnson v. Avery*, 393 U.S. 483 (1969).

18. *Ex parte Hull*.

19. *Younger v. Gilmore*, 404 U.S. 15 (1971).

20. *Wolff v. McDonnell*.

21. *Bounds v. Smith*, 430 U.S. 817, 827–829 (1977).

22. *Gagnon v. Scarpelli*.

23. *Meachum v. Fano*, 427 U.S. at 225.

24. See Michael Millerman, "Prison Disciplinary Hearings and Procedural Due Process," 31 *Md. L. Rev.* 27 (1971).

25. Cf. *Sastre v. McGinnis*, 442 F.2d 178 (1971).

26. *Jackson v. Bishop*, 404 F.2d 571 (1968).

27. *Jordan v Fitzharris*, 257 F. Supp. 674 (1966).

28. *Holt v. Sarver*, 309 F. Supp. 362 (E.D. Ark. 1970).

29. *Holt v. Sarver*, aff'd sub nom. *Hutto v. Finney*, 437 U.S. 678 (1978).

30. *Task Force Report: Corrections*, p. 58.

31. *Pell v. Procunier*, 417 U.S. 817 (1974).

32. *Cruz v. Beto*, 405 U.S. 319 (1972).

33. *Procunier v. Martinez*, 416 U.S. 396 (1974).

34. *Procunier v. Hillery*.

35. *Jones v. North Carolina Prisoners' Labor Union, Inc.*, 433 U.S. 119 (1977).

36. Ibid. at 145.

JUDICIAL DECISIONS

The Loss of Political Rights:
Richardson v. Ramirez, 418 U.S. 24 (1974)

Mr. Justice REHNQUIST delivered the opinion of the Court.

. . .

Unlike most claims under the Equal Protection Clause, for the decision of which we have only the language of the Clause itself as it is embodied in the Fourteenth Amendment, respondents' claim implicates not merely the language of the Equal Protection Clause of § 1 of the Fourteenth Amendment, but also the provisions of the less familiar § 2 of the Amendment:

> "Representatives shall be apportioned among the several States according to their respective numbers, counting the whole number of persons in each State, excluding Indians not taxed. But when the right to vote at any election for the choice of electors for President and Vice President of the United States, Representatives in Congress, the Executive and Judicial officers of a State, or the members of the Legislature thereof, is denied to any of the male inhabitants of such State, being *twenty-one years of age,* and citizens of the United States, or in any way abridged, *except for participation in rebellion, or other crime,* the basis of representation therein shall be reduced in the proportion which the number of such male citizens shall bear to the whole number of male citizens twenty-one years of age in such State." (Emphasis supplied.)

Petitioner contends that the italicized language of § 2 expressly exempts from the sanction of that section disenfranchisement grounded on prior conviction of a felony. She goes on to argue that those who framed and adopted the Fourteenth Amendment could not have intended to prohibit outright in § 1 of that Amendment that which was expressly exempted from the lesser sanction of reduced representation imposed by § 2 of the Amendment. This argument seems to us a persuasive one unless it can be shown that the language of § 2, "execpt for participation in rebellion, or other crime," was intended to have a different meaning than would appear from its face.

The problem of interpreting the "intention" of a constitutional provision is, as countless cases of this Court recognize, a difficult one. Not only are there deliberations of congressional committees and floor debates in the House and Senate, but an amendment must thereafter be ratified by the necessary number of States. The legislative history bearing on the meaning of the relevant language of § 2 is scant indeed; the framers of the Amendment were primarily concerned with the effect of reduced representation upon the States, rather than with the two forms of disenfranchisement which were exempted from that consequence by the language with which we are concerned here. Nonetheless, what legislative history there is indicates that this language was intended by Congress to mean what it says.

. . .

Further light is shed on the understanding of those who framed and ratified the Fourteenth Amendment, and thus on the meaning of § 2, by the fact that at the time of the adoption of the Amendment, 29 States had provisions in their constitutions which prohibited, or authorized the legislature to prohibit, exercise of the franchise by persons convicted of felonies or infamous crimes.

More impressive than the mere existence of the state constitutional provisions disenfranchising felons at the time of the adoption of the Fourteenth Amendment is the congressional treatment of States readmitted to the Union following the Civil War. For every State thus readmitted, affirmative congressional action in the form of an enabling act was taken, and as a part of the readmission process the State seeking readmission was required to submit for the approval of the Congress its proposed state constitution. In March 1867, before any State was readmitted, Congress passed "An act to provide for the more efficient Government of the Rebel States," the so-called Reconstruction Act. Act of Mar. 2, 1867, c. 153, 14 Stat. 428. Section 5 of the Reconstruction Act established conditions on which the former Confederate States would be readmitted to representation in Congress. It provided:

> "That when the people of any one of said rebel States shall have formed a constitution of government in conformity with the Constitution of the United States in all respects, framed by a convention of delegates elected by the male citizens of said State, twenty-one years old and upward, of whatever race, color, or previous condition, who have been resident in said State for one year previous to the day of such election, *except such as may be disenfranchised for participation in the rebellion or for felony at common law* . . . said State shall be declared entitled to representation in Congress, and senators and representatives shall be admitted therefrom on their taking the oath prescribed by law, and then and thereafter the preceding sections of this act shall be inoperative in said State. . . ." (Emphasis supplied.)

. . .

This convincing evidence of the historical understanding of the Fourteenth Amendment is confirmed by the decisions of this Court which have discussed the constitutionality of provisions disenfranchising felons. Although the Court has never given plenary consideration to the precise question of whether a State may constitutionally exclude some or all convicted felons from the franchise, we have indicated approval of such exclusions on a number of occasions. . . .

Despite this settled historical and judicial understanding of the Fourteenth Amendment's effect on state laws disenfranchising convicted felons, respondents argue that our recent decisions invalidating other state-imposed restrictions on the franchise as violative of the Equal Protection Clause require us to invalidate the disenfranchisement of felons as well. . . .

As we have seen, however, the exclusion of felons from the vote has an affirmative sanction in § 2 of the Fourteenth Amendment, a sanction which was not present in the case of the other restrictions on the franchise which were invalidated in the cases on which respondents rely. We hold that the understanding of those who adopted the Fourteenth Amendment, as reflected in the express language of § 2 and in the historical and judicial interpretation of the Amendment's applicability to state laws disenfranchising felons, is of controlling significance in distinguishing such laws from those other state limitations on the franchise which have been held invalid under the Equal Protection Clause by this Court. . . .

Pressed upon us by the respondents, and by amici curia, are contentions that these notions are outmoded, and that the more modern view is that it is essential to the process of rehabilitating the ex-felon that he be returned to his role in society as a fully participating citizen when he has completed the serving of his term. We would by no means discount these arguments if addressed to the legislative forum which may properly weigh and balance them against those advanced in support of California's present constitutional provisions. But it is not for us to choose one set of values over the other. If respondents are correct, and the view which they advocate is indeed the more enlightened and sensible one, presumably the people of the State of California will ultimately come around to that view. And if they do not do so, their failure is some evidence, at least, of the fact that there are two sides to the argument.

We therefore hold that the Supreme Court of California erred in concluding that California may no longer, consistent with the Equal Protection Clause of the Fourteenth Amendment, exclude from the franchise convicted felons who have completed their sentences and paroles. . . . Accordingly, we reverse and remand for further proceedings not inconsistent with this opinion.

It is so ordered.

Probation Revocation:
Gagnon v. Scarpelli, 411 U.S. 778 (1973)

Mr. Justice POWELL delivered the opinion of the Court.

This case presents the related questions whether a previously sentenced probationer is entitled to a hearing when his probation is revoked and, if so, whether he is entitled to be represented by appointed counsel at such a hearing.

I

Respondent, Gerald Scarpelli, pleaded guilty in July 1965, to a charge of armed robbery in Wisconsin. The trial judge sentenced him to 15 years' imprisonment, but suspended the sentence and placed him on probation for seven years in the custody of the Wisconsin Department of Public Welfare (the Department). At that time, he signed an agreement specifying the terms of his probation and a "Travel Permit and Agreement to Return" allowing him to reside in Illinois, with supervision there under an interstate compact. On August 5, 1965, he was accepted for supervision by the Adult Probation Department of Cook County, Illinois.

On August 6, respondent was apprehended by Illinois police, who had surprised him and one Fred Kleckner, Jr., in the course of the burglary of a house. After being apprised of his constitutional rights, respondent admitted that he and Kleckner had broken into the house for the purpose of stealing merchandise or money, although he now asserts that his statement was made under duress and is false. Probation was revoked by the Wisconsin Department on September 1, without a hearing. The stated grounds for revocation were that:

"1.   [Scarpelli] has associated with known criminals, in direct violation of his probation regulations and his supervising agent's instructions;
"2.   [Scarpelli] while associating with a known criminal, namely Fred Kleckner, Jr., was involved in, and arrested for, a burglary . . . in Deerfield, Illinois." App. 20.

On September 4, 1965, he was incarcerated in the Wisconsin State Reformatory at Green Bay to begin serving the 15 years to which he had been sentenced by the trial judge. At no time was he afforded a hearing.

Some three years later, on December 16, 1968, respondent applied for a writ of habeas corpus. After the petition had been filed, but before it had been acted upon, the Department placed respondent on parole. The District Court found that his status as parolee was sufficient custody to confer jurisdiction on the court and that the petition was not moot because the revocation carried "collateral consequences," presumably including the restraints imposed by his parole. On the merits, the District Court held that revocation without a hearing and counsel was a denial of due process. 317 F. Supp. 72 (E.D. Wis. 1970). The Court of Appeals affirmed, and we granted certiorari.

<h2 style="text-align:center">II</h2>

Two prior decisions set the bounds of our present inquiry. In *Mempa v. Rhay*, 389 U.S. 128 (1967), the Court held that a probationer is entitled to be represented by appointed counsel at a combined revocation and sentencing hearing. . . .

Of greater relevance is our decision last Term in *Morrissey v. Brewer*, 408 U.S. 471 (1972). There we held that the revocation of parole is not a part of a criminal prosecution. . . .

Even though the revocation of parole is not a part of the criminal prosecution, we held that the loss of liberty entailed is a serious deprivation requiring that the parolee be accorded due process. Specifically, we held that a parolee is entitled to two hearings, one a preliminary hearing at the time of his arrest and detention to determine whether there is probable cause to believe that he has committed a violation of his parole, and the other a somewhat more comprehensive hearing prior to the making of the final revocation decision.

Petitioner does not contend that there is any difference relevant to the guarantee of due process between the revocation of parole and the revocation of probation, nor do we perceive one. Probation revocation, like parole revocation, is not a stage of a criminal prosecution, but does result in a loss of liberty. Accordingly, we hold that a probationer, like a parolee, is entitled to a preliminary and a final revocation hearing, under the conditions specified in *Morrissey v. Brewer*.

<h2 style="text-align:center">III</h2>

The second, and more difficult, question posed by this case is whether an indigent probationer or parolee has a due process right to be represented by appointed counsel at these hearings. In answering that question, we draw heavily on the opinion in *Morrissey*. Our first point of reference is the character of probation or parole. As noted in *Morrissey* regarding parole, the "purpose is to help individuals reintegrate into society as constructive individuals as soon as they are able. . . ." 408 U.S., at 477. . . . Because the probation or parole officer's function is not so much to compel conformance to a strict code of behavior as to supervise a course of rehabilitation, he has been entrusted traditionally with broad discretion to judge the progress of rehabilitation in individual cases, and has been armed with the power to recommend or even to declare revocation.

In *Morrissey*, we recognized that the revocation decision has two analytically distinct components:

"The first step in a revocation decision thus involves a wholly retrospective factual question: whether the parolee has in fact acted in violation of one or more conditions of his parole. Only if it is determined that the parolee did violate the conditions does the second question arise: should the parolee be recommitted to prison or should other steps be taken to protect society and improve chances of rehabilitation?" 408 U.S., at 479–480. . . .

But an exclusive focus on the benevolent attitudes of those who administer the probation/parole system when it is working successfully obscures the modification in attitude which is likely to take place once the officer has decided to recommend revocation. Even though the officer is not by this recommendation converted into a prosecutor committed to convict, his role as counsellor to the probationer or parolee is then surely compromised.

When the officer's view of the probationer's or parolee's conduct differs in this fundamental way from the latter's own view, due process requires that the difference be resolved before revocation becomes final. Both the probationer or parolee and the State have interests in the accurate finding of fact and the informed use of discretion—the probationer or parolee to insure that his liberty is not unjustifiably taken away and the State to make certain that it is neither unnecessarily interrupting a successful effort at rehabilitation nor imprudently prejudicing the safety of the community.

It was to serve all of these interests that *Morrissey* mandated preliminary and final revocation hearings. At the preliminary hearing, a probationer or parolee is entitled to notice of the alleged violations of probation or parole, an opportunity to appear and to present evidence in his own behalf, a conditional right to confront adverse witnesses, an independent decisionmaker, and a written report of the hearing. The final hearing is a less summary one because the decision under consideration is the ultimate decision to revoke rather than a mere determination of probable cause, but the "minimum requirements of due process" include very similar elements. . . .

These requirements in themselves serve as substantial protection against ill-considered revocation, and petitioner argues that counsel need never be supplied. What this argument overlooks is that the effectiveness of the rights guaranteed by *Morrissey* may in some circumstances depend on the use of skills which the probationer or parolee is unlikely to possess. Despite the informal nature of the proceedings and the absence of technical rules of procedure or evidence, the unskilled or uneducated probationer or parolee may well have difficulty in presenting his version of a disputed set of facts where the presentation requires the examining or cross-examining of witnesses or the offering or dissecting of complex documentary evidence.

By the same token, we think that the Court of Appeals erred in accepting respondent's contention that the State is under a constitutional duty to provide counsel for indigents in all probation or parole revocation cases. While such a rule has the appeal of simplicity, it would impose direct costs and serious collateral disadvantages without regard to the need or the likelihood in a particular case for a constructive contribution by counsel. In most cases, the probationer or parolee has been convicted of committing another crime or has admitted the charges against him. And while in some cases he may have a justifiable excuse for the violation or a convincing reason why revocation is not the appropriate disposition, mitigating evidence of this kind is often not susceptible of proof or is so simple as not to require either investigation or exposition by counsel.

The introduction of counsel into a revocation proceeding will alter significantly the nature of the proceeding. If counsel is provided for the probationer or parolee, the State in turn will normally provide its own counsel; lawyers, by training and disposition, are advocates and bound by professional duty to present all available evidence and arguments in support of their clients' positions and to contest with vigor all adverse evidence and views. The role of the hearing body itself, aptly described in *Morrissey* as being "predictive and discretionary" as well as factfinding, may become more akin to that of a judge at a trial, and less attuned to the rehabilitative needs of the individual probationer or parolee. In the greater self-consciousness of its quasi-judicial role, the hearing body may be less tolerant of marginal deviant behavior and feel more pressure to reincarcerate than to continue nonpunitive rehabilitation. Certainly, the decisionmaking process will be prolonged, and the financial cost to the State—for appointed counsel, counsel for the State, a longer record, and the possibility of judicial review—will not be insubstantial.

In some cases, these modifications in the nature of the revocation hearing must be endured and the costs borne because, as we have indicated above, the probationer's or parolee's version of a disputed issue can fairly be represented only by a trained advocate. But due process is not so rigid as to require that the significant interests in informality, flexibility, and economy must always be sacrificed.

. . .

In a criminal trial, the State is represented by a prosecutor; formal rules of evidence are in force; a defendant enjoys a number of procedural rights which may be lost if not timely raised; and, in a jury trial, a defendant must make a presentation understandable to untrained jurors. In short, a criminal trial under our system is an adversary proceeding with its own unique characteristics. In a revocation hearing, on the other hand, the State is represented, not by a prosecutor, but by a parole officer with the orientation described above; formal procedures and rules of evidence are not employed; and the members of the hearing body are familiar with the problems and practice of probation or parole. The need for counsel at revocation hearings derives, not from the invariable attributes of those hearings, but rather from the peculiarities of particular cases.

. . .

We thus find no justification for a new inflexible constitutional rule with respect to the requirement of counsel. We think, rather, that the decision as to the need for counsel must be made on a case-by-case basis in the exercise of a sound discretion by the state authority charged with responsibility for administering the probation and parole system. Although the presence and participation of counsel will probably be both undesirable and constitutionally unnecessary in most revocation hearings, there will remain certain cases in which fundamental fairness—the touchstone of due process—will require that the State provide at its expense counsel for indigent probationers or parolees.

It is neither possible nor prudent to attempt to formulate a precise and detailed set of guidelines to be followed in determining when the providing of counsel is necessary to meet the applicable due process requirements. The facts and circumstances in preliminary and final hearings are susceptible of almost infinite variation, and a considerable discretion must be allowed the responsible agency in making the decision. Presumptively, it may be said that counsel should be provided in cases where, after being informed of his right to request counsel, the probationer or parolee makes such a request, based on a timely and colorable claim (i) that he has not committed the alleged violation of the conditions upon which he is at liberty; or (ii) that, even if the violation is a matter of public record or is uncontested, there are substantial reasons which justified or mitigated the violation and make revocation inappropriate, and that the reasons are complex or otherwise difficult to develop or present. In passing on a request for the appointment of counsel, the responsible agency also should consider, especially in doubtful cases, whether the probationer appears to be capable of speaking effectiveiy for himself. In every case in which a request for counsel at a preliminary or final hearing is refused, the grounds for refusal should be stated succinctly in the record.

IV

We return to the facts of the present case. Because respondent was not afforded either a preliminary hearing or a final hearing the revocation of his probation did not meet the standards of due process prescribed in *Morrissey*, which we have here held applicable to probation revocations. Accordingly, respondent was entitled to a writ of habeas corpus. . . .

Affirmed in part, reversed in part, and remanded.

Parole Revocation:
Morrissey v. Brewer, 408 U.S. 471 (1972)

Mr. Chief Justice BURGER delivered the opinion of the Court.

We granted certiorari in this case to determine whether the Due Process Clause of the Fourteenth Amendment requires that a State afford an individual some opportunity to be heard prior to revoking his parole.

Petitioner Morrissey was convicted of false drawing or uttering of checks in 1967 pursuant to his guilty plea, and was sentenced to not more than seven years' confinement. He was paroled from the Iowa State Penitentiary in June 1968. Seven months later, at the direction of his parole officer, he was arrested in his home town as a parole violator and incarcerated in the county jail. One week later, after review of the parole officer's written report, the Iowa Board of Parole revoked Morrissey's parole, and he was returned to the penitentiary located about 100 miles from his home. Petitioner asserts he received no hearing prior to revocation of his parole.

The parole officer's report on which the Board of Parole acted shows that petitioner's parole was revoked on the basis of information that he had violated the conditions of parole by buying a car under an assumed name and operating it without permission, giving false statements to police concerning his address and insurance company after a minor accident, obtaining credit under an *assumed name, and failing to report his* place of residence to his parole officer. The report states that the officer interviewed Morrissey, and that he could not explain why he did not contact his parole officer despite his effort to excuse this on the ground that he had been sick. Further, the report asserts that Morrissey admitted buying the car and obtaining credit under an assumed name, and also admitted being involved in the accident.

The parole officer recommended that his parole be revoked because of "his continual violating of his parole rules."

. . .

I

Before reaching the issue of whether due process applies to the parole system, it is important to recall the function of parole in the correctional process.

During the past 60 years, the practice of releasing prisoners on parole before the end of their sentences has become an integral part of the penological system. Rather than being an ad hoc exercise of clemency, parole is an established variation on imprisonment of convicted criminals. Its purpose is to help individuals reintegrate into society as constructive individuals as soon as they are able, without being confined for the full term of the sentence imposed. It also serves to alleviate the costs to society of keeping an individual in prison. The essence of parole is release from prison, before the completion of sentence, on the condition that the prisoner abide by certain rules during the balance of the sentence. . . .

The enforcement leverage that supports the parole conditions derives from the authority to return the parolee to prison to serve out the balance of his sentence if he fails to abide by the rules. In practice, not every violation of parole conditions automatically leads to revocation. Typically, a parolee will be counseled to abide by the conditions of parole, and the parole officer ordinarily does not take steps to have parole revoked unless he thinks that the violations are serious and continuing so as to indicate that the parolee is not adjusting properly and cannot be counted on to avoid antisocial activity. The broad discretion accorded the parole officer is also inherent in some of the quite vague conditions, such as the typical requirement that the parolee avoid "undesirable" associations or correspondence. Yet revocation of parole is not an unusual phenomenon, affecting only a few parolees. It has been estimated that 35%–40% of all parolees are subjected to revocation and return to prison. Sometimes revocation occurs when the parolee is accused of another crime; it is often preferred to a new prosecution because of the procedural ease of recommitting the individual on the basis of a lesser showing by the State.

Implicit in the system's concern with parole violations is the notion that the parolee is entitled to retain his liberty as long as he substantially abides by the conditions of his parole. The first step in a revocation decision thus involves a wholly retrospective factual question: whether the parolee has in fact acted in violation of one or more conditions of his parole. Only if it is determined that the parolee did violate the conditions does the second question arise: should the parolee be recommitted to prison or should other steps be taken to protect society and improve chances of rehabilitation? The first step is relatively simple; the second is more complex. The second question involves the application of expertise by the parole authority in making a prediction as to the ability of the individual to live in society without committing antisocial acts. This part of the decision, too, depends on facts, and therefore it is important for the board to know not only that some violation was committed but also to know accurately how many and how serious the violations were. Yet this second step, deciding what to do about the violation once it is identified, is not purely factual but also predictive and discretionary.

If a parolee is returned to prison, he usually receives no credit for the time "served" on parole. Thus, the returnee may face a potential of substantial imprisonment.

II

We begin with the proposition that the revocation of parole is not part of a criminal prosecution and thus the full panoply of rights due a defendant in such a proceeding does not apply to parole revocations. Parole arises after the end of the criminal prosecution, including imposition of sentence. Supervision is not directly by the court but by an administrative agency, which is sometimes an arm of the court and sometimes of the executive. Revocation deprives an individual, not of the absolute liberty to which every citizen is entitled, but only of the conditional liberty properly dependent on observance of special parole restrictions.

We turn, therefore, to the question whether the requirements of due process in general apply to parole revocations. . . . Whether any procedural protections are due depends on the extent to which an individual will be "condemned to suffer grievous loss." *Joint Anti-Fascist Refugee Committee v. McGrath,* 341 U.S. 123, 168 (1951) (Frankfurter, J., concurring). The question is not merely the "weight" of the individual's interest, but whether the nature of the interest is one within the contemplation of the "liberty or property" language of the Fourteenth Amendment. *Fuentes v. Shevin,* 407 U.S. 67 (1972). Once it is determined that due process applies, the question remains what process is due. It has been said so often by this Court and others as not to require citation of authority that due process is flexible and calls for such procedural protections as the particular situation demands. . . .

We turn to an examination of the nature of the interest of the parolee in his continued liberty. The liberty of a parolee enables him to do a wide range of things open to persons who have never been convicted of any crime. The parolee has been released from prison based on an evaluation that he shows reasonable promise of being able to return to society and function as a responsible, self-reliant person. Subject to the conditions of his parole, he can be gainfully employed and is free to be with family and friends and to form the other enduring attachments of normal life. Though the State properly subjects him to many restrictions not applicable to other citizens, his condition is very different from that of confinement in a prison. He may have been on parole for a number of years and may be living a relatively normal life at the time he is faced with revocation. The parolee has relied on at least an implicit promise that parole will be revoked only if he fails to live up to the parole conditions. In many cases, the parolee faces lengthy incarceration if his parole is revoked.

We see, therefore, that the liberty of a parolee, although indeterminate, includes many of the core values of unqualified liberty and its termination inflicts a "grievous loss" on the parolee and often on others. It is hardly useful any longer to try to deal with this problem in terms of whether the parolee's liberty is a "right" or a "privilege." By whatever name, the liberty is valuable and must be seen as within the protection of the Fourteenth Amendment. Its termination calls for some orderly process, however informal.

Turning to the question what process is due, we find that the State's interests are several. The State has found the parolee guilty of a crime against the people. That finding justifies imposing extensive restrictions on the individual's liberty. Release of the parolee before the end of his prison sentence is made with the recognition that with many prisoners there is a risk that they will not be able to live in society without committing additional antisocial acts. Given the previous conviction and the proper imposition of conditions, the State has an overwhelming interest in being able to return the individual to imprisonment without the burden of a new adversary criminal trial if in fact he has failed to abide by the conditions of his parole.

Yet, the State has no interest in revoking parole without some informal procedural guarantees. Although the parolee is often formally described as being "in custody," the argument cannot even be made here that summary treatment is necessary as it may be with respect to controlling a large group of potentially disruptive prisoners in actual custody. Nor are we persuaded by the argument that revocation is so totally a discretionary matter that some form of hearing would be administratively intolerable. A simple factual hearing will not interfere with the exercise of discretion. Serious studies have suggested that fair treatment on parole revocation will not result in fewer grants of parole.

This discretionary aspect of the revocation decision need not be reached unless there is first an appropriate determination that the individual has in fact breached the conditions of parole. The parolee is not the only one who has a stake in his conditional liberty. Society has a stake in whatever may be the chance of restoring him to normal and useful life within the law. Society thus has an interest in not having parole revoked because of erroneous information or because of an erroneous evaluation of the need to revoke parole, given the breach of parole conditions. And society has a further interest in treating the parolee with basic fairness: fair treatment in parole revocations will enhance the chance of rehabilitation by avoiding reactions to arbitrariness.

. . .

III

We now turn to the nature of the process that is due, bearing in mind that the interest of both State and parolee will be furthered by an effective but informal hearing. In analyzing what is due, we see two important stages in the typical process of parole revocation.

(a) Arrest of Parolee and Preliminary Hearing. The first stage occurs when the parolee is arrested and detained, usually at the direction of his parole officer. The second occurs when parole is formally revoked. There is typically a substantial time lag between the arrest and the eventual determination by the parole board whether parole should be revoked. Additionally, it may be that the parolee is arrested at a place distant from the state institution, to which he may be returned before the final decision is made concerning revocation. Given these factors, due process would seem to require that some minimal inquiry be conducted at or reasonably near the place of the alleged parole violation or arrest and as promptly as convenient after arrest while information is fresh and sources are available. . . .

In our view, due process requires that after the arrest, the determination that reasonable ground exists for revocation of parole should be made by someone not directly involved in the case. It would be unfair to assume that the supervising parole officer does not conduct an interview with the parolee to confront him with the reasons for revocation before he recommends an arrest. It would also be unfair to assume that the parole officer bears hostility against the parolee that destroys his neutrality; realistically the failure of the parolee is in a sense a failure for his supervising officer. However, we need make no assumptions one way or the other to conclude that there should be an uninvolved person to make this preliminary evaluation of the basis for believing the conditions of parole have been violated. The officer directly involved in making recommendations cannot always have complete objectivity in evaluating them. . . . It will be sufficient, therefore, in the parole revocation context, if an evaluation of whether reasonable cause exists to believe that conditions of parole have been violated is made by someone such as a parole officer other than the one who has made the report of parole violations or has recommended revocation. A State could certainly choose some other independent decision-maker to perform this preliminary function.

With respect to the preliminary hearing before this officer, the parolee should be given notice that the hearing will take place and that its purpose is to determine whether there is probable cause to believe he has committed a parole violation. The notice should state what parole violations have been alleged. At the hearing the parolee may appear and speak in his own behalf; he may bring letters, documents, or individuals who can give relevant information to the hearing officer. On request of the parolee, a person who has given adverse information on which parole revocation is to be based is to be made available for questioning in his presence. However, if the hearing officer determines that an informant would be subjected to risk of harm if his identity were disclosed, he need not be subjected to confrontation and cross-examination.

The hearing officer shall have the duty of making a summary, or digest, of what occurs at the hearing in terms of the responses of the parolee and the substance of the documents or evidence given in support of parole revocation and of the parolee's position. Based on the information before him, the officer should determine whether there is probable cause to hold the parolee for the final decision of the parole board on revocation. Such a determination would be sufficient to warrant the parolee's continued detention and return to the state correctional institution pending the final decision. . . .

(b) The Revocation Hearing. There must also be an opportunity for a hearing, if it is desired by the parolee, prior to the final decision on revocation by the parole authority. This hearing must be the basis for more than determining probable cause; it must lead to a final evaluation of any contested relevant facts and consideration of whether the facts as determined warrant revocation. The parolee must have an opportunity to be heard and to show, if he can, that he did not violate the conditions, or, if he did, that circumstances in mitigation suggest that the violation does not warrant revocation. The revocation hearing must be tendered within a reasonable time after the parolee is taken into custody. A lapse of two months, as respondents suggest occurs in some cases, would not appear to be unreasonable.

We cannot write a code of procedure; that is the responsibility of each State. Most States have done so by legislation, others by judicial decision usually on due process grounds. Our task is limited to deciding the minimum requirements of due process. They include (a) written notice of the claimed violations of parole; (b) disclosure to the parolee of evidence against him; (c) opportunity to be heard in person and to present witnesses and documentary evidence; (d) the right to confront and cross-examine adverse witnesses (unless the hearing officer specifically finds good cause for not allowing confrontation); (e) a "neutral and detached" hearing body such as a traditional parole board, members of which need not be judicial officers or lawyers; and (f) a written statement by the factfinders as to the evidence relied on and reasons for revoking parole. We emphasize there is no thought to equate this second stage of parole revocation to a criminal prosecution in any sense. It is a narrow inquiry; the process should be flexible enough to consider evidence including letters, affidavits, and other material that would not be admissible in an adversary criminal trial.

We do not reach or decide the question whether the parolee is entitled to the assistance of retained counsel or to appointed counsel if he is indigent.

We have no thought to create an inflexible structure for parole revocation procedures. The few basic requirements set out above, which are applicable to future revocations of parole, should not impose a great burden on any State's parole system. Control over the required proceedings by the hearing officers can assure that delaying tactics and other abuses sometimes present in the traditional adversary trial situation do not occur. Obviously a parolee cannot relitigate issues determined against him in other forums, as in the situation presented when the revocation is based on conviction of another crime.

In the peculiar posture of this case, given the absence of an adequate record, we conclude the ends of justice will be best served by remanding the case to the Court of Appeals for its return of the two consolidated cases to the District Court with directions to make findings on the procedures actually followed by the Parole Board in these two revocations. . . .

We reverse and remand to the Court of Appeals for further proceedings consistent with this opinion.

Reversed and remanded.

Prison Transfers:
Meachum v. Fano, 427 U.S. 215 (1976)

Mr. Justice WHITE delivered the opinion of the Court.

The question here is whether the Due Process Clause of the Fourteenth Amendment entitles a state prisoner to a hearing when he is transferred to a prison the conditions of which are substantially less favorable to the prisoner, absent a state law or practice conditioning such transfers on proof of serious misconduct or the occurrence of other events. We hold that it does not.

I

During a 2½-month period in 1974, there were nine serious fires at the Massachusetts Correctional Institution at Norfolk—a medium-security institution. Based primarily on reports from informants, the six respondent inmates were removed from the general prison population and placed in the Receiving Building, an administrative detention area used to process new inmates. Proceedings were then had before the Norfolk prison Classification Board with respect to whether respondents were to be transferred to another institution—possibly a maximum-security institution, the living conditions at which are substantially less favorable than those at Norfolk. Each respondent was notified of the classification hearing and was informed that the authorities had information indicating that he had engaged in criminal conduct.

Individual classification hearings were held, each respondent being represented by counsel. Each hearing began by the reading of a prepared statement by the Classification Board. The Board then heard, *in camera* and out of the respondent's presence, the testimony of petitioner Meachum, the Norfolk prison superintendent, who repeated the information that had been received from informants. Each respondent was then told that the evidence supported the allegations contained in the notice but was not then—or ever—given transcripts or summaries of Meachum's testimony before the Board. Each respondent was allowed to present evidence in his own behalf; and each denied involvement in the particular infraction being investigated. Some respondents submitted supportive testimony or written statements from correction officers. A social worker also testified in the presence of each respondent, furnishing the respondent's criminal and custodial record, including prior rule infractions, if any, and other aspects of his performance and "general adjustment" at Norfolk.

The Board recommended that Royce be placed in administrative segregation for 30 days; that Fano, Dussault, and McPhearson be transferred to Walpole, a maximum-security institution where the living conditions are substantially less favorable to the prisoners than those at Norfolk and that DeBrosky and Hathaway be transferred to Bridgewater which has both maximum- and medium-security facilities. The reasons for its actions were stated in the Board's reports, which, however, were not then available to respondents. Although respondents were aware of the general import of the informants' allegations and were told that the recommendations drew upon informant sources, the details of this information were not revealed to respondents and are not included in the Board's reports which are part of the record before us.

. . .

We granted . . . certiorari in order to determine whether the Constitution required petitioners to conduct a factfinding hearing in connection with the transfers in this case where state law does not condition the authority to transfer on the occurrence of specific acts of misconduct or other events and, if so, whether the hearings granted in this case were adequate. In light of our resolution of the first issue, we do not reach the second.

II

The Fourteenth Amendment prohibits any State from depriving a person of life, liberty, or property without due process of law. The initial inquiry is whether the transfer of respondents from Norfolk to Walpole and Bridgewater infringed or implicated a "liberty" interest of respondents within the meaning of the Due Process Clause. Contrary to the Court of Appeals, we hold that it did not. We reject at the outset the notion that *any* grievous loss visited upon a person by the State is sufficient to invoke the procedural protections of the Due Process Clause. . . . We cannot agree that *any* change in the conditions of confinement having a substantial adverse impact on the prisoner involved is sufficient to invoke the protections of the Due Process Clause. The Due Process Clause by its own force forbids the State from convicting any person of crime and depriving him of his liberty without complying fully with the requirements of the Clause. But given a valid conviction, the criminal defendant has been constitutionally deprived of his liberty to the extent that the State may confine him and subject him to the rules of its prison system so long as the conditions of confinement do not otherwise violate the Constitution. The Constitution does not require that the State have more than one prison for convicted felons; nor does it guarantee that the convicted prisoner will be placed in any particular prison, if, as is likely, the State has more than one correctional institution. The initial decision to assign the convict to a particular institution is not subject to audit under the Due Process Clause, although the degree of confinement in one prison may be quite different from that in another. The conviction has sufficiently extinguished the defendant's liberty interest to empower the State to confine him in *any* of its prisons.

Neither, in our view, does the Due Process Clause in and of itself protect a duly convicted prisoner against transfer from one institution to another within the state prison system. Confinement in any of the State's institutions is within the normal limits or range of custody which the conviction has authorized the State to impose. That life in one prison is much more disagreeable than in another does not in itself signify that a Fourteenth Amendment liberty interest is implicated when a prisoner is transferred to the institution with the more severe rules.

Our cases hold that the convicted felon does not forfeit all constitutional protections by reason of his conviction and confinement in prison. He retains a variety of important rights that the courts must be alert to protect. . . . To hold as we are urged to do that *any* substantial deprivation imposed by prison authorities triggers the procedural protections of the Due Process Clause would subject to judicial review a wide spectrum of discretionary actions that traditionally have been the business of prison administrators rather than of the federal courts.

Transfers between institutions, for example, are made for a variety of reasons and often involve no more than informed predictions as to what would best serve institutional security or the safety and welfare of the inmate. Yet under the approach urged here, any transfer, for whatever reason, would require a hearing as long as it could be said that the transfer would place the prisoner in substantially more burdensome conditions than he had been experiencing. We are unwilling to go so far.

Wolff v. McDonnell, on which the Court of Appeals heavily relied, is not to the contrary. Under that case, the Due Process Clause entitles a state prisoner to certain procedural protections when he is deprived of good-time credits because of serious misconduct. But the liberty interest there identified did not originate in the Constitution, which "itself does not guarantee good-time credit for satisfactory behavior while in prison." Id., at 557. The State itself, not the Constitution, had "not only provided a statutory right to good time but also specifies that it is to be forfeited only for serious misbehavior." Ibid. . . . The liberty interest protected in *Wolff* had its roots in state law, and the minimum procedures appropriated under the circumstances were held required by the Due Process Clause "to insure that the state-created right is not arbitrarily abrogated." Id., at 557. This is consistent with our approach in other due process cases. . . .

Here, Massachusetts law conferred no right on the prisoner to remain in the prison to which he was initially assigned, defeasible only upon proof of specific acts of misconduct. Insofar as we are advised, transfers between Massachusetts prisons are not conditioned upon the occurrence of specified events. On the contrary, transfer in a wide variety of circumstances is vested in prison officials. The predicate for invoking the protection of the Fourteenth Amendment as construed and applied in *Wolff v. McDonnell* is totally nonexistent in this case.

Even if Massachusetts has not represented that transfers will occur only on the occurrence of certain events, it is argued that charges of serious misbehavior, as in this case, often initiate and heavily influence the transfer decision and that because allegations of misconduct may be erroneous, hearings should be held before transfer to a more confining institution is to be suffered by the prisoner. That an inmate's conduct, in general or in specific instances, may often be a major factor in the decision of prison officials to transfer him is to be expected unless it be assumed that transfers are mindless events. A prisoner's past and anticipated future behavior will very likely be taken into account in selecting a prison in which he will be initially incarcerated or to which he will be transferred to best serve the State's penological goals.

A prisoner's behavior may precipitate a transfer; and absent such behavior, perhaps transfer would not take place at all. But, as we have said, Massachusetts prison officials have the discretion to transfer prisoners for any number of reasons. Their discretion is not limited to instances of serious misconduct. As we understand it no legal interest or right of these respondents under Massachusetts law would have been violated by their transfer whether or not their misconduct had been proved in accordance with procedures that might be required by the Due Process Clause in other circumstances. Whatever expectation the prisoner may have in remaining at a particular prison so long as he behaves himself, it is too ephemeral and insubstantial to trigger procedural due process protections as long as prison officials have discretion to transfer him for whatever reason or for no reason at all.

Holding that arrangements like this are within reach of the procedural protections of the Due Process Clause would place the Clause astride the day-to-day functioning of state prisons and involve the judiciary in issues and discretionary decisions that are not the business of federal judges. We decline to so interpret and apply the Due Process Clause. The federal courts do not sit to supervise state prisons, the administration of which is of acute interest to the States. The individual States, of course, are free to follow another course, whether by statute, by rule or regulation, or by interpretation of their own constitutions. They may thus decide that prudent prison administration requires pretransfer hearings. Our holding is that the Due Process Clause does not impose a nationwide rule mandating transfer hearings.

The judgment of the Court of Appeals accordingly is

Reversed.

Mr. Justice STEVENS, with whom Mr. Justice BRENNAN and Mr. Justice MARSHALL join, dissenting.

The Court's rationale is more disturbing than its narrow holding. If the Court had merely held that the transfer of a prisoner from one penal institution to another does not cause a sufficiently grievous loss to amount to a deprivation of liberty within the meaning of the Due Process Clause of the Fourteenth Amendment I would disagree with the conclusion but not with the constitutional analysis. The Court's holding today, however, appears to rest on a conception of "liberty" which I consider fundamentally incorrect.

The Court indicates that a "liberty interest" may have either of two sources. According to the Court, a liberty interest may "originate in the Constitution" or it may have "its roots in state law." Apart from those two possible origins, the Court is unable to find that a person has a constitutionally protected interest in liberty.

If a man were a creature of the state, the analysis would be correct. But neither the Bill of Rights nor the laws of sovereign States create the liberty which the Due Process Clause protects. The relevant constitutional provisions are limitations on the power of the sovereign to infringe on the liberty of the citizen. The relevant state laws either create property rights, or they curtail the freedom of the citizen who must live in an ordered society. Of course, law is essential to the exercise and enjoyment of individual liberty in a complex society. But it is not the source of liberty, and surely not the exclusive source.

I had thought it self-evident that all men were endowed by their Creator with liberty as one of the cardinal unalienable rights. It is that basic freedom which the Due Process Clause protects, rather than the particular rights or privileges conferred by specific laws or regulations.

A correct description of the source of the liberty protected by the Constitution does not, of course, decide this case. For, by hypothesis, we are dealing with persons who may be deprived of their liberty because they have been convicted of criminal conduct after a fair trial. We should therefore first ask whether the deprivation of liberty which follows conviction is total or partial.

At one time the prevailing view was that deprivation was essentially total. The penitentiary inmate was considered "the slave of the State." See *Ruffin v. Commonwealth*, 62 Va. 790, 796 (1871). Although the wording of the Thirteenth Amendment provided some support for that point of view, "courts in recent years have moderated the harsh implications of the Thirteenth Amendment."

The moderating trend culminated in this Court's landmark holding that notwithstanding the conditions of legal custody pursuant to a criminal conviction, a parolee has a measure of liberty that is entitled to constitutional protection.

> "We see, therefore, that the liberty of a parolee, although indeterminate, includes many of the core values of unqualified liberty and its termination inflicts a 'grievous loss' on the parolee and often on others. It is hardly useful any longer to try to deal with this problem in terms of whether the parolee's liberty is a 'right' or a 'privilege.' By whatever name, the liberty is valuable and must be seen as within the protection of the Fourteenth Amendment. Its termination calls for some orderly process, however informal." *Morrissey v. Brewer*, 408 U.S. 471, 482.

Although the Court's opinion was narrowly written with careful emphasis on the permission given to the parolee to live outside the prison walls, the Court necessarily held that the individual possesses a residuum of constitutionally protected liberty while in legal custody pursuant to a valid conviction. . . . It demeans the holding in *Morrissey*—more importantly it demeans the concept of liberty itself—to ascribe to that holding nothing more than a protection of an interest that the State has created through its own prison regulations. For if the inmate's protected liberty interests are no greater than the State chooses to allow, he is really little more than the slave described in the 19th century cases. I think it clear that even the inmate retains an unalienable interest in liberty—at the very minimum the right to be treated with dignity—which the Constitution may never ignore.

This basic premise is not inconsistent with recognition of the obvious fact that the

State must have wide latitude in determining the conditions of confinement that will be imposed following conviction of crime. To supervise and control its prison population, the State must retain the power to change the conditions for individuals, or for groups of prisoners, quickly and without judicial review. In many respects the State's problems in governing its inmate population are comparable to those encountered in governing a military force. Prompt and unquestioning obedience by the individual, even to commands he does not understand, may be essential to the preservation of order and discipline. Nevertheless, within the limits imposed by the basic restraints governing the controlled population, each individual retains his dignity and, in time, acquires a status that is entitled to respect.

Imprisonment is intended to accomplish more than the temporary removal of the offender from society in order to prevent him from committing like offenses during the period of his incarceration. While custody denies the inmate the opportunity to offend, it also gives him an opportunity to improve himself and to acquire skills and habits that will help him to participate in an open society after his release. Within the prison community, if my basic hypothesis is correct, he has a protected right to pursue his limited rehabilitative goals, or at the minimum, to maintain whatever attributes of dignity are associated with his status in a tightly controlled society. It is unquestionably within the power of the State to change that status, abruptly and adversely; but if the change is sufficiently grievous, it may not be imposed arbitrarily. In such case due process must be afforded.

That does not mean, of course, that every adversity amounts to a deprivation within the meaning of the Fourteenth Amendment. There must be grievous loss, and that term itself is somewhat flexible. I would certainly not consider every transfer within a prison system, even to more onerous conditions of confinement, such a loss. On the other hand, I am unable to identify a principled basis for differentiating between a transfer from the general prison population to solitary confinement and a transfer involving equally disparate conditions between one physical facility and another.

In view of the Court's basic holding, I merely note that I agree with the Court of Appeals that the transfer involved in this case was sufficiently serious to invoke the protection of the Constitution.

I respectfully dissent.

Disciplinary Proceedings:
Wolff v. McDonnell, 418 U.S. 539 (1974)

Mr. Justice WHITE delivered the opinion of the Court.

We granted the petition for writ of certiorari in this case because it raises important questions concerning the administration of a state prison.

Respondent, on behalf of himself and other inmates of the Nebraska Penal and Correctional Complex, Lincoln, Nebraska, filed a complaint under 42 U.S.C. § 1983 challenging several of the practices, rules, and regulations of the Complex. For present purposes, the pertinent allegations were that disciplinary proceedings did not comply with the Due Process Clause of the Fourteenth Amendment to the Federal

Constitution; that the inmate legal assistance program did not meet constitutional standards, and that the regulations governing the inspection of mail to and from attorneys for inmates were unconstitutionally restrictive. Respondent requested damages and injunctive relief.

. . .

I

We begin with the due process claim. An understanding of the issues involved requires a detailing of the prison disciplinary regime set down by Nebraska statutes and prison regulations.

Section 16 of the Nebraska Treatment and Corrections Act, as amended, Neb. Rev. Stat. § 83–185 (Cum. Supp. 1972), provides that the chief executive officer of each penal facility is responsible for the discipline of inmates in a particular institution. The statute provides for a range of possible disciplinary action. "Except in flagrant or serious cases, punishment for misconduct shall consist of deprivation of privileges. In cases of flagrant or serious misconduct, the chief executive officer may order that a person's reduction of term as provided in section 83–1,107 [good-time credit] be forfeited or withheld and also that the person be confined in a disciplinary cell." Each breach of discipline is to be entered in the person's file together with the disposition or punishment therefor.

As the statute makes clear, there are basically two kinds of punishment for flagrant or serious misconduct. The first is the forfeiture or withholding of good-time credits, which affects the term of confinement, while the second, confinement in a disciplinary cell, involves alteration of the conditions of confinement. If the misconduct is less than flagrant or serious, only deprivation of privileges results.

The only statutory provision establishing procedures for the imposition of disciplinary sanctions which pertains to good time, § 38 of the Nebraska Treatment and Corrections Act, as amended, Neb. Rev. Stat. § 83–1,107 (Cum. Supp. 1972), merely requires that an inmate be "consulted regarding the charges of misconduct" in connection with the forfeiture, withholding, or restoration of credit. But prison authorities have framed written regulations dealing with procedures and policies for controlling inmate misconduct.

. . . By regulation, misconduct is classified into two categories: major misconduct is a "serious violation" and must be formally reported to an Adjustment Committee. . . . This Committee is directed to "review and evaluate all misconduct reports" and, among other things, to "conduct investigations, make findings, [and] impose disciplinary actions." If only minor misconduct, "a less serious violation," is involved, the problem may either be resolved informally by the inmate's supervisor or it can be formally reported for action to the Adjustment Committee. Repeated minor misconduct must be reported. The Adjustment Committee has available a wide range of sanctions. "Disciplinary action taken and recommended may include but not necessarily be limited to the following: reprimand, restrictions of various kinds, extra duty, confinement in the Adjustment Center [the disciplinary cell], withholding of statutory good time and/or extra earned good time, or a combination of the elements listed herein."

. . .

III

Petitioners assert that the procedure for disciplining prison inmates for serious misconduct is a matter of policy raising no constitutional issue. If the position implies that prisoners in state institutions are wholly without the protections of the Constitution and the Due Process Clause, it is plainly untenable. Lawful imprisonment necessarily makes unavailable many rights and privileges of the ordinary citizen, a "retraction justified by the considerations underlying our penal system." *Price v. Johnston,* 334 U.S. 266, 285 (1948). But though his rights may be diminished by the needs and exigencies of the institutional environment, a prisoner is not wholly stripped of constitutional protections when he is imprisoned for crime. There is no iron curtain drawn between the Constitution and the prisons of this country. Prisoners have been held to enjoy substantial religious freedom under the First and Fourteenth Amendments. *Cruz v. Beto,* 405 U.S. 319 (1972). They retain right of access to the courts. *Younger v. Gilmore,* 404 U.S. 15 (1971). Prisoners are protected under the Equal Protection Clause of the Fourteenth Amendment from invidious discrimination based on race. *Lee v. Washington,* 390 U.S. 333 (1968). Prisoners may also claim the protections of the Due Process Clause. They may not be deprived of life, liberty, or property without due process of law. *Haines v. Kerner,* 404 U.S. 519 (1972).

Of course, as we have indicated, the fact that prisoners retain rights under the Due Process Clause in no way implies that these rights are not subject to restrictions imposed by the nature of the regime to which they have been lawfully committed. Prison disciplinary proceedings are not part of a criminal prosecution, and the full panoply of rights due a defendant in such proceedings does not apply. In sum, there must be mutual accommodation between institutional needs and objectives and the provisions of the Constitution that are of general application.

We also reject the assertion of the State that whatever may be true of the Due Process Clause in general or of other rights protected by that Clause against state infringement, the interest of prisoners in disciplinary procedures is not included in that "liberty" protected by the Fourteenth Amendment. It is true that the Constitution itself does not guarantee good-time credit for satisfactory behavior while in prison. But here the State itself has not only provided a statutory right to good time but also specifies that it is to be forfeited only for serious misbehavior. Nebraska may have the authority to create, or not, a right to a shortened prison sentence through the accumulation of credits for good behavior. . . . But the State having created the right to good time and itself recognizing that its deprivation is a sanction authorized for major misconduct, the prisoner's interest has real substance and is sufficiently embraced within Fourteenth Amendment "liberty" to entitle him to those minimum procedures appropriate under the circumstances and required by the Due Process Clause to insure that the state-created right is not arbitrarily abrogated. This is the thrust of recent cases in the prison disciplinary context. . . .

We think a person's liberty is equally protected, even when the liberty itself is a statutory creation of the State. The touchstone of due process is protection of the individual against arbitrary action of government, *Dent v. West Virginia,* 129 U.S. 114, 123 (1889). Since prisoners in Nebraska can only lose good-time credits if they are guilty of serious misconduct, the determination of whether such behavior has occurred becomes critical, and the minimum requirements of procedural due process appropriate for the circumstances must be observed.

. . .

We have often repeated that "the very nature of due process negates any concept of inflexible procedures universally applicable to every imaginable situation." *Cafeteria & Restaurant Workers v. McElroy*, 367 U.S., at 895. . . . Viewed in this light it is immediately apparent that one cannot automatically apply procedural rules designed for free citizens in an open society, or for parolees or probationers under only limited restraints, to the very different situation presented by a disciplinary proceeding in a state prison.

. . .

In striking the balance that the Due Process Clause demands, however, we think the major consideration militating against adopting the full range of procedures suggested by *Morrissey* for alleged parole violators is the very different stake the State has in the structure and content of the prison disciplinary hearing. That the revocation of parole be justified and based on an accurate assessment of the facts is a critical matter to the State as well as the parolee; but the procedures by which it is determined whether the conditions of parole have been breached do not themselves threaten other important state interests, parole officers, the police, or witnesses—at least no more so than in the case of the ordinary criminal trial. Prison disciplinary proceedings, on the other hand, take place in a closed, tightly controlled environment peopled by those who have chosen to violate the criminal law and who have been lawfully incarcerated for doing so. Some are first offenders, but many are recidivists who have repeatedly employed illegal and often very violent means to attain their ends. They may have little regard for the safety of others or their property or for the rules designed to provide an orderly and reasonably safe prison life. Although there are very many varieties of prisons with different degrees of security, we must realize that in many of them the inmates are closely supervised and their activities controlled around the clock. Guards and inmates co-exist in direct and intimate contact. Tension between them is unremitting. Frustration, resentment, and despair are commonplace. Relationships among the inmates are varied and complex and perhaps subject to the unwritten code that exhorts inmates not to inform on a fellow prisoner.

It is against this background that disciplinary proceedings must be structured by prison authorities; and it is against this background that we must make our constitutional judgments, realizing that we are dealing with the maximum security institution as well as those where security considerations are not paramount. The reality is that disciplinary hearings and the imposition of disagreeable sanctions necessarily involve confrontations between inmates and authority and between inmates who are being disciplined and those who would charge or furnish evidence against them. . . .

V

Two of the procedures that the Court held should be extended to parolees facing revocation proceedings are not, but must be, provided to prisoners in the Nebraska Complex if the minimum requirements of procedural due process are to be satisfied. These are advance written notice of the claimed violation and a written statement of the factfinders as to the evidence relied upon and the reasons for the disciplinary action taken. As described by the Warden in his oral testimony, on the basis of which the District Court made its findings, the inmate is now given oral notice of the charges against him at least as soon as the conference with the Chief Corrections Supervisor and charging party. A written record is there compiled and the report read to the inmate at the hearing before the Adjustment Committee where the charges are discussed and pursued. There is no indication that the inmate is ever given a written statement by the Committee as to the evidence or informed in writing or otherwise as to the reasons for the disciplinary action taken.

Part of the function of notice is to give the charged party a chance to marshal the facts in his defense and to clarify what the charges are, in fact. Neither of these functions was performed by the notice described by the Warden. Although the charges are discussed orally with the inmate somewhat in advance of the hearing, the inmate is sometimes brought before the Adjustment Committee shortly after he is orally informed of the charges. . . . We hold that written notice of the charges must be given to the disciplinary-action defendant in order to inform him of the charges and to enable him to marshal the facts and prepare a defense. At least a brief period of time after the notice, no less than 24 hours, should be allowed to the inmate to prepare for the appearance before the Adjustment Committee.

We also hold that there must be a "written statement by the factfinders as to the evidence relied on and reasons" for the disciplinary action. Although Nebraska does not seem to provide administrative review of the action taken by the Adjustment Committee, the actions taken at such proceedings may involve review by other bodies. . . . Written records of proceedings will thus protect the inmate against collateral consequences based on a misunderstanding of the nature of the original proceeding. Further, as to the disciplinary action itself, the provision for a written record helps to insure that administrators, faced with possible scrutiny by state officials and the public, and perhaps even the courts, where fundamental constitutional rights may have been abridged, will act fairly. Without written records, the inmate will be at a severe disadvantage in propounding his own cause to or defending himself from others. . . .

We are also of the opinion that the inmate facing disciplinary proceedings should be allowed to call witnesses and present documentary evidence in his defense when permitting him to do so will not be unduly hazardous to institutional safety or correctional goals. Ordinarily, the right to present evidence is basic to a fair hearing; but the unrestricted right to call witnesses from the prison population carries obvious potential for disruption and for interference with the swift punishment that in individual cases may be essential to carrying out the correctional program of the institution. We should not be too ready to exercise oversight and put aside the judgment of prison administrators. It may be that an individual threatened with serious sanctions would normally be entitled to present witnesses and relevant documentary evidence; but here we must balance the inmate's interest in avoiding loss of good time against the needs of the prison, and some amount of flexibility and accommodation is required. Prison officials must have the necessary discretion to keep the hearing within reasonable limits and to refuse to call witnesses that may create a risk of reprisal or undermine authority, as well as to limit access to other inmates to collect statements or to compile other documentary evidence. . . . There is this much play in the joints of the Due Process Clause, and we stop short of imposing a more demanding rule with respect to witnesses and documents.

Confrontation and cross-examination present greater hazards to institutional interests. If confrontation and cross-examination of those furnishing evidence against the inmate were to be allowed as a matter of course, as in criminal trials, there would be considerable potential for havoc inside the prison walls. Proceedings would inevitably be longer and tend to unmanageability. . . . Although some States do seem to allow cross-examination in disciplinary hearings, we are not apprised of the conditions under which the procedure may be curtailed; and it does not appear that confrontation and cross-examination are generally required in this context. We think that the Constitution should not be read to impose the procedure at the present time and that adequate bases for decision in prison disciplinary cases can be arrived at without cross-examination.

. . . Although the dangers posed by cross-examination of known inmate accusers, or guards, may be less, the resentment which may persist after confrontation may still be substantial. Also, even where the accuser or adverse witness is known, the disclosure of third parties may pose a problem. There may be a class of cases where the facts are closely disputed, and the character of the parties minimizes the dangers involved. However, any constitutional rule tailored to meet these situations would undoubtedly produce great litigation and attendant costs in a much wider range of cases. . . .

As to the right to counsel, the problem as outlined in *Scarpelli* with respect to parole and probation revocation proceedings is even more pertinent here. . . .

The insertion of counsel into the disciplinary process would inevitably give the proceedings a more adversary cast and tend to reduce their utility as a means to further correctional goals. There would also be delay and very practical problems in providing counsel in sufficient numbers at the time and place where hearings are to be held. At this stage of the development of these procedures we are not prepared to hold that inmates have a right to either retained or appointed counsel in disciplinary proceedings.

Where an illiterate inmate is involved, however, or where the complexity of the issue makes it unlikely that the inmate will be able to collect and present the evidence necessary for an adequate comprehension of the case, he should be free to seek the aid of a fellow inmate, or if that is forbidden, to have adequate substitute aid in the form of help from the staff or from a sufficiently competent inmate designated by the staff. . . .

Our conclusion that some, but not all, of the procedures specified in *Morrissey* and *Scarpelli* must accompany the deprivation of good time by state prison authorities is not graven in stone. As the nature of the prison disciplinary process changes in future years, circumstances may then exist which will require further consideration and reflection of this Court. It is our view, however, that the procedures we have now required in prison disciplinary proceedings represent a reasonable accommodation between the interests of the inmates and the needs of the institution.

. . .

VII

The issue of the extent to which prison authorities can open and inspect incoming mail from attorneys to inmates, has been considerably narrowed in the course of this litigation. The prison regulation under challenge provided that "all incoming and outgoing mail will be read and inspected," and no exception was made for attorney-prisoner mail. . . .

Petitioners now concede that they cannot open and *read* mail from attorneys to inmates, but contend that they may open all letters from attorneys as long as it is done in the presence of the prisoners. The narrow issue thus presented is whether letters determined or found to be from attorneys may be opened by prison authorities in the presence of the inmate or whether such mail must be delivered unopened if normal detection techniques fail to indicate contraband.

Respondent asserts that his First, Sixth, and Fourteenth Amendment rights are infringed, under a procedure whereby the State may open mail from his attorney, even though in his presence and even though it may not be read. To begin with, the constitutional status of the rights asserted, as applied in this situation, is far from clear. While First Amendment rights of correspondents with prisoners may protect against the censoring of inmate mail, when not necessary to protect legitimate governmental interests, see *Procunier v. Martinez*, 416 U.S. 396 (1974), this Court has not yet recognized First Amendment rights of prisoners in this context. Furthermore, freedom from censorship is not equivalent to freedom from inspection or perusal. As to the Sixth Amendment, its reach is only to protect the attorney-client relationship from intrusion in the criminal setting, while the claim here would insulate all mail from inspection, whether related to civil or criminal matters. . . . We think it entirely appropriate that the State require any such communications to be specially marked as originating from an attorney, with his name and address being given, if they are to receive special treatment. It would also certainly be permissible that prison authorities require that a lawyer desiring to correspond with a prisoner, *first* identify himself and his client to the prison officials, to assure that the letters marked privileged are actually from members of the bar. As to the ability to open the mail in the presence of inmates, this could in no way constitute censorship, since the mail would not be read. Neither could it chill such communications, since the inmate's presence insures that prison officials will not read the mail. The possibility that contraband will be enclosed in letters, even those from apparent attorneys, surely warrants prison officials' opening the letters. . . .

VIII

The last issue presented is whether the Complex must make available, and if so has made available, adequate legal assistance, under *Johnson v. Avery*, supra, for the preparation of habeas corpus petitions and civil rights actions by inmates. . . .

In *Johnson v. Avery*, an inmate was disciplined for violating a prison regulation which prohibited inmates from assisting other prisoners in preparing habeas corpus petitions. The Court held that "unless and until the State provides some reasonable alternative to assist inmates in the preparation of petitions for post-conviction relief," inmates could not be barred from furnishing assistance to each other. 393 U.S., at 490. The court emphasized that the writ of habeas corpus was of fundamental importance in our constitutional scheme, and since the basic purpose of the writ "is to enable those unlawfully incarcerated to obtain their freedom, it is fundamental that access of prisoners to the courts for the purpose of presenting their complaints may not be denied or obstructed." Id., at 485. Following *Avery*, the Court, in *Younger v. Gilmore*, supra, affirmed a three-judge court judgment which required state officials to provide indigent inmates with access to a reasonably adequate law library for preparation of legal actions.

Petitioners contend that *Avery* is limited to assistance in the preparation of habeas corpus petitions and disputes the direction of the Court of Appeals to the District Court that the capacity of the inmate adviser be assessed in light of the demand for assistance in civil rights actions as well as in the preparation of habeas petitions. Petitioners take too narrow a view of that decision.

First, the demarcation line between civil rights actions and habeas petitions is not always clear. The Court has already recognized instances where the same constitutional rights might be redressed under either form of relief. Second, while it is true that only in habeas actions may relief be granted which will shorten the term of confinement, *Preiser*, supra, it is more pertinent that both actions serve to protect basic constitutional rights. . . .

Finding no reasonable distinction between the two forms of actions, we affirm the Court of Appeals on this point, and as the Court of Appeals suggested, the District Court will assess the adequacy of legal assistance under the reasonable-alternative standard of *Avery*.

Affirmed in part, reversed in part.

Disciplinary Proceedings:
Baxter v. Palmigiano, 425 U.S. 308 (1976)

Mr. Justice WHITE delivered the opinion of the Court.

These cases present questions as to procedures required at prison disciplinary hearings and as to the reach of our recent decision in *Wolff v. McDonnell*, 418 U.S. 539 (1974).

I

A.   No. 74–1194

Respondents are inmates of the California penal institution at San Quentin. They filed an action under 42 U.S.C. § 1983 seeking declaratory and injunctive relief and alleging that the procedures used in disciplinary proceedings at San Quentin violated their rights to due process and equal protection of the laws under the Fourteenth Amendment of the Constitution. After an evidentiary hearing, the District Court granted substantial relief. The Court of Appeals for the Ninth Circuit, with one judge dissenting, affirmed. . . .

B.   No. 74–1187

Respondent Palmigiano is an inmate of the Rhode Island Adult Correction Institution serving a life sentence for murder. He was charged by correctional officers with "inciting a disturbance and disrupt[ion] of [prison] operations, which might have resulted in a riot." App. 197 (No. 74–1187). He was summoned before the prison Disciplinary Board and informed that he might be prosecuted for a violation of state law, that he should consult his attorney (although his attorney was not permitted by the Board to be present during the hearing), that he had a right to remain silent during the hearing but that if he remained silent his silence would be held against him. Respondent availed himself of the counsel-substitute provided for by prison rules and remained silent during the hearing. The Disciplinary Board's decision was that respondent be placed in "punitive segregation" for 30 days and that his classification status be downgraded thereafter.

Respondent filed an action under 42 U.S.C. § 1983 for damages and injunctive relief, claiming that the disciplinary hearing violated the Due Process Clause of the Fourteenth Amendment of the Constitution. The District Court held an evidentiary hearing and denied relief. The Court of Appeals for the First Circuit, with one judge dissenting, reversed, holding that respondent "was denied due process in the disciplinary hearing only insofar as he was not provided with use immunity for statements he might have made within the disciplinary hearing, and because he was denied access to retained counsel within the hearing. . . .

II

. . .

We see no reason to alter our conclusion so recently made in *Wolff* that inmates do not "have a right to either retained or appointed counsel in disciplinary hearings." 418 U.S., at 570. Plainly, therefore, state authorities were not in error in failing to advise Palmigiano to the contrary, i.e., that he was entitled to counsel at the hearing and that the State would furnish counsel if he did not have one of his own.

III

Palmigiano was advised that he was not required to testify at his disciplinary hearing and that he could remain silent but that his silence could be used against him. The Court of Appeals for the First Circuit held that the self-incrimination privilege of the Fifth Amendment, made applicable to the States by reason of the Fourteenth Amendment, forbids drawing adverse inferences against an inmate from his failure to testify. The State challenges this determination, and we sustain the challenge.

As the Court has often held, the Fifth Amendment "not only protects the individual against being involuntarily called as a witness against himself in a criminal prosecution but also privileges him not to answer official questions put to him in any other proceeding, civil or criminal, formal or informal, where the answers might incriminate him in future criminal proceedings." *Lefkowitz v. Turley*, 414 U.S. 70, 77 (1973). Prison disciplinary hearings are not criminal proceedings; but if inmates are compelled in those proceedings to furnish testimonial evidence that might incriminate them in later criminal proceedings, they must be offered "whatever immunity is required to supplant the privilege" and may not be required to "waive such immunity." . . .

The Court has also plainly ruled that it is constitutional error under the Fifth Amendment to instruct a jury in a criminal case that it may draw an inference of guilt from a defendant's failure to testify about facts relevant to his case. *Griffin v. California*, 380 U.S. 609 (1965). . . .

The Rhode Island prison rules do not transgress the foregoing principles. No criminal proceedings are or were pending against Palmigiano. The State has not, contrary to *Griffin*, sought to make evidentiary use of his silence at the disciplinary hearing in any criminal proceeding. Neither has Rhode Island insisted or asked that

Palmigiano waive his Fifth Amendment privilege. He was notified that he was privileged to remain silent if he chose. He was also advised that his silence could be used against him, but a prison inmate in Rhode Island electing to remain silent during his disciplinary hearing, as respondent Palmigiano did here, is not in consequence of his silence automatically found guilty of the infraction with which he has been charged. Under Rhode Island law, disciplinary decisions "must be based on substantial evidence manifested in the record of the disciplinary proceeding." *Morris v. Travisono*, 310 F. Supp. 857, 873 (R.I. 1970). It is thus undisputed that an inmate's silence in and of itself is insufficient to support an adverse decision by the Disciplinary Board. In this respect, this case is very different from the circumstances before the Court in the *Garrity-Lefkowitz* decisions, where refusal to submit to interrogation and to waive the Fifth Amendment privilege, standing alone and without regard to the other evidence, resulted in loss of employment or opportunity to contract with the State. There, failure to respond to interrogation was treated as a final admission of guilt. Here, Palmigiano remained silent at the hearing in the face of evidence that incriminated him; and, as far as this record reveals, his silence was given no more evidentiary value than was warranted by the facts surrounding his case. This does not smack of an invalid attempt by the State to compel testimony without granting immunity or to penalize the exercise of the privilege. The advice given inmates by the decisionmakers is merely a realistic reflection of the evidentiary significance of the choice to remain silent.

Had the State desired Palmigiano's testimony over his Fifth Amendment objection, we can but assume that it would have extended whatever use immunity is required by the Federal Constitution. Had this occurred and had Palmigiano nevertheless refused to answer, it surely would not have violated the Fifth Amendment to draw whatever inference from his silence that the circumstances warranted. Insofar as the privilege is concerned, the situation is little different where the State advises the inmate of his right to silence but also plainly notifies him that his silence will be weighed in the balance.

. . .

The short of it is that permitting an adverse inference to be drawn from an inmate's silence at his disciplinary proceedings is not, on its face, an invalid practice; and there is no basis in the record for invalidating it as here applied to Palmigiano.

IV

In *Wolff v. McDonnell*, we held that "the inmate facing disciplinary proceedings should be allowed to call witnesses and present documentary evidence in his defense when permitting him to do so will not be unduly hazardous to institutional safety or correctional goals." 418 U.S., at 566. We noted that "ordinarily, the right to present evidence is basic to a fair hearing; but the unrestricted right to call witnesses from the prison population carries obvious potential for disruption and for interference with the swift punishment that in individual cases may be essential to carrying out the correctional program of the institution." Ibid. . . .

We were careful to distinguish between this limited right to call witnesses and other due process rights at disciplinary hearings. We noted expressly that, in comparison to the right to call witnesses, "confrontation and cross-examination present greater hazards to institutional interests." Id., at 567. We said:

> "If confrontation and cross-examination of those furnishing evidence against the inmate were to be allowed as a matter of course, as in criminal trials, there would be considerable potential for havoc inside the prison walls. Proceedings would inevitably be longer and tend to unmanageability." Ibid.

We therefore concluded that "the better course at this time, in a period where prison practices are diverse and somewhat experimental, is to leave these matters to the sound discretion of the officials of state prisons." Id., at 569.

Although acknowledging the strictures of *Wolff* with respect to confrontation and cross-examination, the Court of Appeals for the Ninth Circuit, on rehearing in No. 74-1194, went on to require prison authorities to provide reasons in writing to inmates denied the privilege to cross-examine or confront witnesses against them in disciplinary proceedings; absent explanation, failure to set forth reasons related to the prevention of one or more of the four concerns expressly mentioned in *Wolff* would be deemed prima facie abuse of discretion.

This conclusion is inconsistent with *Wolff*. We characterized as "useful," but did not require, written reasons for denying inmates the limited right to call witnesses in their defense. We made no such suggestion with respect to confrontation and cross-examination which, as was there pointed out, stand on a different footing because of their inherent danger and the availability of adequate bases of decisions without them. See 418 U.S., at 567–568. Mandating confrontation and cross-examination, except where prison officials can justify their denial on one or more grounds that appeal to judges, effectively preempts the area that *Wolff* left to the sound discretion of prison officials. We add that on the record before us there is no evidence of the abuse of discretion by the state prison officials.

. . .

We said in *Wolff v. McDonnell*: "As the nature of the prison disciplinary process changes in future years, circumstances may then exist which will require further consideration and reflection of this Court. It is our view, however, that the procedures we have now required in prison disciplinary proceedings represent a reasonable accommodation between the interests of the inmates and the needs of the institution." 418 U.S., at 572. We do not retreat from that view. However, the procedures required by the Courts of Appeals . . . are either inconsistent with the "reasonable accommodation" reached in *Wolff*, or premature on the bases of the records before us. The judgments . . . accordingly are

Reversed.

Conditions of Confinement:
Hutto v. Finney, 437 U.S. 678 (1978)

Mr. Justice STEVENS delivered the opinion of the Court.

After finding that conditions in the Arkansas penal system constituted cruel and unusual punishment, the District Court entered a series of detailed remedial orders.

On appeal to the United States Court of Appeals for the Eighth Circuit, petitioners challenged . . . an order placing a maximum limit of 30 days on confinement in punitive isolation. . . . The Court of Appeals affirmed. . . . We granted certiorari and now affirm.

This litigation began in 1969; it is a sequel to two earlier cases holding that conditions in the Arkansas prison system violated the Eighth and Fourteenth Amendments. Only a brief summary of the facts is necessary to explain the basis for the remedial order.

The routine conditions that the ordinary Arkansas convict had to endure were characterized by the District Court as "a dark and evil world completely alien to the free world." 309 F. Supp., at 381. That characterization was amply supported by the evidence.* The punishments for misconduct not serious enough to result in punitive isolation were cruel,† unsual,‡ and unpredictable.§ It is the discipline known as "punitive isolation" that is most relevant for present purposes.

Confinement in punitive isolation was for an indeterminate period of time. An average of four, and sometimes as many as 10 or 11, prisoners were crowded into windowless 8′ × 10′ cells containing no furniture other than a source of water and a toilet that could only be flushed from outside the cell. At night the prisoners were given mattresses to spread on the floor. Although some prisoners suffered from infectious diseases such as hepatitis and venereal disease, mattresses were removed and

---

* The administrators of Arkansas' prison system evidently tried to operate their prisons at a profit. Cummins Farm, the institution at the center of this litigation, required its 1,000 inmates to work in the fields 10 hours a day, six days a week, using mule-drawn tools and tending crops by hand. The inmates were sometimes required to run to and from the fields, with a guard in an automobile or on horseback driving them on. They worked in all sorts of weather, so long as the temperature was above freezing, sometimes in unsuitably light clothing or without shoes.

The inmates slept together in large, 100-man barracks and some convicts, known as "creepers," would slip from their beds to crawl along the floor, stalking their sleeping enemies. In one 18-month period, there were 17 stabbings, all but one occurring in the barracks. Homosexual rape was so common and uncontrolled that some potential victims dared not sleep; instead they would leave their beds and spend the night clinging to the bars nearest the guards' station.

† Inmates were lashed with a wooden-handled leather strap five feet long and four inches wide. Although it was not official policy to do so, some inmates were apparently whipped for minor offenses until their skin was bloody and bruised.

‡ The "Tucker telephone," a hand-cranked device, was used to administer electrical shocks to various sensitive parts of an inmate's body.

§ Most of the guards were simply inmates who had been issued guns. Although it had 1,000 prisoners, Cummins employed only eight guards who were not themselves convicts. Only two nonconvict guards kept watch over the 1,000 men at night. While the "trusties" maintained an appearance of order, they took a high toll from the other prisoners. Inmates could obtain access to medical treatment only if they bribed the trusty in charge of sick call. As the District Court found, it was "within the power of a trusty guard to murder another inmate with practical impunity," because trusties with weapons were authorized to use deadly force against escapees. "Accidental shootings" also occurred; and one trusty fired his shotgun into a crowded barracks because the inmates would not turn off their TV. Another trusty beat an inmate so badly the victim required partial dentures.

jumbled together each morning, then returned to the cells at random in the evening. Prisoners in isolation received fewer than 1,000 calories a day; their meals consisted primarily of 4-inch squares of "grue," a substance created by mashing meat, potatoes, oleo, syrup, vegetables, eggs, and seasoning into a paste and baking the mixture in a pan.

After finding the conditions of confinement unconstitutional, the District Court did not immediately impose a detailed remedy of its own. Instead, it directed the Department of Correction to "make a substantial start" on improving conditions and to file reports on its progress. *Holt I*, 300 F. Supp., at 833–834. When the Department's progress proved unsatisfactory, a second hearing was held. The District Court found some improvements, but concluded that prison conditions remained unconstitutional. *Holt II*, 309 F. Supp., at 383. Again the court offered prison administrators an opportunity to devise a plan of their own for remedying the constitutional violations, but this time the court issued guidelines, identifying four areas of change that would cure the worst evils: improving conditions in the isolation cells, increasing inmate safety, eliminating the barracks sleeping arrangements, and putting an end to the trusty system. Id., at 385. The Department was ordered to move as rapidly as funds became available. Ibid.

After this order was affirmed on appeal, *Holt v. Sarver*, 442 F.2d 304 (C.A.8 1971), more hearings were held in 1972 and 1973 to review the Department's progress. Finding substantial improvements, the court concluded that continuing supervision was no longer necessary. The court held, however, that its prior decrees would remain in effect and noted that sanctions, as well as an award of costs and attorney's fees, would be imposed if violations occurred. *Holt III*, 363 F. Supp., at 217.

The Court of Appeals reversed the District Court's decision to withdraw its supervisory jurisdiction, *Finney v. Arkansas Board of Correction*, 505 F.2d 194 (C.A.8 1974), and the District Court held a fourth set of hearings. *Finney v. Hutto*, 410 F. Supp. 251 (E.D. Ark. 1976). It found that, in some respects, conditions had seriously deteriorated since 1973, when the court had withdrawn its supervisory jurisdiction. Cummins Farm, which the court had condemned as overcrowded in 1970 because it housed 1,000 inmates, now had a population of about 1,500. Id., at 254–255. The situation in the punitive isolation cells was particularly disturbing. The court concluded that either it had misjudged conditions in these cells in 1973 or conditions had become much worse since then. Id., at 275. There were still twice as many prisoners as beds in some cells. And because inmates in punitive isolation are often violently antisocial, overcrowding led to persecution of the weaker prisoners. The "grue" diet was still in use, and practically all inmates were losing weight on it. The cells had been vandalized to a "very substantial" extent. Id., at 276. Because of their inadequate numbers, guards assigned to the punitive isolation cells frequently resorted to physical violence, using nightsticks and Mace in their efforts to maintain order. Prisoners were sometimes left in isolation for months, their release depending on "their attitudes as appraised by prison personnel." Id., at 275.

The court concluded that the constitutional violations identified earlier had not been cured. It entered an order that placed limits on the number of men that could be confined in one cell, required that each have a bunk, discontinued the "grue" diet, and set 30 days as the maximum isolation sentence. The District Court gave detailed consideration to the matter of fees and expenses, made an express finding that petitioners had acted in bad faith, and awarded counsel "a fee of $20,000.00 to be paid out of [the] Department of Correction funds." Id., at 285. The Court of Appeals affirmed and assessed an additional $2,500 to cover fees and expenses on appeal. 548 F.2d, at 743.

I

The Eighth Amendment's ban on inflicting cruel and unusual punishments, made applicable to the States by the Fourteenth Amendment, "proscribes more than physically barbarous punishments." *Estelle v. Gamble*, 429 U.S. 97. It prohibits penalties that are grossly disproportionate to the offense, *Weems v. United States*, 217 U.S. 349, 367, as well as those that transgress today's "broad and idealistic concepts of dignity, civilized standards, humanity, and decency." *Estelle v. Gamble*. Confinement in a prison or in an isolation cell is a form of punishment subject to scrutiny under Eighth Amendment standards. Petitioners do not challenge this proposition; nor do they disagree with the District Court's original conclusion that Arkansas' prisons, including its punitive isolation cells, constituted cruel and unusual punishment. Rather, petitioners single out that portion of the District Court's most recent order that forbids the Department to sentence inmates to more than 30 days in punitive isolation. Petitioners assume that the District Court held that indeterminate sentences to punitive isolation always constitute cruel and unusual punishments. This assumption misreads the District Court's holding.

Read in its entirety, the District Court's opinion makes it abundantly clear that the length of isolation sentences was not considered in a vacuum. In the court's words, punitive isolation "is not necessarily unconstitutional, but it may be, depending on the duration of the confinement and the conditions thereof." 410 F. Supp., at 275. It is perfectly obvious that every decision to remove a particular inmate from the general prison population for an indeterminate period could not be characterized as cruel and unusual. If new conditions of confinement are not materially different from those affecting other prisoners, a transfer for the duration of a prisoner's sentence might be completely unobjectionable and well within the authority of the prison administrator. Cf. *Meachum v. Fano*, 427 U.S. 215. It is equally plain, however, that the length of confinement cannot be ignored in deciding whether the confinement meets constitutional standards. A filthy, overcrowded cell and a diet of "grue" might be tolerable for a few days and intolerably cruel for weeks or months.

The question before the trial court was whether past constitutional violations had been remedied. The court was entitled to consider the severity of those violations in assessing the constitutionality of conditions in the isolation cells. The court took note of the inmates' diet, the continued overcrowding, the rampant violence, the vandalized cells, and the "lack of professionalism and good judgment on the part of maximum security personnel." 410 F. Supp., at 277 and 278. The length of time each inmate spent in isolation was simply one consideration among many. We find no error in the court's conclusion that, taken as a whole, conditions in the isolation cells continued to violate the prohibition against cruel and unusual punishments.

. . .

The judgment of the Court of Appeals is accordingly affirmed.

Affirmed.

Freedom of Religion:
Cruz v. Beto, 405 U.S. 319 (1972)

PER CURIAM.

The complaint, alleging a cause of action under 42 U.S.C. § 1983, states that Cruz is a Buddhist, who is in a Texas prison. While prisoners who are members of other religious sects are allowed to use the prison chapel, Cruz is not. He shared his Buddhist religious material with other prisoners and, according to the allegations, in retaliation was placed in solitary confinement on a diet of bread and water for two weeks, without access to newspapers, magazines, or other sources of news. He also alleged that he was prohibited from corresponding with his religious advisor in the Buddhist sect. Those in the isolation unit spend 22 hours a day in total idleness.

Again, according to the allegations, Texas encourages inmates to participate in other religious programs; providing at state expense chaplains of the Catholic, Jewish, and Protestant faiths, providing also at state expense copies of the Jewish and Christian Bibles, conducting weekly Sunday school classes and religious services. According to the allegations, points of good merit are given prisoners as a reward for attending orthodox religious services, those points enhancing a prisoner's eligibility for desirable job assignments and early parole consideration. Respondent answered, denying the allegations and moving to dismiss.

The Federal District Court denied relief without a hearing or any findings. . . . The Court of Appeals affirmed.

Federal courts sit not to supervise prisons but to enforce the constitutional rights of all "persons," including prisoners. We are not unmindful that prison officials must be accorded latitude in the administration of prison affairs, and that prisoners necessarily are subject to appropriate rules and regulations. But persons in prison, like other individuals, have the right to petition the Government for redress of grievances which, of course, includes "access of prisoners to the courts for the purpose of presenting their complaints." *Johnson v. Avery*, 393 U.S. 483. . . .

If Cruz was a Buddhist and if he was denied a reasonable opportunity of pursuing his faith comparable to the opportunity afforded fellow prisoners who adhere to conventional religious precepts, then there was palpable discrimination by the State against the Buddhist religion, established 600 B.C., long before the Christian era. The First Amendment, applicable to the States by reason of the Fourteenth Amendment, prohibits government from making a law "prohibiting the free exercise [of religion]." If the allegations of this complaint are assumed to be true, as they must be on the motion to dismiss, Texas has violated the First and Fourteenth Amendments.

The motion for leave to proceed *in forma pauperis* is granted. The petition for certiorari is granted, the judgment is vacated, and the cause remanded for a hearing and appropriate findings.

Vacated and remanded.

Mail Censorship:
Procunier v. Martinez, 416 U.S. 396 (1974)

Mr. Justice POWELL delivered the opinion of the Court.

This case concerns the constitutionality of certain regulations promulgated by appellant Procunier in his capacity as Director of the California Department of Corrections. Appellees brought a class action on behalf of themselves and all other inmates of penal institutions under the Department's jurisdiction to challenge the rules relating to censorship of prisoner mail. . . .

I

First we consider the constitutionality of the Director's rules restricting the personal correspondence of prison inmates. Under these regulations correspondence between inmates of California penal institutions and persons other than licensed attorneys and holders of public office was censored for nonconformity to certain standards. Rule 2401 stated the Department's general premise that personal correspondence by prisoners is "a privilege, not a right. . . ." More detailed regulations implemented the Department's policy. Rule 1201 directed inmates not to write letters in which they "unduly complain" or "magnify grievances." Rule 1205(d) defined as contraband writings "expressing inflammatory political, racial, religious or other views or beliefs. . . ." Finally, Rule 2402(8) provided that inmates "may not send or receive letters that pertain to criminal activity; are lewd, obscene, or defamatory; contain foreign matter, or are otherwise inappropriate."

Prison employees screened both incoming and outgoing personal mail for violations of these regulations. No further criteria were provided to help members of the mailroom staff decide whether a particular letter contravened any prison rule or policy. When a prison employee found a letter objectionable, he could take one or more of the following actions: (1) refuse to mail or deliver the letter and return it to the author; (2) submit a disciplinary report, which could lead to suspension of mail privileges or other sanctions; or (3) place a copy of the letter or a summary of its contents in the prisoner's file, where it might be a factor in determining the inmate's work and housing assignments and in setting a date for parole eligibility.

The District Court held that the regulations relating to prisoner mail authorized censorship of protected expression without adequate justification in violation of the First Amendment and that they were void for vagueness. The court also noted that the regulations failed to provide minimum procedural safeguards against error and arbitrariness in the censorship of inmate correspondence. Consequently, it enjoined their continued enforcement.

. . .

We begin our analysis of the proper standard of review for constitutional challenges to censorship of prisoner mail with a somewhat different premise from that taken by the other federal courts that have considered the question. For the most part, these courts have dealt with challenges to censorship of prisoner mail as involving broad questions of "prisoners' rights." This case is no exception. The District Court stated the issue in general terms as "the applicability of First Amendment rights to prison inmates . . . ," 354 F. Supp., at 1096, and the arguments of the parties reflect the assumption that the resolution of this case requires an assessment of the extent to which prisoners may claim First Amendment freedoms. In our view this inquiry is unnecessary. In determining the proper standard of review for prison restrictions on inmate correspondence, we have no occasion to consider the extent to which an individual's right to free speech survives incarceration, for a narrower basis of decision is at hand. In the case of direct personal correspondence between inmates and those who have a particularized interest in communicating with them, mail censorship implicates more than the right of prisoners.

Communication by letter is not accomplished by the act of writing words on paper. Rather, it is effected only when the letter is read by the addressee. Both parties to the correspondence have an interest in securing that result, and censorship of the communication between them necessarily impinges on the interest of each. Whatever the status of a prisoner's claim to uncensored correspondence with an outsider, it is plain that the latter's interest is grounded in the First Amendment's guarantee of freedom of speech. And this does not depend on whether the nonprisoner correspondent is the author or intended recipient of a particular letter, for the addressee as well as the sender of direct personal correspondence derives from the First and Fourteenth Amendments a protection against unjustified governmental interference with the intended communication. *Lamont v. Postmaster General*, 381 U.S. 301 (1965). We do not deal here with difficult questions of the so-called "right to hear" and third-party standing but with a particular means of communication in which the interests of both parties are inextricably meshed. The wife of a prison inmate who is not permitted to read all that her husband wanted to say to her has suffered an abridgement of her interest in communicating with him as plain as that which results from censorship of her letter to him. In either event, censorship of prisoner mail works a consequential restriction on the First and Fourteenth Amendments rights of those who are not prisoners.

Accordingly, we reject any attempt to justify censorship of inmate correspondence merely by reference to certain assumptions about the legal status of prisoners. Into this category of argument falls appellants' contention that "an inmate's rights with reference to social correspondence are something fundamentally different than those enjoyed by his free brother." Brief for Appellants 19. This line of argument and the undemanding standard of review it is intended to support fail to recognize that the First Amendment liberties of free citizens are implicated in censorship of prisoner mail. . . .

The case at hand arises in the context of prisons. One of the primary functions of government is the preservation of societal order through enforcement of the criminal law, and the maintenance of penal institutions is an essential part of that task. The identifiable governmental interests at stake in this task are the preservation of internal order and discipline, the maintenance of institutional security against escape or unauthorized entry, and the rehabilitation of the prisoners. While the weight of professional opinion seems to be that inmate freedom to correspond with outsiders advances rather than retards the goal of rehabilitation, the legitimate governmental interest in the order and security of penal institutions justifies the imposition of certain restraints on inmate correspondence. Perhaps the most obvious example of justifiable censorship of prisoner mail would be refusal to send or deliver letters concerning escape plans or containing other information concerning proposed criminal activity, whether within or without the prison. Similarly, prison officials may properly refuse to transmit encoded messages. Other less obvious possibilities come to mind, but it is not our purpose to survey the range of circumstances in which particular restrictions on prisoner mail might be warranted by the legitimate demands of prison administration as they exist from time to time in the various kinds of penal institutions found in this country. Our task is to determine the proper standard for deciding whether a particular regulation or practice relating to inmate correspondence constitutes an impermissible restraint of First Amendment liberties.

Applying the teachings of our prior decisions to the instant context, we hold that censorship of prisoner mail is justified if the following criteria are met. First, the regulation or practice in question must further an important or substantial governmental interest unrelated to the suppression of expression. Prison officials may not censor inmate correspondence simply to eliminate unflattering or unwelcome opinions or factually inaccurate statements. Rather, they must show that a regulation authorizing mail censorship furthers one or more of the substantial governmental interests of security, order, and rehabilitation. Second, the limitation of First Amendment freedoms must be no greater than is necessary or essential to the protection of the particular governmental interest involved. Thus a restriction on inmate correspondence that furthers an important or substantial interest of penal administration will nevertheless be invalid if its sweep is unnecessarily broad. This does not mean, of course, that prison administrators may be required to show with certainty that adverse consequences would flow from the failure to censor a particular letter. Some latitude in anticipating the probable consequences of allowing certain speech in a prison environment is essential to the proper discharge of an administrator's duty. But any regulation or practice that restricts inmate correspondence must be generally necessary to protect one or more of the legitimate governmental interests identified above.

. . . On the basis of this standard, we affirm the judgment of the District Court. The regulations invalidated by that court authorized, inter alia, censorship of statements that "unduly complain" or "magnify grievances," expression of "inflammatory political, racial, religious or other views," and matter deemed "defamatory" or "otherwise inappropriate." These regulations fairly invited prison officials and employees to apply their own personal prejudices and opinions as standards for prisoner mail censorship. Not surprisingly, some prison officials used the extraordinary latitude for discretion authorized by the regulations to suppress unwelcome criticism. For example, at one institution under the Department's jurisdiction, the checklist used by the mailroom staff authorized rejection of letters "criticizing policy, rules or officials," and the mailroom sergeant stated in a deposition that he would reject as "defamatory" letters "belittling staff or our judicial system or anything connected with Department of Corrections." Correspondence was also censored for "disrespectful comments," "derogatory remarks," and the like.

Appellants have failed to show that these broad restrictions on prisoner mail were in any way necessary to the furtherance of a new governmental interest unrelated to the suppression of expression. Indeed, the heart of appellants' position is not that the regulations are justified by a legitimate governmental interest but that they do not need to be. This misconception is not only stated affirmatively; it also underlies appellants' discussion of the particular regulations under attack. . . .

We also agree with the District Court that the decision to censor or withhold delivery of a particular letter must be accompanied by minimum procedural safeguards. The interest of prisoners and their correspondents in uncensored communication by letter, grounded as it is in the First Amendment, is plainly a "liberty" interest within the meaning of the Fourteenth Amendment even though qualified of necessity by the circumstance of imprisonment. As such, it is protected from arbitrary governmental invasion. See *Board of Regents v. Roth*, 408 U.S. 564 (1972). The District Court required that an inmate be notified of the rejection of a letter written by or addressed to him, that the author of that letter be given a reasonable opportunity to protest that decision, and that complaints be referred to a prison official other than the person who originally disapproved the correspondence. These requirements do not appear to be unduly burdensome, nor do appellants so contend. Accordingly, we affirm the judgment of the District Court with respect to the Department's regulations relating to prisoner mail.

Affirmed.

Access to the Press:
Pell v. Procunier, *417 U.S. 817 (1974)*

Mr. Justice STEWART delivered the opinion of the Court.

. . . The plaintiffs in the District Court were four California prison inmates— Booker T. Hillery, Jr., John Larry Spain, Bobby Bly, and Michael Shane Guile. . . . The defendants were Raymond K. Procunier, Director of the California Department of Corrections, and several subordinate officers in that department. The plaintiffs brought the suit to challenge the constitutionality, under the First and Fourteenth Amendments, of § 415.071 of the California Department of Corrections Manual, which provides that "press and other media interviews with specific individual inmates will not be permitted." . . .

The facts are undisputed. Pell, Segal, and Jacobs [three professional journalists] each requested permission from the appropriate corrections officials to interview inmates Spain, Bly, and Guile, respectively. In addition, the editors of a certain periodical requested permission to visit inmate Hillery to discuss the possibility of their publishing certain of his writings and to interview him concerning conditions at the prison. Pursuant to § 415.071, these requests were all denied. The plaintiffs thereupon sued to enjoin the continued enforcement of this regulation. The inmate plaintiffs contended that § 415.071 violates their rights of free speech under the First and Fourteenth Amendments. Similarly, the media plaintiffs asserted that the limitation that this regulation places on their newsgathering activity unconstitutionally infringes the freedom of the press guaranteed by the First and Fourteenth Amendments.

. . .

We start with the familiar proposition that "lawful incarceration brings about the necessary withdrawal or limitation of many privileges and rights, a retraction justified by the considerations underlying our penal system." *Price v. Johnston*, 334 U.S. 266, 285 (1948). In the First Amendment context a corollary of this principle is that a prison inmate retains those First Amendment rights that are not inconsistent with his status as a prisoner or with the legitimate penological objectives of the corrections system. Thus, challenges to prison restrictions that are asserted to inhibit First Amendment interests must be analyzed in terms of the legitimate policies and goals of the corrections system, to whose custody and care the prisoner has been committed in accordance with due process of law.

An important function of the corrections system is the deterrence of crime. The premise is that by confining criminal offenders in a facility where they are isolated from the rest of society, a condition that most people presumably find undesirable, they and others will be deterred from committing additional criminal offenses. This isolation, of course, also serves a protective function by quarantining criminal offenders for a given period of time while, it is hoped, the rehabilitative processes of the corrections system work to correct the offender's demonstrated criminal proclivity. Thus, since most offenders will eventually return to society, another paramount objective of the corrections system is the rehabilitation of those committed to its custody. Finally, central to all other correction goals is the institutional consideration of internal security within the corrections facilities themselves. It is in the light of these legitimate penal objectives that a court must assess challenges to prison regulations based on asserted constitutional rights of prisoners.

The regulation challenged here clearly restricts one manner of communication between prison inmates and members of the general public beyond the prison walls. But this is merely to state the problem, not to resolve it. For the same could be said of a refusal by corrections authorities to permit an inmate temporarily to leave the prison in order to communicate with persons outside. Yet no one could sensibly contend that the Constitution requires the authorities to give even individualized consideration to such requests. In order properly to evaluate the constitutionality of § 415.071, we think that the regulation cannot be considered in isolation but must be viewed in the light of the alternative means of communication permitted under the regulations with persons outside the prison. . . .

One such alternative available to California prison inmates is communication by mail. Although prison regulations, until recently, called for the censorship of statements, inter alia, that "unduly complain" or "magnify grievances," that express "inflammatory political, racial, religious or other views," or that were deemed "defamatory" or "otherwise inappropriate," we recently held that "the Department's regulations authorized censorship of prisoner mail far broader than any legitimate interest of penal administration demands," and accordingly affirmed a district court judgment invalidating the regulations. *Procunier v. Martinez*, 416 U.S. 396, 416 (1974). In addition, we held that "the interests of prisoners and their correspondents in uncensored communication by letter, grounded as it is in the First Amendment, is plainly a 'liberty' interest within the meaning of the Fourteenth Amendment even though qualified of necessity by the circumstance of imprisonment." Accordingly, we concluded that any "decision to censor or withhold delivery of a particular letter must be accompanied by minimal procedural safeguards." Id., at 417, 418. Thus, it is clear that the medium of written correspondence affords inmates an open and substantially unimpeded channel for communication with persons outside the prison, including representatives of the news media.

Moreover, the visitation policy of the California Corrections Department does not seal the inmate off from personal contact with those outside the prison. Inmates are permitted to receive limited visits from members of their families, the clergy, their attorneys, and friends of prior acquaintance. The selection of these categories of visitors is based on the Director's professional judgment that such visits will aid in the rehabilitation of the inmate while not compromising the other legitimate objectives of the corrections system. This is not a case in which the selection is based on the anticipated content of the communication between the inmate and the prospective visitor. If a member of the press fell within any of these categories, there is no suggestion that he would not be permitted to visit with the inmate. More importantly, however, inmates have an unrestricted opportunity to communicate with the press or any other member of the public through their families, friends, clergy, or attorneys who are permitted to visit them at the prison. Thus, this provides another alternative avenue of communication between prison inmates and persons outside the prison.

We would find the availability of such alternatives unimpressive if they were submitted as justification for governmental restriction of personal communication among members of the general public. We have recognized, however, that "the relationship of state prisoners and the state officers who supervise their confinement is far more intimate than that of a State and a private citizen," and that the "internal problems of state prisons involve issues . . . peculiarly within state authority and expertise." *Preiser v. Rodriguez,* 411 U.S. 475, 492 (1973).

. . . When . . . the question involves the entry of people into the prisons for face-to-face communication with inmates, it is obvious that institutional considerations, such as security and related administrative problems, as well as the accepted and legitimate policy objectives of the corrections system itself, require that some limitation be placed on such visitations. So long as reasonable and effective means of communication remain open and no discrimination in terms of content is involved, we believe that, in drawing such lines, "prison officials must be accorded latitude." *Cruz v. Beto,* 405 U.S., at 321.

. . . The "normal activity" to which a prison is committed—the involuntary confinement and isolation of large numbers of people, some of whom have demonstrated a capacity for violence—necessarily requires that considerable attention be devoted to the maintenance of security. Although they would not permit prison officials to prohibit all expression or communication by prison inmates, security considerations are sufficiently paramount in the administration of the prison to justify the imposition of some restrictions on the entry of outsiders into the prison for face-to-face contact with inmates.

In this case the restriction takes the form of limiting visitations to individuals who have either a personal or professional relationship to the inmate—family, friends of prior acquaintance, legal counsel, and clergy. In the judgment of the state corrections officials, this visitation policy will permit inmates to have personal contact with those persons who will aid in their rehabilitation, while keeping visitations at a manageable level that will not compromise institutional security. Such considerations are peculiarly within the province and professional expertise of corrections officials, and, in the absence of substantial evidence in the record to indicate that the officials have exaggerated their response to these considerations, courts should ordinarily defer to their expert judgment in such matters. Courts cannot, of course, abdicate their constitutional responsibility to delineate and protect fundamental liberties. But when the issue involves a regulation limiting one of several means of communication by an inmate, the institutional objectives furthered by that regulation and the measure of judicial deference owed to corrections officials in their attempt to serve those interests are relevant in gauging the validity of the regulation.

Accordingly, in light of the alternative channels of communication that are open to prison inmates, we cannot say on the record in this case that this restriction on one manner in which prisoners can communicate with persons outside of prison is unconstitutional. So long as this restriction operates in a neutral fashion, without regard to the content of the expression, it falls within the "appropriate rules and regulations" to which "prisoners necessarily are subject," *Cruz v. Beto,* supra, 405 U.S., at 321, and does not abridge any First Amendment freedoms retained by prison inmates.

II

. . .

For the reasons stated, we reverse the District Court's judgment that § 415.071 infringes the freedom of speech of the prison inmates and affirm its judgment that that regulation does not abridge the constitutional right of a free press. Accordingly, the judgment is vacated, and the cases are remanded to the District Court for further proceedings consistent with this opinion.

It is so ordered.

Judgment vacated and case remanded.

The Right to Organize:
Jones v. North Carolina Prisoners' Labor Union, Inc.,
_____ U.S. _____ (1979)

Mr. Justice REHNQUIST delivered the opinion of the Court.

Pursuant to regulations promulgated by the North Carolina Department of Correction, appellants prohibited inmates from soliciting other inmates to join appellee, the North Carolina Prisoners' Labor Union, Inc. (the Union), barred all meetings of the Union, and refused to deliver packets of Union publications that had been mailed in bulk to several inmates for redistribution among other prisoners. The Union instituted this action, based on 42 U.S.C. § 1983, to challenge these policies. It alleged that appellants' efforts to prevent the operation of a prisoners' union violated the First and Fourteenth Amendment rights of it and its members and that the refusal to grant the Union those privileges accorded several other organizations operating within the prison system deprived the Union of equal protection of the laws. A three-judge court was convened. After a hearing, the court found merit in the Union's free speech, association, and equal protection arguments, and enjoined appellants from preventing inmates from soliciting other prisoners to join the Union and from "refus[ing] receipt of the Union's publications on the ground that they are calculated to encourage membership in the organization or solicit joining." The court also held that the Union "shall be accorded the privilege of holding meetings under such limitations and control as are neutrally applied to all inmate organizations. . . ." We noted probable jurisdiction to consider whether the First and Fourteenth Amendments extend prisoner labor unions such protection. We have denied that they do not, and we accordingly reverse the judgment of the District Court.

I

Appellee, an organization self-denominated as a Prisoners' Labor Union, was incorporated in late 1974, with a stated goal of "the promotion of charitable labor union purposes" and the formation of a "prisoners' labor union at every prison and jail in North Carolina to seek through collective bargaining . . . to improve . . . working . . . conditions. . . ." It also proposed to work towards the alteration or elimination of practices and policies of the Department of Correction which it did not approve of, and to serve as a vehicle for the presentation of and resolution of inmate grievances. By early 1975, the Union had attracted some 2,000 inmate "members" in 40 different prison units throughout North Carolina. The State of North Carolina, unhappy with these developments, set out to prevent inmates from forming or operating a "union." While the State tolerated individual "membership," or belief, in the Union, it sought to prohibit inmate solicitation of other inmates, meetings between members of the Union, and bulk mailings concerning the Union from outside sources. Pursuant to a regulation promulgated by the Department of Correction on March 26, 1975, such solicitation and group activity was proscribed. . . .

II

A

The District Court, we believe, got off on the wrong foot in this case by not giving appropriate deference to the decisions of prison administrators and appropriate recognition to the peculiar and restrictive circumstances of penal confinement. While litigation by prison inmates concerning conditions of confinement, challenged other than under the Eighth Amendment, is of recent vintage, this Court has long recognized that "lawful incarceration brings about the necessary withdrawal or limitation of many privileges and rights, a retraction justified by the considerations underlying our penal system." *Price v. Johnston*, 334 U.S. 266, 285 (1948). The fact of confinement and the needs of the penal institution impose limitations on constitutional rights, including those derived from the First Amendment, which are implicit in incarceration. . . . Perhaps the most obvious of the First Amendment rights that are necessarily curtailed by confinement are those associational rights that the First Amendment protects outside of prison walls. The concept of incarceration itself entails a restriction on the freedom of inmates to associate with those outside of the penal institution. Equally as obviously, the inmate's "status as a prisoner" and the operational realities of a prison dictate restrictions on the associational rights among inmates. . . .

B

State correctional officials uniformly testified that the concept of a prisoners' labor union was itself fraught with potential dangers, whether or not such a union intended, illegally, to press for collective-bargaining recognition. Appellant Ralph Edwards, the Commissioner of the Department of Correction, stated in his affidavit that

> "The creation of an inmate union will naturally result in increasing the existing friction between inmates and prison personnel. It can also create friction between union inmates and non-union inmates." . . .

The District Court did not reject these beliefs as fanciful or erroneous. It, instead, noted that they were held "sincerely," and were arguably correct. Without a showing that these beliefs were unreasonable, it was error for the District Court to conclude that appellants needed to show more. In particular, the burden was not on appellants to show affirmatively that the Union would be "detrimental to proper penological objectives" or would constitute a "present danger to security and order." . . . The necessary and correct result of our deference to the informed discretion of prison administrators permits them, and not the courts, to make the difficult judgments concerning institutional operations in situations such as this.

The District Court, however, gave particular emphasis to what it viewed as appellants' tolerance of membership by inmates in the Union as undermining appellants' position. . . .

But appellants never acquiesced in, or permitted, group activity of the Union in the nature of a functioning organization of the inmates within the prison, nor did the District Court find that they had. It is clearly not irrational to conclude that individuals may believe what they want, but that concerted group activity, or solicitation therefor, would pose additional and unwarranted problems and frictions in the operation of the State's penal institutions. The ban on inmate solicitation and group meetings, therefore, was rationally related to the reasonable, indeed to the central, objectives of prison administration.

C

The invocation of the First Amendment, whether the asserted rights are speech or associational, does not change this analysis. In a prison context, an inmate does not retain those First Amendment rights that are "inconsistent with his status as a prisoner or with the legitimate penological objectives of the corrections system." *Pell v. Procunier*, 417 U.S., at 822. Prisons, it is obvious, differ in numerous respects from free society. They, to begin with, are populated, involuntarily, by people who have been found to have violated one or more of the criminal laws established by society for its orderly governance. In seeking a "mutual accommodation between institutional needs and objectives [of prisons] and the provisions of the Constitution that are of general application," *Wolff v. McDonnell*, 418 U.S., at 556, this Court has repeatedly recognized the need for major restrictions on a prisoner's rights. These restrictions have applied as well where First Amendment values were implicated.

An examination of the potential restrictions on speech or association that have been imposed by the regulations under challenge, demonstrate that the restrictions imposed are reasonable, and are consistent with the inmates' status as prisoners and with the legitimate operational considerations of the institution. To begin with, First Amendment speech rights are barely implicated in this case. Mail rights are not themselves implicated; the only question respecting the mail is that of *bulk* mailings. The advantages of bulk mailings to inmates by the Union are those of cheaper rates and convenience. . . .

Nor does the prohibition on inmate-to-inmate solicitation of membership trench untowardly on the inmates' First Amendment speech rights. Solicitation of membership itself involves a good deal more than the simple expression of individual views as to the advantages or disadvantages of a Union or its views; it is an invitation to collectively engage in a legitimately prohibited activity. If the prison officials are otherwise entitled to control organized union activity within the prison walls, the prohibition on solicitation for such activity is not then made impermissible on account of First Amendment considerations, for such a prohibition is then not only reasonable but necessary. *Pell v. Procunier,* 417 U.S., at 822.

First Amendment associational rights, while perhaps more directly implicated by the regulatory prohibitions, likewise must give way to the reasonable considerations of penal management. As already noted, numerous associational rights are necessarily curtailed by the realities of confinement. They may be curtailed whenever the institution's officials, in the exercise of their informed discretion, reasonably conclude that such associations, whether through group meetings or otherwise, possess the likelihood of disruption to prison order or stability, or otherwise interfere with the legitimate penological objectives of the prison environment. As we noted in *Pell v. Procunier,* 417 U.S., "central to all other correctional goals is the institutional consideration of internal security within the correctional facilities themselves."

Appellant prison officials concluded that the presence, perhaps even the objectives, of a prisoners' labor union would be detrimental to order and security in the prisons. It is enough to say that they have not been conclusively shown to be wrong in this view. The interest in preserving order and authority in the prisons is self-evident. Prison life, and relations between the inmates themselves and between the inmates and prison officials or staff, contain the ever-present potential for violent confrontation and conflagration. *Wolff v. McDonnell,* 418 U.S., at 561–562. Responsible prison officials must be permitted to take reasonable steps to forestall such a threat, and they must be permitted to act before the time when they can compile a dossier on the eve of a riot. The case of a prisoners' union, where the focus is on the presentation of grievances to, and encouragement of adversary relations with, institution officials surely would rank high on anyone's list of potential trouble spots. If the appellants' views as to the possible detrimental effects of the organizational activities of the Union are reasonable, as we conclude they are, then the regulations are drafted no more broadly than they need to be to meet the perceived threat—which stems directly from group meetings and group organizational activities of the Union. When weighed against the First Amendment rights asserted, these institutional reasons are sufficiently weighty to prevail.

. . .

Reversed.

Mr. Justice MARSHALL, with whom Mr. Justice BRENNAN joins, dissenting.

There was a time, not so very long ago, when prisoners were regarded as "slave[s] of the State," having "not only forfeited [their] liberty, but all [their] personal rights . . ." *Ruffin v. Commonwealth,* 62 Va. 790, 792 (1871). In recent years, however, the courts increasingly have rejected this view, and with it the corollary which holds that courts should keep their "hands off" penal institutions. Today, however, the Court, in apparent fear of a prison reform organization that has the temerity to call itself a "union," takes a giant step backwards towards that discredited conception of prisoners' rights and the role of the courts. I decline to join in what I hope will prove to be a temporary retreat.

. . .

The reason courts cannot blindly defer to the judgment of prison administrators—or any other officials for that matter—is easily understood. Because the prison administrator's business is to maintain order, "there inheres the danger that he may well be less responsive than a court—part of an independent branch of government—to the constitutionally protected interests in free expression." *Freedman v. Maryland*, 380 U.S. 51, 57–58 (1965). A warden seldom will find himself subject to public criticism or dismissal because he needlessly repressed free speech; indeed, neither the public nor the warden will have any way of knowing when repression was unnecessary. But a warden's job can be jeopardized and public criticism is sure to come should disorder occur. Consequently, prison officials inevitably will err on the side of too little freedom. . . .

I do not mean to suggest that the views of correctional officials should be cavalierly disregarded by courts called upon to adjudicate constitutional claims of prisoners. Far from it. . . . My point is simply that the ultimate responsibility for evaluating the prison officials' testimony, as well as any other expert testimony, must rest with the courts, which are required to read an independent judgment concerning the constitutionality of any restriction on expressive activity.

. . .

II

. . . Appellants' fears that the leaders of an operating Union "would be in a position to misuse their influence" and that the Union itself could engage in disruptive, concerted activities or increase tension within the prisons are not entirely fanciful. It is important to note, however, that appellee's two expert witnesses, both correctional officers who had dealt with inmate reform organizations, testified that such groups actually play a constructive role in their prisons. The weight of professional opinion seems to favor recognizing such groups. Moreover, the risks appellant fears are inherent in any inmate organization, no matter how innocuous its stated goals; indeed, even without any organizations some inmates inevitably will become leaders capable of "misus[ing] their influence," and some concerted activity can still occur.

But even if the risks posed by the Union were unique to it, and even if appellants' fear of the Union were more widely shared by other professionals, the prohibition on Union meetings still could not survive constitutional attack. The central lesson of over a half-century of First Amendment adjudication is that freedom is sometimes a hazardous enterprise, and that the Constitution requires the State to bear certain risks to preserve our liberty. As the ABA Joint Committee put it, "the doubts and risks raised by creating a humane and open prison must be accepted as a cost of our society; democracy is self-definitionally a risk taking form of government." To my mind, therefore, the fact that appellants have not acted wholly irrationally in banning union meetings is not dispositive. Rather, I believe that where, as here, meetings would not pose an immediate and substantial threat to the security or rehabilitative functions of the prisons, the First Amendment guarantees Union members the right to associate freely, and the Fourteenth Amendment guarantees them the right to be treated as favorably as members of other inmate organizations. The State can surely regulate the time, place, and manner of the meetings, and perhaps can monitor them to assure that disruptions are not planned, but the State cannot outlaw such assemblies altogether.

III

. . . I . . . believe that the tension between today's decision and our prior cases ultimately will be resolved not by the demise of the earlier cases, but by the recognition that the decision today is an aberration, a manifestation of the extent to which the very phrase "prisoner union" is threatening to those holding traditional conceptions of the nature of penal institutions.

I respectfully dissent.

Epilogue
The
Supreme Court
and
Criminal Justice

One of the truly amazing features of the American system of criminal procedure has been the durability of its principles and standards, many of which are now well over three hundred years old. Standards such as double jeopardy, trial by jury, no compulsory self-incrimination, and reasonable doubt are not the products of some golden age, but rather the practical maxims of men and women who came to realize that unchecked power was at least as dangerous to personal freedom as was unchecked crime.

Our system of criminal justice rests on an old and bedrock conviction that unchecked power will be abused; that is, the liberties of a free people will suffer at the hands of officers of the state if we do not in some measure tie the hands of those who work to make us safe from crime. This conviction does not rest on any assumption that the officers of the state will act out of malice; indeed, they are far more likely to act in pursuit of an honest dedication to what they consider to be the best interests of the community. Rather the conviction rests on a set of assumptions about the frailty of honest people and the temptations of power. For all of the progress of humanity over the past three centuries, these assumptions still appear prudent.

The task, then, for the legislatures and courts, especially the Supreme Court, is to strike an appropriate balance between the prudence of constitutional restraints and the needs of government. Constitutions are instruments of government, and the goals of governing cannot be lost to fears of power. To borrow from Alexander Hamilton, we must be far gone in utopian speculation to believe that our liberties can be made secure only in the restraint of power rather than in its exercise. The difficult and often delicate task is ensuring that neither the constitutional grants of power nor the Bill of Rights becomes a suicide pact.

To that end, we have allowed the weakest branch of government to strike the balance between power and procedural restraints, and the judiciary is sometimes not equal to the task. With neither the power of the purse nor the power of the sword, it must persuade by words, hoping that the words reach into the far-flung recesses of the loosely joined federal system.

The well-crafted judicial opinion cannot hawk a naively libertine view nor sell the tough-minded views of the law enforcement establishment. Americans have rarely accepted judicial fiats. Instead, the attentive public expects that judicial decisions involving basic constitutional arrangements between individuals and the state will rest on convincing and compelling rationales. In the long run, courts, especially the Supreme Court, are judged by the results of their decisions. In the short run, however, courts are judged by the merits of the rationale they offer in support of a position. Given the nature of judicial power, the decisions of appellate bodies are intellectual exercises, demanding evidence of reasoned elaboration and attention to traditional legal criteria, including, of course, the principles of the Bill of Rights.

We could argue that this standard of intellectual excellence is so vague and subjective that few, if any, judicial opinions in fact satisfy its unknown contours. Still, the measurement of quality is often a subjective process, and this subjectivity only lends caution to the enterprise.

The Supreme Court is not an ordinary appellate body. Not only is it the highest judicial tribunal in the United States, but it also has virtually complete discretion over its docket. The Court's lofty constitutional position in our system of government, coupled with the freedom to control its own docket, creates certain expectations. When the Court takes jurisdiction in a criminal procedure case, we presume that the case raises an important constitutional question about which there is significant, if not substantial, division of opinion.[1] In turn, we expect that the Court's resolution of the question will be at once clear and compelling.

If Supreme Court decisions are to have significance in guiding criminal justice, then the rules must be clear to the legal community—to judges, lawyers, prosecutors, and police. But clarity is possible only within the constraints imposed by the Court's traditional setting. For example, judicial rule making is constrained by the common-law tradition that limits rules to the facts of an instant case. The Court is also constrained by the potential political implications of a given rule. Thus, in *Argersinger,* a bright-line rule that indigent defendants are entitled to counsel in all criminal cases was avoided. In part, the reason for this was the Court's recognition that a clear ruling in *Argersinger* would extend the right to counsel to a host of minor criminal areas (traffic cases, for example), creating considerable resource problems for other agencies of the government and consequently propelling the Court into an arena where legislatures and executives have far greater competence.

In other areas, we cannot excuse the Court's lack of clarity. Its most glaring failure is in the area of search and seizure. Constitutional rules as they relate to probable cause have moved back and forth like a pendulum over the past quarter of a century, leaving the police with no reasonably defined parameters within which to operate. Admittedly, probable cause is not a standard that can be or should be reduced to some positive state of clarity; because the rule deals in probabilities rather than legal certainties, a degree of ambiguity necessarily obtains. Still, the Court has failed to provide reasonably clear indications of the quantity and quality of information necessary to establish prior probable cause. Furthermore, the problem has been compounded by the Courts' decision to divorce street encounters from the normal constitutional requirements.

These observations are not intended to apply across the board. There are areas where the Court has spoken clearly, among them its outstanding performance regarding the death penalty. Although the Court began with only a per curiam decision,[2] one that clarified virtually nothing, it soon handed down a series of rules that has brought a measure of clarity to a troubled area. The performance of the Court in the death penalty cases is all the more commendable because of the political thicket that has surrounded the use of the penalty in recent years. Although the justices may have been unwilling to risk the certain wrath of the more vocal and politically visible supporters of capital punishment, and although this may have conditioned their responses somewhat, nonetheless, the cases illustrate the independence of the judicial power. The mandates of the Court in the death penalty cases surely provided less independent legislators with a politically safe excuse to work for reform in the area.

The second measure of judicial quality is the rationales the Court can marshall in support of its decisions. Unfortunately, in recent years, insufficient arguments abound. There is probably no more striking example of this than the Court's opinions in the cases involving the size of the trial jury and the unanimity requirement. We may agree that simply because the twelve-person jury and the unanimity rule date back to the Middle Ages is not a compelling reason for their continuing today. Still, a decent regard for the wisdom of the past requires that new departures offer more convincing rationales than those of economy and efficiency. There is something shocking, even arrogant, when rules that heretofore were assumed to have constitutional significance can be toppled by the demands of economy and efficiency in the administration of justice.

Of course, we should not generalize solely on the basis of the jury cases. However, to the jury cases we can add numerous other opinions that offer one-dimensional arguments. The *Kirby* decision (1972), limiting the right to pretrial counsel, the several decisions that have restricted the *Miranda* rule, and the plethora of opinions that have expanded the police power over the search of automobiles are all striking examples of the failure of the Court to offer convincing evidence that it has wrestled with all sides of these issues.

Certainly, the changes in Supreme Court personnel that came after the presidential election in 1968 have resulted in a marked change in the direction of the Court's decisions. The Burger Court has demonstrated sympathy for the demands of criminal law enforcement not only by the direction of its decisions, but additionally by its inattention to a host of problems that must be addressed. The Court has virtually abandoned the problems of compulsory process; similarly, it has done little to clarify the problems surrounding the hearsay rule and the cross-examination of witnesses. Nor has the Court been willing to grapple with double-jeopardy problems that stem from legislative decisions to offer prosecutors increasing freedom to prosecute separately the elements of the same criminal offense. To this list of unresolved problems, we could add that of standards for appellate review of sentencing and the continuing inequalities that confront the poor in such areas as bail and ancillary services.

We have come to accept, indeed expect, judicial leadership in the area of criminal procedure, but it would be a mistake to conclude that the responsibility for reform is solely a judicial task. Some areas of criminal procedure are particularly suited to legislative review, as are bail reform and sentencing procedures. It is unrealistic to expect the weakest branch of government to address itself to a broad range of politically sensitive issues. And too, reversing convictions and imposing exclusionary rules are often the least viable methods for resolving problems in criminal procedure. The fact remains, however, that law enforcement agencies are not particularly anxious to obtain legislative authorization and oversight of their internal practices. It seems equally apparent that legislatures are generally indifferent to reforms of criminal procedure, especially at the pretrial stage, and these reforms do not have a political constituency, at least one with clout.

The consequence, then, has been that the judiciary, particularly the Supreme Court, has assumed leadership by default in the area of criminal procedure. What the Court sometimes fails to recognize is that its leadership is often the only oversight that our system of government provides. Given the low visibility of criminal law enforcement, of prosecutorial decisions, and of most criminal trials, a constitutional state must guarantee some measure of review and control over the imposition of the criminal sanction. In consequence, the Supreme Court can ill afford to rubber-stamp assumptions of unreviewable power by the police, prosecutors, and trial judges. Prudence dictates today, as it did at the time of the adoption of the Bill of Rights, the need for reasonable checks and restraints on the exercise of criminal power.

Again, we do not suggest that the Supreme Court is the most effective restraint on this power, but rather that somewhere in our system of government we must keep alive the principles of the Bill of Rights. Not only is the Supreme Court competent to discharge this responsibility, but, further, it can be argued that it is uniquely situated to do so. The Court has long assumed a special role as interpreter of the Constitution, and over the past quarter of a century it has adopted an even more specific role as guardian of the Bill of Rights. Of course, there are pitfalls to the assumption of such roles for the judiciary, not the least of which is that it may offend majoritarian principles of democratic theory. But American government has not been constructed on the basis of pure majoritarian theory: American government, at its inception and throughout its history, has often found it necessary to adopt institutional devices that have been found in practice to be at once workable and consonant with the broader goals of individual freedom.

The special role of the Supreme Court as guardian of the Bill of Rights is politically workable. The judiciary's independence means that it is free of many of the normal political constraints imposed on the executive and legislative branches. The Supreme Court is generally more free to adopt positions supportive of the procedural rights of criminal defendants than are the executive and legislative branches. These positions are often unpopular, but the Court is not immediately responsible, at least in the electoral sense, to the bar of public opinion. In consequence, the Court has the unique opportunity to provide a degree of support for procedural justice that the other branches of our government cannot and do not provide. The role of the Court, then, is not simply to legitimate the practices of the police, prosecutors, and trial judges, as it so often does in other areas. No agency in our government operates with greater freedom, with more discretion, with less visibility, and with so little oversight as do the police departments, prosecutors, and trial judges. The special role of the Supreme Court must be prudential. Of course, this does not mean that the Court is free to adopt simple minded prodefendant stances. But it does mean that the Supreme Court has a special obligation to examine cases in criminal procedure critically to ensure that the principles of the Bill of Rights retain their vitality.

NOTES

1. Excluding, of course, those federal cases that involve only statutory questions or questions arising under the Federal Rules of Criminal Procedures.

2. *Furman v. Georgia*, 408 U.S. 238 (1972).

The Constitution of the United States of America

We, the People of the United States, in order to form a more perfect union, establish justice, insure domestic tranquility, provide for the common defence, promote the general welfare, and secure the blessings of liberty to ourselves and our posterity, do ordain and establish this Constitution for the United States of America.

ARTICLE I

Sect. 1. All legislative powers herein granted shall be vested in a Congress of the United States, which shall consist of a Senate and House of Representatives.

Sect. 2. The House of Representatives shall be composed of members chosen every second year by the people of the several states, and the electors in each state

The *Constitution* is reprinted in the typographic style of the final draft printed by (John) Dunlap & Claypoole at Philadelphia for the Federal Convention of 1787 on 15 September 1787. The original text was printed in small Caslon italic and the old style "f" has been changed to "s." This text is reprinted from U.S. Congress, House, 94th Cong., 2d sess., H. Doc. 94–497, 1976.

shall have the qualifications requisite for electors of the most numerous branch of the state legislature.

No person shall be a representative who shall not have attained to the age of twenty-five years, and been seven years a citizen of the United States, and who shall not, when elected, be an inhabitant of that state in which he shall be chosen.

*[Representatives and direct taxes shall be apportioned among the several states which may be included within this Union, according to their respective numbers, which shall be determined by adding to the whole number of free persons, including those bound to service for a term of years, and excluding Indians not taxed, three-fifths of all other persons.] The actual enumeration shall be made within three years after the first meeting of the Congress of the United States, and within every subsequent term of ten years, in such manner as they shall by law direct. The number of representatives shall not exceed one for every thirty thousand, but each state shall have at least one representative; and until such enumeration shall be made, the state of New-Hampshire shall be entitled to chuse three, Massachusetts eight, Rhode-Island and Providence Plantations one, Connecticut five, New-York six, New-Jersey four, Pennsylvania eight, Delaware one, Maryland six, Virginia ten, North-Carolina five, South-Carolina five, and Georgia three.

When vacancies happen in the representation from any state, the Executive authority thereof shall issue writs of election to fill such vacancies.

The House of Representatives shall chuse their Speaker and other officers; and shall have the sole power of impeachment.

Sect. 3.   The Senate of the United States shall be composed of two senators from each state, **[chosen by the legislature thereof,] for six years; and each senator shall have one vote.

Immediately after they shall be assembled in consequence of the first election, they shall be divided as equally as may be into three classes. The seats of the senators of the first class shall be vacated at the expiration of the second year, of the second class at the expiration of the fourth year, and of the third class at the expiration of the sixth year, so that one-third may be chosen every second year; †[and if vacancies happen by resignation, or otherwise, during the recess of the Legislature of any state, the Executive thereof may make temporary appointments until the next meeting of the Legislature, which shall then fill such vacancies.]

No person shall be a senator who shall not have attained to the age of thirty years, and been nine years a citizen of the United States, and who shall not, when elected, be an inhabitant of that state for which he shall be chosen.

The Vice-President of the United States shall be President of the senate, but shall have no vote, unless they be equally divided.

The Senate shall chuse their other officers, and also a President pro tempore, in the absence of the Vice-President, or when he shall exercise the office of President of the United States.

The Senate shall have the sole power to try all impeachments. When sitting for that purpose, they shall be on oath or affirmation. When the President of the United

---

*The part enclosed by brackets was changed by section 2 of Amendment XIV.
**The clause enclosed by brackets was changed by clause 1 of Amendment XVII.
†The part enclosed by brackets was changed by clause 2 of Amendment XVII.

States is tried, the Chief Justice shall preside: And no person shall be convicted without the concurrence of two-thirds of the members present.

Judgment in cases of impeachment shall not extend further than to removal from office, and disqualification to hold and enjoy any office of honor, trust or profit under the United States; but the party convicted shall nevertheless be liable and subject to indictment, trial, judgment and punishment, according to law.

Sect. 4.   The times, places and manner of holding elections for senators and representatives, shall be prescribed in each state by the legislature thereof; but the Congress may at any time by law make or alter such regulations, except as to the places of chusing Senators.

The Congress shall assemble at least once in every year, and such meeting shall *[be on the first Monday in December,] unless they shall by law appoint a different day.

Sect. 5.   Each house shall be the judge of the elections, returns and qualifications of its own members, and a majority of each shall constitute a quorum to do business; but a smaller number may adjourn from day to day, and may be authorized to compel the attendance of absent members, in such manner, and under such penalties as each house may provide.

Each house may determine the rules of its proceedings, punish its members for disorderly behaviour, and, with the concurrence of two-thirds, expel a member.

Each house shall keep a journal of its proceedings, and from time to time publish the same, excepting such parts as may in their judgment require secrecy; and the yeas and nays of the members of either house on any question shall, at the desire of one-fifth of those present, be entered on the journal.

Neither house, during the session of Congress, shall, without the consent of the other, adjourn for more than three days, nor to any other place than that in which the two houses shall be sitting.

Sect. 6.   The senators and representatives shall receive a compensation for their services, to be ascertained by law, and paid out of the treasury of the United States. They shall in all cases, except treason, felony and breach of the peace, be privileged from arrest during their attendance at the session of their respective houses, and in going to and returning from the same; and for any speech or debate in either house, they shall not be questioned in any other place.

No senator or representative shall, during the time for which he was elected, be appointed to any civil office under the authority of the United States, which shall have been created, or the emoluments whereof shall have been encreased during such time; and no person holding any office under the United States, shall be a member of either house during his continuance in office.

Sect. 7.   All bills for raising revenue shall originate in the house of representatives; but the senate may propose or concur with amendments as on other bills.

Every bill which shall have passed the house of representatives and the senate, shall, before it become a law, be presented to the president of the United States; if he approve he shall sign it, but if not he shall return it, with his objections to that house in which it shall have originated, who shall enter the objections at large on their journal, and proceed to reconsider it. If after such reconsideration two-thirds of that house shall agree to pass the bill, it shall be sent, together with the objec-

*The clause enclosed by brackets was changed by section 2 of Amendment XX.

tions, to the other house, by which it shall likewise be reconsidered, and if approved by two-thirds of that house, it shall become a law. But in all such cases the votes of both houses shall be determined by yeas and nays, and the names of the persons voting for and against the bill shall be entered on the journal of each house respectively. If any bill shall not be returned by the President within ten days (Sundays excepted) after it shall have been presented to him, the same shall be a law, in like manner as if he had signed it, unless the Congress by their adjournment prevent its return, in which case it shall not be a law.

Every order, resolution, or vote to which the concurrence of the Senate and House of Representatives may be necessary (except on a question of adjournment) shall be presented to the President of the United States; and before the same shall take effect, shall be approved by him, or, being disapproved by him, shall be repassed by two-thirds of the Senate and House of Representatives, according to the rules and limitations prescribed in the case of a bill.

Sect. 8.   The Congress shall have power

To lay and collect taxes, duties, imposts and excises, to pay the debts and provide for the common defence and general welfare of the United States; but all duties, imposts and excises shall be uniform throughout the United States;

To borrow money on the credit of the United States;

To regulate commerce with foreign nations, and among the several states, and with the Indian tribes;

To establish an uniform rule of naturalization, and uniform laws on the subject of bankruptcies throughout the United States;

To coin money, regulate the value thereof, and of foreign coin, and fix the standard of weights and measures;

To provide for the punishment of counterfeiting the securities and current coin of the United States;

To establish post offices and post roads;

To promote the progress of science and useful arts, by securing for limited times to authors and inventors the exclusive right to their respective writings and discoveries;

To constitute tribunals inferior to the supreme court;

To define and punish piracies and felonies committed on the high seas, and offences against the law of nations;

To declare war, grant letters of marque and reprisal, and make rules concerning captures on land and water;

To raise and support armies, but no appropriation of money to that use shall be for a longer term than two years;

To provide and maintain a navy;

To make rules for the government and regulation of the land and naval forces;

To provide for calling forth the militia to execute the laws of the union, suppress insurrections and repel invasions;

To provide for organizing, arming, and disciplining, the militia, and for governing such part of them as may be employed in the service of the United States, reserving to the States respectively, the appointment of the officers, and the authority of training the militia according to the discipline prescribed by Congress;

To exercise exclusive legislation in all cases whatsoever, over such district (not exceeding ten miles square) as may, by cession of particular States, and the acceptance of Congress, become the seat of the government of the United States, and to exercise like authority over all places purchased by the consent of the legislature of the state in which the same shall be, for the erection of forts, magazines, arsenals, dock-yards, and other needful buildings;—And

To make all laws which shall be necessary and proper for carrying into execution the foregoing powers, and all other powers vested by this constitution in the government of the United States, or in any department or officer thereof.

Sect. 9.   The migration or importation of such persons as any of the states now existing shall think proper to admit, shall not be prohibited by the Congress prior to the year one thousand eight hundred and eight, but a tax or duty may be imposed on such importation, not exceeding ten dollars for each person.

The privilege of the writ of habeas corpus shall not be suspended, unless when in cases of rebellion or invasion the public safety may require it.

No bill of attainder or ex post facto law shall be passed.

No capitation, or other direct, tax shall be laid, unless in proportion to the census or enumeration herein before directed to be taken.*

No tax or duty shall be laid on articles exported from any state. No preference shall be given by any regulation of commerce or revenue to the ports of one state over those of another: nor shall vessels bound to, or from, one state, be obliged to enter, clear, or pay duties in another.

No money shall be drawn from the treasury, but in consequence of appropriations made by law; and a regular statement and account of the receipts and expenditures of all public money shall be published from time to time.

No title of nobility shall be granted by the United States:—And no person holding any office of profit or trust under them, shall, without the consent of the Congress, accept of any present, emolument, office, or title, of any kind whatever, from any king, prince, or foreign state.

Sect. 10.   No state shall enter into any treaty, alliance, or confederation; grant letters of marque and reprisal; coin money; emit bills of credit; make any thing but gold and silver coin a tender in payment of debts; pass any bill of attainder, ex post facto law, or law impairing the obligation of contracts, or grant any title of nobility.

No state shall, without the consent of the Congress, lay any imposts or duties on imports or exports, except what may be absolutely necessary for executing its inspection laws; and the net produce of all duties and imposts, laid by any state on imports or exports, shall be for the use of the Treasury of the United States; and all such laws shall be subject to the revision and controul of the Congress. No state shall, without the consent of Congress, lay any duty of tonnage, keep troops, or ships of war in time of peace, enter into any agreement or compact with another state, or with a foreign power, or engage in war, unless actually invaded, or in such imminent danger as will not admit of delay.

II.

Sect. 1.   The executive power shall be vested in a president of the United States of America. He shall hold his office during the term of four years, and, together with the vice-president, chosen for the same term, be elected as follows.

*See also Amendment XVI.

Each state shall appoint, in such manner as the legislature thereof may direct, a number of electors, equal to the whole number of senators and representatives to which the state may be entitled in the Congress: but no senator or representative, or person holding an office of trust or profit under the United States, shall be appointed an elector.

*[The electors shall meet in their respective states, and vote by ballot for two persons, of whom one at least shall not be an inhabitant of the same state with themselves. And they shall make a list of all the persons voted for, and of the number of votes for each; which list they shall sign and certify, and transmit sealed to the seat of the government of the United States, directed to the president of the senate. The president of the senate shall, in the presence of the senate and house of representatives, open all the certificates, and the votes shall then be counted. The person having the greatest number of votes shall be the president, if such number be a majority of the whole number of electors appointed; and if there be more than one who have such majority, and have an equal number of votes, then the house of representatives shall immediately chuse by ballot one of them for president; and if no person have a majority, then from the five highest on the list the said house shall in like manner chuse the president. But in chusing the president, the votes shall be taken by states, the representation from each state having one vote; a quorum for this purpose shall consist of a member or members from two-thirds of the states, and a majority of all the states shall be necessary to a choice. In every case, after the choice of the president, the person having the greatest number of votes of the electors shall be the vice-president. But if there should remain two or more who have equal votes, the senate shall chuse from them by ballot the vice-president.]

The Congress may determine the time of chusing the electors, and the day on which they shall give their votes; which day shall be the same throughout the United States.

No person except a natural born citizen, or a citizen of the United States, at the time of the adoption of this constitution, shall be eligible to the office of president; neither shall any person be eligible to that office who shall not have attained to the age of thirty-five years, and been fourteen years a resident within the United States.

**In case of the removal of the president from office, or of his death, resignation, or inability to discharge the powers and duties of the said office, the same shall devolve on the vice-president, and the Congress may by law provide for the case of removal, death, resignation or inability, both of the president and vice-president, declaring what officer shall then act as president, and such officer shall act accordingly, until the disability be removed, or a president shall be elected.

The president shall, at stated times, receive for his services, a compensation, which shall neither be encreased nor diminished during the period for which he shall have been elected, and he shall not receive within that period any other emolument from the United States, or any of them.

Before he enter on the execution of his office, he shall take the following oath or affirmation:

"I do solemnly swear (or affirm) that I will faithfully execute the office of president of the United States, and will to the best of my ability, preserve, protect and defend the constitution of the United States."

*This paragraph has been superseded by Amendment XII.
**This clause has been affected by Amendment XXV.

Sect. 2.   The president shall be commander in chief of the army and navy of the United States, and of the militia of the several States, when called into the actual service of the United States; he may require the opinion, in writing, of the principal officer in each of the executive departments, upon any subject relating to the duties of their respective offices, and he shall have power to grant reprieves and pardons for offences against the United States, except in cases of impeachment.

He shall have power, by and with the advice and consent of the senate, to make treaties, provided two-thirds of the senators present concur; and he shall nominate, and by and with the advice and consent of the senate, shall appoint ambassadors, other public ministers and consuls, judges of the supreme court, and all other officers of the United States, whose appointments are not herein otherwise provided for, and which shall be established by law. But the Congress may by law vest the appointment of such inferior officers, as they think proper, in the president alone, in the courts of law, or in the heads of departments.

The president shall have power to fill up all vacancies that may happen during the recess of the senate, by granting commissions which shall expire at the end of their next session.

Sect. 3.   He shall from time to time give to the Congress information of the state of the union, and recommend to their consideration such measures as he shall judge necessary and expedient; he may, on extraordinary occasions, convene both houses, or either of them, and in case of disagreement between them, with respect to the time of adjournment, he may adjourn them to such time as he shall think proper; he shall receive ambassadors and other public ministers; he shall take care that the laws be faithfully executed, and shall commission all the officers of the United States.

Sect. 4.   The president, vice-president and all civil officers of the United States, shall be removed from office on impeachment for, and conviction of, treason, bribery, or other high crimes and misdemeanors.

III.

Sect. 1.   The judicial power of the United States, shall be vested in one supreme court, and in such inferior courts as the Congress may from time to time ordain and establish. The judges, both of the supreme and inferior courts, shall hold their offices during good behaviour, and shall, at stated times, receive for their services, a compensation, which shall not be diminished during their continuance in office.

Sect. 2.   The judicial power shall extend to all cases, in law and equity, arising under this constitution, the laws of the United States, and treaties made, or which shall be made, under their authority; to all cases affecting ambassadors, other public ministers and consuls; to all cases of admiralty and maritime jurisdiction; to controversies to which the United States shall be a party; to controversies between two or more States, between a state and citizens of another state,° between citizens of different States, between citizens of the same state claiming lands under grants of different States, and between a state, or the citizens thereof, and foreign States, citizens or subjects.

In all cases affecting ambassadors, other public ministers and consuls, and those

°This clause has been affected by Amendment XI.

in which a state shall be party, the supreme court shall have original jurisdiction. In all the other cases before mentioned, the supreme court shall have appellate jurisdiction, both as to law and fact, with such exceptions, and under such regulations as the Congress shall make.

The trial of all crimes, except in cases of impeachment, shall be by jury; and such trial shall be held in the state where the said crimes shall have been committed; but when not committed within any state, the trial shall be at such place or places as the Congress may by law have directed.

Sect. 3. Treason against the United States, shall consist only in levying war against them, or in adhering to their enemies, giving them aid and comfort. No person shall be convicted of treason unless on the testimony of two witnesses to the same overt act, or on confession in open court.

The Congress shall have power to declare the punishment of treason, but no attainder of treason shall work corruption of blood, or forfeiture except during the life of the person attainted.

IV.

Sect. 1. Full faith and credit shall be given in each state to the public acts, records, and judicial proceedings of every other state. And the Congress may by general laws prescribe the manner in which such acts, records and proceedings shall be proved, and the effect thereof.

Sect. 2. The citizens of each state shall be entitled to all privileges and immunities of citizens in the several states.

A person charged in any state with treason, felony, or other crime, who shall flee from justice, and be found in another state, shall, on demand of the executive authority of the state from which he fled, be delivered up, to be removed to the state having jurisdiction of the crime.

*[No person held to service or labour in one state, under the laws thereof, escaping into another, shall, in consequence of any law or regulation therein, be discharged from such service or labour, but shall be delivered up on claim of the party to whom such service or labour may be due.]

Sect. 3. New states may be admitted by the Congress into this union; but no new state shall be formed or erected within the jurisdiction of any other state; nor any state be formed by the junction of two or more states, or parts of states, without the consent of the legislatures of the states concerned as well as of the Congress.

The Congress shall have power to dispose of and make all needful rules and regulations respecting the territory or other property belonging to the United States; and nothing in this Constitution shall be so construed as to prejudice any claims of the United States, or of any particular state.

Sect. 4. The United States shall guarantee to every state in this union a Republican form of government, and shall protect each of them against invasion; and on application of the legislature, or of the executive (when the legislature cannot be convened) against domestic violence.

*This paragraph has been superseded by Amendment XIII.

V.

The Congress, whenever two-thirds of both houses shall deem it necessary, shall proposed amendments to this constitution, or, on the application of the legislatures of two-thirds of the several states, shall call a convention for proposing amendments, which, in either case, shall be valid to all intents and purposes, as part of this constitution, when ratified by the legislatures of three-fourths of the several states, or by conventions in three-fourths thereof, as the one or the other mode of ratification may be proposed by the Congress; Provided, that no amendment which may be made prior to the year one thousand eight* hundred and eight shall in any manner affect the first and fourth clauses in the ninth section of the first article; and that no state, without its consent, shall be deprived of its equal suffrage in the senate.

VI.

All debts contracted and engagements entered into, before the adoption of this Constitution, shall be as valid against the United States under this Constitution, as under the confederation.

This constitution, and the laws of the United States which shall be made in pursuance thereof; and all treaties made, or which shall be made, under the authority of the United States, shall be the supreme law of the land; and the judges in every state shall be bound thereby, any thing in the constitution or laws of any state to the contrary notwithstanding.

The senators and representatives beforementioned, and the members of the several state legislatures, and all executive and judicial officers, both of the United States and of the several States, shall be bound by oath or affirmation, to support this constitution; but no religious test shall ever be required as a qualification to any office or public trust under the United States.

VII.

The ratification of the conventions of nine States, shall be sufficient for the establishment of this constitution between the States so ratifying the same.

[Signatures omitted]

---

*Misprinted "seven" in the original broadside of September 17, 1787, when the figures of the preceding draft were spelled out. Corrected by Dunlap & Claypoole in their Pennsylvania Packet reprint of September 19, 1787. It was the only error of text in the original print. Noted in Edmund Pendleton's copy. Correct in engrossed copy.

Amendments
to the
Constitution

Articles in addition to, and Amendment of the Constitution of the United States of America, proposed by Congress, and ratified by the Legislatures* of the several States, pursuant to the fifth Article of the original Constitution.

ARTICLE [I]**

*All the amendments except the Twenty-first Amendment were ratified by State Legislatures. The Twenty-first Amendment, by its terms, was ratified by "conventions in the several States." Only the Thirteenth, Fourteenth, Fifteenth, and Sixteenth Amendments had numbers assigned to them at the time of ratification.

**The first 10 amendments (termed articles), together with 2 others that failed of ratification, were proposed to the several States by resolution of Congress on September 25, 1789. The ratifications were transmitted by the Governors to the President and by him communicated to Congress from time to time. The first 10 amendments were ratified by 11 of the 14 States. Virginia completed the required three fourths by ratification on December 15, 1791, and its action was communicated to Congress by the President on December 30, 1791. The legislatures of Massachusetts, Georgia and Connecticut ratified them on March 2, 1939, March 18, 1939, and April 19, 1939, respectively.

Congress shall make no law respecting an establishment of religion, or prohibiting the free exercise thereof; or abridging the freedom of speech, or of the press; or the right of the people peaceably to assemble, and to petition the Government for a redress of grievances.

ARTICLE [II]

A well regulated Militia, being necessary to the security of a free State, the right of the people to keep and bear Arms, shall not be infringed.

ARTICLE [III]

No Soldier shall, in time of peace be quartered in any house, without the consent of the Owner, nor in time of war, but in a manner to be prescribed by law.

ARTICLE [IV]

The right of the people to be secure in their persons, houses, papers, and effects, against unreasonable searches and seizures, shall not be violated, and no Warrants shall issue, but upon probable cause, supported by Oath or affirmation, and particularly describing the place to be searched, and the persons or things to be seized.

ARTICLE [V]

No person shall be held to answer for a capital, or otherwise infamous crime, unless on a presentment or indictment of a Grand Jury, except in cases arising in the land or naval forces, or in the Militia, when in actual service in time of War or public danger; nor shall any person be subject for the same offence to be twice put in jeopardy of life or limb; nor shall be compelled in any criminal case to be a witness against himself, nor be deprived of life, liberty, or property, without due process of law; nor shall private property be taken for public use, without just compensation.

ARTICLE [VI]

In all criminal prosecutions, the accused shall enjoy the right to a speedy and public trial, by an impartial jury of the State and district wherein the crime shall have been committed, which district shall have been previously ascertained by law, and to be informed of the nature and cause of the accusation; to be confronted with the witnesses against him; to have compulsory process for obtaining witnesses in his favor, and to have the Assistance of Counsel for his defence.

ARTICLE [VII]

In Suits at common law, where the value in controversy shall exceed twenty dollars, the right of trial by jury shall be preserved, and no fact tried by a jury, shall be otherwise re-examined in any Court of the United States, than according to the rules of the common law.

ARTICLE [VIII]

Excessive bail shall not be required, nor excessive fines imposed, nor cruel and unusual punishments inflicted.

ARTICLE [IX]

The enumeration in the Constitution, of certain rights, shall not be construed to deny or disparage others retained by the people.

ARTICLE [X]

The powers not delegated to the United States by the Constitution, nor prohibited by it to the States, are reserved to the States respectively, or to the people.

ARTICLE [XI]*

The Judicial power of the United States shall not be construed to extend to any suit in law or equity, commenced or prosecuted against one of the United States by Citizens of another State, or by Citizens or Subjects of any Foreign State.

ARTICLE [XII]**

The Electors shall meet in their respective states, and vote by ballot for President

---

*The Eleventh Amendment was proposed by resolution of Congress on March 4, 1794. It was declared by the President, in a message to Congress dated January 8, 1798, to have been ratified by three fourths of the several States. Records of the National Archives show that the 11th Amendment was ratified by 13 of the 16 States. It was not ratified by New Jersey or Pennsylvania.

**The Twelfth Amendment was proposed in lieu of the original third paragraph of section 1 of article II, by resolution of Congress on December 9, 1803. It was declared in a proclamation of the Secretary of State, dated September 25, 1804, to have been ratified by three fourths of the States. Records of the National Archives show that it was ratified by 14 States and rejected by Connecticut and Delaware.

and Vice-President, one of whom, at least, shall not be an inhabitant of the same state with themselves; they shall name in their ballots the person voted for as President, and in distinct ballots the person voted for as Vice-President, and they shall make distinct lists of all persons voted for as President, and of all persons voted for as Vice-President, and of the number of votes for each, which lists they shall sign and certify, and transmit sealed to the seat of the government of the United States, directed to the President of the Senate;—The President of the Senate shall, in the presence of the Senate and House of Representatives, open all the certificates and the votes shall then be counted;—The person having the greatest number of votes for President, shall be the President, if such number be a majority of the whole number of Electors appointed; and if no person have such majority, then from the persons having the highest numbers not exceeding three on the list of those voted for as President, the House of Representatives shall choose immediately, by ballot, the President. But in choosing the President, the votes shall be taken by states, the representation from each state having one vote; a quorum for this purpose shall consist of a member or members from two-thirds of the states, and a majority of all the states shall be necessary to a choice.

*[And if the House of Representatives shall not choose a President whenever the right of choice shall devolve upon them, before the fourth day of March next following, then the Vice-President shall act as President, as in the case of the death or other constitutional disability of the President.]—The person having the greatest number of votes as Vice-President, shall be the Vice President, if such number be a majority of the whole number of Electors appointed, and if no person have a majority, then from the two highest numbers on the list, the Senate shall choose the Vice-President; a quorum for the purpose shall consist of two-thirds of the whole number of Senators, and a majority of the whole number shall be necessary to a choice. But no person constitutionally ineligible to the office of President shall be eligible to that of Vice-President of the United States.

ARTICLE XIII**

Section 1.   Neither slavery nor involuntary servitude, except as a punishment for crime whereof the party shall have been duly convicted, shall exist within the United States, or any place subject to their jurisdiction.

Section 2.   Congress shall have power to enforce this article by appropriate legislation.

---

*The part enclosed by brackets has been superseded by section 3 of Amendment XX.

**The Thirteenth Amendment was proposed by resolution of Congress on January 31, 1865. It was declared in a proclamation of the Secretary of State, dated December 18, 1865, to have been ratified by 27 States. Subsequent records of the National Archives show that the 13th Amendment was ratified by 7 additional States. It was rejected by Kentucky and Mississippi.

ARTICLE XIV*

Section 1.   All persons born or naturalized in the United States, and subject to the jurisdiction thereof, are citizens of the United States and of the State wherein they reside. No State shall make or enforce any law which shall abridge the privileges or immunities of citizens of the United States; nor shall any State deprive any person of life, liberty, or property, without due process of law; nor deny to any person within its jurisdiction the equal protection of the laws.

Section 2.   Representatives shall be apportioned among the several States according to their respective numbers, counting the whole number of persons in each State, excluding Indians not taxed. But when the right to vote at any election for the choice of electors for President and Vice President of the United States, Representatives in Congress, the Executive and Judicial officers of a State, or the members of the Legislature thereof, is denied to any of the male inhabitants of such State, being twenty-one years of age, and citizens of the United States, or in any way abridged, except for participation in rebellion, or other crime, the basis of representation therein shall be reduced in the proportion which the number of such male citizens shall bear to the whole number of male citizens twenty-one years of age in such State.

Section 3.   No person shall be a Senator or Representative in Congress, or elector of President and Vice-President, or hold any office, civil or military, under the United States, or under any State, who, having previously taken an oath, as a member of Congress, or as an officer of the United States, or as a member of any State legislature, or as an executive or judicial officer of any State, to support the Constitution of the United States, shall have engaged in insurrection or rebellion against the same, or given aid or comfort to the enemies thereof. But Congress may by a vote of two-thirds of each House, remove such disability.

Section 4.   The validity of the public debt of the United States, authorized by law, including debts incurred for payment of pensions and bounties for services in suppressing insurrection or rebellion, shall not be questioned. But neither the United States nor any State shall assume or pay any debt or obligation incurred in aid of insurrection or rebellion against the United States, or any claim for the loss of emancipation of any slave; but all such debts, obligations and claims shall be held illegal and void.

Section 5.   The Congress shall have power to enforce, by appropriate legislation, the provisions of this article.

*The Fourteenth Amendment was proposed by resolution of Congress on June 13, 1866. By a concurrent resolution of Congress adopted July 21, 1868, it was declared to have been ratified by "three fourths and more of the several States of the Union," and the Secretary of State was required duly to promulgate the amendment as a part of the Constitution. He accordingly issued a proclamation, dated July 28, 1868, declaring the amendment to have been ratified by 30 States, "being more than three fourths." Records of the National Archives show that the 14th Amendment was subsequently ratified by 8 additional States. It was rejected by Kentucky.

ARTICLE XV*

Section 1.   The right of citizens of the United States to vote shall not be denied or abridged by the United States or by any State on account of race, color, or previous condition of servitude.

Section 2.   The Congress shall have power to enforce this article by appropriate legislation.

ARTICLE XVI**

The Congress shall have power to lay and collect taxes on incomes, from whatever source derived, without apportionment among the several States, and without regard to any census or enumeration.

ARTICLE [XVII]†

The Senate of the United States shall be composed of two Senators from each State, elected by the people thereof, for six years; and each Senator shall have one vote. The electors in each State shall have the qualifications requisite for electors of the most numerous branch of the State legislatures.

When vacancies happen in the representation of any State in the Senate, the executive authority of such State shall issue writs of election to fill such vacancies: *Provided,* That the legislature of any State may empower the executive thereof to make temporary appointments until the people fill the vacancies by election as the legislature may direct.

This amendment shall not be so construed as to affect the election or term of any Senator chosen before it becomes valid as part of the Constitution.

*The Fifteenth Amendment was proposed by resolution of Congress on February 26, 1869. It was declared in a proclamation of the Secretary of State, dated March 30, 1870, to have been ratified by 29 States, which "constitute three fourths." Records of the National Archives show that the 15th Amendment was subsequently ratified by 6 more of the States. It was rejected by Kentucky, Maryland, and Tennessee.

**The Sixteenth Amendment was proposed by resolution of Congress on July 12, 1909. It was declared in a proclamation of the Secretary of State, dated February 25, 1913, to have been ratified by 38 States, which "constitute three fourths." Subsequent records of the National Archives show that the 16th Amendment was ratified by 4 additional States. It was rejected by Connecticut, Florida, Rhode Island, and Utah.

†The Seventeenth Amendment was proposed by resolution of Congress on May 13, 1912. It was declared in a proclamation of the Secretary of State, dated May 31, 1913, to have been ratified by 36 States, which "constitute three fourths." Records of the National Archives show that the 17th Amendment was subsequently ratified by 1 additional State. It was rejected by Utah and Delaware.

ARTICLE [XVIII]*

[Section 1.   After one year from the ratification of this article the manufacture, sale, or transportation of intoxicating liquors within, the importation thereof into, or the exportation thereof from the United States and all territory subject to the jurisdiction thereof for beverage purposes is hereby prohibited.

[Section 2.   The Congress and the several States shall have concurrent power to enforce this article by appropriate legislation.

[Section 3.   This article shall be inoperative unless it shall have been ratified as an amendment to the Constitution by the legislatures of the several States, as provided in the Constitution, within seven years from the date of the submission hereof to the States by the Congress.]

ARTICLE [XIX]**

The right of citizens of the United States to vote shall not be denied or abridged by the United States or by any State on account of sex.

Congress shall have power to enforce this article by appropriate legislation.

ARTICLE [XX]†

*The Eighteenth Amendment was proposed by resolution of Congress on December 18, 1917. It was declared in a proclamation of the Acting Secretary of State, dated January 29, 1919, to have been ratified by 36 States, which "constitute three fourths." Subsequent records of the National Archives show that the 18th Amendment was ratified by 10 additional States. It was rejected by Rhode Island. By its own terms the 18th Amendment became effective one year after its ratification, which was consummated on January 16, 1919, and therefore went into effect on January 16, 1920.

Repeal of the 18th Amendment on December 5, 1933, was proclaimed by the President in his proclamation of that date, when the ratification of the 21st Amendment was certified by the Acting Secretary of State.

**The Nineteenth Amendment was proposed by resolution of Congress on June 4, 1919. It was declared in a proclamation of the Secretary of State, dated August 26, 1920, to have been ratified by 36 States, which "constitute three fourths." Subsequent records of the National Archives show that the 19th Amendment was ratified by 5 additional States. It was rejected by Georgia, South Carolina, Mississippi, Delaware, and Louisiana.

†The Twentieth Amendment was proposed by resolution of Congress on March 2, 1932. It was declared in a proclamation of the Secretary of State, dated February 6, 1933, to have been ratified by 39 States, which "constitute more than the requisite three fourths." Subsequent records of the National Archives show that the 20th Amendment was ratified by all 48 States before sections 1 and 2 became effective on October 15, 1933. The other sections of the amendment became effective on January 23, 1933, when its ratification was consummated by three fourths of the States.

Section 1. The terms of the President and Vice President shall end at noon on the 20th day of January, and the terms of Senators and Representatives at noon on the 3d day of January, of the years in which such terms would have ended if this article had not been ratified; and the terms of their successors shall then begin.

Sec. 2. The Congress shall assemble at least once in every year, and such meeting shall begin at noon on the 3d day of January, unless they shall by law appoint a different day.

Sec. 3. If, at the time fixed for the beginning of the term of the President, the President elect shall have died, the Vice President elect shall become President. If a President shall not have been chosen before the time fixed for the beginning of his term, or if the President elect shall have failed to qualify, then the Vice President elect shall act as President until a President shall have qualified; and the Congress may by law provide for the case wherein neither a President elect nor a Vice President elect shall have qualified, declaring who shall then act as President, or the manner in which one who is to act shall be selected, and such person shall act accordingly until a President or Vice President shall have qualified.

Sec. 4. The Congress may by law provide for the case of the death of any of the persons from whom the House of Representatives may choose a President whenever the right of choice shall have devolved upon them, and for the case of the death of any of the persons from whom the Senate may choose a Vice President whenever the right of choice shall have devolved upon them.

Sec. 5. Sections 1 and 2 shall take effect on the 15th day of October following the ratification of this article.

Sec. 6. This article shall be inoperative unless it shall have been ratified as an amendment to the Constitution by the legislatures of three-fourths of the several States within seven years from the date of its submission.

ARTICLE [XXI]*

Section 1. The eighteenth article of amendment to the Constitution of the United States is hereby repealed.

Sec. 2. The transportation or importation into any State, Territory, or possession of the United States for delivery or use therein of intoxicating liquors, in violation of the laws thereof, is hereby prohibited.

Sec. 3. This article shall be inoperative unless it shall have been ratified as an amendment to the Constitution by conventions in the several States, as provided in the Constitution, within seven years from the date of the submission hereof to the States by the Congress.

*The Twenty-first Amendment was proposed by resolution of Congress on February 20, 1933. It was certified in a proclamation of the Acting Secretary of State dated December 5, 1933, to have been ratified by conventions of 36 States, which "constitute the requisite three fourths of the whole number of States." Subsequent records of the National Archives show that the 21st Amendment was ratified by 2 additional States. It was rejected by the convention of South Carolina. North Carolina voted against holding a convention.

ARTICLE [XXII]*

Section 1.   No person shall be elected to the office of the President more than twice, and no person who has held the office of President, or acted as President, for more than two years of a term to which some other person was elected President shall be elected to the office of the President more than once. But this Article shall not apply to any person holding the office of President when this Article was proposed by the Congress, and shall not prevent any person who may be holding the office of President, or acting as President, during the term within which this Article becomes operative from holding the office of President or acting as President during the remainder of such term.

Sec. 2.   This article shall be inoperative unless it shall have been ratified as an amendment to the Constitution by the legislatures of three-fourths of the several States within seven years from the date of its submission to the States by the Congress.

ARTICLE [XXIII]**

Section 1.   The District constituting the seat of Government of the United States shall appoint in such manner as the Congress may direct:

A number of electors of President and Vice President equal to the whole number of Senators and Representatives in Congress to which the District would be entitled if it were a State, but in no event more than the least populous State; they shall be in addition to those appointed by the States, but they shall be considered, for the purposes of the election of President and Vice President, to be electors appointed by a State; and they shall meet in the District and perform such duties as provided by the twelfth article of amendment.

Section 2.   The Congress shall have the power to enforce this article by appropriate legislation.

*The Twenty-second Amendment was proposed by resolution of Congress on March 24, 1947. Ratification was completed on February 27, 1951, when the thirty-sixth State (Minnesota) approved the amendment. On March 1, 1951, the Administrator of General Services certified that "the States whose Legislatures have so ratified the said proposed Amendment constitute the requisite three-fourths of the whole number of States in the United States." Records of the National Archives show that the 22nd Amendment was subsequently ratified by 5 additional States.

**The Twenty-third Amendment was proposed by resolution of Congress on June 16, 1960. The Administrator of General Services certified the ratification and adoption of the amendment by three-fourths of the States on April 3, 1961. It was rejected by Arkansas.

ARTICLE [XXIV]*

Section 1.   The right of citizens of the United States to vote in any primary or other election for President or Vice President, for electors for President or Vice President, or for Senator or Representative in Congress, shall not be denied or abridged by the United States or any State by reason of failure to pay any poll tax or other tax.

Section 2.   The Congress shall have power to enforce this article by appropriate legislation.

ARTICLE [XXV]**

Section 1.   In case of the removal of the President from office or of his death or resignation, the Vice President shall become President.

Sec. 2.   Whenever there is a vacancy in the office of the Vice President, the President shall nominate a Vice President who shall take office upon confirmation by a majority vote of both Houses of Congress.

Sec. 3.   Whenever the President transmits to the President pro tempore of the Senate and the Speaker of the House of Representatives his written declaration that he is unable to discharge the powers and duties of his office, and until he transmits to them a written declaration to the contrary, such powers and duties shall be discharged by the Vice President as Acting President.

Sec. 4.   Whenever the Vice President and a majority of either the principal officers of the executive departments or of such other body as Congress may by law provide, transmit to the President pro tempore of the Senate and the Speaker of the House of Representatives their written declaration that the President is unable to discharge the powers and duties of his office, the Vice President shall immediately assume the powers and duties of the office as Acting President.

Thereafter, when the President transmits to the President pro tempore of the Senate and the Speaker of the House of Representatives his written declaration that no inability exists, he shall resume the powers and duties of his office unless the Vice President and a majority of either the principal officers of the executive department or of such other body as Congress may by law provide, transmit within four days to the President pro tempore of the Senate and the Speaker of the House of Representatives their written declaration that the President is unable to discharge the powers

---

*The Twenty-fourth Amendment was proposed by resolution of Congress on August 27, 1962. It was declared in a Proclamation of the Administrator of General Services dated February 4, 1964, to have been ratified by three-fourths of the States. It was rejected by the legislature of Mississippi on December 20, 1962.

**The Twenty-fifth Amendment to the Constitution was proposed by the Congress on July 6, 1965. It was declared in a certificate of the Administrator of General Services, dated February 23, 1967, to have been ratified by the legislatures of 39 of the 50 States.

Ratification was completed on February 10, 1967.

The amendment was subsequently ratified by Connecticut, Montana, South Dakota, Ohio, Alabama, North Carolina, Illinois, and Texas.

and duties of his office. Thereupon Congress shall decide the issue, assembling within forty-eight hours for that purpose if not in session. If the Congress, within twenty-one days after receipt of the latter written declaration, or, if Congress is not in session, within twenty-one days after Congress is required to assemble, determines by two-thirds vote of both Houses that the President is unable to discharge the powers and duties of his office, the Vice President shall continue to discharge the same as Acting President; otherwise, the President shall resume the powers and duties of his office.

ARTICLE [XXVI]*

Sec. 1.   The right of citizens of the United States, who are eighteen years of age or older, to vote shall not be denied or abridged by the United States or by any State on account of age.

Sec. 2.   The Congress shall have power to enforce this article by appropriate legislation.

*The Twenty-sixth Amendment was proposed by resolution of Congress on March 8, 1971. It was declared in a certificate of the Administrator of General Services, dated July 5, 1971, to have been ratified by the legislatures of 39 of the 50 States.

Ratification was completed on July 1, 1971.

The amendment was subsequently ratified by Virginia and Wyoming.

Table
of
Cases

AMERICAN

Italic page numbers indicate an extended discussion.

ENGLISH

Index